D0818504

CONCISE DICTIONARY OF MODERN JAPANESE HISTORY

CONCISE DICTIONARY OF MODERN JAPANESE HISTORY

Compiled by
Janet Hunter

University of California Press

Berkeley · Los Angeles · London

University of California Press
Berkeley and Los Angeles, California

University of California Press, Ltd.
London, England

Printed in the United States of America

3 4 5 6 7 8 9

Library of Congress Cataloging in
Publication Data

Hunter, Janet.
Concise dictionary of modern
Japanese history.

Includes index.
1. Japan—History—1868—
—Dictionaries.
I. Title.
DS881.9.H86 1983 952.03 82-17456
ISBN 0-520-04557-2 (alk. paper)

The paper used in this publication meets the
minimum requirements of American
National Standard for Information
Sciences—Permanence of Paper for Printed
Library Materials, ANSI Z39.48–1984. ∞

In memory of my father

CONTENTS

MAPS

PREFACE

Historical dictionaries and other similar reference works are widely accepted and widely used in Japan and are an integral part of modern Japanese historiography. As a part of English-language historiography, however, the historical dictionary, as a general listing of people, places, and events, is far less used. It is therefore especially important to say something about the aims and limitations of this *Concise Dictionary of Modern Japanese History.*

Japanese history is relatively unknown in the West. Linguistic difficulties, the fact that the study of Japan traditionally has little place within Western historiography, and the trend toward academic specialization have all contributed to this neglect. Yet the importance of Japan in our lives today is such as to merit a deeper awareness and understanding. Japanese history deserves to be better known because it is intrinsically of as much interest as the history of any other country, because of its importance for world history in the modern period, and because of the comparative insights it has to offer. The aim of this book is to provide a handy source of information on the individuals, events, and organizations that have played a significant role in Japan's modern history. It is aimed primarily at non-Japanese speakers and nonspecialists or students just embarking on the study of Japanese history, in fact, anyone in search of further information on a topic they may have come across in their reading. This need is not met by the existing English-language historical dictionaries of Japan compiled by E. Papinot and Joseph M. Goedertier. Specialists in Japan and others with a good knowledge of Japanese would obviously turn to the large number of existing Japanese-language historical dictionaries, many of which are far larger and more comprehensive than the present volume and on a scale that can only be attempted with multiple authorship.

The aim of this work is to supply only basic information. It has not been conceived as an encyclopedic compendium of facts and figures. In accordance with this intention, the length of each entry and of the text as a whole has been kept as brief as possible. To do otherwise would suggest a work of a different scale. Especially in view of the curtailments imposed by length, therefore, the selection of information for such a volume does present enormous problems. A major aim has been to reflect the priorities of Japanese as well as Western historians; the factual details of biographical notes, for example, are based largely on the work of Japanese historians, and it is these very facts that are in many cases so difficult to obtain if one has no knowledge of Japanese. Conflicting statements and dates have been checked as far as possible. Purely in terms of factual information, therefore, this work tries to fill a considerable lacuna in English-language writings.

Japanese historians, however, interpret these facts for the Japanese. The Western approach is often very different. Where interpretation of an event, movement, or idea is regarded as essential to the understanding of an entry, I have tried to provide a précis of available information on such topics and to take a balanced view, giving either the "normally accepted" interpretation or, where two or more major, conflicting interpretations exist, making the reader aware of this fact.

The focus of the work, for reasons both of length and of personal interest, is on political, diplomatic, and socioeconomic developments. Items of importance in intellectual history have been included only where they are regarded as having a direct and important bearing on such developments. Literary personalities and events also find no place except where they are of prime importance in this sphere. The need for brevity has also, perhaps regretfully, resulted in the exclusion of items which are of undoubted importance but which are less central to the main focus of the work, for example, the new religions, of which the only one covered is Sōka Gakkai.

The time span covered by the entries in the dictionary is from 1853 through 1980. These dates are, however, subject to certain provisos. Although 1853, the year when the West breached Japan's national isolation for the first time in over 200 years, is frequently given as the starting date for Japan's modern history, it is commonplace that no single year ever marks a total transformation in historical events of any great significance. Any such date is somewhat arbitrary, and in many ways the developmental watershed of 1868 was much greater than that of 1853. Many of the dictionary entries, therefore, refer either in whole or in part to pre-1853 ideas, systems, and individuals where the significance of these without doubt extended into the modern period.

Similarly, it is impossible to bring a reference work satisfactorily up to the present, and the post-1945 period has been given relatively less coverage than the earlier years, in part reflecting the greater difficulty of assessing the true significance of events close to the present. The intention has been to cover those items of major importance in Japan's postwar development—the events that caught the public eye, the governments, economic developments—but the gaps are far greater than those in the earlier period. Furthermore, the most recent facts and figures will be rapidly overtaken, and the reader in search of up-to-the minute information about contemporary Japan will turn instead to the latest yearbooks and white papers. In other words, the book is tailored primarily to those seeking information about historical rather than contemporary developments.

The information contained in the various items has been drawn from a large number of both English and Japanese secondary and reference works. Most important have been the many Japanese historical dictionaries and reference books. Particularly worth mentioning of the more concise works are M. Takayanagi and R. Takeuchi, eds., *Kakugawa Nihonshi Jiten,* 11th ed. (Tokyo, 1968); Nihon Kingendaishi Jiten Henshū Iinkai, ed., *Nihon Kingendaishi Jiten* (Tokyo, 1978); Kyōto Daigaku Bungakubu Kokushi Kenkyūshitsu, ed., *Nihon Kindaishi Jiten* (Tokyo, 1958); and Nihon Rekishi Daijiten Henshū Iinkai, ed., *Nihonshi Nenpyō* (Tokyo, 1976). These works are of varying quality, and their interpretations are often questionable; nevertheless, they do attempt to give the basic facts (though it is surprising how often they conflict even on these). This information has in some cases been supplemented by information from and checked against other reference works and English- and Japanese-language monographs as far as possible. The interpretation and selection of facts, however, is such as I hope will be of value and interest particularly to Western readers.

The books and articles cited at the end of most entries are intended to suggest where the reader with no knowledge of the Japanese language may find more detailed information about that particular item. In some cases where no reference is given, the author has been unable to trace any English-language sources on the subject. The citing of a source is not necessarily to be regarded as a wholehearted recommendation of it. The English-language literature on Japan is still sufficiently limited so that it is frequently possible only to cite one or two sources on an item, and these may sometimes be hopelessly outdated or of dubious value. Only in cases where the English-language literature on a subject is sufficiently large that reasons of length render citation of all relevant sources impossible have I provided a selection of references, taking what I regard as the most valuable, informative, or representative. These references are cited in alphabetical order, not in order of value. The references thus cited do not include the fairly considerable number of general works on the modern period, some of which are extremely good and should be constantly borne in mind as a background for the study of modern Japanese history. It should be added that the range of subject matter of this dictionary is so wide that most of it lies outside the author's own field of expertise. Comments on entries and bibliography from those with more specialized knowledge will be greatly welcomed.

Stylistic conventions are in accordance with the University of Chicago Press *Manual of Style,* 12th ed. (Chicago, 1969). Japanese words have been romanized in accordance with the modified Hepburn system as found in Kenkyūsha's *New Japanese-English Dictionary,* 4th ed. (Tokyo, 1974). This system uses a macron to denote a long vowel (e.g., ō), but this has been omitted in the case of a few very well-known place names such as Tokyo, Osaka, and Kyoto. Japanese words that are not proper nouns or titles have been italicized, with the exception again of a small number of words which have in effect passed into the English language, for example, samurai and Bakufu. Japanese names are given in the normal Japanese manner with family name preceding given name. Japanese characters are included in the entry titles, glossary, and index with the aim of assisting beginners in the use of Japanese sources. Those with a reasonable level of proficiency in written Japanese will, as mentioned above, naturally be assumed to turn to Japanese-language reference works for their information.

As should be the case with all reference works, the aim of this book is to help the reader in his or her studies; it is not intended as a substitute for study, and its use is essentially a limited one. If it assists the reader, and perhaps stimulates him or her to probe further into an important but neglected field, it will have gone a long way toward serving its purpose.

A professional fellowship from the Japan Foundation in 1977 enabled me to collect reference works by Japanese historians, which were of great use in compiling this volume. I would like to thank in particular the following, who have read all or parts of the manuscript: Professor Ian Nish of the London School of Economics and Political Science; Professor Richard Storry of St. Antony's College, Oxford; Dr. Michael Connors, Lesley Connors, Dr. Gordon Daniels, Graham Healey, and Dr. Hamish Ion of the Center of Japanese Studies, University of Sheffield, all of whose comments and advice were of great value. I would also like to express my gratitude to the members of Dawson Publishing, which originally commissioned this work, and to the staff of the University of California Press, which took over its publication. Finally, I would like to thank Ethel Curley, who typed the manuscript for me, and Rosemary Duncan, of the Geography Department, University of Sheffield, who drew the maps.

GUIDE TO USE OF THE DICTIONARY

The aims and limitations of this dictionary are set out in the preface; the following notes are intended to assist the reader.

The romanization used for Japanese is the modified Hepburn system as used in Kenkyūsha's *New Japanese-English Dictionary*, 4th ed. (Tokyo, 1974). Long vowels are indicated by the use of macrons, e.g., Kyūshū, Hokkaidō. The romanization used for Chinese is the Wade-Giles system.

Entries are arranged alphabetically, with their headings in boldface letters. Biographical entries are in the order of the subject's family name. Where two or more individuals have the same family name, they are in alphabetical order of given name, e.g., **Kido Kōichi** precedes **Kido Kōin**. The same alphabetical principle applies to nonbiographical entries, e.g., **Shakai Minshūtō** precedes **Shakai Taishūtō**. Letters with macrons are treated exactly as those without, except where both exist side by side, when that without precedes that with the macron, e.g., **Shakai Minshutō** precedes **Shakai Minshūtō**.

Japanese names are given throughout in the Japanese order, i.e., family name preceding given name. Where the Japanese character for a given name has more than one possible reading in common use, the alternative forms are given in parentheses in the biographical entry headings, e.g., **Hara Kei (Satoshi, Takashi)**. Alternative family names are also given in this manner, e.g., **Heco, Joseph (Hamada Hikozō)**.

English is used for entry headings wherever a generally accepted or unambiguous translation of a Japanese title or phrase exists. Where appropriate, the

Japanese term or title is given in parentheses following the English. However, the Japanese phrase given after such an English entry heading is not necessarily the direct translation of that heading: different phrases are often used in the two languages to refer to the same thing, e.g., **Siberian Intervention** (Shiberia shuppei).

Within the text of an entry (*q.v.*) is used to guide the reader to another entry containing related material. Such cross-referencing is not exhaustive; (*q.v.*) is inserted only where reference to the related material is considered indispensable to the understanding of an entry or where an unfamiliar term or concept is referred to. Persons and political parties are generally not cross-referenced. Related material is also indicated by See . . . at the end of an entry. Some headings are also cross-references, e.g., **Hitotsubashi Keiki.** See TOKUGAWA KEIKI.

The brief English-language bibliographies at the end of entries are arranged in alphabetical order by author.

The information in the text, bibliographies, and appendices is based on data available up to the end of 1980.

The glossary of Japanese words and phrases is arranged in alphabetical order. The index of Japanese characters is arranged in ascending order of the number of strokes in the first character of an entry. Where more than one entry starts with the same character, the order is based on the number of strokes in the second character, and so on. Characters with the same number of strokes are arranged in the order found in Nelson's *Japanese-English Character Dictionary*.

ABBREVIATIONS

BAJS	*British Association for Japanese Studies*
CJ	*Contemporary Japan*
FEQ	*Far Eastern Quarterly*
HPJ	*Harvard University East Asian Research Center Papers on Japan*
JAH	*Journal of Asian History*
JAS	*Journal of Asian Studies*
JJS	*Journal of Japanese Studies*
JQ	*Japan Quarterly*
MAS	*Modern Asian Studies*
MN	*Monumenta Nipponica*
PHR	*Pacific Historical Review*

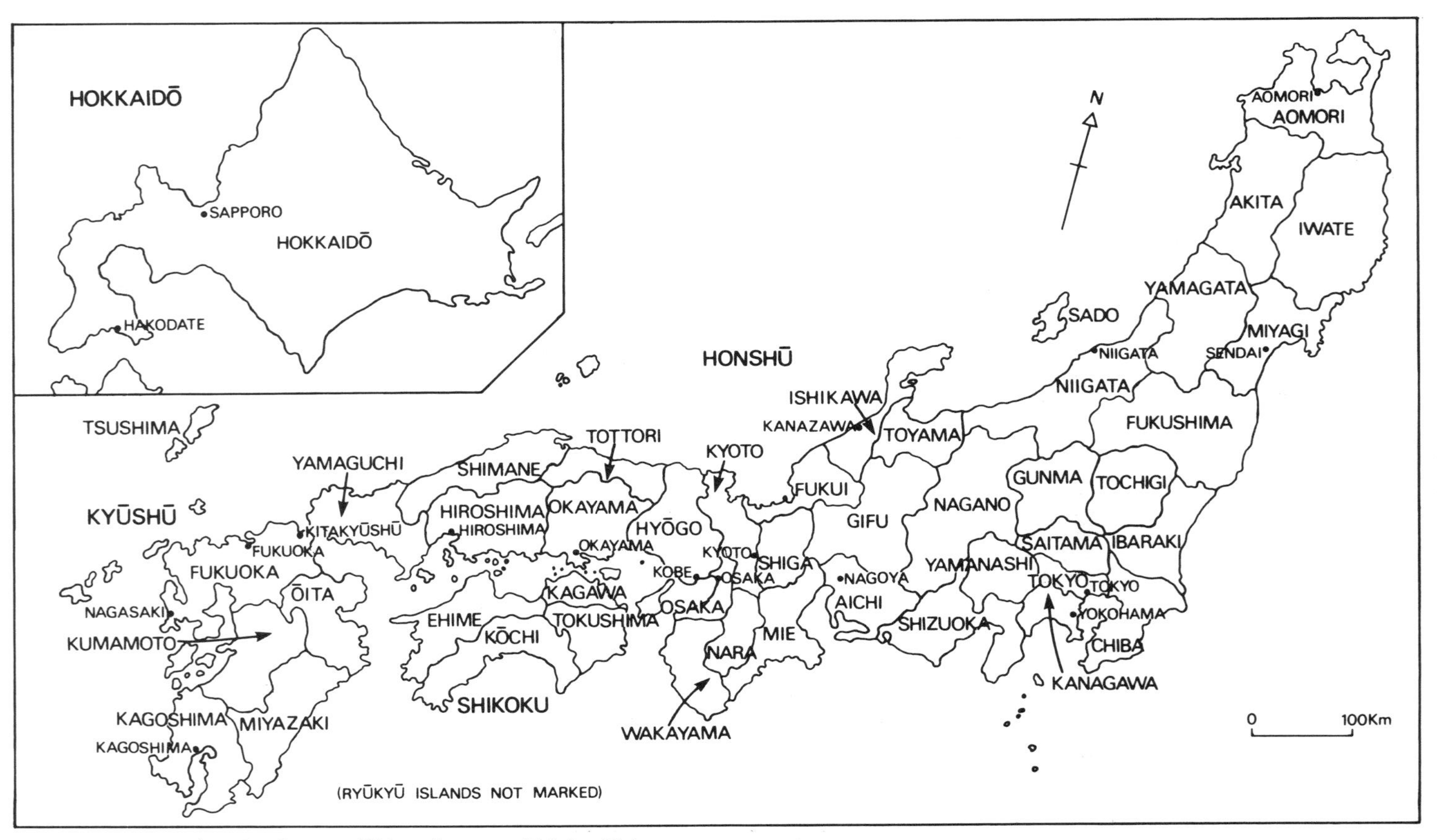

Map 1. JAPAN. Modern Prefectures, Urban Areas, and Major Cities

CONCISE DICTIONARY OF MODERN JAPANESE HISTORY

A

Abe Isoo 1865–1949 安部磯雄
Native of Fukuoka Prefecture, Abe studied at Dōshisha and became a Christian; after studying in the West, he returned to Japan and became a Unitarian preacher. From 1899 he taught at Tokyo College (later Waseda University). He participated in the early Socialist movement, becoming a member of the Society for the Study of Socialism in 1898 and then president of the Socialist Society in 1900; in 1901 he was one of the founders of the Shakai Minshutō. Abe maintained a pacifist stance throughout the Russo-Japanese War, and his subsequent publication of the journal *Shin Kigen* (New Era) with Ishikawa Sanshirō marked his continuing activity as one of Japan's leading Christian Socialists. Though withdrawing from Socialist activity after 1910, Abe reemerged in 1924 to become president of the Japan Fabian Society. As a member of the Labor Farmer Party in 1926, then chairman of the Shakai Minshūtō, and finally as chairman of the Shakai Taishūtō from 1932, he remained a leading figure among right-wing Socialists until the war. In 1928 he was elected to the Diet. Abe withdrew from political activity in 1940 but postwar acted as adviser to the Japan Socialist Party.

Powles, C. H. "Abe Isoo: The Utility Man," in N. Bamba and J. F. Howes, eds. *Pacifism in Japan* (Kyoto, 1978).

Abe Nobuyuki 1875–1953 阿部信行
Native of Ishikawa Prefecture, graduating from the Military Academy, Abe rose to

the rank of general before being placed on the reserve list in 1936. In August 1939 he succeeded Hiranuma as prime minister and in this post advocated the formation of a new Chinese government under Wang Ching-wei and nonintervention in the war in Europe. Abe's cabinet failed to curb rampant inflation; other measures incurred the hostility of the Privy Council, Foreign Ministry, and Diet. Bereft of army support, the cabinet resigned in January 1940. Abe subsequently served as special envoy to China and in 1942 joined the House of Peers. His other official posts included the presidency of the Imperial Rule Assistance Political Association and from July 1944 the governorship of Korea.

Berger, G. M. *Parties Out of Power in Japan, 1931–1941* (Princeton, 1977).
Iwabuchi, T. "Japan's New Premier, General Nobuyuki Abe," *CJ* 8, no. 8 (Oct. 1939).
Shigemitsu, M. *Japan and Her Destiny* (London, 1958).

Abolition of the Domains (haihan chiken) 廃藩置県
During the Tokugawa period daimyō (feudal lords) ruled over semiautonomous areas known as *han* (domains), whose continuing existence after the Meiji Restoration was an obstacle to the creation of a centralized state. In 1869 many daimyō, following the lead of the ruling domains of Satsuma, Chōshū, Tosa, and Hizen, offered to surrender the domain registers to the emperor (*hanseki hōkan*), and the daimyō of all *han* subsequently became imperial governors of their former domains. The years 1869–1871 brought an increasing need for government intervention in the autonomy of the domains, and in August 1871 the prefectural system was extended to the whole of Japan (*haihan chiken*). Although something of a political gamble, the move met with relatively little opposition. The former daimyō were guaranteed stipend and nobility status, and the government took over the income and debts of the domain. The domains were replaced by urban districts (*fu*) and prefectures (*ken*) governed by officials sent out from Tokyo. This system of units of local administration under the central government had already been adopted in lands formerly held by the Tokugawa. In 1873 real local autonomy was virtually ended by the establishment of the new Home Ministry (*q.v.*), and in subsequent reorganizations the domains largely lost their identities.

Beasley, W. G. *The Meiji Restoration* (London, 1973).

Abolition of the Han. See ABOLITION OF THE DOMAINS; FEUDAL SYSTEM

Adachi Kenzō 1864–1948 安達謙蔵
Native of Kumamoto, in 1895 Adachi was involved in the murder of the Korean queen, Min, but was acquitted. He was a founder member of the Kumamoto National Party (Kokkentō). A member of the House of Representatives from 1902, from 1913 Adachi was active in the Rikken Dōshikai and later as a leading member of the Kenseikai and Minseitō. His political maneuverings caused him to be known as *senkyo no kamisama* (god of elections). Adachi was communications minister 1925–1927 and home minister 1929–1931, but his advocacy of a coalition cabinet after the Manchurian Incident split the Wakatsuki cabinet and helped bring it down. Adachi left the Minseitō and in 1932 formed and became president of the Kokumin Dōmei (National League).

Berger, G. M. *Parties Out of Power in Japan, 1931–1941* (Princeton, 1977).
Duus, P. *Party Rivalry and Political Change in Taishō Japan* (Cambridge, Mass., 1968).

Admonition to Soldiers and Sailors. See TAKEHASHI RISING

Advisory Council on Foreign Relations (Rinji Gaikō Chōsa Iinkai) 臨時外交調査委員会

In June 1917 the Terauchi cabinet, on the advice of Miura Gorō and Gotō Shinpei, established the Advisory Council on Foreign Relations in an attempt to unify the making of foreign policy and eliminate party strife over it. The council, which was directly responsible to the emperor, was presided over by the prime minister. Its membership comprised the home, foreign, war and navy ministers, three members of the Privy Council (Makino Nobuaki, Itō Miyoji, and Hirata Tōsuke), Hara Kei of the Seiyūkai, and Inukai Tsuyoshi of the Kokumintō. The Kenseikai leader, Katō Takaaki, refused to participate. The council was less influential after the war in view of Hara's large parliamentary majority, but it discussed the Siberian Intervention (*q.v.*) and had a strong voice in policy concerning the Versailles Peace Treaty (*q.v.*) and Washington Conference (*q.v.*). Until its abolition in September 1922, the council continued to be a forum where opposition leaders could be consulted, and it considerably restricted the foreign minister's influence in originating Japan's foreign policy.

Nish, I. H. *Japanese Foreign Policy, 1869–1942* (London, 1977).

Agrarianism. See NŌHONSHUGI

Agriculture

Agriculture was the main occupation during the Tokugawa period, with rice (*q.v.*) the major crop. In 1872 75% of the population was still engaged in farming, but by 1920 this proportion had fallen to 50%, and in 1977 to 19%. In 1975 farming households comprised 23 million people, of whom 13.5 million were engaged in agriculture, many of them part time. Reform of the land tax in the 1870s allowed peasants to possess land, and tax paid by cultivators still amounted to 60% of government income in 1894. Agricultural modernization after the Restoration increased yields although the actual growth rate of agriculture remains a matter of controversy. Products diversified (e.g., dairy products in Hokkaidō), and agriculture became more commercialized, but shortage of land, excess population, and the widespread cultivation of rice meant that plots remained small and intensively cultivated. During the Meiji period the agricultural sector was a source of labor, capital, and a potential market for industrialization, and it provided exports, especially raw silk (*q.v.*) (by 1913 one-third of total exports by value) in the early stages of industrialization. The difficulty of subsistence farming and heavy taxes created economic distress, leading to an increase in tenancy (by 1910 over 40% of land was tenanted) and fragmentation of land holdings. The rate of increase in agricultural production slowed after 1918, with population growth and rice imports marking a transition to an industrial economy. From 1920 rural areas increasingly suffered from a fall in the price of rice, and the situation was worsened by a slump in silk prices from the late 1920s. Rural distress was especially bad in northern areas, and awareness of intense rural poverty played a role in ultranationalist ideology both inside and outside the army. The postwar land reform (*q.v.*) increased agricultural efficiency, and technical change again increased rice production levels. Products have become much diversified, but in 1974 rice production, valued at ¥2,822,600 million, still amounted to 37% of agricultural production by value, followed by stock raising and then fruit and vegetables. Although the government has recently attempted to divert farmers into the production of other crops, continuing government subsidies for rice production suggest that its cultivation will remain profitable, but the increasing depopulation of farming villages is a matter of growing concern.

Hayami, Y. *A Century of Agricultural Growth in Japan* (Tokyo, 1975).
International Society for Educational

Information. *Postwar Japanese Agriculture* (Tokyo, 1973).
O.E.C.D. *Agricultural Policy in Japan* (Paris, 1974).

Aikoku Kōtō 愛国公党

The Aikoku Kōtō (Patriotic Public Party) was a political society founded in January 1874 by Itagaki Taisuke (*q.v.*) in Tokyo. Members included Gotō Shōjirō, Etō Shinpei, and Soejima Taneomi, all of whom had resigned from the government over the invasion of Korea (*q.v.*). The group advocated the equality of men and popular rights and submitted to the government a memorial for an elected assembly, but it had no popular support nor organizational structure and was soon disbanded. Itagaki founded a second political party of the same name in May 1890, but after the August 1890 election it merged with the Jiyūtō (*q.v.*) and the Daidō Club to form the Rikken Jiyūtō.

Cody, C. E. "A Study of the Career of Itagaki Taisuke, 1837–1919," Ph.D. diss., University of Washington, 1965.
Scalapino, R. A. *Democracy and the Party Movement in Prewar Japan* (Berkeley, 1967).

Aikokusha 愛国社

The Aikokusha was the name given to Japan's first national political party. It was founded at Osaka in February 1875 at a conference of local popular rights groups called by Itagaki Taisuke's Risshisha (*q.v.*). The Aikokusha's aim was constitutional parliamentary government. It resolved to establish a Tokyo headquarters and hold a biennial conference, but funds were nonexistent and membership very small, so with Itagaki's return to the government after the Osaka Conference (*q.v.*), the Aikokusha virtually ceased to exist. When the popular rights movement later spread among farmers, the Risshisha ressuscitated the Aikokusha; it held conferences in 1878 and 1879, and at the fourth conference in March 1880, where delegates claimed to represent 96 organizations with a total membership of over 98,000, the Aikokusha voted to initiate a nationwide petition movement and changed its name to Kokkai Kisei Dōmei (League for the Establishment of a Diet) (*q.v.*).

Ike, N. *The Beginnings of Political Democracy in Japan* (Baltimore, 1958).

Ainu

The indigenous population of Hokkaidō, the Ainu traded with Japanese during the Tokugawa period. Many were also hired as fishing labor and were frequently badly treated. From the early 19th century the Japanese adopted a sporadically executed assimilation policy, but the Ainu suffered through the post-Restoration reforms, and many fell into dire poverty. Their lack of any concept of the private ownership of land meant that under these reforms all communal land passed to the government, and the Ainu kept only the land on which they lived. With many Ainu forced to abandon hunting, this land proved insufficient to provide a living from farming. Increasingly, the Ainu also lost the special treatment they had received in the early years after the Restoration. Ainu numbers decreased rapidly in relation to Japanese immigrants. In 1873 the Ainu constituted 95% of Hokkaidō's population, but by 1897 this figure had fallen to only 22%. By 1900 only 17,500 Ainu remained; they failed even to maintain their numbers because of medical problems, especially alcoholism, tuberculosis, and venereal disease. Sporadic and unsuccessful attempts had been made to educate the Ainu, but these were largely dependent on missionaries. By the 1890s the state of the Ainu had become a topic of national discussion, which provoked the 1899 Ainu Protection Law. This law, which remained in force until 1937, rationalized the hitherto sporadic policies relating to the Ainu and had wide provisions relating to employment, relief, medical treatment, education, and communal property owning; nevertheless, it failed to make any fundamental difference to the condition of the Ainu. The government's basic policy remained assimilation, and this was mostly supported by the Ainu leaders. In 1937 the Ainu Protection Law was revised, abolishing land grants and special primary education for the Ainu, and other provisions were merged with general welfare legislation. In 1960 there were still some 17,000 Ainu, but few were pure-blooded. Ainu language and culture have undergone a severe decline, and the few remaining Ainu communities are now no more than tourist attractions.

"Ainu Rights," *JQ* 21, no. 3 (July-Sept. 1974).
Batchelor, J. *Ainu Life and Lore* (rprt. New York, 1971).
Hilger, M. I. *Together with the Ainu: A Vanishing People* (Norman, Okla., 1971).
Sala, G. C. "Protest and the Ainu of Hokkaido," *Japan Interpreter* 10, no. 1 (Summer 1975).
Takakura, S. "The Ainu of Northern Japan, a Study in Conquest and Acculturation," *Transactions of the American Philosophical Society* (1960).

Aizawa Incident (Aizawa jiken) 相沢事件

On 12 August 1935 Major-General Nagata Tetsuzan, head of the Military Affairs Bureau, was assassinated by Lieutenant-Colonel Aizawa Saburō. Aizawa had protested against the enforced resignation of Masaki Jinzaburō as inspector of military education earlier that year and had been posted to Formosa. A member of the *kōdō* faction (*q.v.*), he believed that Nagata was responsible both for Masaki's resignation and for other moves against the faction. Complicated by political factors, the trial was delayed by the February 26 Rising (*q.v.*), but Aizawa was eventually executed in July 1936.

Byas, H. *Government by Assassination* (London, 1943).
Storry, R. *The Double Patriots* (London, 1957).

Aizu 会津

Han in northeast Honshū now part of Fukushima Prefecture. During the last years of the Tokugawa period, Aizu, whose ruling family was related to the Tokugawa, was one of the Bakufu's strongest supporters. At the time of the coup of January 1868 the Aizu daimyō, Matsudaira Katamori, was military governor of Kyoto, and Aizu forces participated in the first Bakufu defeat at Toba-Fushimi. In May 1868 Aizu, supported by an alliance of northeastern *han*, became a focus of resistance to the imperial forces. The castle at its capital, Aizu-Wakamatsu, eventually fell in autumn 1868 after heavy Aizu losses; the domain was laid waste, and the Matsudaira family and retainers transferred to a small fief at the northern tip of Honshū, which proved inadequate to support them.

Bolitho, H. "Aizu, 1853–1868," in G. Daniels and P. Lowe, eds. *BAJS Proceedings* 2, pt. 1 (Sheffield, 1977).

Akahata Incident. See Red Flag Incident

Akita Incident (Akita jiken) 秋田事件

In spring 1881 members of the Akita Risshikai, a union of samurai and farmers formed in 1880 as part of the popular rights movement, devised a plot to overthrow the government. Under the leadership of Shibata Asagorō the group stole funds to carry out their conspiracy, but the plot was discovered and the participants convicted of treason. The national popular rights movement disclaimed any involvement in the plot.

Alcock, Sir Rutherford 1809–1897

After serving as a consul in China, Alcock arrived in Japan in 1859 to head the British diplomatic mission. With Townsend Harris (*q.v.*) he played a major role in the early development of Japan's foreign relations as well as in promoting British interests in Japan and became one of the most influential of the foreign diplomatic representatives of the time. Alcock went to England on leave in March 1862, but on his return to Japan in March 1864 he strongly urged the bombardment of Shimonoseki (*q.v.*). He was recalled later in 1864 but was British minister in China 1865–1871.

Alcock, R. *The Capital of the Tycoon: A Narrative of Three Years' Residence in Japan*, 2 vols. (London, 1863).
Beasley, W. G. *Select Documents on Japanese Foreign Policy, 1853–1868* (London, 1967).
McMaster, J. "Alcock and Harris: Foreign Diplomacy in Bakumatsu Japan," *MN* 22, nos. 3–4 (1967).

All Japan General Federation of Labor. See LABOR MOVEMENT

All Japan Industrial Labor Unions Conference. See LABOR MOVEMENT

All Japan Labor Unions Conference. See LABOR MOVEMENT

All Japan Proletarian Youth League. See YOUTH ORGANIZATIONS

Allied Council for Japan (Rengōkoku Tainichi Rijikai) 連合国対日理事会
The allied foreign ministers conference in Moscow in December 1945 established the Allied Council for Japan, which was to meet in Tokyo. Consisting of representatives from the U.S., U.S.S.R., Nationalist China, and the British Commonwealth and chaired by SCAP (*q.v.*) or his representative, the council was to consult with and advise SCAP over the implementation of surrender terms and the Occupation and administration of Japan. From April 1946 two meetings a month were held, and in the early stages of the Occupation the council played an active part in promoting such matters as land reform (*q.v.*), but its establishment had been opposed by Douglas MacArthur, who rarely attended after the first meeting, and the exercise of its function was hindered both by his obstructiveness and by increasing U.S.-U.S.S.R. mistrust. The San Francisco Peace Treaty brought its existence to an end.

Ball, W. M. *Japan, Enemy or Ally?* (New York, 1949).
Daniels, G. "Nationalist China in the Allied Council: Policies Toward Japan, 1946–1952," *Hokkaidō Law Review* 27, no. 2 (Nov. 1976).

Allied Powers GHQ. See SCAP

Amakasu Incident. See ŌSUGI SAKAE

Amamiya Silk Mill Dispute (Amamiya Seishi sōgi) 雨宮製糸争議
In February 1886 the owners of 73 silk mills in the Kōfu (Yamanashi) area employing some 4,500 female workers formed an organization to tighten their joint control over their labor force. The resulting attempt to enforce harsher working conditions provoked over 100 women at the Amamiya mill, one of the largest in the area, into refusing to work until conditions were improved. The withdrawal of labor on 14 June 1886 is regarded as Japan's first factory strike. The dispute was ended in two days by the employer's granting concessions, and it triggered off a succession of similar disputes in the area. But its significance was small and localized; its importance lies in its existence as a historical event rather than as the precursor of a successful and organized labor movement.

Amur River Society. See KOKURYŪKAI

Ana-Boru Dispute. See ANARCHISM

Anarchism
Anarchist ideas were first openly expounded in Japan by Kōtoku Shūsui after 1905; he rejected authority and argued that socialism must be achieved through direct action of organized workers since the Diet would always be the weapon of the propertied classes. A split within the Socialist movement followed between anarchists and social democrats. The dominant form of anarchism in Japan was anarcho-syndicalism; adherents aimed at the liberation of the working class but did not recognize parliamentary activity and the leadership of political parties, instead wishing to bring down capitalism by direct action of unions through general strikes, boycotts, and sabotage. They also regarded organized workers at plant level as the basic unit not only of revolutionary struggle but also of production and distribution in any new society. After Kōtoku's death in 1911, the anarcho-syndicalist group was led by Ōsugi Sakae, and his doctrines dominated the labor movement 1921–1922. After the Russian Revolution the popularity of Bolshevik ideas grew, and by 1922 a conflict between the Bolsheviks and anarcho-syndicalists had split the labor and Socialist movements. This was the so-called Ana-Boru dispute. The anarcho-syndicalists still rejected the leadership of political parties, advocating a loose confederation based on autonomous plant unions and direct economic action through strikes to achieve workers' control over production. The Bolsheviks advocated the building of strong united labor organizations, obtaining public support, and raising political issues. The split was worsened by the anarchists' problems in the Soviet Union and the anarchists' use of offensive tactics in a period of recession. After the founding of the Japan Communist Party and the murder of Ōsugi in 1923, anarcho-syndicalism yielded its dominance of the labor movement to communism. Government suppression meant the loss of successive leaders, and with the manifest failure of anarcho-syndicalism as a revolutionary tactic, as opposed to the obvious success of Bolshevism, it lost most of its influence. In 1926 there occurred a split between anarchists and syndicalists, and they have not reemerged as a united movement. Postwar activities by anarchists have been minimal despite some revival among the Zengakuren (*q.v.*) from 1958.

Notehelfer, F. G. *Kōtoku Shūsui: Portrait of a Japanese Radical* (Cambridge, 1971).
Totten, G. O. *The Social Democratic Movement in Prewar Japan* (New Haven, 1966).

Anarcho-Syndicalism. See ANARCHISM

Anglo-Japanese Alliance (Nichiei Dōmei) 日英同盟
Some Japanese, notably Itō Hirobumi, wished for a Russian alliance to effect a local compromise over Russo-Japanese relations, and the Germans had pushed for a triple alliance with Britain and Japan, but following negotiations between Hayashi Tadasu, Japanese envoy in London, and Lord Lansdowne an Anglo-Japanese alliance was concluded, to be effective from 30 January 1902. The terms of the alliance recognized a common interest in opposing Russian expansion, promising mutual help for the preservation of U. K. rights and interests in China, and of Japan's interests in China and Korea. If either signatory power engaged in hostilities with one power in the Far East area, the other would remain neutral, but hostilities with two or more powers would oblige the other signatory power to participate. The treaty's term was five years. The British regarded the alliance as an end to "Splendid Isolation" and a warning to Russia; the Japanese regarded it as a triumph, putting her on an equal footing with the great powers and enabling her to fight Russia without fear of Russia's invoking her alliance with France. In August 1905 the alliance terms were revised and broadened to provide for the defense of British interests in India and a more precise recognition of Japan's hegemony in Korea, and its term was ex-

tended to 10 years. Improved relations with Russia, deteriorating relations with Germany, and Japan's annexation of Korea rendered further revision desirable, and renewal in 1911 also excluded the U. S. from the sphere of application. Japan invoked the alliance in order to declare war on Germany in 1914. It remained legally in force until the effecting of the Washington Four-Power Treaty, which replaced it in August 1923.

Lowe, P. C. *Great Britain and Japan, 1911–1915* (London, 1969).
Nish, I. H. *Alliance in Decline* (London, 1972).
______. *The Anglo-Japanese Alliance: The Diplomacy of Two Island Empires* (London, 1966).
Pooley, A. M. *Secret Memoirs of Count Tadasu Hayashi* (London, 1915).

Annexation of Korea. See KOREA, COLONY OF

Anpo. See U.S.-JAPAN SECURITY TREATY

Ansei Purge (Ansei no Taigoku) 安政の大獄
A series of measures carried out by Ii Naosuke 1858–1859 to suppress powerful rivals and opponents inside and outside the Bakufu. Opposition had centered on the twin problems of the shōgunal succession dispute (*q.v.*) and conclusion of the U. S.-Japan Treaty of Amity and Commerce (*q.v.*). Ii removed from office many of his main opponents within the Bakufu; he forced daimyō from both *fudai* and *tozama han* into retirement and banned Hitotsubashi Keiki from public life. The purge extended to the court, members of the antiforeign, pro-emperor movement and others connected with the Hitotsubashi party. Over 100 people were affected and eight executed, including Yoshida Shōin.

Beasley, W. G. *The Meiji Restoration* (London, 1973).

Ansei Treaties. See U. S.-JAPAN TREATY OF AMITY AND COMMERCE

Anti-Bakufu Movement (Tōbaku undō) 討幕運動
The downfall of the Bakufu and restoration of power to the emperor was in many ways the logical corollary of *sonnō* (*q.v.*) ideas, and the term *anti-Bakufu movement* embraces both those who, during the 1860s, aimed at the overthrow of the Tokugawa regime by force (the *tōbaku* [destroy the Bakufu] faction) and those who wished for a peaceful transference of the responsibility for national rule from Bakufu to emperor. From the early 1860s Chōshū openly defied the Bakufu, but it was only after the conclusion of an alliance in 1866 with Satsuma, which had hitherto advocated *kōbu gattai* (*q.v.*) policies, that successful armed struggle to overthrow the Bakufu became a possibility. Advocates of peaceful transition, led by Tosa, achieved the shōgun's resignation late in 1867, but Satsuma and Chōshū, and other more hostile to the Bakufu, seized power at court, and their victory in the subsequent hostilities gave them dominance in the new government.

Beasley, W. G. *The Meiji Restoration* (London, 1973).
Craig, A. *Chōshū in the Meiji Restoration* (Cambridge, Mass., 1961).
Harootunian, H. *Toward Restoration* (Berkeley, 1970).
Jansen, M. B. *Sakamoto Ryōma and the Meiji Restoration* (Princeton, 1961).

Anti-Bolshevism League (Sekka Bōshidan) 赤化防止団
Violent right-wing group founded October 1922 by lawyer and Kokuryūkai member Yonemura Kaichirō. The league aimed at the eradication of socialism and had branches throughout the country carrying on "patriotic" campaigns and intimidating strikers and leftist organizations. Its membership never exceeded 2,000, and in 1923 Yonemura stabbed to death a Communist who had attacked the

league's headquarters, and he was imprisoned. The group soon afterwards ceased to exist, but there is a postwar organization of the same name. It is also known as the Anti-Red League.

Storry, R. *The Double Patriots* (London, 1959).
Tanin, O., and E. Yohan. *Militarism and Fascism in Japan* (London, 1934).

Anti-Comintern Pact (Nichidokui Bōkyō Kyōtei) 日独伊防共協定
Concluded in Berlin between Japan and Germany 25 November 1936. In Japan there was strong army pressure to conclude the pact, and a leading role was played by Ōshima Hiroshi, Japan's military attaché in Berlin. The two countries agreed to exchange information concerning the Comintern and to take measures to oppose its activities. A secret additional protocol provided for mutual consultation and the cessation of activity beneficial to the U.S.S.R. by one signatory should the other open hostilities with Russia. The pact was extended in November 1937 to include Italy. For Japan the pact was a step away from her international isolation since the Manchurian Incident (*q.v.*) and toward the Tripartite Pact (*q.v.*) of 1940.

Boyd, C. "The Role of Hiroshi Oshima in the Preparation of the Anti-Comintern Pact," *JAH* 11, no. 1 (1977).
Ikle, F. W. *German-Japanese Relations, 1936–1940* (New York, 1956).
Ohata, T. "The Anti-Comintern Pact, 1935–1939," in J. W. Morley, ed., *Deterrent Diplomacy: Japan, Germany, and the U.S.S.R., 1935–1940* (New York, 1976).
Presseisen, E. L. *Germany and Japan: A Study in Totalitarian Diplomacy, 1933–1941* (The Hague, 1958).

Anti-Japanese Movement (China)
The first boycott of Japanese goods by the Chinese was in 1908, but from 1914 anti-Japanese feeling expressed in boycotts and demonstrations gained momentum in response to such incidents as Japan's occupation of former German concessions in China (1914), the Twenty-One Demands (1915) (*q.v.*), and the Nishihara Loans (*q.v.*). After 1918 Chinese students returning en masse from Japan in protest and resentment at the failure of China's calls at the Paris Peace Conference for cancellation of the Twenty-One Demands and return of the Shantung Peninsula initiated the so-called May 4 Movement when demonstrations, boycotts, and strikes prevented China's signing the peace treaty. From the early 1920s Japan shifted toward a policy of economic infiltration, and tariff disputes led to strikes in Japanese-owned plants 1925–1926. The 1927 Shantung Expeditions (*q.v.*) marked the revival of more open Japanese intervention in Chinese affairs, and attempts to organize a nationwide boycott of Japanese goods inflicted severe economic damage on Japan. The Chinese populace was further inflamed by the Wanpaoshan Incident of July 1931, when a dispute between local Korean and Chinese farmers in Wanpaoshan, Manchuria, led to anti-Chinese riots in Korea. After the Manchurian Incident (*q.v.*) Shanghai became the center of an increasingly strong nationwide movement of strikes and boycotts, but continuing Japanese encroachments gradually led the Chinese to try to resist further aggression by force. Initially the Kuomintang government gave little strong support to the resistance movement, preferring to fight its internal battle against the Communists before tackling Japan, but it was pressurized by increasing Chinese nationalism and worsening Japanese aggression; in 1937 a united front to oppose the Japanese was formed after the kidnapping of Chiang Kai-shek at Sian. The Chinese Communist Party had been the dominant element in the anti-Japanese movement in Manchuria since 1935. The united military front against Japan was in principle maintained until 1945.

Chow, T. T. *The May Fourth Movement: Intellectual Revolution in Modern China* (Cambridge, Mass., 1960).

Coox, A. D., and H. Conroy eds. *China and Japan: Search for Balance Since World War I* (Santa Barbara, 1978).
Jansen, M. B. *China and Japan* (Chicago, 1975).

Anti-Japanese Movement (Korea). See KOREAN INDEPENDENCE MOVEMENT

Antimonopoly Law. See ZAIBATSU DISSOLUTION

Antinuclear Movement. See PEACE MOVEMENT

Anti-Red League. See ANTI-BOLSHEVISM LEAGUE

April 16 Arrests. See JAPAN COMMUNIST PARTY

Arahata Kanson (Katsuzō) 1887–1981 荒畑寒村(勝三)
Native of Yokohama, Arahata became interested in socialism and in 1904 joined the Heiminsha (*q.v.*). Remaining active in the Socialist movement after the Heiminsha's demise, he was influenced by Kōtoku Shūsui and turned to anarcho-syndicalism; imprisoned after the 1908 Red Flag Incident (*q.v.*), he subsequently published the journal *Kindai Shisō* (Modern Thought) with Ōsugi Sakae. Turning to Bolshevism in 1922, he sat on the first central committee of the new Japan Communist Party; he was subsequently imprisoned several times for his adherence. He opposed the dissolution of the party in 1924 and subsequently broke with it because of his opposition to Fukumotoism (*q.v.*), becoming a leading figure in the Rōnō faction in the debate over Japanese capitalism. He moved away from communism toward social democracy and was arrested late 1937 for united front activities. In 1946–1948 he was a member of the central executive committee of the Japan Socialist Party and a Diet member 1946–1949, but he left politics to spend his time as a writer and critic. His works include histories of the Socialist and labor movements in Japan and translations into Japanese.

Beckmann, G. M., and G. Okubo. *The Japanese Communist Party, 1922–1945* (Stanford, 1969).
Colbert, E. *The Left Wing in Japanese Politics* (New York, 1952).

Araki Sadao 1877–1966 (Baron, 1935) 荒木貞夫
Native of Tokyo, graduating from the Military Academy, Araki held various army posts including those of military attaché in Russia and section head at the General Staff. Briefly inspector-general of military education in 1931, he became war minister the same year, retaining the post until his resignation in 1934 on grounds of ill health; he was subsequently appointed to the Supreme Military Council. As war minister Araki conducted a major army reshuffle, establishing members of his own personal clique in dominant positions; he took a strong stand on the matter of the military budget and supported the establishment of an independent Manchurian state. Strongly identified with the reform movement among the young officers, he was regarded as one of the leaders of the *kōdō* faction (*q.v.*) and was placed on the reserve list in 1936 after the February 26 Rising (*q.v.*). As minister of education under Konoe and Hiranuma 1938–1939 Araki reinforced the military slant of education and culture. Tried after the war as a class "A" war criminal, he was sentenced to life imprisonment but was released in 1955 due to illness.

Fukuda, I. "Araki—the Man of the Crisis," *CJ* 1, no. 3, (Dec. 1932).
Shillony, B. A. *Revolt in Japan: The Young Officers and the February 26, 1936, Incident* (Princeton, 1973).
Williston, H. "General Araki's Contribution to Japanese Militarism and Ultra-Nationalism in the 1930s," M.A. thesis, University of California, 1951.

Army

An imperial guard (*goshinpei*, later *ko-noehei*) for the personal protection of the emperor and under his command was formed by volunteers from Satsuma, Chōshū, and Tosa in 1871, but the basis of Japan's modern army was established by the introduction of conscription after 1872. Initially organized for domestic security, members of the army inherited the prestige formerly accruing to samurai, and the army became an instrument of national unity. Influenced by French and German models, a separate War Ministry was established in 1872 to be headed by someone of at least major-general rank. In 1878 a new independent General Staff took over military command matters, leaving military administration to the War Ministry. Major reforms at this time led to the formation of a professional military establishment in the 1880s, although initial Chōshū dominance of the army was only very slowly eroded. The Meiji constitution placed the army outside Diet and cabinet control by making the emperor supreme commander of the armed forces and by recognizing the right of military leaders to appeal directly to the throne. A supreme military council and military advisers were appointed to advise the emperor. Matters such as martial law lay outside the jurisdiction of the regular courts. In 1898 the Department of Military Education (Kyōiku Sōkanbu) was established. The army controlled various educational establishments including preparatory schools, specialist colleges, the War College, and the Military Academy (1873), whose graduates became the officer elite. It also controlled factories engaged in military production. During time of war an imperial headquarters (*daihon'ei*) was established, directly responsible to the emperor; this happened in 1894–1895, 1904–1905, and 1937–1945. By 1894 the strength of the army was seven divisions; victories gave it increasing prestige, and by 1907 there were 19, but attempts to expand further contributed to the Taishō Political Crisis (*q.v.*), and further expansion came only during the 1914–1918 war. Pressure for disarmament reduced the army's strength to 17 divisions (250,000 men) in 1925, but tanks, artillery, and planes were invested in and considerable rationalization and modernization took place. The army grew from the late 1920s, and in 1945 there were nearly 200 divisions comprising over 5½ million men. From the start the army played an important role in spreading not only practical skills and knowledge but also nationalist ideology. Under the influence of Yamagata Aritomo the army developed as a stronghold of conservative and nationalist values, and after 1900 its political influence increased. In 1900 it was stipulated that the war minister must be a general on the active list, and although this provision was abolished in 1913, it was reintroduced in 1936. At all times the war minister was in a difficult position between army and cabinet. From the 1920s the three most important figures in the army, the war minister, the chief of staff, and the inspector-general of military education, consulted on the appointment of a war minister, and in effect the army could bring a cabinet down by a refusal to appoint a representative. In conjunction with the so-called "independence of the supreme command"—the fact that the command function was potentially free of political checks applied through the cabinet—this gave the army a base for extending its influence into nonmilitary affairs. Although in the Meiji period there had been strict limitations imposed on the military's involvement in politics, the growth of radicalism among younger officers from the 1920s and the legal independence of the military from civilian authority stimulated it to play an increasingly dominant role in national politics. The civilian authorities had no say in the affairs of the military. Independent army moves in Manchuria in the early 1930s indicated that civilian governments were unable to dictate foreign policy. Military influence throughout the country was helped by three decades of inculcation of conservative and nationalist values through the Imperial Reservists' Association (*q.v.*) and other local organizations, and also by military training for all those above middle-school age, which was introduced in 1925 partly to alleviate military unemployment due to disarmament. Despite internal dissent, after 1936 the army achieved considerable control of foreign and domestic policymaking, and its authority was not challenged until the closing stages of the war. The army and those institutions connected with it were disbanded by the Occupation authorities, and military forces were disallowed under the 1947 constitution. The Self-Defense Force (*q.v.*) has since been established.

Crowley, J. B. "From Closed Door to Empire: The Formation of the Meiji Military Establishment," in B. S. Silberman and H. Harootunian, eds., *Modern Japanese Leadership* (Tucson, 1966).
______. "Japan's Military Foreign Policies," in J. W. Morley, ed., *Japan's Foreign Policy, 1868–1941: A Research Guide* (New York, 1974).
Hackett, R. F. "The Military: Japan," in R. E. Ward and D. Rustow, eds., *Political Modernization in Japan and Turkey* (Princeton, 1964).
______. *Yamagata Aritomo in the Rise of Modern Japan, 1838–1922* (Cambridge, Mass., 1971).
Presseisen, E. L. *Before Aggression* (Tucson, 1965).
Smethurst, R. J. *A Social Basis for Prewar Japanese Militarism* (Berkeley, 1974).

Asahi Shinbun. See NEWSPAPERS

Asano Sōichirō 1848–1930
浅野総一郎

A samurai from Toyama region, in 1871 Asano went to Tokyo after failing in business at home. Possessing no capital, he engaged in the sale of coke and firewood. He developed contacts with Shibusawa Eiichi, and with his help rented and later purchased (1884) the government-owned, loss-making Fukagawa Cement Works. Renamed Asano Cement, the business prospered with the assistance of government orders, and from there Asano, known as the "Cement King," diversified his interests. An almost reckless innovator, much of his financial support came from Yasuda Zenjirō. By his death Asano had built up a huge business empire founded on cement, metals, and shipping interests. After 1918 the business was controlled by a family partnership and known as one of the smaller *zaibatsu*, but unlike most *zaibatsu* builders Asano's attempts at banking were unsuccessful, and much of the funding continued to be done through the Yasuda group. After a decline in the 1920s the concern revived after the Manchurian Incident and at its peak controlled (directly or indirectly) 87 companies with capital of ¥500 million. Postwar connections between the various companies were dissolved, but many of them remain influential.

Hirschmeier, J. *The Origins of Entrepreneurship in Meiji Japan* (Cambridge, Mass., 1964).

Asano Zaibatsu. See ASANO SŌICHIRŌ

Ashida Hitoshi 1887–1959 芦田均

Native of Kyoto, Ashida graduated from Tokyo Imperial University and entered the Foreign Ministry but resigned after the Manchurian Incident over policy disagreements. He then entered the Diet as a Seiyūkai member. Despite his opposition to militarist policies, Ashida was elected nine times subsequently, including once in 1942 as a non-government-sponsored candidate. He also lectured at Keiō University and was president of the *Japan Times* 1933–1940. In 1945 he became minister of welfare. He subsequently helped Hatoyama to form the Japan Liberal Party but in March 1947 participated in the founding of the Democratic Party, of which he became president in May. Advocating moderate policies, he cooperated with the Socialist Party and in June 1947 became foreign minister and deputy prime minister under Katayama. In March 1948 he succeeded Katayama as prime minister, heading a coalition cabinet of Democratic Party, Socialist Party, and Kokumin Kyōdōtō (National Cooperative Party) members. Ashida promoted the import of foreign capital to aid economic recovery and vigorously opposed communism. On the orders of SCAP he removed the right of strike and collective bargaining from public and government unions. However, Ashida's cooperation with the Socialists alienated the conservative wing of his own party; the Socialists also became divided, and the cabinet resigned in October 1948 over accusations of corruption among cabinet members in connection with the Shōwa Electrical Company. Ashida himself was acquitted in 1958. He remained active in politics during the early 1950s but spent much of his time writing on diplomatic history, notably a history of World War II.

Colbert, E. S. *The Left Wing in Japanese Politics* (New York, 1952).
Quigley, H. S., and J. E. Turner *The New Japan* (Minneapolis, 1956).
Yamaura, K. "Prime Minister Hitoshi Ashida: Portrayal," *CJ* 17, nos. 1–3 (Jan.-Mar. 1948).

Ashio Copper Mine 足尾銅山
In Tochigi Prefecture. Owned by the Bakufu in the Tokugawa period, in 1877 the mine was taken over by Furukawa Ichibei and subsequently became the focal enterprise of his mining empire. Furukawa undertook mechanization and management reforms, and by the later Meiji period the mine was producing over 40% of Japan's total copper production; a large proportion was exported. From the 1880s the mine was notorious as a source of pollution. Effluent in the Watarase and Tone rivers killed fish, massive deforestation led to widespread flooding with polluted waters, and the livelihood of many was threatened. A petition movement for the mine to be closed was led in the Diet by Tanaka Shōzō from 1891, but it had little effect, and pollution worsened. Renewed protest from 1897 led to mass demonstrations in Tokyo, on occasion bringing clashes with police, and the pollution became a national issue. The government directed the mine to enforce the antipollution measures agreed in 1897, but results were slow. In December 1901 Tanaka made a direct appeal to the throne. The protest movement subsequently declined although the Copper Pollution Law, which was passed, proved inadequate. Due to the pollution problem and to fierce labor disputes in the late Meiji and Taishō periods, the mine's production declined, and copper ceased to be mined at Ashio in 1973.

Notehelfer, F. G. "Japan's First Pollution Incident," *JJS* 1, no. 2 (Spring 1975).
Strong, K. *Ox Against the Storm* (Tenterden, Kent, 1977).
———. "Tanaka Shōzō: Meiji Hero and Pioneer Against Pollution," *Japan Society of London Bulletin* 67 (June 1972).

Asō Hisashi 1891–1940 麻生久
A farmer's son from Ōita Prefecture, Asō read law at Tokyo University, where he became interested in socialism. After graduating, he became a reporter, but in 1919 he joined the Yūaikai (*q.v.*) as head of its mining section and founded a national organization for miners. He participated in the Shinjinkai (*q.v.*). He was subsequently among the leaders of the Sōdōmei and active in the proletarian party movement where he was among the leadership of moderate parties such as the Nihon Rōnōtō (Japan Labor Farmer Party) of 1926, the Nihon Taishūtō (Japan Masses' Party), and the Shakai Taishūtō. He was elected to the Diet in 1936. From the early 1930s he began to support alignment with reformist elements and the army to oppose the existing political parties and to move toward support of the war. This made him willing to cooperate with Konoe in forming a single, national renovationist party, and he was actively participating in the New Structure Movement (*q.v.*) at the time of his death.

Wray, W. D. "Asō Hisashi and the Search for Renovation in the 1930s," *HPJ* 5 (1970).

Atomic Bomb. See HIROSHIMA; NAGASAKI

Automobile Industry. See CAR INDUSTRY

Ayukawa Yoshisuke. See NISSAN ZAIBATSU

B

Baba Tatsui 1850–1888 馬場辰猪
Member of a Tosa samurai family, in 1866–1870 Baba studied at Keiō and in 1870–1878 in England, where he concentrated on law. During this stay he wrote a Japanese grammar (*Nihongo Bunten*), organized an association of Japanese students, and advocated treaty revision, writing *The Treaty Between Japan and England* and *The English in Japan*. After his return he became active in the popular rights movement. He became vice-president of the Jiyūtō in 1881 but resigned in 1882 over Itagaki's trip abroad. He wrote in the *Kyōson Zasshi* (Live and Let Live), the *Jiyū Shinbun*, and the *Chōya Shinbun*. He was interested in legal education, founding the Meiji Gijuku, and started a legal advice bureau. In 1885 he was detained for six months on an explosives charge and on acquittal in June 1886 went to America, where he died in Philadelphia.

Soviak, E. "An Early Meiji Intellectual in Politics: Baba Tatsui and the Jiyūtō," in B. S. Silberman and H. D. Harootunian, eds., *Modern Japanese Leadership* (Tucson, 1966).

Baibunsha. See SAKAI TOSHIHIKO

Bakufu-Han System. See TOKUGAWA BAKUFU

Bakuhan System. See TOKUGAWA BAKUFU

Banchōkai. See IMPERIAL RAYON SCANDAL

Banking
Exchange companies had existed in the Tokugawa period, and in the early Meiji period many quasi-banks and exchange companies carried on small-scale banking and related activities. The word *bank* (*ginkō*) was used first in 1876 by Mitsui and subsequently by other private banking institutions. In 1872 the government, with the aim of setting up an American-style banking system and also assisting the samurai class, passed regulations to encourage the establishment of currency-issuing national banks, but only after the regulations were modified in 1876 did national banks develop on any scale; they remained highly dependent on government funds. Under Matsukata Masayoshi, banking policy shifted toward adoption of an English model. The Bank of Japan was established in 1882, and eventually all note issue was centralized. Under the 1890 Banking Regulations all other banks ultimately became ordinary banks. National banks had disappeared by 1899. In addition, the government established special banks to promote specific aims, such as the Yokohama Specie Bank (started business 1880) to finance foreign trade and the Japan Hypothec Bank (1896) for long-term investment in industry and agriculture. Overall banks were important in funding productive activity, especially in industry, because little capital was raised elsewhere, but the degree of their contribution to economic development remains a matter of controversy. Banks played a crucial role in *zaibatsu*

development (*q.v.*), and some grew to a great size, but there remained many small banks vulnerable in times of financial panic. After the 1927 financial crisis (*q.v.*) the government passed the Bank Law to control banking activities; its provisions included a prohibition on banks with under ¥1 million capital. Special banks were abolished by the Occupation authorities, but otherwise banks were little affected by the reforms. They continue to play an extremely influential role in funding economic activity of all kinds (relatively little capital is raised on the open market) and in forging links between various enterprises. Some bank specialization in function has also recurred.

Patrick, H. "Japan 1868–1914," in R. Cameron, ed., *Banking in the Early Stages of Industrialization* (New York, 1967).
Pressnell, L. S., ed. *Money and Banking in Japan* (London, 1973).
Yamamura, K. "Japan 1868–1930," in R. Cameron, ed., *Banking and Economic Development* (New York, 1972).

Bansho Torishirabejo. See KAISEIJO

Besshi Copper Mine. See SUMITOMO ZAIBATSU

Bikini Incident (Bikini hibaku jiken) ビキニ被爆事件
On 1 March 1954 the U.S. exploded a hydrogen bomb at Bikini Atoll in the Marshall Islands. The crew of a Japanese fishing vessel 125 miles (200 kilometers) from the site, outside the designated danger area, all suffered from radiation sickness. One man died, and hundreds of tons of contaminated fish had to be destroyed. Although legal responsibility for the damage was not assigned, the U.S. government awarded $2 million compensation in January 1955. This incident, in conjunction with uncertainty caused by further tests, caused considerable anxiety to the Japanese and provided a stimulus to the peace movement, especially that element of it calling for a ban on nuclear weapons. Nuclear tests in the Pacific also harmed Japanese interests by making certain fishing areas out of bounds.

Lapp, R. E. *The Voyage of the Lucky Dragon* (New York, 1958).
Tanaka, S. "'Death Ash': Experience of 23 Japanese Fishermen," *JQ* 2, no. 1 (Jan.–Mar. 1955).

Black Dragon Society. See KOKURYŪKAI

Blood League Incident (Ketsumeidan jiken) 血盟団事件
After the failure of the October Incident (*q.v.*) Inoue Nisshō organized a terrorist group known as the Blood League (Ketsumeidan). The group, which mostly consisted of young peasants from Ibaragi, took an oath to eliminate those public figures whom they regarded as having betrayed their country internationally or as having enriched themselves at the expense of farmers and peasants. The league had connections with the naval group which carried out the May 15 Incident (*q.v.*). Their slogan was "one man, one death." On 9 February 1932 Inoue Junnosuke, Minseitō leader and former finance minister, was shot dead, and on March 5 the same fate befell Dan Takuma, managing director of Mitsui enterprises. The assassins' arrest revealed the league's existence, and 14 members were arrested, including Inoue. He and three others were sentenced to life imprisonment, the rest to shorter terms.

Butow, R. *Tojo and the Coming of War* (Stanford, 1961).
Storry, R. *The Double Patriots* (London, 1957).

Bluestocking Society. See SEITŌSHA

Boissonade, Gustave Emile 1825–1910
Boissonade taught law at Grenoble and Paris universities and came to Japan in 1873 on the invitation of the Japanese

government. He pioneered Western legal education in Japan, teaching French legal theory, criminal and civil law. A strong adherent of natural law theories, Boissonade advised the government on legal aspects of both domestic and foreign affairs; he also drafted new criminal and civil codes on the French pattern, but the latter was never implemented. He was active in the movement to abolish torture and opposed the presence of foreign judges in Japanese courts as envisaged by the treaty revision proposals of 1887. From the late 1880s Prussian legal theories became influential in Japan, and Boissonade returned to France in 1895.

Von Mehren, A. T. *Law in Japan* (Cambridge, Mass., 1963).

Bombardment of Kagoshima. See NAMAMUGI INCIDENT

Bombardment of Shimonoseki

Following the Bakufu's failure to expel all foreigners by June 1863, as it had agreed to do under pressure from the court, Chōshū immediately initiated attacks on Western ships passing through the straits of Shimonoseki. The attacks persisted despite U.S. and French retaliation against the Shimonoseki forts, and in summer 1864 ships from Great Britain, the U.S., France, and Holland bombarded the forts and landed troops. A peace agreement was quickly signed between Chōshū and the powers, and the event marked a shift of emphasis in domain policies away from antiforeignism toward a single-minded opposition to the Bakufu.

Craig, A. *Chōshū in the Meiji Restoration* (Cambridge, Mass., 1961).
Satow, E. *A Diplomat in Japan* (London, 1921).

Bonin Islands (Ogasawara Shotō)
小笠原諸島

Known by the Japanese as the Ogasawara Islands, the Bonins are a chain of islands running due south of Tokyo Bay. Almost uninhabited until the 19th century, from the 1820s British and U.S. colonists lived on the islands. A Japanese colony was started in 1861. Both Bakufu and Meiji government asserted Japanese ownership of the islands, which were a center for sugar growing and fishing, and these claims were eventually recognized by Britain and the U.S. In 1875 Japan declared ownership of the islands, and in 1880 they were placed under the jurisdiction of the Tokyo metropolitan authorities. Most of the islanders left for the mainland during 1945, and after Japan's defeat the rest were also forcibly removed there. The islands were placed under U.S. military control, which under the San Francisco Peace Treaty was replaced by American exercise of U.N. trusteeship, although Japan's residual sovereignty was recognized. Only those with Western ancestry were permitted to return to live in the islands, and during the 1960s there was increasing agitation for the islands' return to Japan. An agreement for their return was signed between Japan and the U.S. in April 1968 and took effect in June. The islands are again part of the Tokyo local government area.

Cholmondely, L. B. *The History of the Bonin Islands, 1827–1876* (London, 1915).
Kublin, H. "The Ogasawara Venture (1861–1863)," *Harvard Journal of Asiatic Studies* 14 (1951).
Mendel, D. H. *The Japanese People and Foreign Policy* (Berkeley, 1961).

Boshin War (Boshin sensō)
戊辰戦争

Name given to the 1868–1869 civil war between former supporters of the Bakufu and troops of the anti-Bakufu movement fighting to unify the country in the name of the emperor. In January 1868 a court decree stripped the shōgun of his title and lands, and Tokugawa Keiki withdrew to Osaka with his forces. On January 26 forces from Aizu and Kuwana *han* (without the shōgun's permission) marched on Kyoto, determined to subdue Satsuma and the other "rebels." The following day they clashed with Satsuma and Chōshū forces at Toba-Fushimi. Although outnumbered three to one by the Bakufu force of 15,000, the "imperial" troops drove the Bakufu's supporters back toward Osaka, achieving victory in the first battle of the war. His support waning, the shōgun withdrew to Edo. In May, following negotiations between Saigō Takamori and Katsu Kaishū, he surrendered Edo castle without a fight to the newly formed "imperial" army, although the elite of the old shōgunate army, the Shōgitai, held out for several weeks at Ueno. The strongest resistance came from an alliance of northeastern *han* led by Aizu (*q.v.*), which yielded only in November after bitter fighting and considerable devastation. Enomoto Takeaki pursued isolated resistance in Hokkaidō until July 1869. The foreign powers maintained neutrality in the fighting.

Daniels, G. "The Japanese Civil War (1868)—A British View," *MAS* 1 (July 1967).
Satow, E. *A Diplomat in Japan* (London, 1921).
Sheldon, C. D. "The Politics of the Civil War of 1868," in W. G. Beasley, ed., *Modern Japan: Aspects of History, Literature, and Society* (London, 1975).

Boxer Rebellion (Giwadan undō)
義和団運動

After the Sino-Japanese War (*q.v.*) antiforeign resentment increased in China, and the activities of the Boxers, a violent antiforeign group who attacked missionaries, converts, and Chinese with foreign connections, spread in the last years of the century. By 1900 the movement threatened Peking. In June members laid siege to the Peking legations, killing the German ambassador. The empress dowager at first supported the movement and declared war on the powers but then, fearing antidynastic tendencies, tried to suppress it. A seven-power force whose largest contingent was 8,000 Japanese eventually relieved the legations in mid-August; they were joined slightly after by a German contingent. Much of the city was laid waste. In 1901 China was forced to pay out massive compensation and accept the stationing of foreign troops. Russia used the situation to advance her influence in Manchuria, which indirectly hastened the Anglo-Japanese Alliance and the Russo-Japanese War. Japan also made moves to strengthen her position in China.

Clements, P. H. *The Boxer Rebellion* (New York, 1967).
Lensen, G. A., ed. *Korea and Manchuria Between Russia and Japan* (Tallahassee, Fla., 1966).
Nish, I. H. "Japan's Indecision During the Boxer Disturbances," *JAS* 20, no. 4 (Aug. 1961).
Purcell, V. *The Boxer Uprising* (Cambridge, 1963).

Broadcasting

Experimental radio transmitting was carried out in Japan from 1905. The first radio stations were licensed in Tokyo, Nagoya, and Osaka in 1924 and started broadcasting in 1925. In March 1926 these were consolidated into the Japan Broadcasting Association (Nihon Hōsō Kyōkai-N.H.K.), a half-private, half-public body, which had a monopoly of all radio broadcasting. Further regional broadcasting stations were established, and the whole organization came under the supervision of the Communications Ministry. Until 1945 this government-controlled service was an important propaganda weapon, and during the Occupation as well radio transmission was subject to considerable censorship. Under the 1950 Broadcasting Law N.H.K. was reorganized as a public corporation, and commercial radio stations financed by advertising started operating in 1951. Although experiments had been carried out before the war, television transmission by N.H.K. and private companies did not begin until 1953. The growth of television led to a decline in radio audiences, but, subsequently, they revived because of such technological advances as stereo and transistors; by the mid-1960s almost all households had radios. In 1968 the radio license was abolished, and a differential color/black-and-white licensing system for television now funds N.H.K. By late 1975 91% of households had color televisions. Educational broadcasting has been carried out since the late 1920s and is now very widespread, though N.H.K. remains the most important educational broadcaster. As of 1977 there were 91 television broadcasting organizations and 51 radio broadcasting organizations.

Itō, M. *Broadcasting in Japan* (London, 1978).
Katō, H. *Japanese Research on Mass Communication* (Honolulu, 1974).
Nishimoto, M. *The Development of Educational Broadcasting in Japan* (Tokyo, 1969).

Buddhism

Buddhism, originally introduced into Japan from the 6th century, had become popularized during the 13th – 14th centuries and continued to flourish during the early Tokugawa period. It was patronized by the state but was closely subordinated to shōgunal authority and essentially used as a political tool for maintaining social order and control. The Tokugawa's emphasis on certain Neo-Confucian doctrines to support the status quo and revival of interest in Shintō from the 18th century were potentially damaging to Buddhism's official status, but the fusion of Buddhist and Shintō practices as an integral part of the life of the people maintained the position of Buddhist beliefs, when, with the exception of Zen, perhaps, doctrines were prone to stultification and Buddhism's official position was weak. The government's attempts after the Meiji Restoration to establish Shintō as a state religion led to the disestablishment of Buddhism in 1868. The government's attempts to sever all ties between Buddhism and Shintō following the partial fusion that had occurred during the Edo period always discriminated in favor of Shintō both in the sphere of religious practices and in the case of physical endowments such as buildings. Many priests were secularized. For a few years virulent anti-Buddhism at a lower level led to violence and rioting. Attempts to interfere with Buddhism largely ceased from the mid-1870s, but attempts to reform and revive organized Buddhism were not particularly successful, even after its theoretical equality with Shintō was pronounced by the 1889 constitution. Few Buddhist sects flourished in the period up to 1945 although the Japanese still retained many Buddhist rituals and a strong identification with Buddhism. Dissatisfaction with Buddhism as an organized religion contributed to the growth of new sects in Japan, and although these are considered by the Japanese to come under the category of the so-called "new religions," several of them have basically Buddhist beliefs. The most conspicuously successful in the postwar period has been Sōka Gakkai (Value-Creating Study Society), which is a lay organization of the traditionally nationalistic Nichiren Shōshū sect. The Sōka Gakkai, originally founded in the 1930s by Makiguchi Tsunesaburō, was revived in 1947 following suppression during the war and is now the largest voluntary organization of any kind in Japan. Much of its growth has been under the presidency of Ikeda Daisaku 1960 – 1979. In 1977 Nichiren Shōshū claimed over 16 million adherents, the majority of whom were in Sōka Gakkai; it also has members outside Japan. The Kōmeitō (*q.v.*) was established as its political wing in 1964, and although the formal connection has been severed, much of Kōmeitō's support is still drawn from Sōka Gakkai members, giving the sect considerable political influence. The traditional sects have been less successful, but figures in 1977 showed that over 84 million Japanese, some 75% of the population, declared an affiliation to some form of Buddhism. This affiliation is not necessarily institutionalized, but Buddhist rituals remain an integral part of the life of most Japanese.

Dator, J. A. *Sōka Gakkai: Builders of the Third Civilization* (Seattle, 1969).
Morioka, K. *Religion in Changing Japanese Society* (Tokyo, 1975).
Murakami, S. *Japanese Religion in the Modern Century* (Tokyo, 1980).
Saunders, E. D. *Buddhism in Japan* (Philadelphia, 1964).

White, J. W. *The Sōka Gakkai and Mass Society* (Stanford, 1970).

Bunmei Kaika. See CIVILIZATION AND ENLIGHTENMENT

Buraku Emancipation Movement
(Buraku kaihō undō)
部落解放運動

The *burakumin* (*eta* and *hinin*), the outcast class of Japan, trace their origins to ancient times. They were given legal equality in 1871, but discrimination in work, place of residence, and marriage continued. An increasing awareness of this continuing social discrimination stimulated the formation of *burakumin* organizations after 1903, advocating improvement of the conditions of life through self-help. In March 1922 the national Suiheisha (Leveling Society) was formed; its first conference attracted some 2,000 participants. It condemned all discrimination, advocated political, economic, and social freedom by national solidarity and the *burakumin*'s own efforts, and aimed to attract both liberals and radicals. After 1925 the Suiheisha was increasingly dominated by Bolshevik ideas; many members believed that status discrimination could only be overcome by proletarian revolution, and the Suiheisha became a major element in the proletarian movement. Under the leadership of Matsumoto Jiichirō, who was elected to the Diet in 1936, the society was active throughout the 1920s and 1930s, but even at its peak membership was only 35,000 – 40,000, some 4% of all *burakumin*. Grass-roots activities remained weak, and many leaders were lost in the suppression of the late 1920s. The Suiheisha was never officially dissolved during the war but became completely inactive. Late in 1946 its tradition was revived by Matsumoto in the National Committee for Buraku Emancipation, which after 1950 developed into a mass organization whose attempts to improve the life of the *burakumin* have received the support of many left-wing groups. In 1955 it was renamed the Buraku Emancipation League (Buraku Kaihō Dōmei). A large number of *burakumin* communities have been organized into the league, but its strong left-wing tendencies stimulated the founding of a more moderate organization, the Dōwakai, and rivalry between the two organizations has impeded the progress toward emancipation. Discrimination still persists on a wide scale.

Brameld, T. *Japan: Culture, Education, and Change in Two Communities* (New York, 1968).
Neary, I. "Tenkō of an Organization: The Suiheisha in the Late 1930s," in D. W. Anthony, ed., *BAJS Proceedings* 2, pt. 2 (Sheffield, 1977).
De Vos, G., and H. Wagatsuma. *Japan's Invisible Race* (Berkeley, 1966).

Bureaucracy

A status-based bureaucracy existed under the Tokugawa shōgunate, but this was already breaking down by the late Tokugawa period. In the early years after the Meiji Restoration there was no formal recruitment practice for the higher bureaucracy; enrollment was based on individual factors such as attitude to the Restoration, personal connections, and Western knowledge. Through the 1870s and 1880s the higher bureaucracy was dominated by men from Satsuma and Chōshū. From 1887 higher civil service examinations were instituted, and after 1893 all but the highest offices were subject to exam appointment, but despite this the top bureaucracy remained the province of a trained elite, some 75% of whom came from Tokyo Imperial University's law department. During the period of Taishō Democracy (*q.v.*) members of political parties had more access to the highest appointments, and top bureaucrats could be more easily dismissed, but after 1932 all senior dismissals had to be brought before a status committee, which in effect provided considerable guarantee of position for top bureaucrats. The Meiji constitution strengthened the position of the bureaucracy; its regulation by imperial ordinance rather than by law permitted the political parties and Diet only limited control over it. It retained its position as the core of the executive branch, and the practice of bureaucratic, transcendental cabinets further strengthened its position vis-à-vis the legislature. The bureaucracy was not regarded as a body of politically neutral, professional public servants carrying out the decisions of a democratically elected government and responsible to the people but as chosen servants of the emperor responsible to him alone. A tradition of respect for officialdom was continued by this concept. Due to a lack of legislature from 1868 to 1890, the executive wing was supreme, and bureaucracy was synonymous with government, but even after the Meiji period the higher bureaucracy had major political influence. This influence rested largely on the tradition of such political involvement, the weakness of the legislature, and the genuinely essential administrative role of the bureaucracy. Contacts with the nonproletarian political parties were close, many ex-bureaucrats holding high office within them. Overall, the bureaucracy prewar was a powerful conservative force; the so-called "reformist" bureaucrats especially assisted the triumph of reactionary policies in the 1930s. Nevertheless, the Occupation authorities did not subject the bureaucracy to punitive action, although a few individuals were purged. Postwar public employees have been appointed according to the 1947 State Employees Law and the 1950 Regional Employees Law. Members of the bureaucracy are regarded as servants of the whole community, and constitutional limits are placed on their power, notably by the position of the Diet as the highest organ of state. No civil servant is allowed the right to strike. However, the role of the bureaucracy during the Occupation and the fact that most of its traditional practices were unchanged permitted its continuing prestige, and the subservience of the higher bureaucracy to the Diet and its responsibility to the people is not always established in fact. The higher civil service largely remains the province of a few university departments and is still legally politically powerful, influencing affairs through Diet committees and cabinet bureaus. The tradition of executive supremacy is hard to break. Many senior bureaucrats enter politics after early retirement, reinforcing an already strong identification with the ruling Liberal Democratic Party. The entry of other bureaucrats into business reinforces the existence of a government-politics-big-business nexus. In various ways, therefore, entry into the bureaucracy is still the key to political influence.

Inoki, M. "The Civil Bureaucracy—Japan," in R. E. Ward and D. Rustow, eds., *Political Modernization in Japan and Turkey* (Princeton, 1964).

Silberman, B. S. "The Bureaucratic Role in Japan 1900–1945: The Bureaucrat as Politician," in B. S. Silberman and H. Harootunian, eds., *Japan in Crisis* (Princeton, 1974).

Spaulding, R. M. *Imperial Japan's Higher Civil Service Examinations* (Princeton, 1967).

Yanaga, C. *Big Business in Japanese Politics* (New Haven, 1968).

C

Cabinet system

The cabinet system was initiated in December 1885 to replace the Dajōkan system (*q.v.*). The national administration was separated from the imperial household, and the cabinet was its highest organ. The cabinet consisted of the heads of various ministries presided over by a prime minister with an imperial mandate to form a government, and although the power of the prime minister was somewhat controlled by the Meiji constitution (*q.v.*), cabinets for long remained transcendental, not responsible to the Diet. Participation by party politicians in cabinets did increase after the Meiji period, but until the 1920s the *genrō* (*q.v.*) remained responsible for choosing the prime minister; after that it was done by consensus. The prime minister's power was greatly restricted by the existence of the Privy Council (*q.v.*) and the increasing influence of the armed forces. Prewar cabinets included among their members the director of the Legislative Bureau and the chief of the Cabinet Secretariat. Also under cabinet control were the Information Bureau (1940–1945), which coordinated news, propaganda, and control of thought and speech, and the Statistics Bureau (founded in 1898). During the years of the Sino-Japanese and Pacific wars (1937–1945) the cabinet appointed cabinet advisers for consultation on important policy matters. Under the 1947 constitution the cabinet has executive power. It consists of 15 to 20 members, all of whom must be civilians and a majority of whom are chosen from the majority party in the Diet. It bears collective responsibility toward the Diet, especially the House of Representatives. The prime minister's powers have been correspondingly increased although he has to maximize support behind his own position within his party. His own office, equivalent to the Cabinet Office in the U.K., is now very large, to some extent reducing the prime minister's dependency on the bureaucracy of the various ministries. The Bureau of Legislation, after some changes, was reconstituted under that name in 1952, but neither its head nor the chief of the Cabinet Secretariat (formerly *shokikanchō*, now *kanbō chōkan*) is by right a cabinet member, although they may well be ministers of state, as are the heads of many of the agencies controlled by the cabinet. Despite the changes, the cabinet maintains close contacts with the bureaucracy while the Liberal Democratic Party holds power and is also subject to checks from elements within the party.

Colegrove, K. "The Japanese Cabinet," *American Political Science Review* 30, no. 5 (Oct. 1936).

Steven, R. P. G. "Cabinet Responsibility: The Separation of Powers and the Makers and Breakers of Cabinets in Japanese Politics 1890–1940," Ph.D. diss., University of British Columbia, 1974.

Ward, R. E. *Japan's Political System* (Englewood Cliffs, N.J., 1967).

Cairo Declaration (Kairo sengen) カイロ宣言

After talks in Cairo in November 1943 Roosevelt, Churchill, and Chiang Kai-shek issued a joint declaration stating that the war against Japan would be pursued until Japan surrendered unconditionally and that in order to restrain and punish Japanese aggression Japan would be divested of all Pacific islands seized or occupied since 1914. Manchuria, Taiwan, and the Pescadores would be returned to China, and Korea would become independent. The declaration was the first statement of the war concerning Japanese-held territory, and its stipulations were later subsumed under the Potsdam Declaration (*q.v.*).

Haring, D. G., ed., *Japan's Prospect* (Cambridge, Mass., 1946).

Capitalism (Japanese). See JAPANESE CAPITALISM DEBATE

Car Industry

The first cars were imported into Japan in the late 1890s, and in 1907 Japan produced her first petrol engine car, but despite government assistance after 1914 (due to the military importance of the industry) few companies were successful. The cars produced were technologically primitive and expensive due to the underdevelopment of the machine-tool and other related industries; they could not compete with American manufacturers such as Ford and General Motors who were already engaged in mass production and who set up factories in Japan in the 1920s. In 1930 only 500 Japanese vehicles were produced. Government protection of domestic vehicle production through tax and exchange measures increased steadily after the Manchurian Incident, and in 1941 nearly 44,000 vehicles were produced. During the Pacific War many facilities were diverted to produce ships and airplanes, but concentration on the production of small and medium-sized vehicles brought rapid revival in the years after the Korean War. In recent years the export success of the Japanese car industry, dominated by a few large firms, has become legendary, with exports expanding faster than domestic sales. In 1976 some 8 million vehicles were produced, of which close on 3 million were exported, and further expansion since then has caused considerable problems in Japan's trading relations with the United States and the E.E.C.

Chang, C. S. "The Japanese Motor Vehicle Industry," Ph.D. diss., American University, Washington, 1974.

Carolines. See MANDATED TERRITORIES

Central Review. See CHŪŌ KŌRON

Chang Tso-lin, Assassination of (Chōsakurin bakusatsu jiken) 張作霖爆殺事件

During 1928 the Tanaka cabinet, fearful of Chinese unification under the Nationalists (Kuomintang) after the failure of the Shantung Expeditions (*q.v.*), urged Marshall Chang Tso-lin, the Manchurian warlord, to forestall his defeat by the Kuomintang by retreating from Peking and consolidating his position in Manchuria. There the Japanese hoped that under Japanese tutelage he would act as the ruler of a Manchuria cut off from the main body of Kuomintang China. Members of the Kwantung Army (*q.v.*), however, wished to depose Chang in favor of his son and occupy Manchuria. On 4 June 1928, as Chang was retreating toward Mukden, his train was blown up just outside the city in a plot engineered by Kōmoto Daisaku and other staff officers of the Kwantung Army. Chang was killed instantly, but the incident did not initiate wider hostilities. The explosion was attributed by the Japanese to nonuniformed members of the Kuomintang, but the real circumstances soon emerged and the hush-up and the failure to punish the conspirators forced the Japanese cabinet to resign in July 1929. The army's report on the affair was not published and the conspirators were never charged with the assassination, many of them remaining active in radical circles. Chang was succeeded by his son, Chang Hsüeh-liang, who by December 1928 had joined with the Kuomintang in vigorous resistance to the Japanese.

Dull, P. S. "The Assassination of Chang Tso-lin," *FEQ* 11, no. 4 (Aug. 1952).
Iriye, A. "Chang Hsüeh-liang and the Japanese," *JAS* 20, no. 1 (Nov. 1960).
McCormack, G. *Chang Tso-lin in Northeast China, 1911–1928: China, Japan, and the Manchurian Idea* (Stanford, 1977).

Changkufeng Incident (Chōkohō jiken) 張鼓峰事件

On 29 July 1938, following previous border incidents, fighting erupted between Russian and Japanese troops at Changkufeng near the convergence of the Soviet, Korean, and Manchukuo borders. Fighting was bitter, and by the time a cease-fire negotiated in Moscow came into force on August 11 there had been several thousand casualties on both sides. The Tokyo war crimes tribunal declared the incident to be aggressive war on the part of Japan.

Blumenson, M. "The Soviet Power Play at Changkufeng," *World Politics* 12 (Jan. 1950).
Coox, A. D. *The Anatomy of a Small War—The Soviet-Japanese Struggle for Changkufeng/Khasan, 1938* (Westport, Conn., 1977).
Hata, I. "The Japanese-Soviet Confrontation, 1935–1939," in J. W. Morley, ed., *Deterrent Diplomacy: Japan, Germany, and the U.S.S.R., 1935–1940* (New York, 1976).
Pritchard, R. J. "Changkufeng—New Evidence of Japan's Military Victory Against Soviet Russia in 1938," in G. Daniels, ed., *BAJS Proceedings* 3, pt. 1 (Sheffield, 1978).

Charter Oath (Gokajō no Seimon)
五ヵ条の誓文

The name given to an imperial declaration issued 6 April 1868 aimed at using imperial influence to reassure both the domains and Westerners concerning the aims of the new government. The oath, consisting of five clauses, was first drafted by Yuri Kimimasa and then revised to varying degrees by Fukuoka Kōtei, Kido Kōin, Iwakura Tomomi, and Sanjō Sanetomi. Its provisions: (1) all classes to unite in promoting the nation's economy and welfare, (2) the establishment of an assembly and matters of state to be decided by public discussion, (3) all classes to be allowed to fulfill their just aspirations to avoid discontent, (4) discontinuance of former base customs and all actions to conform to the principles of international justice, and (5) knowledge to be sought throughout the world to strengthen the foundations of the imperial rule.

Beasley, W. G. *The Meiji Restoration* (London, 1973).

Chemical Industry

Apart from fertilizers and the manufacture of explosives, soda, and sulphuric acid for military use, Japan had little chemical industry in the Meiji period. During World War I the cutting of imports stimulated domestic production, and by 1937 11% total factory employment was in chemicals. Especially during the 1930s the industry grew rapidly. Bigger plants reduced costs, and growth was helped by military demand, industrial construction, export expansion, and the development of synthetic textiles. Ammonium sulphate—Japan was the second biggest producer in 1937—and artificial dyestuffs—over 50% of the 1939 production of 28,000 tons was exported—were especially successful, although production of other chemicals was still largely for the home market. Prewar, most chemical production was in the hands of the *zaibatsu* (*q.v.*) because of the large amounts of capital required and organic interconnectedness. The industry recovered slowly after the war but was stimulated by increasing production of foodstuffs and artificial fibres, and by the late 1950s prewar levels had been exceeded. Rapid expansion followed in the late 1960s and early 1970s, and by 1974 chemicals comprised over 7% exports by value. There has been considerable diversification in the industry with huge pharmaceutical and petrochemical industries developing. In 1974 petrochemicals comprised 40% of all chemical products. Since 1974 a decline in demand has led to some stagnation in the industry. Much Japanese chemical production is now concentrated in huge complexes on the Japanese coast such as those at Yokkaichi and Kitakyūshū.

Chemulpo, Treaty of. See JINGO INCIDENT

Cherry Society. See SAKURAKAI

Chian Iji Hō. See PEACE PRESERVATION LAW

Chichibu Incident (Chichibu jiken)
秩父事件

The economic crisis of the 1880s led to the rise of several local peasant parties, and in Chichibu (Saitama) and surrounding areas, which were hit by agricultural depression due to their dependence on raw silk production, these campaigned for debt deferment and reduced taxes. Some of these party members had connections with the Jiyūtō (*q.v.*), but Ōi Kentarō of the Jiyūtō failed to halt a mass uprising in the Chichibu area following the lack of success of the debt deferment campaign. On 1-2 November 1884 some 7,000–10,000 rioters broke into and burned offices and the homes of moneylenders and soon controlled most of Chichibu *gun*. The local authorities were taken unaware, but the rising was crushed within a couple of days. Three hundred rebels escaped to Nagano, but all were rounded up within a week. In 1886 four of the rising's leaders were executed and 3,000 others sentenced to fines or imprisonment. The attempted rising further discredited the Jiyūtō and reinforced police vigilance.

Bowen, R. W. *Rebellion and Democracy in Meiji Japan* (Berkeley, 1980).
Ike, N. *The Beginnings of Political Democracy in Japan* (Baltimore, 1950).

China Incident. See MARCO POLO BRIDGE INCIDENT; SINO-JAPANESE WAR, 1937-1945

Chōshū 長州

A *tozama* domain in southwest Honshū, with its castle town at Hagi. A focus of the *sonnō jōi* movement (*q.v.*) in the early 1860s, Chōshū attacks on foreigners in 1863 led to the bombardment of Shimonoseki (*q.v.*). Strong Chōshū influence at the Kyoto court was temporarily ousted by the dominance of *kōbu gattai* policies (*q.v.*), but from 1865 Chōshū regained and increased its influence in national politics as a leader of the anti-Bakufu movement (*q.v.*). The Bakufu mounted two military expeditions against Chōshū. The first, undertaken in 1864 after declaring Chōshū an imperial rebel, ended virtually without fighting after a declaration of submission by the *han*. The second in 1866, over Chōshū intransigence, saw the Bakufu unsupported by other domains and faced by domestic disturbances. The obvious failure of the expedition totally undermined Bakufu authority. In 1866 Chōshū concluded an alliance with Satsuma (*q.v.*) to bring down the Bakufu by force and subsequently played a major part in the 1868 coup. Members of the fief after 1868 dominated the army and with Satsuma formed the nucleus of the Meiji government.

Craig, A. *Chōshū in the Meiji Restoration* (Cambridge, Mass., 1961).
______. "The Restoration Movement in Chōshū," *JAS* 18, no. 2 (Feb. 1959).

Chōya Shinbun. See NEWSPAPERS

Christianity

Catholicism, introduced into Japan during the 16th century, was banned during the Tokugawa period and continued to exist only underground on a very small scale. Protestant and Catholic missionaries began to arrive during the *bakumatsu*, but the ban on Catholicism, which had in effect been extended to apply to Christianity as a whole, was not lifted until 1873. Its eventual removal was due to strong Western pressure on the Meiji government following its fierce persecution of Christians at Urakami. Although there were some Catholics, the majority of missionaries continued to be American and Canadian Protestants. Most converts were members of the middle and upper classes. Their number was not large, but the influence of Christianity as a vehicle for the introduction of Western ideas, especially through educational and charitable institutions, was immense. Christian schools such as Dōshisha produced leading thinkers in the Meiji period and exerted a strong influence on writers and intellectuals. Many of the early leaders of the Socialist and labor movements were also Christian. The influence of Christianity waned in the face of positive persecution in the years before the Pacific War. In 1941 over 30 Protestant sects were united into the Japan Christian Order (Nihon Kirisuto Kyōdan), which, despite splits in the early 1970s and the rise of other groupings, is still the biggest Protestant group. Christianity remains influential in such fields as education, but numerically its membership is small. In 1972 0.8% of the Japanese population was registered as Christian with 361,000 Catholics and 429,000 Protestants, and the figure is still under 1%.

Iglehart, C. W. *A Century of Protestant Christianity in Japan* (Tokyo, 1959).
Laures. J. *The Catholic Church in Japan* (Rutland, Vt., 1954).
Ministry of Education, Japan. *Religions in Japan* (Tokyo, 1963).
Morioka, K. *Religion in Changing Japanese Society* (Tokyo, 1975).
Murakami, S. *Japanese Religion in the Modern Century* (Tokyo, 1980).

Chūō Kōron 中央公論
A Kyoto-based monthly publication developed into a general magazine and in 1899 was renamed *Chūō Kōron* (Central Review). Although it had a strong literary emphasis, its range of subject matter was considerable, and by the end of the Meiji period *Chūō Kōron* rivaled *Taiyō* (Sun) (*q.v.*) in its influence. *Chūō Kōron* continued to flourish through the years of World War I, when it was regarded as the leading journal of Taishō Democracy (*q.v.*). It suffered a decline in the 1920s but was revived along its traditional liberal lines and during the 1930s was highly influential. *Kaizō* (Reconstruction) (*q.v.*) was the only journal to equal this influence. Increasingly subject to official disapproval, after 1942 many connected with *Chūō Kōron* were arrested on charges of Communist sympathies (the so-called Yokohama incident), and the magazine was eventually closed in July 1944. It was restarted in January 1946 and still has a wide circulation and considerable influence. In 1961 there was an assassination attempt on the editor, Shimanaka Hōji, following the publication of an article considered by the right-wing disrespectful toward the emperor.

Havens, T. R. H. *Valley of Darkness* (New York, 1978).

Chūritsu Rōdō Kumiai Renraku Kaigi. See LABOR MOVEMENT

Chūritsu Rōren. See LABOR MOVEMENT

Civil Code (minpō) 民法
In 1890 the government promulgated the first sections of a new civil code drafted under the advice of Gustave Boissonade, with the aim of implementing it from 1893. The code, which was modeled on the French pattern and based on natural rights, met with strong opposition both from lawyers of other schools and on the grounds that it would undermine traditional Japanese values, and in 1892 the government indefinitely postponed its implementation. A new committee established in 1893 drafted a new code on the German model, which came into force in 1898. The family law of this code was a codification of the then-prevailing custom of the patriarchal family system, giving the family precedence over the individual, men over women, etc. Despite moves for reform in the early 1920s this code remained in force until 1947. Its provisions were considered incompatible with the respect for the individual and equality of the sexes stipulated by the new constitution, and a provisional reform of the sections relating to relatives and inheritance was implemented. A complete reform followed in 1948 when the present civil code was implemented, providing for the legal abolition of the *ie*, free choice of spouse and domicile, sexual equality, etc.

Epp, R. "The Challenge from Tradition: Attempts to Compile a Civil Code in Japan, 1866–1878," *MN* 22 (1967).
Steiner, K. "The Revision of the Civil Code of Japan: Provisions Affecting the Family," *FEQ* 9, no. 2 (Feb. 1950).
Von Mehren, A. T. *Law in Japan* (Cambridge, Mass., 1963).

Civil Service. See BUREAUCRACY

Civil War of 1868. See BOSHIN WAR

Civilization and Enlightenment (bunmei kaika) 文明開化
The phrase *civilization and enlightenment* was used in the 1870s, often in conjunction with the slogan "rich country strong army." It referred to the introduction of Western social systems, ways of life, ways of thinking, and values in such fields as education, i.e., the state of development reached by Western society by the late 19th century. The policy of ***bunmei kaika*** was encouraged by the government and personified by intellectual groups such as the Meirokusha (*q.v.*), who sought to convey Western ideas to the people. Such attempts at the introduction of Western culture, by their very nature piecemeal,

were later often criticized as excessive Westernization.

Blacker, C. *The Japanese Enlightenment* (Cambridge, 1964).

Clean Government Party. See KŌMEITŌ

Coal Mining. See MINING

Communism. See JAPAN COMMUNIST PARTY

Communist Party. See JAPAN COMMUNIST PARTY

Commutation of Stipends
(chitsuroku shobun) 秩禄処分
After 1868 daimyō continued to pay rice stipends to their samurai retainers although reforms in the system meant that many stipends were considerably reduced. Samurai were also encouraged to engage in commerce and industry and to receive salaries rather than stipends. After the abolition of the domains in 1871, the government took over these payments, but it was a considerable drain on government income, and in December 1873 it announced the taxation of stipends and the optional commutation of lower stipends for a lump sum. The system was gradually extended, and in August 1876 commutation of the annual stipend for a lump sum became compulsory. Some ¥174 million was paid out to 313,000 individuals, almost all of it in the form of government bonds, many of which were later used for investments in land, commerce, and industry. The commutation relieved the economic burden on the government and marked a change in the whole socioeconomic structure of the country.

Beasley, W. G. *The Meiji Restoration* (London, 1973).

Concordia Association. See MANCHUKUO

Confucianism
Confucian ideas were influential in Japan from about the 6th century, but during the Tokugawa period the Neo-Confucian doctrines of the Chinese philosopher Chu Hsi, which had entered Japan during the Kamakura period, became the core of the official orthodoxy of the Tokugawa Bakufu system, under the initial promotion of scholars such as Fujiwara Seika and Hayashi Razan. Neo-Confucianism was fundamentally secular and rational in character; its rationalism promoted the study of history and other disciplines. It had absorbed from Confucianism an emphasis on agrarianism, which found favor with the Bakufu, as did an emphasis on national superiority, which led naturally to isolationism. The ethnocentrism of Neo-Confucianism played a vital part in the later development of nationalism, but the aspect of the doctrine most stressed in Tokugawa Japan was the humanistic emphasis on personal loyalties and relationships, i.e., Neo-Confucianism as a social ethic. The defined relationships, of which the most important was perhaps *taigi meibun,* the true relationship between ruler and subject, embraced an emphasis on hierarchy, loyalty, and service suited to the society desired by the regime. Neo-Confucianism thus served to rationalize and perpetuate the fixed social relationships fundamental to the politicoeconomic system. Neo-Confucian doctrines retained official backing throughout the Tokugawa period, influencing both governmental practice and every aspect of the life of the people at large, but heterodox ideologies did develop during the course of the period. Among the most important of these was the Wang Yang-ming (Ōyōmei) ideology, a branch of Neo-Confucianism originally introduced by Nakae Tōjū (1608–1648) and later supported by Kumazawa Banzan (1619–1691). Unlike Chu Hsi, the Chinese scholar Wang Yang-ming emphasized the importance of personal intuition and moral sense over

rationality and intellect, an idea which appealed to all classes of society. Under Kumazawa the political applicability of a doctrine that stressed the importance of practice over theory became obvious, and the ideas of Wang Yang-ming not only influenced Tokugawa statesmen such as Arai Hakuseki, but their emphasis on deeds rather than words had a major influence in bringing about the Restoration. Under Yamaga Sokō (1622–1685) and Itō Jinsai (1627–1705) there was also some reassertion of Confucianism. This *kogaku* (ancient learning), reached its peak under Ogyū Sorai (1666–1728), who through study of ancient China asserted that the improvement of society was to be achieved through the nature of its institutions and administration rather than through the moral training of the individual, an essentially practical and utilitarian doctrine, which could not but come into conflict with Neo-Confucianism. Nevertheless, the views of Ogyū Sorai achieved a certain amount of official approval and played a crucial role in the revival of interest in Japan's own past, thereby ensuring his position as a major intellectual influence long after his death. The strength of such heterodox ideas led to limited suppression from the late 18th century and a not very successful reassertion of Chu Hsi Neo-Confucianism. Following the Restoration institutionalized Neo-Confucianism was put aside. It declined as a system of thought, but from the 1880s "Confucian" ethical values such as loyalty and filial piety were reasserted by the ruling elite as a fundamental part of the official emperor system (*q.v.*) ideology; the increasing identification of such values with the Shintō tradition, which had occurred during the Tokugawa period, made easier their consideration as an integral part of the traditional Japanese heritage. As in the Tokugawa period this was an adoption of Confucian ideas for the achievement of certain desired ends, their mobilization in the service of the state. As a major prop of the nationalistic ideas prevalent in Japan during the pre-1945 period, therefore, Confucianism was discredited at official levels after 1945. Nevertheless, the influence of Confucian ideas on the moral and social attitudes of all Japanese still remains very strong.

Anesaki, M. *The Religious Life of the Japanese People* (Tokyo, 1938).
Lidin, O. G. *The Life of Ogyū Sorai, a Tokugawa Confucian Philosopher* (Sweden, 1973).
McEwen, J. R. *The Political Writings of Ogyū Sorai* (Cambridge, 1962).
Smith, W. W. *Confucianism in Modern Japan: A Study of Conservatism in Modern Japanese Intellectual History* (Tokyo, 1959).
Tsunoda, R., W. T. de Bary, and D. Keene. *Sources of the Japanese Tradition* (New York, 1958).

Conscription

During the Tokugawa period military activity was the exclusive right of the samurai although peasant militia were sometimes raised to deal with local disturbances, and irregular forces (*shotai*) were organized during the *bakumatsu*. The new government after 1868 found itself in control of disparate forces. Although some requisitioning of troops occurred before 1873, only in November 1872 did an imperial rescript and Dajōkan notification announce the introduction of conscription. This decision to recruit regardless of social origins constituted a rejection of the basis of Tokugawa society and was therefore a revolutionary move by the Meiji government. The government's aim was the establishment of a strong central army to maintain its own power as well as for protection against foreign attacks. The Conscription Law was promulgated in January 1873 and was effective from April of that year. The use of conscription for the establishment of a modern, regular army was opposed both by samurai, deprived of their prerogative of military service, and by the peasantry, who misconstrued the word "blood tax" in the Dajōkan notification, and, more importantly, could often ill afford the diversion of the strongest element of its labor force. Initially, the system also permitted exemption and service by proxy, which meant both evasion and also unfair distribution of the burden, again mostly to the detriment of the peasantry. Widespread peasant riots occurred, especially in the west of Japan. The system was reformed in 1879, 1883, and 1889; the abolition of exemption and service by proxy established the obligation of all men to military service, and their equal right to promotion was stated. The conscription system continued to be modified up to the Military Service Law of 1927 but in essence remained unchanged. Conscription was abolished in 1945.

Hackett, R. F. "The Military—Japan," in R. E. Ward and D. A. Rustow, eds., *Political Modernization in Japan and Turkey* (Princeton, 1964).
Norman, E. H. *Soldier and Peasant in Japan: The Origins of Conscription* (New York, 1943).
Ogawa, G. *The Conscription System in Japan* (London and New York, 1921).

Constitution, Meiji. See MEIJI CONSTITUTION

Constitution of Japan, 1947
(Nihon Koku Kenpō) 日本国憲法
The present constitution of Japan was promulgated on 3 November 1946 and became effective on 3 May 1947. In October 1945 SCAP (*q.v.*) instructed the Japanese government to draft a new constitution, and a plan was produced by Matsumoto Jōji, minister of state in the Shidehara cabinet. This draft was rejected by SCAP as being only a partial amendment of the old constitution, sovereignty still resting with the emperor. SCAP finally produced its own draft, which was promulgated after approval by the Far Eastern Commission (*q.v.*). While it was nominally a revised version of the Meiji constitution carried out under stipulated revision procedures, the new constitution in fact embraced radical changes. Among the most important provisions: (1) sovereignty to rest with the people, not with the emperor, who should remain merely a symbol of the state; (2) the Diet to be the highest organ of the state, with the cabinet responsible to the Diet; (3) an independent judiciary; (4) local autonomy; (5) guarantee of basic human rights; (6) equal rights for men and women; and (7) renunciation of war as a means of settling international disputes and of the right to possess military potential. Despite this last provision (clause 9) Japan from 1950 possessed a Police Reserve Force, which has developed into a Self-Defense Force, and many have called for the amendment of this clause. In July 1964 the Committee on the Constitution advocated its reform, but constitutional amendment requires a two-thirds majority in the Diet and is strongly opposed by the opposition left-wing parties. No other clause of the constitution has aroused similar controversy, but there are spheres where the stipulations of the constitution prevail neither in spirit nor in fact.

Henderson, D. F. *The Constitution of Japan: Its First Twenty Years, 1947–1967* (Seattle, 1968).
SCAP, Government Section. *The Political Reorientation of Japan,* 2 vols. (Washington, 1960).
Ward, R. E. "The Commission on the Constitution and Prospects for Constitutional Change in Japan," *JAS* 24, no. 3 (May 1965).
______. "The Origins of the Present Japanese Constitution," *American Political Science Review* 50, no. 4 (Dec. 1956).

Constitutional Democratic Party. See MINSEITŌ

Constitutional Government. See MOVEMENT FOR THE PROTECTION OF CONSTITUTIONAL GOVERNMENT

Constitutional Imperial Party. See TEISEITŌ

Constitutional Progressive Party. See KAISHINTŌ

Consular Courts. See EXTRATERRITORIALITY

Control Faction. See TŌSEI FACTION

Cotton Industry

Raw cotton was produced in Japan during the Tokugawa period, but production declined rapidly from the 1860s, unable to compete with Indian and American imports. Cotton spinning and weaving had been a supplementary occupation for farmers, but from the *bakumatsu* production could not compete in quality or quantity with the imported yarn, which constituted a high proportion of total imports. Attempts were made to introduce mechanized cotton spinning into Japan from 1866, but only after 1878, when the government initiated direct assistance to promote mechanized spinning in order to cut imports, did large-scale factories begin to appear. The first major private mill was Shibusawa Eiichi's Osaka Spinning Company, which started operating in 1883; the steam-powered mill produced better quality yarn and was highly successful. The industry subsequently expanded fast on a private enterprise basis. Its development was helped by cheap female labor and the accessibility of the Korean and Chinese markets. Raw cotton was imported from India and the U.S. Cotton spinning was the first industry in Japan to achieve large-scale capitalist production and began to export in the 1890s. Cotton weaving developed slightly later, but by 1914 Japan was self-sufficient in cotton cloth, and finished cloth manufactured from imported raw cotton was becoming a staple Japanese export. During World War I Japan's cotton exports invaded the previously British-dominated world markets, and Japan increasingly manufactured her own cotton spinning and weaving machinery. During the 1920s Japanese spinners invested in China and owned 40% of China's spindleage by 1930. At home the industry responded to depression with massive rationalization, and its export success during the 1930s led to accusations of social dumping followed by protective measures by other countries. Nevertheless, Japan remained the world's second biggest cotton producer. Until 1937, when it came under government control, the industry was dominated by a powerful employers' association which controlled labor, promoted mergers, and acted as a cartel. Cotton production suffered severely due to subsequent emphasis on war production, and much equipment was scrapped. Small-scale spinners especially revived in the postwar years, but the industry has suffered from loss of the China market, the development of synthetic materials, and the development of cotton production in developing countries. It has never regained its dominant export position, and during the 1970s production has declined and imports increased.

Kroese, W. T. *The Japanese Cotton Industry* (Leiden, 1950).
Seki, K. *The Cotton Industry of Japan* (Tokyo, 1956).
Shindō, T. *Labor in the Japanese Cotton Industry* (Tokyo, 1961).

Criminal Code (keihō) 刑法

A national criminal code was adopted in 1870, but Japan's first modern criminal code was drawn up under the guidance of Gustave Boissonade and promulgated in 1880 (effective 1882). Based on the Code Napoleon but incorporating certain traditional Japanese elements, the new code embraced such fundamental principles as individual guilt, public courts, right of appeal, and legality of punishment and introduced the category of offenses against the imperial household. From 1890–1908 considerable modification by statutes altered the law along German lines. From 1926 the government embarked on a thoroughgoing reform of criminal law, but this process was suspended by the war. In 1947, in accordance with the new constitution, a partial amendment of the code included the abolition of the crimes of lese majesty and adultery, and a new criminal procedure code was adopted in 1949. Since 1956 officials have been engaged on a complete revision of the penal code, and in 1974 the Ministry of Justice completed a preparatory draft of a revised code but some of the proposed changes have met with considerable opposition.

Clifford, W. *Crime Control in Japan* (Lexington, Mass., 1976).
Sebald, W. J. *The Criminal Code of Japan* (Kobe, 1936).
Von Mehren, A. T., ed., *Law in Japan* (Cambridge, Mass., 1963).

Currency

During the Tokugawa period gold and silver coins and notes issued by feudal authorities and merchants circulated. Under the treaties signed with the West from 1858 a de facto silver standard operated in the open ports due to the circulation of Mexican silver dollars for international trade, but lack of parity between gold and silver caused an outflow of specie in the 1860s. After 1868 the government attempted to standardize the coinage. A mint was set up in Osaka under the supervision of an Englishman, William Kinder; minting of coins started in late 1870. From 1868 the new government issued various inconvertible paper notes, but the value of these rapidly declined, and currency confusion continued. Only from 1871, with the abolition of the domains, did the government have sole charge of currency throughout the nation. The yen was first issued in 1872 as the new national currency. ¥1 was equivalent to 1 *ryō* of the old currency; it consisted of 100 *sen*, each *sen* consisting of 10 *rin*, but these smaller units have passed out of use due to inflation. The 1871 Currency Regulations ostensibly adopted a gold standard, but a de facto silver standard operated due to the outflow of gold because of a world fall in the price of silver, the inconvertibility of notes, and the continuing circulation of silver in the ports. From 1876 national banks issued inconvertible notes and rampant inflation was worsened by the Satsuma Rebellion (*q.v.*). In 1878 the government adopted bimetallic principles, making silver legally the dominant medium of circulation. Matsukata's deflationary policy reduced the number of notes in circulation, and from 1885 the Bank of Japan alone had the right of note issue, notes being convertible into silver. Gradual withdrawal of the inconvertible notes achieved considerable domestic currency stabilization. The indemnity gained from China after the Sino-Japanese War assisted Japan to go on the gold standard in 1897. This was maintained until an embargo was placed on gold exports in 1917. Japan's subsequent return to gold was delayed by the postwar depression and the 1923 earthquake, and it was eventually achieved in January 1930 by the retrenchment and rationalization policies of the Hamaguchi cabinet. The prevailing world depression immediately led to a flight of specie, and the embargo was reimposed in December 1931, leading to a drastic fall in the previously overvalued yen, which during the 1920s had an exchange rate of circa ¥10 = £1 (ca. 46 cents = ¥1). During the 1930s inflationary monetary policies were adopted for military acquisition and to combat depression, but all monetary matters became subject to central control during the war period. To curb rampant postwar inflation, deposits were frozen and circulation limited, and in December 1949 a new inconvertible yen currency was adopted with a fixed exchange rate of ca. ¥1,000 = £1 (¥360 = $1). The exchange rate was to be based not on gold but was to be artificially supported by exchange controls. Despite considerable domestic inflation, since the 1950s the international value of the yen has appreciated. It was permitted to "float" in February 1973, and its value appreciated still further although its international value has fluctuated since 1979. As of July 1981, £1 was equivalent to ca. ¥435 and $1 to ¥235.

Adams, T. F. M. *A Financial History of Modern Japan* (Tokyo, 1964).
Adams, T. F. M., and I. Hoshii. *Financial History of the New Japan* (Tokyo, 1972).
Pressnell, L. S. *Money and Banking in Japan* (London, 1973).
Shinjo, H. *History of the Yen* (Kobe, 1962).

D

Daidō Club. See DAIDŌ DANKETSU MOVEMENT

Daidō Danketsu Movement (Daidō Danketsu undō) 大同団結運動
In October 1886 former Jiyūtō sympathizers started a campaign against the government's alleged mishandling of treaty revision (*q.v.*), and in 1887 disaffected elements united to form the nationwide Daidō Danketsu (Unionist League) movement against the government. Gotō Shōjirō assumed leadership of the movement, which called for treaty revision on equal terms, reduction of the land tax (*q.v.*), and freedom of speech and assembly. Public agitation increased, and a memorial was submitted to the government, but the Peace Regulations (*q.v.*) of December 1887 excluded many of the Daidō Danketsu's leaders from Tokyo. It was also weakened by Ōkuma Shigenobu's return to the government in February 1888, but Gotō remained active, and the movement continued throughout the country. In March 1889, however, Gotō joined the Kuroda cabinet, and in May the movement split into the Daidō Kyōwakai, a "nonpolitical party" group, which developed into the new Jiyūtō in January 1890, and the Daidō Club, a political association led by Kōno Hironaka and Inukai Tsuyoshi. The latter gained 50 members in the first Diet and joined with other liberal elements to form the Rikken Jiyūtō in October 1890.

Mason, R. H. P. *Japan's First General Election, 1890* (Cambridge, 1969).

Daidō Kyōwakai. See DAIDŌ DANKETSU MOVEMENT

Daijōkan. See DAJŌKAN SYSTEM

Dainihon Fujinkai. See WOMEN'S MOVEMENT

Dainihon Rōdō Kyōkai. See LABOR MOVEMENT

Dainihon Sangyō Hōkokukai. See LABOR MOVEMENT

Dainihon Seinendan. See YOUTH ORGANIZATIONS

Dainihon Seisantō. See GREATER JAPAN PRODUCTION PARTY

Dajōkan System (Dajōkan sei) 太政官制
The Dajōkan system of government in operation 1868–1885 was based on a system originated in 702 but underwent various reforms in the early Meiji years. The years 1868–1869 were a transitional period when the whole government was called the Dajōkan, but from 1869 the Dajōkan was the highest executive organ alone; it existed in conjunction with the Jingikan (Bureau of Shrines), which controlled spiritual affairs and which was theoretically above the Dajōkan. At this time the Dajōkan was headed by ministers of the Left and the Right *(sadaijin* and *udaijin),* consisted of state councillors *(sangi* and *dainagon),* and controlled six ministries (Civil Affairs, Official Affairs, Foreign Affairs, Finance, War, and Justice). There was also a legislative body, the Shūgiin, which had little authority or influence and which never met after 1870. After the abolition of the *han* in 1871 the system was reformed with spiritual affairs in a subordinate position. The Dajōkan now consisted of the *seiin,* which was the executive and highest decision-making organ and consisted of state councillors

(*sangi*) headed by the *dajō daijin,* who discussed policy and advised the emperor; the Department of the Left (*sain*), which replaced the Shūgiin as a legislative advisory organ under *seiin* control with limited powers and functions; and the Department of the Right (*uin*), a council of the heads of the administrative departments who were mostly already members of the *seiin* and who controlled policy and administration through the various ministries (*shō*). In 1871 there were eight ministries (Finance, Foreign Affairs, War, Public Works, Justice, Education, Religious Affairs, and Imperial Household), but there were several changes during the 1870s. In 1873 the powers of the *seiin* were formally enlarged and the combination of the post of state councillor with that of minister made the *seiin* the highest administrative organ as well. In 1875 the departments of the Left and the Right were abolished, and in 1877 the *seiin* itself; it was replaced by a conference of councillors, which remained in existence until 1885. In 1869–1871 the post of minister of the Left was never filled; minister of the Right was Sanjō Sanetomi. From 1871 Sanjō was *dajō daijin* and in theory supreme commander of the armed forces, adviser to the emperor, and final arbiter on national affairs, but power gradually passed to the state councillors, who, with their additional role as ministers, held considerable influence, and then to the ministers themselves. The Dajōkan system was superseded by the cabinet system (*q.v.*) in 1885.

Akita, G. *The Origins of Constitutional Government in Japan* (Cambridge, Mass., 1967).
Beckmann, G. M. *The Making of the Meiji Constitution* (Lawrence, Kans., 1957).
Wilson, R. A. *The Genesis of the Meiji Government in Japan, 1868–1871* (Berkeley, 1957).

Dan Takuma 1858–1932 (Baron, 1928)
団琢磨
Member of a Fukuoka samurai family, in 1871 Dan went with the Iwakura Mission (*q.v.*) to study mining science in the U. S. and returned in 1878. After teaching in Osaka and at Tokyo University, in 1884 he joined the Ministry of Industry, becoming engineer at the state-owned Miike Coal Mine. In 1888 the mine was sold to the Mitsui family. Dan joined Mitsui (*q.v.*) as the mine's manager, and under his management it flourished. He directed all Mitsui's mining enterprises from 1894 and became managing director of the Mitsui partnership in 1914. In this position he controlled the *zaibatsu*'s subsequent expansion. He was a leading figure in the economic world, dominating business and employers' organizations such as the Nihon Keizai Renmei (Japan Economic Federation) and Nihon Kōgyō Kurabu (Japan Industrial Club), and in 1921 heading a business mission to Britain and America. In 1929 he led the successful opposition to the proposed Labor Union Law. On 5 March 1932 he was assassinated by a member of the Blood League (*q.v.*).

Dark Ocean Society. See GENYŌSHA

Date Munenari (Muneki) 1818–1892
伊達宗城
Tozama daimyō of Uwajima *han* (100,000 *koku*) in northern Shikoku 1844–1858. As one of the "reforming" daimyō, Date was an active supporter of Tokugawa Keiki in the shogunal succession dispute (*q.v.*) and a strong critic of the Ansei treaties and was forced into retirement in the Ansei Purge (*q.v.*). From retirement he supported the *kōbu-gattai* movement (*q.v.*), then increasingly opposed the Bakufu though he was somewhat reluctant to become involved in national politics. Nevertheless, he wielded considerable influence at Kyoto. Date promoted Western studies in Uwajima in the 1860s; he constructed gun installations, adopted an English-style military system, and traded directly with foreign countries through Nagasaki. After the Restoration he held very senior government posts prior to the abolition of the domains (*q.v.*) but played no major role in post-Restoration politics.

Beasley, W. G. *The Meiji Restoration* (London, 1973).

Deconcentration Law. See ZAIBATSU DISSOLUTION

Defense Agency. See SELF-DEFENSE FORCE

Democratic Liberal Party. See LIBERAL DEMOCRATIC PARTY

Democratic Socialist Party (Minshu Shakaitō [Minshatō]) 民主社会党

The D. S. P. was founded in January 1960 after moderates of the Japan Socialist Party under Nishio Suehiro had split off from the main party in autumn 1959. The D. S. P. opposes "dictatorship of the left and right" and advocates the achievement of socialism by democratic, legal means; to this end members call for the expansion of welfare programs, progressive taxation, cooperative management, and special assistance in the modernization of small and medium enterprises. Its emphasis on a national, rather than a purely working-class, basis for socialism often brings it into conflict with the Communist Party. Support for the party comes largely from the moderate labor organizations, white-collar workers, and small manufacturers. In its early years the party was dominated by veterans of the prewar legal left calling for labor to act through D. S. P. representatives in the Diet; its formation possibly strengthened moderate elements in the J. S. P. The D. S. P. has suffered from weak local and regional organization and the problem of how to play a distinctive role between the J. S. P. and the Liberal Democratic Party (*q.v.*), both of whom it supports on occasions. In the November 1960 election the D. S. P. failed to establish itself as a liberal center, and its Lower House membership fell from 40 to 17. It somewhat recovered during the 1960s, and autumn 1979 it had 35 members in the House of Representatives, 11 in the House of Councillors. National membership was 40,000. At the June 1980 election Lower House representation fell to 32.

Cole, A. B., G. O. Totten, and C. H. Uyehara. *Socialist Parties in Postwar Japan* (New Haven, 1966).
Nishio, S. "The Democratic Socialist Party: Its Status and Policy," *CJ* 27, no. 1 (May 1961).

Depression (sekai daikyōkō) 世界大恐慌

Japan was caught up in world depression from 1930. As elsewhere there was a price slump and massive unemployment, but the Japanese situation was exacerbated by the severe agricultural depression already existing and government retrenchment policies aimed at a return to the gold standard. In both 1930 and 1931 wholesale prices and interest rates fell drastically. There was a flight of specie, and many smaller banks and companies suspended business, hastening concentration of economic interests. By adopting a cheap money policy after abandoning the gold standard in December 1931 and by increasing military expenditure after the Manchurian Incident, the Japanese stumbled comparatively quickly upon reflationary policies, enabling Japan's industry to recover more quickly than was the case in many other countries. Agricultural depression continued through much of the 1930s.

Chō, Y. "The Depression in Japan and Its Consequences for the 1930s: The Financial Policy of Takahashi Korekiyo," in P. C. Lowe, ed., *BAJS Proceedings* 1, pt. 1 (Sheffield, 1976).
______. "From the Shōwa Economic Crisis to Military Economy," *Developing Economies* 5, no. 4, (Dec. 1967).
Shidachi, T. *The Depression of 1930 as It Affected Japan* (Tokyo, 1931).

Deshima (Dejima). See NAGASAKI

Diet

Under the Meiji constitution (*q.v.*) the Diet, first convened in November 1890, was called the Imperial Diet *(teikoku gikai)*. It consisted of the House of Representatives, with 300 members elected after 1925 by universal male suffrage (before then by limited suffrage), and the House of Peers, composed of members of the imperial family and nobility, imperial appointees, and representatives of the highest taxpayers. The number of the latter fluctuated, but by the 1930s had grown to something over 400. The Diet's role was to sanction imperial legislation. Apart from the right to prior deliberation on the budget (the previous year's budget automatically came into force if a budget was not passed), the powers of the lower house were equal to those of the House of Peers. The democratic function of the Diet was limited by the principle of nonresponsible transcendental cabinets, by the Imperial House Law, and by the emperor's prerogative to declare war, make peace, conclude treaties, command the armed forces, and impose legislation by imperial edict. Its influence was also limited by the existence and authority of such bodies as the Privy Council (*q.v.*) and the *genrō* (*q.v.*). The emperor controlled the convening, opening, closing, and extension of Diet sessions. The Imperial Diet reached the peak of its limited powers during the Taishō period, but its influence faded with the political parties from 1932. It had little effective power from 1940 although it was never suspended. In 1945–1947 it passed Occupation policies, and was reconstituted in 1947 as the National Assembly *(kokkai)* of the new constitution. The new assembly derives its authority from the people and is the highest organ of state power and sole legislative organ. It is bicameral: the House of Representatives *(shūgiin)*, a lower house of 491 members, has greater powers than the House of Councillors *(sangiin)*, an upper house consisting of 252 members. Both houses are elected by all citizens over 20, but whereas the maximum term for the lower house is four years, members of the upper house are elected for six-year terms, half of them facing election every three years. The cabinet is responsible to the Diet, which controls budgetary matters and all prerogatives formerly belonging to the emperor. The Diet is backed up by a system of standing and special committees to consider legislation in which all members participate.

Baerwald, H. H. *Japan's Parliament* (Cambridge, 1974).
Misawa, S., and S. Ninomiya. "The Role of the Diet and Political Parties," in D. Borg and S. Okamoto, eds., *Pearl Harbor as History* (New York, 1973).
Stockwin, J. A. A. *Divided Politics in a Growth Economy* (London, 1975).
Ward, R. E. *Japan's Political System* (Englewood Cliffs, N. J., 1967).

Divine Soldiers Incident. See SHINPEITAI INCIDENT

Dodge Line. See ECONOMIC STABILIZATION PROGRAM

Doihara Kenji. See MANCHURIAN INCIDENT

Domains. See ABOLITION OF DOMAINS

Dōmei. See LABOR MOVEMENT

Dōshikai. See RIKKEN DŌSHIKAI

Dōshisha. See NIIJIMA JŌ

Dutch Learning (Rangaku) 蘭学

Dutch learning was the term given to Western learning gained through the medium of the Dutch language during the Tokugawa period. Some Dutch-language books were available through Nagasaki from the 17th century, but in 1720 the shōgun Yoshimune relaxed the ban on the import of Dutch books, encouraging "practical" learning. Study of the West increased, concentrating on medicine, astronomy, calendars, and other natural sciences. As the problem of Western contact became pressing in the early 19th century, Western knowledge stimulated some scholars to criticize the political and social order, leading the Bakufu to purge some in 1839. After 1853 the Bakufu encouraged Western learning; study was extended to military science and even political and social matters, and books in other languages became available.

Boxer, C. R. *Jan Compagnie in Japan, 1600–1850* (The Hague, 1950).
Center for East Asian Studies. *Acceptance of Western Cultures in Japan* (Tokyo, 1964).
Goodman, G. K. *The Dutch Impact on Japan, 1650–1853* (Leiden, 1967).
Keene, D. *The Japanese Discovery of Europe, 1720–1830* (Stanford, 1969).
Krieger, C. C. *The Infiltration of European Civilization in Japan During the 18th Century* (Leiden, 1940).
Numata, J. "Dutch Learning (Rangaku) in Japan—A Response Pattern to the Foreign Impact," *Acta Asiatica* 22 (1972).

E

Eastern Conference (Tōhō Kaigi) 東方会議
The name given to a conference convened by the Tanaka cabinet 27 June–7 July 1927 to discuss Japan's basic policy toward China after the first Shantung Expedition (*q.v.*). The meetings were presided over by Prime Minister Tanaka and were attended by 22 members of the Foreign, War, and Navy ministries, representatives from the colonies, members of the Kwantung Army (*q.v.*) and General Staff, consular officials, and others concerned with Japan's China policy. On July 7 Tanaka issued a policy statement declaring the need for Japan to take decisive action to protect her interests in China, and for positive interventionary measures in Manchuria and Mongolia. This statement embodied the so-called Tanaka diplomacy of a "strong" policy toward China although it has been suggested that the conference itself was more to sanction existing policies than to define a new one.

The same term is also used to refer to a meeting convened by the Hara cabinet in May 1921 to discuss continental policy, which resulted in a decision to help the Chinese warlord Chang Tso-lin.

Bamba, N. *Japanese Diplomacy in a Dilemma: New Light on Japan's China Policy, 1924–1929* (Kyoto, 1972).
Iriye, A. *After Imperialism* (Cambridge, Mass., 1965).

Ebina Danjō 1856–1937 海老名弾正
A samurai from Kyūshū, Ebina studied at a Western school in Kumamoto. Converted to Christianity, he became a member of Kumamoto Christian Band and then studied at Dōshisha under Niijima Jō. After entering the church, he worked throughout Japan to spread Christianity, but it was especially as pastor of the Hongō church in Tokyo 1897–1920 that he became known as a preacher and evangelist. He also founded a Christian journal *Shinjin* (New Man). At Hongō and as head of Dōshisha 1920–1928 he was a leading figure in the Japanese Congregational Church, but his advocacy of a liberal and progressive Christianity that could accommodate traditional Japanese values and emphases led him to clash with his more orthodox colleagues. His personal and religious influence over both Christians and non-Christians was considerable.

Mitsui, H. "Dōshisha and the Kumamoto Band," *Japan Christian Quarterly* 25, no. 2 (Apr. 1959).
Notehelfer, F. G. "Ebina Danjō: A Christian Samurai of the Meiji Period," *HPJ* 2 (1963).
Scheiner, I. *Christian Converts and Social Protest in Meiji Japan* (Berkeley, 1970).

Economic Stabilization Program

(keizai antei kyūgensoku)
経済安定9原則

At the end of the war Japan was in a state of economic prostration with inflation rampant. Subsequent recovery was slow. From mid-1948 the U.S. government pressed for economic stabilization through wage and price control in order to relieve the burden of supporting Japan borne by the U.S. taxpayer and to establish a strong Japan against the background of the worsening cold war. In December 1948 a program for the rapid achievement of fiscal, monetary, price, and wage stability was recommended to the Japanese government. This called for balanced budgets, efficient taxation, credit restriction, wage stabilization, price controls, improved trade and exchange control, export expansion, increased production of essential raw materials, and improvement in food supplies. In February 1949 the American banker Joseph Dodge was sent to Japan as special adviser, and these austerity measures, known as the "Dodge Line," were adopted in the 1949 "Dodge" budget. The yen was given a fixed exchange rate to help exports, and a general policy of balanced budgets and control of inflation was followed. This economic stabilization prepared the way for industrial recovery, which was given a further stimulus by the Korean War. Dodge continued as adviser on the Japanese economy until 1951.

Cohen, J. B. *Japan's Postwar Economy* (Bloomington, Ind., 1960).
Kil, S. H. "The Dodge Line and the Japanese Conservative Party," Ph.D. diss., University of Michigan, 1977.
Lu, D. J. *Sources of Japanese History*, vol. 2 (New York, 1974).

Edo. See TOKYO

Edo Bakufu. See TOKUGAWA BAKUFU

Education

In the Tokugawa period there existed domain schools for samurai and *terakoya* (temple schools) widely attended by all classes of the population, as well as education specifically geared to trade and commerce. It is estimated that by the Restoration nearly 50% of the population had some degree of literacy. The first move toward a modern education system was the announcement of the Education Law (*gakusei*) in 1872, which asserted the importance of education for developing a modern nation and that all people had a right to such education. A pyramid system of education with the according administrative machinery was to be established, with eight university areas, each served by 32 middle schools, each middle school fed by 210 primary schools. There would also be specialist schools, and teacher training was to be provided. This education policy did stimulate the arrival of many foreign teachers and the development of primary schools out of existing *terakoya*, but the system was too large to be implemented quickly. The overall attendance rate was only 30%. In 1879 the Education Law was replaced by the Education Ordinance (*kyōikurei*), which laid the basis for the prewar school education system and for the first time made education compulsory (16 months over a four-year period). Simultaneously, conservative ideas began to reassert themselves against the more liberal educational ideas initially dominant. Although the original ordinance allowed regions considerable freedom in choosing their own education system, it was modified in 1880 to allow for a more centralized system. The details of the prewar system were laid by Mori Arinori's school education ordinances of the 1880s, which provided for an elitist, two-channel education system, with a specialist course of education for those aiming at the few imperial universities, and a "mainstream" for the majority of children. An increasing emphasis on moral education and the national spirit led to the statement of basic educational principles in the Imperial Rescript on Education (*q.v.*) of 1890. From 1886 compulsory schooling was raised to four years, and in 1907 to six, where it remained until 1947. After all payment for such schooling was abolished in 1904, over 90% of the population completed such education, and the existence of an educated workforce in conjunction with a trained elite made a major contribution to modernization. This basic education system remained unchanged until after the war although private educational institutions grew up especially in the 1920s. Military training in educational institutions was introduced from the Taishō period, and in the 1930s education became increasingly geared to the immediate needs of the state and nationalist ideology. The Basic Law on Education of 1947 set down the basic aims and concepts of a democratic education to reflect the principles of the new constitution (*q.v.*) and a new system, based on the American one, was accordingly introduced. Compulsory education consists of six years of primary school and three of middle school. High school (three years) and further education (two to four years) are optional. Elected education committees were established to control all educational decisions at prefectural and local level, but since 1956 these committees have been appointed, and increasingly the system has become more centralized. Private schools flourish at all levels. The rate of attendance beyond the primary level is extremely high, with nearly 90% of children proceeding to high school. Although in some ways education is egalitarian, being a major route to success, there are considerable problems in education, notably the dominance of a few universities, the disparity between public and private education, educational competition, and conflict between the government and the Japan Teachers' Union (*q.v.*). The government's educational spending remains a lower percentage of GNP than is the case in many other countries.

Dore, R. P. *Education in Tokugawa Japan* (London, 1965).
Hall, I. P. *Mori Arinori* (Cambridge, Mass., 1973).
Kaigo T. *Japanese Education: Its Past and Present* (Tokyo, 1965).
Passin, H. *Society and Education in Japan* (New York, 1965).

Education, Imperial Rescript. See IMPERIAL RESCRIPT ON EDUCATION

1881 Political Crisis (Meiji jūyonen no seihen) 明治14年の政変

Early in 1881 leading members of the Meiji government disagreed over constitutional proposals, Itō Hirobumi advocating transcendental cabinets after 10 years and Ōkuma Shigenobu advocating party governments within two years. Itō threatened to resign over Ōkuma's unforeseen radical proposals, but the quarrel was, with difficulty, patched up, to be reopened soon after by the Hokkaidō colonization assets scandal (*q.v.*). Ōkuma openly opposed the sale of the assets, thereby identifying himself with anti-Satsuma and Chōshū elements and violating apparent government unity. By consensus of other government members he was forced to resign on October 12; 15 senior bureaucrats resigned with him. The same month the government announced the establishment of a Diet in 1890 and cancellation of the sale of the Hokkaidō assets. The crisis firmly established the dominance of Itō and the other *hanbatsu* politicians.

Akita, G. *The Foundations of Constitutional Government in Modern Japan, 1868–1900* (Cambridge, Mass., 1967).
Fraser, A. "The Expulsion of Ōkuma from the Government in 1881," *JAS* 26, no. 2 (Feb. 1967).
Lebra, J. C. *Ōkuma Shigenobu* (Canberra, 1973).
——— "Ōkuma Shigenobu and the 1881 Political Crisis," *JAS* 18, no. 4 (Aug. 1959).

Electoral System

Japan has had a national election system since February 1889 when an open ballot system was introduced for Diet elections. Males over 25 paying over ¥15 annually in direct national taxes could vote, and those over 30 could be elected. This meant an electorate of 450,000 out of a population of 40 million. The property qualification for regional and local elections also existed, at ¥10 for prefectural assemblies down to ¥2 for town assemblies. Small electoral districts meant that politicians of local standing could be elected. In 1900 the property qualification nationally was amended to ¥10, and the system changed from small to large electoral districts with single-member secret ballot. In 1919 the qualification was reduced to ¥3 and small electoral districts reintroduced. The 1925 Suffrage Law granted universal male suffrage over 25, excluding the homeless, those unable to support themselves, and citizens of the colonies. The property qualification for local elections, already modified in preceding years, was abolished in 1926. In April 1945 males over 25 paying over ¥15 taxes in Korea and Taiwan were also admitted to the vote. From December 1945 a large electoral districts system with multiple candidature and single vote was introduced, and practically all men and women over 20 possessed the vote. All those over 25 were eligible for election. Election districts were after 1947 reduced in size, but otherwise the system has not been fundamentally changed. Elections at all levels were standardized in the Public Offices Election Law of April 1950. With the changed role of the Diet in postwar Japan, elections have taken on a much greater significance than previously. There have been considerable calls for modification of the system especially in view of the overrepresentation of less populous rural districts. It has also been argued that the multicandidature works in favor of weaker parties and candidates and increases disunity within the larger parties.

Curtis, G. L. *Election Campaigning Japanese Style* (New York, 1971).
Ike, N. *Japanese Politics* (New York, 1957).

Emigration
Japanese were legally permitted to emigrate to work abroad from 1884. During the Meiji period most emigration was to Hawaii, where Japanese laborers worked on sugar and pineapple plantations and to the western U.S. The number emigrating rose up to 1907, declined briefly, then rose again from 1913. There were over 80,000 Japanese in the U.S. by 1910, and the success of Japanese immigrants in conjunction with their failure to be assimilated on the West Coast evoked increasing opposition, resulting in local and diplomatic problems. After 1907 Japan and the U.S. came to a mutual agreement over stricter control of Japanese immigration (the so-called Gentlemen's Agreement [*q.v.*]), as Japan had done with some other countries, and this relaxed tension for a while, but U.S. discontent increased, and in 1924 Japanese immigration was effectively banned. Nevertheless, in 1930 there were an estimated 140,000 Japanese residents in the U.S. Partly due to a decline in emigration to other countries, from the Taishō period the government encouraged farmers to emigrate to South America, and nearly 200,000 had done so by 1935. The other main emigration destination was the Asian continent; here also the government promoted emigration, especially after the Manchurian Incident in its effort to develop Manchukuo. By 1937 there were half a million Japanese in Manchuria and more in China proper. Emigrants also went in small numbers to the Japanese colonies. In total some 2 million Japanese emigrated up to 1935, but there was a general unwillingness to emigrate, and emigration was not sufficient to solve Japan's population problems. There was also a high rate of returning emigrants, so in 1936 only about a million were resident abroad. Postwar emigration was banned until 1952, and in addition over 3 million Japanese were repatriated from previously occupied territories. Since 1952 small numbers of Japanese have left, mostly to go to Brazil.

Conroy, H., and T. S. Miyakawa, eds., *East Across the Pacific* (Santa Barbara, 1972).
Neu, C. E. *An Uncertain Friendship* (Cambridge, Mass., 1967).
Stanford, P. *Pioneers in the Tropics* (London, 1973).

Emperor Organ Theory
(tennō kikan setsu) 天皇機関説
Conflicting with the traditional interpretation of the Meiji constitution (*q.v.*) by Hozumi Yatsuka and others that sovereignty rested with the emperor, the emperor organ theory contended that sovereign power rested with the state and that the emperor exercised power only as the highest organ of the state under the constitution. The theory was widely held by academics and politicians during the period of Taishō Democracy (*q.v.*), but increasing criticism of it came from conservative and patriotic groups in academic, military, and bureaucratic circles. In 1935 Minobe Tatsukichi, the theory's leading exponent, was publicly denounced, forced to resign all public posts, and narrowly escaped prosecution. His writings were banned. The controversy became a national issue nearly bringing the cabinet down. Attack on the theory was part of the movement for "clarification of the national polity" (*kokutai meichō*), the widespread call for Shōwa restoration and the establishment of a new order.

Miller, F. O. *Minobe Tatsukichi—Interpreter of Constitutionalism in Japan* (Berkeley, 1965).

Emperor System (tennōsei) 天皇制
The name given to Japan's prewar political system whereby the emperor wielded the highest authority. The move toward a revival of traditional imperial authority was used before the Restoration to unite forces against the Bakufu, and this authority was used subsequently to promote a national unity, which would survive the rapid changes taking place. The official ideology was a mixture of Shintō and Confucian elements, which placed the emperor in the position of highest authority and which promoted the idea of an unbroken imperial line of divine descent to act as the axis of a unified Japanese state. The emperor's position was legally established by the Meiji constitution, which declared his inviolability and allowed him wide powers, limiting those of such organs as the Diet and cabinet. The emperor, however, did not normally make political decisions himself although everything was done in his name, and prewar politics is sometimes referred to as a struggle for the body of the emperor. The official ideology stressed loyalty and piety within the family, and this was transferred upward to the nation, which was regarded as one large family (*kazoku kokka*—family state) presided over by the emperor to whom loyalty at all levels was promoted. These ideas were increasingly reinforced after the Manchurian Incident. In 1945 the emperor system was abolished as a ruling structure, and the emperor renounced his divinity on 1 January 1946. Under the new constitution the emperor became "the symbol of the state and of the unity of the people, deriving his position from the will of the people with whom resides sovereign power."

Fridell, W. M. "Family State (*Kazoku Kokka*): An Imperial Ideology for Meiji Japan," in H. J. Lamley, ed., *East Asian Occasional Papers* 2 (Honolulu, 1970).
Hall, R. K. *Shūshin: The Ethics of a Defeated Nation* (New York, 1949).
Ōkubo, G. *The Problems of the Emperor System in Postwar Japan* (Tokyo, 1948).
Titus, D. A. *Palace and Politics in Prewar Japan* (New York, 1974).

Enomoto Takeaki (Buyō) 1836–1908
(Viscount, 1887) 榎本武揚
Member of Bakufu retainer family in Edo, Enomoto studied Dutch learning and seamanship in the 1850s and in 1862–1867 studied in Holland. He subsequently joined the Bakufu's naval department, becoming deputy head. In 1868 he refused to surrender to imperial forces and fled with Bakufu warships to Hokkaidō where he resisted the new government at the Goryōkaku fortress in Hakodate. In 1869 he surrendered and was imprisoned but was pardoned in 1872 and joined the Hokkaidō Colonization Board. In 1874 he was appointed vice-admiral and as special envoy to Russia concluded the treaty exchanging Sakhalin for the Kurile Islands (*q.v.*). He was navy minister 1880–

1881, and as special envoy to China 1882–1883 and 1884–1885 he assisted Itō Hirobumi in concluding the 1885 Tientsin Treaty. He was afterwards minister of communications 1885–1888, agriculture and commerce 1888 and 1894–1897, education 1889–1890, and foreign affairs 1891–1892. He was privy councillor 1890–1891 and 1892–1894.

EROA Funds. See RELIEF FUNDS

Eta. See BURAKU EMANCIPATION MOVEMENT

Etō Shinpei 1834–1874 江藤新平
Member of lower samurai family of Saga *han,* in the 1860s Etō was placed under house arrest for participating in the anti-foreign and pro-emperor movements but was released at the time of the Restoration. He held important posts in the new government and in April 1872 was appointed justice minister. In this capacity he worked to introduce a modern legal system, and a year later was appointed *sangi* but soon resigned over the invasion of Korea (*q.v.*). With Itagaki Taisuke he pressed for an elected assembly in Tokyo, but then returned to Saga, where in 1874 he led disaffected samurai against the government in the so-called Saga Rebellion. After the rebellion failed, Etō was arrested and executed.

Evacuation
Despite the isolated Doolittle raid of April 1942, as long as the war was going well the Japanese authorities were not inclined to make plans for the dispersal of factories and evacuation of citizens from urban areas. Some evacuation by persuasion of those not needed in war plants was proposed in autumn 1943, with more concrete plans from December on, but the evacuation of children and other persons from cities threatened by bombing was slow. The government aimed to maintain household units and utilize rural relatives as destinations for evacuees. From July 1944 a policy of enforced evacuation from 13 major cities was applied to children in 3rd to 6th grades of elementary school. Those without relatives or friends in the country were sent in groups to be looked after by teachers or housemothers in shrines, inns, and halls. Some younger children were later included, and by March 1945 over 450,000 had been moved, but many children and adults still remained in the cities, where casualties from bombing reached hundreds of thousands. Safety from bombing meant that such evacuation as took place was a qualified success, but many children suffered intense homesickness, and their living conditions were little better than they might otherwise have been. After the March 1945 bombings many fled from the cities—some 10 million in all—but this was purely voluntary rather than being the result of state planning, and the mass exodus caused considerable problems in the countryside.

Daniels, B. "The Evacuation of School Children in Wartime Japan," in G. Daniels and P. C. Lowe, eds., *BAJS Proceedings* 2, pt. 2 (Sheffield, 1977).
Havens, T. R. H. *Valley of Darkness* (New York, 1978).

Exhibitions
Japan first sent exhibits to the Paris International Exposition of 1867, and by 1885 had exhibited at 20 other foreign exhibitions in the hope of increasing exports. More important were the five domestic industrial exhibitions sponsored by the government in Tokyo (1877, 1881, 1890), Kyoto (1895), and Osaka (1903), which aimed at the encouragement of industry by exhibiting domestically produced goods. In 1877 over 80,000 items were exhibited, and there were nearly half a million visitors. Although craft goods were initially dominant, machinery and other Western-style goods increasingly appeared, and in conjunction with competitions and shows sponsored by local government and private enterprise after 1880, these exhibitions played a considera-

ble role in advancing industrial technology and improving its quality.

Extraterritoriality
The freedom from jurisdiction of the territory of residence or stay and the exercise by one state of judicial authority and sovereignty within the territories of another was an old custom but was enjoyed by Westerners in many countries of Asia and Africa in the 19th century. In Japan this right was initiated by the first treaties with the West in 1854 but was made explicit in the Ansei Treaties of 1858 (*q.v.*), which provided for foreigners to be tried by their own consuls according to their own laws in both civil and criminal cases. Consulates established in open ports and cities held consular courts. The Japanese had no reciprocal rights abroad, and the abolition of extraterritoriality became a basic issue of treaty revision (*q.v.*). Japan achieved the abolition of extraterritoriality in 1899 when new treaties, signed 1894 (and subsequently), came into effect. From 1876 Japan herself exercised extraterritorial rights in Korea and from 1895 in China.

Jones, F. C. *Extraterritoriality in Japan and the Diplomatic Relations Resulting in Its Abolition, 1853–1899* (New Haven, 1931).

F

Factory Legislation
In the early Meiji period there were few provisions for the protection of workers, only covering individual industries such as mining. After 1881 the Industry Department of the Agriculture and Commerce Ministry began to investigate working conditions in the increasing number of factories, and in 1902 an outline factory act was published. Submitted to the Diet in 1909, after much opposition it was passed in March 1911. Its provisions included prohibition of the employment of children under 12, prohibition of night work (10 P.M. to 4 A.M.) by women and young workers and a 12-hour day for women and those under 15. Although the act was to come into force in 1916, the ban on night work and the 12-hour day were only to be enforced from 1926. Many of the other stipulations fell below international standards, the act was not applied to factories of less than 15 workers (except for those doing dangerous or unhealthy work), and inspection was inadequate. The act had very limited impact although the fact that the initiative for it had come from the government was significant. The revised act of 1926 included among its modifications application to factories of over 10 workers and further limitations on some working hours, but many of the provisions were never enforced absolutely. Outside factories some protection of other employments such as seafaring was available, but as late as 1933 protection was almost nonexistent in the primary sector, except for mining. After 1923 a limited degree of workmen's compensation and accident insurance was also introduced. In 1947 the existing factory legislation was replaced by the Labor Standards Act and its concomitant laws.

Ayusawa, I. *A History of Labor in Modern Japan* (Honolulu, 1966).
Dore, R. P. "The Modernizer as a Special Case: Japanese Factory Legislation, 1882–1911," *Studies in Society and History* 11 (Oct. 1969).
Harari, E. *The Politics of Labor Legislation in Japan* (Berkeley, 1973).

Family Law. See CIVIL CODE

Far Eastern Commission (Kyokutō Iinkai) 極東委員会
This supreme organ of allied policy formulation toward Occupied Japan was established as a result of the Moscow foreign ministers conference of December 1945. The commission, which met regularly in

Washington from February 1946, consisted of representatives of the 11 countries at war with Japan, joined in 1949 by Burma and Pakistan. The commission was charged with formulating the basic principles of Occupation policy and scrutiny of SCAP (*q.v.*) activities and directives via the U.S. government. Its prior approval was necessary for fundamental changes in Japan's administrative system and constitutional structure. At the same time the Allied Council for Japan (*q.v.*) was established to advise the Occupation authorities in Tokyo. The U.S., Russia, China, and Britain had veto power in the commission, but the U.S.'s entitlement to issue interim directives to SCAP in fact gave the U.S. considerable freedom in policy making. The commission was initially active in decision making, but its effectiveness was hindered by delays in passing needed policy decisions, failure to settle some important policy matters, especially with increasing Soviet-U.S. disagreement after 1948, and inadequate liaison with Douglas MacArthur, and its importance decreased. It was abolished in 1952.

Ball, W. M. *Japan: Enemy or Ally?* (New York, 1949).
Blakeslee, G. H. *The Far Eastern Commission* (Washington, 1953).

Farmers' Movement
Peasant uprisings against local hardships were very frequent in the later Tokugawa period and continued into the early Meiji period. Some of these uprisings opposed the execution of new government policies such as reform of the land tax and conscription; others demanded local tax and rent reductions, but by and large most disturbances were spontaneous and had limited aims. During the 1880s some peasant discontent was manifested in participation in the popular rights movement. The rapid increase in tenancy (*q.v.*) during the Meiji period meant that from about 1900 tenancy disputes became a major element in the farmers' protest movement. These became especially numerous after World War I, and in 1922 the first national farmers' organization, the Japan Farmers' Union (Nihon Nōmin Kumiai), was founded by Kagawa Toyohiko and Sugiyama Motojirō with the aim of coordinating tenant protest and improving the welfare and status of farmers. The union expanded fast and played a major role in disputes and in wider agitation, but it suffered from the ideological and personal divisions that beset much of the left-wing movement at this time. This, in conjunction with government oppression and rural depression, meant that from the mid-1920s national leadership of the farmers' movement was split and ineffective, despite the existence of a variety of farmers' organizations. Overall union membership remained a minute percentage of Japan's total farming population. Small-scale tenancy disputes remained numerous through the 1930s, but national coordination was nonexistent although the right-wing elements of the movement led by Hirano Rikizō maintained a semblance of national organization up to the time of the Pacific War. Farmers' organizations revived postwar, with the unifying Japan Farmers' Union being formed in 1946. Protest concentrated on matters of tax and grain quotas, but the land reform removed many of the farmers' grievances, and activity waned. The united front presented by the J.F.U. did not last long, and since 1947 the farmers' movement has suffered from divided leadership. Increasing prosperity has also removed most of the prewar sources of discontent.

Dore, R. P. *Land Reform in Japan* (London, 1959).
Waswo, A. *Japanese Landlords: The Decline of a Rural Elite* (Berkeley, 1977).
______. "The Origins of Tenant Unrest," in B. S. Silberman and H. D. Harootunian, eds., *Japan in Crisis: Essays in Taishō Democracy* (Princeton, 1974).

February 26 Rising (Ni-ni-roku jiken) 2.26事件
Following the trial of Aizawa Saburō (*q.v.*) and the measures taken to disperse the army's *kōdō* faction (*q.v.*), on 26 Febru-

ary 1936 young *kōdō* faction officers led an attempted coup. In the early morning some 1,400 soldiers from three regiments took over the center of Tokyo, occupying such places as the Diet building and War Ministry. Finance Minister Takahashi Korekiyo, Lord Privy Seal Saitō Makoto, and Inspector General of Military Education Watanabe Jōtarō were killed, and other leading public figures were attacked and wounded, including Grand Chamberlain Suzuki Kantarō. Through the War Ministry the rising's leaders called for a Shōwa Restoration (*q.v.*), the establishment of a new domestic order. Martial law was declared, but initially the military authorities took no measures to put down the mutiny. Only on February 28, when it had become clear that a coup lacked support from the navy, financial circles, and people at large, as well as from the emperor, did the military authorities refer to the mutineers as rebels and move in other forces to quell the rising. Most rebel soldiers were persuaded to return to their barracks; some of the leaders committed suicide, and on February 29 the others were arrested. One hundred twenty-four were prosecuted, and after a quick trial 13 officers and four civilians were sentenced to death. Collaborators were also tried, and in August 1937 Kita Ikki and Nishida Mitsugu, whose ideas had strongly influenced the young officers, were executed. After the rising the Okada cabinet fell. Many *kōdō* faction members were placed on reserve or scattered among new posts, and the incident ultimately served to strengthen the *tōsei* faction's (*q.v.*) influence.

Shillony, B. A. *Revolt in Japan: The Young Officers and the February 26, 1936, Incident* (Princeton, 1973).

Federation of Economic Organizations (Keizai Dantai Rengōkai) 経済団体連合会

Keidanren for short, this federation was founded in 1946 as a central body to assist liaison between individual economic organizations, but since 1952 it has had a wide role and membership. Affiliation is classified by industry, and membership comprises economic organizations, enterprises, and individuals. Apart from linking various economic organizations, Keidanren coordinates opinion in the business world and communicates it to both government and Diet; it has thus come to exercise a strong influence over the policy of the Liberal Democratic government.

Feudal System (hōken seido) 封建制度

Notwithstanding the widespread use of the term *feudal* in relation to Japan, its application in Japanese historiography poses considerable problems. Originally used in China to denote a centralized administrative system, the term *hōken seido* (domain-building system) was used in Japan in the Tokugawa period to denote the separatist, decentralized political character of the Tokugawa's *baku-han* system, in contrast to the *gunken* (prefectural) system of administration based on local units under officials of a central government, such as existed in contemporary China. Following renewed contact with the West, the term came to be translated into English as "feudalism" or "feudal system," thereby initiating use of the term also to imply certain socioeconomic characteristics of European feudalism. Since the term is also used in materialist historiography to denote the whole socioeconomic structure of a society at a certain stage of development, application of the term to Japan is frequently vague and apt to lead to confusion. However, the term is normally broadly used to refer to Japan under military governments in the years from the Kamakura period to the fall of the Tokugawa Bakufu (1185–1867) although within this time span there is a multiplicity of subdivisions. The influence of Western concepts of feudalism means that *hōken seido* is used to denote not just the administrative system but the whole socioeconomic structure during this period, and therefore "the abolition of feudalism" is loosely used in the case of Japan to refer to the series of measures by which the Meiji government dismantled the apparatus of Tokugawa rule and the socioeconomic structure on which it was based, replacing it by a politically centralized state headed by the emperor. The major steps of this radical change were return of the land and people to the emperor and the ultimate conversion of feudal fiefs into prefectures; reform of the class structure from samurai, farmers, artisans, merchants, and outcasts to nobility, warriors, and common people (1869–1872), and the eventual abolition of warrior status; the introduction of conscription (1873); the commutation of samurai stipends (1873–1875), and reform of the land tax (1872–1877). Nevertheless, the continued existence of "feudal" influences and elements long after these reforms has remained the object of considerable debate among Japanese historians. (See also JAPANESE CAPITALISM DEBATE.)

Anderson, P. *Lineages of the Absolutist State* (London, 1974).
Beasley, W. G. *The Meiji Restoration* (London, 1973).
Duus, P. *Feudalism in Japan* (New York, 1969).
Hall, J. W. "Feudalism in Japan—A Reassessment," *Comparative Studies in Society and History* 5, no. 1 (Oct. 1962).
Reischauer, E. O. "Japanese Feudalism," in R. Coulborn, ed., *Feudalism in History* (Princeton, 1956).

Financial Crisis, 1927. See 1927 FINANCIAL CRISIS

Foreign Relations Advisory Council. See ADVISORY COUNCIL ON FOREIGN RELATIONS

Formosa. See TAIWAN

Formosan Expedition (Seitai no eki) 征台の役

In 1871 Ryūkyūans landing on Formosa were killed by natives. Ownership of the Ryūkyū islands (*q.v.*) was in dispute at this time, but Japan demanded that China take punitive action and provide compensation. In 1873 China did acknowledge Japan's claim that the Ryūkyūans were Japanese citizens, but her failure to indemnify Japan led to a Japanese resolution to send a punitive expedition to Formosa. Disagreement within the government following objections by the U.S. delayed the expedition, but its appointed leader, Saigō Tsugumichi, went ahead on his own. In spring 1874 he landed on Formosa with over 3,500 men and occupied part of it. The troops were eventually withdrawn after Ōkubo Toshimichi reached agreement with the Chinese in October. The Chinese agreed to pay some of Japan's expenses for the expedition and openly recognized that the Ryūkyūans were Japanese citizens. The expedition also acted as something of a safety valve for samurai discontent.

Atkins, E. H. "General Charles LeGendre and the Japanese Expedition to Formosa, 1874," Ph.D. diss., University of Florida, 1953.
House, E. H. *The Japanese Expedition to Formosa* (Tokyo, 1875).

Franco-Japanese Agreement (1907) (Nichi-Futsu Kyōyaku) 日仏協約

In June 1907 France and Japan concluded an agreement in Paris by which both countries testified to the independence and territorial integrity of China and agreed to respect each other's territorial rights and position in Asia. For France the agreement guaranteed friendly relations with Japan, which was now strong in Asia; Japan was brought closer to the Triple Entente countries, especially in support of communal interests in China and neighboring areas. The agreement in effect supported spheres of influence in China despite assertions of an "open door" policy.

Pooley, A. M., ed. *The Secret Memoirs of Count Tadasu Hayashi* (London, 1915).

Freedom and People's Rights Movement (jiyū minken undō) 自由民権運動

This was the name given to the antigovernment movement of 1874–1890, which called for a Diet and a democratic constitution. In January 1874 Gotō Shōjirō and Itagaki Taisuke submitted a petition for an elected assembly and founded the Aikoku Kōtō (*q.v.*). The movement was initially dominated by dissatisfied *shizoku* acting through the Risshisha (*q.v.*) and other regional organizations and through national groups such as the Aikokusha (*q.v.*), but in the later 1870s it increasingly gained support from the richer members of the farming community. Government attempts to suppress opposition after 1875 by restrictive press and assembly laws hindered activity 1875–1878, but the movement then revived on a nationwide basis. By 1881 its main organization, the Kokkai Kisei Dōmei (League for Founding a National Assembly) (*q.v.*), claimed to represent 200,000 people. Pressure from the movement contributed to the government's promise of a Diet and constitution in 1881. In the early 1880s the movement was led by the Jiyūtō and the Kaishintō (*q.v.*). Its preoccupations were now the nature of the Japanese constitution and the problem of treaty revision, but at local levels there was an increasing involvement with the problems of impoverished farmers; the movement called for land tax reduction. From 1882 Jiyūtō members were involved in several violent incidents over which party leadership had no control. Government suppression grew worse, and after 1884 there was little activity at national or local levels. An antigovernment movement revived in 1887 with a petition movement for treaty revision, reduction in the land tax, and freedom of speech. Until 1889 this was embodied in the Daidō Danketsu movement (*q.v.*), but after that mass interest again declined. Opposition to the government after 1890 could be largely expressed through political parties in the Diet.

Akita, G. *The Foundations of Constitutional Government in Japan, 1868–1900* (Cambridge, Mass., 1967).
Ike, N. *The Beginnings of Political Democracy in Japan* (Baltimore, 1950).

Friendly Society. See YŪAIKAI

Fujita Denzaburō 1841–1912 (Baron, 1911) 藤田伝三郎
The son of a sake brewer in Chōshū, Fujita participated in the anti-Bakufu movement (*q.v.*). After the Restoration he engaged in business, and he utilized his strong Chōshū connections, especially that with Inoue Kaoru, to gain for his Osaka based trading company contracts for supplies to the army. From 1881 the company was known as the Fujita Group (*gumi*). It benefited from the sale of government enterprises, and the group's interests subsequently expanded and diversified although they remained concentrated in mining, farming, forestry, and transport. Fujita himself, known as a political merchant (*seishō*) (*q.v.*) par excellence, became a leader of the Osaka business world and dominated the group until his death. Although expansion continued subsequently and the group founded its own bank, it suffered severely during the economic fluctuations of the 1920s and never became one of the biggest *zaibatsu* (*q.v.*). After a revival in the late 1930s existing enterprise connections were dissolved under the postwar deconcentration measures.

Hirschmeier, J. *The Origins of Entrepreneurship in Meiji Japan* (Cambridge, Mass., 1964).

Fujita Group. See FUJITA DENZABURŌ

Fukuchi Gen'ichirō 1841–1906 福地源一郎
A samurai from Nagasaki, Fukuchi studied Dutch and English and twice acted as interpreter on Bakufu missions to the U.S. In 1870 he joined the new government and accompanied Itō and Iwakura on foreign missions 1871–1872. Returning to Japan in 1874, he left the government and until January 1888 was editor of the pro-government *Tokyo Nichi Nichi* newspaper. He was also active in the stock exchange and Tokyo city government and led the short-lived, pro-government Rikken Teiseitō (Constitutional Imperialist Party) (*q.v.*) 1882–1883, when he clashed bitterly with advocates of

popular rights. From 1887 he managed the Kabuki theater and devoted himself to writing plays, novels, and historical works, the latter mostly concerning the Bakufu's demise. He was elected to the Diet in 1904.

Huffman, J. L. "Fukuchi Gen'ichirō, Journalist-Intellectual in Early Meiji Japan," Ph.D. diss., University of Michigan, 1972.

Fukuda (Kageyama) Hideko 1865–1927 福田(景山)英子

Kageyama Hideko was the daughter of a lower samurai of Okayama *han*. At 17 she established a school for girls with her mother and, inspired by Kishida Toshiko, began to work for women's rights. Increasingly involved in the popular rights movement, after her school was banned in 1884 by the prefectural authorities she went to Tokyo and joined the Jiyūtō (*q.v.*) but in 1885 was arrested and imprisoned for participating in the Osaka incident (*q.v.*). After leaving prison in 1889, she lived with Ōi Kentarō but subsequently separated from him and married Fukuda Yūsaku, who died in 1900. During the 1890s and 1900s she twice established schools in Tokyo to provide a practical education for girls to help them to economic independence. In 1904 she completed an autobiography *Warawa no Hanshōgai* (Half My Life). Her fight for women's political rights led her to become interested in socialism. She joined the Heiminsha (*q.v.*) and in 1907 became editor of the newly founded *Sekai Fujin* (World Women), a Socialist women's rights publication. *Sekai Fujin* was suppressed in 1908 and despite Fukuda's early fame, she spent much of the rest of her life in poverty and comparative obscurity.

Fukuda Takeo 1905– 福田赳夫

A native of Gunma prefecture, Fukuda graduated in law from Tokyo Imperial University and entered the Finance Ministry where he held top offices after the war. In 1948 he was accused of corruption in connection with the Shōwa Electric Company (*q.v.*) but was acquitted in 1958. In 1952 he was elected to the Diet and subsequently became a member of Kishi's faction in the Liberal Democratic Party. After serving as minister of agriculture and forestry 1959–1960, he was head of the party's political affairs section under Ikeda and a strong supporter of Satō Eisaku. Despite his criticisms of factionalism he took over former Kishi adherents to create his own faction. He served as finance minister 1965–1966 and 1968–1970 and foreign minister 1971–1972. He was beaten by Tanaka Kakuei in the 1972 leadership ballot but served under him as finance minister 1973–1974 when he had to cope with the effects of the oil shock. In 1974–1976 Fukuda was deputy prime minister and director of the Economic Planning Agency under Miki Takeo. In December 1976 he was eventually successful in a leadership ballot and became prime minister. Fukuda has close contacts both with the bureaucracy and with the financial world and is regarded as being among the more conservative elements in his party. His "bureaucratic" image has contributed to lack of popularity, and he resigned as prime minister and party leader in December 1978 after a nationwide ballot of the L.D.P. membership expressed a preference for the leadership of Ōhira Masayoshi. Fukuda's greatest achievement as prime minister was probably the Peace and Friendship Treaty with the People's Republic of China.

Fukumotoism 福本イズム

The theories of the Marxist intellectual Fukumoto Kazuo, known as Fukumotoism, replaced the previously influential views of Yamakawa Hitoshi (Yamakawaism) as the dominant influence in the ideology of the Japanese Communist movement 1925–1927. Fukumoto stressed the importance of theory over practical means and experience, the need to establish a correct theoretical base for any mass movement, and the separation of "correct" from "false" Marxists. This in effect amounted to an attack on other members of the left wing. Fukumoto was increasingly criticized by the Comintern and some Japanese Communists on the grounds that his ideas alienated the party from the masses, placed excessive emphasis on intellectuals, and failed to understand the role of the party as distinct from labor unions. The 1927 thesis approved by the Comintern in July of that year marked the end of the dominance of Fukumoto's ideas in the movement, and he subsequently lost his position on the central committee of the Japan Communist Party.

Beckmann, G. M., and G. Okubo. *The Japanese Communist Party, 1922–1945* (Berkeley, 1969).
Scalapino, R. A. *The Japanese Communist Movement, 1920–1966* (Berkeley, 1967).

Fukushima Incident (Fukushima jiken) 福島事件

In 1882 Mishima Michitsune was appointed governor of Fukushima prefecture and immediately tried to enforce a compulsory labor program for a road-building program round Aizu. The Jiyūtō-dominated prefectural assembly, led by Kōno Hironaka, opposed the proposals, and from July when Mishima attempted to impose tax in lieu of labor, resistance spread among the people of Aizu. Backed by the Home Ministry, Mishima disregarded the opposition and in November arrested the leaders of the protest movement. A mob of about 10,000 attacked and destroyed the police station at Kitakata where those arrested were being held, and on November 29 over 2,000 farmers and Jiyūtō members were arrested. Of the Jiyūtō members Kōno was sentenced to seven years imprisonment for crimes against the state, and several others to six years. The incident, which was symptomatic of growing radical and violent tendencies in the democratic movement, considerably undermined the Jiyūtō's influence in the north.

Bowen, R. W. *Rebellion and Democracy in Meiji Japan* (Berkeley, 1980).
Ike, N. *The Beginnings of Political Democracy in Japan* (Baltimore, 1950).

Fukuzawa Yukichi 1835–1901 福沢諭吉

A lower samurai from Nakatsu domain (now Fukuoka Prefecture), by his own account Fukuzawa from early on hated the feudal system. He studied Dutch and Western sciences in Nagasaki and from 1854 in Osaka under Ogata Kōan. In 1858 he opened his own school in Edo and subsequently introduced the teaching of English, which he had studied by himself. In 1860, 1862, and 1867 he went to Europe and America on Bakufu service, and the knowledge of the West gained from these trips appeared in his famous introduction to Western civilization *Seiyō Jijō* (Conditions in the West), first published in 1866 (subsequently modified), as well as other books. In 1868 he renamed his school Keiō Gijuku, and after moving to Mita (Tokyo) in 1871 it developed into the famous Keiō University (*q.v.*). Renouncing samurai status, Fukuzawa refused requests to join the new government and devoted himself to the provision of "practical" education, stressing the value of science and a spirit of independence. He wrote and spoke on a wide range of topics and was a major influence in the spread of Western ideas in Japan. From 1873 he was active in the Meirokusha (*q.v.*). Influenced by English utilitarianism, Fukuzawa strongly attacked feudal mores and advocated the people's possession of rights as well as duties. His support of independence and self-respect for both individual and state led him to support the government policy of "rich country/strong army." In 1882 he founded a paper, the *Jiji Shinpō,* aimed, as were his educational efforts, at disseminating the principle of independence. From the 1880s some of his ideas became less radical; he criticized the freedom and people's rights movement (*q.v.*), advocated harmony between government and people, and gave qualified support to an aggressive continental policy. Despite this Fukuzawa is considered the most important "enlightened" thinker of the early Meiji period and wielded tremendous influence through his educational achievements, his speeches, and his numerous writings. Other best known works include *The Encouragement of Learning* (1872–1876) and *An Outline of a Theory of Civilization* (1875).

Blacker, C. *The Japanese Enlightenment* (Cambridge, 1964).
Fukuzawa, Y. (tr. and intro. D. A. Dilworth). *An Encouragement of Learning* (Tokyo, 1969).
______. (tr. and ed. D. A. Dilworth and G. C. Hurst). *An Outline of a Theory of Civilization* (Tokyo, 1973).
Kiyooka, E., tr. and ed. *The Autobiography of Fukuzawa Yukichi* (Tokyo, 1960).

Furukawa Ichibei 1832–1903
古河市兵衛

Member of a merchant family in Kyoto, Furukawa worked for the Ono Group (*q.v.*) in the silk trade but went independent after the group's bankruptcy. In 1877, with the help of a loan and aided by Shibusawa Eiichi, he purchased the Ashio copper mine, where his radical innovations produced commercial success. In 1885 he bought up the great Innai and Ani silver mines and by 1897 was manager of 12 copper mines (producing 40% domestic copper production), eight silver mines, one gold mine, and several other related enterprises; these interests caused him to be called "the mining king." Furukawa avoided the joint stock form of enterprise, and on his death his companies passed directly into the ownership of his family. Successive reorganizations led the enterprises to take on the form of a *zaibatsu* (*q.v.*),and interests expanded into metal processing, chemicals, and machinery. The Furukawa interests remained concentrated on heavy industry, and despite more organic interconnectedness its enterprises were less tied to each other than those of most other *zaibatsu;* although the group founded its own bank in 1917, it remained dependent on Shibusawa's Daiichi Bank. The economic conditions of the early 1930s forced the group into retrenchment, but its fortunes revived under the ensuing military impetus. Despite dissolution postwar many of the prewar links have been retained or renewed.

Hirschmeier, J. *The Origins of Entrepreneurship in Meiji Japan* (Cambridge, Mass., 1964).

Furukawa Zaibatsu. See FURUKAWA ICHIBEI

G

Gakusei. See EDUCATION

GARIOA Funds. See RELIEF FUNDS

Genrō 元老

Name applied to a group of senior statesmen who advised the emperor and exercised considerable influence in political affairs even when no longer holding high office. Initially the *genrō* (elder statesmen) consisted of Inoue Kaoru, Itō Hirobumi, Kuroda Kiyotaka, Matsukata Masayoshi, Ōyama Iwao, Saigō Tsugumichi, and Yamagata Aritomo, all of whom were Satsuma and Chōshū men who had dominated the administration in the 1870s to 1890s. Later Katsura Tarō and Saionji Kinmochi joined the group. Although as a group the *genrō* had no constitutional existence, formal rank, or even official title (although individually they may also have held office), they played a crucial role in political affairs from the 1890s to the 1930s, intervening in all major political decisions; their role included advising the emperor on the appointment of a new prime minister, and they acted as a link between the emperor and the formal government. Although after 1924 Saionji was the only living *genrō*, he remained extremely influential into the 1930s. The *genrō*'s role was in part filled during the 1930s by conferences of so-called "senior statesmen" (*jūshin*).

Bailey, J. "The Origin and Nature of the *Genrō*," in R. K. Sakai, ed., *Studies on Asia* (Lincoln, Nebr., 1965).
Hackett, R. F. "Political Modernization and the Meiji *Genrō*," in R. E. Ward, ed., *Political Development in Modern Japan* (Princeton, 1968).
Okamoto, S. *The Japanese Oligarchy and the Russo-Japanese War* (New York, 1970).

Genrōin 元老院

Established as a result of the Osaka Conference (*q.v.*) in April 1875, the Genrōin (senate) replaced the *sain* and was an advisory organ on legislation, preparatory to a division of administrative, legislative, and judicial powers. Presided over by ministers of the Left and Right who headed the Dajōkan system, Genrōin members were appointed by the emperor from the nobility, high-ranking bureaucrats, etc. Although constituted to discuss legislation, the Genrōin discussed matters referred to it only by imperial command, and the government was permitted to take measures which were only afterwards discussed by it. In addition to its weak powers the composition of the Genrōin was not such as was likely to disagree with the government on major matters, and in terms of legislation it could be largely disregarded. It published a draft constitution in 1880, but this came to nothing. The Genrōin was abolished in October 1890.

Center for East Asian Cultural Studies. *Meiji Japan Through Contemporary Sources,* vol. 1 (Tokyo, 1969).
Teters, B. J. "The Genrōin and the National Essence Movement," *PHR* 31 (Nov. 1962).

Gentlemen's Agreement
(Nichibei shinshi kyōyaku)
日米紳士協約

Name given to an agreement reached after lengthy negotiations between Japan and America in February 1908 relating to Japan's voluntary restriction of Japanese emigration to the U.S. The agreement eased the strain in American-Japanese relations, avoiding immediate exclusion legislation, and made way for the Root-Takahira Agreement (*q.v.*), but the immigrant problem continued to arouse tensions, and the 1924 Quota Law had the effect of halting virtually all Japanese immigration into the U.S.

Esthus, R. A. *Theodore Roosevelt and Japan* (Seattle, 1966).
Neu, C. E. *An Uncertain Friendship* (Cambridge, Mass., 1967).

Genyōsha 玄洋社

An ultranationalist society founded in 1881. The first president was Hiraoka Kōtarō, and subsequent leading members were Tōyama Mitsuru and Uchida Ryōhei. The Genyōsha (Dark Ocean Society) was begun by Fukuoka samurai who had opposed the government following the dispute over the invasion of Korea (*q.v.*) and initially called for democratic politics, but during the 1880s the society moved away from the popular rights movement, advocating advance on the continent and a strong foreign policy. A Genyōsha member injured Ōkuma Shigenobu because of his treaty revision proposals in 1889. Members had strong connections with the army and engaged in clandestine activity in Manchuria, Korea, and China, where they were referred to as "continental adventurers" (*tairiku rōnin*). The society also developed strong connections with the government and on occasions allied with it to suppress liberal and left-wing movements at home. As the society's real leader, Tōyama wielded tremendous influence not only among the right wing but at highest government levels. The Genyōsha was abolished 1946.

Norman, E. H. "The Genyōsha: A Study in the Origins of Japanese Imperialism," *Pacific Affairs* 17, no. 3 (Sept. 1944).
Sabey, J. W. "The Gen'yōsha, the Koku-

ryūkai and Japanese Expansionism," Ph.D. diss., University of Michigan, 1972.

GHQ. See SCAP

Gold Standard. See CURRENCY

Godai Tomoatsu 1836–1885
五代友厚
A Satsuma samurai, Godai studied in Nagasaki from 1857 and after a secret visit to Shanghai began to advocate Japan's opening to foreign trade and Western influences. He was captured by the English during their confrontation with Satsuma in 1863 but escaped, and in 1865, by order of his domain, he went to study in the West. Returning the following year he worked to expand trade in Satsuma but in 1868 joined the new government, only to leave the following year to devote himself to private business. Retaining strong connections with members of the government and receiving considerable help from them, he became famous as a *seishō* (political merchant) (*q.v.*) and was involved in the Hokkaidō Colonization Assets scandal of 1881 (*q.v.*). His main business interests were in metals, mining, indigo, and railways, but he also helped to lay the basis of the Osaka financial world by working for the establishment in the city of a stock exchange, a rice exchange, a chamber of commerce, and an assay office. He also established a private commercial training school as part of an attempt to break down conservative business attitudes.

Hirschmeier, J. *The Origins of Entrepreneurship in Meiji Japan* (Cambridge, Mass., 1964).
Hoover, W. D. "Crisis Resolution in Early Meiji Diplomatic Relations: The Role of Godai Tomoatsu," *JAH* 9, no. 1 (1975).
———. "Godai Tomoatsu (1836–1885)—An Economic Statesman of Early Meiji Japan," Ph.D. diss., University of Michigan, 1973.

Gondō Seikyō (Seikei, Nariaki) 1868–1937 権藤成卿
Gondō, the son of a Fukuoka Prefecture samurai/owner-farmer, traveled widely in mainland Asia in his youth but in 1900 settled in Tokyo. He had joined the Kokuryūkai (*q.v.*) and soon established a reputation as a nationalist and agrarianist (*nōhonshugi*) ideologue. He rejected bureaucratic government, capitalism, and urbanization, urging a return to an agrarian-centered economy based on rural communes self-sufficient economically and politically. His ideas appealed especially to landlords and wealthy peasants. His followers participated in farmers' protest movements especially from the late 1920s when acute rural depression set in. From the late Taishō period his views were influential among the right wing and young army officers, especially among those with first-hand experience of the problems faced by the rural areas, and he was a major influence on the ideology of nationalism in Japan between the wars. Gondō was arrested after the Blood League and May 15 Incidents (*q.v.*) for which he was the ideological inspiration but was released. He wrote and lectured widely on his views.

Havens, T. R. H. *Farm and Nation in Modern Japan—Agrarian Nationalism, 1870–1940* (Princeton, 1974).
Tanin, O. and E. Yohan. *Militarism and Fascism in Japan* (rprt. Westport, Conn., 1973).

Gotō-Joffe Talks (Gotō-Yoffe kaidan)
後藤・ヨッフェ会談
In spring 1923, A. Joffe, the Soviet representative in China, was in Japan ostensibly on a cure at Atami, and March-June he had a series of informal meetings with Gotō Shinpei with a view to solving the problem of Japanese recognition of the U.S.S.R. In June these talks developed into informal negotiations between Joffe and Kawakami of the Japanese Foreign Ministry, but the major obstacles of the Japanese occupation of northern Sakhalin and settlement of the Nikolaevsk massacre (*q.v.*) prevented the opening of formal

negotiations at this point, and relations were not established until 1925.

Lensen, G. A. *Japanese Recognition of the U.S.S.R.: Soviet-Japanese Relations, 1921–1930* (Tokyo, 1970).

Gotō Shinpei 1857–1929 (Baron, 1906; Viscount, 1922; Count, 1928)
後藤新平
A native of Sendai domain, Gotō studied medicine and in 1881 became head of Aichi Hospital and Medical School. In 1883 he joined the Home Ministry and after studying in Germany was the head of its new Sanitation Bureau 1890–1892 and 1895–1898; here his interests lay in the social and administrative aspects of public health. As head of the civil administration of Taiwan under General Kodama 1898–1906, Gotō laid the basis for the administration of the colony; he founded the Bank of Taiwan, made opium and camphor state monopolies, and adopted a "strong" policy toward the island's indigenous population. In 1906 he became the first president of the Manchurian Railway. 1908–1910 and 1912–1913 he was communications minister and head of the Railways Bureau with responsibility for colonial affairs. 1916–1918 he was home minister and also in charge of railways and then in 1918 foreign minister during the Siberian Expedition (*q.v.*). Appointed mayor of Tokyo in 1920, during 1923–1924 he was again home minister, with responsibility for rebuilding the city after the Kantō earthquake (*q.v.*). Gotō was throughout an advocate of Asian unity but also advocated improving Japan's relations with the powers; during the early 1920s he held a series of private conversations with the Soviet representative in China, Joffe, with a view to restoring Russo-Japanese relations. An interest in relations with Russia was maintained until his death. After retiring in 1924, Gotō was involved in the development of broadcasting, youth organizations, and the movement agitating for greater morality in politics.

Hayase, Y. "The Career of Gotō Shinpei: Japan's Statesman of Research, 1857–1929," Ph.D. diss., Florida State University, 1974.
Lensen, G. A. *Japanese Recognition of the U.S.S.R.: Soviet-Japanese Relations, 1921–1930* (Tokyo, 1970).
Tsurumi, E. P. "Taiwan Under Kodama Gentarō and Gotō Shinpei," *HPJ* 4 (1967).

Gotō Shōjirō 1838–1897 (Count, 1887)
後藤象二郎
Member of Tosa samurai family, Gotō studied at the Kaiseijo (*q.v.*) and subsequently played a major role in *han* government. Influenced by Sakamoto Ryōma, he became a leading advocate of a peaceful restoration of imperial rule. In 1868 he joined the new government and worked in foreign affairs, industry, and as governor of Osaka before becoming *sangi* but resigned in 1873 over the invasion of Korea (*q.v.*). For the rest of his life, Gotō retained a strong interest in the Korean problem. He subsequently participated in the founding of the Aikoku Kōtō (*q.v.*) and campaigned for an elected assembly, although returning briefly to the government after the Osaka Conference (*q.v.*). In 1881 he became a founder-member of the Jiyūtō, but the following year the government persuaded him to leave and travel abroad with Itagaki Taisuke. After 1887 he led the Daidō Danketsu movement (*q.v.*) against the government but was persuaded to abandon his opposition and act as communications minister 1889–1892. In 1892 he was appointed minister of agriculture and commerce but resigned in 1894.

Ike, N. *The Beginnings of Political Democracy in Japan* (Baltimore, 1950).

Government Enterprises
At the time of the Restoration the government took over munitions factories, shipyards, and mines formerly owned by the Bakufu and from them built up military production industries. As well as such infrastructure as railways and telegraphs, the government tried to promote industrial development and reduce imports and during the 1870s set up model

factories to introduce new Western techniques and to encourage the development of private enterprise in such fields as shipbuilding, textiles, cement, glass, and bricks. During the 1870s, therefore, government engagement in direct production, much of it administered by the Ministry of Industry, was considerable and contributed greatly to the introduction of modern industry. Among the most famous enterprises were the Tomioka Silk Mill and shipyards at Yokosuka, Hyōgo, and Nagasaki. Many of these operations were highly unprofitable and were sold off very cheaply to private enterprise as part of the deflationary policy after 1880. Among the purchasers were Mitsui, Mitsubishi, Asano, and Furukawa, the later *zaibatsu (q.v.)*. Apart from nonproductive industries, such as communications, the government retained control over the core of the munitions industry. It also later played a crucial part in the development of heavy industry by founding the Yawata Iron Works, which dominated iron and steel production up to 1945.

Smith, T. C. *Political Change and Industrial Development in Japan: Government Enterprise, 1868–1880* (Stanford, 1955).

Great Kantō Earthquake. See KANTŌ EARTHQUAKE

Greater East Asia Conference
(Daitōa Kaigi) 大東亜会議

A conference held in Tokyo 5–6 November 1943 with the aim of strengthening support for and cooperation with Japan in the territories under her control. The conference was presided over by Prime Minister Tōjō Hideki, who called for discussion on a successful conclusion to the war and the creation of a new order in East Asia free of Western colonial exploitation. The conference was attended by representatives from Manchukuo, the Nanking (Wang Ching-wei) regime in China, Thailand, Philippines, Burma, and the Provisional Government of Free India. There were no concrete results although a joint declaration was issued subscribing to vague ideals such as coexistence and cooperation, friendly relations with all countries, and the abolition of racial discrimination.

Lebra, J. C. *Japan's Greater East Asia Co-Prosperity Sphere in World War II* (Kuala Lumpur, 1975).

Greater East Asia Co-Prosperity Sphere
(Daitōa kyōeiken) 大東亜共栄圏

The idea of Pan-Asianism dated back to the Meiji period, but in November 1938 the Konoe cabinet declared its aim of building a New Order in East Asia (*q.v.*) based on the banding together of Japan, Manchukuo, and China. The concept was expanded to include countries in Southeast Asia, and in August 1940 Matsuoka Yōsuke, the foreign minister, first spoke of Japan's aim of creating a Greater East Asia co-prosperity sphere. The term was used to designate an economically self-sufficient sphere "of coexistence and co-prosperity" among the countries of East and Southeast Asia under Japanese leadership. The projected area covered Japan, China, Manchukuo, and the former Dutch, French, and British colonies in Southeast Asia. It was later extended to cover the Philippines, and some Japanese even included countries such as Australia and New Zealand. Subsequently, the Greater East Asia Ministry was established to promote the idea. A certain amount of economic integration was achieved in the area, but despite Japan's claim that the sphere meant Asia for the Asiatics, her efforts to gain support for the plan from participant countries under Japanese control, by such means as the Greater East Asia Conference (*q.v.*), were unsuccessful as most of them regarded the Japanese as just another imperialist.

Grajdanzev, A. J. "Japan's Co-Prosperity Sphere," *Pacific Affairs* 16, no. 3 (Sept. 1943).
Lebra, J. C. *Japan's Greater East Asia Co-Prosperity Sphere in World War II* (Kuala Lumpur, 1975).

Greater East Asia Ministry
(Daitōashō) 大東亜省
Established in November 1942 by an amalgamation of those agencies within existing ministries which dealt with affairs in Manchuria, China, and Japanese-controlled Southeast Asia. The establishment of the ministry was aimed at promoting the Greater East Asia co-prosperity sphere (*q.v.*) by unifying army and navy policies in these areas and coordinating central policy toward them. The move brought the resignation of Foreign Minister Tōgō Shigenori. Due to the war's turning against Japan and the dominant position of the armed forces on the spot, the desired policy coordination was never achieved. The ministry was abolished in August 1945.

Lebra, J. C. *Japan's Greater East Asia Co-Prosperity Sphere in World War II* (Kuala Lumpur, 1975).
Togo, S. *The Cause of Japan* (New York, 1956).

Greater East Asia War. See PACIFIC WAR

Greater Japan Industrial Patriotic Association. See LABOR MOVEMENT

Greater Japan Labor Association. See LABOR MOVEMENT

Greater Japan National Defense Women's Association. See WOMEN'S MOVEMENT

Greater Japan Production Party
(Dainihon Seisantō) 大日本生産党
A right-wing organization established by members of the Kokuryūkai (*q.v.*) June 1931 in Osaka. It moved to Tokyo in October. The party gained the allegiance of various nationalist groups and "patriotic" labor organizations. The first president was Uchida Ryōhei, and Tōyama Mitsuru was adviser. The party called for respect for the Meiji constitution (*q.v.*), reform or abolition of laws incompatible with the *kokutai (q.v.)*, a state-controlled economy, and a strong foreign policy based on Japanese guidance of Asia. After unsuccessful efforts to secure direct representation in the Diet, many members turned to illegal and violent activities, and it declined as a political force after the Shinpeitai incident (*q.v.*), but recorded membership 1939–1940 was still 150,000. Reorganized in 1942 as the Greater Japan Renovation Association (Dainihon Isshinkai) it was purged in 1946. Its tradition was revived postwar by an organization founded in 1954 which took the same name and called for respect for the emperor, a strong defense policy, and the promotion of traditional ethics.

Morris, I. *Nationalism and the Right Wing in Japan* (London, 1960).
Storry, R. *The Double Patriots* (London, 1957).

Greater Japan Women's Association. See WOMEN'S MOVEMENT

Greater Japan Youth Association. See YOUTH ORGANIZATIONS

Gumma Incident. See GUNMA INCIDENT

Gunbatsu. See MILITARY CLIQUE

Gunjin Chokuyu. See TAKEHASHI RISING

Gunjin Kunkai. See TAKEHASHI RISING

Gunma Incident (Gunma jiken)
群馬事件
Early in 1884 leaders of the Gunma Jiyūtō mobilized impoverished peasants for an antigovernment uprising. A planned attack on senior government officials assembled for the opening of the Takasaki

railway was thwarted because the ceremonies were postponed, but because the rank and file were restless, the leaders decided to go ahead with the uprising. Some 3,000 peasants assembled, and in the violence of May 16–17 a moneylender's house and godown were destroyed and a police station and substation occupied. The mob moved on to the local barracks at Takasaki, but many dispersed due to tiredness and lack of food, and the remainder were ordered by the leaders to disband. Forty-two people were subsequently arrested, and the uprising's leaders received lengthy prison sentences.

Ike, N. *The Beginnings of Political Democracy in Japan* (Baltimore , 1950).

H

Hagi Rebellion. See MAEBARA ISSEI

Haihan Chiken. See ABOLITION OF DOMAINS

Hamada Hikozō. See HECO, JOSEPH

Hamaguchi Osachi (Yūkō) 1870–1931 浜口雄幸

Native of Kōchi Prefecture, graduating from Tokyo University in 1895, Hamaguchi entered the Finance Ministry before joining the Rikken Dōshikai in 1913. He was elected to the Diet in 1915 and as a leader of the Kenseikai subsequently was finance minister 1924–1926 and home minister 1926–1927. In 1927 he became president of the newly formed Minseitō and in July 1929 formed his own cabinet. He pursued a policy of economic retrenchment and industrial rationalization with a view to restoring the gold standard, but although this was achieved in 1930, the cutbacks exacerbated the prevailing depression and caused even more widespread distress. A conciliatory foreign policy, with Shidehara as foreign minister, culminated in the forcing through of the ratification of the treaty agreed at the London Naval Conference (*q.v.*). This aroused further hostility from the armed forces and right-wing opinion, and in November 1930 Hamaguchi was shot by a member of the civilian right wing at Tokyo Station. The cabinet resigned in April 1931 due to Hamaguchi's worsening health, and he himself died in August.

Tiedemann, A. E. "The Hamaguchi Cabinet, First Phase July 1929–February 1930: A Study in Japanese Parliamentary Government," Ph.D. diss., Columbia University, 1959.
Young, A. M. *Imperial Japan, 1926–1938* (London, 1938).

Han. See ABOLITION OF DOMAINS; TOKUGAWA BAKUFU

Hanbatsu Politics (hanbatsu seiji) 藩閥政治

Four domains (Satsuma, Chōshū, Tosa, and Hizen) played a central role in the Meiji Restoration, and it was men from Satsuma and Chōshū who dominated the government for decades afterwards. Real political power during this period was wielded by a small number of men from these clans. Until the 1890s the dominance of the two *han* was due to personal participation in the anti-Bakufu struggle, but increasingly the tradition was continued under the protégés of the original protagonists, and this monopoly of political power by men from Satsuma and Chōshū was referred to by their opponents as *hanbatsu* (clan-faction) politics. Although there was some divergence between army and navy factions and between Satsuma and Chōshū, the existence of common interests meant that they maintained sufficient unity to retain dominance into the 1920s despite increasing political party influence. *Hanbatsu* politics, which reached its peak 1890–1918, was supported by the provisions of the Meiji constitution (*q.v.*),the pursuit of transcendental cabinets, and the informal institution of the *genrō* (*q.v.*).

Hanseki Hōkan. See ABOLITION OF DOMAINS

Hanyehping Company (Kanyahyō Konsu) 漢冶萍公司
A Chinese company extracting and refining iron ore and coal formally incorporated in 1908. From an early stage it was highly dependent on Japanese loans, by which the Japanese attempted to secure the supply of iron ore for the Yawata Iron Works. A 1912 plan to place the company under joint control of the two countries failed, but China was forced to make this concession (to be implemented at a "convenient" time) in the Twenty-One Demands (*q.v.*). Meanwhile China could not nationalize the company nor permit investment in it by a third power without Japan's approval. The company declined. It was taken over by the Japanese during the Sino-Japanese War of 1937–1945 but has revived under state ownership since then.

Jansen, M. B. *Japan and China: From War to Peace, 1894–1972* (Chicago, 1973).
———. "Yawata, Hanyehping, and the Twenty-One Demands," *PHR* 23 (1954).

Hara Kei (Satoshi, Takashi) 1856–1921 原敬
Member of samurai family of Nanbu domain (now Iwate Prefecture), Hara worked briefly as a journalist before working in the ministries of Foreign Affairs and Agriculture and Commerce after 1882. He had strong contacts with Inoue Kaoru and Mutsu Munemitsu and became deputy foreign minister in 1895 but resigned in 1897 after Mutsu's death to become president of the Osaka Mainichi Company. Although retaining certain business interests, from 1900 Hara played a leading part in the development of the Seiyūkai (*q.v.*); 1900–1901 he was communications minister. He sat in the Diet from August 1902 until his death. After being home minister 1906–1908, 1911–1912, and 1913–1914, in June 1914 he became leader of the Seiyūkai. In 1918 he became the first prime minister to head a majority party cabinet and hold a seat in the lower house, giving him the name of the "commoner" prime minister. Hara's cabinet enlarged the franchise but rejected universal male suffrage and undertook no major institutional reform. Suppressive policies were adopted toward domestic social and labor movements and the Korean independence movement (*q.v.*). Abroad Hara was unable to extricate Japan from the Siberian intervention (*q.v.*). Increasing accusations of government corruption and scandal culminated in Hara's being stabbed to death in Tokyo November 1921. His diary is an important historical source.

Duus, P. *Party Rivalry and Political Change in Taishō Japan* (Cambridge, Mass., 1968).
Hara, T. "Harmony Between East and West," in K. Kawakami, ed., *What Japan Thinks* (New York, 1921).
Najita, T. *Hara Kei in the Politics of Compromise* (Cambridge, Mass., 1967).
Olson, L. A. "Hara Kei—A Political Biography," Ph.D. diss., Harvard University, 1954.

Harmonization Society. See KYŌCHŌKAI

Harris, Townsend 1804–1878
Having spent much of his life trading in East and Southeast Asia, in August 1856 Harris landed at Shimoda (Izu) as the first American consul-general in Japan. In 1857 he concluded the Treaty of Shimoda (*q.v.*) and subsequently negotiated with the Bakufu for the conclusion of a more comprehensive treaty. Imperial approval was not forthcoming for such a treaty, but Harris used the threat posed by the imperialist powers' recent victory in China to force the conclusion of the U.S.-Japan Treaty of Amity and Commerce (*q.v.*), which was signed without imperial permission in July 1858. This led to similar treaties with other powers. Harris was promoted to minister and from 1859 resided in Edo. He left Japan in 1862.

Cosenza, M. E. *The Complete Journal of Townsend Harris, First American Consul and Minister to Japan* (Rutland, Vt., 1959).
Griffis, W. E. *Townsend Harris* (rprt. New York, 1971).
Kublin, H. "A Salute to Townsend Harris," *JQ* 5, no. 3 (July–Sept. 1958).
McMaster, J. "Alcock and Harris: Foreign Diplomacy in Bakumatsu Japan," *MN* 22, nos. 3–4 (1967).

Harris Treaty. See U.S.-JAPAN TREATY OF AMITY AND COMMERCE

Hashimoto Kingorō 1890–1957
橋本欣五郎
A native of Okayama, Hashimoto graduated from the Military Academy. He worked at the General Staff before becoming a colonel and regimental commander in 1934. Strongly influenced by Kita Ikki and Ōkawa Shūmei, he was active in the young officers' movement for national reform from early on, and in 1927 he was involved with a clandestine group, the Kinkikai, in planning a coup. He founded the Sakurakai (*q.v.*) in 1930 and was the leader of its militant faction, playing a major role in the unsuccessful March and October incidents of 1931 (*q.v.*). Within the army he was associated with the *kōdō* faction (*q.v.*). Hashimoto was retired from active service in 1936 but was reinstated in 1937 because of the war; he attempted to force hostilities with Britain by shelling a Royal Navy vessel on the Yangtze. He was recalled to Japan in 1938 and retired a second time. As a civilian he founded the Greater Japan Youth Party and was influential in the Imperial Rule Assistance Association (*q.v.*) and as a Diet member. Postwar he was tried as a class "A" war criminal and sentenced to life imprisonment.

Storry, R. *The Double Patriots* (London, 1957).

Hatoyama Ichirō 1883–1959 鳩山一郎
Native of Tokyo and eldest son of the lawyer and politician Hatoyama Kazuo, graduating from Tokyo Imperial University, Hatoyama practiced law before entering the Diet as a member for Tokyo in 1915. In 1927 he became secretary to the Seiyūkai, then was chief cabinet secretary 1927–1929 and education minister 1931–1934. Later he opposed the formation of the Imperial Rule Assistance Association (*q.v.*) and was elected to the Diet in 1942 despite being an "unofficial" candidate. The Japan Liberal Party founded by Hatoyama postwar became the biggest party in the Diet in 1946, but Hatoyama was prevented from becoming prime minister by being purged by SCAP. He was replaced by Yoshida Shigeru. Hatoyama was depurged in 1951, but his conflict with Yoshida over leadership of the party split the Liberal Party. In 1954 he became president of the new Japan Democratic Party and in December succeeded Yoshida as prime minister. He headed three cabinets, the first as a minority party with Socialist support, the second as the single biggest party, and the third as the leader of the new conservative coalition, the Liberal Democratic Party. Hatoyama revised various Occupation reforms and was criticized for his strengthening of the police and of central control over education and for his advocation of rearmament. His attempts to revise clause 9 of the constitution (the disarmament clause) were unsuccessful, as were his attempts to gain electoral reform to ensure a two-party system. In 1956 he achieved the restoration of diplomatic relations with Russia, and Japan joined the United Nations. A popular premier, Hatoyama resigned in December 1956.

Berger, G. M. *Parties Out of Power in Japan, 1931–1941* (Princeton, 1977).
Quigley, H. S., and J. E. Turner. *The New Japan* (Minneapolis, 1956).

Hawaii
In 1871 Japan signed a Treaty of Commerce and Friendship with the kingdom of Hawaii. From the early 1880s Japanese emigrated to Hawaii in large numbers, mostly on a contract system to work in sugar plantations. By 1894 over 28,000 had gone to the islands, 20,000 of whom

still remained. Over half of these immigrants were no longer under contract but had remained in the islands and built up their own community. Immigration was liberalized after 1894, and the inrush of Japanese led to increasing local antagonism and problems over the jurisdiction and status of Japanese immigrants. In 1897 the U.S. and Hawaii concluded an annexation agreement, and Japan had to discuss the immigration issue with America. The 1900 census enumerates over 61,000 Japanese residing in Hawaii. Despite subsequent restrictions on Japanese immigration, by the time immigration was effectively halted in 1924, the Japanese population of Hawaii was over 125,000, roughly one-third of the population.

Conroy, F. H. *The Japanese Frontier in Hawaii, 1868–1898* (Berkeley, 1953).

Hayashi Senjūrō 1876–1943 林銑十郎
Native of Kanazawa, Hayashi graduated from the Military Academy and held various posts in military education. He was commander of the Imperial Guards and then army commander in Korea, where his arbitrary decision to send troops across the border during the Manchurian Incident (*q.v.*) raised considerable problems. In 1932 he became a full general and inspector of military education and 1934–1935 served as war minister, when he participated in the attack on the emperor organ theory (*q.v.*). Hayashi's dismissal of Masaki Jinzaburō as inspector of military education in 1935 aroused strong hostility within the army and led to his being regarded as a figurehead of the *tōsei* faction (*q.v.*). He was placed on the reserve list in 1936 but headed a short-lived cabinet in 1937 whose policies alienated both public opinion and the Diet.

Fukuda, I. "Hayashi, the Strong Silent Minister," *CJ* 3, no. 1 (June 1934).

Hayashi Tadasu 1850–1913
(Baron, 1895; Viscount, 1902; Count, 1907) 林董
A samurai from Sakura *han* (now Chiba Prefecture), Hayashi was sent by the Bakufu to study in London 1867–1868 but returned to fight with Enomoto Takeaki and was captured at Goryōkaku in 1869. In 1871 he joined the new government and acted as interpreter on the Iwakura Mission (*q.v.*). As an official his main contribution was in the field of foreign affairs. In 1891 he became deputy foreign minister under Mutsu and was then special envoy to China and ambassador to Russia. In 1900–1906 he was ambassador to Britain, where he worked successfully for the conclusion of the Anglo-Japanese Alliance (*q.v.*). As foreign minister 1906–1908 Hayashi tried to stabilize Japan's position in Asia by concluding agreements with France and Russia.

Pooley, A. M., ed., *The Secret Memoirs of Count Tadasu Hayashi* (London, 1915).

Hayashi Yūzō 1842–1921 林有造
Native of Tosa, active in the anti-Bakufu movement (*q.v.*), after the Restoration Hayashi worked in the central bureaucracy but resigned in 1873 over the invasion of Korea (*q.v.*). He returned to Tosa where he was active in the Risshisha (*q.v.*). He provided arms for the rebels in the Satsuma rebellion (*q.v.*) and was imprisoned for plotting against the government. He was pardoned in 1886 but was barred from Tokyo under the 1887 Peace Regulations (*q.v.*) following opposition to the government's treaty revision proposals. In 1890 Hayashi was elected to the Diet for the Jiyūtō and became communications minister in 1898. In 1900 he participated in the founding of the Seiyūkai and was minister of agriculture and commerce 1900–1901 but later resigned from his position among the party's leadership. He left the political world in 1908 and lived in retirement in Kōchi.

Heco, Joseph (Hamada Hikozō)
1837–1897 浜田彦造
Hamada Hikozō, a native of Harima (now Hyōgo Prefecture), was shipwrecked in 1850 on a voyage from Hyōgo to Edo, rescued by an American ship, and taken

to the U.S. Educated there under the name of Joseph Heco he took American citizenship and in 1859 returned to Japan as interpreter for the U.S. consulate in Yokohama, in which role he contributed to the development of American-Japanese relations. From 1863 Heco was engaged in private business, and in 1864–1866 he participated in the publication of the first Japanese-language newspaper, the *Kaigai Shinbun* (Overseas Newspaper). In 1872–1874 he worked in the Finance Ministry but subsequently returned to private business, devoting his efforts to the expansion of foreign trade.

Chikamori, H. *Joseph Heco* (Tokyo, 1963).
Heco, J. (ed. J. Murdoch) *The Narrative of a Japanese,* 2 vols. (Yokohama, 1895).

Heimin Shinbun. See HEIMINSHA

Heiminsha 平民社
A Socialist group formed November 1903 by Sakai Toshihiko and Kōtoku Shūsui after their break with the *Yorozu Chōhō* (*q.v.*) over war with Russia. They were joined by Ishikawa Sanshirō and Nishikawa Kōjirō, and from early 1904 the group constituted the mainstream of the Japanese Socialist movement. The group's main activity was the publication of the weekly *Heimin Shinbun* (Commoner's Paper), which advocated socialism, commonerism *(heiminshugi),* and pacifism based on liberty, equality, and humanity but which, nevertheless, embraced a diversity of ideological positions. The Heiminsha also carried on propaganda and book publishing activities, acting in general as a Socialist focus. In January 1905 publication of the *Heimin Shinbun* ceased following government oppression and financial problems. Its work was carried on in the weekly *Chokugen* (Plain Speaking), but this was banned in September 1905. The Heiminsha itself was split between Christian and non-Christian Socialists and disbanded in October. In January 1907 a reunion of the two Socialist wings resulted in the publication of the daily *Heimin Shinbun,* which briefly acted as the organ of the Japan Socialist Party (*q.v.*), but the reunion was short-lived, and the paper was banned in April.

Kublin, H. "The Japanese Socialists and the Russo-Japanese War," *Journal of Modern History* 22, no. 4 (Dec. 1950).
Notehelfer, F. G. *Kōtoku Shūsui—Portrait of a Japanese Radical* (Cambridge, 1971).

Hepburn, James Curtis 1815–1911
Hepburn was an American Presbyterian missionary and doctor who had worked in China and arrived in Japan in October 1859. He worked in the Kanagawa-Yokohama area until 1892, when he returned to America. As well as his missionary work, Hepburn provided free treatment for huge numbers of patients and also taught English and mathematics. He studied the Japanese language and in 1867 completed the first Japanese-English dictionary, shortly followed by an English-Japanese one. The system of romanization he developed is named after him and is the most widely used today. Hepburn subsequently translated many Christian texts into Japanese. He was also closely involved with the development of English and girls' education.

Griffis, W. E. *Hepburn of Japan* (Philadelphia, 1913).
Hepburn, J. C. (ed. M. Takaya). *Letters* (Tokyo, 1955).

Heusken, Henry 1832–1861
A native of Amsterdam, Heusken emigrated to the U.S. in 1853 and in August 1856 arrived at Shimoda as Townsend Harris's secretary and interpreter. He subsequently learned Japanese. Apart from assisting Harris, he also acted as translator for the treaty negotiations conducted by Britain in 1858 and by Prussia in 1861. In 1860 Heusken became first secretary of the U.S. Legation in Edo, but while returning from the Prussian Legation one night in January 1861, he was assassinated by antiforeign samurai. His murder brought resentment at attacks on

foreigners to a head. Many foreigners withdrew to Yokohama, but Harris eventually reached an agreement with the Bakufu, and compensation was paid.

Alcock, R. *The Capital of the Tycoon* (London, 1863).
Heusken, H. (tr. and ed. J. C. van der Corput and R. A. Wilson). *Japan Journal, 1855–1861* (New Brunswick, N.J., 1964).

Hibiya Riots (Hibiya yakiuchi jiken) 日比谷焼打事件

As part of the nationwide resentment at the terms of the Portsmouth Treaty (*q.v.*), on 5 September 1905 a mass protest meeting in contravention of a police ban was held in Hibiya Park, Tokyo. The vast crowd clashed with police, and after the meeting mobs attacked and burned the offices of the *Kokumin Shinbun* (a pro-government paper), the home minister's residence and other official buildings, churches, police stations, trams, and huge numbers of police boxes. The meeting's organizers were unable to control the violence, which continued the next day. The army was called out, and late on September 6 martial law was declared in the Tokyo area. Many magazines and newspapers were suspended. By late on September 7 the rioting had ended. In all 17 people were recorded killed, about 500 wounded; 2,000 were arrested, of whom 308 were charged; most of the 87 found guilty were unskilled workers, and those who had organized the meeting were released. The movement calling for the peace terms to be revoked and the cabinet censured spread throughout the country. Although the treaty was ratified by the emperor on October 14, martial law was retained until November 29.

Okamoto, S. *The Japanese Oligarchy and the Russo-Japanese War* (New York, 1970).

Higashikuni Naruhiko
1887– (Prince) 東久邇稔彦

A member of the imperial family, Higashikuni made his career in the army. In August 1945 he headed an unprecedented "imperial" cabinet; it was hoped that having an imperial prince as prime minister would enable the emperor's authority to be utilized to suppress opposition to peace within the army and avoid general confusion. Higashikuni was considered a suitable candidate as he was relatively liberal and despite his army career was reputed to oppose militarism. The Higashikuni cabinet signed the surrender instrument and initiated the disbanding of the army and such other matters relating to the surrender and peace, but it was forced by SCAP (*q.v.*) to resign in October on the grounds that its members included war criminals, it was reluctant to release political prisoners and abolish the Peace Preservation Law (*q.v.*), and it would not have implemented the changes desired by SCAP. Higashikuni was under a purge order until 1952. He severed his connection with the imperial family in 1947, and his subsequent activities included the founding of a new religion.

High Treason Incident
(taigyaku jiken) 大逆事件

During May-June 1910 several hundred Socialists and anarchists throughout Japan were interrogated by the police. Of these 26 were eventually charged with plotting to assassinate the emperor. In the secret trial December 1910 – January 1911 most of the defendants denied the existence of such a plot, and it was argued in defense that the Katsura government's suppression of socialism was itself responsible for the growth of any extremist plots that might exist. Kōtoku Shūsui, who was among those arrested, testified to his withdrawal from any possible conspiracy. Despite this, 24 of those charged were sentenced to death and two to imprisonment. Twelve of the death sentences were commuted to life imprisonment, but the other 12, including Kōtoku, Kanno Sugako, and Morichika Unpei, were executed on 24 January 1911. The trial was a major blow to the whole left-wing movement and initiated the so-called "winter period" of socialism, which lasted until after World War I.

Notehelfer, F. G. *Kōtoku Shūsui, Portrait of a Japanese Radical* (Cambridge, 1971).
Plotkin, I. L. "A Question of Treason: The Great Treason Conspiracy of 1911," Ph.D. diss., University of Michigan, 1974.

Hinin. See BURAKU EMANCIPATION MOVEMENT

Hiranuma Kiichirō 1867–1952 (Baron, 1926) 平沼騏一郎
Native of Okayama, Hiranuma graduated in law from Tokyo Imperial University and rose to become head of the Supreme Court and a leading figure of the legal world. He was minister of justice 1923–1924 and in 1924 became a member of the House of Peers and Privy Council. He was vice-president of the Privy Council 1925–1936 and president 1936–1939. This was a time when the Privy Council was vocal in national affairs and conflicted with the government over such matters as the London Naval Conference (*q.v.*). Hiranuma's position in the Privy Council and his presidency of the nationalist Kokuhonsha (*q.v.*) 1924–1936 made him a leading figure among right-wing politicians. In January 1939 he succeeded Konoe as prime minister and, despite his previous conflicts with the Diet, declared his intention of working with the political parties and not instituting a new ruling structure. During Hiranuma's premiership Japan's rift with America and Britain widened, and the conclusion of the German-Soviet Non-Aggression Pact caused negotiations over the conclusion of a military alliance with Germany to be broken off. The cabinet resigned in August 1939. After acting as home minister and minister of state 1940–1941, Hiranuma was briefly again president of the Privy Council in 1945. He was subsequently sentenced to life imprisonment as a class "A" war criminal and died in prison.

Berger, G. M. *Parties Out of Power in Japan, 1931–1941* (Princeton, 1977).
Yasko, R. "Hiranuma Kiichirō and Conservative Politics in Prewar Japan," Ph.D. diss., University of Chicago, 1973.
______. "Hiranuma Kiichirō and the New Structure Movement, 1940–1941," *Asian Forum* 5, no. 2 (Apr.–June 1973).

Hiratsuka Raichō 1886–1971 平塚らいてう
Hiratsuka, whose real given name was Haruko, came from Tokyo and in 1906 graduated from Japan Women's University. In 1911 she founded the women's organization, the Seitōsha (*q.v.*), and in its publication, *Seitō* (Bluestocking), wrote widely on the history and position of women, especially in relation to literature. In 1913 she went to live with the painter Okumura Hiroshi, which led to a break with her family. Poverty and harassment led her to hand over the management of *Seitō* to Itō Noe in 1915. In 1919 Hiratsuka was one of the founders of the New Women's Association (*Shin Fujin Kyōkai*), which campaigned for an extension of women's rights, higher education, and welfare. The repeal of clause 5 of the Peace Police Law (*q.v.*), which forbade political activity by women, was eventually achieved, but the association then disbanded. Hiratsuka retired from the mainstream of the women's movement until the 1930s, when she again became openly involved, being especially interested in the promotion of consumer unions. After the war she remained active and was until her death influential as a leader and symbol not only of the women's movement but also of the peace movement, both in Japan and internationally.

Andrew, N. "The Seitōsha: An Early Japanese Women's Organization, 1911–1916," *HPJ* 6 (1972).

Hirohito. See SHŌWA EMPEROR

Hirose Saihei 1828–1914 広瀬宰平
Native of Shiga, at the age of 11 Hirose

started work at the Sumitomo family's Besshi Copper Mine near Osaka and eventually became its manager in 1865. His introduction of new techniques and other reforms helped it to survive the difficult period of the Restoration and to prosper, and from there Hirose worked to extend Sumitomo interests into other fields. He initially benefited from government contacts, but these played little part after the 1870s. By his retirement in 1894 he had built up the foundations of the Sumitomo *zaibatsu* (*q.v.*). Hirose also possessed extensive personal business interests in such fields as shipping and was a leading figure in the Osaka business world.

Hirschmeier, J. *The Origins of Entrepreneurship in Meiji Japan* (Cambridge, Mass., 1964).

Hiroshima 広島
The city of Hiroshima lies on the northern side of the Inland Sea in western Honshū and during the Tokugawa period was the castle town of the domain of the *tozama* Asano family. It grew after the Restoration and by 1945 had a registered population of something over 300,000. In the early morning of 6 August 1945 the city was devastated by the first atomic bomb to be dropped. Some 100,000 people were estimated ultimately to have died from the effects of the bomb, and the city center was completely destroyed. Since 1945 the city has been rebuilt and is now a prosperous shipping, fishing, and manufacturing center with a population of nearly 880,000 as of late 1979. Designated a city of international peace and civilization, the city has become a symbol and focus for the antinuclear movement, and its Peace Park and Museum are major attractions.

Feis, H. *Japan Subdued: The Atomic Bomb and the End of the War in the Pacific* (Princeton, 1961).
Hersey, J. *Hiroshima* (New York, 1946).
Lifton, R. J. *Death in Life: Survivors of Hiroshima* (New York, 1967).

Hirota Kōki 1878–1948 広田弘毅
Native of Fukuoka, from his youth Hirota had connections with the Genyōsha (*q.v.*). Graduating from Tokyo Imperial University, he joined the Foreign Ministry and served as envoy to Holland 1927–1930 and to the Soviet Union 1930–1932. During his term of office as foreign minister 1933–1936 Hirota attempted to improve Japan's position on the continent although simultaneously advocating improvement in Sino-Japanese relations. Appointed prime minister in 1936 after the February 26 rising (*q.v.*), he presided over a cabinet of "national unity" noted for its strong connections with the *tōsei* faction (*q.v.*) of the army. The cabinet promoted an aggressive foreign policy, planning for a Japanese advance into Southeast Asia and concluding the Anti-Comintern Pact (*q.v.*). At home its legislation against subversive writing and thought, its promotion of deficit shipbuilding and reimplementation of the system whereby the service ministers were officers on the active list reinforced war preparedness and army influence. Hirota's cabinet resigned January 1937 due to open conflict between the army and the political parties, but Hirota served as foreign minister 1937–1938. The failure of his initial attempts to localize the conflict with China eventually led to a Japanese refusal to deal with the Nationalist government. Hirota subsequently withdrew from the forefront of political affairs but remained until 1945 a highly influential figure. In 1945 he attempted unsuccessfully to secure Soviet mediation for peace in discussions with Malik, the Soviet envoy in Tokyo. Postwar Hirota was tried as a class "A" war criminal and was the only civilian to receive the death sentence; this sentence was the subject of considerable controversy as many considered that he had been powerless in the face of the military.

Baba, T. "Hirota's 'Renovation' Plans," *CJ* 5, no. 2 (Sept. 1936).
Farnsworth, L. "Hirota Kōki: The Diplomacy of Expansionism," in R. D. Burns and E. M. Bennett, eds., *Diplomats in Crisis: United States-Chinese-Japanese Relations, 1919–1941* (Santa

Barbara, 1974).
Shiroyama, S. (tr. J. Bester) *War Criminal: The Life and Death of Hirota Kōki* (Tokyo, 1977).

Hitachi Company. See NISSAN ZAIBATSU

Hitotsubashi Keiki (Yoshinobu). See TOKUGAWA KEIKI (YOSHINOBU)

Hōchi Shinbun. See NEWSPAPERS

Hokkaidō 北海道

The northernmost of the four main Japanese islands, Hokkaidō was known as Ezo in the Tokugawa period. The indigenous population was the Ainu (*q.v.*), but some Japanese did live there during this time. The Bakufu took an interest in Hokkaidō from the early 19th century, with the aim of checking Russia's southward expansion. In July 1869 the Hokkaidō Colonization Board (*kaitakushi*) was established by the new government with the aim of developing Hokkaidō for political and military reasons. In 1871 – 1876 the board was also responsible for Sakhalin and from 1876 for the Kuriles. Under the leadership of Kuroda Kiyotaka through the 1870s the board's activities were concentrated on the development of natural resources (coal, minerals, timber, and fishing), Western-style farming, and railways. An American agriculturist, Horace Capron, was engaged as special adviser and the Sapporo Agricultural College (later Hokkaidō University) established. The board also aimed to increase the island's productive population by encouraging immigration. Despite such official encouragement immigration was initially slow, and in 1874 the *tondenhei* system was instituted, whereby ex-samurai could fuse militia and farming activities. This continued into the 20th century. Immigration did subsequently increase, much of it from northern Japan, but agricultural settlement lagged behind that in the towns. The harsh climatic and natural conditions meant that many other destinations were more attractive to potential immigrants. Huge amounts of money were invested in the island's development, and attempts to sell off the board's interests led to the Hokkaidō colonization assets scandal (*q.v.*) of 1881. In 1882 the board was abolished, and Hokkaidō ceased to have colonial status. From 1886 a Hokkaidō Bureau directly under the cabinet had administrative powers over the whole island to unify policy, but even after that there were administrative changes which did not always work in the best interests of the island. Autonomy was granted to Hokkaidō far later than other areas of Japan, and the frontier conditions persisted into the Taishō period in the more remote northern areas of the island, although they had disappeared by the 1930s. From 1901 a series of long-term development plans successfully established cold climate wet rice agriculture, dairy farming, coal mining, fishing, and forestry. Development was helped by emphasis on communications, facilitating the exploitation of resources, and a network of commercial centers appeared. The Hokkaidō Development Bank was founded in 1900 to assist funding. By the 1930s its natural resources had made Hokkaidō of crucial importance to the Japanese economy. The island escaped serious destruction in the war, and in 1948 was integrated into the national regional autonomy system. In 1951 the Hokkaidō Development Office was established to supervise the development of the island as a whole. Postwar development plans have emphasized industrial expansion, but targets have only been partially fulfilled, and the primary sector remains of vital importance to the island's economy. The population of the island in 1979 was some 5½ million, and that of the capital, Sapporo, approaching 1½ million.

Anthony, D. F. "The Administration of Hokkaidō Under Kuroda Kiyotaka, 1870 – 1882," Ph.D. diss., Yale University, 1951.
Harrison, J. A. *Japan's Northern Frontier* (Gainesville, Fla., 1953).
Jones, F. C. *Hokkaidō* (London, 1958).

Hokkaidō Colonization Assets Scandal (Hokkaidō kaitakushi kanyūbutsu haraisage jiken) 北海道開拓使官有物払下事件
In 1869–1881 the Hokkaidō Colonization Board (*kaitakushi*) invested some ¥14 million in the development of Hokkaidō, and in 1881 the board's head, Kuroda Kiyotaka, gained imperial approval for the sale of the assets, now valued at ¥30 million, to a group of Osaka businessmen with strong Satsuma and Chōshū connections and led by Godai Tomoatsu. The price was ¥387,082 payable over 30 years at no interest. The news of the sale leaked out in July and increased agitation from the popular rights movement, leading to widespread criticism of *hanbatsu* politics (*q.v.*) and "political merchants" *(seishō)* (*q.v.*) from outside the government. Within the government opposition to the sale was led by Ōkuma Shigenobu. The sale of the assets was eventually canceled, but the scandal contributed to the 1881 political crisis (*q.v.*) and the resignation of Ōkuma.

Akita, G. *The Foundations of Constitutional Government in Modern Japan, 1868–1900* (Cambridge, Mass., 1967).
Fraser, A. "The Expulsion of Ōkuma from the Government in 1881," *JAS* 26, no. 2 (Feb. 1967).
Harrison, J. A. *Japan's Northern Frontier* (Gainesville, Fla., 1953)

Home Ministry (Naimushō) 内務省
The Home Ministry was established in 1873 with the aim of political integration but also acted as a major center of innovation during the 1870s. Under its first head, Ōkubo Toshimichi, it had jurisdiction over domestic administration, communications, law and order, civil engineering works, and much of the economic development in agriculture, light industry, and commerce. Despite subsequent changes which reduced its jurisdiction, the home minister retained until the Pacific War a highly influential position within the government due to his control of police, law and order legislation, freedom of speech and assembly, mass movements, organization of elections, and virtually every other aspect of the life of the people. The ministry was disbanded in 1947 as part of the dismantling of the "militaristic" state.

Brown, S. D. "Ōkubo Toshimichi and the First Home Ministry Bureaucracy," in B. S. Silberman and H. D. Harootunian, eds., *Modern Japanese Leadership* (Tucson, 1966).

Hoshi Tōru 1850–1901 星亨
Native of Tokyo, after studying law in London, he practiced as a lawyer before joining the Jiyūtō (*q.v.*) in 1881. He played a leading role in the party's propaganda and fund-raising activities and after the party's dissolution was imprisoned for insulting government officials. In 1887 he was banned from Tokyo under the Peace Regulations (*q.v.*). In 1892 he was elected to the Diet and became speaker but was struck off the register of Diet members after a no-confidence motion from anti-Hoshi Jiyūtō members. Hoshi was closely identified with Mutsu Munemitsu and subsequently with Itō Hirobumi. He served as ambassador to America 1896–1898. In 1900 Hoshi participated in the founding of the Seiyūkai (*q.v.*) and was communications minister the same year but resigned under suspicion of corruption. He was assassinated while president of Tokyo City Council.

Hotta Masayoshi 1810–1864 堀田正睦
As daimyō of Sakura domain (now Chiba Prefecture), Hotta held leading posts in the Bakufu's central administration and was an elder (*rōjū*) 1841–1843, but he resigned to reform his own fief, where he encouraged Dutch learning and the adoption of Western armaments. In 1855 he succeeded Abe Masahiro as chief Bakufu elder. Hotta believed that it was impossible to close the country and negotiated with Townsend Harris (*q.v.*) over the conclusion of a commercial treaty. His move provoked a national crisis, and despite a visit to Kyoto Hotta failed to gain imperial approval for a treaty. He also backed Hitotsubashi Keiki in the shōgunal succession dispute (*q.v.*) and

after the appointment of Ii Naosuke as regent in 1858 was dismissed from office. He handed over the domain to his son and from 1862 was under permanent house arrest for his dealings in foreign affairs.

Satoh, H. *Lord Hotta, the Pioneer Diplomat of Japan* (Tokyo, 1908).

Hozumi Nobushige 1856–1926 (Baron, 1915) 穂積陳重
Samurai from Uwajima domain (Ehime) and brother of Hozumi Yatsuka, in 1876–1881 Hozumi studied as a government student in Germany and England and 1882–1912 was a professor of law at Tokyo Imperial University. In 1888 he became Japan's first Doctor of Laws. Appointed to the House of Peers in 1890, from 1916 Hozumi was a member of the Privy Council, becoming its president in 1925. Hozumi strongly opposed the civil code (*q.v.*) promulgated in 1890, on the grounds that it undermined the traditional Japanese family system. He introduced the study of English and German legal theory to Japan and both directly, by committee membership, and more indirectly, exercised considerable influence on legislation, especially commercial law. He wrote widely on all aspects of law, in particular on comparative law.

Hozumi, N. *Ancestor Worship and Japanese Law* (Tokyo, 1913).

Hozumi Yatsuka 1860–1912 穂積八束
Samurai from Uwajima domain, brother of Hozumi Nobushige, Hozumi studied law at Tokyo Imperial University 1879–1884 and then in Germany until 1888. In 1889 he became professor of public law and administrative law at Tokyo. In 1889 he was appointed to the House of Peers and from 1908 was adviser to the emperor. He also served on government committees relating to the imperial house and to education. Hozumi's main field of expertise was constitutional law; his interpretation of the constitution was based on Japanese tradition, and he was known as the chief legal theorist of the "emperor system" (*q.v.*). His legal identification of the emperor with the government of Japan led to sharp criticism of Minobe Tatsukichi's emperor organ theory (*q.v.*) when it was first enunciated. He also led the opposition to the French-influenced civil code (*q.v.*), which was promulgated in 1890. Hozumi wrote widely on the constitution and constitutional law.

Hozumi, Y. *Lectures on the New Japanese Civil Code* (Tokyo, 1912).
Minear, R. H. *Japanese Tradition and Western Law—Emperor, State, and Law in the Thought of Hozumi Yatsuka* (Cambridge, Mass., 1970).

Hyōgikai. See LABOR MOVEMENT

I

Ichikawa Fusae 1893–1981 市川房枝
Native of Nagoya, Ichikawa worked as a primary school teacher and reporter and was briefly involved with the Yūaikai (*q.v.*) in 1919. In 1920–1922 she worked with Hiratsuka Raichō in the Shinfujin Kyōkai (New Women's Association) to raise the social and political position of women in Japan. In December 1924 she founded the Women's Suffrage League and remained the leading figure in the women's suffrage movement until the league was disbanded in 1940. In 1945 Ichikawa organized and became president of the Shin Nihon Fujin Dōmei (New Japan Women's League) an organization aimed at improving the legal status of Japanese women, but in 1947–1950 she was banned from public office because of associations with state-sponsored women's organizations during the war. Resigning from women's organizations in 1953, Ichikawa was elected to the House of Councillors as an independent and, except

for 1971–1974, remained there until her death. She consistently campaigned against money politics and for "clean" elections. She wrote widely on the women's movement and her part in it and on politics.

Molony, K. S. "One Woman Who Dared: Ichikawa Fusae and the Japanese Women's Suffrage Movement," Ph.D. diss., University of Michigan, 1980.
Murray, P. "Ichikawa Fusae and the Lonely Red Carpet," *Japan Interpreter* 10, no. 2 (Autumn 1975).
Vavich, D. A. "The Japanese Women's Movement: Ichikawa Fusae, a Pioneer in Women's Suffrage," *MN* 22, nos. 3–4 (1967).

Ii Naosuke 1815–1860 井伊直弼
In 1850 Ii became daimyō of Hikone *han* (now Shiga Prefecture) and subsequently advocated the opening of the country. In June 1858 he was appointed *tairō* (regent) and solved the prevailing political impasse by having the Bakufu conclude the Treaty of Amity and Commerce with the U.S. without imperial sanction and by deciding the shōgunal succession dispute (*q.v.*) in favor of Tokugawa Yoshitomi of Kii. These acts were followed by the Ansei purge (*q.v.*). Ii continued to pursue a strong policy in an attempt to reestablish Bakufu supremacy until he was assassinated outside the Sakurada Gate of Edo castle by Mito and Satsuma samurai in March 1860.

Beasley, W. G. *The Meiji Restoration* (London, 1973).
Lee, E. B. "The Political Career of Ii Naosuke," Ph.D. diss., Columbia University, 1960.
Nakamura, K. *Lord Ii Naosuke and the New Japan* (Tokyo, 1909).
Satoh, H. *Agitated Japan: The Life of Baron Ii Kamon-no-kami Naosuke* (Tokyo, 1896).

Ikeda Hayato 1899–1965 池田勇人
Native of Hiroshima, Ikeda studied law at Kyoto Imperial University, entered the Finance Ministry and became deputy finance minister 1947–1948. In 1949 he was elected to the Diet and as finance minister 1949–1952 was responsible for implementing the economic stabilization program (*q.v.*). He was close to Yoshida and attended the San Francisco conference as a delegate. Briefly minister of international trade and industry in 1952 he resigned after a no-confidence motion. Ikeda remained influential in the Liberal Democratic Party and from 1956 built up his own faction. In 1956–1957 he was finance minister and then minister of international trade and industry 1959–1960. In July 1960 he succeeded Kishi as president of the L.D.P. and prime minister. Domestically, Ikeda maintained a "low profile" as compared with Kishi and concentrated on procuring a high rate of economic growth with his famous income-doubling plan. Abroad he promoted close relations with the U.S. There was also a resumption of the trend toward increasing commerce and trade with the People's Republic of China, although formal relations were not reestablished. Ikeda resigned in November 1964 due to ill health.

Waldner, G. W. "Japanese Foreign Policy and Economic Growth: Ikeda Hayato's Approach to the Liberalization Issue," Ph.D. diss., Princeton University, 1975.

Imperial Conference (gozen kaigi) 御前会議
The term *imperial conference* was used to refer to a conference of national leaders on major matters of state policy held in the presence of the emperor. Although from the Meiji period the emperor occasionally attended cabinet, Privy Council, and Imperial Headquarters meetings, an *imperial conference* was used to mean one not provided for by law. It was attended by *genrō*, cabinet and military leaders. In this sense the first imperial conference occurred in 1894 before the declaration of war on China. Such meetings were subsequently held at times of crisis, such as the Triple Intervention (*q.v.*) and the Russo-Japanese War. The system lapsed in the

early Showā period but was revived in 1938, and between then and 1945 over ten such conferences took place to discuss war policy and other such important matters. Although the emperor was regarded as the highest authority, he was not normally expected to speak, but his decision in favor of accepting the Potsdam Declaration (*q.v.*) at a conference in August 1945 is generally regarded as crucial in ending the war.

Butow, R.J.C. *Japan's Decision to Surrender* (Stanford, 1954).

Imperial Guard. See ARMY

Imperial House
During the Tokugawa period the imperial house was isolated from almost every governing office, but toward the end of the period the court acted as a focus for discontent and began to reemerge onto the national political scene. Its income came from privately owned estates. After the Restoration, when the emperor moved to Tokyo, these estates were abolished, and the imperial family was economically dependent on the state. Nevertheless, it gradually amassed private assets such as state forests and shareholding in major banks and companies. The position of the imperial house was strengthened by a series of reforms and laws upon which the "emperor system" (*q.v.*) was based. The Imperial Household Ministry was established, which, with its related departments, was clearly separate from other administrative departments. The imperial family was not subject to normal laws, and matters relating to them were the prerogative of the emperor as the head of the house, advised when necessary by the Lord Keeper of the Privy Seal (*naidaijin*). The legal base for the imperial position was provided by the Meiji constitution (*q.v.*) and the 1889 Imperial Household Law, which controlled accession, marriage, and regency without reference to the Diet. In 1946 a new Imperial Household Law was enacted, and the imperial family became subject to the constitution and normal laws. Its assets were frozen, and in 1947 some ¥3,300 million out of ¥3,700 million was paid as property tax. The remainder was ruled state property. The imperial family has since remained economically dependent on the state, the receipt or purchase of any property being subject to Diet approval. Important matters relating to the imperial family or its finances are discussed by imperial house conferences attended by members of the imperial family, prime minister, Lord Privy Seal, leaders of the houses of the Diet, and judges.

Titus, D. *Palace and Politics in Prewar Japan* (New York, 1974).
Webb, H. *The Japanese Imperial Institution in the Tokugawa Period* (New York, 1968).

Imperial Japanese Constitution. See MEIJI CONSTITUTION

Imperial Rayon Scandal (Teijin jiken) 帝人事件
The Imperial Rayon Company (Teijin) was largely owned by the Suzuki firm, and on Suzuki's bankruptcy in 1927 some 220,000 shares passed to the Bank of Taiwan in payment of debts. A boom in the rayon industry led to strong competition to buy the shares during 1933, and it was rumored that a group of young businessmen known as the Banchōkai had obtained some cheaply through bribing Finance Ministry officials. Following revelations in the *Jiji Shinpō* various Banchōkai members and senior government officials were arrested; the outcry led to the resignation of the Saitō cabinet in July 1934. Shortly afterwards former Commerce Minister Nakajima Kumakichi was arrested, and former Railway Minister Mitsuchi Chūzō was among those charged with corruption, but in 1937 all those accused were acquitted.

Imperial Rescript (chōchoku) 詔勅
From the Meiji period the term *imperial*

rescript was used to mean a declaration by the emperor regarding important imperial family or state matters. There were various kinds of rescript, relating both to specific events, like declarations of war, and to general lines of state policy, of which the most well known are probably those to soldiers and sailors of 1882 and on education of 1890. Rescripts were not subject to the Diet nor even to cabinet control yet had the force of law. Rescripts were abolished under the 1947 constitution, although the sovereign's name is still used for decreeing the opening and dissolution of the Diet.

Imperial Rescript on Education
(kyōiku chokugo) 教育勅語
Promulgated on 30 October 1890, the Imperial Rescript on Education affirmed the basic traditionalist principles of prewar education and came to be regarded as an ideological support of the "emperor system" (*q.v.*). Drafted mainly by Inoue Kowashi and Motoda Eifu, the rescript stated that loyalty to the emperor and patriotism were the ultimate virtues of the people and propagated the idea of the state as one family under the emperor, its morality based on traditional Confucian values. Copies of the rescript were distributed to all schools and hung alongside the emperor's portrait. Ceremonial readings and worship of it were used until 1945 to instill its ideas into students.

Hall, R. K. *Shūshin: The Ethics of a Defeated Nation* (New York, 1949).
Passin, H. *Society and Education in Japan* (New York, 1965).
Tsunoda, R., W. T. de Bary, and D. Keene, eds., *Sources of the Japanese Tradition*, vol. 2 (New York, 1958).

Imperial Rescript to Soldiers and Sailors. See TAKEHASHI RISING

Imperial Reservists' Association. See RESERVISTS' ASSOCIATION

Imperial Rule Assistance Association
(Taisei Yokusankai) 大政翼賛会
A national organization founded in October 1940 under government sponsorship as the nuclear body of the "new political structure." Although its purpose was the concentration of national political power and the establishment of a strong political structure and although political organizations dissolved themselves in its favor, the various constituent groups (government, bureaucracy, parties, army, right wing, etc.) could not agree on the nature of the association. It was eventually founded with the vague aim of "fulfilling the way of the subject in assisting imperial rule." The prime minister was automatically president of the association, and there was a national branch network, local administrators being branch heads. The various groups fought to dominate the association and the wider movement; although many had intended the association to have the function of a mass political party, this character failed to materialize, although it did have its own political association. Especially under the Tōjō cabinet the association increasingly functioned as an instrument of national control. From June 1942 it took over the responsibility for many national organizations and local government units from government ministries. Its lack of autonomy ultimately weakened it, and it was abolished in a domestic reorganization in June 1945.

Berger, G. M. *Parties Out of Power in Japan, 1931–1941* (Princeton, 1977).
Quigley, H. S., and J. E. Turner. *The New Japan* (Minneapolis, 1956).

Imperial University. See TOKYO UNIVERSITY

Imperial Way Faction. See KŌDŌ FACTION

Independence of the Supreme Command (tōsuiken no dokuritsu) 統帥権の独立

Under the Meiji constitution (*q.v.*) the military authorities were given considerable autonomy by the fact that the emperor was supreme commander of the armed forces, whose leaders had the right of direct appeal to the throne. Although the war minister as a member of the cabinet could rule on administrative matters, operational decisions were regarded as the prerogative of the chief of staff. This dichotomy initially caused little problem as the same group controlled both the cabinet and the highest army and navy positions, but conflict arose later when the army leadership defined operational matters as including the level of armament needed for defense. In 1926 the Katō cabinet forced a cut of four divisions in the army. More seriously, during the ratification process of the London Naval Treaty (*q.v.*) in 1930 the naval chief of staff, who objected to the treaty, was overruled and ultimately forced to resign on the grounds that legally the prime minister could make the final decision on matters affecting national security. The issue of this "violation of the right of the supreme command" to operational decisions assumed major political proportions, and the outcry became a factor in the later attack on Hamaguchi, who had enforced ratification. The independence of the supreme command was invoked in 1931 to allow the Kwantung Army (*q.v.*) to define the limits of its operations in South Manchuria. With the increasing influence of the army, cabinets became increasingly disinclined, or unable, to contest decisions of the supreme command, although constitutional ambiguity remained until 1945.

Crowley, J. B. *Japan's Quest for Autonomy* (Princeton, 1966).

Industrial Exhibitions. See EXHIBITIONS

Industrialization

There was some industry in Japan before the Meiji Restoration, but most was on a very small scale, much of it farming sidework. There existed a few "manufactories" where several processes were conducted by hand on one site. From the 1860s, and especially after the Restoration, a conscious effort was made by the government and a few entrepreneurs to modernize the production of goods and to introduce totally new Western manufacturing processes.The idea that industrialization was a prerequisite to national and international strength was fundamental to the policies of the Meiji government, which promoted industry by direct involvement, indirect encouragement, and the provision of an efficient economic infrastructure. Military motives and expenditure also influenced the pattern of Japan's industrialization. Initial expansion and modernization took place in the traditional industries. The expansionary impetus passed to light industry, and, then, in the period after World War I, manufacturing and heavy industry expanded rapidly. This developmental pattern emerged from a situation where capital was expensive, labor cheap, most raw materials had to be imported, and the constraints imposed on Japan from outside permitted little protection to her infant industries. She was therefore forced to concentrate on the lines of greatest comparative advantage, and from the beginning her trading position had an important influence on her industrial development. Western technology was introduced both by hiring foreigners and by sending Japanese to be trained abroad. During the Meiji period the availability of cheap labor (despite local shortages), the size of the internal market, and government-created demand helped expansion, but even by 1900 some 70% of the population gained its income from agriculture. Of those industries that did develop, textiles were the most important. Although silk and cotton products were slow to provide competition with the West, by the turn of the century large-scale production on a factory basis was widespread in these industries. After 1900 development in all sectors of industry was rapid; heavy industry and machinery production began to expand, and a considerable stimulus to development was provided by World War I. By the late 1920s the secondary sector had overtaken the primary in terms of real national income. Factory operatives (those in workplaces of over five people) increased from some 800,000 in 1909 to nearly 3 million in 1937, but over half the population remained in the primary sector up to the Pacific War. As diversification and rapid technological advances took place during the 1930s, Japan became increasingly self-sufficient in her own industrial needs and reduced her imports of finished goods. Finished goods began to amount to over 50% of Japan's own exports by value. However, textiles still accounted for over 50% total factory employment up to 1930, and textiles and other light manufactures remained dominant in exports despite advances in heavy industry and machine tools. Viewed overall, the pace of industrial expansion in this period was remarkable. Indices of production show that the volume of textile production in the late 1930s was some ten times that of the late 1890s. That of metals and machinery was thirty-six times as great. From the mid-1930s the industrial structure was distorted to cope with the war effort. Since the beginning of industrialization Japan had been vulnerable in terms of raw material supply, and this problem became acute in the years following 1937. Diversion of resources, war damage, and lack of raw materials meant that by 1946 industrial production had fallen to some 30% of the 1934–1936 level, which was not regained until 1953. Postwar industrial growth has concentrated on heavy industry, chemicals, and machinery of all kinds, which together accounted for 60% total factory employment by the late 1950s. In 1977 manufacturing accounted for 20% GNP, services 55%, and agricultural and fishing only 5% whereas in 1978 manufactured goods accounted for 69% of exports. The same year Japan ranked second in the world in industrial production. (See also individual industries; GOVERNMENT ENTERPRISES.)

Allen, G. C. *A Short Economic History of Modern Japan* (London, 1962).
Lockwood, W. W. *The Economic Development of Japan* (expanded ed., Princeton, 1968).
Schumpeter, E. B., ed., *The Industrialization of Japan and Manchukuo, 1930–1940* (New York, 1940).

Industry Ministry. See GOVERNMENT ENTERPRISES

Inoue Junnosuke 1869–1932
井上準之助
Native of Ōita, Inoue graduated in law from Tokyo Imperial University and worked for the Bank of Japan, spending considerable periods abroad. In 1913 he became president of the Yokohama Specie Bank, then in 1919–1923 was governor of the Bank of Japan. As finance minister 1923–1924 he had to deal with the financial problems following the Kantō earthquake (*q.v.*), and he was then recalled as governor of the Bank of Japan at the time of the 1927 financial crisis. In 1928 Inoue entered the Minseitō and served as finance minister 1929–1931. He enforced a strict deflationary policy in order to return Japan to the gold standard; this exacerbated the already worsening depression in Japan. Inoue was assassinated by a member of the Blood League (*q.v.*) while electioneering in February 1932.

Inouye, J. *Problems of the Japanese Exchange, 1914–1926* (London, 1931).

Inoue Kaoru (Bunda) 1835–1915
(Count, 1884; Prince, 1907)
井上馨(聞多)
Inoue, a Chōshū samurai, studied Western learning but initially joined the antiforeign movement, participating in an attack on the British Legation. In 1863 he went to England but returned with Itō Hirobumi to try and mediate in Chōshū's dispute

with the foreign powers. Rejecting anti-foreignism, Inoue survived an assassination attempt by conservatives and went on to fight against the Bakufu and to play a leading part in its demise. In 1868 he joined the new government and after working in foreign affairs became deputy finance minister in 1871. His efforts to stabilize the government's finances included the reform of the land tax and stipend commutation. Resigning 1873 over disagreement with the government's financial policy, he was briefly engaged in business but returned to the government 1875 after the Osaka Conference (*q.v.*). He acted as special envoy to Korea, concluding a Friendship Treaty in 1876, and was appointed *sangi* in 1878. After serving as industry minister 1878–1879, Inoue then became foreign minister; he retained the position after the introduction of the cabinet system in 1885. In this capacity he worked toward treaty revision (*q.v.*) but was criticized for his excessive Europeanization policies and the new draft treaties and resigned in September 1887. He was afterwards minister of Agriculture and Commerce 1888–1889, home minister 1892–1894, and finance minister 1898. He then retired from active politics but remained influential as a *genrō*. Throughout his life he worked for the development of transport and industry and had strong connections with the world of business, especially with Mitsui.

Akita, G. *The Foundations of Constitutional Government in Modern Japan, 1868–1900* (Cambridge, Mass., 1967).
Morris, J. *Makers of Japan* (London, 1906).

Inoue Kowashi 1843–1895
(Viscount, 1895) 井上毅
Samurai from Kumamoto Prefecture, Inoue joined the Justice Ministry in 1871. He traveled to Europe in 1872 and through the 1870s researched into foreign constitutions and legal codes. He was close to leading members of the government and helped to draft Iwakura Tomomi's statement of opinion on a constitution, which included many principles later embodied in the Meiji constitution (*q.v.*). In the 1880s he worked closely with Itō Hirobumi in drafting the Meiji constitution and the Imperial Household Law. In 1888–1891 Inoue was chief of the Cabinet Legislative Bureau and in 1890–1893 secretary to the Privy Council. He strongly supported Mori Arinori's educational principles, played a major role in drafting the Imperial Rescript on Education (*q.v.*), and despite only a brief term as education minister 1893–1894 had a far reaching influence on educational development.

Beauchamp, E. R., ed., *Learning to Be Japanese* (Hamden, Conn., 1978).
Pittau, J. "Inoue Kowashi, 1843–1895, and the Formation of Modern Japan," *MN* 20, nos 3–4 (1965).
______ . *Political Thought in Early Meiji Japan, 1868–1889* (Cambridge, Mass., 1967).

Inoue Nisshō (Akira) 1886–1967
井上日召(昭)
Native of Gunma, Inoue traveled in China following the 1911 revolution and acted as a secret agent of the Japanese Army in Manchuria. After returning in 1916, he became a Nichiren Buddhist priest. An ardent nationalist, he believed in national "renovation" through the abolition of capitalism and the elimination of those he regarded as traitors. His ideas received support from young village people in his local Ibaraki who were hard hit by agrarian depression. Inoue also had strong connections with Gondō Seikyō and his followers. He was highly regarded by radical young naval officers, and after the failure of the army-led October incident (*q.v.*) of 1931 Inoue's followers caused the Blood League incident (*q.v.*) and supported a proposed naval uprising. Inoue was subsequently sentenced to life imprisonment but was released in a general amnesty in 1940. He was purged postwar but in the 1950s reemerged into political activity and founded an extremist nationalist group with some of his former followers.

Morris, I. *Nationalism and the Right Wing in Japan* (London, 1960).
Storry, R. *The Double Patriots* (London, 1957).

Inoue Tetsujirō 1856–1944 井上哲次郎
The son of a physician in Fukuoka, Inoue graduated in Oriental philosophy from Tokyo Imperial University in 1880. After studying in Germany he became the university's first Japanese professor of philosophy and taught there until 1923. He played a major part in promoting the study of philosophy in Japan and was also a major thinker in his own right. The fundamental aim of combining and unifying Eastern and Western philosophical concepts dominated all his ideas, and he wrote widely on both philosophical method and ethical philosophy, which led him to develop the idea of a national morality. His political ideology was strongly pro-establishment; he stressed the need for loyalty to the emperor and love for Japan as the essentials of national morality, and in his official commentary on the Imperial Rescript on Education (*q.v.*) he attacked Christianity as opposing this morality. This theme was continued in later writings, which became increasingly nationalistic.

Piovesana, G. K. *Recent Japanese Philosophical Thought, 1862–1912* (Tokyo, 1968).
Yamazaki, M. and T. Miyakawa. "Inoue Tetsujirō: The Man and His Works," in Japan Commission for UNESCO, *The Modernization of Japan*, vol. 7 (Tokyo, 1969).

International Military Tribunal for the Far East (kyokutō kokusai gunji saiban) 極東国際軍事裁判
According to the Potsdam declaration (*q.v.*), in January 1946 SCAP (*q.v.*) ordered that a military court be established in Tokyo to try as class "A" war criminals those members of the government and military authorities of Japan charged with crimes against peace and planning and initiating aggressive war since the Manchurian Incident (*q.v.*). The proceedings opened in May 1946. There were 11 judges, one each from the nine countries signing the surrender document and also from India and the Philippines; the presiding judge was William Webb of Australia. Twenty-eight individuals were charged, but one was ruled unfit to stand, and two others died during proceedings. In November 1948 the remaining 25 were all found guilty, mostly of conspiracy to wage aggressive war. Seven were sentenced to death, 16 to life imprisonment, one to 20 years' imprisonment, and one to seven years' imprisonment. The death sentences were carried out December 1948. All those remaining in prison were paroled after the San Francisco Peace Treaty (*q.v.*), and in April 1958 all were unconditionally released. After discussion the emperor was excluded from trial. Other classes of war crimes were tried outside Japan.

International Military Tribunal for the Far East. *Transcript of Proceedings.*
Minear, R. H. *Victors' Justice—The Tokyo War Crimes Trial* (Princeton, 1971).

International Trade and Industry Ministry. See MITI

Inukai Tsuyoshi 1855–1932 犬養毅
A native of Okayama Prefecture, Inukai studied at Keiō and in 1880 helped to found the economic journal *Tōkai Keizai Shinpō* (Tōkai Economic Journal), in whose pages he advocated trade protection. He entered the government in 1881 only to resign in the political crisis of that year, and he subsequently participated in the Kaishintō and the Daidō Danketsu movement (*q.v.*), writing in antigovernment papers such as the *Hōchi.* In 1890 Inukai was elected to the Diet, and his strong local base, so-called "iron" *jiban* (constituency), enabled him to remain a member until his death. After serving as

education minister in 1898, he remained in opposition for over 20 years. He was strongly anti-*hanbatsu* (*q.v.*) and attempted to unite the parties in the Diet in opposition to the *hanbatsu* politicians, but for a long period his efforts were unsuccessful. During this time Inukai was a member of various parties and in 1910–1922 was the leader of the Kokumintō. He played a leading role in the movements for the protection of constitutional government in 1912 and 1924 (*q.v.*) and was a supporter of universal suffrage. In 1922 he formed the Kakushin Club, which in 1925 merged with the Seiyūkai. Inukai was communications minister 1923–1924 and 1924–1925. In 1929 he became president of the Seiyūkai and prime minister in December 1931. He was faced both with the effects of the prevailing depression and with the difficult post-Manchurian Incident (*q.v.*) situation. He adopted a policy of deficit financing to stimulate the economy, but his economic, diplomatic, and other policies met with constant opposition, and Inukai was assassinated in the May 15 incident (*q.v.*).

Duus, P. *Party Rivalry and Political Change in Taishō Japan.* (Cambridge, Mass., 1968).

Najita, T. "Inukai Tsuyoshi: Some Dilemmas in Party Development in Pre-World War II Japan," *American Historical Review* 74, no. 2 (Dec. 1968).

Invasion of Korea. See KOREA, INVASION OF

Iron and Steel Industry

Some iron was produced from iron sand during the Tokugawa period, but although modern techniques began to be introduced after the Restoration, Japan was deficient in both ore and coking coal and was flooded with Western imports of pig iron and steel. Government and private attempts to set up large-scale production were generally unsuccessful because of the vast capital investment necessary, and in 1896 Japan supplied only 40% domestic pig iron consumption and almost no steel. Realizing the need for increased production, the government established the Yawata (Yahata) Iron Works, which started production in 1901, and although private firms subsequently developed, it for long retained its dominance of pig iron production assisted by state sponsorship and subsidy. In 1913 Japan produced 243,000 tons of pig iron and 255,000 steel (48% and 34% consumption, respectively). Raw materials came increasingly from China and Korea. Production expanded considerably during the 1920s although private growth was slow and the industry remained dominated by Yawata and a few *zaibatsu*-owned companies. Diversification and expansion in the 1930s was greater. From 2 million tons of steel in 1929 Japan produced 5½ million tons in 1936, and during the same period pig iron production nearly doubled. Techniques also improved noticeably. This development considerably reduced import dependence. The government-controlled Japan Iron and Steel Company (Nihon Seitetsu) formed from an amalgamation of Yawata and six other big works in 1934 placed most pig iron and much steel capacity under government control. Total government control followed in the war and lasted until 1945. Postwar the industry suffered from loss of markets, raw materials, and military demand, but steel especially revived from the time of the Korean War. With the aid of massive investment and new techniques, production in 1960 reached almost 12 million tons of pig iron and over 22 million tons of steel. Production is now on a purely private basis. There is still a high dependence on imported ores or scrap, most ore coming from Australia, Brazil, and India. In 1974 Japan produced 17% world steel production with 117 million tons, but because of world recession, production of both iron and steel has declined. In 1978 Japan produced only 102 million tons of steel. Approximately one-third of output is exported, and Japan remains the world's third largest producer of iron and steel.

British Iron and Steel Federation. *The*

Iron and Steel Industry of Japan (London, 1963).
Burton, W. D. "The Origins of the Modern Japanese Iron and Steel Industry with Special Reference to Mito and Kamaishi, 1853–1907," Ph.D. diss., University of London, 1972.
Kawahito, K. *The Japanese Steel Industry* (New York, 1972).

Ishibashi Tanzan 1884–1973 石橋湛山
Native of Tokyo, Ishibashi became a journalist after graduating from Waseda University in 1907. In 1911 he joined the *Tōyō Keizai Shinpō* (Oriental Economic Journal) and acted as its editor 1925–1946 and from 1941 also as its president. He became well known as a liberal economist and exponent of Keynesian ideas. In 1946–1947 Ishibashi was finance minister under Yoshida and tried to use his theories to rebuild the economy. He was elected to the Diet in 1947 but was soon purged by SCAP (*q.v.*). Returning to sit in the Diet 1952–1963, conflict with Yoshida developed; Ishibashi built up his own faction and served as minister of international trade and industry under Hatoyama 1954–1956. He then became president of the Liberal Democratic Party in the first election to be held at the party assembly and consequently prime minister in December 1956. His policies were at the liberal end of the L. D. P. spectrum, and he hoped to reflate the economy by tax reduction and initiate relations of friendship and commerce with the People's Republic of China. However in February 1957 Ishibashi resigned due to ill health. The Ishibashi faction virtually ceased to exist after Ishibashi failed to get elected in 1963, but until his death Ishibashi worked to promote relations with the People's Republic of China and the Soviet Union, although he argued for Japan's independent defense capability.

Kimura, K. "Ishibashi Tanzan, the Man and His Policy," *CJ* 15, nos. 5–8 (May–Aug. 1946).

Ishihara Kanji. See ISHIWARA KANJI

Ishii Kikujirō 1866–1945 (Baron, 1911; Viscount, 1916) 石井菊次郎
Native of Chiba, Ishii graduated in law from Tokyo Imperial University in 1890 and entered the Foreign Ministry, where his posts included that of ambassador to France 1912–1915. As foreign minister 1915–1916 he concluded an agreement with Russia aimed at forestalling a separate peace with Germany. In 1916 he was also appointed to the House of Peers. As special envoy to America in 1917, he concluded the Lansing-Ishii agreement (*q.v.*). In 1920–1927 Ishii was ambassador to France and also Japan's chief delegate to the League of Nations. He represented Japan at several international conferences including the 1927 Geneva Arms Limitation Conference. From 1929 until his death he was a member of the Privy Council and played the role of elder statesman in Japan's diplomatic affairs. He left extensive diplomatic commentaries *(Gaikō Yoroku)*.

Ishii, K. (tr. and ed. F. C. Langdon). *Diplomatic Commentaries* (Baltimore, 1936).
Nish, I. H. *Alliance in Decline* (London, 1972).

Ishii-Lansing Agreement. See LANSING—ISHII AGREEMENT

Ishikawa Sanshirō 1876–1956 石川三四郎
Native of Saitama Prefecture, after studying law, Ishikawa joined the *Yorozu Chōhō* (*q.v.*) as a reporter and then became a member of the Heiminsha (*q.v.*). As a leading Christian Socialist he worked with Abe Isoo and Kinoshita Naoe on *Shin Kigen* (New Era), the magazine of the moderate wing of the Socialist movement. Ishikawa spent the years 1912–1920 in Europe and during this time turned from active politics and labor agitation to political theorizing, and from Christian socialism to anarchism. After the death of Ōsugi Sakae he was regarded as Japan's leading anarchist theorist. His works include histories of Japanese and Western social movements, socialism, and Socialists.

Ishiwara Kanji 1889–1949 石原莞爾
Native of Yamagata Prefecture, Ishiwara studied at the Military Academy and Staff College and was in Germany 1922–1924. In October 1928 he became operations officer on the Kwantung Army (*q.v.*) staff and in this position played a leading role in the Manchurian Incident (*q.v.*) and the founding of Manchukuo. A leading ideologist in army circles, he came to have considerable influence over young officers. After a posting to Sendai he became chief of the operations section at the General Staff in 1935 and then in March 1937 major general and chief of the operations division at the General Staff. In September 1937 he became deputy chief of staff of the Kwantung Army, but his strong anti-Russian stance, his desire for an East Asian League, and his criticism of Japanese policy in Manchukuo led to a declining influence, and he returned to Japan August 1938 as a regional commander. Although promoted again in 1939, his views on Asian affairs increasingly clashed with those of Tōjō Hideki, and in March 1941 he retired and was placed on the reserve list. In 1941–1942 he lectured at Ritsumeikan University, but although he remained ideologically influential among some right-wing elements, he was largely isolated and under suspicion throughout the war. He reemerged into public life 1945 but was purged 1946. Although he testified at the Tokyo war crimes trial 1947, the remainder of his life was spent in ill health and retirement in Yamagata.

Peattie, M. R. *Ishiwara Kanji and Japan's Confrontation with the West* (Princeton, 1975).

Itagaki Seishirō. See MANCHURIAN INCIDENT

Itagaki Taisuke 1837–1919 (Count, 1887) 板垣退助
A samurai from Tosa, Itagaki participated in the anti-Bakufu movement (*q.v.*) and fought in the Boshin War. After the Restoration he worked in the administration of Tosa and 1871 became *sangi* in the central government but resigned in 1873 over the invasion of Korea (*q.v.*), returning to the government briefly after the 1875 Ōsaka Conference (*q.v.*). In 1874 with Gotō Shōjirō, Soejima Taneomi, and Etō Shinpei he submitted a petition for an elected assembly. He called for the end of *hanbatsu* (*q.v.*) government and the extension of popular rights; to this end he founded the Tosa Risshisha and the national Aikoku Kōtō (*q.v.*) and in 1876–1881 was the effective leader of the popular rights movement. In October 1881 Itagaki founded the Jiyūtō (*q.v.*) and despite going abroad on government expenses in 1882 remained its head until the party disbanded in 1884. He survived an assassination attack in Gifu in 1882. He retained strong connections with the antigovernment movement and became Jiyūtō leader in the Diet at its inception; however, he served as home minister under Itō in 1896 and also in 1898 under Ōkuma. Itagaki left politics on the formation of the Seiyūkai in 1900 and devoted the rest of his life to welfare work.

Cody, C. E. "A Study of the Career of Itagaki Taisuke (1837–1919), a Leader of the Democratic Movement in Meiji Japan," Ph.D. diss., University of Washington, 1955.
Ike, N. *The Beginnings of Political Democracy in Japan* (Baltimore, 1950).

Itō Hirobumi 1841–1909 (Count, 1884; Marquis, 1895; Prince, 1907) 伊藤博文
Member of Chōshū lower samurai family, Itō secretly visited England in 1863, returning 1864 in an attempt to mediate over the bombardment of Shimonoseki (*q.v.*). He rejected his former anti-Western views and participated in the anti-Bakufu movement (*q.v.*). After 1868 Itō held posts in the new government including governor of Hyōgo and within the ministries of Finance, Civil Affairs, and Industry. He was a member of the Iwakura mission (*q.v.*). In 1873 he became *sangi* and minister of industry and as minister of home affairs from 1878 was, along with Ōkuma Shigenobu, the most influential member

of the government. The 1881 political crisis (*q.v.*) made his position within the government unchallenged, and he remained one of the leading figures in Japanese politics until his death. In 1882 Itō visited Europe to study Western constitutions, and on his return he was the leading architect of the peerage system and the new cabinet system (*q.v.*). The Meiji constitution (*q.v.*) is regarded largely as Itō's work. As Japan's first prime minister 1885–1888 Itō devoted most of his efforts to the new constitution, but unrest over treaty revision caused his cabinet to implement the Peace Regulations (*q.v.*). In 1888–1890 he was president of the Privy Council where he led discussion on the constitutional proposals. In 1890 he became president of the House of Peers but was again prime minister 1892–1896 (the time of the Sino-Japanese War), in 1898, and 1900–1901, this last time as leader of the Seiyūkai. Again president of the Privy Council 1903–1905, from December 1905 to June 1909, Itō acted as resident-general of the protectorate of Korea; during this time the internal as well as external affairs of Korea were increasingly brought under Japanese control, although Itō himself was not a strong advocate of annexation. In October 1909 he was assassinated by a Korean at Harbin.

Hamada, K. *Prince Itō* (Tokyo, 1936).
Ladd, G. T. *In Korea with Marquis Itō* (New York, 1908).
Nakamura, K. *Prince Itō—The Man and Statesman* (New York, 1910).

Itō Miyoji 1857–1934 (Baron, 1895; Viscount, 1907; Count, 1922) 伊藤巳代治

Son of a Nagasaki townsman, Itō studied languages and joined the bureaucracy in 1877. He was closely identified with Itō Hirobumi, whom he accompanied to Europe in 1882; and as private secretary to Itō after returning in 1883, he helped in the formation of the cabinet system and drafting of the constitution. In 1889 he became chief secretary to the Privy Council, 1890 a member of the House of Peers, and 1892–1896 was chief of the cabinet secretariat. After serving as agriculture and commerce minister January–April 1898, he subsequently avoided public politics but as a member of the Privy Council from 1899 became a leader of the "bureaucratic" conservative faction, terming himself the "guardian of the constitution"; although unpopular, he wielded a major, if covert, influence on Japanese politics until his death. Itō conflicted often with both Diet and cabinet and was partly responsible for the fall of the Wakatsuki cabinet in the 1927 financial crisis (*q.v.*). In 1891–1904 he was owner and president of the *Tokyo Nichi Nichi Shinbun.*

Akita, G. "The Other Itō: A Political Failure," in A. M. Craig and D. H. Shively, eds., *Personality in Japanese History* (Berkeley, 1970).

Itō Noe 1895–1923 伊藤野枝

A native of Fukuoka, Itō graduated from high school in Tokyo. Fleeing an arranged marriage, in 1913 she joined the Seitōsha (*q.v.*), where she edited its magazine and reinforced its emphasis on the women's rights struggle. In 1916 she left the group and went to live with Ōsugi Sakae, working thereafter as an anarchist leader. After the 1923 earthquake she was arrested with Ōsugi and murdered by the police.

Large, S. S. "The Romance of Revolution in Japanese Anarchism and Communism During the Taishō Period," *MAS* 11, no. 3 (July 1977).
Miyamoto, K. "Itō Noe and the Bluestockings," *JI* 10, no. 2 (Autumn 1975).

Iwakura Mission (Iwakura kengai shisetsu) 岩倉遣外使節

In 1871 a delegation led by Iwakura Tomomi and including government leaders such as Kido Kōin, Ōkubo Toshimichi, and Itō Hirobumi left for the U.S. and Europe in an effort to secure treaty revision (*q.v.*) and study the West. The group also included lower-level officials and students going to study abroad. Treaty revision negotiations with the U.S. were unsuccessful, but the group's leaders made extensive observations of Western civilization, and their report was of great importance in determining subsequent policy. All the delegates had returned home by September 1873 and most of them strongly opposed the invasion of Korea (*q.v.*) during the government crisis of 1873.

Mayo, M. "The Iwakura Mission to the U.S. and Europe 1871–1873." Columbia University East Asian Institute, *Researches in the Social Sciences on Japan*, vol. 2 (New York, 1959).
______. "Rationality in the Meiji Restoration: The Iwakura Embassy," in B. S. Silberman and H. D. Harootunian, eds., *Modern Japanese Leadership* (Tucson, 1966).
Soviak, E. "On the Nature of Western Progress: The Journal of the Iwakura Embassy," in D. H. Shively, ed., *Tradition and Modernization in Japanese Culture* (Princeton, 1971).

Iwakura Tomomi 1825–1883 (Prince) 岩倉具視

Court noble, Iwakura opposed the early treaties with the West and although subsequently supporting *kōbu gattai* policies (*q.v.*) was exiled from the court 1862–1867. He increasingly opposed the Bakufu, had strong connections with leaders of the anti-Bakufu movement (*q.v.*) in the domains, and in 1867 participated in the anti-Bakufu coup as one of the leaders of the court faction. He held top offices in the new administration, becoming minister of the Right in 1871, and 1871–1873 he led a mission to the West in an unsuccessful attempt to negotiate treaty revision. On his return he opposed plans for the invasion of Korea (*q.v.*) and in 1874 was wounded in an assassination attempt by Tosa samurai. Until his death Iwakura remained one of the most influential figures in the government. He devoted his efforts to the development of a strong state headed by the emperor, and his statement on the fundamental principles of an emperor-given constitution (drafted by Inoue Kowashi) foreshadowed the basic lines of the Meiji constitution (*q.v.*). Iwakura also promoted the founding of economic enterprises which would mitigate the effects of impoverishment and unemployment among the nobility and samurai.

Morris, J. *Makers of Japan* (London, 1906).

Iwasaki Yatarō 1835–1885 岩崎弥太郎

Son of a Tosa peasant who bought the title of *gōshi* in 1854, Iwasaki entered the service of his domain, became friendly with Gotō Shōjirō, and then acted as agent in Nagasaki for Tosa's trading company. With the abolition of the domains in 1871 he inherited the capital and ships formerly owned by Tosa to form his own Tsukumo Trading Company and quickly expanded his shipping business, competing successfully with the government's Postal Steamship Company. The company was renamed Mitsubishi in 1873. In 1874 Iwasaki was commissioned by the government to carry troops and arms for the Formosan Expedition and subsequently cheaply purchased the ships formerly owned by the Postal Steamship Company. With the aid of massive government subsidies aimed at promoting a strong merchant marine, by 1877 Iwasaki had successfully combated foreign competition to dominate the seas round Japan. With government support Iwasaki expanded his business interests to include exchange, marine insurance, mining, and shipbuilding and was known as one of the leading *seishō* ("political merchants") (*q.v.*). His ruthless monopoly practices and commercial success drew strong criticism. Iwasaki had strong contacts with Fukuzawa Yukichi and employed many of his Keiō students. After Ōkuma—Mitsubishi's main supporter in the government—was ousted in 1881, the government helped the founding of a new competitor, the Kyōdo Unyū Company; cut-throat competition ensued but in 1885 the two companies merged into the Nihon Yūsen Kaisha (Japan Shipping

Company) with Mitsubishi interests remaining dominant. Iwasaki dominated the company until his death shortly before the merger, and his brother, Yanosuke, continued the family's dominance in the Mitsubishi *zaibatsu* (*q.v.*).

Hirschmeier, J. *The Origins of Entrepreneurship in Meiji Japan* (Cambridge, Mass., 1964).
Hirschmeier, J., and T. Yui. *The Development of Japanese Business, 1600–1973* (London, 1975).
Yamamura, K. *A Study of Samurai Income and Entrepreneurship* (Cambridge, Mass., 1974).

J

Japan-China Basic Treaty (Nikka Kihon Jōyaku) 日華基本条約

In an attempt to provide an alternative to the hostile Chiang Kai-shek regime in China, in March 1940 Japan installed Wang Ching-wei as president of a new national government in Nanking. Wang was a Kuomintang leader who saw no possibility of defeating the Japanese and feared Communist influence in China. In November 1940 Japan concluded the Basic Treaty with the Wang regime, which was recognized in the treaty by Japan as the legitimate government of China. In return Japan received wide powers, including permission to station troops in north China, nominally for anti-Communist purposes, responsibility for maintaining law and order, permission for warship patrols, and privileges relating to the exploitation of natural resources. An accompanying protocol and secret agreements also stipulated the use of Japanese advisers. Wang's regime never gained any credibility in China. The Japanese failed to grant any concessions which might have assisted this, such as abandonment of extraterritorial privileges and troop withdrawal, and northern China was virtually autonomous under Japanese control. The Basic Treaty, which was opposed both in China and abroad, was replaced in October 1943 by a pact of alliance following Wang's agreement to declare war on the allies. From that year Japan began to abandon some of her privileges, but it was too late to help either Japan or Wang, who died in late 1944.

Boyle, J. H. *China and Japan at War, 1937–1945: The Politics of Collaboration* (Stanford, 1972).
Bunker, G. E. *The Peace Conspiracy: Wang Ching-wei and the China War, 1937–1941* (Cambridge, Mass., 1972).
Lin, H. S. "A New Look at Chinese Nationalist 'Appeasers,'" in A. D. Coox and H. Conroy, eds., *China and Japan: Search for Balance Since World War I* (Santa Barbara, 1978).
Miwa, K. "The Wang Ching-wei Regime and Japanese Efforts to Terminate the China Conflict," in J. Roggendorf, ed., *Studies in Japanese Culture* (Tokyo, 1963).

Japan-China Joint Defense Agreement (Nikka Kyōdō Bōteki Gunji Kyōtei) 日華共同防敵軍事協定

In view of the situation in Siberia in 1918 Japan persuaded China to accept her proposals for a military agreement. Notes were exchanged in March 1918 and specific army and navy agreements concluded in May. The agreement stipulated that China would help in every possible way Japanese forces passing through Manchuria to Lake Baikal and the Amur River region as part of the Siberian intervention (*q.v.*) and that Chinese forces in the area would be under Japanese control. This agreement provided a legal basis for Japanese deployment in China, and Japan used this privilege to move her troops as she wished in northern Manchuria. The agreement was widely resented in China, where it turned public opinion against Tuan Ch'i-jui, who had negotiated the agreement. It was abrogated January 1921 when Japan started negotiations with the Soviet Far Eastern Republic concerning recognition of the area.

Shao, H-P. "From the Twenty-One Demands to the Sino-Japanese Military Agreements, 1915–1918: Ambivalent Relations," in A. D. Coox and H. Conroy, eds., *China and Japan: Search for Balance Since World War I* (Santa Barbara, 1978).

Japan Communist Party (Nihon Kyōsantō) 日本共産党

Following the existence of small underground Communist groups, on the directive of Comintern an illegal Communist party was founded in Japan 15 July 1922. It was headed by Sakai Toshihiko, Yamakawa Hitoshi, Arahata Kanson, and Tokuda Kyūichi. The party's activities were initially largely propagandistic and educational, but it was hampered by factionalism and government suppression. After arrests in June 1923 there was a move to disband the party, and this was done March 1924, although both Comintern and some party members objected to the dissolution. Activity by Communists continued, and in December 1926 the party was formally reestablished. In 1926–1927 the doctrines of Fukumotoism (*q.v.*) dominated party thinking, replacing previous support for the views of Yamakawa, but the J.C.P. returned to Comintern guidance late in 1927. From 1928 it began to publish its own newspaper *Akahata* (Red Flag) and attempted to secure wider support, but its success led to increased government suppression. On 15 March 1928 police carried out wholesale arrests of Communists and sympathizers throughout Japan. Out of over 1,000 arrested for violating the Peace Preservation Law (*q.v.*), some 500 were charged. Although the authorities missed some key figures, the arrests severely damaged the Communist movement, and three Communist-related organizations were banned in April of that year. A second raid, aimed at stopping a rebuilding of the J.C.P., followed on 16 April 1929, after which some 250 persons were held for trial. Leaders such as Nabeyama Sadachika and Sano Manabu were arrested soon afterwards. These arrests smashed the party organization and undermined its influence. Subsequent ideological splits ended any semblance of unity and the *tenkō* (*q.v.*) of Nabeyama and Sano in 1933, and of other leading Communists, was a severe blow. Arrests afterwards totally destroyed the party's national leadership, and those who did not revoke their views remained imprisoned until 1945. With the freeing of these men in October 1945, the J.C.P. was reconstituted by Tokuda Kyūichi and Shiga Yoshio, for the first time a legal political party. Under the leadership of Nosaka Sanzō from 1946 the J.C.P. played a leading role in popular protest and the labor movement, but in 1950 it split over Cominform criticism of its attitudes toward the Occupation reforms. In addition SCAP suppression from 1948 culminating in the "Red Purge" (*q.v.*) of 1950 sent many ideologues underground and overall party influence was considerably weakened. Extreme militancy with a few minor terrorist acts in the early 1950s lost the party mass support, so from 1955 attempts were made to reunite factions and rebuild the party. Subsequently, unity remained threatened by ideological disagreements over the criticism of Stalin and the Sino-Soviet split and in 1964 produced a major split in the party and its related organizations. Despite this the party increased its appeal through the late 1960s and early 1970s and was highly successful in the 1974 elections. However, in the December 1976 elections representation in the Lower House fell from 39 to 19, and in July 1977 in the Upper House from 20 to 16. Reported membership in 1978 was 440,000. In October 1979 Lower House representation rose again to 39 but fell to 29 in the June 1980 election when Upper House representation also fell to 12.

Beckmann, G. M. and G. Ōkubo. *The Japanese Communist Party, 1922–1945* (Stanford, 1969).
Emmerson, J. K. "The Japanese Communist Party After 50 Years," *Asian Survey* 12, no. 7 (July 1972).

Langer, P. F. *Communism in Japan* (Stanford, 1972).
Scalapino, R. A. *The Japanese Communist Movement, 1920–1966* (Berkeley, 1967).

Japan Democratic Party. See LIBERAL DEMOCRATIC PARTY

Japan Farmers' Union. See FARMERS' MOVEMENT

Japan Federation of Employers' Associations (Nihon Keieisha Dantai Renmei) 日本経営者団体連盟
The Japan Federation of Employers' Associations was initially founded in 1948 to strengthen the position of management in response to the labor problems of the late 1940s. Nikkeiren carries out research into and collects information on economic and labor problems and attempts to coordinate and strengthen management response to such things as wage demands, especially in the case of the "spring offensive." Nikkeiren, which in 1978 consisted of 125 industrial associations and 793 corporations, embracing in all thousands of enterprises, has had considerable success in recommending productivity agreements and wage rise levels.

Japan Federation of Labor. See LABOR MOVEMENT

Japan Labor Farmer Party (Nihon Rōnōtō) 日本労農党
The Japan Labor Farmer Party was a proletarian party formed in December 1926 by leaders of Sōdōmei and the Japan Farmers' Union claiming to stand for a middle course between anti-Communist social democrats and pro-Communist elements. The group consisted largely of intellectuals and former students and gave its name to the Japan Labor clique *(nichirōkei)*, one of the major strands in the interwar labor and Socialist movements. The party called for emancipation of the proletariat, reform by legal means, and class solidarity of the masses, as well as nonintervention in China. Its leader 1927–1928 was Asō Hisashi. In December 1928 the party became part of the Nihon Taishūtō, but its leadership maintained continuity as a group through the 1930s.

Totten, G. O. *The Social Democratic Movement in Prewar Japan* (New Haven, 1966).

Japan Labor Unions Council. See LABOR MOVEMENT

Japan Labor Unions General Council. See LABOR MOVEMENT

Japan Liberal Party. See LIBERAL DEMOCRATIC PARTY

Japan-Manchukuo Protocol (Nichiman Giteisho) 日満議定書
Signed on 15 September 1932 with immediate effect and followed immediately by Japan's formal recognition of Manchukuo (*q.v.*). The agreement was hurried through to make recognition of Manchukuo a fait accompli before publication of the Lytton commission's report (*q.v.*). In return for Japan's recognition of the independent status of Manchukuo, Manchukuo was to respect Japan's rights and interests according to former agreements with China. Japanese troops were to be stationed in Manchukuo for mutual defense purposes, and the protocol in effect acknowledged the dependent status of Manchukuo.

Ogata, S. *Defiance in Manchuria* (Berkeley, 1964).

Japan Progressive Party. See LIBERAL DEMOCRATIC PARTY

Japan Socialist League. See SOCIALIST MOVEMENT

Japan Socialist Party (Nihon Shakaitō) 日本社会党

The name *Japan Socialist Party* was given to Japan's first legal Socialist party formed in January 1906. Its leadership included Sakai Toshihiko, Nishikawa Kōjirō, and Katayama Sen, and there were initially some 200 members, embracing Socialists of all kinds. The party's organ was the magazine *Hikari* (Light) and later the daily *Heimin Shinbun* (Commoners' Newspaper). It engaged mostly in educational and propaganda activities. From early 1907 fierce conflict arose within the party between advocates of direct action, led by Kōtoku Shūsui, and those desiring to work through parliamentary means; and the Katsura administration, regarding the direct actionists as dangerous, banned the party on February 22.

The name *Japan Socialist Party* was also given to the postwar Socialist party founded 2 November 1945 and led by prewar social democrats such as Katayama Tetsu and Nishio Suehiro. At the April 1947 election the party became the biggest single party with 143 seats in the Diet, and with the support of the Democratic Party (Minshutō) and the Kokumin Kyōdōtō (National United Party) Katayama formed a cabinet. His lack of ability to implement Socialist policies led to strong criticism of Katayama from the party's left wing, and in March 1948 the whole cabinet resigned. The J.S.P. also supported the Ashida cabinet, but Nishio's involvement with the Shōwa Electrical scandal (*q.v.*) damaged the party's reputation. Its popularity declined, and in the 1949 election its Diet strength was reduced to 48. The leadership of the party became inclined to more left-wing policies, and the party split over the security treaty with the U.S. in 1951. The left-wing J.S.P. was led by Suzuki Mosaburō and supported by Sōhyō; it opposed the peace and security treaties and rearmament and advocated international neutrality. The right-wing J.S.P., led by Asanuma Inejirō, increased its influence in the early 1950s but less so than its left-wing competitor. Formal reunification into one party took place in October 1955. The party strongly opposed renewal of the security treaty in 1960, and this led to the defection of Nishio and his followers to form the new Democratic Socialist Party (*q.v.*), initially reinforcing left-wing dominance of the party. The party has maintained its position as the second largest party in the Diet, but it has failed to shake the monopoly of the Liberal Democratic Party. It is damaged by its strong Marxist heritage and the unlikelihood of gaining power in the foreseeable future; its failure to propose policies appealing to broad sections of the electorate is shown in its low national membership figure of 50,000 (as of 1979). The year 1977 was a disastrous one for the party, with major ideological disagreements within it, a poor showing in the House of Councillors' elections, and the resignation of the party chairman of nine years, Narita Tomomi. Lack of a willing successor led to a three-month interregnum before the appointment of Asukata Ichio, former mayor of Yokohama, in December 1977; and despite Asukata's skill in bringing together the party's factions, the party's fortunes have not yet noticeably revived. Lower House representation was maintained in the June 1980 election at 107, but Upper House representation fell from 56 to 47.

Colbert, E. S. *The Left Wing in Japanese Politics* (New York, 1952).
Cole, A. B., G. O. Totten, and C. H. Uyehara. *Socialist Parties in Postwar Japan* (New Haven, 1966).
Stockwin, J. A. A. *The Japanese Socialist Party and Neutralism* (Melbourne, 1968).
Totten, G. O. *The Social Democratic Movement in Prewar Japan* (New Haven, 1966).

Japan Teachers' Union (Nihon Kyōshokuin Kumiai) 日本教職員組合

A national body formed June 1947 by a merger of existing teachers' organizations representing some half million teachers at all levels. At first the union concentrated on educational matters such as teachers' living standards and the educational budget, but it extended its political activity to include opposition to rearmament, support of the peace movement, etc.

Nikkyōso, as it was known, was strongly influenced by communism, but many teachers were affected by the "red purge" (*q.v.*), and moderate elements reasserted themselves. From 1952 the government acted to curb political activity by teachers and to centralize education by such measures as the appointment rather than election of local education councils. Although Nikkyōso lost its official status as a national union in 1950 when teachers were designated local civil servants, this did not prevent fierce union-government hostility. Teachers were especially united in opposition to the efficiency rating system forced through by the government 1957–1959, but the violent and unsuccessful struggle weakened the union. It rebuilt its strength during the 1960s and increasingly concentrated on economic goals, but it has become increasingly militant in support of these.

Duke, B. C. *Japan's Militant Teachers* (Honolulu, 1973).
Thurston, D. R. *Teachers and Politics in Japan* (Princeton, 1973).

Japanese Capitalism Debate (Nihon shihonshugi ronsō 日本資本主義論争

A controversy among Japanese Marxists over the nature of prewar capitalism in Japan and the character of the coming revolution developed in the late 1920s under the stimulus of the 1927 financial crisis (*q.v.*). The Kōza group, which was identified with the Japan Communist Party (as shown in the Moscow-approved theses issued by the J. C. P. in 1927 and 1932), was represented by such historians as Hattori Shisō and Hani Gorō and emphasized the persistence of feudalism in Japan as evidenced by the landlord-dominated agrarian economy and the emperor system (*q.v.*). Its members believed that a two-stage revolution was necessary and that Japanese Marxists must initially work toward a bourgeois-democratic/agrarian revolution. The Rōnō group, whose members were labeled Trotskyist by their opponents, included Yamakawa Hitoshi, Arahata Kanson, Ōuchi Hyōe, and Tsuchiya Takao. They argued that the Meiji Restoration had been an incomplete bourgeois revolution and elements of feudal agrarian relations in the countryside did persist, but the existence of such factors as the dominance of financial capital and the "semiproletarianization" of the peasantry by the 1920s meant that Marxists should work toward a Socialist revolution in Japan. The debate was tied up with the whole position of the Japan Communist Party and was carried on vigorously through the early 1930s. It inspired leading historians to extensive research to substantiate the theoretical issues. The dispute was largely brought to a halt by the suppression of the late 1930s, but it has continued to be a major controversy among Japanese Marxists postwar.

Beckmann, G. M. "Japanese Adaptations of Marx-Leninism," *Asian Cultural Studies* 3 (I. C. U., Tokyo, 1962).
Beckmann, G. M., and G. Okubo. *The Japanese Communist Party, 1822–1945* (Stanford, 1969).
Borton, H. "Modern Japanese Economic Historians," in W. G. Beasley and E. G. Pulleyblank, eds., *Historians of China and Japan* (Oxford, 1961).
Yasuba, Y. "Anatomy of the Debate on Japanese Capitalism," *JJS* 2, no. 1 (Autumn 1975).

Japanese Invasion of Southeast Asia

In autumn 1940 the Vichy government signed an agreement which enabled Japan to move her troops and use air bases in northern Indochina in return for guarantees of territorial integrity and French sovereignty in the area. Japan subsequently occupied the area as part of her strategy against China, but Japan's aim to create a "new order in East Asia" and an autarkic economic sphere necessitated further control in Southeast Asia. During early 1941 Japan carried on negotiations with Thailand and Indochina in an attempt to ingratiate herself and secure economic privileges, but negotiations to secure economic and political rights in the resource-rich Dutch East Indies, regarded as an essential part of the Greater East Asia co-prosperity sphere (*q.v.*), were broken off in June 1941. In July, following a further agreement with the Vichy regime, Japan occupied southern French Indochina on the grounds of forestalling the encirclement of Japan and safeguarding her basic supplies. The threat posed to the Philippines by the end of July caused the U.S. government to freeze Japanese assets in the U. S. and place a total embargo on all exports to Japan. This virtually halted the supply of oil to Japan. An impasse in U. S.-Japanese negotiations to solve the problem resulted in Japan's attack on Pearl Harbor and further advance into Southeast Asia. Manila fell in January, Kuala Lumpur and Singapore by mid-February, Burma and the Dutch East Indies in March. Encouraged by these victories, Japan believed she could even threaten Australia. Indochina was nominally left in French hands, and Thailand, by signing a treaty of alliance, retained her monarchy and administration. Burma and the Philippines later achieved nominal independence while Malaya and the Dutch Indies were retained under military control. These territories were gradually removed from Japanese control in the closing stages of the Pacific War and after Japan's surrender.

Aziz, M. A. *Japan's Colonialism and Indonesia* (The Hague, 1955).
Goodman, G. K. *Imperial Japan and Asia* (New York, 1967).
Ike, N. *Japan's Decision for War* (Stanford, 1967).

Jiji Shinpō. See NEWSPAPERS

Jingo Incident (Jingo no hen) 壬午の変

In July 1882 rioting was started by soldiers in Seoul in response to increasing foreign influence under the Korean Min regime. The main figures of the Min faction were killed, Japanese legation and military personnel were attacked and killed, and the Japanese legation was burned and remaining Japanese fled, escaping by a small boat from Inchon. Power was seized by the conservative opposition Taewonkun. Both China and Japan sent troops to Korea. The Chinese restored the Min regime and negotiated with Japan. Under the Treaty of Chemulpo concluded in September Korea promised to apologize; to punish all offenders; to compensate Japan for loss of life, buildings, and the cost of sending an expedition (these provisions were much later canceled); to permit Japanese troops to be stationed at the legation; to permit Japanese officials unrestricted travel in Korea; to allow greater freedom for Japanese residents of open ports; and to open one additional port. The incident received its name after the designation of the year 1882 in the Japanese-Chinese calendar.

Conroy, H. *The Japanese Seizure of Korea, 1868–1910* (Philadelphia, 1960).
Kim, C. I. E., and H-K. Kim. *Korea and the Politics of Imperialism, 1876–1910* (Berkeley, 1967).

Jiyū Minshutō. See LIBERAL DEMOCRATIC PARTY

Jiyūtō 自由党

The Jiyūtō (Liberal Party) was one of the leading parties of the 1880s freedom and people's rights movement (*q.v.*) and was led by Itagaki Taisuke and Gotō Shōjirō. Founded in October 1881 its 101 members included Baba Tatsui, Nakajima Nobuyuki, and Kōno Hironaka. Its ideology was influenced by French revolutionary and Rousseauan theories and the ideas of Herbert Spencer; members pledged the extension of liberty, guarantee of popular rights, promotion of happiness, establishment of sound constitutional government, and cooperation with others to meet these objectives. They called for treaty revision and a decrease in the land tax. The party's organ was the *Jiyū Shinbun*. Leaders undertook many speech tours, and the party gained considerable support in all classes, forming a national network of loosely affiliated groups. Initial support came especially from merchants and rural industrialists, but more and more, this came from impoverished peasants, tenant farmers, and wage workers. Throughout its existence the Jiyūtō maintained its rural base. Depression sparked off divisions in the party and a tendency toward violence; government oppression increased, the party was short of funds, and Itagaki and Gotō were persuaded by government funds to make extended trips abroad, a move which worsened already bitter disputes with the Kaishintō (*q.v.*). The party leadership could not control the involvement of local members with impoverished peasants in violent antigovernment incidents such as those at Gunma and Kabasan (*q.v.*). Caught between government oppression and pressure from the poor peasants, the party was dissolved by its leaders October 1884. Its disappearance left the democratic movement without effective leadership.

In January 1890 the Daidō Kyōwakai wing of the Daidō Danketsu movement (*q.v.*) reformed. In August it fused with other liberal groups to form the Rikken Jiyūtō (Constitutional Liberal Party) under the guidance of Ōi Kentarō. In March 1891, it was renamed the Jiyūtō, and Itagaki Taisuke became leader. The party strongly attacked the government in the Diet but gradually began to cooperate with it, to the extent that Itagaki served as home minister in 1895. In 1898 it fused with the Shinpotō (Progressive Party) to form the Kenseitō, which supported the Ōkuma cabinet, but this party reverted to its former factions in June 1898. In 1900 the former Jiyūtō faction became part of the Seiyūkai (*q.v.*).

Ike, N. *The Beginnings of Political Democracy in Japan* (Baltimore, 1950).
Mason, R. H. P. *Japan's First General Election, 1890* (Cambridge, 1969).

Jiyūtō (1950). See LIBERAL DEMOCRATIC PARTY

Justice Ministry (Shihōshō) 司法省 (Hōmushō) 法務省

First established as the Shihōshō in 1871. Under the Meiji constitution (*q.v.*) the Justice Ministry had extensive powers over all matters relating to courts and law, being able to appoint personnel and control trials. The courts were in effect an arm of the national government administered by the Justice Ministry. In 1947 the ministry was replaced by a legal office, and many of its powers were transferred to the Supreme Court in order to create an independent judiciary. In 1952 a Justice Ministry (Hōmushō) was reconstituted, but its function is only to draft laws and treaties, deal with actions involving the government, and oversee the whole legal system, thus maintaining the principle of an independent judiciary.

K

Kabasan Incident (Kabasan jiken) 加波山事件

One of a series of abortive armed uprisings which occurred in 1882–1884, stimulated largely by the prevailing economic difficulties, and in which local supporters of the Jiyūtō (*q.v.*) were often involved. In the months after the Fukushima incident (*q.v.*) in 1883 Fukushima supporters of the Jiyūtō planned to assassinate Governor Mishima Michitsune in revenge for his autocratic behavior. In conjunction with others from Tochigi and Ibaraki they planned also to make bombs, assassinate other leading officials, and ultimately to overthrow the government. After an abortive assassination attempt in July 1884, discovery of the plot by Kabasan (Ibaraki) police sparked off a premature rising by a few men in September. These fled after a battle with police, but all were later arrested. In 1886 seven were sentenced to death and others to lengthy terms of imprisonment.

Bowen, R. W. *Rebellion and Democracy in Meiji Japan* (Berkeley, 1980).

Kagawa Toyohiko 1888–1960 賀川豊彦
Native of Kobe and a Christian, Kagawa studied theology in Japan and the U. S. and was ordained in 1917. He worked for many years in the Kobe slums, where his experiences roused an interest in social problems. He joined the Yūaikai (*q.v.*) and subsequently as a Christian Socialist played a leading role in labor and farmer union organization, labor disputes, and the formation of cooperatives. Kagawa's accounts of life in the Kobe slums aroused great acclaim, and during his life he produced many books on Christianity, labor, and social problems, the income from which helped him to continue his activities. For his views, with their emphasis on love and harmony, for his actions, and for his speech tours, Kagawa became world famous although his reputation within Japan was less great. After the war he was involved in political and religious activities but from 1948 went into semiretirement.

Bikle, G. B., Jr. *The New Jerusalem: Aspects of Utopianism in the Thought of Kagawa Toyohiko* (Tucson, 1976).
Davey, C. J. *Kagawa of Japan* (London, 1960).

Kagoshima, Bombardment of. See NAMAMUGI INCIDENT

Kaisei Gakkō. See KAISEIJO

Kaiseijo 開成所
In 1857 the Bakufu's first institute for Western learning started work in Edo under the name of Bansho Torishirabejo (Institute for the Study of Barbarian Books). After various name changes it was renamed the Kaiseijo (Institute for Development) in 1863. Tuition was ultimately provided in all fields of Western learning including languages, natural science, and military studies. Until 1868 the institute was Japan's main center of Western education, although it failed in the attempt it embodied to bring Western learning under total Bakufu control. Among the school's teachers were Katō Hiroyuki, Nishi Amane, Kanda Kōhei, and Tsuda Mamichi. The Kaiseijo was temporarily closed with the fall of the Bakufu but reopened as the Kaisei Gakkō and became the parent organization both of the Numazu Military School and of Tokyo University.

Jansen, M. B. "New Materials for the Intellectual History of Nineteenth-Century Japan," *Harvard Journal of Asiatic Studies* 20 (1957).

Kaishintō 改進党
The Rikken Kaishintō (Constitutional Progressive Party) was founded in March 1882 under Ōkuma Shigenobu, bringing together progressive intellectual groups led by Ono Azusa, Yano Fumio, and Numa Morikazu and bureaucrats such as Ozaki Yukio, Kōno Togama, Inukai Tsuyoshi, and Maejima Hisoka who had resigned from the government with Ōkuma in the 1881 political crisis (*q.v.*). The party was strongly influenced by British utilitarianism and opposed the radicalism of the Jiyūtō (*q.v.*), instead expounding moderate, gradualist views. Members advocated a two-chamber parliament of the English type and a constitutional monarchy. Its main support came from the urban middle class and intellectuals and it had strong connections with Mitsubishi (*q.v.*). The party extended its influence through membership in prefectural assemblies, but following conflict with the Jiyūtō and suppression of the popular rights movement by the government, Ōkuma and much of the party's leadership resigned in 1884. However, the remnant of the party continued to exist and supported Ōkuma during his term as foreign minister 1887–1889. Name and organizational changes occurred during the 1890s, but continuity of leadership, membership, and principles was maintained. In 1896 the Kaishintō combined with other groups to form the Shinpotō (Progressive Party), which in 1898 became part of the Kenseitō (*q.v.*).

Itō, I. "The Constitutional Reform Party and Ōkuma Shigenobu," *Sophia Law*

Review 7, nos. 1–2 (Autumn 1963).
Lebra, J. C. "The Kaishintō as a Political Elite," in B. S. Silberman and H. D. Harootunian, eds., *Modern Japanese Leadership* (Tucson, 1966).
Mason, R. H. P. *Japan's First General Election, 1890* (Cambridge, 1969).

Kaitakushi. See HOKKAIDŌ

Kaizō 改造

Kaizō (Reconstruction) was a monthly journal first published in 1919. It contained articles on all aspects of politics, economics, society, and ideas, many by eminent foreign thinkers, and its influence on the intelligentsia in the interwar period was equaled only by *Chūō Kōron* (Central Review). During the 1920s, *Kaizō* became identified with Socialist ideas and as such came increasingly under official disapproval from the late 1930s. In autumn 1942 *Kaizō* was forced to sack senior staff following the publication of a so-called "Communist" article, and staff of *Kaizō* were among those arrested in Yokohama the same year on the grounds of procommunism (the so-called Yokohama incident). Eventually closed down July 1944, *Kaizō* was revived in January 1946, but internal disputes led to final closure in March 1955.

Havens, T. R. H. *Valley of Darkness* (New York, 1978).

Kakushin Club (Kakushin Kurabu) 革新倶楽部

The Kakushin Club (Reform Club) was a political party formed in November 1922 under the leadership of Inukai Tsuyoshi. It consisted of 45 Diet members from the Kokumintō (National Party), Kenseikai, and independents, including Shimada Saburō, Nakano Seigō, and Ozaki Yukio. The party called for reform of the political world and eradication of existing evils in party politics, universal male suffrage, arms limitation, and removal of conditions for eligibility for the post of war minister. In 1924 the Kakushin Club participated in the movement for the protection of constitutional government (*q.v.*), and Inukai joined Katō's ensuing coalition cabinet as the main stimulus behind the retrenchment program. In May 1925 most of the party's members were absorbed into the Seiyūkai, from within which they hoped to achieve political reform.

Duus, P. *Party Politics and Political Change in Taishō Japan* (Cambridge, Mass., 1968).

Kanagawa, Treaty of (Kanagawa jōyaku) 神奈川条約 (Nichibei washin jōyaku) 日米和親条約

The treaty breaking Japan's seclusion policy was signed with Commodore Matthew Perry (*q.v.*) in March 1854 with a more detailed supplement in May. Among the stipulations of the treaty were the opening of Shimoda and Hakodate for the purchase of necessities such as coal, water, and food, better treatment for shipwrecked Americans, and the permitting of an American consul at Shimoda. All dealings were to be made through the Japanese authorities, and there was no provision for private free trade. Similar agreements were subsequently concluded with other countries. The Kanagawa Treaty (U.S.-Japan Treaty of Friendship) was followed by further agreements in 1857 and then by full commercial treaties (the Ansei Treaties) after 1858.

Beasley, W. G. *Select Documents on Japanese Foreign Policy, 1853–1868* (London, 1955).

Kaneko Kentarō 1853–1942 (Baron 1900; Viscount, 1907; Count, 1934) 金子堅太郎

Samurai from Fukuoka *han*, in 1871–1878 Kaneko studied law at Harvard and from 1880 worked as a secretary in the Genrōin (*q.v.*). In 1885 he became private secretary to Itō Hirobumi and in this capacity contributed to the drafting of the Meiji constitution (*q.v.*). In 1890 he became a member of the House of Peers and 1894 deputy minister of agriculture and commerce. He served as agriculture and commerce minister in 1898 and justice minister 1900–1901. Kaneko was sent to America on the outbreak of the Russo-Japanese War and was an important figure in Japanese-American relations. He was appointed privy councillor in 1906 and remained one until his death but withdrew from a major role in politics after Itō's death in 1911.

Akita, G. *The Foundations of Constitutional Government in Modern Japan, 1868–1900* (Cambridge, Mass., 1967).

Kanghwa, Treaty of
(Nitchō shūkō jōki) 日朝修好条規
(Kōka jōyaku) 江華条約

After the decision not to invade Korea in 1873, the Japanese government attempted unsuccessfully to negotiate the opening of Western-style relations with Korea. In 1875 Japanese ships maneuvering off Kanghwa Island, near Inchon, were fired upon, leading to an armed clash. Japan discussed the matter with China, and Kuroda Kiyotaka and Inoue Kaoru were appointed as envoys to negotiate a solution. They went to Korea accompanied by 4,000 soldiers, and on 26 February 1876 the Treaty of Kanghwa was signed. The Koreans agreed to exchange diplomatic representatives, open Pusan, Inchon, and Wonsan to trade, to give Japan the right to survey Korean waters, and extraterritorial rights. Korea was recognized as a completely independent state. An additional commercial agreement was negotiated and trade expanded.

Conroy, H. *The Japanese Seizure of Korea, 1868–1910* (Philadelphia, 1960).
Deuchler, M. *Confucian Gentlemen and Barbarian Envoys: The Opening of Korea, 1875–1885* (Seattle, 1977).
Kim, C. I. E., and H-K. Kim. *Korea and the Politics of Imperialism, 1876–1910* (Berkeley, 1967).

Kanno Sugako (Suga) 1881–1911
管野スガ

Native of Kyoto, after an unhappy childhood and youth and a brief marriage at 20, Kanno became a reporter in Osaka and then Tokyo. In 1904, influenced by Sakai Toshihiko, she became a Socialist and joined the Heiminsha (*q.v.*), living with Arahata Kanson 1906–1908. She was arrested in the 1908 Red Flag incident (*q.v.*) but released. She subsequently became an anarchist and lived with Kōtoku Shūsui. Kanno was arrested in the 1910 High Treason incident (*q.v.*) and executed in January 1911.

Notehelfer, F. G. *Kōtoku Shūsui, Portrait of a Japanese Radical* (Cambridge, 1971).

Kantō Earthquake (Kantō daishinsai)
関東大震災

Earthquakes occur frequently in Japan, and the worst one in the modern period was that occurring in the Kantō plain and surrounding areas on 1 September 1923. Much of the damage was done by fires which swept Tokyo, Yokohama, and other cities after the earthquake. Over 100,000 died and over 550,000 buildings were destroyed, rendering over 2 million homeless. Rumors abounded of plots by Koreans and Socialists, and hundreds were killed by mobs. The government declared martial law. Ōsugi Sakae, the anarchist leader, was among left-wing intellectuals arrested and secretly killed by police. The disaster threw the financial world into confusion and was a major setback to economic advance. Recovery was reasonably fast, but the government's measures to help were instrumental in bringing about the 1927 financial crisis (*q.v.*).

Home Office, Bureau of Reconstruction. *The Outline of the Reconstruction Work in Tokyo and Yokohama* (Tokyo, 1929).
Home Office, Bureau of Social Affairs. *The Great Earthquake of 1923 in Japan*, 2 vols. (Tokyo, 1926).
Poole, O. M. *The Death of Old Yokohama* (London, 1968).

Karafuto. See SAKHALIN

Kataoka Kenkichi 1844–1903 片岡健吉
Tosa samurai, Kataoka fought in the 1868 civil war but resigned all connections with the new government in 1873 following the argument over the invasion of Korea (*q.v.*). He joined Itagaki Taisuke in the popular rights movement and became president of the Risshisha (*q.v.*), submitting a petition for an elected assembly to the government in 1877 on its behalf. He became president of Tosa prefectural assembly in 1879 and as a leading member of the Aikokusha and Kokkai Kisei Dōmei (*q.v.*) in 1880 submitted a further petition in conjunction with Kōno Hironaka. He was a leading member of the Jiyūtō and then participated in the 1887 petition movement but was imprisoned for contravening the Peace Regulations (*q.v.*). Pardoned on the occasion of the promulgation of the constitution, he served as a Diet member for the Jiyūtō and Kenseitō and from 1900 for the Seiyūkai. Kataoka was president of the Diet 1898–1903.

Katayama Sen 1860–1933 片山潜
Member of an Okayama farming family, Katayama studied and worked in Tokyo and then was from 1884 in the U.S., where he majored in divinity at Yale, returning to Japan 1896. From 1897 he became a leader of the early trade union movement, edited the magazine *Rōdō Sekai* (Labor World), and campaigned for factory legislation. As a leading Christian Socialist he was involved in the 1900 Shakaishugi Kenyūkai (Society for the Study of Socialism) and the abortive Shakai Minshutō (*q.v.*) of 1901. As Japanese representative at the Second International in Amsterdam during the Russo-Japanese War, Katayama joined with the Russian delegate in taking an antiwar stance. After a period in the U.S. he returned to Japan for the founding of the Japan Socialist Party (*q.v.*) in 1906 but clashed with Kōtoku Shūsui over the latter's advocacy of anarcho-syndicalism, calling for parliamentary reforms; he became increasingly ideologically isolated from more radical members of the movement. He was imprisoned for several months for involvement in strike organization 1911–1912, and in 1914 went to the U.S. His views became gradually more left wing, and he eventually became a Communist. After the Russian Revolution Katayama worked for the Comintern in Mexico and from 1921 until his death lived in Moscow, playing a major role in Comintern activities. His writings include works on the Japanese labor movement, socialism, and an autobiography.

Katayama, S. *The Labor Movement in Japan* (Chicago, 1918).
Kublin, H. *Asian Revolutionary, the Life of Sen Katayama* (Princeton, 1964).

Katayama Tetsu 1887–1978 片山哲
Native of Wakayama, Katayama graduated in law from Tokyo Imperial University in 1912. A Christian, he was a friend of Abe Isoo. From 1920 he acted as legal adviser to Sōdōmei and then became head of its legal section. He was also legal adviser to the Japan Farmers' Union and was involved in several disputes. A leading social democrat, he became secretary of the Shakai Minshūtō (*q.v.*) in 1926 and was the architect of its "anticommunism, anticapitalism, antifascism" slogan. He was elected to the Diet for the first time in 1930. In 1932 the party became part of the new Shakai Taishūtō, and Katayama remained a Diet member until 1940; his refusal to sanction the exclusion of a member who had made an antiwar speech led to his resignation. Postwar he became chief secretary of the Japan Socialist Party (*q.v.*), and its president 1946. In May 1947 he headed a coalition cabinet with members of the Democratic Party and the Kokumin Kyōdōtō. As a Christian Katayama was welcomed by SCAP (*q.v.*) and with SCAP's backing passed laws to implement the new constitution as well as some aimed at economic and social democratization. However, Katayama had little strength to implement radical reform, and intraparty conflict over wage and

price control measures forced him to resign in February 1948. Katayama also lost his Diet seat in 1949 and in 1950 declined reelection as J.S.P. president, although he remained a leading figure on the party's right wing through the 1950s. He devoted his efforts to the prevention of constitutional revision, opposed renewal of the security treaty with the U.S. in 1960, and advocated a "one-China" policy. From 1960 he supported the new Democratic Socialist Party (*q.v.*) but severed his connection with it in 1965. In 1963 he failed to get elected and withdrew from the front line of politics.

Cole, A. B., G. O. Totten, and C. H. Uyehara. *Socialist Parties in Postwar Japan* (New Haven, 1966).
Kakehi, M. "Tetsu Katayama, A Christian Socialist," *CJ* 16, nos. 1–3 (Jan.–Mar. 1947).
Quigley, H. S., and J. E. Turner. *The New Japan* (Minneapolis, 1956).

Katō Hiroyuki 1836–1916 (Baron, 1900) 加藤弘之

Samurai from Tajima, now Hyōgo Prefecture, Katō studied Western learning and military science and in 1860 was sent by the Bakufu to the Bansho Torishirabejo (*q.v.*), where he studied German. He secretly wrote a book on modern constitutions and produced other works on the West. He also advocated development of foreign trade. Katō joined the government after the Restoration and was a member of the Meirokusha (*q.v.*). Well known as a political philosopher, he was early on a strong supporter of natural rights, but he increasingly moved toward a less radical position. By the 1880s his ideas included that of a restricted electorate; his strong adherence to Social Darwinism and conservative German-influenced theories from this time found him favor with the government. From 1881–1893 Katō was president of Tokyo University. He became a member of the Genrōin, as well as sitting in the House of Peers, and was a member of the Privy Council 1906–1916. He was also adviser to the emperor.

Abosch, D. "Katō Hiroyuki and the Introduction of German Political Thought in Modern Japan, 1868–1883," Ph.D. diss., University of California, Berkeley, 1964.
Kosaka, M. *Japanese Thought in the Meiji Era* (Tokyo, 1958).

Katō Takaaki (Kōmei) 1860–1926 (Baron, 1911; Viscount, 1916) 加藤高明

Member of a samurai family from Ōwari domain (now Aichi Prefecture), Katō graduated in law from Tokyo Imperial University in 1881. He entered Mitsubishi (*q.v.*), was sent by the company to study in England 1883–1885 and 1886 married Iwasaki Yatarō's eldest daughter. In 1886 he joined the bureaucracy and worked in both Foreign and Finance ministries. He was Japanese envoy in England 1895–1899 and then foreign minister 1900–1901. He sat in the Diet 1902–1904 and was again briefly foreign minister in 1906. In 1906–1908 he unsuccessfully managed the *Tōkyō Nichi Nichi* and was again Japan's representative in Britain 1909–1913. Despite poor relations with Katsura, Katō became foreign minister in early 1913 and in April 1913 joined the Rikken Dōshikai, the political party originally proposed by Katsura. As foreign minister again 1914–1915 Katō promoted Japan's involvement in World War I and the Twenty-One Demands (*q.v.*), but he was a strong supporter of the two-party system and criticized *hanbatsu* politics (*q.v.*) and the political influence of the *genrō* (*q.v.*), and this attitude led to his resignation. In 1916 he became president of the Kenseikai, successor to the Dōshikai, but his hostility to the *genrō* meant that despite the Kenseikai's Diet majority, Katō was not asked to form a cabinet. He therefore remained in opposition until the second movement for the protection of constitutional government (*q.v.*) brought him to power with a coalition cabinet in June 1924. The cabinet enacted universal male suffrage, counterbalanced by the Peace Preservation Law (*q.v.*), and normalized relations with Russia, but its attempts at peerage reform were largely ineffectual. Financial retrenchment was not as much as Katō had desired; in the case of the army it led to the introduction of military training in schools and modernization and increased efficiency in the fighting forces. The cabinet resigned in August 1925 with the collapse of the coalition, but despite worsening health Katō headed a Kenseikai cabinet. He was soon taken ill, and with his death in January 1926 the whole cabinet resigned.

Dull, P. S. "Count Katō Kōmei and the Twenty-One Demands," *PHR* 19, no. 2 (May 1950).
Duus, P. *Party Rivalry and Political Change in Taishō Japan* (Cambridge, Mass., 1968).
Yang, E. S. "Katō Kōmei (1860–1926): Ethics vs. Power in Political Leadership," Ph.D. diss., Claremont Graduate School, 1971.

Katō Tomosaburō 1861–1923
(Baron 1920; Viscount, 1923)
加藤友三郎

Native of Hiroshima Prefecture, Katō joined the navy and after serving as chief of staff to Admiral Tōgō in the Russo-Japanese War became an admiral in 1915. As navy minister 1915–1923 he initially promoted naval expansion; but when appointed chief delegate to the Washington Conference (*q.v.*), he became leader of the "treaty" faction within the navy which supported naval arms limitation. In June 1922 Katō was appointed prime minister and with Seiyūkai support headed a nonparty cabinet. Withdrawal from Siberia and a solution to the Shantung problem were achieved; at home naval and administrative retrenchment was carried out, but the Katō cabinet opposed universal suffrage. The cabinet resigned after Katō's death in August 1923.

Asada, S. "Japanese Admirals and the Politics of Naval Limitation," in G. Jordan, ed. *Naval Warfare in the Twentieth Century* (London, 1977).
Duus, P. *Party Rivalry and Political Change in Taishō Japan* (Cambridge, Mass., 1968).

Katsu Kaishū (Awa, Rintarō),
1823–1899 (Count, 1887)
勝海舟(安房)(麟太郎)

A native of Edo and Bakufu retainer, Katsu trained in Dutch studies and Western military science. In 1855 he became an official translator of Western books, then a naval student at Nagasaki. In 1860 he captained the *Kanrinmaru* on the first Japanese crossing of the Pacific. On his return he taught gunnery and naval affairs and worked successfully for the establishment of a naval school at Hyōgo in 1863. As Tokugawa naval commissioner Katsu worked to build up a Bakufu navy. The naval school took students from various *han*, and among Katsu's followers here was Sakamoto Ryōma. This was the start of Katsu's strong contacts with loyalists. The degree of modernization which he propounded and the divergence of his views from many servants of the Bakufu led conservatives to press successfully for his dismissal in 1864, but he was restored to favor under Tokugawa Keiki and served as the Bakufu's major contact with its opponents. In 1868 he negotiated successfully with Saigō Takamori for the peaceful surrender of Edo. Katsu acted as deputy navy minister 1872–1873 and state councillor and navy minister 1873–1875. He was subsequently a member of the Genrōin and then privy councillor 1888–1899. His later years were devoted to writing, and his works included histories of the army and navy, of the Bakufu, of the opening of the country, and personal memoirs.

Clark, E. W. *Katz Awa, Bismarck of Japan, A Story of a Noble Life* (New York, 1904).
Jansen, M. B. *Sakamoto Ryōma and the Meiji Restoration* (Princeton, 1961).
Steele, M. W. "Katsu Kaishū and the Collapse of the Tokugawa Bakufu," Ph.D. diss., Harvard University, 1976.

Katsura-Taft Agreement. See TAFT-KATSURA AGREEMENT

Katsura Tarō 1848–1913 (Count, 1902; Marquis 1907; Prince, 1911) 桂太郎
Member of a Chōshū samurai family, Katsura became a member of the Kiheitai (*q.v.*) and fought in the 1868 civil war. He studied in Europe and under the aegis of Yamagata Aritomo rose through the army ranks to become vice-minister of war, divisional commander in the Sino-Japanese War, and then governor of Formosa in 1896. After serving as war minister 1898–1900, as Yamagata's protégé Katsura became prime minister June 1901. For the next 11 years he alternated as prime minister with Saionji Kinmochi. Katsura's first ministry, when he headed a bureaucratic cabinet, saw him often at odds with the political parties, especially due to his desire to raise taxes for military expansion, but it achieved the signing of the Anglo-Japanese Alliance (*q.v.*), the Taft-Katsura Agreement (*q.v.*), and the successful waging of the Russo-Japanese War. Despite his hostility to the political parties Katsura was forced to compromise on many occasions. The cabinet resigned December 1905 after the Hibiya riots (*q.v.*). Katsura's second cabinet of July 1908–August 1911 tried to expand Japan's interests in Asia, a policy culminating in the annexation of Korea in 1910. At home an oppressive policy toward left-wing and social movements culminated in the High Treason incident (*q.v.*) of 1910. On his retirement Katsura was recognized as a *genrō* and became Lord Privy Seal, but in December 1912 he was recalled as prime minister. Katsura had throughout his political career supported transcendental cabinets, but his awareness of the hostility now greeting *hanbatsu* politics (*q.v.*) and nonparty cabinets led him for the first time to act contrary to Yamagata's wishes and to decide to form his own political party. However, the cabinet was brought down by the movement for the protection of constitutional government (*q.v.*) before Katsura could act, and he died shortly afterwards.

Hackett, R. F. *Yamagata Aritomo in the Rise of Modern Japan, 1838–1922* (Cambridge, Mass., 1971).
Najita, T. *Hara Kei in the Politics of Compromise* (Cambridge, Mass., 1967).

Kawaji Toshiyoshi. See POLICE

Kawakami Hajime 1879–1946 河上肇
A native of Yamaguchi Prefecture, Kawakami graduated in 1902 from Tokyo Imperial University and then taught economics there until 1905. He became known for his writings on economics and socialism. In 1907–1908 he published the *Nihon Keizai Shinshi* (New Journal of the Japanese Economy), which argued for nationalist economics. In 1908 Kawakami became lecturer at Kyoto University and after studying in Europe 1914–1915 became full professor there. He was regarded as an authority on classical economics, but an increasing interest in social policy and comparative sociology moved him toward Marxist economics. The founding of his journal *Shakai Mondai Kenkyū* (Research into Social Problems) in 1919 marked a conversion to Marxism, and through his writings and translations Kawakami played a major role in spreading Marxist doctrines. The unorthodoxy of his Marxism led to criticism from people such as Fukumoto Kazuo, and from the late 1920s he joined more actively in the proletarian movement, eventually joining the Japan Communist Party in 1932. In 1928 Kawakami was forced to resign from Kyoto following the wholesale Communist arrests of March 25. In January 1933 he was arrested and sentenced to five years' imprisonment. He did not commit *tenkō* (*q.v.*) but on release in 1937 agreed to refrain from political activity. From 1930 to his death most of his time was spent on writing and translating. He left many works on economics, social problems, and history as well as an autobiography.

Bernstein, G. L. *Japanese Marxist: A Portrait of Kawakami Hajime, 1879–1946*

(Cambridge, Mass., 1976).
______. "Kawakami Hajime: A Japanese Marxist in Search of the Way," in B. S. Silberman and H. D. Harootunian, eds., *Japan in Crisis* (Princeton, 1974).

Kawamoto Daisaku. See CHANG TSO-LIN, ASSASSINATION OF

Keidanren. See FEDERATION OF ECONOMIC ORGANIZATIONS

Keiō University (Keiō Gijuku) 慶応義塾

In 1858 Fukuzawa Yukichi founded a college for Western studies in Edo. In 1868 it was given the name Keiō Gijuku (Keiō private school). In 1871 it was moved to the Mita area of Tokyo and from then expanded rapidly. Under the guidance of Fukuzawa until his death, throughout the Meiji period the school made every positive effort to assert its independence from the government and officialdom. It attracted many of the government's opponents and produced many of the leaders of the business world. In 1904 it was renamed Keiō Gijuku University and in 1920 was, with Waseda, the first private university to receive official accreditation as a university. The university remains one of Japan's leading private universities, maintaining its nongovernmental, pro-business tradition.

Kellogg Pact (Keroggu fusen jōyaku) ケロッグ不戦条約 (Sensō hōki ni kansuru jōyaku) (戦争放棄に関する条約)

The Kellogg Pact (Kellogg-Briand Pact) was a declaration renouncing war as an instrument of national policy signed by 65 countries in all, of which Japan became a signatory in August 1928. The pact was backed only by the sanction of public disapproval and deprivation of the slight benefits furnished by the treaty, and it in no way curbed Japan's subsequent aggression.

Ferrell, R. H. *Peace in Their Time: The Origins of the Kellogg-Briand Pact* (New Haven, 1952).

Kenpeitai. See POLICE

Kensei Hontō. See KENSEITŌ

Kenseikai 憲政会

In 1913 Katsura Tarō announced his intention of forming a political party, and this was founded after his death under the name of the Rikken Dōshikai; it consisted of elements from the Chūō Club, the Rikken Kokumintō, and the bureaucracy. In October 1916 members of the Dōshikai became the major element in the new Kenseikai (Constitutional Government Party). With 197 members in the Diet the Kenseikai was the majority party, but it remained in opposition until 1924 under the leadership of Katō Takaaki. It nominally opposed the influence of the *genrō* (*q.v.*) and subscribed to constitutional government, extension of the suffrage, and civil rights, but it was split between its ruling clique and a liberal minority. In 1924 the Kenseikai gained power when Katō became prime minister following the successful movement for the protection of constitutional government (*q.v.*) and the Universal Manhood Suffrage Act and Peace Preservation Law were passed. Kenseikai members also comprised the second Katō and Wakatsuki cabinets. In 1927 the Kenseikai merged with the Seiyū Hontō to form the Minseitō (*q.v.*).

Duus, P. *Party Rivalry and Political Change in Taishō Japan* (Cambridge, Mass., 1968).
Turner, J. E. "The Kenseikai (Constitutional Party) of Japan, 1913–1927: A Study of Its History, Organization and Domestic and Foreign Policies," Ph.D. diss., University of Minnesota, 1950.

Kenseitō 憲政党

In an attempt to check the influence of the *hanbatsu* (*q.v.*), in June 1898 the Jiyūtō and Shinpotō merged to form a new party, the Kenseitō (Constitutional Government Party). The move led Itō Hirobumi to resign, and the *genrō* eventually called on Ōkuma Shigenobu and Itagaki Taisuke, the new party's leaders, to form a cabinet in which all except the forces' ministers were Kenseitō members, causing it sometimes to be referred to as the first true party cabinet. The party gained a majority at the election in August 1898 on a platform of constitutional party cabinets, but it had incurred the hostility of bureaucracy, military, and oligarchs, and internal dissent led to its splitting again into two parties in October, the inevitable result of this union of political expediency. The former Jiyūtō members retained the name Kenseitō and after Ōkuma's resignation in December for a while supported the Yamagata cabinet. In 1900 the Kenseitō became part of the Seiyūkai (*q.v.*). The former Shinpotō elements under Ōkuma took the name Kensei Hontō in November 1898. Its lack of success against the Seiyūkai and an increasing inclination to compromise with the *hanbatsu* politicians led to dissent within the party. In 1907 Inukai Tsuyoshi succeeded Ōkuma as president, and in 1910 the Kensei Hontō became part of the new Rikken Kokumintō (Constitutional National Party).

Akita, G. *The Foundations of Constitutional Government in Modern Japan* (Cambridge, Mass., 1967).
Najita, T. *Hara Kei in the Politics of Compromise* (Cambridge, Mass., 1967).

Ketsumeidan Incident. See BLOOD LEAGUE INCIDENT

Kido Kōichi 1889–1977 (Marquis, 1917)
木戸幸一

Grandson of Kido Kōin, Kido studied at the Gakushūin and Kyoto University and after his peerage in 1917 became a member of the House of Peers. In 1915–1930 he worked as a bureaucrat and then 1930–1936 as chief private secretary to the Lord Privy Seal. In this capacity he was the main contact between the Lord Privy Seal and affairs outside the court and was personally close to such people as Saionji Kinmochi and Konoe Fumimaro. In 1937–1938 he was education minister under Konoe and 1939 home minister under Hiranuma. In 1940 Kido became the Lord Privy Seal and retained the post until the office was abolished in November 1945, playing a key political role. Kido was tried as a class "A" war criminal and sentenced to life imprisonment but was released in 1953 due to illness. His diary of the period 1930–1955 is a valuable historical source.

Butow, R. J. C. *Tojo and the Coming of War* (Princeton, 1961).
Titus, D. A. *Palace and Politics in Prewar Japan* (New York, 1974).

Kido Kōin (Takayoshi) 1833–1877
木戸孝允

Member of a Chōshū samurai family, Kido was originally known as Katsura Kogorō. He studied with Yoshida Shōin and after a spell in Edo held important posts in his *han*. He played a leading role in the antiforeign and later the anti-Bakufu movement (*q.v.*), and in 1866 acted as Chōshū's representative in concluding an alliance with Satsuma. Following his role as one of the most important protagonists of the Meiji Restoration, from 1868 Kido held top government posts and was *sangi* (state councillor) from 1871. He contributed to the drafting of the Charter Oath (*q.v.*) and worked for the spread of education, the abolition of the domains (*q.v.*), and the establishment of a centralized state. He at first advocated the invasion of Korea (*q.v.*), but after going on the Iwakura Mission 1871–1873 (*q.v.*), he opposed invasion, believing that priority should go to domestic development. In 1874 he became education minister but soon resigned, opposing the Formosan expedition (*q.v.*). Although Kido rejoined the government as *sangi* in 1875 after the Osaka Conference (*q.v.*), he resigned in 1876 due to illness. His death in 1877 removed a leading progressive and idealist influence from the political scene.

Brown, S. D. "Kido Takayoshi (1833–1877): Meiji Japan's Cautious Revolutionary," *PHR* 25 (May 1956).
______"Kido Takayoshi and the Meiji Restoration: A Political Biography, 1833–1877," Ph.D. diss., University of Wisconsin, 1952.
Craig, A. M. *Chōshū in the Meiji Restoration* (Cambridge, Mass., 1961).
______"Kido Kōin and Ōkubo Toshimichi: A Psychohistorical Analysis," in A. M. Craig and D. H. Shively, eds., *Personality in Japanese History* (Berkeley, 1970).

Kiheitai 奇兵隊

After 1863 various auxiliary units (*shotai*) were formed to reinforce regular Chōshū troops in case of foreign or Bakufu attack. The most famous was the Kiheitai, a body of 300 to 500 men founded 1863 by Takasugi Shinsaku and later commanded by Yamagata Aritomo. The auxiliary units broke with tradition in that they included not only samurai but also farmers and townspeople, and in theory neither recruitment nor promotion depended on social status. Weapons and pay were supplied on a semipermanent basis, unlike with the local militia traditionally recruited at times of emergency. The units became a major force behind *sonnō jōi* (*q.v.*) views and in 1864 helped to overthrow conservative dominance in the *han*. The Kiheitai subsequently played a major role in resistance to the second Chōshū expedition of 1866 and the Boshin War (*q.v.*). It was disbanded early 1870.

Norman, E. H. *Soldier and Peasant in Japan: The Origins of Conscription* (New York, 1943).

Kinoshita Naoe 1869–1937 木下尚江

Christian and native of Nagano Prefecture, after graduating from Tokyo College (later Waseda University), Kinoshita worked as a reporter and lawyer in Nagano, where he was imprisoned for participation in the suffrage movement. In 1899 he joined the *Mainichi* paper in Tokyo. He became interested in social problems and wrote in especially strong terms of the Ashio copper mine pollution (*q.v.*). This led him toward socialism, and he participated in the founding of the 1901 Shakai Minshutō and was involved with the *Heimin Shinbun* from 1903. His *Pillar of Fire* (1904) was the first real Socialist novel. A strong pacifist at the time of the Russo-Japanese War, he stood unsuccessfully as a Socialist candidate in the 1905 election. After the closure of the *Heimin Shinbun* Kinoshita wrote for the Christian Socialist journal *Shin Kigen* (New Era). His enthusiasm for Socialist activism and his Christian beliefs gradually weakened and many of his later years were devoted to Buddhist meditation. Kinoshita is now famous for his novels rather than his political activity.

Kosaka, M. *Japanese Thought in the Meiji Era* (Tokyo, 1958).
Nishida, T. "Kinoshita Naoe: Pacifism and Religious Withdrawal," in N. Bamba and J. F. Howes, eds., *Pacifism in Japan* (Kyoto, 1978).

Kishi Nobusuke 1896– 岸信介

Native of Yamaguchi Prefecture and brother of Satō Eisaku, Kishi graduated in 1920 from Tokyo University where his political inclinations tended toward traditionalism. He then rose through the bureaucratic hierarchy at the Commerce and Industry Ministry before becoming deputy head of the Manchukuo government's business section in 1936. The nominal head of the department was a Chinese, and Kishi was in fact second only to Manchukuo's director of general affairs and played a major role in implementing the five-year plan for industrial development. As commerce and industry minister 1941–1943 and minister of state and deputy munitions minister 1943–1944 he was involved in providing economic support for the war effort. Kishi was listed as a class "A" war criminal but was never charged but released December 1948. His anti-Communist stance and support for constitutional revision gradually increased his influence among conservatives, and his strong financial connections as well meant that he successfully achieved a base for a return to politics after being depurged in 1952. That year he was elected to the Diet for the Liberal Party. He opposed Yoshida within the party and subsequently promoted consolidation of the various conservative parties, becoming secretary general of the new Liberal Democratic Party. He was defeated for the party presidency in 1956 but was briefly foreign minister under Ishibashi before succeeding him as prime minister in February 1957. In this capacity Kishi worked to promote domestic industry and Japanese commercial interests in Southeast Asia. His strong conservative and anti-Communist leanings were shown in such measures as the introduction of efficiency rating for teachers and the proposed Police Duties Law, which aroused such opposition that it was abandoned. Kishi's efforts to forge closer links with the U.S. ended in his resignation in July 1960 after the crisis over the security treaty with the U.S. (*q.v.*). Kishi has since remained a staunch anti-Communist and influential in conservative and right-wing groups.

Kurzman, D. *Kishi and Japan* (New York, 1960).
Packard, G. R. *Protest in Tokyo* (Princeton, 1966).

Kishida Toshiko 1864–1901 岸田俊子
Daughter of a Kyoto clothing merchant, Kishida was briefly employed at court, but from 1882 was active in the popular rights movement. She gained considerable support by making speeches throughout western Japan on popular rights and equality for men and women. In 1885 she married Nakajima Nobuyuki, one of the leaders of the Jiyūtō, and played no further part in radical or antigovernment movements after the 1887 Peace Regulations (*q.v.*), but she played an important role both in the popular rights movement and as one of the forerunners of the women's rights movement.

Kita Ikki 1883–1937 北一輝
Native of Sado island, initially a Socialist, Kita published in 1906 *Theory of the Kokutai and Pure Socialism*, which rejected contemporary analysis of the *kokutai* (*q.v.*) and also criticized contemporary socialism. The book was well received by intellectuals but was immediately banned. Kita associated with Japanese working for revolution in China, and his interest led to a close relationship with Sung Chiao-jen. He went to China in 1911 but was expelled in 1913. In 1915–1916 he worked on *Private History of the Chinese Revolution*, which called on Japan to promote the revolution in China to expel the West from Asia. He was converted to Nichiren Buddhism. In 1916 he returned to China, but his disillusionment with anti-Japanese feeling and the conflict between Chinese and Japanese interests led him to believe that domestic reform was necessary before Japan could achieve the foreign policy that he desired. The result of this attitude was *An Outline Plan for the Reconstruction of Japan* (1919), which called for a military coup d'état, suspension of the constitution, and three years of martial law locally policed by the army. A major reorganization during this time would eliminate large private concentrations of land and capital, introduce sharing of profits and worker participation in management, eliminate from national life all financial, military, bureaucratic, and political party elites who stood between the emperor and the people, and establish something along the lines of a welfare state. This Kita regarded as a transitional period during which Japan could be transformed into a state capable of performing her prescribed Asian mission, i.e., the liberation of China and India from the West. Kita was persuaded to return to Japan in 1919 and in 1920 joined the nationalist Yūzonsha, but in 1923 he conflicted with Ōkawa Shūmei over policy toward Russia. Kita subsequently played a more withdrawn role, financially supported by the Mitsui *zaibatsu*, but his writings had considerable influence on younger army officers, and he is regarded as one of the major nationalist ideologues of the 1930s. Although his

ideas differed greatly from those of the officers involved, Kita was accused of being an accessory to the February 26 rising (*q.v.*). His subsequent execution meant that the government had rid themselves of a leading anti-*kokutai* radical and nationalist.

Tanin, O., and E. Yohan *Militarism and Fascism in Japan* (London, 1934).
Wilson, G. M. *Radical Nationalist in Japan: Kita Ikki, 1883–1937* (Cambridge, Mass., 1969).

Kiyoura Keigo 1850–1942 (Baron, 1902; Viscount, 1907; Count, 1928) 清浦奎吾

Native of Kumamoto Prefecture and lawyer, Kiyoura was employed in local government and then in the central bureaucracy, where, as chief of the Police Bureau and deputy justice minister, he was closely identified with Yamagata Aritomo. He served as justice minister 1896–1898, 1898–1900, and 1901–1903. He was then agriculture and commerce minister 1903–1906 and concurrently home minister 1905–1906. He was appointed to the House of Peers and was also a member of the Privy Council 1906–1917. Kiyoura was asked to form a cabinet in 1914, but the navy refused to provide a minister. He was president of the Privy Council 1922–1924. He did head a short-lived nonparty cabinet January-June 1924, but his appointment stimulated the second movement for the protection of constitutional government, which brought his political career to an end.

Duus, P. *Party Rivalry and Political Change in Taishō Japan* (Cambridge, Mass., 1968).

Kobe Incident (Kōbe jiken) 神戸事件

An attack on foreign troops by Okayama *han* samurai on 4 February 1868 led to the occupation of Kobe by foreign troops to forestall further attacks and their holding of all ships in the harbor. The new government quickly undertook to protect the lives and property of all foreigners at Kobe and ordered the punishment of the samurai responsible. The foreign troops were withdrawn and the ships restored to the Japanese, but similar anti-foreign feeling was shown in the Sakai incident (*q.v.*).

Satow, E. M. *A Diplomat in Japan* (London, 1921).

Kōbu Gattai 公武合体

The idea of shoring up the *Bakufu-han* system by tying it to the traditional powers of the court had existed since the mid-Tokugawa period, but in the crisis situation of the 1860s the slogan *kōbu gattai* (unity of court and Bakufu) was adopted by those inside and outside the Bakufu, who, often to enhance their own power, sought a basis of accommodation between the Bakufu and the great daimyō. The movement achieved a marriage between the shōgun, Iemochi, and Kazunomiya, sister of the emperor, in March 1862. *Kōbu gattai* advocates conflicted with Chōshū-led opponents of the Bakufu but remained influential after the anti-Chōshū coup in Kyoto late 1863. A conference of leading daimyō was established, but this quickly split, and from 1865 the movement lost ground in the face of the strengthening anti-Bakufu movement (*q.v.*). It was moderate successors of the *kōbu gattai* movement, led by Matsudaira Keiei and Yamanouchi Yōdō, who in 1867 called unsuccessfully for rule by a deliberative assembly of the leading *han*.

Beasley, W. G. *The Meiji Restoration* (London, 1973).
Lee, C. B. "Alliance Between the Court and Bakufu: The Kazunomiya Marriage," *MN* 22, nos. 3-4 (1967).
Totman, C. "Tokugawa Yoshinobu and Kōbu Gattai: A Study of Political Inadequacy," *MN* 30, no. 4 (1975).

Kodama Gentarō 1852–1906 (Baron, 1895; Viscount, 1906) 児玉源太郎

Samurai from Tokuyama domain (now Yamaguchi Prefecture), Kodama fought in the Boshin War (*q.v.*) and then joined the army, rising to be deputy war minister and chief of the Military Affairs Bureau 1892–1898, where he was a strong proponent of German military methods. He was governor of Taiwan 1898–1906 and with Gotō Shinpei established a basis for Japanese rule of the island. He also served as war minister 1900–1902 and as home and education minister in 1903. In 1903 he became vice-chief of staff and the following year became a full general. During the Russo-Japanese War he was chief of staff of the Manchurian forces. In 1906 he was appointed chief of the General Staff but died shortly afterwards.

Tsurumi, E. P. "Taiwan Under Kodama Gentarō and Gotō Shinpei," *HPJ* 4 (1967).

Kodama Yoshio 1911– 児玉誉士夫
A native of Fukushima, Kodama was from 1928 active in various right-wing and nationalist societies and was arrested several times for violent ultranationalist activities, including an abortive plot to kill Prime Minister Saitō Makoto. From 1937 he spent most of his time in China and Manchuria where he was attached in a semiofficial capacity to the Japanese army and acted as guard/adviser to Wang Ching-wei. He resigned over a disagreement with Tōjō but later returned to Shanghai as navy procurement agent. In this capacity he accumulated a vast fortune through his Kodama *kikan* (agency), allegedly by purchasing looted goods. At the end of the war he was appointed adviser to Prime Minister Higashikuni but was then tried and sentenced as a class "A" war criminal; he was released from prison only in 1948, when he used some of his vast wealth to help rebuild the conservative parties. He developed close relations with conservative leaders such as Hatoyama Kazuo and Ogata Taketora and is still highly, if sometimes surreptitiously, influential in conservative and business circles. He has remained a leading figure of the right wing. In 1976 Kodama was accused of involvement in the Lockheed scandal (*q.v.*).

Hanzawa, H. "Two Right-Wing Bosses: A Comparison of Sugiyama and Kodama," *JQ* 23, no. 3 (July-Sept. 1976).
Kodama, Y. *I Was Defeated* (Tokyo, 1951).
Morris, I. *Nationalism and the Right Wing in Japan* (London, 1960).

Kōdansha. See NOMA SEIJI

Kōdō Faction (kōdōha) 皇道派
A leading faction within the army in the 1930s grouping around Araki Sadao and Mazaki Jinzaburō. Araki was appointed war minister in December 1931 and replaced members of the previously dominant Ugaki faction with his own personal supporters. This group was supported by younger officers, mostly those of field officer ranks. Many of them were influenced by Kita Ikki; they fervently espoused the principles of the *kokutai* and aimed at internal reconstruction by direct action. Abroad they regarded Russia as Japan's main enemy. Military personnel personally or ideologically hostile to Araki's supporters formed the *tōsei* faction; and after Araki ceased to be war minister in 1934, struggle between the two factions grew fiercer. Members of the *kōdō* faction were responsible for the 1935 Aizawa incident (*q.v.*) and the February 26 (1936) rising (*q.v.*). After the latter, strong punitive measures marked its decline as a separate force.

Crowley, J. B. *Japan's Quest for Autonomy* (Princeton, 1966).
______"Japanese Army Factionalism in the 1930s," *JAS* 21, no. 3 (May 1962).
Lory, H. *Japan's Military Masters* (New York, 1943).
Storry, R. *The Double Patriots* (London, 1957).
Wald, R. J. "The Young Officers' Movement in Japan ca. 1925–1935: Ideology and Actions," Ph.D. diss., University of California, Berkeley, 1948.

Koiso Kuniaki 1880–1955 小磯国昭
Native of Yamagata Prefecture, graduating from the Military Academy, Koiso rose

quickly in the army to become a full general in 1937, serving as deputy war minister and commander of the Japanese forces in Korea. He was a member of the Kokuhonsha (*q.v.*). He was involved with the March incident of 1931 (*q.v.*) and was subsequently known as a leading member of the *tōsei* faction. He was minister for colonization in 1939 and 1940 and then governor of Korea May 1942 – July 1944. That month Koiso and Yonai were requested to cooperate in forming a cabinet, and Koiso succeeded Tōjō as prime minister. From the start he believed the war to be already lost, but he established the Supreme War Guidance Council to be the liaison between the cabinet and the supreme command, which in effect became an inner war cabinet. Koiso attempted to control the war and munitions supply without becoming war minister, but his attempts to wrest control of the war from the army made for bad relations with the military, and in fact he had little success in directing the war. There was also criticism within the cabinet of his strategy vis-à-vis China, and Koiso resigned in April 1945. Postwar he was tried as a class "A" war criminal and in November 1948 was sentenced to life imprisonment. He died of illness in prison in November 1950. He left an autobiography.

Akashi, Y. "A Botched Peace Effort: The Miao Pin Kōsaku, 1944 – 1945," in A. D. Coox and H. Conroy, eds., *China and Japan: Search for Balance Since World War I* (Santa Barbara, 1978).
Butow, R. J. C. *Japan's Decision to Surrender* (Stanford, 1954).
Komai, T. "Koiso, the Man and his Policy," *CJ* 8, no. 5 (July 1939).

Kokkai Kisei Dōmei 国会期成同盟
The Kokkai Kisei Dōmei (League for Founding a National Assembly) succeeded the Aikokusha (*q.v.*) in March 1880. It was agreed that Kōno Hironaka and Kataoka Kenkichi, leaders of the league, should initiate a national movement for the establishment of a Diet by submitting a petition to the government. Despite lack of success the league's second conference November 1880 was attended by 64 members claiming to represent 130,000 people. It resolved to expand its activities, research into a draft constitution, and plan for a broader party. It demanded a national assembly, reduction in land tax, and treaty revision. It continued to exist until October 1881 when the government promised the establishment of a Diet.

Ike, N. *The Beginnings of Political Democracy in Japan* (Baltimore, 1950).
Scalapino, R. *Democracy and the Party Movement in Prewar Japan* (Berkeley, 1967).

Kokugaku. See NATIVISM

Kokuhonsha 国本社
The Kokuhonsha (National Foundation Society) was founded in 1924 with Hiranuma Kiichirō as president. The society stressed the unique religious character of Japan, Japan's mission in Asia, and the necessity of implementing reform in Japan in accordance with "the basic principles of the state." The society's members included Saitō Makoto, Koiso Kuniaki, Ugaki Kazushige, Araki Sadao, and other leading politicians, soldiers, bureaucrats, and *zaibatsu* leaders. It expanded its membership and at one time claimed 170 branches and 200,000 members. The Kokuhonsha was the stronghold of traditional conservative ideas at very high levels and was in many ways not distant from right-wing nationalism. Hiranuma resigned as president following his appointment as president of the Privy Council in 1936, and the Kokuhonsha was dissolved in June of that year.

Storry, R. *The Double Patriots* (London, 1957).

Kokumin no Tomo. See MINYŪSHA

Kokumin Shinbun. See MINYŪSHA

Kokuryūkai 黒龍会

The Kokuryūkai (Amur River Society, also known as the Black Dragon Society) was a "patriotic" society connected with the Genyōsha (*q.v.*) and founded in 1901 by Uchida Ryōhei, who headed it until his death in 1937. Tōyama Mitsuru was also closely identified with it. The Kokuryūkai subscribed to such ideas as harmony between East and West, revival of the martial spirit, educational reform, and overseas expansion. In effect, it aimed at extending Japanese influence in Manchuria. Members of the society had close relations with the army and civilian businessmen and during the Russo-Japanese War and after worked in close contact with the army as intelligence agents and interpreters. Members active in China became known as "continental adventurers" (*tairiku rōnin*). The society supported the annexation of Korea and worked for revolution in China. Containment of Russia and the fall of the Manchu dynasty were regarded as enhancing Japan's continental influence. Some of the society's members had considerable influence on Japan's China policy, maintaining close contacts with leading politicians. After World War I the society in addition turned its attentions to internal reconstruction and the suppression of labor and Socialist movements. In 1931 its members became a major element in the Greater Japan Production Party (*q.v.*). In January 1946 the Kokuryūkai was purged by SCAP.

Jansen, M. B. *The Japanese and Sun Yat-sen* (Cambridge, Mass., 1954).

Sabey, J. W. "The Gen'yōsha, the Kokuryūkai and Japanese Expansionism," Ph.D. diss., University of Michigan, 1972.

Storry, R. *The Double Patriots* (London, 1957).

Kokusuishugi. See ULTRANATIONALISM

Kokutai 国体

Attempts to fit the new Meiji constitution into a framework of Japanese tradition led to the formulation of a political orthodoxy comprised of several related theories of the Japanese state. The major point in common to these various theories was the belief in the uniqueness of Japan's *kokutai,* a term normally translated "national polity" and used in prewar Japan to refer to the fundamental character of the Japanese state. Much of what the *kokutai* embraced remained at times nebulous, and its interpretation differed according to the individual, but fundamental to the concept was, first, the existence of the emperor as the highest power in the state and, second, the statement of a morality of filial piety and loyalty governing the relationship between the emperor and his people which made the nation an organic whole. The attempt to merge prevailing sociopolitical forms with Japanese tradition also involved for some their reconciliation with the traditional ethical standards and religious beliefs of Confucianism and Buddhism. The accommodation of the imperial Japanese state to the Confucian view of the world order, the long-cherished idea of the Japanese state and people as one family under the unbroken line of emperors, the merging of Shintō mythology with Japan's early history to suggest divine descent—each were added to the concept of the *kokutai,* which came to epitomize the ideology of the "emperor system." As early as the 1890s Christianity was criticized as being irreconcileable with the *kokutai,* and the idea was increasingly emphasized after the Russo-Japanese War by conservatives wishing to stress Japan's unique traditions, but although the whole concept of *kokutai* and these different attitudes were fundamental to political activity, it was only in the 1930s that the differences erupted into open theoretical controversy, although the contradictions had certainly existed previously. The political implications of Minobe Tatsukichi's emperor organ theory (*q.v.*), which regarded the emperor as subordinate to the state and subject to the law, led to its being criticized as contrary to the *kokutai* and promoted calls for a clarification of the fundamental nature of the Japanese state (*kokutai meichō*). In response to this, in 1937 the Ministry of Education published *Kokutai no Hongi* (Principles of the National Polity) with the aim of setting out the orthodox ideological course for the Japanese people. It is on the basis of these principles that rests the concept of the *kokutai* as a nationalist imperial state where individualism was extremely difficult (and certainly undesirable) and service to the state the supreme virtue. Largely using extracts from the ancient Japanese classics, the *Kojiki*, and the *Nihon Shoki*, the *Kokutai no Hongi* defined the *kokutai*, talked of its manifestations, and spoke of Japan's historical mission in East Asia. It became the main ethics text in schools and the formal basis of the official ideology, as well as reinforcing use of the word *kokutai* as a nationalist slogan. After Japan's defeat many Japanese desired to preserve the emperor as the essence of Japan's *kokutai*; radical reforms changed the institutional position of the emperor in relation to his people, and the ethical aspects of the emperor-subject relationship no longer received official or widespread unofficial support. Much of the prewar ideology was discredited by Japan's failure, and the idea of the *kokutai* ceased to exert its former influence. Some attempts to reassert the importance of the concept have come from the right wing and conservatives, but these have not received great support from the postwar generation.

Brown, D. M. *Nationalism in Japan* (Berkeley, 1955).
Hall, R. K. *Shūshin: the Ethics of a Defeated Nation* (New York, 1949).
Hall, R. K., ed., and J. O. Gauntlett, tr., *Kokutai no Hongi: Cardinal Principles of the National Entity of Japan* (Cambridge, Mass., 1949).
Maruyama, M. *Thought and Behavior in Modern Japanese Politics* (Oxford, 1963).
Miller, F. O. *Minobe Tatsukichi: Interpreter of Constitutionalism in Japan* (Berkeley, 1965).

Kokutai no Hongi. See KOKUTAI

Kōmeitō 公明党

The Kōmeitō (Clean Government Party) was officially constituted in 1964 as the political wing of the Buddhist organization Sōka Gakkai, which had been involved in politics since the mid-1950s. The party advocated the renovation of society on the basis of religious premises and the purification of politics; it called for welfare policies and the abolition of income tax and opposed the use of nuclear power. On the basis of the mass membership of Sōka Gakkai rather than these vague policies, it secured 25 representatives in the 1967 lower house elections. From the early 1970s it has reduced its formal connection with Sōka Gakkai, although this former dependence no doubt remains a major factor in its support. Advocating "humanitarian socialism" and strongly anti-Communist, Kōmeitō aims at being the center of a coalition of centrist elements. It draws much of its support from office workers, the self-employed, and those connected with small business and by 1979 claimed a national membership of 142,000. The 1979 lower house elections gave it 57 Diet members, making it the third largest party, but in the June 1980 election this number fell to 33.

Aruga, H. "Kōmeitō: Its Political Characteristics," *Annals of the Institute of Social Science, Tokyo* 9 (1968).
Ingram, P. O. "Sōka Gakkai and the Kōmeitō: Buddhism and Political Power in Japan," *Contemporary Religions in Japan* 10, nos. 3–4 (Sept.-Dec. 1969).
Lee, J. "Kōmeitō-Sōkagakkai-ism in Japanese Politics," *Asian Survey* 10, no. 6 (June 1970).
Palmer, A. *Buddhist Politics—Japan's Clean Government Party* (The Hague, 1971).
White, J. W. *The Sōka Gakkai and Mass Society* (Stanford, 1970).

Komura Jūtarō 1855–1911 (Baron, 1902; Count, 1907; Marquis, 1911)
小村寿太郎

A samurai from Obi domain (now Miyazaki Prefecture), Komura joined the Justice Ministry after graduating from Harvard but in 1884 moved to the Foreign Ministry. His offices included that of Japan's representative in Korea 1895–1896, deputy foreign minister 1896–1898, ambassador to the U.S. 1898–1900, to Russia 1900, and to China 1901. As foreign minister 1901–1905 Komura supported the conclusion of the Anglo-Japanese Alliance (*q.v.*) and was Japan's representative at the Portsmouth Conference, which followed the Russo-Japanese War (*q.v.*). He was then briefly privy councillor in 1906 and ambassador to Britain 1906–1908 before again serving as foreign minister 1908–1911. This term saw the annexation of Korea and Japan's recovery of tariff autonomy. Komura's diplomatic skill in utilizing conflict between the powers to improve Japan's weak position assisted a strengthening of Japan's international position, especially in Asia.

Komura, S. "Jūtarō Komura, My Father," *CJ* 1, no. 4 (Mar. 1933).

Komura-Weber Memorandum
(Komura Uēbā kyōtei)
小村・ウェーバー協定
On 14 May 1896 Komura Jūtarō, Japan's representative in Korea, and K. I. Weber, the Russian envoy there, concluded an agreement terminating Japan's attempts to dominate Korea. The emphasis of the agreement was on mutual advice to Korea. It was agreed that both countries would advise the Korean king on the appointment of his ministers, that Japan would be permitted military police to guard the Seoul-Pusan telegraph, and that both countries would station an agreed number of troops at Seoul, Pusan, and Wonsan. Japan hoped that her assurances would persuade the Korean king, currently sheltering in the Russian Legation following the murder of Queen Min, to return to his palace, and he subsequently did so. This agreement, which was made public in February 1897, was confirmed by the Yamagata-Lobanov agreement (*q.v.*).

Kajima, M. *The Diplomacy of Japan, 1894–1922,* vol. 1, *Sino-Japanese War and the Triple Intervention* (Tokyo, 1976).
Rockhill, W. W., ed. *Treaties and Conventions With or Concerning China and Korea, 1894–1904* (Washington, 1904).

Kōno Hironaka 1849–1923 河野広中
A native of Fukushima, Kōno fought against the Bakufu in the Boshin War (*q.v.*). After playing a leading role in the popular rights movement through the 1870s, he joined the Jiyūtō in 1881. He became president of Fukushima prefectural assembly the same year but conflicted with Governor Mishima Michitsune in the Fukushima incident (*q.v.*) and was imprisoned in 1883. Released in 1889 with a pardon, from 1890 Kōno was elected 14 successive times to the Diet and was to be found among the leadership of the Jiyūtō, Kensei Hontō, Rikken Kokumintō, Rikken Dōshikai, and Kenseikai. He was president of the Diet in 1903, but his opening speech calling for impeachment of the government provoked the immediate dissolution of the Diet. Kōno was arrested in 1905 after the Hibiya riots (*q.v.*) but released the following year. He remained throughout in opposition except for a term as agriculture and commerce minister 1915–1916.

Ike, N. *The Beginnings of Political Democracy in Japan* (Baltimore, 1950).

Kōno Togama (Binken) 1844–1895
(Viscount, 1893) 河野敏鎌
A Tosa samurai, Kōno was active in the loyalist movement and through the mediation of Etō Shinpei joined the new government in 1869. From 1875 he was a leading figure in the Genrōin and became agriculture and commerce minister in spring 1881, only to resign later that year in the 1881 political crisis (*q.v.*). Close to both Ōkuma and Numa Morikazu, he became vice-president of the Kaishintō in 1882. In 1884 he was the main advocate of the Kaishintō's dissolution, and when this was not accepted, he resigned, as did Ōkuma. Kōno was privy councillor 1888–1892 and in 1893, home, justice and

agriculture/commerce minister in 1892, and education minister 1892–1893.

Lebra, J. *Ōkuma Shigenobu* (Canberra, 1973).

Konoe Fumimaro 1891–1945 (Prince) 近衛文麿
Native of Tokyo and member of the court nobility, Konoe studied at Kyoto Imperial University. A protégé of Saionji, in 1919 he attended the Paris Peace Conference and later criticized the peace as an effort by the West to preserve the status quo. In 1916 he took his seat in the House of Peers and became its president in 1933. He had good relations with both military and civilian leaders, and although he declined an offer to become prime minister after the February 26 (1936) rising (*q.v.*), in June 1937 he did form a cabinet. Konoe made little attempt to stop the spread of fighting with China and in January 1938 declared that Japan would not deal with the nationalist government. In November he announced Japan's founding of a new order in East Asia (*q.v.*) but resigned the following January over the protraction of the China war and disputes concerning alliance with Germany and Italy. After acting as president of the Privy Council January 1939–June 1940, Konoe was reappointed prime minister in July 1940 with the aim of promoting the new structure movement (*q.v.*) and the new order in East Asia; to this end he founded the Imperial Rule Assistance Association (*q.v.*). The alliance with Germany was signed September 1940. Konoe hoped that the new structure movement could counterbalance the influence of the army, but it remained politically weak and acted as little more than an organ for mobilization of the energies and enthusiasm of people for waging the war. Many, although by no means all, of Konoe's actions were the result of army pressure he was not strong enough to resist. In July 1941 he succeeded in dropping Foreign Minister Matsuoka from his cabinet due to the latter's opposition to negotiations with the U.S., but in October 1941 Konoe's cabinet resigned following conflict with War Minister Tōjō over the army's refusal to withdraw from China and French Indochina. From 1944 Konoe worked for an end to the war. August–October 1945 he was minister of state and subsequently embarked upon a plan for constitutional reform but in December 1945 was designated a class "A" war criminal and took his own life.

Berger, G. M. "Japan's Young Prince: Konoe Fumimaro's Early Political Career, 1916–1931," *MN* 29, no. 4 (Winter 1974).
______. *Parties Out of Power, 1931–1941* (Princeton, 1977).
Crowley, J. B. *Japan's Quest for Autonomy* (Princeton, 1966).
Storry, R. "Konoe Fumimaro: 'The Last of the Fujiwara,'" in G. F. Hudson, ed., *St. Antony's Papers,* vol. 7, *Far Eastern Affairs,* no. 2 (London, 1960).

Korea, Colony of
Japan increased its dominance over Korea as a protectorate from 1905, and the country was annexed in 1910. The resident general (*tōkan*) was replaced by a governor general (*sōtoku*) appointed by the emperor from among army and navy chiefs. The governor general had wide powers over political and other affairs and controlled a comprehensive administration with specialist offices to advise on such things as justice and railways. Terauchi Masatake (first governor 1910–1916) advocated strict control of thought and speech and ran what was virtually a military government. He was followed by Hasegawa Yoshimichi. Rising political and economic discontent led to the March First independence movement, and under Saitō Makoto (1919–1927, 1929–1931) a policy of relative appeasement was adopted. The worst excesses of military-type government were removed, with greater freedom of speech, writing and assembly; the governorship became open to civil officials (though in practice mostly reserve members of the forces); the military police were abolished; and the administrative offices were modified and increased. However, security remained tighter than

ever. During this period Japan developed Korea as the granary of Japan; by the late 1920s over 50% of Korea's rice production was exported to Japan, despite the fact that many Koreans were still ill-provided for. Poverty drove many Koreans to emigrate to Japan. Subsequent governors were Ugaki Kazushige (1927, 1931–1936), Yamanashi Hanzō (1927–1929—accused of corruption in office but acquitted), Minami Jirō (1936–1942), Koiso Kuniaki (1942–1944), and Abe Nobuyuki (1944–1945). After the Manchurian Incident (*q.v.*), and especially after 1937, Korea was gradually transformed into a supply base for Japanese troops in Manchuria, leading to almost total government economic control and enforced conscription of labor and requisitioning of food. These policies led to worsening economic difficulties. A program of heavy industrialization, especially for armaments production, was pushed forward, mostly in northern Korea. Suppression measures by the Japanese became increasingly severe; in an effort to secure total support for the war, assimilation measures were accelerated. These included attempts to eradicate Korean names and the Korean language, the recruitment of young Koreans for military service, and the enforced introduction of Shintō. Korea remained in Japanese hands until 1945, when it was occupied by U.S. and Russian troops. In 1948 it was divided along the 38th parallel into the Korean Democratic People's Republic (North Korea) and the Republic of Korea (South Korea).

Brudnoy, D. "Japan's Experiment in Korea," *MN* 25 (1970).
Kim, C. I. E., and Mortimore, D. E. eds., *Korea's Response to Japan: The Colonial Period, 1910–1945* (Kalamazoo, 1975).
Nahm, A. C., ed. *Korea Under Japanese Colonial Rule* (Kalamazoo, 1973).

Korea, Invasion of (seikanron)
征韓論
After the Restoration there were increasing calls for an invasion of Korea should that country refuse to cooperate with Japan in resisting the West. Korea's refusal to recognize or accept the documents of the new Meiji government was regarded as an insult to Japan and meant that the calls for an invasion (or *seikanron*, as it was known) were supported by many of the Meiji leaders. It was also considered that the invasion would act as an outlet for samurai discontent. Attempts to breach Korea's seclusion failed, and during the absence of the Iwakura mission (*q.v.*) the arguments for invasion gained strength. In August 1873 the government, led by Saigō Takamori and Itagaki Taisuke, resolved to send Saigō as an envoy to Korea on the assumption that he would be killed and his death could be used to initiate hostilities. After the return of members of the Iwakura mission led by Ōkubo and Iwakura, who now stressed that internal development should precede foreign aggression, the decision to invade Korea was overruled in October 1873. This marked the first major split in the Meiji leadership, and Saigō, Itagaki, Soejima Taneomi, Etō Shinpei, and Gotō Shōjirō all resigned. Their subsequent opposition to the government came in the form of both military rebellion and democratic movements. By 1876 Japan had established relations with Korea under the Treaty of Kanghwa (*q.v.*). The Formosan expedition (*q.v.*) was used as an outlet for samurai discontent.

Conroy, H. *The Japanese Seizure of Korea, 1868–1910* (Philadelphia, 1960).
Ike, N. "The Triumph of the Peace Party in Japan in 1873," *JAS* 2 (May 1943).
Limb, B. Q. "Seikan-ron: A Study in the Evolution of Expansionism in Modern Japan, 1868–1873," Ph.D. diss., St. John's University, 1979.
Mayo, M. J. "The Korean Crisis of 1873 and Early Meiji Foreign Policy," *JAS* 31, no. 4 (Aug. 1972).

Korea, Protectorate of
From the first day of Russo-Japanese hostilities in 1904 Korea was under the military control of Japan, but a series of agreements negotiated 1904–1905 culminated in the establishment of a formal protectorate. During 1904 Korea accepted

Japanese advisers for consultation on financial, diplomatic, and other matters. Recognition of Japan's special position in Korea by the U.S., Britain, and Russia under the Taft-Katsura agreement (*q.v.*), the renewed Anglo-Japanese Alliance, and the Portsmouth Treaty (*q.v.*) enabled Japan to conclude the November 1905 protectorate agreement arrogating to Japan Korea's foreign policy making. It was negotiated by Itō Hirobumi but in effect imposed on Korea. A residency was established in Seoul with agencies in the main open ports. It was headed by a resident general *(tōkan)* directly responsible to the Japanese emperor. The post was held by Itō Hirobumi (1905–1909), Sone Arasuke (1909–1910), and Terauchi Masatake (1910). Japan's powers were further extended by a 1907 agreement, which abolished the Korean army and allowed Japanese guidance in all administrative matters. Japanese gradually replaced Koreans in administrative posts. Korean appeals abroad against Japanese domination met with little support, and the anti-Japanese movement was ruthlessly suppressed in as far as this could be done without provoking criticism abroad. The establishment of such organs as the Bank of Korea (1909) and the Oriental Colonization Company (1908) paved the way for economic as well as political domination. The failure of this policy to meet what many considered the demands of Japanese security led to increasing demands for complete Japanese hegemony in Korea, and this resulted in annexation in 1910.

Conroy, H. *The Japanese Seizure of Korea, 1868–1910* (Philadelphia, 1960).
Kim, C. I. E. "Japan in Korea 1905–1910: The Techniques of Political Power," Ph.D. diss., Stanford University, 1959.
Ladd, G. T. *In Korea with Marquis Itō* (New York, 1908).

Korea, Relations with Japan to 1905
The Japanese had attempted to open diplomatic relations with Korea since the late Tokugawa period. Calls for an invasion of Korea (*q.v.*) were thwarted in 1873, but under the 1876 Kanghwa Treaty (*q.v.*) relations were established. Contacts increased, and there was a Japanese mission in Seoul by 1880. Due to its geographical position and Japan's economic and political situation, Korea was regarded as having a strong bearing on Japanese interests, and Japan tried to extend her influence there. China, however, still claimed suzerainty, and the area was one of potential conflict. Japanese liberals had strong connections with Korean progressives by the early 1880s, and Japan was involved in the 1882 Jingo incident (*q.v.*) and the 1884 Kōshin incident, which resulted in the Tientsin Treaty (*q.v.*). Although the Kanghwa Treaty had declared Korea's independent status, the Chinese attitude meant that Korea's real status was not clarified. By the early 1880s Japan was pressing for international guarantees of Korean independence, believing that turbulent conditions and international rivalries in Korea threatened Japan's security. Chinese influence in Korea remained politically and economically dominant until Sino-Japanese rivalry in the area culminated in the Sino-Japanese War (*q.v.*). During the war Korea was under Japanese control; concessions and wholesale reforms were enforced by the Japanese, but lack of support from Korea's rulers forced modifications in the policy, and Japanese influence declined. The complicity of the Japanese envoy, Miura, in the murder of the Korean Queen Min and the unsuccessful putsch of October 1895 also fueled anti-Japanese feeling and led to an increase of Russian influence in the country. The Yamagata-Lobanov and Komura-Weber agreements (*q.v.*) were attempts to reach an agreement with Russia over Korea on equal terms, but the Nishi-Rosen agreement of 1898 (*q.v.*) shifted toward an increase of Japan's influence in Korea. Russia and Japan remained suspicious of each other and competed in the struggle for concessions, but Japan achieved increasing economic dominance in Korea. The conclusion of the Anglo-Japanese Alliance (*q.v.*) played an important role in keeping Russia out of Korea, and a 1903 policy statement by the Japanese govenment stated that the independence of Korea was essential

since Korea was an outpost of Japan's line of defense and that Japan was unwilling to surrender her paramount political, commercial, and industrial interests in Korea. The outbreak of the Russo-Japanese War marked the beginning of exclusive Japanese control over Korea, and agreements between the two countries led to the forming of a protectorate in 1905.

Conroy, H. *The Japanese Seizure of Korea, 1868–1910* (Philadelphia, 1960).
Deuchler, M. *Confucian Gentlemen and Barbarian Envoys: The Opening of Korea, 1875–1885* (Seattle, 1977).
Kim, C. I. E., and H-K. Kim. *Korea and the Politics of Imperialism, 1876–1910* (Berkeley, 1967).
Lensen, G. A., ed. *Korea and Manchuria Between Russia and Japan* (Tallahassee, Fla., 1966).

Korean Independence Movement (Chōsen dokuritsu undō) 朝鮮独立運動

Unarmed and armed resistance to Japanese influence in Korea after the country became a protectorate in 1905 included an unsuccessful attempt to gain independent Korean representation at the 1907 Hague Peace Conference. A resistance movement active in the years after annexation was harshly suppressed. There was a limited focus of resistance among Koreans in Manchuria, and anti-Japanism among intellectuals and writers within Korea also continued. Korean discontent culminated in mass demonstrations in Seoul in March 1919 calling for independence, which spread throughout the country. This was known as the March First movement. These demonstrations were brutally suppressed by Japanese forces, several thousands were killed and injured, and tens of thousands were arrested. In April 1919 exiled Koreans in Shanghai set up a provisional government under Syngman Rhee; an increasingly strong movement in Manchuria, from 1935 under the leadership of Kim Il-sung, became tied up with the anti-Japanese movement in China. Within Korea radical nationalists and Communists united into one organization in 1927 to oppose the Japanese, but this organization was dissolved in 1931, and subsequent resistance was disorganized. During the Pacific War the allies committed themselves to postwar Korean independence, and this was attained in 1945, although the variety of nationalist groups led to a struggle within the country.

Baldwin, F. "The March First Movement: Korean Challenge and Japanese Response," Ph.D. diss., Columbia University, 1969.
Lee, C-S. *The Politics of Korean Nationalism* (Berkeley, 1963).
Wales, N., and S. Kim. *Song of Ariran: A Korean Communist in the Chinese Revolution* (rprt. San Francisco, 1972).

Korean War (Chōsen sensō) 朝鮮戦争

Fighting between troops from the Democratic Republic of Korea (North Korea) backed by the People's Republic of China and those from the Republic of Korea (South Korea) and the United Nations lasted from June 1950–July 1953. The impact of the war on Japan was immense. Politically, it drew Japan further into the American camp during the cold war, which stimulated such developments as the founding of the National Police Reserve, the "red purge" (*q.v.*), the San Francisco Peace Treaty (*q.v.*), and the U.S.-Japan Security Treaty (*q.v.*) and was also a stimulus toward rearmament. Japan acted as a military base for the U.N. forces, and economically the "special procurements" (*q.v.*) created by war demand provided a stimulus for economic recovery and initiated the trend toward rapid economic growth.

Rees, D. *Korea: The Limited War* (London, 1964).
Simmons, R. R. *The Strained Alliance* (New York, 1975).

Kōseishō. See WELFARE MINISTRY

Kōshin Incident. See TIENTSIN TREATY

Kōtoku Shūsui 1871–1911
幸徳秋水
Member of samurai family from Kōchi Prefecture, given name Kōtoku Denjirō, Kōtoku participated in the popular rights movement from 1887 and was banned from Tokyo under the Peace Regulations (*q.v.*). From 1888 he studied under Nakae Chōmin before acting as a reporter on the *Jiyū Shinbun* 1893–1894 and the *Chūō Shinbun* 1895–1898. In 1898–1903 he worked on the *Yorozu Chōhō* (*q.v.*), during which time he gradually became known as a Socialist and pacifist. In 1898 he joined the Society for the Study of Socialism and in 1901 participated in the short-lived Shakai Minshutō. In 1903 he resigned from *Yorozu Chōhō* over the issue of war with Russia and with Sakai Toshihiko founded the Heiminsha (*q.v.*). Kōtoku turned to anarchism while in America 1905–1906 and after his return became the leading theorist among advocates of direct action within the left wing. He was arrested in June 1910 in the High Treason incident (*q.v.*) and, despite his assertions that he had abandoned his connections with any such plot, was executed in January 1911. Apart from articles and an anti-Christian treatise, Kōtoku's best-known works are *Imperialism: Spectre of the Twentieth Century* (1901) and *The Quintessence of Socialism* (1903).

Elison, G. "Kōtoku Shūsui: 'The Change in Thought,'" *MN* 22, nos. 3-4 (1967)
Ike, N. "Kōtoku: Advocate of Direct Action," *FEQ* 3, no. 3 (May 1944).
Notehelfer, F. G. *Kōtoku Shūsui: Portrait of a Japanese Radical* (Cambridge, 1971).

Kōza Faction. See JAPANESE CAPITALISM DEBATE

Kurile (Kuril) Islands (Chishima)
千島
The Kurile Islands lie off northeastern Hokkaidō. In February 1855 a Russo-Japanese treaty placed the Russo-Japanese border between the islands of Etorofu (Iturup) and Uruppu (Urup), and in 1869 the southern Kuriles became one of the provinces of Hokkaidō. In May 1875 the Sakhalin-Kurile Exchange Treaty gave Japan jurisdiction over the whole chain of islands. Attempts to develop the islands subsequently largely consisted of promoting fishing. Since the islands held a strategic position near Alaska and the Aleutians, from the 1930s they were developed as an important military/naval base. The islands were invaded by Soviet troops in August 1945 under the terms of the Yalta agreement (*q.v.*). Japan abandoned her claim to the islands in the San Francisco Peace Treaty (*q.v.*), but who did own them was not stated. Russia, who was meanwhile developing the islands, was not a signatory of the treaty and asserted sovereignty over the whole chain. The Japanese were themselves split on ownership of the islands but in negotiations with Russia 1955–1956 asserted that Etorofu and islands south of it were original Japanese territory and not included in those abandoned under the peace treaty. The controversy over the so-called "northern territories problem" meant that a peace declaration, rather than a peace treaty, was signed in 1956. The U.S.S.R. agreed that Habomai and Shikotan, the southernmost islands, should be handed back after a full treaty, but this has yet to be signed. In Japan there is considerable irredentist agitation clamoring for the return of Etorofu and Kunashiri, but the issue remains a major problem in Russo-Japanese relations, with little prospect of a solution.

Lensen, G. A. *The Russian Push Toward Japan* (Princeton, 1959).
Ōmori, S. "Japan's Northern Territories," *JQ* 17, no. 1 (Jan.-Nov. 1970).
Stephan, J. J. *The Kuril Islands* (Oxford, 1974).
Swearingen, R. *The Soviet Union and Postwar Japan* (Stanford, 1978).

Kuroda Kiyotaka 1840–1900
(Count, 1884) 黒田清隆
Satsuma samurai, Kuroda participated in the anti-Bakufu movement (*q.v.*) and fought in the Boshin War (*q.v.*). He became lieutenant-general and then deputy head of the Hokkaidō Colonization

Board in 1870, its head in 1874. He continued in this post until the board was abolished in 1882, despite criticism over the Hokkaidō colonization assets scandal (*q.v.*) in 1881. As special envoy to Korea in 1876 Kuroda concluded the Kanghwa Treaty (*q.v.*). He also fought against the Satsuma rebellion. In 1882 he became state councillor and then cabinet adviser, then agriculture and commerce minister 1887–1888. As prime minister 1888–1889 Kuroda headed a *hanbatsu* cabinet openly committed to transcendentalism. The cabinet presided over the promulgation of the constitution but eventually fell over Foreign Minister Ōkuma's treaty revision proposals. Kuroda was subsequently privy councillor 1888–1892, communications minister 1892–1895, and president of the Privy Council 1895–1900.

Anthony, D. F. "The Administration of Hokkaidō Under Kuroda Kiyotaka, 1870–1882," Ph.D. diss., Yale University, 1951.

Kuroiwa Ruikō. See YOROZU CHŌHŌ.

Kurozumikyō. See SHINTŌ

Kwantung Army (Kantōgun) 関東軍
From 1907 Japanese troops were permitted in Kwantung province in Manchuria to guard the South Manchurian Railway and the Liaotung peninsula leased by Japan. In 1919 these troops were given independent status as the Kwantung Army. The army consisted of one division to guard the leased territory and railway zone, plus military police, and was an important agent in promoting the development of Manchuria. Despite its small size, during the 1920s the army became highly politicized and attracted the cream of younger officers. In 1928 the army's headquarters were moved from Port Arthur to Mukden, and it played an increasingly assertive role in policy toward Manchuria. Many officers believed the promotion of Japanese interests necessitated the use of force to separate Manchuria from China. It was members of the Kwantung Army who murdered Chang Tso-lin (*q.v.*) and initiated the Manchurian Incident (*q.v.*). After the Manchurian Incident the commander of the Kwantung Army became ambassador to Manchukuo and head of the Kwantung Office. In effect, he governed the state of Manchukuo, largely free of control from Tokyo. The strength of the Kwantung Army was increased to five divisions in 1937 and 13 in 1941. With the aim of containing communism, the cream of the army was placed on the Soviet-Manchukuo border, resulting in major clashes at Changkufeng (1938) and Nomonhan (1939) (*q.v.*). Following Germany's declaration of war on Russia in 1941, the Kwantung Army was prepared for conflict with the U.S.S.R., but most of the best forces were gradually moved to the southern front, and the Russian attack of August 1945 met with little resistance. The Kwantung Army was disbanded with other Japanese forces.

Ogata, S. *Defiance in Manchuria* (Berkeley, 1964).
Weland, J. E. "The Japanese Army in Manchuria: Covert Operations and the Roots of Kwantung Army Insubordination," Ph.D. diss., University of Arizona, 1977.
Yoshihashi, T. *Conspiracy at Mukden* (New Haven, 1963).

Kyōchōkai 協調会
As the first government attempt to co-opt major sections of the labor movement in the hope of counteracting its growing strength, during 1919 Home Minister Tokonami Takejirō suggested the formation of an organization of business, labor, and government representatives to mediate in labor disputes when so requested, research into labor problems, and make policy recommendations to the government. The idea was rejected by organized labor in the form of the Yūaikai (*q.v.*), which suspected Tokonami's motivations,

but despite labor's refusal to participate, the Kyōchōkai (Harmonization Society) was founded in December 1919 to promote "harmony" in the industrial world. It was supported by both government and business; sponsors included Shibusawa Eiichi and Kiyoura Keigo. The association had branches in factories regionally federated and controlled by a central coordinating organization, but its mediation in disputes was rarely very successful. Despite its defects the association conducted extensive and valuable research into labor and social problems, fostered educational work, and had some influence on government policy in such developments as the growth of labor exchanges. Apart from research reports the Kyōchōkai published the periodicals *Shakai Seisaku Jihō* (Social Policy Review) and *Rōdō Nenkan* (Labor Yearbook). It was disbanded in June 1946.

Harari, E. *The Politics of Labor Legislation in Japan* (Berkeley, 1973).
I. L. O. *Industrial Labor in Japan* (Geneva, 1933).

Kyōikurei. See EDUCATION

Kyoto University (Kyōto daigaku) 京都大学
Kyoto was established as Kyoto Imperial University in 1897. It was initially science-based but added faculties of law and medicine in 1899 and humanities in 1906. As opposed to the bureaucracy-oriented training traditionally supplied by Tokyo, the emphasis at Kyoto was more on the pursuit of learning for its own sake. By the 1920s it had developed a strongly liberal academic tradition—although during the heyday of the student movement in the early 1920s it was Tokyo students who were more radical—which eventually led it to clash with the government. In 1928 the university was forced to dismiss Professor Kawakami Hajime due to his Communist beliefs, and when, in 1933, the home minister demanded the dismissal of law professor Takigawa for alleged Communist sympathies (the so-called Takigawa incident), many leading members of the university resigned. In 1947 the university was renamed Kyoto University and absorbed into the new system as a national university, but it retains some element of its prewar characteristics.

L

Labor Farmer Party. See RŌDŌ NŌMINTŌ

Labor Movement
During the early Meiji period the industrial labor force remained small, and despite poor working conditions there was little organized protest over matters affecting workers. In 1897–1901 Takano Fusatarō and Katayama Sen ran the Rōdō Kumiai Kiseikai (League for Founding Labor Unions) and made limited attempts to organize iron workers, printers, and railway employees. Ōi Kentarō's Dainihon Rōdō Kyōkai (Greater Japan Labor Association) of 1899–1901 attempted to research into labor problems and provide welfare facilities for workers as well as encouraging labor unions. The late 1890s, therefore, saw a real advance toward labor organization, but government suppression, including the 1900 Peace Police Law (*q.v.*), virtually brought its development to a halt. In 1912 Suzuki Bunji founded the Yūaikai (*q.v.*), which during the 1914–1918 war became the main voice of organized labor and increasingly militant. In the postwar upsurge of disputes it changed its name to Nihon Rōdō Sōdōmei (Japan Federation of Labor). Initially militant and Communist-influenced, Sōdōmei played a major role in the strikes and disturbances of 1919–1921, but after 1923 dominance passed to its right wing, led by Nishio Suehiro, Suzuki Bunji, and Matsuoka Komakichi. In 1925 Sōdōmei expelled its leftist ele-

ments, who formed their own labor organization, Nihon Rōdō Kumiai Hyōgikai (Japan Labor Unions Council). Hyōgikai was strongly influenced by communism and extended its influence by such organizations as factory councils; it boasted 32,000 members by 1926. It played a leading role in labor disputes and antigovernment agitation, but it was weakened by doctrinal conflict and government oppression before its final dissolution in April 1928. In contrast, Sōdōmei adopted a strongly anti-Communist line in the hope of avoiding government suppression, devoting its attention to campaigns for labor legislation rather than open agitation. It remained the mainstream of the legal labor movement through the 1930s (it merged with a smaller centrist organization, Zenrō [National Labor Unions Federation] in 1936) but increasingly denied much of its own raison d'être by compromising with political trends and the status quo in the vague hope of thereby reforming it. After the upsurge of labor activity in the early 1920s, organized labor failed to sustain its early momentum, although it undoubtedly played a major role in the founding of the early proletarian parties. Even at its prewar peak only some 8% of the industrial labor force was organized, and even the larger national organizations had little political or economic influence, especially during the 1930s. The smaller ones could be almost totally ignored. The movement was further weakened by doctrinal and personal conflicts and fragmentation reflected in the proletarian party movement, by depression, by employers' paternalistic policies and promotion of company unions, by government oppression, and finally by the growing success of the so-called "patriotic" labor unions sponsored by the government. In 1940 all remaining labor union organizations were dissolved, and the Dainihon Sangyō Hōkokukai (Greater Japan Industrial Patriotic Association) was established as a unifying body to control and mobilize each company's "patriotic" union and labor force according to the needs of the state. This remained in existence until September 1945. After Japan's defeat Occupation policy was to encourage a labor movement in the hope of promoting democracy. Following the December 1945 Labor Union Law, which guaranteed the right of collective activity by workers, labor organizations grew to embrace some 40% of the industrial labor force during 1946. The two main organizations of these early postwar years were the moderate Sōdōmei (reviving the earlier name) and the Communist-dominated Sanbetsu Kaigi (All Japan Industrial Labor Unions Conference). It was the left wing which dominated labor organization at this time; strikes and disputes were widespread, and a general strike in February 1947 was avoided only by SCAP's intervention. The increasing anticommunism of the authorities, including extensive revision of labor legislation, weakened Sanbetsu Kaigi and the influence of communism among organized labor. Many unionists called for the formation of an anti-Communist democratic alliance, and in July 1950 elements from all groups combined together to form the Nihon Rōdō Kumiai Sōhyōgikai (Sōhyō) (Japan Labor Unions General Council). Sōdōmei was disbanded, only to be reformed a year later as Sōhyō too became increasingly dominated by the Left. Sōhyō remained the focus of national labor union activity even after secessions in 1954 and played a leading role in opposing government policies. In 1978 it numbered some 4½ million members, about one-third of all organized labor. It has strong connections with the left wing of the Japan Socialist Party, providing the party's main source of support, and draws much of its membership from government and public corporation employees. In 1954 four major unions, including the seamen and textile workers, seceded from Sōhyō to form Zennihon Rōdō Kumiai Kaigi (Zenrō Kaigi) (All Japan Labor Unions Conference) in conjunction with members of Sōdōmei. This gained further support from public employees, and in November 1964 the two organizations merged completely to form the Zennihon Rōdō Sōdōmei (Dōmei) (All Japan General Federation of Labor), which has since been the other focal organization for organized labor. Dōmei is anti-Communist and supports the right wing of the J. S. P. and the Democratic Socialist Party. Its membership is not as large as that of Sōhyō, numbering around 2½ million in 1979, but it is more powerful in private enterprise. The other two major national labor organizations are the moderate Chūritsu Rōdō Kumiai Renraku Kaigi (Chūritsu Rōren) (Neutral Labor Unions Liaison Conference) with 1½ million members in 1975, and the much smaller, Communist-dominated Zenkoku Sangyōbetsu Rōdō Kumiai Rengō (Shinsanbetsu) (National Industrial Labor Unions Federation). Most individual unions are affiliated to only one of these national organizations, which means that organized labor as a whole lacks unity, although there is concerted action on some issues. At local level many unions are company unions, and many unionists are inclined to think of the interests of the company rather than those of unionists in other enterprises. Nevertheless, the annual spring offensive (*shuntō*) has become a powerful factor in establishing wage rises. Overall, however, organized labor remains underrepresented in decision making at the highest political and economic levels.

Ayusawa, I. F. *A History of Labor in Modern Japan* (Honolulu, 1966).
Katayama, S. *The Labor Movement in Japan* (Chicago, 1918).
Notar, E. J. "Labor Unions and the Sangyō Hōkoku Movement, 1930–1945: A Japanese Model for Industrial Relations," Ph.D. diss., University of California, Berkeley, 1979.
Shiota, S. *Some Aspects of the History of the Labor Movement in Japan* (Tokyo, 1961).
Taira, K. *Economic Development and the Labor Market in Japan* (New York, 1970).

Labor Standards Law
(Rōdō Kijun Hō) 労働基準法

The Labor Standards Law aimed at securing minimum standards for working conditions was passed in April 1947 (taking effect from September) as part of SCAP's democratization policy. Provisions included an eight-hour day and 48-hour week, paid weekly and annual holidays, accident compensation, monthly and maternity leave for women, no full-time workers under 15, limited overtime by women and minors, and men and women to receive equal pay for equal work. The Labor Standards Bureau was established within the Labor Ministry to supervise implementation of the law. The standards set were fairly high, but since the 1960s there have been calls to raise them in the hope of putting greater pressure on employers to improve working conditions. As it is, although large enterprises generally adhere to the law, conditions in many small and medium enterprises fall short; the law cannot control those working at home nor those in the large number of household or family undertakings, and in respect of women real equality has not been achieved. No minimum wage level has been implemented. Attempts to modify the law to accord with these realities have been unsuccessful.

Levine, S. B. *Industrial Relations in Postwar Japan* (Urbana, Ill., 1958).

Land Reform (nōchi kaikaku)
農地改革

Land reform to ameliorate the tenancy problem (*q.v.*) had been under discussion in Japan before the war, and although the position of the landlord declined during the war, SCAP (*q.v.*) still considered reform necessary, believing that agrarian problems had contributed to Japanese aggression. Initial reform proposals were prepared under the Shidehara cabinet and submitted to the Diet in December 1945, but they were weak suggestions and were watered down still further by the Diet. Recommendations by the Allied Council for Japan (*q.v.*) led to an Occupation draft passing the Diet in October 1946. The reform stipulated the compulsory purchase of all land belonging to absentee landlords and of all land owned by resident landlords and owner-farmers over three *chō* (7.35 acres) (12 *chō* in

Hokkaidō). Of this remaining land, not more than one-third could be rented out although there were extra provisions for uncultivated and residential land. The surplus land was to be purchased by the government at fixed 1945 prices. It was sold mostly to existing tenants at the same price. For those who remained tenants, moderate rents paid in cash and security of tenure replaced high rents often paid in kind. Some inequalities remained, largely due to lack of thoroughgoing reform of forest land, and smaller landlords continued to exist, but landlords were hit both by the loss of their land and the depreciated level of compensation due to rampant inflation. Tenanted land, which had amounted to some 46% cultivated land in 1941, fell to less than 10%. The remaining 90% was owned by owner-cultivators. The main provisions of the reform were embodied permanently in the Agricultural Land Law of 1952. The land reform genuinely reduced rural unrest in Japan to a low level. It made most Japanese farmers into better-off owner-cultivators and increased productivity, although this may not continue with such small-scale production. It also led to a considerable decline in paternalism and the traditional status system in the villages.

Dore, R. P. *Land Reform in Japan* (London, 1959).
Grad, A. J. "Land Reform in Japan," *Pacific Affairs* 21, no. 2 (June 1948).

Land Tax (chiso) 地租
Before the Restoration most land was owned by daimyō or Bakufu, and the income they received from it in the form of crops supported the samurai class and was the basis of the Bakufu-*han* system. After the Restoration the government desired to create a unified, centralized tax system to give a regular, stable revenue essential to a national government. Their main source of tax was inevitably the land. Private ownership of land was recognized by the issue of title deeds. In 1872 the government removed the ban on the sale, purchase, and mortgage of land and ruled that there should be a fixed tax payable in money. To this end a nation-wide survey to establish the ownership and value of land was provided for in the July 1873 land tax reform regulations. The regulations stated that 3% of the monetary value of the land should be annually paid in cash as tax by the individual landholder. Later a 1% supplement for local government or village levy was added. This ended the traditional system of fixing the land tax at a certain percentage of the crop yield and levying it on the village as a unit, all or part of it payable in kind. Progress in the reform was slow, so in 1875 the Land Tax Reform Bureau was established under the joint jurisdiction of the Finance and Home ministries to enforce the measure. Despite the change farmers continued to pay heavy taxes, and the often violent resistance to the high tax levels meant that in January 1877 the tax rate was reduced to 2.5% land value (village supplement 0.5%). The reform bureau was abolished in 1881 with the completion of the reform. The land tax was a major element in the Meiji government's revenue, comprising 80–90% in the 1870s–1880s. The reform of the 1870s aimed at maintaining overall tax income at roughly the same level as previously, but although the reform did provide stable government revenue, it meant a heavy burden on cultivators. Many farmers paid up to a third of their harvest in tax, and there was no reduction at times of poor harvests. Tenancy rates therefore also remained high, bringing a marked increase in tenancy and impoverishment, especially during the deflation of the 1880s. Later, when rises in the price of rice lightened the tax burden, parasitic landholding became common. On the government side the failure to revise land values regularly led to a progressive reduction in the value of the tax. Revenue from other sources increased, and by 1902 the land tax supplied only 20% government revenue. Although the issue of whether land tax should go to central or local government remained a problem during the 1920s, by 1940 it comprised only 3%

government income. In 1950 land became one of the assets subject to the general tax on fixed assets.

Chambliss, W. J. *Chiaraijima Village* (Tucson, 1965).
Dore, R. P. *Land Reform in Japan* (London, 1959).
Waswo, A. *Japanese Landlords* (Berkeley, 1977).

Landlordism. See TENANCY

Language Problem (kokugo mondai) 国語問題

Some interest was shown in the Japanese language and script from the mid-Tokugawa period, but after contact with the West was reopened, there were increasing calls for rationalization of the language and script. In 1867 Maejima Hisoka petitioned the shōgun on the need to abolish characters to promote Japan's development, and from then on many others, including Nishi Amane and Mori Arinori, called for language reform to assist general education and national advancement. Some called for the establishment of a national, standard language, for abolition of the various written forms of Japanese, and unification of the written and spoken forms of the language. Others called for an improvement in the script by the abolition of characters (or restriction of the number in use), use of *kana* only, use of Roman letters, or the invention of a totally new script. Some even advocated the use of English as the national language. Each group founded organizations to promote its point of view, but little headway was made. As academic study of the language increased in the late Meiji period, emphasis was placed more on the unification of the written and spoken languages, the so-called *genbun itchi* movement. Official research into the language problem was carried out from 1899, and some simplification was achieved in the use of spoken-form Japanese in textbooks and in limiting the number of characters in use for specific purposes, but overall there was little major progress up to the Pacific War. After the war the aim was the "democratization" of the language. *Kana* orthography was simplified, the number of characters in everyday use restricted, and a simpler form of written Japanese close to the spoken language was spread throughout the country by newspapers and official documents. The so-called "standard language" (*hyōjungo*) is now used throughout the country although local dialects of course remain. Despite these improvements the Japanese script remains a subject of controversy, but further radical improvements appear unlikely at present.

Twine, N. R. "The Genbunitchi Movement: A Study in the Development of Modern Colloquial Style in Japan," Ph.D. diss., University of Queensland, 1975.

Lansing-Ishii Agreement (Ishii-Ranshingu kyōtei) 石井・ランシング協定

The name given to the exchange of formal notes between special envoy Ishii Kikujirō and U.S. Secretary of State Robert Lansing in November 1917. The notes, which amounted to a joint U.S.-Japanese declaration, recognized Japan's special interests in China while also affirming Chinese territorial integrity, an open door policy, and equal opportunity in commerce and industry. Disagreement subsequently arose over the interpretation of the notes as the U.S. maintained that Japan's "special interests" were not political, merely economic. The declaration was abrogated at the request of the U.S. in April 1923.

Beers, B. F. *Vain Endeavor: Robert Lansing's Attempt to End the American-Japanese Rivalry* (Durham, N. C., 1962).
Ishii, K. (tr. and ed. F. C. Langdon) *Diplomatic Commentaries* (Baltimore, 1936).
Prescott, F. C. "The Lansing-Ishii Agreement," Ph.D. diss., Yale University, 1949.

League for the Establishment of a Diet. See KOKKAI KISEI DŌMEI

League for the Founding of Labor Unions. See LABOR MOVEMENT

League of Nations (Kokusai Renmei) 国際連盟

Japan received a permanent seat on the council of the League of Nations from its formal founding in January 1920 although she had failed at Versailles to get a racial equality declaration inserted in the league's charter. She remained in the league until announcing her withdrawal in February 1933 after the report of the Lytton commission (*q.v.*) was adopted.

Nish, I. H. *Japanese Foreign Policy, 1869–1942* (London, 1977).
Thorne, C. *The Limits of Foreign Policy* (London, 1972).

Leased Territories. See LIAOTUNG PENINSULA

Legal System

The initial written legislation after the Meiji Restoration was piecemeal, but from early on hopes of treaty revision (*q.v.*) acted as a stimulus to bring Japanese judicial practice in line with Western standards. Major legal reforms continued to be implemented until the turn of the century, some under foreign tutelage. During the 1870s Gustave Boissonade, a French legal adviser, drafted a criminal code based on elements of Japanese feudal law and the Code Napoleon; it was modified by the Japanese and came into effect in 1882, but in 1907 it was replaced by a new German-influenced code. A criminal procedure code was also first promulgated in 1882, but this too was reformed along German lines after 1890; its form was finalized only in 1922. The enactment of a civil code drafted by Boissonade in the 1880s and promulgated in 1890 was postponed due to considerable opposition, much of it from those who believed that it departed too far from traditional concepts of such things as the family and property. A similar criticism attended many sections of a newly drafted commercial code, and both codes were referred to special committees, which modified them extensively along German lines before their final implementation 1898–1899. The civil procedure code implemented after 1891 was also along German lines, although it was modified in 1926. Early moves toward constitutional law culminated in the 1889 Meiji constitution (*q.v.*). This gave the Justice Ministry extensive powers over all matters relating to courts and the law. Post-1945 reforms considerably modified the Japanese legal system. The judiciary was made totally independent of the executive. Administrative supervision of courts was transferred from the Justice Ministry to the Supreme Court, which appoints judges (except its own members) and pronounces on the constitutionality of laws, making it the guardian of the human rights promised in the 1947 constitution. All codes have been modified to comply with the new constitution, and in 1948 a new criminal procedure code replaced the existing one, protecting the rights of suspects and accused and forbidding preliminary investigations. Despite major legal reforms since 1945 the principle of an independent judiciary has been maintained.

Ishii, R. *Japanese Legislation in the Meiji Era* (Tokyo, 1958).
Oppler, A. C. *Legal Reform in Occupied Japan* (Princeton, 1976).
Toshitani, N. "Japan's Modern Legal System: Its Formation and Structure," *Annals of the Institute of Social Science, Tokyo* 17 (1976).
Von Mehren, A. T. *Law in Japan: The Legal Order in a Changing Society* (Cambridge, Mass., 1963).

Li-Itō Convention. See TIENTSIN TREATY

Liaotung Peninsula (Ryōtō hantō) 遼東半島

The Liaotung Peninsula lies off the Manchurian coast west of Korea. Port Arthur (Lushun) on its southern tip was a shipping center and base for the north China fleet in the 19th century. The area was occupied by Japan during the Sino-Japanese War, and under the Treaty of Shimonoseki the whole peninsula south of a line from Yingkou (Newchwang) to the mouth of the Yalu River was ceded to Japan, but the Triple Intervention (*q.v.*) forced Japan to abandon the concession. In 1898 Russia leased the area of Kwantung Province round Port Arthur and Dairen, stationed its Far Eastern fleet at Port Arthur, which was ice-free in winter, and built a branch line from there to the Chinese Eastern Railway. The territory was again occupied by Japan in the Russo-Japanese War, and under the 1905 Portsmouth Treaty the railway and leased territories were transferred to Japan. The railway was renamed the South Manchurian Railway. The Japanese established a Kwantung Office (Kantōchō) and stationed forces there, and the territory became a foothold for advances in Manchuria. The lease of the territories was extended from 25 to 99 years under the Twenty-One Demands (*q.v.*), and in 1932 became part of the state of Manchukuo. The territories were among those occupied by Russia at the end of World War II and returned to China.

Asakawa, K. *The Russo-Japanese Conflict* (London, 1904).
Lensen, G. A., ed., *Korea and Manchuria Between Russia and Japan* (Tallahassee, Fla., 1966).

Liberal Democratic Party (Jiyū Minshutō) 自由民主党

In the years after 1945 the conservative wing of the political spectrum, dominated by politicians from the prewar era, formed a succession of conservative parties, starting with the Japan Liberal Party (Nihon Jiyūtō) and the Japan Progressive Party (Nihon Shinpotō) of November 1945. While Yoshida Shigeru, with the support of the Japan Liberal Party, Democratic Liberal Party (Minshu Jiyūtō), the Liberal Party (Jiyūtō), and other conservative elements, retained power for most of the Occupation period, conservative politics remained deeply divided by ideological and personal differences, notably that between Yoshida and Hatoyama. After the end of the Occupation conservative elements opposed to Yoshida worked together to bring him down, and he eventually resigned in December 1954. Pressure from the business world and fear of the real threat now posed by the opposition parties stimulated an amalgamation of conservative forces; the Liberal Party (former Yoshida supporters) and the Japan Democratic Party (Nihon Minshutō) merged in November 1955 to form the new Liberal Democratic Party (Jiyū Minshutō). At the time of its formation the party had 298 members in the lower house and 118 in the upper. Its formation meant that there was no opposition party with a chance of assuming power. With the support of so-called "independent" conservatives the L. D. P. has retained an absolute majority in the Diet since that time, although it has never gained the two-thirds majority necessary for constitutional revision. Its retention of power has been assisted by such factors as the heavy weight given to the rural vote and the support of big business. Despite its apparent unity, however, the L. D. P. has remained little more than a coalition of personal factions, with leadership of the party (and therefore the premiership) remaining the subject of extensive negotiations between factions. Various party leaders have attempted to abolish the factions, but the fact that their own position has rested on factionalism renders these attempts unconvincing and unsuccessful. Though nominally a people's party, much of the party's finance comes from business, and it also has strong bureaucratic connections. The U.S.-Japan Security Treaty, the strengthening of the Self-Defense Force, and a high rate of economic growth accompanied by capital exports have supplied the basic framework within which all L. D. P. policies have been executed. Since the 1960s the problems of pollution, urbanization, energy supply, and inflation have made wholehearted pursuit of the "economic growth first" policy more difficult, but the L. D. P. remains the party of big business intent on economic expansion within a framework of close cooperation with the U.S. and her allies. Party membership in 1978 was 1.5 million. A small group left the L. D. P. in June 1976 to form the New Liberal Club but this conservative group has failed to shake the position of the L. D. P. In the October 1979 election the L. D. P.'s representation in the lower house fell to 248, but this figure rose to 284 in the June 1980 election, when upper house representation also increased.

Fukui, H. *Party in Power* (Canberra, 1970).
Quigley, H. S., and J. E. Turner *The New Japan* (Minneapolis, 1956).
Thayer, N. B. *How the Conservatives Rule Japan* (Princeton, 1969).

Liberal Party. See Jiyūtō; Liberal Democratic Party

Lobanov-Yamagata Agreement. See Yamagata-Lobanov Agreement

Local Assemblies (chihō kaigi) 地方会議

Some village and town councils existed from 1872, but most of their members were chosen either by government or by mutual agreement among local heads. Largely under the stimulus of the popular rights movement, elected prefectural assemblies were created by the government in 1878, elected town and city assemblies in 1880, but their powers were restricted. Property qualifications attended the right to vote and to be elected; the ballot was not secret. The assembly once elected could only discuss matters largely relating to local finances; state-appointed bureaucrats initiated bills, vetoed recommendations, and suspended or dissolved assembly sittings. Although the parties of the popular rights movement did achieve some influence through these prefectural assemblies, they were essentially concessions in form rather than reality. During the early 1880s town councils did have some autonomy, but this was gradually reduced by the centralization of administration. The system of advisory prefectural and city assemblies was retained by the Meiji constitution, and subsequent moves toward assembly autonomy were largely counterbalanced by new central controls. In 1929 assembly powers were extended to include some legislation, but this too was curbed as the war with China developed. Under the extension of local autonomy postwar, prefectural and municipal assemblies have been given considerable powers, but such is the power retained by the local executive branch that these assemblies rarely do more than approve matters already settled by the central government.

Steiner, K. *Local Government in Japan* (Stanford, 1965).

Local Government

From 1871 a comprehensive system of local government areas was established in Japan; this was modified and consolidated up to 1890. After the abolition of the domains (*q.v.*) the country was divided into cities and prefectures. In the early 1870s a system of local officials was established, and in 1875 their titles, authority, and functions were legally defined. Local authorities had a wide range of responsibilities, including the control of police in the area, but the prefectural governor and his staff were subordinate to the Home Ministry (*q.v.*). Prefectural governors were career government administrators who subsequently went on to central government, so increasingly the local bureaucracy became part of a single national bureaucracy. The governor's power was rarely affected by the post-1878 establishment of local assemblies. The system of local government was perfected during the 1880s, under the influence of Yamagata Aritomo, and under the Meiji constitution it remained largely unchanged up to the Pacific War. Local officials were hamstrung by restrictive financial and legal regulations, their prestige was slight compared with that accruing to officials of the national bureaucracy, and the only progress was toward increasing centralization of decision making. The neighborhood associations (*q.v.*) were used during the war for even stricter control and centralization. After 1945 local autonomy was regarded as an integral part of the democratization policies. Immediate modifications in local government included the abolition of the Home Ministry and dispersal of many of its functions to prefectural and city administrations headed by elected governments and mayors. The 1947 Local Autonomy Law consolidated these measures by providing for public election of local government heads and the recall system. Matters dispersed from central to local government included education, and each local unit had its own police and civil service paid for out of local taxes. There were attempts to increase local taxes for this purpose. Some of these units proved to be too small for financial viability and easily controlled by political bosses. This sort of factor, combined with the political inclinations of subsequent Japanese governments, contributed to a growing trend toward centralization since the Occupation.

Braibanti, R. J. D. "Executive Power in Japanese Prefectural Government," *FEQ* 9, no. 3 (May 1950).
Steiner, K. *Local Government in Japan* (Stanford, 1965).

Lockheed Scandal (Rokkiido jiken)
ロッキード事件

In February 1976 it was revealed in the U.S. that the Lockheed Corporation had used bribery to sell its Tristars in Japan. Investigations in Japan resulted in charges of tax evasion and/or corrupt dealings being laid against senior officials of Marubeni, Lockheed's agent in Japan, and of All Nippon Airways; against high government officials including former Prime Minister Tanaka Kakuei and former Transport Minister Hashimoto Tomisaburō and against the right-wing leader Kodama Yoshio. Revelations as to the extent of corruption in the ruling Liberal Democratic Party caused friction within the party, and increasing party dissatisfaction with Prime Minister Miki, who desired to expose the whole scandal, contributed to his resignation in December 1976. Proceedings against Tanaka, Hashimoto, and the Marubeni and A.N.A. officials started in January 1977 and those against Kodama in June 1977 and still continue.

Baerwald, H. H. "Lockheed and Japanese Politics," *Asian Survey* 16, no. 9 (Sept. 1976).
Blaker, M. "Japan 1976: The Year of Lockheed," *Asian Survey* 17, no. 1 (Jan. 1977).
Imazu, H. "Power Mosaic: Hotbed of the Lockheed Case," *JQ* 23, no. 3 (July-Sept. 1976).
Kitazawa, M. "The Lockheed Incident and Japanese Culture," *Japan Interpreter* 11, no. 2 (Autumn 1976).

London Naval Conference
(Rondon kaigun gunshuku kaigi)
ロンドン海軍軍縮会議

January-April 1930 a naval arms limitation conference was held in London. It was attended by Britain, the U.S., Japan, France, and Italy. The leading Japanese delegates were Wakatsuki Reijirō and Navy Minister Takarabe Takeshi. The Japanese hoped for 70% of the British and U.S. level in auxiliary warships, but the final treaty signed on April 21 extended the 5:5:3 ratio on capital ships agreed at the Washington Conference (*q.v.*) to auxiliary ships and extended the stop on the building of capital ships until 1935. Many in the navy considered that this level was an insult to Japan, that it limited Japan's freedom in East Asia and the Pacific and should not be accepted. The Hamaguchi cabinet forced through the ratification in the face of intense opposition from the naval chief of staff, who resigned, and the Privy Council. This increased resentment because many considered that the civilian government was infringing the prerogative of the supreme command to operational decisions, which were regarded as including the level of armaments necessary for Japan's defense. This outcry of the so-called "independence of the supreme command" was a factor in the shooting of Hamaguchi in November 1930. A second conference was opened in London in December 1935, but agreement proved impossible, and Japan withdrew the following month. The expiration of the Washington and London agreements in December 1936 ended attempts at naval arms limitations.

Itō, T. "Conflicts and Coalitions in Japan 1930: Political Groups and the London Naval Disarmament Conference," in S. Groennings, E. W. Kelley, and M. Leiserson, eds., *The Study of Coalition Behavior: Theoretical Perspectives and Cases from Four Continents* (New York, 1970).
Mayer Oakes, T. F., tr. *Fragile Victory, Saionji-Harada Memoirs* (Detroit, 1968).
Pelz, S. E. *Race to Pearl Harbor* (Cambridge, Mass., 1974).

London Naval Treaty. See London Naval Conference

Lytton Commission (Ritton chōsadan) リットン調査団
Following Chinese protests after the Manchurian Incident (*q.v.*), in December 1931 the League of Nations appointed a four-man commission headed by Lord Lytton to investigate the state of affairs in China, Manchuria, and Japan. The survey was carried out during the first half of 1932. Japan established the "independent" state of Manchukuo (*q.v.*) in March and had recognized it before the commission's report was published in October 1932. Although the Lytton report was intended to be conciliatory to Japan, blaming both countries, it rejected Japan's arguments concerning the course of events in Manchuria. It received approval in the West but was condemned by the Japanese, who rejected its proposals for a settlement. The acceptance of the report by the league in February 1933 made the nonrecognition of Manchukuo inevitable outside Japan and brought Japan's withdrawal from the league.

League of Nations. *Report on the Sino-Japanese Dispute* (Geneva, 1932).
Ogata, S. *Defiance in Manchuria* (Berkeley, 1964).
Thorne, C. *The Limits of Foreign Policy* (London, 1972).

M

MacArthur, Douglas 1880–1964
MacArthur was commander in chief of U.S. forces in the Far East during the Pacific War. After Japan's surrender he was appointed Supreme Commander for the Allied Powers (SCAP) and took charge of the Occupation of Japan. Although his decisions and policy execution were made on the orders of the U.S. government, which transmitted allied policy as decided by the Far East Commission (*q.v.*), and MacArthur was advised by the Allied Council for Japan (*q.v.*), in practice he had increasing discretion in policy and wielded tremendous power. He was responsible for executing the radical demilitarization and democratization policies and also influenced the increasing anti-Communist line of policies after 1947. In 1950 MacArthur became commander of the U.N. forces in the Korean War, but disagreement over policy in Korea meant that he was relieved of his command in the Far East in April 1951. (See also Occupation of Japan; SCAP.)

MacArthur, D. *Reminiscences* (London, 1964).
Whitney, C. *MacArthur, His Rendezvous*

with History (New York, 1956).
Willoughby, C. A., and J. Chamberlain, *MacArthur, 1941–1951: Victory in the Pacific* (London, 1956).

Machida Chūji 1863–1946 町田忠治
Native of Akita Prefecture, Machida worked as a bureaucrat and journalist, then as a banker achieved considerable influence in the financial world. He was elected to the Diet 10 times from 1912. Strong connections with Ōkuma and Inukai led him to join the Dōshikai, Kenseikai, and Minseitō. He was agriculture and forestry minister 1926–1927 and 1929–1931, minister of commerce and industry 1934–1936, and finance minister in 1936. Machida succeeded Wakatsuki as president of the Minseitō in 1935 and retained this post until the party's dissolution in 1940. He continued to exercise considerable influence outside the Diet even after this and was minister of state 1944–1945. Postwar he founded the Japan Progressive Party but was purged and died soon afterwards.

Berger, G. M. *Parties Out of Power in Japan, 1931–1941* (Princeton, 1977).

Maebara Issei 1834–1876 前原一誠
A samurai from Chōshū, Maebara studied under Yoshida Shōin. He was close to Takasugi Shinsaku and acted as leader of one of Chōshū's auxiliary units (*shotai*). A leading figure in the anti-Bakufu movement (*q.v.*), Maebara fought in the Boshin War (*q.v.*) and gained high office in the new government after the Restoration. Disagreements with Ōkubo and Kido led to his resignation in 1870, and he returned to Hagi. In October 1876 he launched a revolt of discontented samurai, which was aimed to coincide with uprisings at Kumamoto and Akizuki in Kyūshū. This uprising, known as the Hagi rebellion, was quickly quelled by forces from Hiroshima commanded by Miura Gorō. Maebara tried to escape to Shimane but was arrested and sentenced to death.

Craig, A. *Chōshū in the Meiji Restoration* (Cambridge, Mass., 1961).

Maejima Hisoka 1835–1919 (Baron, 1902) 前島密
Member of samurai family of Takada (now Niigata Prefecture), Maejima traveled widely throughout Japan in his youth, studied Western and traditional learning, then became a Bakufu retainer in 1866. He joined the new government in 1870 and, after a trip to England, in 1871 was appointed head of the Communications Bureau, where he was responsible for founding a modern postal and postal savings system and for promoting communications in general. He rose to become deputy home minister but resigned in the 1881 political crisis (*q.v.*), returning to office only 1888–1891 as deputy communications minister. In 1882–1884 he was among the leadership of the Kaishintō and 1886–1890 was president of Tokyo College (later Waseda University). Maejima had wide business interests, especially in railways, and participated in various educational and charitable activities. From the 1860s he advocated the abolition of characters in favor of *kana* and retained a deep interest in the language problem the rest of his life.

Hunter, J. "A Study of the Career of Maejima Hisoka, 1835–1919," D.Phil. diss., Oxford University, 1976.

Makino Nobuaki 1861–1949 (Baron, 1907; Viscount, 1920; Count 1925) 牧野伸顕
Native of Satsuma, second son of Ōkubo Toshimichi, and father-in-law of Yoshida Shigeru, Makino studied in the U.S. 1871–1878 and in 1880 joined the Foreign Ministry. He worked in London and was also ambassador to Italy and Austria before acting as education minister 1906–1908. He was then privy councillor 1909–1911, education minister and agriculture and commerce minister 1911–1912, and foreign minister 1913–1914. In 1914 Makino was appointed to the House of Peers and rejoined the Privy Council. He

sat on the Advisory Council on Foreign Relations (*q.v.*) from 1917 and was also a delegate to the Paris Peace Conference. As imperial household minister 1921–1925 and Lord Privy Seal 1925–1935 Makino played a key "elder statesman" role; he was closely identified with the Satsuma faction and with Saionji and regarded as pro-British and pro-American. He was fortunate to escape with his life in the February 26 rising in 1936 (*q.v.*) and thereafter retired from politics.

Manchōhō. See YOROZU CHŌHŌ

Manchukuo (Manchoukuo) (Manshū-koku) 満州国

Manchukuo was the name given to the Japanese puppet state established in Manchuria in March 1932 after the Manchurian Incident (*q.v.*). With the addition of Jehol Province in 1933 Manchukuo consisted of four provinces with a population of about 30 million and its capital at Changchun. The country was headed by a chief executive presiding over a state council and advised by a privy council; these bodies included Japanese. The country was headed by Pu Yi, the last emperor of China, who in March 1934 was made emperor of Manchukuo. Japan formally recognized Manchukuo in September 1932, simultaneously concluding the Japan-Manchukuo Protocol (*q.v.*), but following acceptance of the Lytton Commission's report (*q.v.*) by the League of Nations, only Germany, Italy, and one or two other countries awarded it recognition. There was no elected assembly, and real power was wielded by Japanese in key posts in the administration under the ultimate guidance of the commander of the Kwantung Army (*q.v.*). Political associations were forbidden with the exception of the official Hsieh Ho Hui (Concordia Association), which acted as a government propaganda organ. Manchukuo was a major source of industrial raw materials for Japan. Economic development, in which a crucial role was played by the South Manchurian Railway Company (*q.v.*), concentrated on large-scale mining and heavy manufacturing superimposed on a primitive agriculture. Manchukuo's development as an extension of Japan's own industrial economy was strictly controlled, especially after the Five-Year Plan of 1936. Under pressure of war, Japan attempted to speed up the development of heavy (military) industries and communications by the formation of the Manchukuo Heavy Industries Development Corporation in October 1937. This corporation, funded half by Nissan (*q.v.*) and half by the Manchukuo government, was to take over all industrial matters from the South Manchurian Railway Company and coordinate their development, but the results were not as successful as had been hoped. Progress was hindered by the war in China, and there was insufficient capital for the required development. Japan's economic and political policies in Manchukuo led to increasing discontent from residents faced with labor conscription, heavy taxes, low wages, enforced purchase of land for Japanese immigrants, and subsequent inflation. On the Japanese side, emigration to Manchuria failed to reach hoped-for levels. After 1937 anti-Japanese guerrilla activities increased, often under the guidance of the local Communists. In August 1945 Manchukuo was occupied by Russian troops. The state was disbanded, the area returned to China, and Japanese repatriated.

Jones, F. C. *Manchuria Since 1931* (New York, 1949).
Kawakami, K. K. *Manchukuo, Child of Conflict* (New York, 1933).
Myers, R. H. "The Japanese Economic Development of Manchuria 1932–1945," Ph.D. diss., University of Washington, 1959.
Schumpeter, E. B., ed. *The Industrialization of Japan and Manchukuo, 1930–1940* (New York, 1940).

Manchuria (Manshū) 満州

From the 1870s Japan purchased Manchuria's staple products such as soya beans. Trade grew especially rapidly from 1889, but Japan exported little in return to

Map 2. Japan and Northeast Asia, 1936

Manchuria. The area was the scene of much of the fighting in the Sino-Japanese War, and in the peace settlement Japan attempted to acquire rights and interests there; the most major of these, the cession of the Liaotung Peninsula, was blocked by the Triple Intervention (*q.v.*). Japan nevertheless became increasingly aware of the importance of Manchuria as a source of agricultural products and industrial raw materials and took steps to open it to Japanese commerce. After leasing the Liaotung area in 1898, Russia occupied much of Manchuria following the Boxer Rebellion (*q.v.*). Japan feared that a permanent Russian occupation of Manchuria would threaten her position in Korea and also block her route into China, let alone prevent expansion of Japan's own interests in Manchuria. It was the Russian failure to withdraw her troops against the background of a more widespread conflict of interests in northeast Asia which ultimately led to the Russo-Japanese War, which was again mostly fought on Manchurian territory. Under the Portsmouth Treaty Japan took over the Russian lease of southern Liaotung and the South Manchurian Railway, which was subsequently administered by the South Manchurian Railway Company (*q.v.*). From August 1906 this area was under the control of the governor general of Kwantung Province, normally the commander of the Kwantung Army (*q.v.*). The other powers acquiesced in Japan's privileges, and her economic and political interests expanded fast even outside the Liaotung Peninsula. Extra privileges were secured under the Twenty-One Demands (*q.v.*), and successive Japanese governments worked toward Japanese political and economic domination of the area. Japanese argued that control in Manchuria was necessary for the security of Japan in case of a Russian attack and also for China's own security. Economically, Manchuria was seen as a source of valuable industrial raw materials and as an emigration destination for Japan's growing population. The course of the Chinese revolution in the 1920s was potentially damaging to Japan's influence in Manchuria. The threat of China's unification under Chiang Kai-shek led members of the politicized Kwantung Army, objecting to what they considered an excessively conciliatory government policy toward China, to assassinate Chang Tso-lin, the Manchurian warlord (*q.v.*), in 1928. The continuing resistance to Japanese influence and control eventually led to the Manchurian Incident of 1931 (*q.v.*), followed by the establishment of Manchukuo (*q.v.*) in 1932.

Bix, H. P. "Japanese Imperialism in Manchuria, 1890–1931," Ph.D. diss., Harvard University, 1972.

McCormack, G. *Chang Tso-lin in Northeast China, 1911–1928: Japan and the Manchurian Idea* (Stanford, 1977).

Spinks, C. N. "The Origin of Japanese Interests in Manchuria," *FEQ* 2, no. 3 (May 1943).

Sun, K. C. *The Economic Development of Manchuria in the First Half of the Twentieth Century* (Cambridge, Mass., 1969).

Young, C. W. *Japan's Special Position in Manchuria* (rprt. New York, 1971).

Manchurian Incident (Manshū jihen) 満州事変

After the murder of Chang Tso-lin (*q.v.*) in 1928, his son, Chang Hsüeh-liang, increasingly opposed Japanese influence in Manchuria, and there was a strong move among members of the Kwantung Army (*q.v.*) to initiate an "incident" and occupy Manchuria. A plot was engineered by a group led by Lieutenant-Colonel Ishiwara Kanji, Colonel Itagaki Seishirō, and Colonel Doihara Kenji. Despite attempts by the authorities in Tokyo to halt it, this was implemented on the night of 18 September 1931. An explosion occurred on the South Manchurian railway line just outside Mukden. Claiming that it was caused by Chinese troops and that they were acting in self-defense, Kwantung Army forces occupied Mukden. Reinforcements were sent from Korea without government permission, and within four days Changchun and Kirin had been occupied as well. The government in Tokyo was powerless to stop the fighting and, faced with a fait accompli, announced that its policy was nonexpansion of the conflict. However, government instructions were largely ignored by field officers on the grounds of operational necessity, and at each advance the government was increasingly forced to act as an apologist for the military's acts. By early 1932 almost the whole of the three provinces of eastern Manchuria had been occupied with the backing of the War Ministry and General Staff in Tokyo. In February 1932 the puppet "independent" state of Manchukuo (*q.v.*) was established. China appealed to the League of Nations, and Japan's failure to withdraw her troops led to the establishment of the Lytton Commission (*q.v.*) and Japan's subsequent withdrawal from the league. Early in 1933 the Japanese also occupied Jehol Province. Japan continued to make small advances and clashed frequently with Chinese troops up until the outbreak of full-scale war in 1937.

Ogata, S. *Defiance in Manchuria: The Making of Japanese Foreign Policy, 1931–1932* (Berkeley, 1964).
Storry, R. "The Mukden Incident of September 18–19, 1931," *St. Antony's Papers* 2, *Far Eastern Affairs* 1 (London, 1957).
Yoshihashi, T. *Conspiracy at Mukden* (New Haven, 1963).

Manchurian Railway. See SOUTH MANCHURIAN RAILWAY COMPANY

Mandated Territories (inin tōchi ryōdo) 委任統治領土
After her declaration of war on Germany in October 1914, Japan occupied the German-owned islands in the Pacific north of the equator, the Carolines, Marianas, and Marshalls. After the war the League of Nations awarded her the islands under a "C" category mandate, which meant they could be administered as an integral part of the domain of the country granted the mandate but could not be fortified or used for military purposes of any kind. The islands came under Japanese civil administration in 1922. An increasing number of Japanese moved to the islands, which were developed as a source of copra, phosphates, and sugar, and by 1933 there were over 32,000 Japanese as well as 50,000 indigenous inhabitants. Japan retained the islands after withdrawing from the League of Nations in 1933. They held a strategic position in the western Pacific and were developed for naval purposes. Since 1945 the islands have been controlled by the U.S. as U.N. trust territories.

Clyde, P. H. *Japan's Pacific Mandate* (New York, 1935).
Purcell, D. C. "Japanese Expansion in the South Pacific 1890–1935," Ph.D. diss., University of Pennsylvania, 1967.
Yanaihara, T. *Pacific Islands Under Japanese Mandate* (London, 1940).

March 15 Arrests. See JAPAN COMMUNIST PARTY

March First Movement. See KOREAN INDEPENDENCE MOVEMENT

March Incident (Sangatsu jiken) 3月事件
Hashimoto Kingorō and other members of the Sakurakai (*q.v.*) planned a coup d'état for 20 March 1931 with the support of members of the civilian right wing including Ōkawa Shūmei. Several senior army officers were privy to the plot, including Koiso Kuniaki. The intention was that civilian mobs armed by the conspirators would provoke rioting, surround the Diet, and carry out bomb attacks on party offices and the prime minister's residence. Under the guise of "protection" the army would then declare martial law, force the government to resign, and establish a military government under War Minister Ugaki Kazushige which could carry out major domestic reforms. The plan was called off due to disagreements between the conspirators and the reluctance of Ugaki to see it through, but it was not openly revealed until after the war, and even at the highest

levels it was known to many only a few months later. None of the participants was punished, and the same group was involved in planning the October incident (*q.v.*).

Crowley, J. B. *Japan's Quest for Autonomy* (Princeton, 1966).
Storry, R. *The Double Patriots* (London, 1957).

Marco Polo Bridge Incident (Rokōkyō jiken) 蘆溝橋事件
From 1935 Japanese and Chinese troops in China conflicted several times on a small scale, and on 7 July 1937 Japanese troops conducting night maneuvers at Marco Polo Bridge, near Peking, clashed with the Chinese garrison in the area. A cease-fire was arranged, and the Japanese government announced its intention of reaching a local settlement of the dispute, but the Chinese, reacting more strongly than in any previous incident, moved troops to the area. On July 11 the Japanese cabinet approved mobilization of troops in Japan. Delay in implementing a local agreement led the two governments to pursue their conflicting policies, and fighting continued, more seriously from July 27. The outbreak of hostilities in Shanghai led to full-scale war lasting until 1945.

Chinese Delegation to the League of Nations. *Japanese Aggression and the League of Nations 1937* (Geneva, 1937).
Crowley, J. B. *Japan's Quest for Autonomy* (Princeton 1966).
______"A Reconsideration of the Marco Polo Bridge Incident," *JAS* 22, no. 3 (May 1963).

Maria Luz Incident (Maria Rusugō jiken) マリア・ルス号事件
In July 1872 a Peruvian ship, the *Maria Luz*, carrying some 230 Chinese coolies, put into Yokohama due to bad weather. The escape of some of the coolies to an English warship aroused suspicions of maltreatment, and at the suggestion of the British the Japanese investigated the matter. A provisional court was set up under Ōe Taku, governor of Kanagawa Prefecture; the court impounded the ship, ruled that the captain had subjected his alleged "passengers" to cruel treatment and that the coolies were free to return to China if they so wished. As Japan had no treaty relations with Peru, which since 1870 had been represented by the U.S. in dealings with Japan, strong objections were raised by Peru, which demanded compensation and an apology. Subsequent arbitration by Russia upheld Japan's decision, and in 1873 diplomatic relations were established with Peru.

Gardener, C. H. *The Japanese and Peru, 1873–1973* (Albuquerque, 1975).
Stewart, W. *Chinese Bondage in Peru: A History of the Chinese Coolie in Peru, 1849–1874* (Durham, N.C., 1951).

Marianas. See MANDATED TERRITORIES

Marshalls. See MANDATED TERRITORIES

Martial Law (kaigenrei) 戒厳令
Under the Meiji constitution the declaration of martial law was the prerogative of the emperor. Apart from army control in certain cities at times of war, on three occasions full martial law was declared to cope with domestic crises: in 1905 after the Hibiya riots (*q.v.*), in 1923 after the Kantō earthquake (*q.v.*), and in 1936 after the February 26 rising (*q.v.*). The postwar constitution has no provision for martial law although there is provision for a state of emergency.

Masuda Takashi 1848–1938 (Baron, 1918) 益田孝
A samurai from Sado Island, Niigata Prefecture, Masuda studied in the West and after the Restoration joined the Finance Ministry. He resigned in 1873 to engage in private business and after 1874 worked for Mitsui (*q.v.*). As president of

Mitsui Trading from its founding until his retirement in 1892, Masuda initially concentrated on the development of foreign trading interests and then turned to the development of industrial interests, commercial training, and agricultural education. After leaving Mitsui in 1913, he devoted his time to sponsoring farming and fruit growing. He was also known as an art collector and tea ceremony expert.

Hirschmeier, J. *The Origins of Entrepreneurship in Meiji Japan* (Cambridge, Mass., 1964).

Matsuda Masahisa 1845–1914 (Baron, 1914) 松田正久
Samurai from Hizen, Matsuda was sent by the army to study in France but after his return worked for the *Tōyō Jiyū Shinbun* (Oriental Liberal Paper) 1881–1882. He was active in the popular rights movement through the 1870s and was elected to the Diet for the Jiyūtō in 1890. He became finance minister in 1898. After the formation of the Seiyūkai in 1900, Matsuda led its influential Kyūshū faction and especially under the presidency of Saionji was, with Hara Kei, the most powerful figure in the party. As education minister 1900—1901, president of the Diet in 1904, finance minister in 1908, and justice minister 1906–1908, 1911–1912, and 1913, he wielded tremendous influence. He remained a symbol of the early popular rights movement and was far more popular than Hara, but his death in 1914 permitted Hara to take over the Seiyūkai presidency.

Najita, T. *Hara Kei in the Politics of Compromise* (Cambridge, Mass., 1967).

Matsukata Masayoshi 1835–1924 (Count, 1884; Marquis, 1907; Prince, 1922) 松方正義
Satsuma samurai, Matsukata's involvement with *han* politics and the anti-Bakufu movement (*q.v.*) brought him into early contact with Westerners. He was close to Ōkubo Toshimichi and after the Restoration was governor of Nagasaki before joining the central bureaucracy. Working in the Finance and Home ministries he played a leading role in the commutation of stipends, land tax reform, and the encouragement of industry and after Ōkubo's death became the leader of the Satsuma faction in government. After the 1881 political crisis (*q.v.*) he became state councillor and finance minister, retaining the latter post after the institution of the cabinet system in 1885. Matsukata enforced government retrenchment, instituting a wide-ranging deflationary policy named after him, which was so successful that by 1885 the rampant inflation was well under control. With the exception of 1892–1896 and 1898 Matsukata retained the post of finance minister until 1900, serving altogether 15 years in this capacity. He was also home minister 1888–1889. As finance minister Matsukata was the architect of Japan's modern financial system, establishing a banking system with a central bank with sole right of note issue, a convertible currency, and a regularized budget, accounting, and tax system. By 1900 he had put Japan on the gold standard and achieved financial stability. Matsukata also served as prime minister 1891–1892 and 1896–1897. His first "bureaucratic" cabinet conflicted with the Diet, which it then dissolved. Home Minister Shinagawa Yajirō's interference in the ensuing election aroused criticism, which ultimately forced the cabinet's resignation. Matsukata's second cabinet was initially established with Shinpotō support, but an increase in the land tax and restrictions on freedom of speech contributed to a complete loss of support, so Matsukata dissolved the Diet and simultaneously resigned. He was regarded as a *genrō* from 1900, was a privy councillor 1903–1917 and Lord Privy Seal 1917–1922, but his political influence declined after the end of the Meiji period.

Morris, J. *Makers of Japan* (London, 1906).

Matsukawa Incident. See SHIMOYAMA INCIDENT

Matsuoka Komakichi 1888–1958
松岡駒吉

Born of a peasant family in Tottori, Matsuoka worked in industry and in 1914 joined the Yūaikai (*q.v.*). In 1917 he formed its Osaka federation and the following year became one of the Yūaikai's leaders. He remained active in the later Sōdōmei, becoming the head of its Kantō federation in 1925, and was Sōdōmei president 1932–1940. Matsuoka tried hard to extend the influence of labor union organizations by union recognition, collective bargaining, and strike funding. The dominant figure on Sōdōmei's right wing, he was strongly anti-Communist. As a leading member of the "sociodemocratic" group he played a leading role in the proletarian political parties, the Shakai Minshūtō and Shakai Taishūtō. Postwar Matsuoka worked successfully to revive organized labor and was active in the Japan Socialist Party. He was elected to the Diet six times after 1946 and was the Diet's first Socialist president. His influence in the labor movement declined after he turned his attention to politics, but he remained active in labor organization.

Totten, G. O. *The Social Democratic Movement in Prewar Japan* (New Haven, 1966).

Matsuoka Yōsuke 1880–1946
松岡洋右

A native of Yamaguchi Prefecture, Matsuoka worked his way through school in America and graduated from Oregon University. Returning to Japan he worked as a diplomat 1904–1921; during this time he developed close connections with the Seiyūkai, businessmen, and leading members of the army and navy. In 1921–1926 he was a director of the South Manchurian Railway (*q.v.*) and then its vice-president 1927–1929. In 1930 he entered the Diet as a Seiyūkai member, where he was a strong opponent of Shidehara's China policy. As Japan's delegate to the League of Nations in 1933 his walkout over acceptance of the Lytton Commission report (*q.v.*) was followed by Japan's withdrawal from the league. Matsuoka left the Seiyūkai in December 1933, advocating the abolition of all political parties. In 1935–1938 he was president of the South Manchurian Railway Company and also cabinet adviser 1937–1940. As foreign minister 1940–1941 Matsuoka took a strong pro-Axis stance, committing Japan to alliance with Germany and Italy and the neutrality pact with Soviet Russia. After the initiation of Russo-German hostilities he advocated war with Russia and also opposed further negotiations with the U.S. Matsuoka alienated his colleagues by his attitudes and ambition, and the Konoe cabinet resigned to enable Konoe to form a second cabinet without Matsuoka. Illness led Matsuoka to retire from politics, and although he was arrested postwar as a class "A" war criminal, he died before any verdict was reached.

Huizenga, J. "Yōsuke Matsuoka and the Japanese-German Alliance," in G. A. Craig and F. Gilbert, eds., *The Diplomats, 1919–1939* (Princeton, 1953).
Lu, D. J. *From the Marco Polo Bridge to Pearl Harbor* (Washington, 1961).
Teters, B. "Matsuoka Yōsuke: The Diplomacy of Bluff and Gesture," in R. D. Burns and E. M. Bennett, eds., *Diplomats in Crisis: United States-Chinese-Japanese Relations, 1919–1941* (Santa Barbara, 1974).

May 15 Incident (go-ichi-go jiken)
5・15事件

From 1930 there were growing calls from a group of junior naval officers for national renovation by direct action. They procured financial and other help from Ōkawa Shūmei and promises of participation from army cadets. In concerted action on 15 May 1932 one group shot Prime Minister Inukai Tsuyoshi; others attacked the residence of Lord Privy Seal Makino Nobuaki, Seiyūkai headquarters, and other buildings including the Mitsubishi Bank. *Nōhonshugi (q.v.)* supporters of Tachibana Kōzaburō, mobilized through the group's strong connections with agrarian nationalists, attempted unsuccessfully to put suburban power stations out of action. The rebels hoped that in the resulting confusion martial law could be declared. They called on the people to rise in the bringing about of a Shōwa Restoration (*q.v.*), but their ideas contained few concrete proposals. The army failed to rise in sympathy although most regarded the rebels as patriots and all participants in the attempted coup were eventually arrested. There was a public court-martial, but most of the rebels received light sentences. This attempted coup and Inukai's death marked the demise of party cabinets.

Shillony, B-A. *Revolt in Japan* (Princeton, 1973).
Storry, R. *The Double Patriots* (London, 1957).

May 4 Movement. See ANTI-JAPANESE MOVEMENT (CHINA)

May Day

Mass celebration of May Day first took place in Japan in Tokyo in 1920 and was attended by over 1,000 people. Celebrations continued every year until 1935 although participation varied according to the strength of the labor movement. Celebrations were normally under police surveillance, and arrests were frequent, as well as clashes between different sections of the labor movement. May Day celebrations were banned after the February 26 rising in 1936. From 1946 May Day was revived as an annual celebration for workers, although at times different political groups have sponsored different parades. In 1952 opposition to the new peace treaty, security treaty and resentment at the ban on use of the square in front of the imperial palace—the traditional site for May Day celebrations—led to violent clashes between demonstrators and police, who used tear gas and pistols. Two demonstrators were killed, many others wounded, and hundreds arrested.

Meiji Constitution (Meiji kenpō)
明治憲法
(Dainihon teikoku kenpō)
大日本帝国憲法

Calls for a constitution in Japan began in the 1870s. Spurred on by the need for international prestige and also by popular agitation, in 1881 the government announced that both a constitution and an elected assembly would operate from 1890. During the early 1880s Itō Hirobumi studied other government systems in Europe. Also taking into account the views of his government colleagues, he subsequently drafted a Japanese constitution with the aid of Inoue Kowashi, Itō Miyoji, and Kaneko Kentarō, advised by Hermann Roesler and Albert Mosse. Prior to implementation, a peerage, cabinet system, and privy council were established. The Privy Council approved the final constitutional draft in 1888. The constitution, properly the Imperial Japanese Constitution, but known as the Meiji constitution, was promulgated in February 1889 and became operative in November 1890. Iwakura Tomomi had earlier pressed for an "emperor-given" constitution, and that of 1889 was stated as having been granted by the emperor. The influence of the Prussian monarchical model was clear. Only the emperor could initiate amendments to the constitution. Its basic premise was the inviolable sovereignty of the emperor, who controlled supreme political power. The cabinet and two-house Diet could operate independently of each other; the cabinet was appointed by the emperor and was responsible to him. The emperor had legislative superiority over the Diet and many legislative methods, such as emergency imperial decrees, were reserved to him; he also had the sole right to some executive powers, such as that to conclude treaties. The army and navy were directly responsible only to the emperor, outside the control of the cabinet and Diet. Nonresponsible bodies, such as the Privy Council and the House of Peers, also had special powers. The Diet had only limited financial control over emperor and government and proved exceptionally weak under the Meiji constitution. In addition, although the rights and duties of the people were clearly laid down, they could be limited by law. The Meiji constitution is regarded as having provided the legal basis for the "emperor system" (*q.v.*) by establishing the framework within which nonparliamentary elites such as the bureaucracy and armed forces could legally dominate national politics. Many of its provisions were suspended after the war, and it was replaced by a new constitution in 1947. The motivations of the drafters of the constitution are shown in Itō Hirobumi's commentaries of 1889.

Akita, G. *The Foundations of Constitutional Government in Modern Japan* (Cambridge, Mass., 1967).
______. "The Meiji Constitution in Practice: The First Diet," *JAS* 22, no. 1 (Nov. 1962).
Beckmann, G. M. *The Making of the Meiji Constitution: The Oligarchs and the Constitutional Development of Japan, 1868–1891* (Lawrence, Kans., 1957).
Pittau, J. *Political Thought in Early Meiji Japan, 1868–1889* (Cambridge, Mass., 1967).
Siemes, J. *Hermann Roesler and the Making of the Meiji State* (Tokyo, 1968).
Uyehara, G. E. *The Political Development of Japan, 1867–1909* (London, 1910).

Meiji Emperor (Meiji tennō)
1852–1912 明治天皇

Mutsuhito, the 122nd emperor, succeeded his father Kōmei in February 1867. From 1868 his reign was designated "Meiji" (enlightened rule), and he is normally referred to by this name. The Meiji Restoration of that year returned formal responsibility for administration to the emperor, establishing him as the holder of sovereign power, commander of the armed forces, and center of national morality. During Mutsuhito's long reign Japan progressed from a semifeudal, agrarian state to a rapidly industrializing, imperialist power; and although real power was largely held by government officials working in his name, there is no doubt that the Meiji emperor was a strong-minded man and wielded considerable personal influence.

Griffis, W. E. *The Mikado: Institution and Person* (Princeton, 1915).
Morris, J. *Makers of Japan* (London, 1906).

Meiji Restoration (Meiji ishin)
明治維新

Following a palace coup on 3 January 1868, a group of anti-Tokugawa court nobles led by Iwakura Tomomi and samurai from *han* such as Satsuma and Tosa (later joined by Chōshū) declared the shōgunate to be abolished, its lands confiscated, and the responsibility for the administration of the country to have been formally returned to the emperor. The coup was followed by a brief civil war (the Boshin War) (*q.v.*), but by spring 1869 complete national unity under the emperor had been achieved. The young emperor adopted the reign name of Meiji (enlightened rule), and this change is the essence of what in English is known as the Meiji Restoration (the Japanese term is *renovation* [*ishin*] rather than restoration). Nevertheless, the Restoration was in many ways only the pivotal point in a process of historical change lasting several decades, for the events of 1868 marked both a fundamental transfer of political power and the inception of a wide-reaching program of modernization which was carried out by the new leaders. For some historians the process of change which culminated in the Restoration begins as early as the 1830s, when the internal strains which were later compounded by external pressures to contribute to the downfall of the shōgunate first became widely apparent. The 1868 coup followed an apogee in political opposition to the Bakufu 1864-1867. Following the Restoration, the immediate changes which it engendered continued into the 20th century. These changes, normally summed up by the slogans *bunmei kaika* (civilization and enlightenment) and *fukoku kyōhei* (rich country and strong army) radically changed all aspects of the country's politics, economy and society. This forceful change of power and the fundamental changes which followed lead many historians to talk of the Meiji Revolution. Potential difficulties in historical interpretation of the Restoration have always been posed by the inherent contrast between the idea of return to the past, summed up by the phrase *ōsei fukko* (restoration of imperial rule as in ancient times) and that of renovation (*ishin*) and reform to strengthen Japan against the foreign threat; more recently, interpretation of the event has become the object of far deeper historical controversy. During the Meiji period historians viewed the event as a straightforward restoration of imperial rule in political and ideological terms, logically followed by a program of reform, and there is no doubt that the imperial institution was used as an ideological basis for change. Students of the Restoration became increasingly interested in economic causation, and then from the 1920s historians increasingly tried to fit the Restoration within the framework of Marxist historiography. For the first time historians became openly critical of the Restoration and the "absolutist" society which had resulted from it. Even among Marxists, though, there was no agreed interpretation, and assessment of whether or not the Restoration was a bourgeois revolution became a crucial factor in the so-called Japanese capitalism debate (*q.v.*). A materialist interpretation of modern Japanese history is still widespread among Japanese historians, but many Western historians of Japan tend to deny that the Meiji Restoration can be usefully interpreted within the concepts of materialist historiography. Arguing that the leadership for change came from within the ruling samurai class, but from men with differing backgrounds and motivations, something of a consensus has been reached as to the Restoration's being brought about by a combination of nationalist fears aroused by the foreign threat, political strife among the ruling class, and pressures released by social and economic change.

Akamatsu, P. *Meiji 1868* (London, 1972).
Beasley, W. G. *The Meiji Restoration* (London, 1973).
Norman, E. H. *Japan's Emergence as a Modern State* (New York, 1940).

Meirokusha 明六社
A society of Japanese scholars of the West founded at the instigation of Mori Arinori in 1874. There were 10 founding members, most of whom were formerly connected to the Bakufu, including Nishimura Shigeki, Tsuda Mamichi, Nishi Amane, Nakamura Masanao, Katō Hiroyuki, Fukuzawa Yukichi, and Mitsukuri Rinshō. Membership was later expanded. The society met twice a month to discuss aspects of society, politics, economics, natural science, religion, and morality and also aimed to disseminate members' views more widely. March 1874 – November 1875 it published a journal, the *Meiroku Zasshi* (Meiji Six Journal), with articles mostly by members. The society not only brought together many of the enlightened minds of the period but played a major role in disseminating and promoting new ideas. Although the Meirokusha was politically relatively conservative, the journal ceased publication after the Libel Laws and Newspaper Regulations of 1875 since members considered that some political comment was unavoidable. The society ceased to play a major role as an agent of enlightenment, though formally existing until 1910. Its tradition was formalized in the Tokyo (later Imperial) Academy of 1879.

Braisted, R., tr. and ed., *Meiroku Zasshi* (Cambridge, Mass., 1976).
Huish, D. J. "The Meirokusha: Some Grounds for Reassessment," *Harvard Journal of Asiatic Studies* 32 (1972).

Merchant Shipping
Although the construction of ocean-going ships was banned in the Tokugawa period, small-scale coastal shipping was widespread, and this remained important after the Restoration when operators gradually changed to Western-style ships.

The new government initially attempted to run its own shipping company with ships taken over from the Bakufu and *han* in an attempt to break into the Western monopoly of the carriage of goods, but from 1874 its policy was to promote the development of a Japanese merchant marine by sponsoring the Mitsubishi Company (*q.v.*). So successful was this that before long Mitsubishi was dominating both coastal and ocean routes. Rival companies were established, notably the Kyōdō Unyū, whose cut-throat competition with Mitsubishi ended in a government-promoted merger in 1885. The resulting company was known as Nippon Yūsen Kaisha (N.Y.K.) (Japan Shipping Company), and it continued to dominate the industry even after the disappearance of any government involvement in the field. Other competitors did appear, but up to the 1930s N.Y.K. ranked as one of the largest shipping companies in the world. A brief slump in merchant shipping following the Sino-Japanese War was halted by subsidy legislation in 1896. Expansion of trade and increase in Japanese rights and interests abroad led to further expansion, and by 1913 Japanese ships carried 50% of Japan's exports and imports and operated on ocean routes throughout the world. In 1914–1918 the tonnage of steamships and motor vessels doubled due to foreign demand for carrying trade, but this boom was followed by an acute postwar slump, from which recovery was slow. Expansion in merchant shipping accompanied the trade expansion, which Japan achieved in the 1930s despite restrictive trading practices. From 1937 the industry was requested to regulate itself in response to the worsening international situation, and full state supervision was subsequently introduced, with a central regulating authority from 1941. Much of the merchant fleet was requisitioned for military purposes during the war, and the destruction was such that carrying capacity was only one-tenth of its prewar level in 1945, and some of the remaining ships were damaged or obsolescent. Replacement of shipping capacity was slow after the war, but in 1950 all ships were returned to private ownership. The Korean War and a ship-building boom helped rapid expansion thereafter. In 1978 24.5% of Japan's exports was carried in Japanese ships and 44.4% of imports.

Furuta, R. and Y. Hirai (tr. D. MacFarlane) *Short History of Japanese Merchant Shipping* (Tokyo, 1967).

Wray, W. D. "Mitsubishi and the N.Y.K. Line: The Beginnings of the Modern Japanese Merchant Shipping Industry," Ph.D. diss., Harvard University, 1977.

Miki Kiyoshi 1897–1945 三木清

Native of Hyōgo Prefecture, Miki studied philosophy at Kyoto University and in Europe 1922–1925. From 1927 he was professor at Hōsei University. He worked closely with the historian Hani Gorō, and a deep involvement with Marxist philosophy led in 1930 to his being arrested and held for six months as a Communist sympathizer. Miki's work during the 1930s concentrating on the philosophy of history made him a major influence on philosophical thought in modern Japan. He was a member of Konoe's Shōwa Kenkyūkai (*q.v.*) and in 1942 was sent to Manila as an army journalist, but his lack of enthusiasm for the war led him to return to philosophy. In March 1945 he was again arrested and died in prison in September. Miki left numerous works on various aspects of philosophy.

Kim, Y. M. "Miki Kiyoshi: A Representative Thinker of His Times," Ph.D. diss., University of California, Berkeley, 1974.

Piovesana, G. K. "Miki Kiyoshi: Representative Thinker of an Anguished Generation," in J. Roggendorf, ed., *Studies in Japanese Culture* (Tokyo, 1963).

Miki Takeo 1907– 三木武夫

Native of Tokushima Prefecture, Miki was educated at Meiji University and in the U.S. In 1937 he was elected to the Diet as its youngest member and has remained a member ever since. As chief secretary of the Kokumin Kyōdōtō (National Cooperative Party) he was communications minister 1947–1948 and was then in the Kokumin Minshutō (National Democratic Party) and the Kaishintō before becoming secretary of the Liberal Democratic Party in 1956. In 1958 he became a minister of state and head of the Economic Planning Agency under Kishi, but his opposition to the Police Duties Law and disagreement over revision of the security treaty led to his resignation in 1959. In the early 1960s Miki held important posts within the party, and although he was not regarded as belonging to the "mainstream" bureaucratic faction of the party, he served as international trade and industry minister 1965–1966 and foreign minister 1966–1968. In both 1968 and 1970 he was defeated by Satō in the election for party president and again by Tanaka in 1972, but he was deputy prime minister 1972–1974. After Tanaka's resignation in December 1974, Miki did become prime minister. His party base was weak, and his election was to avoid a major split between Ōhira and Fukuda within the party. Miki's "clean government" ticket rendered him initially very popular, but his plans to reform antimonopoly legislation failed because of business opposition; he alienated party members by proposing new political funding laws and the right wing by his Korean policy. His attempts to purge the party after the Lockheed (*q.v.*) revelations provoked even more hostility, but although Miki had lost all support within the party, he battled on, supported by public opinion, until eventually resigning in December 1976.

Arima, S. "The Emergence of Prime Minister Miki Takeo," *JQ* 22, no. 2 (Apr.-June 1975).

Johnson, C. "Japan 1975: Mr. Clean Muddles Through," *Asian Survey* 16, no. 1 (Jan. 1976).

Militarism. See MILITARY CLIQUE; ARMY

Military Academy Incident. See NOVEMBER INCIDENT

Military Clique (gunbatsu) 軍閥

From the early Meiji period men from Satsuma and Chōshū domains dominated the army and navy as well as the civilian government, and military objectives were always of the greatest importance. From the 1890s victories over China and Russia and military control in Japan's colonies increased military prestige, and these military leaders and their successors increasingly seized political privileges, a process assisted by rights awarded them under the Meiji constitution (*q.v.*) and the traditional respect for the military. The words *gunbatsu* (military clique) and *gunbu* (the military) came into use to denote army and navy leaders as an independent political grouping. The political power of the military and the influence of men from Satsuma and Chōshū waned during the period of Taishō Democracy, but the *gunbatsu*, strongly influenced by right-wing ideology, reemerged as a major political elite from the mid-1920s. The Manchurian Incident (*q.v.*) marked the military's usurpation of foreign policy making, and several attempts were made to interfere in domestic policy making through direct action. By the mid-1930s the military's political control was considerable. (See also ARMY.)

Military Police. See POLICE

Minamata Disease (Minamatabyō) 水俣病

The name given to the illness caused by methyl mercury poisoning which first appeared in Minamata, Kumamoto Prefecture, in the years after 1953. The mercury, entering the body by the consumption of poisoned fish from Minamata Bay, attacked the central nervous system, in many cases causing death or severe mental and physical disability. At Minamata scientists regarded the local factory of the Chisso (Nitrogen) Corporation as responsible for discharging the mercury effluent into the bay, but it was only in 1973, after years of government delay and protest and legal action by sufferers and their relatives that the corporation was found legally responsible for the pollution and ordered to pay compensation. In 1965 a similar outbreak occurred in Niigata, and in 1967 the government officially recognized the disease as pollution-related. In August 1975 there were 860 registered sufferers in Kumamoto Prefecture (including 132 deaths), and in March 1975 in Niigata 516 were registered (including 23 deaths). Hundreds of others were still applying for registration. The outbreak has made Minamata a worldwide symbol of the horrors of industrial pollution.

Takeuchi, T. "Distribution of Mercury in the Environment of Minamata Bay and the Inland Ariake Sea," in R. Hartung and B. D. Dinman, eds., *Environmental Mercury Contamination* (Ann Arbor, 1972).

Thurston, D. R. "Aftermath in Minamata," *Japan Interpreter* 9, no. 1 (Spring 1974).

Tsuru, S. "Environmental Pollution Control in Japan," in S. Tsuru, ed., *Proceedings of the International Symposium on Environmental Disruption: A Challenge to the Social Sciences* (Tokyo, 1970).

Mining

During the Tokugawa period gold, silver, copper, and coal were the most important minerals; important mines were owned by the Bakufu, others by domain authorities. After the Restoration the government took over many major mines and operated them as directly owned enterprises, often working them with convict labor, but these were sold off to private enterprise from the 1880s. Among their purchasers were Mitsui, Mitsubishi, Furukawa, and Fujita, and in some cases mines became the core enterprise for *zaibatsu* development (*q.v.*). The large Miike coal mine in Kyūshū, for example, was purchased by Mitsui. *Zaibatsu* continued to dominate mining up to the Pacific War. Most of these companies modernized the mines they took over, especially in the case of coal and copper, where most of the subsequent expansion took place. Up to 1914 some 60% copper production was exported, and it was only after 1918 that copper began to be imported. Most coal in Japan was brown, bituminous coal with limited uses and difficult to work, but despite high production costs in 1913 coal still accounted for half of mineral production by value. After World War I coal was increasingly imported from Shantung (China) and Manchuria largely because of overall increased demand and the need for coking coal. Although depressed in the late 1920s, the mining industry in Japan recovered after the Manchurian Incident, but increasingly production was insufficient to meet Japan's needs. Control of Manchukuo after 1931, however, ensured that domestic supplies of coal could be supplemented. Production in the 1930s increased under state control, but exhaustive mining of all minerals during the Pacific War laid waste many mines, and it was only in 1954 that prewar production levels were reached (except for silver). Coal was given considerable protection in the early postwar period, but with the shift to oil as a major source of energy, the mining of coal has rapidly declined. Japan is now dependent on imports for most minerals and to secure her raw material base has made various long-term agreements with exporting countries.

Lockwood, W. W. *The Economic Development of Japan* (Princeton, 1968).

Uyehara, S. *The Industry and Trade of Japan* (London, 1926).

Minobe Affair. See EMPEROR ORGAN THEORY

Minobe Tatsukichi 1873–1948
美濃部達吉

Son of a Hyōgo Prefecture physician, Minobe graduated from Tokyo Imperial University in 1897 and 1899–1902 studied comparative legal systems in Europe. In 1902 he was appointed professor of law at

Tokyo and lectured there in comparative legal history and administrative and constitutional law until his retirement in 1934. He wrote widely on law and politics and was a major proponent of the emperor organ theory (*q.v.*), which deeply divided experts on constitutional law and which was widely subscribed to by intellectuals and politicians during the Taishō and early Shōwa periods. However, Minobe's description of the emperor as an organ of state was later attacked as lese majesty, and in 1935 his books were banned. He was forced to resign his honors and resign from the House of Peers, to which he had been appointed in May 1932. Early in 1936 he was wounded in an assassination attempt. Minobe subsequently withdrew from public life and devoted his attention to subjects of less political controversy but postwar returned to public office as adviser on the constitution and privy councillor. He wrote commentaries on the new constitution before his death. Minobe's son, Ryōkichi, has been mayor of Tokyo and is now a member of the House of Councillors.

Miller, F. O. *Minobe Tatsukichi* (Berkeley, 1965).

Minomura Rizaemon 1821–1877
三野村利左衛門
Native of Nagano Prefecture, after working in various businesses in Edo, he was adopted into the Minomura family, who traditionally worked for Mitsui (*q.v.*). As one of Mitsui's chief clerks Minomura salvaged Mitsui's financial fortunes before the Restoration and was largely responsible for the company's providing financial support for the imperial government in the Boshin War (*q.v.*) and afterwards, which gained it special privileges. After the Restoration Minomura worked to develop Mitsui's trading, exchange, and banking interests, and it is largely due to him that the company was able to survive the difficult period of the Restoration and establish a base from which the later *zaibatsu* developed.

Hirschmeier, J. *The Origins of Entrepreneurship in Meiji Japan* (Cambridge, Mass., 1964).

Minponshugi. See YOSHINO SAKUZŌ

Minseitō 民政党
The Minseitō (Rikken Minseitō) was a political party formed in June 1927 by an amalgamation of the Kenseikai and Seiyū Hontō and which became subsequently the Seiyūkai's main competitor. Leading members were Hamaguchi Osachi, Wakatsuki Reijirō, and, until his defection in 1928, Tokonami Takejirō. The party stressed "liberal" policies and was dependent on urban rather than rural support, being closely allied with business interests. As the party in power under Hamaguchi the Minseitō supported a conciliatory foreign policy and removal of the gold embargo and his enforced ratification of the London Naval Treaty (*q.v.*). After Hamaguchi was replaced by Wakatsuki, increasing criticism of the party's economic and political policies in the face of depression led to the resignation of Home Minister Adachi Kenzō, which split the party. The Minseitō did disastrously in the 1932 elections, and despite its support for the "national unity" cabinets of Saitō and Okada its influence declined. The Minseitō recovered somewhat under the presidency of Machida Chūji from 1935 and achieved a considerable number of seats in the 1936 and 1937 elections. On occasion it cooperated with the Seiyūkai against the government, but it also moved toward compromise with the army and its policies, some of which it had earlier opposed. In 1940 one of the Minseitō members, Saitō Takao, was struck off the party register for an antimilitary speech. There was increasing support for the new structure movement (*q.v.*) within the party, and in August 1940 it was disbanded.

Berger, G. M. *Parties Out of Power in Japan, 1931–1941* (Princeton, 1977).
Holland, H. M. "The Rikken Minseitō (Constitutional Democratic Party) of Japan (1927–1940): Its Antecedents,

Structure, and Operations," Ph.D. diss., George Washington University, 1958.

Minshatō. See DEMOCRATIC SOCIALIST PARTY

Minshu Jiyūtō. See LIBERAL DEMOCRATIC PARTY

Minshu Shakaitō. See DEMOCRATIC SOCIALIST PARTY

Mint. See CURRENCY

Minyūsha 民友社

The Minyūsha was a publishing group founded in 1887 by Tokutomi Sohō (Iichirō) (1863–1957). Leading members included Yamaji Aizan, Takekoshi Yosaburō, and Tokutomi Roka. The Minyūsha published *Kokumin no Tomo* (People's Friend), a weekly journal, and from 1890 also the daily *Kokumin Shinbun*. Reflecting Tokutomi's views, these publications rejected many elements of traditional Japanese society, supported Western-style parliamentary government, pacifism, and internationalism. Articles pressed for reform and a renewal of the impetus of the Restoration and introduced progressive thinkers, new authors, and historians to a wide audience. Changed conditions after the Sino-Japanese War led Tokutomi to espouse more conservative views; the popularity of his papers decreased, and the *Kokumin no Tomo* ceased publication in 1898. The *Kokumin Shinbun*, now advocating expansionism, openly supported the views of Yamagata Aritomo and his followers; it too declined in influence during the Taishō period. Until its demise in 1929 the Minyūsha also published many books, including those of Tokutomi, who wrote widely on history. Tokutomi himself was purged after the war for supporting the government.

Duus, P. "Whig History, Japanese Style: The Minyūsha Historians and the Meiji Restoration," *JAS* 33, no. 3 (May 1974).
Pierson, J. D. "The Journalist Tokutomi Sohō: Problems of Westernization and Modernization in Meiji Japan," Ph.D. diss., Princeton University, 1972.
______. *Tokutomi Sohō, 1863–1957—A Journalist for Modern Japan* (Princeton, 1980).
Pyle, K. *The New Generation in Meiji Japan: Problems of Cultural Identity* (Stanford, 1969).

Mishima Michitsune 1835–1888 (Viscount, 1887) 三島通庸

Samurai from Satsuma, Mishima participated in the anti-Bakufu movement (*q.v.*) and fought in the Boshin War (*q.v.*). He joined the central government and was then governor of Sakata Prefecture from 1874, of Yamagata from 1876, of Fukushima 1882–1884, and concurrently of Tochigi 1883–1884. In Sakata Mishima was known for his ruthless suppression of peasant uprisings, and his efforts in Fukushima to enforce labor and tax contributions for public works led to the Fukushima incident (*q.v.*) and indirectly to the Kabasan incident (*q.v.*) in Tochigi. From 1884 he worked as chief of civil engineering in the central government and was concurrently chief of police from 1885. During Mishima's term of office as police chief the Peace Regulations (*q.v.*) were passed, and he ruthlessly attempted to suppress the antigovernment movement of the late 1880s.

Strong, K. *Ox Against the Storm* (Tenterden, Kent, 1977).

Mitaka Incident. See SHIMOYAMA INCIDENT

MITI (Tsūshō Sangyōshō) 通商産業省

The Ministry of International Trade and Industry (MITI) was established in May 1949 to coordinate and promote the industrial rationalization, increase in production, and export expansion necessary to rebuild the Japanese economy, as suggested in the economic stabilization program (*q.v.*). Taking over many of the functions of the old Ministry of Commerce and Industry, MITI and its various bureaus have since acted as the major force in planning and implementing the national policy of expansion in industry and trade on the basis of the free market economy. Helped by their close ties with big business, MITI bureaucrats are widely regarded as the architects of Japan's highly successful economic policy.

Johnson, C. *Japan's Public Policy Companies* (Washington, 1978).

Mito 水戸

Mito was a Tokugawa *han* northeast of Edo and one of the *sanke*. During the Tokugawa period Mito was a center of Confucian scholarship; its history of early Japan, the *Dainihon Shi*, gained it a reputation for patriotism. During the 19th century Mito scholars, especially Fujita Yūkoku (1774–1826), Fujita Tōko (1806–1855), and Aizawa Seishisai (Yasushi) (1782–1863), developed an interest in current affairs. Their views, which were in effect a restatement of traditional values, noted the unchanging position of the emperor in Japanese society, called for the expulsion of foreigners through reverence for the emperor, and criticized the Bakufu for overstepping the limits of its ordained role. Although these ideas were intended to strengthen and reform the Bakufu rather than be subversive—Mito thinkers stressed that despite the emperor's preeminence, efficient rule was dependent on the rule of the shōgun—they were influential in the anti-Tokugawa movement, and their views led to increasing emphasis being placed on imperial rule. They had a strong influence also on Tokugawa Nariaki, daimyō of Mito to 1860, and his ensuing reform and modernization policies brought him into conflict with the Bakufu although their purpose was resistance to the West rather than subversion of the Bakufu.

Earl, D. M. *Emperor and Nation in Japan: Political Thinkers of the Tokugawa Period* (Seattle, 1964).
Harootunian, H. D. *Toward Restoration* (Berkeley, 1970).
Webb, H. *The Japanese Imperial Institution in the Tokugawa Period* (New York, 1968).

Mitsubishi Zaibatsu 三菱財閥

A shipping company founded by Iwasaki Yatarō was named Mitsubishi in 1873. With government patronage it achieved a virtual monopoly and then became the major element in the 1885 Japan Shipping Company (N.Y.K.), which dominated merchant shipping throughout the prewar period. Using this company as a base, Iwasaki extended his interests into other spheres, notably insurance and shipbuilding. He purchased the government's Nagasaki Shipyard in 1884. From 1880 he was also engaged in banking. Iwasaki's successors after his death in 1885 continued to expand and diversify the interests of the group. In 1893 a limited partnership was set up to control the interests. After World War I this was changed into a holding company, centralizing ownership and control of the concern's many interests. The *zaibatsu*'s activities remained concentrated on shipping, insurance, and shipbuilding, but heavy industry interests also grew. It never attained the size of Mitsui, but it was more progressive in such things as chemicals and engineering. By 1930 the holding company controlled about 120 companies with ¥900 million capital. The nature of Mitsubishi's interests meant that it had considerable significance for the war economy of the 1930s–1940s. After the war the Iwasaki family lost control of the group, which was split up into its separate units, but prewar connections have to a large extent been reforged by the revival of commercial interests based on the Mitsubishi Bank and, from the 1960s, by the rebuilding of heavy industry interests.

Hirschmeier, J. and T. Yui. *The Development of Japanese Business, 1600–1973* (London, 1975).
Morikawa, H. "The Organizational Structure of Mitsubishi and Mitsui *Zaibatsu*, 1868–1922," *Business History*

Review 44, no. 1 (1970).
Yamamura, K. "The Founding of Mitsubishi," *Business History Review* 41, no. 2 (1967).

Mitsui Zaibatsu 三井財閥
Mitsui were a leading merchant family in the Tokugawa period. Under the clerkship of Minomura Rizaemon the Mitsui house gave financial support to the new government at the time of the Restoration and afterwards became one of the government's official exchange brokers, which put them in a favorable position to expand their interests. Survival over the difficult period of the Restoration was largely due to the genius of Minomura. In 1872 the house's dry goods store became independent under the name of Mitsukoshi, and Mitsui itself concentrated on exchange and banking. In 1876 the Mitsui Bank was established; it received a high rate of government deposits and made loans on the security of rice. The same year Mitsui Bussan (Products, or Trading) was set up under Masuda Takashi; it had a monopoly on the handling of exports from the government's Miike coal mine and expanded Mitsui's trading interests. Mitsui benefited from the sale of government enterprises in the 1880s. Its purchases, which included the Miike Mine, became the nucleus of the producing sector of Mitsui's interests. Mitsui Mining was established in 1893, and expansion of manufacturing interests during the 1890s included machinery, textiles, and paper. Under Nakamigawa Hikojirō's organizational reforms in 1892 a family council was established to centralize decision making. This was replaced in 1909 by an unlimited partnership (largely family-owned) with capital of ¥50 million to act as a holding company to centralize control over the various enterprises. This in fact marked an increasing divergence between management and ownership; unlike many other *zaibatsu* owners the Mitsui family were highly dependent on their managers. The combine developed rapidly in the 1920s, and by 1931 the Mitsui Partnership controlled well over 100 companies directly or indirectly, with over ¥1,000 million capital. Adverse political trends in the early 1930s and accusations of speculation during the depression, of corrupt political involvement, and of being, as it were, a state within a state, led to the murder of Dan Takuma, Mitsui's manager, in 1932, and caused the *zaibatsu* to modify its policies, the so-called "change of direction." Family activity lessened, some shares were sold off, and contributions made to "appropriate" organizations. Mitsui's initial cooperation with the military was unenthusiastic and only due to fear for its trading interests, but through increasing accommodation with the army and its policies, Mitsui continued to extend its interests. The *zaibatsu* was dissolved postwar with the Mitsui family losing control, but the continuing existence of Mitsui Bank has enabled some previous connections to resurface, and individual enterprises are still large and powerful.

Morikawa, H. "The Organizational Structure of Mitsubishi and Mitsui *Zaibatsu*, 1868–1922," *Business History Review* 44, no. 1 (1970).
Roberts, J. G. *Mitsui* (New York, 1973).
Russell, O. D. *The House of Mitsui* (Westport, Conn., 1970).

Mitsukuri Rinshō 1846–1897
箕作麟祥
Native of Edo, Mitsukuri attended the Bakufu's Western learning institute and became a translator. After visiting France in 1867, he worked in the Justice Ministry in the new government. From 1873 he was a member of the Meirokusha (*q.v.*), as was his uncle, the educational specialist Mitsukuri Shūhei. Mitsukuri was a member of the Genrōin from 1880, deputy justice minister 1888–1891, and a member of the House of Peers from 1890. In these posts and through his membership of various specialist committees, Mitsukuri played a major role in the discussion and drafting of many of Japan's laws. He was also head of the Japanese-French Law School, later Hōsei University, and wrote and translated widely on law.

Braisted, W. R., ed. and tr., *Meiroku Zasshi* (Cambridge, Mass., 1976).

Miura Gorō 1847–1926
(Viscount, 1884) 三浦梧楼
Samurai from Chōshū, Miura participated in the anti-Bakufu movement (*q.v.*) and fought in the Kiheitai (*q.v.*). After the Restoration he had a career in the army, then was appointed to the House of Peers in 1890. In 1895 he succeeded Inoue Kaoru as envoy to Korea but was recalled after the murder of the anti-Japanese Korean queen, Min. Miura was tried for complicity in the murder but was never convicted. He was subsequently involved with the Kensei Hontō and was a privy councillor 1910–1924. Despite his Chōshū background and expansionist ideas, Miura was a bitter opponent of *hanbatsu* politics (*q.v.*); his support for constitutional politics led him to mediate on occasions between different party leaders, urging cooperation between them, and he wielded considerable covert political influence.

Conroy, H. *The Japanese Seizure of Korea, 1868–1910* (Philadelphia, 1960).
Critchfield, T. M. "Queen Min's Murder," Ph.D. diss., Indiana University, 1975.
Kim, C. I. E., and H-K. Kim. *Korea and the Politics of Imperialism, 1876–1910* (Berkeley, 1967).

Miyake Setsurei 1860–1945 三宅雪嶺
Samurai from Ishikawa Prefecture, after graduating in philosophy from Tokyo University, Miyake worked briefly in the bureaucracy. From 1887 he worked as a journalist and was especially connected with the journal *Nihonjin* (later translated as *Japan and the Japanese*). Miyake was interested in politics; he strongly opposed the *hanbatsu* (*q.v.*) and was actively involved in politics in the 1880s, but disillusionment with politics led him to devote his time to writing and journalism. Miyake's philosophy was strongly "Japanist." He opposed what he considered excessive Westernization and its concomitant evils such as the pollution at the Ashio mine (*q.v.*) and argued for the preservation of traditional Japanese culture on the grounds that each country had its own contribution to make to world culture. His was a nationalism that perceived Japan in a world context. Miyake wrote widely on his views, and his accounts of prewar Japan, such as *Dōjidai Shi* (Contemporary History), are also a valuable historical source.

Kosaka, M. *Japanese Thought in the Meiji Era* (Tokyo, 1958).
Yanagida, I. "The Thought of Miyake Setsurei," in Japan National Committee for UNESCO. *The Modernization of Japan,* vol. 7 (Tokyo, 1966).

Mobilization. See NATIONAL GENERAL MOBILIZATION LAW; NATIONAL SPIRITUAL MOBILIZATION

Mori Arinori 1847–1889
(Viscount, 1887) 森有礼
Member of a Satsuma samurai family, Mori studied in England and the U.S. and after the Restoration joined the new government, serving as envoy to America 1870–1872, to China 1875–1878, and to England 1879–1884. His pro-Westernization views were early on sufficiently radical to arouse hostility in others; in 1874 he was behind the founding of the Meirokusha (*q.v.*). Mori had long been interested in education, and having persuaded Itō Hirobumi of this interest, he was appointed minister of education in 1885. The radical reforms carried out at all levels of education made Mori the most powerful architect of Japan's prewar education system. The basis of the reforms, behind which was a strong German influence, was that education should be for the purposes of the state, a principle maintained to 1945. Although Mori was by this time by no means the wholehearted "Westernizer" he had been, some of his attitudes roused the opposition of conservative nationalists, and he was assassinated in February 1889. (See also EDUCATION.)

Hall, I. P. *Mori Arinori* (Cambridge, Mass., 1973).
Nagai, M. "Mori Arinori," *JQ* 11, no. 1 (Jan.-Mar. 1964).
Wong, H. C. "Mori Arinori's Mission to China, 1876," *Chung Chi Journal* (Nov. 1963).

Mori Kaku 1883–1932 森格
Native of Osaka, after studying commerce, Mori entered Mitsui Bussan and from 1901 worked for Mitsui (*q.v.*) in China. In 1913 he founded the China Industrial Company (later Sino-Japanese Business Company) aimed at expanding Japanese investment in China and in developing raw material production for Japan's use. In 1920 Mori left Mitsui and joined the Diet as a Seiyūkai member. He had close contacts with Tanaka Giichi and was highly influential in the formation of his China policy, playing a major role in the Eastern Conference of 1927 (*q.v.*). As chief secretary to the Seiyūkai and then cabinet secretary 1931–1932 Mori remained influential, continuing to advocate a policy of continental advance and cooperation with the military to achieve a new political order.

Triplett, L. G. "Mori Kaku (1883–1932): A Political Biography," Ph.D. diss., University of Arizona, 1974.
Yoshihashi, T. *Conspiracy at Mukden* (New Haven, 1963).

Motoda Eifu (Nagazane)
1818–1891 (Baron, 1891) 元田永孚
Samurai from Kumamoto *han*, Motoda studied under Yokoi Shōnan and from 1858 held various offices in the *han* but played no major role in the political events of the 1860s. As reader (1871) and lecturer (1875) to the emperor, however, and as palace councillor from 1886, Motoda came to exert considerable influence over the Meiji emperor. He served as privy councillor 1888–1891. Strongly conservative and an ardent Confucianist, Motoda was a major influence on the Imperial Rescript on Education (*q.v.*). He wrote several books in which he advocated traditional concepts of the kingly way and benevolent government, and his advocacy of a uniquely Japanese ethical and spiritual training and of the strengthening of the imperial institution has caused him to be regarded as a strong upholder of the "emperor system" (*q.v.*).

Shively, D. H. "Motoda Eifu: Confucian Lecturer to the Meiji Emperor," in D. S. Nivison and A. F. Wright, eds., *Confucianism in Action* (Stanford, 1959).

Movement for the Protection of Constitutional Government (kensei yōgo undō) 憲政擁護運動
Twice during the Taishō period, movements arose in opposition to *hanbatsu*-oriented bureaucratic cabinets and military privileges in politics and in defense of political party government.

1. Late in 1912 prominent liberal journalists gained the support of businessmen and veteran party politicians such as Inukai Tsuyoshi and Ozaki Yukio in a movement calling for destruction of the *hanbatsu* (*q.v.*) and implementation of constitutional government. Public meetings and rallies were sponsored, and a massive popular movement developed. It was given fuel by Katsura's appointment as prime minister, and in January 1913 the Seiyūkai also gave its support to the movement, joining with the other parties to propose an anti-Katsura no-confidence motion. On February 10 tens of thousands of people besieged the Diet, pro-government newspaper offices and police stations were attacked, and the following day the Katsura cabinet resigned. The movement subsequently lost momentum.

2. In 1922 the Kenseikai failed in its attempts to initiate a similar popular movement, but it joined with the Kakushin Club in opposing the nonparty Katō and Yamamoto cabinets. In January 1924, with the Kiyoura cabinet in office, elements of the Seiyūkai joined them to form a tripartite league calling for constitutional and political party government. The league advocated universal manhood suffrage, reform of the House of Peers,

and administrative and financial changes. This cooperation was partly the result of the parties' strategy for the coming election, and this was the key to the movement's success. In the May 1924 election the three parties captured an absolute majority and formed a cabinet under Katō Takaaki. As a popular movement this second movement for constitutional government was a failure, but it proved that if the parties united, they could halt the formation of a nonparty cabinet.

Duus, P. *Party Rivalry and Political Change in Taishō Japan* (Cambridge, Mass., 1968).

Mukden Incident. See MANCHURIAN INCIDENT

Mutō Sanji 1867–1934 武藤山治
Native of Gifu Prefecture, Mutō graduated from Keiō and studied in the U.S. before joining the Mitsui Bank in 1893. In 1894 he moved to the Kanegafuchi Spinning Company, of which from 1908 to 1930 he was managing director and then president. The company prospered, and overall Mutō played a leading role in the development of Japan's cotton spinning industry. He was known for his support of mass production methods and paternalistic management. In 1924 Mutō turned to politics and was three times elected to the Diet on a platform of clean politics and free trade. He strongly opposed the prevailing government's economic policies and retired from politics in 1932. The same year he became president of the *Jiji Shinpō* newspaper and was responsible for exposing the Imperial Rayon scandal (*q.v.*) in 1934, but he was attacked at this time by unemployed workers and died of his injuries.

Young, A. *Imperial Japan, 1926–1938* (London, 1938).

Mutsu Munemitsu 1844–1897 (Viscount, 1894; Count, 1895) 陸奥宗光
Samurai of the Tokugawa domain of Wakayama, Mutsu left his fief to join the loyalist movement, forming strong Tosa connections. After the Restoration he held various posts before becoming head of the Land Tax Revision Bureau in 1872 but resigned in 1874. He was appointed to the Genrōin in 1875 but in 1878 was imprisoned for trying to raise an army following the Satsuma Rebellion (*q.v.*). After his release in 1884 he went to Europe. On his return in 1886 Mutsu joined the Foreign Ministry and 1888–1889 served as ambassador to America, where he concluded a trade and commerce treaty with Mexico. Briefly elected to the Diet, he was also agriculture and commerce minister 1890–1892, privy councillor during 1892, and then foreign minister 1892–1896. During this last term of office Mutsu achieved the long hoped-for treaty revision (*q.v.*) and was also one of Japan's representatives at the conference at Shimonoseki after the Sino-Japanese War.

Jansen, M. B. "Mutsu Munemitsu," in A. M. Craig and D. H. Shively, eds., *Personality in Japanese History* (Berkeley, 1970).
Lie, T. "Mutsu Munemitsu, 1844–1897, Portrait of a Machiavelli," Ph.D. diss., Harvard University, 1962.

Mutsuhito. See MEIJI EMPEROR

N

Nabeyama Sadachika 1901–1979 鍋山貞親
Born in Fukuoka Prefecture, Nabeyama was a factory worker who became a Communist through the influence of Arahata Kanson. He was one of the leading figures in the Japan Communist Party from 1927 but was arrested and imprisoned in 1928. In 1933 he announced his *tenkō* (*q.v.*) (conversion) and subsequently played a major role in the ultranationalist movement, acting as a military agent during the war in China. He tried unsuccessfully to join the Japan Socialist Party postwar. He was influential in the postwar organization and leadership of government and company labor unions and had strong contacts with anti-Communist labor groups who have attempted to disunite the left-wing labor camp. Nabeyama also retained strong contacts with Kodama Yoshio and right-wing Socialists and remained until his death keen to expose the activities of the J. C. P. wherever possible.

Nagasaki 長崎
A port on the west coast of Kyūshū, Nagasaki was the only Japanese port open to foreign trade during the Tokugawa period. Dutch merchants on the island of Deshima (Dejima) in Nagasaki Bay had strictly controlled trading contacts, and some trade with China was permitted. Nagasaki was therefore the only real channel by which foreign influences could enter Japan, and especially after the lifting of the ban on the import of Dutch books in 1720, Nagasaki became the center of Dutch learning (*q.v.*) and the destination of scholars interested in the West. Treaties signed with the West 1855–1858 opened Nagasaki fully to Western trade, and it developed as a major center for foreign residence and commerce, although in this respect it was subsequently overtaken by such ports as Yokohama and Kobe. The city was devastated by an atomic bomb on 9 August 1945, but it has since recovered and expanded. Its population is now about half a million.

Boxer, C. R. *Jan Compagnie in Japan, 1600–1850* (The Hague, 1950).
Paske-Smith, M. *Western Barbarians in Japan and Formosa in Tokugawa Days, 1603–1868* (Kobe, 1930).

Nagata Incident. See AIZAWA INCIDENT

Naimushō. See HOME MINISTRY

Nakae Chōmin 1847–1901 中江兆民
A samurai from Tosa, Nakae studied Chinese and Western learning in Nagasaki and Edo. He was sent by the government to study in France 1871–1874 and then opened an institute for French studies. By 1880 Nakae was recognized as the leading Japanese specialist on French thought and known as a leading liberal. He became editor of the *Tōyō Jiyū Shinbun* (Oriental Liberal Paper) in 1881 and through the 1880s was in the forefront of opposition to the government, calling for recognition of human rights and an end to the Satsuma-Chōshū dominance of government. He translated Rousseau's *Social Contract* and other French writings as well as producing his own works on political thought and working as a journalist. In 1887 Nakae was banned from Tokyo under the Peace Regulations (*q.v.*). In 1890 he was elected to the Diet as a Jiyūtō member but resigned in 1891 over the compromises some of his colleagues seemed prepared to make with the government. After an unsuccessful spell in business he returned to writing and political activity. His call for war against Russia in 1900 suggested a strengthening nationalist tendency during his last years.

Dardess, M. B. "The Thought and Politics of Nakae Chōmin (1847–1901)," Ph.D. diss., Columbia University, 1973.
Dardess, M. B., tr. "Nakae Chōmin and His Sansuijin Keirin Mondō, 1847–1901," *East Asian Studies Occasional Papers* 10 (Western Washington State College, 1977).
Ike, N. *The Beginnings of Political Democracy in Japan* (Baltimore, 1950).
Kaji, R. "The Introduction of French Political Ideas—Nakae Chōmin: The Man and His Thought," in Japan Committee for UNESCO. *The Modernization of Japan*, vol. 7 (Tokyo, 1966–1967).

Nakamigawa Hikojirō 1854–1901
中上川彦次郎
Samurai from Nakatsu domain (now Ōita Prefecture) and nephew of Fukuzawa Yukichi, Nakamigawa studied and then taught at Keiō and in 1874–1877 studied in England. His friendship with Inoue Kaoru helped him to posts in the bureaucracy 1878–1881. In 1882–1887 he was manager of the *Jiji Shinpō*. In 1887 Nakamigawa founded the Sanyō Railway Company and acted as its president until 1891. In 1891, again at the suggestion of Inoue, he became vice-president of Mitsui (*q.v.*), whose fortunes were at a low ebb. Nakamigawa started off by rationalizing the Mitsui Bank and streamlining the administration of the *zaibatsu*, then gave his attention to extending the concern's industrial interests. Nakamigawa's policies of reform and innovation included freeing Mitsui of its dependence on government, ruthless financial rationalization, reorganization of central control, and the promotion of a talented management free of traditional business attitudes. It was largely due to him that a firm base was established on which the concern could expand further after his death.

Hirschmeier, J. *The Origins of Entrepreneurship in Meiji Japan* (Cambridge, Mass., 1964).
Yui, T. "The Personality and Career of Nakamigawa Hikojirō, 1887–1901," *Business History Review* 44, no. 1 (Spring 1970).

Nakamura Masanao (Keiu)
1832–1891 中村正直(敬宇)
Native of Edo, Nakamura became an official Confucian teacher and then studied English and Dutch. In 1866–1868 he studied in England under the auspices of the Bakufu and on his return taught in Shizuoka until 1872. During this time he translated into Japanese Samuel Smiles's *Self-Help* and J. S. Mill's *On Liberty*. Both books proved popular and influential and contributed to the spread of ideas of self-help and popular rights. In 1873 Nakamura became a member of the Meirokusha (*q.v.*). In 1874 he was baptized a Christian. After being briefly employed at the Finance Ministry, in 1873 Nakamura opened his private school, the Dōjinsha, whose curriculum emphasized moral education and included Chinese. He was also head of the Girls' Normal School 1875–1880 and professor of Chinese studies at Tokyo University from 1880. In 1886 he became a member of the Genrōin and 1890 a member of the House of Peers. As an educationist and as an agent for the spread of new ideas, Nakamura had a considerable influence during the early Meiji period.

Braisted, W. R., tr. and ed., *Meiroku Zasshi* (Cambridge, Mass., 1976).
Kosaka, M. *Japanese Thought in the Meiji Era* (Tokyo, 1958).

Nakano Seigō 1886–1943 中野正剛
Native of Fukuoka and son-in-law of Miyake Setsurei, Nakano graduated from Waseda University, then worked as a journalist and founded several journals. He was elected to the Diet eight successive times from 1920 and was a member of the Kakushin Club, Kenseikai, and Minseitō. He was increasingly attracted to the solutions proposed by the right wing to Japan's problems and in 1931 cooperated with Adachi Kenzō in attempts to produce a coalition cabinet, helping to bring down the Wakatsuki cabinet. Nakano left the Minseitō and founded the Kokumin Dōmei (National League) and then the

Tōhōkai (Eastern Association). His admiration for Nazi Germany and hopes of realizing an analogous political system in Japan led Nakano to support the new structure movement (*q.v.*). In 1940 he became a director of the Imperial Rule Assistance Association (*q.v.*), which he hoped to convert into a totalitarian party which would replace the cabinet as the central policy-making organ of state, but he resigned his post when his aspirations were not realized. He was elected to the Diet in 1943 as a non-government-sponsored candidate, but his criticism of the Tōjō cabinet led to his arrest. He was released but committed suicide.

Berger, G. M. *Parties Out of Power in Japan, 1931–1941* (Princeton, 1977).

Namamugi Incident (Namamugi jiken) 生麦事件

In September 1862 Charles Richardson, a British merchant from Shanghai, was killed at Namamugi, near Yokohama, by Satsuma samurai. The samurai claimed that Richardson's group had failed to give way to Shimazu Hisamitsu's procession, as was customary. Two other Englishmen were also wounded. The British lodged a strong protest, demanding indemnities from both Satsuma and the Bakufu and execution of the assassins. In June 1863 the Bakufu promised to pay £100,000 indemnity, but Satsuma refused to produce the murderers or pay compensation. In August 1863 a British squadron entered Kagoshima Bay, seized several vessels, and opened a general engagement in which ships were sunk, much of the town destroyed by bombardment, and many people wounded. The squadron then withdrew with a few prisoners and considerable damage to itself. Awareness of military inferiority led Satsuma at subsequent negotiations to agree to the terms and to execute the murderers if found. The money for the indemnity was borrowed from the Bakufu. Satsuma afterwards developed close relations with the British.

Beasley, W. G. *The Meiji Restoration* (London, 1973).
Satow, E. *A Diplomat in Japan* (London, 1921).

Nanking Government. See JAPAN-CHINA BASIC TREATY

Nanking, Rape of. See RAPE OF NANKING

National Foundation Society. See KOKUHONSHA

National Learning. See NATIVISM

National General Mobilization Law (Kokka Sōdōin Hō) 国家総動員法

Passed by the Diet 24 March 1938 and formally decreed on April 1. The law was aimed at the control and management of human and physical resources for war preparedness and war efficiency, and some opposition was raised to the provision that enabled the government to impose wholesale controls over such things as labor, prices, production, and transport by means of imperial ordinance, thereby reducing the authority of the Diet. All ordinances, however, had to be agreed by the National General Mobilization Council, 60% of whose membership came from the Diet. Despite assurances that the law would not be invoked during the current fighting with China, from the summer of 1938 emergency provisions were gradually brought into effect under the provisions of the law to facilitate mobilization of the population and economy toward the war effort. The law was formally rescinded in December 1945.

Berger, G. M. *Parties Out of Power in Japan, 1931–1941* (Princeton, 1977).
Fahs, C. B. *Government in Japan: Recent Trends in Its Scope and Operation* (New York, 1940).

Yanaga, C. *Japan Since Perry* (Hamden, Conn., 1966).

National Industrial Labor Unions Federation. See LABOR MOVEMENT

National Labor Farmer Mass Party. See RŌDŌ NŌMINTŌ

National Labor Unions Federation. See LABOR MOVEMENT

National Police Reserve. See SELF-DEFENSE FORCE

National Polity. See KOKUTAI

National Safety Force. See SELF-DEFENSE FORCE

National Spiritual Mobilization (kokumin seishin sōdōin) 国民精神総動員

In autumn 1937 the Konoe cabinet called for national unity, loyalty, patriotism, and untiring perseverance in the war effort, initiating an official campaign to rally popular awareness of and feeling for the war. In December 1937 the National Spiritual Mobilization Central League was set up as an auxiliary organ of the cabinet, and various national groups such as reservists' and mayors' associations were affiliated to it. In April 1940 the league was reconstituted as the National Spiritual Mobilization Headquarters and continued until its functions were taken over by the Imperial Rule Assistance Association (*q.v.*). During the early years when the war was distant from Japan, the campaign was relatively successful in rallying popular consciousness of and support for the war. As the war continued, emphasis shifted from mental attitudes to more practical contributions to the war effort such as attacks on extravagance as well as spreading increasing antipathy to Western languages and culture. Overall, the spiritual mobilization movement was a major element in a successful program of national indoctrination.

Havens, T. R. H. *Valley of Darkness* (New York, 1978).

Nativism (kokugaku) 国学

Nativism, or "national learning," was a movement which developed during the 18th century and whose main concern was the discovery of the pure Japanese spirit through study of Japan's mythology and the ancient Japanese classics. The ideas of nativism, which had its origins in the increased interest in Shintō among 17th-century intellectuals, were developed by Kamo Mabuchi (1697–1769), whose studies of the *Manyōshū* and other Japanese classics led him to call for a return to the ancient spirit of Japan as it existed prior to the introduction of Buddhism and Confucianism. This reassertion of a native Japanese tradition attained its fullest expression in the works of Kamo's pupil, Motoori Norinaga (1730–1801), who engaged in extensive research, especially into the *Kojiki*, and who perfected an overall philosophy of "return to the past" based on indigenous tradition. Even under Motoori, nativism was concerned primarily with the expression of an indigenous tradition in religious terms and remained basically apolitical; although Motoori regarded the emperor as the bearer of absolute authority, he sought to remove the imperfections in Japanese society not by overthrowing the Tokugawa but by using imperial favor to calm disorders. Hirata Atsutane (1776–1843) expanded certain elements of Motoori's thinking into a full-scale attack on Confucianism, Buddhism, and Western learning, emphasizing the divine origins of the Japanese emperor and people. His nationalistic calls for the restoration of ancient times and assertion of the position of the emperor as the focal point of patriotism and virtue amounted to an attack on the existing status quo, and these ideas, as expounded by his followers, not only inspired religious movements but were a vital theoretical support for the pro-emperor political movement which developed during the 1850s and 1860s. The political influence of nativism was therefore largely a retrospective one during the decades prior to the Restoration. Subsequently its ideas, basically reactionary, became increasingly alienated from political and social reality although the emphasis on the unique Japanese spirit and "polity" remained fundamental to right-wing thought.

Earl, D. M. *Emperor and Nation in Japan* (Seattle, 1964).
Harootunian, H. D. "The Consciousness of Archaic Form in the New Realism of Kokugaku," in T. Najita and I. Scheiner, eds., *Japanese Thought in the Tokugawa Period, 1600 – 1868* (Chicago, 1978).
Maruyama, M. *Studies in the Intellectual History of Tokugawa Japan* (Tokyo, 1974).
Matsumoto, S. *Motoori Norinaga* (Cambridge, Mass., 1970).
Tahara, T. "The Kokugaku Thought," *Acta Asiatica* 25 (1973).

Naval Arms Limitation

Among the "14 Points" for peace in the post-World War I world enunciated by Woodrow Wilson in January 1918 was agreement on reductions in national armaments. This resulted in a series of disarmament conferences, and in addition, at Washington and London, in 1922 and 1930, respectively, the powers negotiated over a naval arms limitation program in the hope of maintaining the status quo and reducing military expenditure. The main signatories of the Washington and London Naval Treaties (*q.v.*) were Britain, the U.S., and Japan. In Japan both agreements met with navy and other opposition and provoked considerable domestic conflict. Attempts after 1930 to extend naval arms limitation failed and with the expiration of the treaties in 1936 there was a full-scale arms race.

Dingman, R. *Power in the Pacific* (Chicago, 1976).
Pelz, S. E. *Race to Pearl Harbor* (Cambridge, Mass., 1974).

Navy

Before the Restoration both Bakufu and domains had initiated the construction and purchase of warships, and the Bakufu's efforts to acquire ships and train personnel, largely under the guidance of Katsu Kaishū, laid the foundations for the Meiji navy. The Meiji government took over the Bakufu's ships and those of some *han*, naval schools, and other facilities, such as the dockyard at Yokosuka. In 1872 all these, including 17 ships, were handed over to the new Navy Ministry. The naval systems of various countries were studied with care, and a building, purchasing, and training program had more than doubled the number of ships by 1894. In preparation for war with Russia a 10-year naval expansion program was launched in 1896; by 1903 Japan possessed 76 major war vessels and total tonnage of over 250,000, including several battleships, which were to play a crucial role in the Russo-Japanese War (*q.v.*). At the end of the war the Japanese navy was indisputably the most powerful fleet in the Far East. Expansion continued until by 1912 the total tonnage was 650,000. Naval building was limited by international naval limitation agreements 1920 – 1936, but after these lapsed, building was pushed forward. Many of Japan's air forces were also under naval control, both army and navy possessing separate air divisions. The navy played a crucial role and was highly successful in the early stages of the Pacific War (*q.v.*). At its peak it numbered 383 vessels, but many were sunk or immobilized later; by the end of the war Japan possessed virtually no naval vessels, merely some 2 million sailors waiting to be demobilized.
Throughout the Meiji and Taishō periods the navy remained dominated by men from Satsuma. In the early Meiji period all naval matters were supervised by the Navy Ministry, but naval command matters were shifted to the General Staff in 1886 and in 1893 to the new Naval General Staff. The Navy Ministry's role was limited to administrative matters, although the navy minister had an additional role to play as a cabinet member. However, the practice that military ministers should be serving officers, which operated 1900 – 1913 and from 1936, gave

the navy considerable potential political leverage. Especially after the 1930 London Naval Treaty (*q.v.*) dissatisfaction grew within the Naval General Staff. The general desire within the navy for political involvement increased, and younger officers influenced by radical nationalistic ideologies became involved in attempted coups d'état such as the May 15 incident (*q.v.*). Although considerably divided by factionalism, the navy's political influence did increase, but it never achieved the political dominance of the army, with which it frequently tended to compete rather than cooperate. The two services were fundamentally divided on strategy; the navy had long planned on the assumption that the U.S. was Japan's major enemy, and its dependence on oil led it to press for a southward advance rather than conflict with Russia. Thoroughgoing disagreements between the two services continued throughout the Pacific War. The navy was disbanded postwar, but the Self-Defense Force (*q.v.*) has a maritime section.

Asada, S. "The Japanese Navy and the United States," in D. Borg and S. Okamoto, eds., *Pearl Harbor as History* (New York, 1973).
Cornwall, P. G. "The Meiji Navy: Training in an Age of Change," Ph.D. diss., University of Michigan, 1970.
Itō, M. *The End of the Imperial Japanese Navy* (London, 1962).

Neighborhood Associations (tonarigumi) 隣組

Descended from the groups used for mutual aid and policing purposes in the Tokugawa period, the neighborhood association was formally revived in September 1940 as a unit of 10 to 20 contiguous households; several of these groups were in turn organized into larger block or village associations. Reorganization in 1942 made the associations an integral part of the Imperial Rule Assistance movement and de facto the lowest level of government. Under this government control the *tonarigumi* were used to mobilize reverence and support for the emperor system and to carry out functions such as air raid protection, distribution of government directives, provision and distribution of supplies, public welfare and relief, forced saving, and training of group leaders. They cooperated closely with other state-sponsored organizations and operated through meetings, notice-boards, and circulars. Apart from its role as the smallest unit of the administrative structure, the associations proved a useful unit for control by government and police. Although they were regarded as politically dangerous by the Occupation authorities, the associations were retained as ration distribution units until 1947, when they were abolished by SCAP, but many survived under the guise of voluntary associations long after, and it was argued that they had democratic potential for the development of an informed electorate.

Braibanti, R. J. D. "Neighborhood Associations in Japan and Their Democratic Potentialities," *FEQ* 7, no. 2 (Feb. 1948).
Havens, T. R. H. *Valley of Darkness* (New York, 1978).
Quigley, H. S., and J. E. Turner. *The New Japan* (Minneapolis, 1956).

Neo-Confucianism. See CONFUCIANISM

Neutral Labor Unions Liaison Conference. See LABOR MOVEMENT

New Labor Farmer Party. See RŌDŌ NŌMINTŌ

New Liberal Club. See LIBERAL DEMOCRATIC PARTY

New Man Society. See SHINJINKAI

New Order in East Asia (Tōa shinchitsujo) 東亜新秩序

In November 1938 Prime Minister Konoe announced plans for a "new order in East Asia" in conjunction with the offering of peace terms to China. The idea of a "new order" was a vague one, subscribing to such ideals as Asia for the Asians, Asian self-sufficiency, anticommunism, world peace, and Asian stability. It was to be manifested in the coordination of military, political, and economic activities in China and Manchukuo under Japanese leadership to build up resistance to the threat of Communist and Western imperialist interference in the affairs of the area. The idea was rejected by the Chinese for what it was—a blueprint for Japan's political and economic hegemony in East Asia. Following the outbreak of war in Europe and increasing calls for Japanese control over the colonies of Southeast Asia, a declaration by Konoe in August 1940 referred to the "new order in Greater East Asia"; the area now envisaged covered much of Southeast Asia. The idea of the Greater East Asia co-prosperity sphere (*q.v.*) was an integral part of the concept of a "new order."

Einzig, P. *The Japanese "New Order" in Asia* (London, 1943).
Jones, F. C. *Japan's New Order in East Asia* (London, 1954).
Lebra, J. C. *Japan's Greater East Asia Co-Prosperity Sphere in World War II* (Kuala Lumpur, 1975).

New Structure Movement (shintaisei undō) 新体制運動

From the late 1930s certain of Japan's political leaders led by Konoe Fumimaro began to call for a "new structure" in Japanese political and economic organization. The "new structure" envisaged was a reorganization of the economic and political life of the nation to produce an advanced defense state to cope successfully with the war with China and bring about the "new order in East Asia" (*q.v.*). Apart from a planned economy, the major plank of political reorganization was the establishment of a new one-party movement, which would facilitate communication between government and people and unite the nation behind the emperor and the war effort. Early in 1940 Konoe's followers secretly canvassed support with a view to this new political structure, and in June Konoe, declaring openly his intention of working toward this end, resigned as president of the Privy Council. When, with widespread support, he became prime minister in July, the aim became official government policy. Political parties and other bodies fearful of being thought unpatriotic dissolved themselves in a wave of enthusiasm, and in October the Imperial Rule Assistance Association (*q.v.*) was formed as the nuclear body of the new political structure. Contrary to Konoe's intentions the association became a bureaucratic instrument for national control, implementation of government policy, and spiritual mobilization, and in the face of the war effort the impetus to achieve the original aims of the new structure movement waned.

Berger, G. M. *Parties Out of Power in Japan, 1931–1941* (Princeton, 1977).
Yasko, R. "Hiranuma Kiichirō and the New Structure Movement, 1940–1941," *Asian Forum* 5, no. 2 (Apr.-June 1973).

New Women's Society. See WOMEN'S MOVEMENT

Newspaper Regulations. See NEWSPAPERS

Newspapers

Some news sheets existed in the Tokugawa period, and although in the 1860s the Bakufu and some foreigners published newspapers, the Japanese ones were all in the form of pamphlets. After a temporary ban on publication in 1868 the new government encouraged private newspaper publication. Most of the early papers to be brought out had strong government connections; apart from the *Nisshin Shinjishi*, edited by the Scotsman J. R. Black, the most famous were the *Tōkyō Nichi Nichi* and the *Yūbin Hōchi* of 1872 and the *Chōya* of 1874, the first to have a regular editorial. While the *Tōkyō Nichi Nichi*, from 1874 under the editorship of Fukuchi Gen'ichirō, advocated a pro-government line, other early newspapers moved away from government control and began to call for popular rights. This vocal opposition brought the government to pass the Libel Law and Newspaper Regulations in 1875. The latter, which were strengthened by revisions up to the late 1880s, provided for harsh punishment for those advocating a change in government or criticizing legislation, and many writers and editors were imprisoned under these two laws. Although some of these leading papers retained their political character through the 1880s by identification with opposition to the government, purely political papers declined and the development of such mass papers as the *Yomiuri* (originally founded 1874), the *Asahi* (1879), and the *Ōsaka Mainichi* (1888) marked a change of emphasis in the direction of information and entertainment. Papers increasingly competed for news items. Apart from the mass circulation dailies there were also less "popular" papers such as the *Jiji Shinpō* founded by Fukuzawa Yukichi in 1882, which aimed at political neutrality and specialized in economic articles. The political emphasis in editorials returned from the late Meiji period, and after 1909 a new, harsher Newspaper Law replaced the existing legislation, which had been relaxed in the years since 1887. During the 1920s the mass circulation dailies and the companies producing them strengthened their hold over the newspaper world, taking over the ownership and control of, and in many cases absorbing, the smaller publications. The process was hastened by the government's wartime policy of promoting the merger of papers for reasons of economy and control. During the war years the content and length of those papers that were permitted to continue publication were strictly controlled. Press restrictions were lifted by the Occupation, with some initial provisos, and since then the press has not been subject to any official, wide-ranging censorship; some self-censorship is engaged in, however. The Japanese read widely, and over 100 dailies are published in Japan; some of these have national distributions, and those with the largest circulation include those that predominated prewar, the *Asahi*, the *Mainichi*, and the *Yomiuri*. Daily circulation of these amounts to several million. There are also large circulation specialist papers such as the *Nihon Keizai Shinbun* (Japan Financial Paper) for economic affairs, and the *Hōchi* for sport.

Hanazono, K. *The Development of Japanese Journalism* (Osaka, 1924).
Nihon Shinbun Kyōkai. *The Japanese Press* (Tokyo, 1977).
Whittemore, E. P. *The Press in Japan Today: A Case Study* (Columbia, S.C., 1961).

Nichiren Shōshū. See BUDDHISM

Nihon Hōsō Kyōkai (N. H. K.). See BROADCASTING

Nihon Jiyūtō. See LIBERAL DEMOCRATIC PARTY

Nihon Keizai Shinbun. See NEWSPAPERS

Nihon Kyōshokuin Kumiai. See JAPAN TEACHERS' UNION

Nihon Minshutō. See LIBERAL DEMOCRATIC PARTY

Nihon Nōmin Kumiai. See FARMERS' MOVEMENT

Nihon Rōdō Kumiai Hyōgikai. See LABOR MOVEMENT

Nihon Rōdō Kumiai Sōhyōgikai. See LABOR MOVEMENT

Nihon Rōdō Sōdōmei. See LABOR MOVEMENT

Nihon Rōnōtō. See JAPAN LABOR FARMER PARTY

Nihon Sekigun. See RED ARMY

Nihon Shakaitō. See JAPAN SOCIALIST PARTY

Nihon Shinpotō. See LIBERAL DEMOCRATIC PARTY

Nihon Yūsen Kaisha (N. Y. K.). See MERCHANT SHIPPING

Niijima Jō 1843–1890 新島襄
Samurai from Annaka domain (now Gunma Prefecture), Niijima worked as a *han* official but after some furtive Western learning fled to America. He became a Christian and was ordained. Niijima developed strong views on education and after graduating in 1874 returned to Japan where he founded a group called the Dōshisha (Society of Like Minds). The Dōshisha started an English school of the same name, and in 1877 a women's school. Niijima's ultimate plan was to develop the school into a Christian university, and he vigorously collected funds to this end. Although it was only after Niijima's death that Dōshisha became the leading Christian university, he was nevertheless the major force behind its founding and the education it offered. Niijima opposed the intellectualism and utilitarianism of state-sponsored education, and education at Dōshisha had a Christian, spiritual emphasis. Among Niijima's students were Abe Isoo and Tokutomi Sohō.

Bonnallie, D. A. "Education in Early Meiji Japan, 1868–1890: Fukuzawa Yukichi, Niijima Jō, and Mori Arinori," Ph.D. diss., Claremont Graduate School, 1976.
Hardy, A. S., ed., *Life and Letters of Joseph Hardy Neesima* (Boston, 1892).
Scheiner, I. *Christian Converts and Social Protest in Meiji Japan* (Berkeley, 1970).

Nikkeiren. See JAPAN FEDERATION OF EMPLOYERS' ASSOCIATIONS

Nikkyōso. See JAPAN TEACHERS' UNION

Nikolaevsk Incident (Nikō jiken)
尼港事件
During the Siberian intervention (*q.v.*) the Japanese and White Russian garrison at Nikolaevsk at the mouth of the Amur River surrendered to partisans. The Japanese broke the surrender agreement to counterattack but were defeated with heavy losses. The 136 remaining Japanese soldiers and some 350 Japanese settlers were taken prisoner. In May 1920 the partisans withdrew when threatened by a Japanese relief force after killing an estimated nearly 700 Japanese prisoners and Russian counterrevolutionaries. Those responsible were later sentenced to death by the revolutionary government, but the Japanese demanded compensation, occupying northern Sakhalin to enforce their demands. Although Japan withdrew from Siberia in 1922, it was only in 1925, when formal relations were resumed, that she withdrew, without compensation, from Sakhalin.

Lensen, G. A. *Japanese Recognition of the U. S. S.R.* (Tokyo, 1970).
Parfenov, V. *The Intervention in Siberia, 1918–1922* (New York, 1941).
White, J. A. *The Siberian Intervention* (Princeton, 1950).

Nine-Point Economic Stabilization Program. See ECONOMIC STABILIZATION PROGRAM

Nine-Power Pact (Chūgoku ni kansuru kyūkakoku jōyaku)
中国に関する9ヵ国条約
The Nine-Power Pact was signed in February 1922 at the Washington Conference by the U. S., Britain, Japan, China, France, Italy, Portugal, Belgium, and Holland. It took effect from August 1925. The signatories of the pact subscribed to

the "open door" policy, agreeing to respect China's sovereignty, territorial integrity, and administrative independence. The pact for a while checked Japan's advance in China, but the powers were slow to abandon their privileges there, and many were unilaterally abrogated by the Chinese. Japan's China policy from the late 1920s was criticized as violating the pact, and her refusal to attend a conference of pact powers in 1938 after the outbreak of war with China proved that the pact had no further force.

Sargent, T. A. "America, Britain, and the Nine-Power Treaty: A Study of Inter-War Diplomacy and Great Power Relationships," Ph.D. diss., Fletcher School of Law and Diplomacy, Tufts University, 1969.

1927 Financial Crisis (kinyū kyōkō) 金融恐慌

In March 1927 an investigation of outstanding government bills issued after the 1923 earthquake (earthquake relief bills) revealed that many banks had vast amounts of unsecured debts. A run on many banks followed. The Bank of Japan intervened to halt a panic, but following the closing of the Bank of Taiwan, during April there was a national run on banks which bankrupted many leading banks and companies. The crisis contributed to the fall of the Wakatsuki cabinet and the Tanaka cabinet, which succeeded it, declared an unprecedented moratorium on payments to avoid further closures. The panic had slackened by May. Apart from short-term relief for the crisis, the Bank Law of 1928 promoted the concentration of banking interests by prohibiting small, less secure, banks.

Chō, Y. "Exposing the Incompetence of the Bourgeoisie: The Financial Panic of 1927," *Japan Interpreter* 8, no. 4 (Winter 1974).

1923 Earthquake. See KANTŌ EARTHQUAKE

Nishi Amane 1829–1897 (Baron, 1897) 西周

Samurai from Tsuwano fief (now Shimane Prefecture), Nishi became a Confucian teacher but at the age of 23 went to Edo and studied Western learning, subsequently joining the Bakufu's Western learning institute. In 1862 the Bakufu sent him to Holland, where he studied politics, economics, law, and philosophy, returning in 1865. He became professor at the Kaiseijo and a close adviser to Tokugawa Keiki. After 1868 he worked at the Tokugawa's Numazu Military Academy and then transferred to the new government, where his main contribution was in the development of Japan's new army. He also sat in the Genrōin and later the House of Peers. In 1873 Nishi became a founder member of the Meirokusha (*q.v.*), and the role for which he is remembered is as an agent for the introduction and spread of Western ideas and philosophy to Japan. His own ideas were strongly influenced by Comte and Mill. Nishi left many books and translations, mostly on philosophy.

Hackett, R. F. "Nishi Amane: A Tokugawa-Meiji Bureaucrat," *JAS* 18, no. 2 (Feb. 1959).
Havens, T. R. H. *Nishi Amane and Modern Japanese Thought* (Princeton, 1970).
Minear, R. H. "Nishi Amane and the Reception of Western Law in Japan," *MN* 28, no. 2 (1973).

Nishi-Rosen Agreement (Nishi-Rōzen kyōtei) 西・ローゼン協定

The Nishi-Rosen agreement between Russia and Japan was signed in April 1898. It reaffirmed the Yamagata-Lobanov and Komura-Weber agreements (*q.v.*), pledging (1) neither country to interfere in Korea's internal affairs since Korea was independent, (2) prior agreement in case of either signatory sending military or financial advisers, and (3) noninterference by Russia in the development of commercial and industrial relations between Japan and Korea. The agreement adjusted Russo-Japanese relations along "Manchuria for Korea" (***Mankan kōkan***) lines, with

Russia recognizing Japan's paramount interests in Korea in return for Japanese recognition of Russia's interests in Manchuria.

Malozemoff, A. *Russian Far Eastern Policy, 1881–1904* (Berkeley, 1958).
Rockhill, W. W. *Treaties and Conventions with or Concerning China and Korea, 1894–1904* (Washington, 1904).

Nishida Kitarō 1870–1945
西田幾多郎
Native of Ishikawa Prefecture, Nishida graduated in philosophy from Tokyo Imperial University in 1894 and taught in various institutions including Kyoto Imperial University 1910–1928. Nishida's basic belief in the need to attain, through zen meditation, an emotional state detached from worldly concerns was formalized in 1911 in *Zen no Kenkyū* (A Study of Good) into the philosophy of "pure experience." Buddhist and traditional concepts throughout remained predominant in Nishida's thought, but his efforts to give a logical structure to traditional ideas marked an attempt to bring together Western and Japanese concepts. Nishida is regarded not merely as the foremost philosopher of modern Japan, but his ideas have had a major influence on contemporary writers and intellectuals.

Arima, T. *The Failure of Freedom* (Cambridge, Mass., 1969).
Nishida, K. (ed. R. Schirzinger) *Intelligibility and the Philosophy of Nothingness* (Tokyo, 1958).
_____ (tr. V. H. Viglielmo) *A Study of Good* (Tokyo, 1960).
Viglielmo, V.H. "Nishida Kitarō," in D. H. Shively, ed., *Tradition and Modernization in Japanese Culture* (Princeton, 1971).

Nishida Mitsugu (Zei, Chikara) 1901–1937 西田税
Native of Tottori Prefecture, Nishida graduated in 1922 from the Military Academy where he was connected with the nationalist Yūzonsha (*q.v.*). He resigned from the army but remained active in nationalist circles, strongly influenced by the ideas of Kita Ikki. He worked with Ōkawa Shūmei in the Kōchisa to spread the idea of a Shōwa Restoration (*q.v.*) among young army and navy officers but withdrew from the society in 1927. Nishida was very close to Kita and was the main agent in promoting the latter's ideas among the young officers, both by formal associations and by personal contacts. Nishida was also closely involved with some civilian rightists and was involved with the October incident of 1931 (*q.v.*). In May 1932 he escaped assassination by other ultranationalists who believed him to have revealed the plans for the October incident. Nishida was sentenced to death after the February 26 rising in 1936 and executed in September 1937.

Storry, R. *The Double Patriots* (London, 1957).

Nishihara Loans (Nishihara shakkan)
西原借款
As part of a conciliatory policy toward the official Chinese government of Tuan Ch'i-jui aimed at promoting Japanese interests in China, the Terauchi cabinet awarded well over ¥200 million of loans to China 1917–1918. Of these some ¥145 million were known as the Nishihara loans after Nishihara Kamezō, a personal envoy sent by Terauchi to promote economic diplomacy. The loans were designated for such things as railways, telegraph, timber, and mining development but in fact were largely consigned to political and military purposes. In China many regarded the loans as a national disgrace, and they fueled anti-Japanese feeling. In Japan they were criticized because of lack of any security; most were swallowed up by fighting between various warlords and, politically, achieved little. In 1919 a new consortium for loans to China, consisting of Japan, France, Britain and America, was formed, and such loans as these were subsequently discontinued.

Jansen, M. B. *Japan and China: From War to Peace, 1894–1972* (Chicago, 1975).

Shao, H-P. "From the Twenty-One Demands to the Sino-Japanese Military Agreements, 1915–1918: Ambivalent Relations," in A. D. Coox and H. Conroy, eds., *China and Japan, Search for Balance Since World War I* (Santa Barbara, 1978).

Nishimura Shigeki 1828–1902
西村茂樹

Samurai from the *fudai* domain of Sakura (now Chiba Prefecture), Nishimura studied both Confucianism and Western learning under Sakuma Shōzan and worked as a domain official. In 1873–1886 he worked at the Ministry of Education where he supervised the editing of textbooks and the compilation of encyclopedias and dictionaries. He was a founding member of the Meirokusha (*q.v.*) and wrote many books and articles aimed at spreading knowledge of the West. For Nishimura the development of individual knowledge and morality was essential, and from the late 1870s he began to emphasize the need for an overall system of morality, a thing he considered to be lacking in unadulterated copying of the West. The strongly traditional, Confucian influence in the synthesis of moral systems that Nishimura advocated has caused him to be regarded overall as a conservative. To promote his ideas, he founded the Nihon Kōdōkai (Japan Society for Promoting the Way), which flourished in the reaction against excessive Westernization and by 1902 claimed 10,000 members. Nishimura also lectured regularly to the emperor 1875–1894 and acted as tutor to the crown prince 1886–1893. In 1888 he became head of the Peeresses' School and in 1890 a member of the House of Peers.

Shively, D. H. "Nishimura Shigeki: A Confucian View of Modernization," in M. B. Jansen, ed., *Changing Japanese Attitudes Towards Modernization* (Princeton, 1965).

Nishio Suehiro 1891– 西尾末広

A native of Kagawa Prefecture, from the age of 14 Nishio worked as a lathe operator and was involved in trade union organization in Osaka. He joined the Yūaikai (*q.v.*) in 1919 and was also among the leadership of its successor, Sōdōmei. He rejected first anarchism and then communism, finally supporting parliamentary socialism; this view resulted in Nishio's being among the leadership of various moderate proletarian parties, including the Shakai Minshūtō and the Shakai Taishūtō. He was elected to the Diet 1928, 1930, and 1937 and continued both labor and parliamentary activities until 1940. Postwar Nishio played a leading part in the founding of the Japan Socialist Party, becoming its chief secretary in 1946. He was cabinet secretary under Katayama and deputy premier under Ashida but resigned in June 1948 after a personal no-confidence vote. His arrest shortly after on corruption charges concerning the Shōwa Electric Company (*q.v.*) led to his exclusion from the party, but he returned as a leading figure of the right-wing J. S. P. in 1952. In 1958 he was eventually acquitted in the Shōwa case. Nishio left the J. S. P. in 1959 over renewal of the security treaty with the U. S. and in 1960 founded the Democratic Socialist Party. He was D. S. P. chairman until his retirement in 1967. Nishio's memoirs are an important record of prewar labor and proletarian movements.

Large, S. S. "Nishio Suehiro and the Japanese Social Democratic Movement, 1920–1940," *JAS* 36, no. 1 (Nov. 1976).

Nissan Zaibatsu 日産財閥
(コンツェルン)

In 1928 Ayukawa (Aikawa) Yoshisuke took over the Kuhara mining business and reorganized it as Nissan (Japan Industries). Ayukawa utilized military demand and government orders to extend his business interests and to build a chain of companies whose major interests lay in heavy chemicals and vehicles. The focal enterprise of the group was the great Hitachi Engineering Works. By 1938 Ayukawa controlled 77 companies and as the biggest of the "new" *zaibatsu* was a serious competitor to the older *zaibatsu* (*q.v.*). Ayukawa also took an active interest in the economic development of Manchukuo (*q.v.*). When the government established the Manchukuo Heavy Industries Development Corporation in 1937, Nissan was chosen to provide much of its capital, favored because it had different financial foundations from the older *zaibatsu* and was unconnected with the great *zaibatsu* families hated by the military. Ayukawa's plans were not terribly successful, and he resigned as president of the corporation in 1942. Nissan's close identification with wartime interests brought its decline toward 1945, and lack of the more solid base attained by many of the older *zaibatsu* meant that as an organization it was hard hit by postwar dissolution measures. However, many of its constituent companies have revived, notably those in vehicle production and the Hitachi group.

Rice, R. B. "Hitachi: Japanese Industry in an Era of Militarism, 1937–1945," Ph.D. diss., Harvard University, 1974.
Schumpeter, E. B., ed. *The Industrialization of Japan and Manchukuo, 1930–1940* (New York, 1940).

Nisshin Shinjishi. See NEWSPAPERS

Nitobe Inazō 1862–1933 新渡戸稲造
A samurai from Morioka, Nitobe studied in Tokyo and then graduated in 1881 from Sapporo Agricultural College, where he knew Uchimura Kanzō. From 1884 he studied in Germany and America, becoming a Quaker and marrying an American, and then returned to Sapporo to teach. He was head of the Industrial Bureau in Taiwan 1901–1903 and retained the connection with Taiwan after returning to be professor at Kyoto University 1903–1906. In 1906–1913 he was head of the First Higher School and as professor at Tokyo 1913–1918 specialized in colonial policy. In 1918–1923 Nitobe was president of Japan Women's University and in 1920–1926 worked for the League of Nations secretariat. He became a member of the Imperial Academy in 1925 and of the House of Peers in 1926 and was also director of the Institute of Pacific Relations from 1929. Nitobe was a strong opponent of militarism and nationalism, and as an internationalist, Christian, and liberal he worked until his death to improve international understanding and inform the outside world about Japan. He wrote widely at a popular and academic level on education, agriculture, and colonial policy and also left several works in English on Japan, the best known of which is *Bushidō—the Soul of Japan*.

Kitasawa, S. *The Life of Dr. Nitobe* (Tokyo, 1953).
Nitobe, I. *Collected Works*, 5 vols. (Tokyo, 1972).

Nogi Maresuke 1849–1912 (Baron, 1895; Count, 1907) 乃木希典
Samurai from Chōshū, Nogi became a member of the Kiheitai (*q.v.*) and fought against the Bakufu, then after the Restoration joined the army. In 1886–1888 he studied in Germany but subsequently illness forced him to retire from active service although he returned to fight in the Sino-Japanese War. He was then governor-general of Formosa 1896–1898. Nogi again retired but in 1904 returned as commander of the imperial guard to lead the fight to take Port Arthur. The same year he became a full general. He subsequently served as military councillor and from 1907 as head of the Peers' School. Nogi was regarded as embodying the traditional samurai spiritual virtues; he and his wife committed suicide following the death of the Meiji emperor.

Peattie, M. R. "The Last Samurai: The Military Career of Nogi Maresuke," in *Princeton Papers in East Asian Studies: Japan* 1 (1972).
Scherer, J. *Three Meiji Leaders: Itō, Tōgō, Nogi* (New York, 1936).

Nōhonshugi 農本主義
During the Tokugawa period agriculture was regarded as the economic and social foundation of the country, but from the

early Meiji period official attempts to promote economic expansion largely favored industrial development. From the 1890s officials such as Tani Kanjō argued for the promotion of agriculture to support industrialization and for military reasons, and this bureaucratic agrarianism continued into the Taishō period. Outside official circles the philosophy of *nōhonshugi* (agriculture as the base of the nation) was first formulated as an ideology in the Meiji period as a reaction against attempts to promote industry and commerce at the expense of agriculture. Physiocratic economic theories combined with advocacy of the traditional values of the family system and paternalism and the spiritual values of rural life marked *nōhonshugi* as a conservative doctrine attempting to keep alive the values of Tokugawa Japan. It was espoused especially by the landlord class who had a vested interest in favorable treatment for agriculture, but in the years after 1900 its basic tenet became the necessity of preserving the existence of small independent farmers whose status was endangered by increasing tenancy. Its principal advocate was Yokoi Tokiyoshi. *Nōhonshugi* thinkers stressed agriculture as a source of economic vitality and spiritual purity. Under the influence of agricultural depression in the post-World War I period the doctrine revived and spread to all classes of the rural community. Despite a variation in their ideas *nōhonshugi* thinkers shared a hatred of urbanism, opposed capitalism, and sought to reestablish the dominance of agriculture in the economy. The leading ideologue was Katō Kanji (1884–1965), who claimed that the soul of Japan's farmers was the spirit of Japan. There were also the more militant leaders Gondō Seikyō and Tachibana Kōzaburō. It was they who popularized the ideas of *nōhonshugi*, denouncing urbanism, capitalism, industrialization, bureaucratization, and the invasion of Japan by foreign cultures. They made common cause with right-wing and army elements in their advocacy of nationalism and the traditional Japanese spirit as embodied in the rural community. Militant followers of Tachibana participated in the May 15 incident (*q.v.*). Toward the mid-1930s *nōhonshugi* ideas became absorbed into the overall nationalist ideology, and many adherents became involved in official educational programs in the villages. *Nōhonshugi* ideas have aroused little interest in postwar industrial Japan.

Dore, R. P. *Land Reform in Japan* (London, 1959).
Havens, T. R. H. *Farm and Nation in Modern Japan* (Princeton, 1974).
——— "Katō Kanji (1884–1965) and the Spirit of Agriculture in Modern Japan," *MN* 25, nos. 3–4 (1970).

Noma Seiji 1878–1938 野間清治
Native of Gunma Prefecture, Noma trained as a teacher and worked in Okinawa but then returned to Tokyo. Taking advantage of the prevailing enthusiasm for debating, from 1910 he published a magazine *Yūben* (Eloquence) and later started his own publishing company, Kōdansha. Kōdansha grew to publish numerous books and magazines geared for a mass audience; the term *Kōdansha culture* was used to mean "mass culture." The business was later extended to include records and from 1930 control of the *Hōchi* newspaper, and it remains one of Japan's largest publishers.

Noma, S. *The Nine Magazines of Kōdansha* (London, 1934).

Nomonhan Incident (Nomonhan jiken) ノモンハン事件
In May 1939 sections of the Kwantung Army near Nomonhan, on the Manchukuo-Outer Mongolia border, clashed with Mongolian forces, who then called on Soviet help. Despite attempts by Tokyo to control the spread of fighting, hostilities took on major proportions, involving tanks and artillery, and by August Japanese forces had suffered a major defeat with heavy losses. The conclusion of the German-Soviet Non-Aggression Pact, and, increasingly, Japan's lack of success in the fighting, brought a diplomatic settlement on September 15. The incident was a severe shock to Japan's

military leaders and stimulated a remodeling and reequipping of many forces.

Moses, L. W. "Soviet-Japanese Confrontation in Outer Mongolia: The Battle of Nomonhan-Khalkin Gol," *JAH* 1 (1967).
Young, K. H. "The Nomonhan Incident—Imperial Japan and the Soviet Union," *MN* 22, nos. 1–2 (1967).

Nonparty Cabinets. See CABINET SYSTEM

North China Incident. See SINO-JAPANESE WAR, 1937–1945

Northern Territories Problem. See KURILE ISLANDS

Nosaka Sanzō 1892– 野坂参三
A native of Yamaguchi Prefecture, Nosaka graduated from Keiō University. He joined the Yūaikai (*q.v.*) and edited its journal *Rōdō oyobi Sangyō* (Labor and Industry). In 1919–1920 he studied in London but was deported because of Communist activities. He returned to Japan via Moscow in 1922 and played a leading role in the founding and early activities of the Japan Communist Party. He remained involved in the Communist and labor movement through the 1920s, was arrested several times, and eventually escaped to Moscow in 1931. In 1935 Nosaka became a member of the executive committee of the Comintern, and his statements were treated by many Japanese Communists as "official." He spent the war years from 1940 in Yenan in China. Nosaka returned to Japan in January 1946 and subsequently played a pivotal role in the new Japan Communist Party, as well as sitting in the Diet. He had a central part in policy formulation, promoting the idea of a "lovable" Communist party; this led to his criticism by Moscow in 1950, and although the Japanese party defended him, he afterwards criticized himself. The party split, and Nosaka was shortly afterwards purged. He returned to open political activity in 1955 and subsequently became secretary and then president of the J. C. P. He was elected to the House of Councillors in 1956. Nosaka has continued to dominate the party and remains on its central committee.

Colbert, E. S. *The Left Wing in Japanese Politics* (New York, 1952).
Scalapino, R. A. *The Japanese Communist Movement, 1920–1966* (Berkeley, 1967).

November Incident (Jūichigatsu jiken) 11月事件
In November 1934 several young *kōdō* faction (*q.v.*) army officers and military cadets were arrested for allegedly conspiring to assassinate senior military and civilian personnel, including the prime minister and Lord Privy Seal. The conspirators were not court-martialed for lack of conclusive evidence, although the officers were suspended and the cadets withdrawn from the academy. *Kōdō* faction members maintained that the whole incident was fabricated by the *tōsei* faction (*q.v.*) to discredit the supposedly sympathetic Mazaki Jinzaburō, inspector general of military education. The incident deepened the rift between the two factions and marginally strengthened the *tōsei* faction.

Storry, R. *The Double Patriots* (London, 1957).

Numa Morikazu 1844–1890 沼間守一
Bakufu retainer from Edo, Numa studied Chinese classics and Western learning in Edo, Nagasaki, and Yokohama and in 1865 entered the Bakufu's military training school. He fought for the Bakufu in the 1868 civil war but was close to some members of the new government, and after studying law in England 1872–1873, he worked in the Finance and Justice ministries and as a judge, as well as in the Genrōin. With Kōno Togama, Numa organized a group to study law and investigate freedom of speech, which in 1877 was renamed the Ōmeisha. Numa resigned

from the bureaucracy in 1879 when officials were banned from political discussion and became active in the popular rights movement, calling for lower taxes, the enactment of a constitution, and establishment of a Diet. He became president of the *Tōkyō Yokohama Mainichi.* Numa was closely involved with Jiyūtō members, but his views were more akin to those of the founders of the Kaishintō, in which the Ōmeisha became a major element. He was a major figure in the party even after Ōkuma's resignation. In 1879–1890 Numa was also a member of the Tokyo metropolitan assembly.

Lebra, J. C. *Ōkuma Shigenobu, Statesman of Meiji Japan* (Canberra, 1973).

O

Occupation of Japan

Following Japan's acceptance of the Potsdam declaration (*q.v.*), the Occupation of Japan formally commenced after the surrender instrument was signed on 2 September 1945. The Occupation was administered by the Supreme Commander for the Allied Powers (SCAP) and his numerous staff at the General Headquarters in Tokyo, with allied troops based throughout the country. This post of SCAP was held initially by General Douglas MacArthur and from April 1951 by General Matthew Ridgeway. Despite the presence of a few Commonwealth troops, the Occupation was essentially a U.S. undertaking although in theory SCAP's orders were issued according to directions from the Far Eastern Commission (*q.v.*) in Washington and with advice from the Allied Council for Japan (*q.v.*). Occupation rule took the form of indirect control with SCAP acting through the Japanese government and Diet. The basic lines of policy were set out by the U.S. government and rested on the fundamental premise of the existence in Japan of a conspiracy to wage aggressive war, which had been assisted by certain economic, political, and social factors; the aim of Occupation policy should be the prevention of Japan's again threatening world peace and stability and the creation of a responsible and peace-loving government in Japan. The two lines of policy were demilitarization and democratization. Initially some 5 million troops at home and abroad were demobilized; all military supplies and installations were destroyed and military production halted; ultranationalist and paramilitary societies were banned; the "political" police were abolished and police powers reduced; an amnesty for political prisoners was declared; the International Military Tribunal of the Far East (*q.v.*) tried Japanese charged with war crimes, and some 200,000 persons active during the war period were purged; the payment of reparations to some countries was organized and Shintō was disestablished. The democratization policies included radical reforms in most areas of Japan's politics, economics, and society. Political parties of all colors were encouraged, and the enactment of the new constitution in 1947 provided a new framework within which they could operate. The emperor, having renounced his divinity, became merely the symbol of the state. The judiciary was clearly separated from the executive. Basic human rights guaranteed by the constitution were enshrined in new laws, which radically affected many aspects of Japanese society. The content of education was changed and the whole system remodeled along less elitist and more accessible lines. Radical reforms in the machinery of government led to a considerable increase in local autonomy. Economic reforms included the dissolution of the *zaibatsu* (*q.v.*), land reform (*q.v.*), and legislation for the encouragement of a labor movement. The constitution included a renunciation of the right to maintain war potential. By 1948 most of the more fundamental reforms had been implemented. The growing rift between the U.S. and Russia and the probability of a Communist victory in China meant that Japan became crucial to U.S. Far Eastern strategy. Occupation policy reflected this shift, stressing economic stabilization and reconstruction, the setting up of Japan as a military, economic, and political bastion in East Asia, in a series of measures and modifications, which is often referred to as the "reverse course." Many of the more radical reforms were modified, increasing suppression of flourishing labor union and left-wing activity culminated in the "red purge" (*q.v.*), and the establishment of the National Police Reserve initiated U.S.-encouraged rearmament. The thousands purged at the end of the war rapidly returned to public activity. This policy of rehabilitating Japan as a U.S. ally was hastened by the Communist victory in China and the outbreak of the Korean War. It culminated in the signing of the San Francisco Peace Treaty (*q.v.*) in 1951 concurrently with the U.S.-Japan Security Treaty (*q.v.*). The implementation of the peace treaty in April 1952 brought the Occupation to an end. (See also individual areas of reform.)

Dower, J. W. *Empire and Aftermath: Yoshida Shigeru and the Japanese Experience, 1878–1954* (Cambridge, Mass., 1979).

Goodman, G. K., ed. *The American Occupation of Japan: A Retrospective View* (Lawrence, Kans., 1968).

Kawai, K. *Japan's American Interlude* (Chicago, 1960).

Nishi, T. "The Politics of Freedom: The American Occupation of Japan, 1945–1952," Ph.D. diss., University of Washington, 1976.

Passin, H. "The Legacy of the Occupation," *Columbia East Asian Institute Occasional Papers* (New York, 1968).

Ward, R. E., and F. J. Shulman. *The Allied Occupation of Japan, 1945–1952: An Annotated Bibliography of Western Language Materials* (Chicago, 1974).

Wildes, H. E. *Typhoon in Tokyo* (New York, 1954).

Williams, J. *Japan's Political Revolution Under MacArthur* (Athens, Ga., 1979).

October Incident (Jūgatsu jiken)
10月事件

After the failure of the March incident (*q.v.*) Hashimoto Kingorō and other members of the Sakurakai (*q.v.*), supported by Ōkawa Shūmei and Nishida Mitsugu of the civilian right wing, plotted a coup d'état for October 1931. Leading cabinet members would be killed by air bombardment, advisers to the throne assassinated, and martial law declared. A new government headed by Araki Sadao would carry out domestic reform and enforce the advantage gained by the Manchurian Incident (*q.v.*). Araki, initially unaware of his role in the intended coup, refused to comply when he became aware of it. On October 17 the plot's army ringleaders were arrested, but on the grounds of "sincere motives" they were not punished although disciplinary action was taken to break up the group. The Sakurakai was shortly after disbanded. The matter was hushed up, but political and economic leaders who heard of it were seriously frightened, and it fueled further rumors. Araki's measures against the plotters enhanced his prestige and paved the way for him to become minister of war the following December.

Storry, R. *The Double Patriots* (London, 1957).

Yoshihashi, T. *Conspiracy at Mukden* (New Haven, 1963).

Ogasawara Islands. See BONIN ISLANDS

Ogata Kōan 1810–1863 緒方洪庵

Ogata studied medicine in Edo and Nagasaki and in 1838 opened a medical practice and school in Osaka. His fame as a doctor of both traditional and Western medicine was considerable, and he is regarded as having laid much of the foundation for the development of Western medicine in Japan, writing several books on the subject and translating others. His interest in Western things extended outside medicine, and he became one of the outstanding Dutch scholars (*rangakusha*) of the 1850s. His fame as a teacher attracted students from all over Japan to study Dutch and science as well as medicine. Among them were Fukuzawa Yukichi, Ōmura Masujirō, Sano Tsunetami, and Ōtori Keisuke. In 1862 the school closed, and Ogata moved to Edo as director of the official Institute of Western Medicine, but he died shortly after.

Bowers, J. Z. *Western Medical Pioneers in Feudal Japan* (Baltimore, 1970).
Kiyooka, E., ed. *The Autobiography of Fukuzawa Yukichi* (Tokyo, 1960).

Ogata Taketora 1888–1956 緒方竹虎
Native of Fukuoka, graduating from Waseda University in 1911, Ogata joined the *Tōkyō Asahi* newspaper and acted both as political editor and general editor before becoming vice-president in 1943. As editor Ogata had maintained a relatively liberal and antimilitarist policy, but from 1940 he participated in the Imperial Rule Assistance Association (*q.v.*) and was minister of state, head of the government's information section, and cabinet secretary during 1944–1945. Ogata was depurged in 1951 and in 1952 was elected to the Diet as a Liberal Party member from Fukuoka. He served as minister of state, cabinet secretary, and deputy prime minister under Yoshida and then succeeded him as president of the Liberal Party. He advocated unification of the various conservative parties and became a leading figure on the more radical wing of the new Liberal Democratic Party. Ogata was widely expected to succeed Hatoyama as the party's president, but this was forestalled by his sudden death.

Ogyū Sorai. See CONFUCIANISM

Ōhara Magosaburō 1880–1943
大原孫三郎
A native of Kurashiki, Okayama Prefecture, Ōhara graduated from Waseda University and in 1906 succeeded his father as president of the Kurashiki Spinning Company. He became highly influential in the business world, where he was known for his unique, Christian idealist management methods, but he is perhaps better known for his sponsorship of welfare, research, and educational institutions. The best known of these are the Kurashiki Museum and the Ōhara Social Problems Research Institute. The latter was founded in Osaka in 1919 following the rice riots (*q.v.*). Under the guidance of Takano Iwasaburō, the institute concentrated on labor problems, and from 1920–1949 it gathered many distinguished scholars, issued regular research publications, and made an outstanding contribution to the development of social science in Japan. The Ōhara Institute was in 1949 made part of Hōsei University.

Ōhira Masayoshi 1910–1980 大平正芳
The son of a Kagawa Prefecture farmer, Ōhira attended Tokyo Commercial College (later Hitotsubashi University) and worked in the Finance Ministry. He was elected to the Diet for the first time in 1952. As foreign minister 1962–1964 he normalized relations with South Korea and subsequently served as minister of international trade and industry 1968–1970. In 1971 Ōhira took over leadership of the old Ikeda faction of the Liberal Democratic Party. He unsuccessfully competed for the party leadership in 1972 but gave his support to Tanaka as foreign minister 1972–1974, when relations with China were restored. On Tanaka's resignation Ōhira again contested the leadership of the party, this time with Fukuda Takeo; the conflict enabled Miki Takeo to become prime minister, and Ōhira again served as finance minister 1974–1976. He was defeated by Fukuda for the party leadership in 1976 but subsequently used his position as L. D. P. chairman to build up nationwide personal support within the party, which enabled him to beat Fukuda for presidency of the L. D. P. and the premiership in December 1978. Ōhira was a member of the "mainstream" faction of the L. D. P. and something of a "dove" in

foreign affairs despite a conservative emphasis on the traditional Japanese values. His nickname of "Papa" (*otōchan*) Ōhira suggested relative popularity. Calls for his resignation followed the October 1979 election, but Ōhira appeared to have little problem in maintaining his leadership. Rivalry within the L. D. P. came increasingly into the open, however, and the government was unexpectedly defeated in a no-confidence motion in May 1980. In the hope of rallying national L. D. P. support and uniting the party, Ōhira called a general election rather than resign but died suddenly in June during the campaign.

Ōi Kentarō 1843–1922 大井憲太郎
Samurai from Buzen (now Ōita Prefecture), Ōi studied Western learning in Nagasaki and Edo and came under the influence of Mitsukuri Rinshō. He worked in Kii *han* and then as a legal translator for the new government until 1876. He was strongly influenced by French political thought and from 1874 played a leading part in the popular rights movement. He joined the Jiyūtō in 1881 and played a leading role in its activities as one of its more radical members. He was sentenced to six years imprisonment after the Osaka incident (*q.v.*) in 1885; the sentence was increased to nine years after an appeal, but Ōi was released in 1889. He returned to political activity and joined the revived Jiyūtō but soon resigned over its compromise with the government. In 1892 he founded and became president of the Tōyō Jiyūtō (Oriental Liberal Party), which attempted to gain mass support by advocating help for tenants, universal suffrage, and land tax reform. Ōi remained a fierce critic of the government but from 1898 spent his time working with labor unions and tenant organizations; his influence in the democratic movement waned. To his death he advocated a "strong" policy abroad. Ōi left many works on politics and economics.

Jansen, M. B. "Ōi Kentarō, Radicalism and Chauvinism," *FEQ* 11, no. 3 (May 1952).

Okada Keisuke 1868–1952 岡田啓介
Samurai from Fukui *han*, Okada entered the navy and rose to become admiral in 1924. He served as navy minister 1927–1929 and 1932–1933 and in July 1934 became prime minister. It was hoped that Okada's bureaucratic cabinet, supported in the Diet by the minority Minseitō, would curb independent activity on the part of the army, but it was unable (and in many cases unwilling) to withstand army and right-wing pressure, especially over rearmament, continental strategy, and criticism of the views of Minobe Tatsukichi. The February 1936 election gave the Minseitō a majority in the Diet, but the February 26 rising (*q.v.*) which quickly followed nearly cost Okada his life and brought the resignation of the whole cabinet. Okada retained some political involvement as an elder statesman and was a major critic of the Tōjō cabinet during the war.

Shillony, B-A. *Revolt in Japan: The Young Officers and the February 26, 1936, Incident* (Princeton, 1973).
Young, A. M. *Imperial Japan, 1926–1938* (London, 1938).

Okakura Tenshin (Kakuzō) 1862–1913 岡倉天心(覚三)
The son of a samurai trader in Yokohama, Okakura graduated from Tokyo University in 1880 and entered the Ministry of Education. Influenced by the American Ernest Fenollosa, Okakura had at the university become interested in the development of fine art in Japan, and his desire to found a school to help the revival of traditional Japanese art forms was realized in the founding of the Tokyo Art School in 1889. As president of the school 1890–1898 and as founder of the Japan Art Academy Okakura played a major role in the revival of Japanese art and as an art theorist. He did not reject Western influences but stressed the need to retain things Japanese and the "oneness" of Asia, a concept showing a strong Buddhist influence. He traveled widely in China, India, and the West and in 1904–1913 was keeper of the Oriental section of the

Boston Art Museum. Okakura's English language works include *The Ideals of the East,* which embodies his theory of art, *The Book of Tea,* and *The Awakening of Japan.*

Horioka, Y. *The Life of Kakuzō* (Tokyo, 1963).
Ikimatsu, K. "Okakura Tenshin," *Developing Economies* 4, no. 4 (Dec. 1966).
Maruyama, M. "Fukuzawa, Uchimura, and Okakura," *Developing Economies* 4, no. 4 (Dec. 1966).
Okakura, K. *The Awakening of Japan* (New York, 1904).
______. *The Ideals of the East* (London, 1903).

Ōkawa Shūmei 1886–1957 大川周明
A native of Yamagata Prefecture, Ōkawa graduated from Tokyo Imperial University in 1911. From early on an advocate of Japan's mission to liberate Asia, from 1918 Ōkawa worked in the research department of the South Manchurian Railway Company (*q.v.*) in both Manchuria and Tokyo. He became a prominent figure in nationalist circles, was a joint founder of the Yūzonsha (*q.v.*) in 1919, and associated with Kita Ikki, but increasingly the views of the two men conflicted and Ōkawa resigned. He formed his own nationalist society, the Kōchisha (Gyōchisha) in 1925, succeeded in 1932 by the Jinmukai. Ōkawa's ideas were closely followed by bureaucrats and young officers of middle rank, and he was connected with the Sakurakai (*q.v.*) and the abortive March and October incidents (*q.v.*) of 1931. He was arrested because of Jinmukai involvement in the May 15 incident (*q.v.*) and in 1935 sentenced to five years' imprisonment but was released in 1937. He then worked in the South Manchurian Railway research department again and in intelligence training. Ōkawa's powerful advocacy of pan-Asianism, the supremacy of the Japanese spirit, and a Shōwa Restoration (*q.v.*) to enable Japan to achieve her rightful place in Asia made him, with Kita, the main theoretical leader of the interwar nationalist movement. This led to his being tried postwar as a class "A" war criminal, but he was released on grounds of insanity; his last years were spent writing and lecturing.

Lieberman, M. E. "Ōkawa Shūmei and Japan's Divine Mission," Ph.D. diss., University of California, Berkeley, 1956.
Storry, R. *The Double Patriots* (London, 1957).

Ōki Takatō 1832–1899 (Count, 1885)
大木喬任
Samurai from Saga domain and cousin of Ōkuma Shigenobu, Ōki gained political prominence after the Restoration and served as governor of Tokyo, minister of civil affairs, religious affairs, and education before becoming state councillor and minister of justice in 1873. He retained this post until 1880 when he headed the committee responsible for drafting a new civil code. In 1885 Ōki became president of the Genrōin. He was then privy councillor from 1888 and president of the Privy Council 1889–1891 and 1892. He served as justice minister 1890–1891 and education minister 1891–1892.

Okinawa. See RYŪKYŪ ISLANDS

Ōkubo Toshimichi 1830–1878
大久保利通
Native of Satsuma, despite low samurai rank, Ōkubo became a leading reformer in *han* government. Abandoning in 1865 his earlier attempts to achieve cooperation between court and Bakufu, Ōkubo subsequently devoted his efforts toward cooperation with Chōshū and the radical faction at court to bring about an imperial restoration by force. Regarded as one of the architects of the Restoration, he held top posts in the new government and from the beginning initiated many of its most revolutionary proposals. In 1871 Ōkubo went on the Iwakura mission (*q.v.*) and on his return in 1873 led opposition to the proposed invasion of Korea (*q.v.*), stressing instead that priority must go to domestic development. To this end he

promoted policies for the encouragement of industry, building up the army, and reforming the land tax to stabilize government revenue. He was in charge of suppressing domestic rebellions in 1874 and 1877 and in 1877 was responsible for a reduction in the land tax rate in an attempt to calm rural disturbances. Despite his stress on internal development Ōkubo encouraged the Formosan expedition (*q.v.*) and acted as Japan's representative at the ensuing negotiations at Peking. As *sangi,* and from 1874 as home minister, Ōkubo remained the focus of, and the most influential figure in, the Meiji government until his assassination by a discontented samurai on 14 May 1878.

Brown, S. D. "Ōkubo Toshimichi: His Political and Economic Policies in Early Meiji Japan," *JAS* 21 (Feb. 1962).
Courant, M. *Okoubo* (Paris, 1904).
Iwata, M. *Ōkubo Toshimichi: The Bismarck of Japan* (Berkeley, 1964).

Ōkuma Shigenobu 1838–1922 (Count, 1887; Marquis, 1916) 大隈重信
Samurai from Saga *han,* Ōkuma studied traditional and Dutch learning and gained commercial expertise in the *han* bureaucracy. He participated in the anti-Bakufu movement (*q.v.*) and joined the new government in 1868. He enhanced his reputation by his handling of diplomatic problems (especially that raised by the persecution of Japanese Christians), and his work in the Finance and Civil Affairs ministries enabled him to attain the rank of *sangi,* despite his non-Satchō background. Ōkuma was a keen advocate of Western ideas and technology and in 1873 opposed the invasion of Korea (*q.v.*). As finance minister 1873–1880 he had to try and establish a firm economic base for the new regime while finding the funds to fight internal rebellions; rampant inflation forced him into unsuccessful attempts at retrenchment from 1878. After 1878 Ōkuma became Itō Hirobumi's major competitor for supreme power within the government and was increasingly faced by hostility from the government's Satsuma and Chōshū members. His effective power was reduced in 1880 although he remained a state councillor supervising several ministries, and he was forced to resign in the 1881 political crisis (*q.v.*). His followers persuaded him to found and lead a new political party, the Kaishintō. Ōkuma left the Kaishintō in 1884, but his contacts with its members remained strong. In 1882 Ōkuma also founded the Tokyo College, later Waseda University. In 1888 the post of foreign minister was offered to Ōkuma in an attempt to mitigate opposition to the government. Ōkuma held the post until 1889 when he lost a leg in a bomb attack following criticism of his treaty revision (*q.v.*) proposals. Despite acting as privy councillor 1889–1891, he remained in party politics, still identified with the Kaishintō and opposition to the oligarchy and a highly popular figure. As leader of the new Shinpotō from 1896, Ōkuma served as foreign minister 1896–1897 and minister of agriculture and commerce in 1897, but Shinpotō conflict with Prime Minister Matsukata led to his resignation. In 1898 Ōkuma and Itagaki allied their parties and formed the first so-called party cabinet; Ōkuma was prime minister and foreign minister from June of that year. The cabinet fell in November due to internal dissent, and the party redivided, but Ōkuma continued as leader of the Kensei Hontō (the Kaishintō faction) until 1907 when disillusionment with party politics led him to resign. As chancellor of Waseda University 1907–1914 he devoted himself to writing and education, but a political impasse resulted in Ōkuma's forming his second cabinet in April 1914, supported by the Dōshikai. During his term of office Japan entered World War I and delivered the Twenty-One Demands (*q.v.*) to China. Foreign Minister Katō Takaaki's attitudes provoked conflict with the *genrō,* and the cabinet resigned in October 1916. Even in retirement Ōkuma remained immensely popular. His writings include histories of post-Restoration Japan and reminiscences.

Iddittie, J. *The Life of Marquis Shigenobu Ōkuma* (Tokyo, 1956).
Lebra, J. C. *Ōkuma Shigenobu* (Canberra, 1973).

Ōkura Kihachirō 1837–1928
(Baron, 1915) 大倉喜八郎
The son of a land-owning merchant family in Niigata Prefecture, Ōkura established an arms business in Edo in the 1850s. He supplied arms to the imperial forces during the 1868 civil war and during the early 1870s extended his business to general trading. However, he remained a major purveyor of arms and other military supplies to the government, making huge profits from the Satsuma rebellion and later the Sino-Japanese and Russo-Japanese wars, and continued to be something of a *seishō* (political merchant) (*q.v.*) throughout his career. Ōkura invested his profits in foreign trade and large-scale industrial enterprises, often in fields where others could not or would not risk their capital. He developed a chain of interests ranging from trade and insurance to mining and construction and also invested in Manchuria and China. The breadth of Ōkura's interests was that of a *zaibatsu* (*q.v.*), but its development as such was impeded by the lack of its own bank. Ōkura was also a pioneer of commercial education.

Hirschmeier, J. *The Origins of Entrepreneurship in Meiji Japan* (Cambridge, Mass., 1964).

Oligarchy. See HANBATSU POLITICS

Ōmeisha. See NUMA MORIKAZU

Ōmura Masujirō 1824–1869
大村益次郎
Lower samurai from Chōshū and the son of a doctor, Ōmura studied medicine (his teachers included Ogata Kōan and later the German Philipp Franz von Siebold) and Western military techniques. In 1853 he became adviser to Date Munenari of Uwajima and then to the Bakufu but in 1856 returned to Chōshū. Ōmura was especially interested in the construction of warships and military administration and apart from teaching at the *han* school and importing weapons, he worked with Takasugi Shinsaku to reform the *han*'s military system, promoting the formation of the *shotai.* He was therefore a major figure behind the Westernization of Chōshū's forces. In 1866 Ōmura led Chōshū forces against the Bakufu; he was also one of the leaders of the imperial forces in the Boshin War (*q.v.*). In the new government Ōmura was a major influence behind plans to build a conscript army on the European model and to abolish the domains and all samurai privileges; he was assassinated by a conservative samurai in October 1869, but many of his ideas were carried out by Yamagata Aritomo. Despite his death Ōmura was therefore an important influence on the Meiji army.

Craig, A. *Chōshū in the Meiji Restoration* (Cambridge, Mass., 1961).
Hackett, R. F. *Yamagata Aritomo in the Rise of Modern Japan, 1838–1922* (Cambridge, Mass., 1971).

Ono Azusa 1852–1886 小野梓
The son of a samurai-merchant in Tosa, Ono attended the domain school and fought in the Tosa forces in the 1868 civil war. He studied Dutch learning and English, then traveled to China and the West, and after returning in 1874, he became a strong advocate of social and political reform. He joined the bureaucracy in 1876 and worked on editing the new civil code, as secretary in the Dajōkan and Genrōin, and in the Finance Ministry, but he was close to Ōkuma and resigned in the 1881 political crisis (*q.v.*). With Yano Fumio, Ono was the major influence on Ōkuma's political ideas, and his leading role in the Kaishintō included the drafting of party manifestoes and statements. Ono left several works and translations on politics, law, and economics.

Davis, S. T. W. "Ono Azusa and the Political Change of 1881," *MN* 25, nos. 1–2 (1970).

Ono Group (Ono-gumi) 小野組

The Ono Group was a Tokugawa merchant house with wide business interests. Ono gave financial support to the new Meiji government and with Mitsui and the Shimada Group became official brokers for the receipt and disbursement of government funds; it also served as financial agent for local authorities. Ono made vast profits from dealing in the government's tax rice. In 1872 the Ono-Mitsui Bank was set up as the official agent of the Finance Ministry, the merchant houses themselves ceasing to be brokers. In 1873 this bank came under the management of Shibusawa Eiichi as the First National Bank, but Ono and Mitsui remained the shareholders. Ono used its official position to enlarge its interests into industry, but its finances became overextended. In 1874, when the group was unable to call in its loans and comply with stricter government regulations concerning securing its deposits, the Ono Group was relieved of all official status and went bankrupt.

Miyamoto, M. *A Study of the Ono-gumi* (Science Council of Japan Economic Series No. 45) (Tokyo, 1969).

Ono-gumi. See ONO GROUP

Osaka 大阪

Osaka developed as a merchant city during the Tokugawa period and by the early 18th century had a population of some 350,000. It was the focus of large-scale commerce and finance for most of central and western Japan. Under the Ansei treaties (*q.v.*) Japan agreed to open Osaka to foreign trade and residence in 1863, but in 1861 the foreign representatives agreed to a postponement until January 1868. After the Restoration it was initially proposed to move the capital to Osaka. It was in fact Edo which became the capital, but although many commercial functions did pass to Tokyo, Osaka continued to develop its industry and commerce and expand rapidly. By 1903 its population was nearly 1 million. Osaka remains a major commercial and industrial center, and in early 1977 Osaka metropolitan area had a population of over 8 million, making it Japan's second largest city.

Osaka Conference (Ōsaka kaigi) 大阪会議

Itagaki Taisuke resigned from the government in 1873 over the invasion of Korea (*q.v.*), and Kido Kōin in 1874 over the Formosan expedition (*q.v.*). For such powerful figures to be outside government was potentially dangerous. Kido's absence especially strained the loyalty of remaining Chōshū members of government, so Itō Hirobumi and Inoue Kaoru arranged a meeting between Kido, Itagaki, and Ōkubo Toshimichi in Osaka. This took place January-February 1875. The participants finally agreed on a pledge to move toward the establishment of constitutional government, which was announced in an imperial rescript in April 1875. As a step toward a national assembly they agreed on the establishment of the Genrōin (*q.v.*) and an assembly of prefectural governors. Moves toward the separation of legislature, judiciary, and executive came with the establishment of a supreme court, and separation of administrative duties and advisory responsibilities by the separate appointment of ministers and state councillors. Itagaki and Kido returned to the government as *sangi* and the conference played a significant role in the continuing Satsuma-Chōshū domination of government, although Kido was in semiretirement from 1876, and Itagaki resigned again in October 1875, dissatisfied with the implementation of the pledges.

Fraser, A. "The Osaka Conference of 1875," *JAS* 26, no. 4 (Aug. 1967).

Osaka Incident (Ōsaka jiken) 大阪事件

The popular rights movement in Japan had a close interest in affairs in Korea, and during 1885 former Jiyūtō members led by Ōi Kentarō raised money and men to support a rising by the Korean Independence Party led by Kim Ok-kyun. They believed that following a successful uprising Korea could be used as a base for agitation against the Meiji government to stimulate it to reform. The group stole funds, purchased arms, and made bombs, but prior to embarcation for Korea its activities were discovered by police, who arrested 130 people, mostly in Osaka, in November 1885; 31 of these, including Ōi himself and Fukuda Hideko, were convicted and imprisoned.

Conroy, H. *The Japanese Seizure of Korea, 1868–1910* (Philadelphia, 1960).
Jansen, M. B. "Ōi Kentarō: Radicalism and Chauvinism," *FEQ* 11, no. 3 (May 1952).

Osaka Mainichi. See NEWSPAPERS

Ōsugi Sakae 1885–1923 大杉栄
Native of Kagawa Prefecture, Ōsugi studied foreign languages in Tokyo and while a student became involved with the Heiminsha (*q.v.*). Under the influence of Kōtoku Shūsui he became a leading advocate of direct action, studying the thought of European anarchists and syndicalists, especially Kropotkin. He was arrested frequently and between 1906 and 1911 spent over three years in prison. During the years after 1911 Ōsugi devoted himself to writing and publishing, his ideas inclining toward individualist anarchism, but after World War I he returned again to active politics and was the focal point of the anarcho-syndicalist-dominated labor movement of the early 1920s. Ōsugi's followers failed to achieve cooperation with other wings of the Socialist movement, and Ōsugi's ideas lost popularity although he remained Japan's leading anarchist theorist. During the chaos after the Kantō earthquake (*q.v.*) Ōsugi, Itō Noe, and Ōsugi's nephew were arrested and murdered by the police in Tokyo (the so-called Amakasu incident). Ōsugi left an autobiography, political writings, and translations of Darwin and Kropotkin.

Arima, T. *The Failure of Freedom* (Cambridge, Mass., 1969).
Large, S. S. "The Romance of Revolution in Japanese Anarchism and Communism During the Taishō Period," *MAS* 11, no. 3 (July 1977).
Simcock, B. "The Anarcho-Syndicalist Thought and Action of Ōsugi Sakae," *HPJ* (1970).

Ōtsu Incident (Ōtsu jiken) 大津事件
On 11 May 1891 the Russian crown prince (from 1894 Tsar Nicholas II) on a visit to Japan was attacked at Ōtsu on Lake Biwa by Tsuda Sanzō, a local policeman who claimed to fear Russian aggression toward Japan. The Japanese government, fearful of a crisis in Russo-Japanese relations, sent a mission of apology. The foreign and home ministers resigned, and the emperor visited the tsarevich's sickbed. The Ōtsu court transferred the case to the Supreme Court, where the government, believing that only the death sentence could avert a crisis, exerted pressure for this sentence. However the court voted 6 to 1 against the death sentence and for life imprisonment in accordance with the criminal code. Tsuda died in prison five months later. The Supreme Court's judgment was important constitutionally as it showed an emphasis on legal rather than political considerations and established for many foreigners the independence of the Japanese judiciary.

Teters, B. "The Ōtsu Affair: The Formation of Japan's Judicial Conscience," in D. Wurfel, ed., *Meiji Japan's Centennial* (Lawrence, Kans., 1971).

Outline Plan for the Reconstruction of Japan. See KITA IKKI

Ōyama Ikuo 1880–1955 大山郁夫
Native of Hyōgo Prefecture, Ōyama studied at Waseda University and abroad. As a writer for the *Ōsaka Asahi* 1917–1918 he was a leading exponent of the *minpon-shugi* ideas of Yoshino Sakuzō and a critic of the Terauchi cabinet and the Siberian intervention (*q.v.*). As a professor at Waseda subsequently, Ōyama remained a

leading exponent of "democratic" ideals, cooperating closely with both Yoshino and, in 1919, with Kawakami Hajime on the journal *Warera* (We). During the 1920s Ōyama was among the leadership of the Rōdō Nōmintō (Labor Farmer Party) and the Shin Rōnōtō (New Labor Farmer Party), both on the left wing of the proletarian movement, but although he was very close to communism until renouncing all connections with it in 1929, he was never a member of the party. He was elected to the Diet in 1930, but subsequent restrictions on his political activity led to his spending the years 1932–1947 in the U.S. After returning, Ōyama again taught at Waseda and was elected to the House of Councillors in 1950. As leader of the peace movement in Japan, Ōyama gained worldwide fame and received the Stalin Peace Prize in 1951.

Totten, G. O. *The Social Democratic Movement in Prewar Japan* (New Haven, 1966).

Ōyama Iwao 1842–1916 (Viscount, 1884; Marquis, 1894; Prince, 1907) 大山巌

Satsuma samurai and cousin of Saigō Takamori, Ōyama participated in the anti-Bakufu movement (*q.v.*) and the ensuing civil war and then studied in France 1871–1874. After his return he became a leading figure in the army and the War Ministry and with Yamagata Aritomo was the major architect of Japan's modern military system. He was deputy chief of staff 1878–1882 and chief of staff 1882–1884, as well as being war minister 1880–1891 and 1892–1894. Ōyama was commander in chief of the Second Army during the Sino-Japanese War and then supreme commander of Japanese forces in Manchuria during the Russo-Japanese War, where the success of Japanese troops made his name world famous. He was again chief of staff 1899–1904, also supreme war councillor 1898–1916, and Lord Privy Seal 1914–1916. Ōyama was numbered among the *genrō* in his later years, but his main ambitions lay in the military rather than political field, and he never attained the political preeminence of his Chōshū counterpart, Yamagata Aritomo.

Morris, J. *Makers of Japan* (London, 1906).

Ōyōmei. See CONFUCIANISM

Ozaki Hotsumi 1901–1944 尾崎秀実

Ozaki was born in Tokyo but spent most of his childhood and youth in Taiwan. He graduated from Tokyo University where he was a member of the Shinjinkai (*q.v.*), then joined the *Tokyo Asahi Shinbun*. He took a keen interest in the Chinese Revolution and its problems and 1928–1932 was special correspondent in Shanghai. From student days Ozaki had studied Marxism and had contact with various left-wing figures although he never joined the Communist Party. Leaving the *Asahi* in 1938, from 1939 Ozaki worked part time in the research department of the South Manchurian Railway Company (*q.v.*). His knowledge of and opinions on China were widely respected, and he became a close adviser of Konoe Fumimaro as a member of the Shōwa Kenkyūkai (*q.v.*). Ozaki was arrested in 1941 in connection with the Sorge incident (*q.v.*) and executed for treason in 1944. Apart from prison letters he left several authoritative works on China.

Deakin, F. W., and G. R. Storry. *The Case of Richard Sorge* (London, 1966).
Johnson, C. *An Instance of Treason: Ozaki Hotsumi and the Sorge Spy Ring* (Stanford, 1964).

Ozaki Yukio 1859–1954 尾崎行雄

A native of Kanagawa Prefecture, Ozaki studied at Keiō and worked as a bureaucrat and journalist. He joined the Kaishintō and also participated in the Daidō Danketsu movement (*q.v.*) but was excluded from Tokyo under the Peace Regulations (*q.v.*) 1887–1889. Ozaki was elected to the Diet in 1890 and was subsequently reelected in 24 successive elections, remaining a member until his death. In June 1898 he became education minister under Ōkuma Shigenobu but resigned in October following criticism of a speech he had made attacking the *zaibatsu* in which republicanism was mentioned. In 1900 he joined the Seiyūkai but left it 1903, criticizing its compromises with the Katsura administration. In 1903–1912 he was mayor of Tokyo. Ozaki rejoined the Seiyūkai in 1909 and played a major role in the first movement for the protection of constitutional government (*q.v.*), but he then resigned again from the party over its compromise with the Yamamoto cabinet. He served as justice minister 1914–1916 and in 1916 joined the Kenseikai. He remained a member until 1921 when he left it, considering its suffrage proposals inadequate. He then joined the Kakushin Club but after 1925 maintained political isolation. Ozaki was throughout a strong critic of the factionalism, corrupt finances, and the difficulty of independent action within the political parties; above all, he criticized the incessant compromise with successive *hanbatsu* governments. His maintenance of political integrity achieved by few others brought him the nickname *kenpō no kamisama* (guardian [god] of the constitution). During the late 1920s and 1930s Ozaki was uncompromisingly antimilitarist, strongly opposing prevailing trends within Japanese politics. He was a strong critic of the Imperial Rule Assistance Association (*q.v.*) and everything it symbolized and in 1942 was charged with lese majesty. He was acquitted by the Supreme Court in 1944 but was barred from the Diet from 1943 although officially a member of it. Postwar Ozaki became something of an elder statesman in the Diet and was eventually made an honorary Diet member. His writings include memoirs and political works.

Mendel, D. H. "Ozaki Yukio: Political Conscience of Modern Japan," *FEQ* 15, no. 3 (May 1956).
Ozaki, Y. "Japan's Defective Constitutional Government," in K. Kawakami, ed., *What Japan Thinks* (New York, 1921).
———. *The Voice of Japanese Democracy* (Yokohama, 1916).

P

Pacific War (Taiheiyō sensō)
大平洋戦争

As Japan's 1937 conflict with China lengthened and she drew closer to Italy and Germany, her relations with the U.S. and Britain worsened. Desperate for a way out of the China war, Japan planned a southward advance in an attempt to restrict aid to China and gain control of resources in Southeast Asia. Encouraged by German victories in Europe, in September 1940 Japan concluded a tripartite pact (*q.v.*) with Germany and Italy and the same month moved into northern French Indochina (through agreement with the Vichy regime). The Japanese hoped that this policy would improve relations with the Soviet Union, isolate the U.S., and avoid war with the U.S., but in fact Japanese moves brought together the European and Asian crises and increased anti-Japanese feeling in the U.S. The U.S. responded to this first advance with economic sanctions while maintaining a policy of military noninvolvement. Negotiation with the U.S. started in April 1941, but Japan continued to prepare for further advances to secure strategic resources and prevent relief supplies reaching China and in July occupied southern French Indochina. In autumn 1941, on the grounds that Japan was now protected from conflict with Russia by the Russo-Japanese Neutrality Pact (*q.v.*), a firm decision was made to pursue a southern advance at the risk of war with Britain and the U.S., which had by now responded with a total embargo on exports to Japan. Negotiations between Japan and the U.S. continued, but Japan failed to get the U.S. to accept her objectives in China and on 8 December 1941 initiated war by attacks on Pearl Harbor and Khota Baru. Japanese control of the sea was almost immediate, and U.S. air power in the Philippines was destroyed. Within six months Japan had occupied the Philippines, Borneo, the Celebes, the Malayan Peninsula, Singapore, Indonesia, and Rangoon, cutting off supplies to China. She subsequently advanced into Guadalcanal, the West Aleutians, and northern New Guinea, threatening Australia. During the years 1942–1944 Japan tried to develop this empire and exploit it on the basis of the economic autarky called for by the idea of the Greater East Asia co-prosperity sphere (*q.v.*). These countries were a major source of raw materials and markets, but Japan also tried to impose a new culture and moral order on these countries to strengthen their support for Japanese aims. With Japan's loss of four aircraft carriers at the Battle of Midway in June 1942, the war tide began to turn against Japan, and in February 1943 Guadalcanal was abandoned. Allied attacks aimed at isolating Japan from her empire by the destruction of her merchant marine, navy, and air force became increasingly effective. Japan lost control of the sea and air, which meant that supplies both to armies abroad and to the domestic population were endangered. Insufficient organization within controlled territories meant that sufficient raw material supplies were not available, and the army and navy conflicted over the use of those materials that were available. Both on the mainland and in the occupied territories the populace became subject to increasing deprivation, and in some of the occupied territories the nationalism originally fostered by Japan turned against her. As many Japanese had predicted, Japan was unable to sustain for long the massive war effort needed. Her only hope had been that the U.S. would agree to peace negotiations while Japan still had the upper hand, and this hope for a short war had proved unfounded. The British mounted a land attack in Indochina, and the U.S. took island after island: the Marshalls in February 1944, Saipan June 1944, Luzon January 1945, and the entire Philippines soon after. The allied offensives converged on Okinawa in April 1945, and the island fell in June with tremendous losses on both sides. Bombing of industrial and residential facilities on the Japanese mainland (with the exception of the isolated Doolittle raid of 1942) started in mid-1944 and became severe from early the following year; the use of incendiary bombs was especially effective. As early as late 1943 Japan made moves toward peace, and disillusionment with the course of the war eventually brought down the Tōjō cabinet in summer 1944, but few Japanese were at this time prepared to countenance the unconditional surrender being demanded by the allies. Calls for surrender were renewed after the fall of Germany in April 1945, but strong objections continued to be voiced by many elements, especially among the military, who called for a fight to the end on Japanese soil. Fear of heavy casualties among allied troops invading Japan led to the dropping of atomic bombs on Hiroshima and Nagasaki on August 6 and 9. Under the Yalta agreement (*q.v.*) Russia declared war on Japan on August 8 and invaded Manchuria and Sakhalin. Against strong military opposition an imperial conference on August 14 decided to accept the Potsdam declaration (*q.v.*), a deadlock at the conference being broken by the emperor's decision in favor of acceptance. On August 15 the emperor broadcast an announcement to this effect. The surrender instrument was signed on September 2, and Japan was governed by an army of Occupation until implementation of the San Francisco Peace Treaty (*q.v.*) in 1952.

Butow, R. J. C. *Japan's Decision to Surrender* (Stanford, 1954).

______. *Tōjō and the Coming of War* (Princeton, 1961).

Calvocoressi, P., and G. Wint *Total War: Causes and Courses of the Second World War* (London, 1972).

Havens, T. R. H. *Valley of Darkness* (New York, 1978).

Ienaga, S. *Japan's Last War* (Oxford, 1979) (published in the U.S. as *The Pacific War*).

Iriye, A. *Power and Culture: The Japanese-American War, 1941–1945* (Cambridge,

Mass., 1981).
Toland, J. *The Rising Sun* (New York, 1970).

Paris Peace Conference. See VERSAILLES PEACE TREATY

Parkes, Sir Harry 1828–1885
Parkes was a British consul in China before being posted as envoy to Japan in 1865. He became well versed in Japan's domestic politics and adopted a conciliatory attitude toward the Bakufu's opponents in strong contrast to the French envoy, Léon Roches. After the Restoration Parkes became the leading figure in the formation of the Western powers' policy toward Japan and was a highly influential man listened to by the Meiji leaders, but his popularity decreased as he increasingly took what Japanese considered to be an overbearing stance toward Japan's development. In 1883 he was transferred to China.

Daniels, G. "Sir Harry Parkes: British Representative in Japan, 1865–1882," D. Phil. diss., Oxford University, 1967.
Lane-Poole, S., and F. V. Dickens *The Life of Sir Harry Parkes* (London, 1894).

Patriotic Labor Unions. See LABOR MOVEMENT

Patriotic Public Party. See AIKOKU KŌTŌ

Patriotic Society. See AIKOKUSHA

Patriotic Women's Association. See WOMEN'S MOVEMENT

Peace Movement
The first exponents of pacifism in Japan appeared from the late 19th century among Christians and Socialists, but up to 1945 there was no widespread adherence to pacifist ideals. After 1945, as part of a worldwide trend, a widespread movement for peace developed in Japan not merely among committed pacifists but also among ordinary Japanese; the suffering of the war years was a major stimulus to this. The yearning for peace was initially fostered by the Occupation authorities and integrated into clause 9 of the constitution, which unconditionally renounced the maintenance of war potential and Japan's right of belligerency. The fight to retain this clause has since remained one of the major concerns of the Japanese peace movement, especially from 1950 when the establishment of the National Police Reserve marked the first step toward Japanese rearmament. In 1951 the peace movement's national organizers collected over 4½ million signatures in favor of peace and nonrearmament but failed to halt the formation of the Self-Defense Force (*q.v.*) in 1952 and the conclusion of the U.S.-Japan Security Treaty (*q.v.*) the following year. The other main preoccupation of the movement has been the abolition of nuclear weapons. Antinuclear feeling, naturally strong after Japan's experiences at Hiroshima and Nagasaki, spread with the inception of the cold war and was further stimulated by the Bikini incident (*q.v.*) of 1954. In August 1955 the first of an intended annual conference on the banning of nuclear weapons was held, and this has continued, but the peace movement as a whole has become tied up with ideological conflicts among the left wing, with which it has for long been closely identified, and has suffered severe organizational fragmentation. Despite this, antiwar feeling has remained relatively strong in Japan, experiencing a peak at the time of the Vietnam war in the late 1960s. The antinuclear lobby especially has tended to act in unity despite organizational disunity, and opposition in the Diet has remained strong enough to prevent revision of the "peace constitution." Both antiwar and antinuclear groups remain closely identified with left-wing groups and are strongly supported by women's organizations. Agitation opposing the strengthening of military cooperation with the U.S.

and calling for abolition of the security treaty remains vocal, but involvement in antiwar protests has declined from a peak in 1978, and the considerable support shown for the Liberal Democratic Party in the 1980 election must cast doubts on the depth of popular antiwar feeling.

Takabatake, M. "Political Consciousness and Citizens' Movements from the 1960s On," in Fukuoka UNESCO Association, *Proceedings of 4th Kyūshū International Cultural Conference* (Fukuoka, 1977).
Totten, G. O., and T. Kawakami. "Gensuikyō and the Peace Movement in Japan," *Asian Survey* 4, no. 5 (May 1964).
Ueda, K. "Tabata Shinobu: Defender of the Peace Constitution," in N. Bamba and J. F. Howes, eds., *Pacifism in Japan* (Kyoto, 1978).

Peace Police Law (chian keisatsu hō) 治安警察法

Enacted in March 1900 to consolidate and supplement existing law and order legislation. It was aimed primarily at antigovernment groups, in particular the nascent labor movement. Its provisions included a ban on political activity by soldiers, police, priests, women, and minors (article 5); a ban on secret associations; the right of the Home Ministry to prohibit any association; compulsory registration of political societies and meetings with police; the right of the police to forbid, attend, or disband meetings, discussions, and demonstrations; and a ban on labor organization and strike activity (article 17). Article 5 remained a persistent obstacle for women. Article 17 was a major blow to the labor movement, and although the clause was abolished in 1926, the new Peace Preservation Law (*q.v.*) could be invoked in its place. The Peace Police Law was modified in 1922 and 1926, and although its significance decreased with the enactment of the Peace Preservation Law, it was not abolished until October 1945.

Ayusawa, I. *A History of Labor in Modern Japan* (Honolulu, 1966).
Mitchell, R. H. *Thought Control in Prewar Japan* (Ithaca, 1976).

Peace Preservation Law (chian iji hō) 治安維持法

Passed as a result of conservative pressure immediately after the enactment of universal male suffrage in March 1925. It was largely a response to the vigorous labor and farmers' movement and the increasing popularity of liberal and left-wing thought. The law forbade the existence of organizations and movements wishing to change the *kokutai* (national polity) (*q.v.*) or to end the private property system, as well as the discussion and execution of such intentions; violation of the law was punishable by up to 10 years hard labor. The law was clearly aimed at the more extreme left-wing movements, but the vagueness of its wording and the possibility of loose interpretation meant that altogether some tens of thousands of people were arrested in its name, including many liberals. Thousands were charged. A 1928 amendment by emergency imperial decree made the law's provisions much harsher, including allowing the death penalty to be imposed, and a 1941 revision broadened its scope to include such things as preventive arrest. The law was rescinded in October 1945. Much of the opposition to the Subversive Activities Law proposed postwar was a result of experience with the earlier Peace Preservation Law.

Mitchell, R. H. *Thought Control in Prewar Japan* (Ithaca, 1976).
Okudaira, Y. "Some Preparatory Notes for the Study of the Peace Preservation Law in Prewar Japan," *Annals of the Institute of Social Science, Tokyo* 14 (1973).

Peace Preservation Ordinance. See PEACE REGULATIONS

Peace Regulations (hoan jōrei) 保安条例

On 26 December 1887 the government without warning issued the Peace Regulations (Peace Preservation Ordinance) aimed at crushing the political activity of the resurgent popular rights movement. The regulations forbade the existence of secret societies or meetings, gave the police authority to ban any mass meeting and the circulation of "dangerous" literature, and, most importantly, allowed the Home Ministry to expel all those judged to be plotting or inciting a disturbance or to be a danger to public peace from within a radius of 3 *ri* (7⅔ miles) of the imperial palace in Tokyo. This enabled the government to keep potential troublemakers from the city center, and by December 28 some 570 people had been forced out of the city, including Ozaki Yukio, Nakae Chōmin, Hoshi Tōru, and other leading figures of the antigovernment movement. The regulations severely hindered the liberal movement for a time, although most of those expelled had returned to Tokyo within two years. The regulations were repealed in June 1898.

Hackett, R. F. *Yamagata Aritomo in the Rise of Modern Japan, 1838–1922* (Cambridge, Mass., 1971).
Ike, N. *The Beginnings of Political Democracy in Japan* (Baltimore, 1950).
McLaren, W. W., ed. "Japanese Government Documents," *Transactions of the Asiatic Society of Japan* 42, no. 1 (May 1914).

Pearl Harbor (Shinjuwan) 真珠湾
Pearl Harbor, the U.S. naval base in Hawaii, was the object of surprise attack by over 100 Japanese planes on 7 December 1941. Although aircraft carriers were out of the harbor, most of the U.S.'s air and naval strength in Hawaii was put out of action, giving Japan a considerable advantage in the early stages of the Pacific War (*q.v.*). The success of the attack indicated lack of preparedness on the American side, but the Japanese had issued no prior declaration of war, and the shock of the attack stimulated the U.S. into an all-out war effort against Japan.

McKechney, J. "The Pearl Harbor Controversy: A Debate Among Historians," *MN* 18, nos. 1–4 (1963).
Melosi, M. *The Shadow of Pearl Harbor* (College Station, Texas, 1977).
Wohlstetter, R. *Pearl Harbor: Warning and Decision* (Stanford, 1962).

Peerage
In 1869 former daimyō and court nobility (*kuge*) were given new status as a single class of nobility (*kazoku*), ranking above former samurai (*shizoku*) and common people (*heimin*). After the abolition of the *han* this nobility had no political power of right although some of its members held high office under the Dajōkan system (*q.v.*). In 1884 the peerage was subdivided into five ranks: prince (*kō*), marquis (*kō*), count (*haku*), viscount (*shi*), and baron (*dan*). Male succession to the title was laid down, and the permission of the Imperial Household Ministry became necessary for marriage or adoption. In addition to the existing nobility, rank was also given to those regarded as having given outstanding service to the country. This custom continued through the Taishō and early Shōwa periods. Under the Meiji constitution (*q.v.*) members of the peerage constituted the major element in the House of Peers; all princes and marquises over 25 were members, and other ranks elected a specified number of their members. They therefore received political privileges as of right, which they continued to exercise throughout the prewar period. The peerage was abolished under the 1947 constitution.

Fahs, C. B. "The Japanese House of Peers," Ph.D. diss., Northwestern University, 1933.

Perry, Matthew C. 1794–1858
Commodore Perry was an American naval officer appointed to command a squadron of four ships with the mission of initiating relations with Japan. The squadron entered Uraga Bay in July 1853. Perry presented presidential letters for transmission to the shōgun, refused to make his proposals at Nagasaki as was customary, and demanded the conclusion of some sort of treaty. The Tokugawa authorities asked for time, and Perry

agreed to return the following year with a larger force. The ultimatum caused a domestic political crisis in Japan with the shōgun taking the unprecedented step of asking the opinions of the various daimyō. Perry returned in February 1854 with a force of nine ships moored off Kanagawa. The threat of military force pressurized the reluctant Japanese into concluding the Treaty of Kanagawa (*q.v.*) in March 1854. Perry left Japan after visiting Shimoda and Hakodate in June 1854 and on his return journey concluded a treaty with the Ryūkyū Islands.

McCauley, E. Y. (ed. A. B. Cole). *With Perry in Japan* (Princeton, 1942).
Morison, S. E. *"Old Bruin" Commodore Matthew C. Perry, 1794–1858* (London, 1958).
Walworth, A. *Black Ships Off Japan* (Hamden, Conn., 1966).

Perry Convention. See KANAGAWA TREATY

Police

A police force as such was established only from 1871 when 3,000 policemen were employed in Tokyo to keep law and order. The organizer of the new system developed during the 1870s and 1880s was Kawaji Toshiyoshi, who had studied the police forces of Europe and who conceived the Japanese force as a centralized, authoritarian force with strong powers. The Japanese police force was from 1873 under the jurisdiction of the Home Ministry, and local governors and mayors had the power to call its members out. From 1890 control was increasingly centralized and the powers wielded by the police extended. The regular police force was supplemented by the Higher Police of 1904 and later the Special Higher Police *(tokkō keisatsu)* of 1911. The Special Higher Police was directly responsible to the Home Ministry and had extensive powers and funds for undercover activities. It was used to investigate and control protest movements and to suppress radicals considered to be spreading dangerous ideologies. This so-called "thought police" became the state's weapon for implementing the legislation available to crush communism and other supposedly dangerous trends although during the war years (1937–1945) this aspect of police activity was mainly carried out by the military police *(kenpeitai)*. The military police had been established in 1881 to inspect and superintend military personnel and civilians in military employment and administrative and legal matters relating to them, but as the influence of the army increased, its activities were gradually expanded to include public law and order and control of thought and mass movements. In Korea the *kenpeitai* had extensive powers, which were used to combat any nationalist activity. In Manchukuo also it wielded considerable control over the lives and activities of the general public. In Japan itself during the China and Pacific wars the *kenpeitai* controlled almost every aspect of daily life. The military police was disbanded in 1945, and under the 1947 Police Law control of the regular police was decentralized as part of the democratization policy; control was placed firmly in the hands of local inhabitants and their elected representatives. Police duties were strictly limited by the 1948 Police Duties Law. Problems in coordinating and financing so many local police units, however, led to reforms consolidated in 1954 legislation, which strengthened central control and police powers while retaining specification of police duties. Before the Occupation many Japanese had regarded the police as the authoritarian arm of the government and the military, and this view contributed to intense opposition inside and outside the Diet, which ultimately blocked a proposal by Prime Minister Kishi in 1958 to widen police powers. Despite increasing centralization of police control, emphasis is still placed on the existence of the neighborhood policeman, which is considered a contributory factor in Japan's relatively low crime rate.

Bayley, D. H. *Forces of Order* (Berkeley, 1976).
Clifford, W. *Crime Control in Japan* (Lex-

ington, Mass., 1976).
Leavell, J. B. "The Development of the Modern Japanese Police System," Ph.D. diss., Duke University, 1975.
Rinalducci, R. J. *The Japanese Police Establishment* (Tokyo, 1972).
Sugai, S. "The Japanese Police System," in R. E. Ward, ed., *Five Studies in Japanese Politics* (Ann Arbor, 1957).

Political Merchants. See SEISHŌ

Political Parties

The first political organizations were formed in the mid-1870s by politicians who had left the government over the invasion of Korea (*q.v.*); they called for the establishment of a national assembly. These groups set the pattern for all early parties in that their origins lay partly in opposition to the government and only partly in a genuine interest in Western political institutions. The first real political parties were the Jiyūtō, Kaishintō, and Rikken Teiseitō formed in the early 1880s in anticipation of the enactment of a constitution. Government oppression reduced their activities from 1883, but activity revived in the late 1880s before the first general election. The powers of political parties were severely limited by the Meiji constitution (*q.v.*), and the struggle by parties to gain control of the budget, and through it of government policy, led to a series of Diet dissolutions and elections 1891–1894. From then on there was an increasing trend toward conciliation and government-party compromise, culminating in Itō Hirobumi's forming his own party, the Seiyūkai, in 1900. There followed a period of bureaucrat-party alliance and compromise. With the exception of the short-lived Ōkuma cabinet of 1898 the first real party cabinet was that of Hara Kei in 1918, but extra-party elites retained considerable influence. The parties attained their maximum power prewar under the era of "Taishō democracy" (*q.v.*) and through the 1920s, but ultimately they proved too weak to withstand an onslaught from any group given competing powers under the constitution. Apart from the restrictive nature of the political framework, the very strong connection with the bureaucracy proved difficult to break, and the parties were also weakened by lack of popular support, rife factionalism, corruption, lack of any clear political ideology, and failure to cooperate with each other to oppose antiparty elements. After 1925 left-wing "proletarian" parties also appeared, but they too lacked popular support, were extensively hampered by police suppression, and suffered considerable fragmentation through ideological and personal differences. They never successfully competed with the traditional political parties in terms of Diet representation. Neither established nor proletarian parties were strong enough to withstand army and right-wing pressure in the 1930s, and those parties which remained were dissolved into the new structure movement (*q.v.*) in 1940. No mass party ever appeared in Japan along the lines of the National Socialists in Germany although attempts were made in that direction. After 1945 political parties reappeared, including the previously illegal Communist Party. Under the new constitution there was a considerable increase in status and real power of parties. With the exception of the late 1940s the conservative political parties, consolidated since 1954 in the Liberal Democratic party, have held power continuously, holding a majority in the Diet and therefore forming the government. Japanese parties retain many of their prewar characteristics. Factionalism, normally built around individuals, remains rampant and divisive, and parties are largely held together by tactical considerations; the left wing, apparently condemned to indefinite opposition, fails to form a united front to combat conservatives; popular support is not widespread, and ideology continues often to be subordinated to practical politics. In addition, as the Lockheed scandal (*q.v.*) has shown, business-political connections are not always free of corruption.

Hayashi, S. "Some Problems of Political Parties in the Meiji Era," *Annals of the*

Institute of Social Science (Tokyo) 10 (1969).
Scalapino, R. A. *Democracy and the Party Movement in Prewar Japan* (Berkeley, 1953).
Scalapino, R. A., and J. Masumi. *Parties and Politics in Contemporary Japan* (Berkeley, 1962).
Yanaga, C. *Japanese People and Politics* (New York, 1956).

Political Studies Association (Seiji Kenkyūkai) 政治研究会
Formed by left-wing intellectuals in June 1924. Leaders included Abe Isoo and Kagawa Toyohiko, and the society published a journal *Seiji Kenkyū* (Political Studies). The society's aim was to study the problems involved in creating a proletarian party and to enlist the support of labor and tenant organizations. By October 1925 it had 6,000 members in 80 branches, encompassing a range of left-wing political tendencies. Domination of the association by its more radical elements led to fragmentation, and its influence waned sharply although it continued to exist 1926–1927 under the name of Taishū Kyōiku Dōmei (League for Mass Education).

Totten, G. O. *The Social Democratic Movement in Prewar Japan* (New Haven, 1966).

Port Arthur. See LIAOTUNG PENINSULA

Portsmouth Treaty (Pōtsumasu jōyaku) ポーツマス条約
After the Battle of the China Sea Japan requested the U.S. to mediate in the Russo-Japanese War (*q.v.*), and a conference was arranged by President Roosevelt at Portsmouth, New Hampshire, in August 1905. A peace treaty was concluded by Komura Jūtarō and Count Sergei Witte, the Russian foreign minister, on September 5. Under the terms of the treaty Russia recognized Japan's dominant military, political, and economic interests in Korea; Russian interests in Manchuria, including Liaotung and the South Manchurian Railway, were to be transferred to Japan; Russian troops were to withdraw from Manchuria; Japanese were to be given coastal fishing rights; and Russia was to cede to Japan Sakhalin south of the 50th parallel. Japan had originally demanded the whole of Sakhalin and an indemnity but despite being the apparent victor was in no state to continue fighting to enforce her demands. The Japanese public had been led to expect more out of the peace treaty, and domestic opposition led to the Hibiya riots (*q.v.*) and the resignation of Prime Minister Katsura.

Okamoto, S. *The Japanese Oligarchy and the Russo-Japanese War* (New York, 1970).
White, J. A. *Diplomacy of the Russo-Japanese War* (London, 1969).

Postal System
During the Tokugawa period couriers had existed, but their use was restricted mainly to feudal officials. In 1871, under the guidance of Maejima Hisoka, a government letter service was inaugurated between Tokyo and Osaka; stamps and letter boxes were started, and by 1872 there were services to many major cities. From 1873 the system came under the Communications Department of the Home Ministry, and through the 1870s the network was expanded. By 1881 there was a comprehensive network for parcel and letter post, with a cheap rate for newspapers; postal savings and postal orders had also been introduced. A uniform rate was introduced in 1873 when the government established a state monopoly, ceasing its dependence on private couriers, who were persuaded to set up a transport company. Foreigners initially refused to recognize the service for foreign mail purposes, but by 1880 Japan had joined the Universal Postal Union, and extraterritoriality in the postal sphere had been abolished. In 1885 a Communications Ministry took over the postal and related

services and the telegraph and subsequently developed interests including the telephone and a post office life insurance system.

Den, K. "Japanese Communications: Post, Telegraph, and Telephone," in S. Ōkuma, ed., *Fifty Years of New Japan* (London, 1909).
Hunter, J. "The Abolition of Extraterritoriality in the Japanese Post Office, 1873–1880," in P. Lowe, ed., *BAJS Proceedings* 1, pt. 1 (Sheffield, 1976).
______. "A Study of the Career of Maejima Hisoka, 1835–1919," D. Phil. diss., Oxford University, 1976.
Maejima, H. "Japanese Communications in the Past," in S. Ōkuma, ed., *Fifty Years of New Japan* (London, 1909).
Osaka Mainichi Publishing Company. *The Development of Postal Enterprise in Japan* (Osaka, 1928).

Potsdam Declaration (Potsudamu sengen) ポツダム宣言
On 26 July 1945 the U.S., Britain, and China issued at Potsdam a declaration concerning Japan's surrender in the Pacific War (*q.v.*). The declaration was afterwards also subscribed to by Russia. The declaration stipulated the unconditional surrender of Japan's armed forces, demilitarization and demobilization, military occupation of Japan until a "new order" was established, punishment of war criminals, removal of obstacles to democratization, and material reparations to be exacted and loss of territory in accordance with the Cairo declaration (*q.v.*). Japan accepted the terms of the declaration and surrendered unconditionally on August 15, but there was considerable hesitation due to doubts as to its stance concerning the fate of the emperor. Occupying forces subsequently issued directives and carried out reforms in accordance with the terms of the declaration.

Butow, R. J. C. *Japan's Decision to Surrender* (Berkeley, 1954).
Haring, D. G., ed. *Japan's Prospect* (Cambridge, Mass., 1946).
Kawai, K. "Mokusatsu: Japan's Response to the Potsdam Declaration," *PHR* 19, no. 4 (Nov. 1950).
Lu, D. J. *Sources of Japanese History*, vol. 2 (New York, 1974).

Press. See NEWSPAPERS

Privy Council (sūmitsuin) 枢密院
Set up in April 1888 as a committee to advise the emperor on major policy matters. Its initial task under its first president, Itō Hirobumi, was deliberation on the draft constitution and related laws. The council consisted of a president, vice-president, and at least 12 members over the age of 40, although membership was normally larger than this. The bureaucracy and peerage were strongly represented, and all ministers also had a right to attend meetings. The sphere of competence of the council was wide, relating to constitutional amendments, declarations of martial law, treaties, and imperial rescripts and ordinances on all matters, and its powers were extended further in the late 1890s. It was nicknamed "the watchdog of the constitution" (*kenpō no bannin*), and its actions in effect preserved the powers of the emperor and restricted those of the political parties and the Diet. Although the Privy Council was not supposed to interfere in cabinet deliberations, it used its powers to direct cabinet decision making on several occasions with success. Its political role was especially conspicuous in the fall of the first Wakatsuki cabinet in 1927 and the ratification of the London Naval Treaty (*q.v.*), and through to the late 1930s the Privy Council exerted a major influence on policy formation. It was abolished in May 1947.

Colegrove, K. "The Japanese Privy Council," *American Political Science Review* 25 (Nov. 1931).

Progressive Party. See SHINPOTŌ

Prostitution Abolition Movement (haishō undō) 廃娼運動

Japan has a long history of licensed (i.e., legal) prostitution, and this has had an important influence on the modern antiprostitution movement. After the Restoration, Christian associations led a movement for the abolition of licensed prostitution. An act of 1872 prohibited human sale or its circumvention by adoption and in some cases permitted prostitutes to leave their employers, but it proved ineffective. The movement grew with support from the popular rights movement and was led by the Women's Christian Temperance Association, and in 1892 Gunma Prefecture became the first area to abolish licensed prostitution. A national antiprostitution organization was formed in 1890 and supported by the Salvation Army from 1899, but the movement achieved little. Private prostitution spread from the mid-Meiji period, and although unlicensed prostitution was forbidden in 1904, by 1925 there were an estimated 178,000 prostitutes. The licensed system was strengthened by a Supreme Court decision of 1904 ordering prostitutes wishing to break their contracts to repay advances made to them. After the Manchurian Incident when everything became subordinated to the war effort, prostitution was even sponsored by the government with the enrollment of "women's volunteer corps." In 1947 an ordinance issued on the orders of SCAP illegalized licensed and involuntary prostitution and the sale of human beings, but because voluntary prostitution was unaffected, it was replaced by organized houses of private prostitutes and a totally new phenomenon in Japan—Western-type street walkers (*panpan*), who were estimated to number 56,000 by 1949. From May 1948 prostitution ceased to be a crime under national law. Although many Japanese regarded it as a necessary evil, prostitution became more conspicuous postwar, and the *panpan* prostitution and mixed blood offspring that were often produced created a considerable social problem. From 1948 female members of the Diet led calls for an antiprostitution bill, and Christian and other groups revived their agitation, but only in May 1956 did all prostitution become illegal. At this time an estimated 150,000 females were engaged in prostitution. The law became effective from 1958, but despite revisions in 1974 it has proved relatively easy to circumvent, and prostitution, often highly organized, continues to exist.

de Becker, J. E. *The Nightless City* (Yokohama, 1899).
Fujita, T. "The Prostitution Prevention Law," *CJ* 24, nos. 7–9 (1956).
National Public Opinion Research Institute. *The Japanese People Look at Prostitution* (Tokyo, 1948).

Protectorate of Korea. See KOREA, PROTECTORATE OF

Public Meeting and Political Societies Law. See PUBLIC MEETING REGULATIONS

Public Meeting Regulations (shūkai jōrei) 集会条例

Promulgated in April 1880 (revised and strengthened 1882) in an attempt to combat the popular rights movement. Political societies and public meetings had to be registered in advance with the police. Outdoor meetings and contact between political associations were forbidden, as well as political activity by teachers, soldiers, and students. Uniformed police sent to meetings could "exercise control" by ordering individuals to leave or the meeting to disband. In 1890 the Public Meeting Regulations were replaced by the Public Meetings and Political Societies Law (*shūkai oyobi seisha hō*). Apart from registration—as opposed to police permission—for public meetings and societies the provisions were substantially similar, although there were extra provisions aimed at controlling political societies taking account of the existence of the Diet. A revised version was passed in 1893, but further attempts by the House of Representatives to change its provisions were unsuccessful. The law was abolished in 1900 and replaced by the Peace Police Law (*q.v.*).

Ike, N. *The Beginnings of Political Democracy in Japan* (Baltimore, 1950).
McLaren W. W., ed. "Japanese Government Documents," *Transactions of the Asiatic Society of Japan* 42 (May 1914).

Public Peace Police Law. See PEACE POLICE LAW

Purge. See OCCUPATION OF JAPAN

R

Radio. See BROADCASTING

Railways (Japan)
The first railway in Japan was a miniature one demonstrated by Commodore Perry in 1853. Foreigners urged the construction of railways after the Restoration, but opinion among Japanese was divided. Eventually a £1 million British loan was taken out to assist in the construction of a line between Shinbashi (Tokyo) and Yokohama, which was opened in September 1872. Initially, the government played a considerable role because the enterprise was unfamiliar—what construction there was relied on foreign technical aid, mostly from Britain—and large amounts of capital were needed. Progress was also hindered by political unrest. Even by 1881 there were only 138 miles of government-owned railway, and until the 1890s the economy was largely dependent on alternative forms of land transport. In 1881 the government sponsored the nobility-run Japan Railway Company to build a private line from Tokyo to Aomori, and this marked the beginning of private railway construction. Largely due to assisting legislation there was a boom in private railway construction in the late 1880s and another in the late 1890s. In 1890 there were 551 miles of government railway and 1,147 miles of private lines, but by 1900 the figures were 952 and 2,902 miles, respectively. However, although in some places railways were a good investment, many private companies found themselves in difficulties. Private ownership led to too great an emphasis on immediate returns; there was also lack of standardization within the national network, and some areas were poorly served. This led to talk of nationalization, and although this step had been rejected in the early 1890s, the desire to achieve the planned, strategic development necessary for economic growth and national defense meant that it was taken in 1906. The government purchased 17 companies owning about 2,700 miles of track, bringing some 90% of the existing 5,000 miles of track under government ownership. In 1908 a Railway Bureau was established directly under the prime minister, but in 1920 – 1943 there was a full minister of railways. By 1913 a reasonably comprehensive network covered the four main islands. In the early Shōwa period emphasis was on expansion and electrification. A massive expansion in private lines provided for suburban commuter travel, and the first underground was opened in 1927. Many railways and stock were damaged or run down during the war, but the network is now even more comprehensive, and railways remain the major method of short and long distance travel throughout the country. By the mid-1970s there were some 25,500 miles of state railways and about 5,500 miles of private railways. In 1964 the Japan National Railway inaugurated its now world famous "bullet train."

Ike, N. "The Pattern of Railway Development in Japan," *FEQ* 14, no. 2 (Feb.

1955).
Tanaka, T. "The Meiji Government and the Introduction of Railways," *CJ* 28, nos. 3–4 (1966–1967).
Watarai, T. *The Nationalization of Railways in Japan* (rprt. New York, 1968).

Railways (Korea)

In 1894 a provisional treaty granted Japan concessions to build railways in Korea. Such railways were regarded as having considerable strategic, economic, and political significance for Japanese influence in Asia and were also seen as Japan's gateway to the Asian continent and ultimately to Europe. Although various problems attended subsequent construction, by 1900 the Seoul-Inchon (Chemulpo) railway had been completed under Japanese ownership and by 1905 that from Seoul to Pusan. Japan's effective control over Korea from 1904 meant control was extended to other railways.

Hunter, J. "Japanese Government Policy, Business Opinion, and the Seoul-Pusan Railway, 1894–1906," *MAS* 11, no. 4 (Oct. 1977).
Inoue, Y. "Russo-Japanese Relations and Railway Construction in Korea, 1894–1904," in P. Lowe, ed., *BAJS Proceedings* 4, pt. 1 (Sheffield, 1979).

Railways (Manchuria). See SOUTH MANCHURIAN RAILWAY COMPANY

Rape of Nanking (Nankin jiken) 南京事件

After the Marco Polo Bridge incident (*q.v.*) in December 1937 Japanese troops entered Nanking. The Chinese army had already withdrawn, but Japanese soldiers ran riot, and for the next two and a half months there was an uncontrolled orgy of murder, rape, and looting. Later estimates suggest that in the first six weeks of Japanese occupation of the city some 200,000 civilians and prisoners of war in Nanking and its vicinity were killed. A third of the city's buildings were burned down. Foreign protests had little effect. In the postwar military tribunal the Japanese commander of the forces taking Nanking, General Matsui Iwane, was sentenced to death for criminal responsibility.

Butow, R. J. C. *Tōjō and the Coming of War* (Berkeley, 1961).
Hsu, S. *The War Conduct of the Japanese* (Shanghai, 1938).

Rationing

As the war begun in 1937 against China continued, the Japanese state was increasingly forced to control the supply and distribution of staple foodstuffs and other commodities. Attempts to curtail rice consumption and encourage a mixed diet began in 1939, and in 1940 the government began to purchase rice for redistribution. Rice rationing started in the six principle cities in 1941 and was subsequently extended to the whole country. The rice ration stipulated remained the same until the last months of the war, but increasingly substitutes were supplied, and as other foodstuffs became rarer the ration proved increasingly inadequate. Less attention was paid to nonstaples although controls on commodities such as fresh fruit and vegetables, salt, sugar, soy sauce, and *miso* (soy bean paste) were introduced from 1940. The February 1942 Foodstuffs Control Law unified existing controls and brought all distribution under government control by a central agency. As production turned from consumer goods, such items as clothing also became scarce and were rationed. A black market in food, clothing, and other goods developed. From October 1942 rations were distributed by the neighborhood associations (*q.v.*), and this system was retained during the severe postwar shortages when government control over supply and distribution was in fact strengthened. Only after 1950 were rationing and quota supply of individual commodities gradually abolished.

Havens, T. R. H. *Valley of Darkness: The Japanese People and World War II* (New

York, 1978).
Johnson, B. F. *Japanese Food Management in World War II* (Stanford, 1953).

Red Army (Sekigun) 赤軍
In the late 1960s the Communist League, left-wing elements opposed to the Japan Communist Party, spawned several extreme groups. One of these, the Red Army faction (Sekigunha) of 1969, was dedicated to achieving its aims by violence and prepared for terrorist activities. In 1970 nine members of the group's leadership hijacked a plane to North Korea. Others formed close contacts with pro-Palestinian terrorists. The group's overseas terrorist activities as part of a world revolutionary movement brought it international notoriety under the name of the Japanese Red Army (Nihon Sekigun). In May 1972 three Red Army members shot and wounded dozens of passengers at Tel Aviv airport. In August 1975 others occupied the U.S. and Swedish embassies in Kuala Lumpur and achieved the release of five activists held in Japan. A further plane hijack in September 1977 achieved the release of nine men held in Japanese prisons and a ransom of $6 million. Those elements remaining in Japan after the commitment to international activity from 1970 merged with other elements to form the United Red Army (Rengō Sekigun), but internal dissent culminated in a violent shoot-out in February 1972. The subsequent arrests virtually destroyed the organization, and revival has been slow. This group too in 1979 reverted to a commitment to international cooperation. Information concerning the membership and activity of the Red Army is sparse; although membership abroad is estimated around 30, this number is generally thought to be increasing, and the organization for support within Japan has also been strengthened.

Red Flag Incident (akahata jiken) 赤旗事件
On 22 June 1908 members of all wings of the Socialist movement held a meeting in Kanda to celebrate the release from prison of the Socialist Yamaguchi Kōken. As the meeting adjourned, several followers of Kōtoku Shūsui brandished red flags bearing the slogans "anarchism" and "anarchist communism" and went into the street chanting "anarchy." A fight with police ensued, which ended in 14 arrests on charges of violating the Peace Police Law (*q.v.*). Ōsugi Sakae was sentenced to two and a half years' imprisonment, Sakai Toshihiko and Yamakawa Hitoshi to two, and most of the others to at least one. The incident brought the resignation of the relatively liberal Saionji cabinet and marked the start of stronger action against Socialists by the government.

Kublin, H. *Asian Revolutionary: The Life of Sen Katayama* (Princeton, 1964).
Notehelfer, F. G. *Kōtoku Shūsui: Portrait of a Japanese Radical* (Cambridge, 1971).

Red Purge レッド・パージ
Following Cominform criticism of the Japan Communist Party, the J.C.P., already highly influential, adopted a more "positive" policy, and against the background of the worsening international situation and the Korean War such an attitude led to increasing SCAP hostility toward Communists. In May 1950 Douglas MacArthur suggested that the J.C.P. be made illegal, and although this was not done, in early June 24 members of the J.C.P. central office and 17 members of the editorial board of *Akahata*, the J.C.P. organ, were purged. *Akahata* was suspended on June 27. The so-called "red purge" was extended to affect many J.C.P. members and supposed sympathizers. By late 1950 some 11,000 workers in private concerns and 1,200 in government service had been purged in an ill-screened and indiscriminate operation affecting many who had little connection with the J.C.P. Little resistance was offered even by Socialists. Many of the J.C.P.'s leaders went underground and resumed public activity only after 1955; the purge reduced J.C.P. influence in the

Diet and in the labor movement where it had formerly been dominant.

Cole, A. B., G. O. Totten, and C. H. Uyehara, *Socialist Parties in Postwar Japan* (New Haven, 1966).

Red Wave Society. See WOMEN'S MOVEMENT

Reform Club. See KAKUSHIN CLUB

Rehabilitation of Samurai (shizoku jusan) 士族授産

At the time of the Restoration many samurai were impoverished by reductions in their previously inadequate stipends, and with the subsequent introduction of conscription (*q.v.*) and the commutation of stipends (*q.v.*) some 400,000 samurai families found themselves without both income and work. Few could support themselves on the interest from their capital alone. Fearing that extensive unemployment and economic distress among samurai would hinder modernization and cause political, economic, and social problems, the government adopted rehabilitation measures. From 1870 some samurai were awarded grants to engage in commerce or agriculture. The policy included encouragement of samurai emigration to and reclamation of new areas, and this program was expanded after 1874 when a new system whereby samurai could fuse militia and farming activities (*tondenhei*) was introduced to encourage emigration to Hokkaidō. In 1876 the commutation of stipends became compulsory, but many samurai were unsuccessful in business enterprises, and others were unwilling to engage in them at all. Fearing discontent, the government further encouraged investment in national banks with commutation bonds, large-scale land reclamation, and the granting of loans to found businesses. The policy was only partially successful but played a considerable role in encouraging both agricultural and industrial development at national and regional level.

Harootunian, H. D. "The Economic Rehabilitation of the Samurai in the Early Meiji Period," *JAS* 19, no. 4 (Aug. 1960).

______. "The Progress of Japan and the Samurai Class," *PHR* 3 (1959).

______. "The Samurai Class During the Early Years of the Meiji Period in Japan," Ph.D. diss., University of Michigan, 1957.

Yamamura, K. *A Study of Samurai Income and Entrepreneurship* (Cambridge, Mass., 1974).

Relief Funds

From September 1945 the U.S. provided Japan with two forms of relief: Government Appropriation for Relief in Occupied Areas (GARIOA) and Economic Rehabilitation in Occupied Areas (EROA). GARIOA funds were for the provision of food, fertilizer, petroleum, and medical supplies necessary to avoid starvation and illness, and Japan received these commodities to the value of $2,140 million. EROA funds were aimed at rehabilitation rather than relief, and $224 million of industrial raw materials, notably raw wool and cotton, was provided. Until 1949 the yen accumulated by the sale of these goods in Japan financed a major part of Japan's unfavorable trade balance. From 1949 under the economic stabilization program (*q.v.*) the money was designated as a special aid counterpart fund, of which some 30% went to the Bank of Japan for repayment of recovery loans, the rest on investment in public and private enterprises such as communications and energy. The fund was closed in 1952, the residue going direct to industrial investment or to the Japan Development Bank. In 1962 the Japanese government concluded an agreement with the U.S. for repayment of this debt. This $2,364 million of direct aid was supplemented by some $4,000 million "special procurements" (*q.v.*) from the time of the Korean War.

Cohen, J. *Japan's Economy in War and Reconstruction* (Minneapolis, 1949).

Reparations

After the Pacific War reparation demands against Japan were made by various countries. Initial proposals by the American E. W. Pauley were that industrial capacity, notably war, heavy and mechanical industry facilities, should be transferred to the countries involved. The Far East Commission (*q.v.*) was unable to agree on the matter, but to meet the pleas of the countries concerned SCAP (*q.v.*) was authorized to make some industrial facilities available as an advance for transfer to countries such as China and the Philippines. Even this sort of reparation proved a severe burden on the Japanese economy; transfer of capacity proved difficult anyway and was halted in 1948. As a result of pressure from the countries demanding reparations, the U.S. promised that guarantees of some sort of reparation should be contained in the San Francisco Peace Treaty (*q.v.*). As a result Japan concluded arrangements with individual countries after 1952. An agreement in 1954 promising to pay Burma $200 million was followed by one with the Philippines ($550 million) in 1956 and with Indonesia ($220 million) in 1958. $140 million was also paid to the former South Vietnam. Payments were completed by 1976.

Bennett, M. T. "Japanese Reparations: Fact or Fantasy," *Pacific Affairs* 21, no. 2 (June 1948).
Cohen, J. *Japan's Economy in War and Reconstruction* (Minneapolis, 1949).

Reservists' Association (Zaigō Gunjinkai) 在郷軍人会

In October 1910 the Imperial Reservists' Association (Teikoku Zaigō Gunjinkai) was established to supervise existing independent local reservist groups. The idea of the association came from a group of Yamagata Aritomo's followers; it is Tanaka Giichi, however, who is known as the father of the reservists. The association became the army's main instrument for ensuring military popularity, spreading nationalist ideology, and building up support for the army. Members carried out military drill and patriotic ceremonies, as well as community service, and also cooperated closely with "official" youth and women's groups, especially in the villages. Association members were often high in the social hierarchy of villages and played a leading part in local community life. The army's aims in establishing the association were so successful that the army dominance and reactionary ideology of the 1930s were easily accepted in rural areas. In 1936 the association had 14,000 branches with 3 million volunteers between 20 and 40 years old, half of whom had never seen service. The association was disbanded in 1945, but since 1953 reservists have again founded a national organization.

Smethurst, R. J. "The Creation of the Imperial Military Reserve Association in Japan," *JAS* 30, no. 4 (Aug. 1971).
______. "The Military Reserve Association and the Minobe Crisis of 1935," in G. M. Wilson, ed., *Crisis Politics in Prewar Japan* (Tokyo, 1970).
______. *A Social Basis for Prewar Japanese Militarism* (Berkeley, 1974).

Revere the Emperor, Expel the Barbarian. See Sonnō Jōi

Rhee Line (Rishōban rain) 李承晩ライン

The Republic of Korea (South Korea) was established in 1948 under President Syngman Rhee. Negotiations to resume normal relations between Japan and the republic commenced in 1952 but foundered over the problems of compensation and the so-called Syngman Rhee line. This was a unilateral declaration by Korea of the extent of Korean territorial waters, with the boundary nearer to Japan than that which had operated during the Occupation. Korea's assertion of sole right to fish within this line was disputed by Japan, and during the 1950s hundreds of Japanese ships and their crews were "arrested" by Korea. In Japan the controversy was used as an argument for rearmament; in Korea it fanned anti-Japanese sentiment. After Syngman Rhee's fall relations were resumed and the boundary problem solved in the December 1965 fishing agreement.

Reeve, W. D. *The Republic of Korea* (London, 1963).

Rice

During the Tokugawa period rice was the staple form of revenue and diet for the ruling samurai class, but for many of Japan's poorer inhabitants it was too expensive, and even after the Restoration some 75% of the population lived on a mixture of rice, barley, and millet. However, throughout the prewar period rice continued to be the main food crop grown, accounting for well over 50% of the total cultivated area. After the Restoration both yields per acre and overall rice production expanded, and up to the early 1880s some rice was even exported, but a rapid subsequent increase in demand led to an import surplus from the early 1890s; this amounted to 4 million *koku* (1 *koku* = 4.96 bushels) annually by World War I. Soaring rice prices during the war led to the 1918 rice riots (*q.v.*), and the government subsequently attempted to increase production in and imports from the colonies of Taiwan and Korea to meet the demand created by the increase in population and the rise in living standards. By the late 1920s Korea and Taiwan exported an amount equivalent to 12 to 14% of Japan's own domestic production; the imports undermined prices for domestically produced rice. Legislation after 1921 attempted to regulate rice prices, but this did not mitigate the increasing domestic agricultural unrest and depression. The world depression only worsened the situation; from ¥29 per *koku* in 1929 the Tokyo wholesale price of rice fell to the region of ¥17.5 per *koku* in November 1930, and the 1929 level was reached again only in 1935. Widespread poverty in the villages led to government measures to control rice production and prices; these measures were continued in the economic controls of the war period and the 1940s. During the war rice production decreased due to diversion of manpower, and only from the early 1950s was rice supply restabilized under the changed conditions brought about by the land reform (*q.v.*). By the late 1950s domestic production supplied most of domestic demand, and rice production subsequently rose to surplus levels under the government's rice price support program. Although rice remains the staple of the Japanese diet, per capita rice consumption is declining, and the government's politically motivated policy of purchasing all rice at an agreed price results in an annual rice surplus. This has led to recent attempts to divert farmers from rice production, but in 1977 total rice production still reached some 13 million tons, accounting for about one-third of the total value of agricultural production, although it has declined slightly since then.

Nasu, S. *Aspects of Japanese Agriculture: A Preliminary Survey* (New York, 1941).
Ogura, T. *Agricultural Development in Modern Japan* (Tokyo, 1970).

Rice Riots (kome sōdō) 米騒動

The inflationary boom of World War I meant that by July 1918 rice prices were about four times the prewar level and 170% higher than in the previous year. Wages had failed to keep pace with this rise, which caused considerable hardship not only to urban workers but also to the poorer farmers and tenants in the countryside. Following a demonstration against rice hoarding in July 1918 by fishermen's wives in Toyama Prefecture, discontent erupted in a nationwide wave of riots and demonstrations affecting over 300 places in 30 prefectures. In many places both police and army were called out to quell the rioting, and disturbances stopped only in September. Tens of thousands of people were arrested and over 7,000 charged, many of them *burakumin;* some received the death penalty. The government responded by immediately halving the price of rice, and the riots stimulated a policy of rice imports, increased domestic production, and the use of substitute grains, but agricultural depression continued through the 1920s. The riots, which were the greatest upsurge of popular discontent since the Hibiya riots (*q.v.*), brought about the fall of the Terauchi cabinet.

Kobayashi, U. *The Basic Industries and Social History of Japan, 1914–1918* (New Haven, 1930).
Lu, D. J. *Sources of Japanese History*, vol. 2 (New York, 1974).

Richardson Incident. See NAMAMUGI INCIDENT

Right-Wing Organizations
Right-wing ideology in the prewar period in effect incorporated elements of the prevailing orthodoxy in more concentrated or more extreme form and was closely identified with Japanese nationalism. During the Meiji period right-wing, nationalist societies such as the Genyōsha and the Kokuryūkai grew out of opposition to the government and its Westernization and foreign policies. These groups emphasized the importance of loyalty to the nation and the emperor, the need to preserve Japan's traditional culture, the existence of a divine mission for Japan in East Asia, and pan-Asianism. After World War I such elements became increasingly hostile to left-wing movements, pacifism, and even democracy. Societies which turned their attention more to domestic reform under the emperor, emphasizing traditional Japanese values such as the family, duties rather than rights, and the need for an authoritarian society, included the Yūzonsha and the Kokuhonsha. From the Meiji period leaders of right-wing societies had close contacts with political and economic leaders, and from the beginning of the Shōwa period ideologists such as Ōkawa Shūmei and Kita Ikki, demonstrating a radicalism common among the right wing, exercised an increasing influence. Rural depression and disarmament assisted their ideas of national reconstruction to gain an ever stronger hold on members of the army. Members of right-wing societies, in some cases encouraged by the rise of fascism in Europe, cooperated with young army officers in a series of attempted coups d'état. During the course of the 1930s the more extreme terrorist right-wing elements were gradually suppressed, but the basic general tenets of the ideology of the right became the official orthodoxy of Japanese militarism and authoritarianism. Japan's defeat dealt a blow to the cause of right-wing ideology although the existence of a degree of ideological vacuum postwar may help revival. All remaining right-wing organizations were purged postwar, and the various Occupation measures attempted to remove the economic, social, and political reasons for widespread support for such ideas. Some right-wing organizations revived in the 1950s although they have never formed any united front; organized support is not widespread, but many Japanese would subscribe to certain elements of the ideology. Support for right-wing ideas is assisted by lack of a stable democratic base and the persistence of various premodern economic and social conditions. Continuation of the right-wing terrorist tradition was shown in the murder of Asanuma Inejirō, Japan Socialist Party chairman, in 1960, and during the Security Treaty crisis the same year. (See also individual societies.)

Itō, T. "The Role of Right-Wing Organizations in Japan," in D. Borg and S. Okamoto, *Pearl Harbor as History* (New York, 1973).
Kinoshita, H. "Uyoku, the Right Wing of Japan," *CJ* 27, nos. 3–4; 28, nos. 1–2; 29, no. 1 (1962–1968).
Morris, I. *Nationalism and the Right Wing in Japan* (London, 1960).
Storry, R. *The Double Patriots* (London, 1957).

Rikken Dōshikai 立憲同志会
In January 1913 Katsura Tarō declared his intention of forming a political party.

This abandonment of transcendental government aroused opposition in the House of Peers and marked a departure from the previous pattern of compromise with Hara Kei and the Seiyūkai. Although Katsura's government was brought down by the Taishō political crisis (*q.v.*), the projected party was a focus for opposition to the Seiyūkai, attracting the support of such politicians as Katō Takaaki, Hamaguchi Osachi, Adachi Kenzō, Kōno Hironaka, and Wakatsuki Reijirō. After Katsura's death the new party came into being in December 1913 under the name Rikken Dōshikai (Constitutional Society of Friends) and was led by Katō. In 1914 the party supported the Ōkuma cabinet; it subsequently increased its strength in the Diet and in September 1916 became a major element in the Kenseikai in a merger of forces opposed to the Seiyūkai.

Duus, P. *Party Rivalry and Political Change in Taishō Japan* (Cambridge, Mass., 1968).
Najita, T. *Hara Kei in the Politics of Compromise* (Cambridge, Mass., 1967).

Rikken Kaishintō. See KAISHINTŌ

Rikken Kokumintō. See KENSEITŌ

Rikken Minseitō. See MINSEITŌ

Rikken Seiyūkai. See SEIYŪKAI

Rikken Teiseitō. See TEISEITŌ

Risshisha 立志社
The Risshisha was a local political organization founded in Tosa in April 1874 by Itagaki Taisuke. Other leading members were Kataoka Kenkichi and Ueki Emori. Initially, the society's main function was the relief of impoverished samurai, but it was strongly opposed to *hanbatsu* politics (*q.v.*) and increasingly campaigned for popular rights. In 1877 it submitted a petition for a Diet, and members played a leading role in the Aikokusha, the Diet petition movement, and the founding of the Jiyūtō. The Risshisha was weakened by government suppression of the popular rights movement, in 1883 changed its name to Kainan Jiyūtō, and subsequently disbanded.

Ike, N. *The Beginnings of Political Democracy in Japan* (Baltimore, 1950).

Roches, Léon 1809–1901
French diplomat appointed as envoy to Japan in 1864. Roches developed close relations with Tokugawa Keiki and other Bakufu leaders and attempted to extend French trade and influence while assisting the Bakufu with French capital, technology, and expertise. Among his more successful efforts was the stimulation of a program of naval and military modernization, in which France played a large part. In March 1867 Roches proposed to the shōgun, Keiki, the reform of the country along Western lines, but the plan was too drastic, and few of the suggestions were implemented. His conspicuous support for the Bakufu led him to clash with Sir Harry Parkes, and Roches left Japan in 1868 after the Restoration had severely undermined his strategy.

Honjō, E. "Leon Roches and Administrative Reform in the Closing Years of the Tokugawa Regime," *Kyoto University Economic Review* 10, no. 1 (1935).
Medzini, M. *French Policy in Japan During the Closing Years of the Tokugawa Regime* (Cambridge, Mass., 1971).
______. "Leon Roches in Japan (1864–1868)," *HPJ* 2 (1963).
Sims, R. "French Policy Toward Japan, 1854–1894," Ph.D. diss., University of London, 1969.

Rōdō Kumiai Kiseikai. See LABOR MOVEMENT

Rōdō Nōmintō 労働農民党
In March 1926 center and right-wing elements of the proletarian movement founded a political party named the

Rōdō Nōmintō (Labor Farmer Party) (Rōnōtō for short), which was dedicated to achieving social equality by parliamentary means. Communist supporters were initially excluded, but in October those in the party opposing the entry of the Left resigned from it. In December it came under the leadership of Ōyama Ikuo and members of the labor organization Hyōgikai, and under the guidance of the Japan Communist Party it became a legal front for the far Left and a supporter of extraparliamentary tactics. Despite government harassment two of its members were elected to the Diet in 1928, but many members were subsequently arrested, and in April 1928 the Rōnōto was dissolved. A second party of the same name, often known as the Shin Rōnōto (New Labor Farmer Party), was founded in November 1929 by Ōyama and Kawakami Hajime, despite doubts on the Left as to the value of a new party. Ōyama was elected to the Diet in 1930, but there was increasing dissent within the party, and it was subject to criticism from both the Left and the Right. Such influence as it had rapidly waned, and in July 1931 it became part of the Zenkoku Rōnō Taishūtō (National Labor Farmer Mass Party).

Totten, G. O. *The Social Democratic Movement in Prewar Japan* (New Haven, 1966).

Roesler, K. F. Hermann 1834–1894
German lawyer and economist who came to Japan in 1878 as legal adviser to the Foreign Ministry. Even before Itō Hirobumi's visit to Germany, Roesler was a strong influence behind proposals to draw up a constitution providing for a monarchy on the Prussian model, and as first legal adviser to the Japanese government from 1881 he was closely involved as helper and adviser to Itō and Inoue Kowashi in drafting the Meiji constitution (*q.v.*). He also advised on commercial and other legislation. Roesler left Japan in 1893.

Pittau, J. *Political Thought in Early Meiji Japan, 1868–1889* (Cambridge, Mass., 1967).
Siemes, J. *Hermann Roesler and the Making of the Meiji State* (Tokyo, 1966).

Rokumeikan 鹿鳴館
The Rokumeikan (Deer Cry Pavilion) was a Western-style hall opened in Tokyo in 1883 to provide a place for social intercourse between Japanese and foreigners. The hall was planned by Inoue Kaoru as part of a "Westernization" policy aimed at achieving treaty revision (*q.v.*), and the social events which took place there marked the peak of Japanese enthusiasm for officially sponsored Westernization; these resulted in the years 1883–1887 being termed the "Rokumeikan era." In 1887 Inoue resigned over criticism of his treaty revision proposals and of his Westernization policies in general, and in subsequent years there was a strong reaction against excessive Westernization. The Rokumeikan was sold off in 1889 and eventually burned down in 1945.

Barr, P. *The Deer Cry Pavilion* (London, 1968).
Sansom, G. B. *The Western World and Japan* (London, 1950).
Shively, D. H. "The Japanization of the Middle Meiji," in D. H. Shively, ed., *Tradition and Modernization in Japanese Culture* (Princeton, 1971).

Rōnō Faction. See JAPANESE CAPITALISM DEBATE

Rōnōtō. See RŌDŌ NŌMINTŌ

Root-Takahira Agreement (Takahira Rūto kyōtei) 高平・ルート協定
On 30 November 1908 notes were exchanged between Japan and the U.S. with the aim of dispelling rumors of ill will between the two countries. They were signed by Takahira, the Japanese ambassador to the U.S., and Elihu Root, the U.S. Secretary of State. The notes provided for maintenance of the status quo in the Pacific, respect for each other's possessions and the independence and territorial integrity of China, equality of opportunity

for commerce and industry in China, and the peaceful development of trade. Japan hoped to gain U.S. acceptance of her policies in China by disclaiming territorial ambitions toward Hawaii and the Philippines, and the U.S. restated that it was not prepared to countenance an increase in Japan's strength in Asia. It was doubtful, however, whether the notes entailed any contractual obligation, and their main significance lay in their effect on public opinion; they were well received in both countries but failed to touch on the basic source of disagreement between the two countries, the immigration issue.

Bailey, T. A. "The Root-Takahira Agreement of 1908," *PHR* 9 (1940).
Esthus, R. A. *Theodore Roosevelt and Japan* (Seattle, 1966).
Neu, C. E. *An Uncertain Friendship* (Cambridge, Mass., 1967).

Russo-Japanese Agreements (Nichiro kyōyaku) 日露協約

A series of open and secret agreements signed 1907–1916 marked a rapprochement in Russo-Japanese relations. The first, of July 1907, subscribed openly to the "open door" in China, China's territorial integrity, and maintenance of the status quo in East Asia, and secretly to the division of Manchuria into spheres of interest, Japan's special interests in Korea and Russia's in Outer Mongolia. That of July 1910, aimed at blocking U.S. proposals to neutralize Manchurian railways, had no reference to China's independence. Publicly it restated railway jurisdiction in Manchuria and secretly restated spheres of influence in the area. The July 1912 secret agreement subscribed to spheres of interest of the two powers in Mongolia. The public text of the final pact of July 1916 stated that neither would be party to any arrangement or political combination directed against the other and that they would confer in the case of any threat to maintenance of rights and interests. Secretly, however, this agreement provided for a defensive alliance under which the two countries would fight together in the case of China falling into the hands of a third power. All these agreements were revealed and renounced by Russia after the 1917 revolution. (Some had in fact been revealed well before this.)

Pooley, A. M., ed. *The Secret Memoirs of Count Tadasu Hayashi* (London, 1915).
Price, E. B. *The Russo-Japanese Treaties of 1907–1916 Concerning Manchuria and Mongolia* (Baltimore, 1933).

Russo-Japanese Neutrality Pact (Nisso chūritsu jōyaku) 日ソ中立条約

Signed in Moscow on 13 April 1941. It stipulated that if one party was attacked by a third power, the other would remain neutral, that peaceful and friendly relations would be maintained, and that the territorial integrity and inviolability of Manchukuo and the Mongolian People's Republic would be respected. The term of the agreement was five years, and any intention not to extend it for a further five years was to be announced one year before expiration. For both powers the pact was a guarantee of short-term security. It enabled Japan to concentrate on a southern advance and gave Russia security at a time when she was potentially threatened from both east and west. Japan had not anticipated Germany's opening hostilities with Russia in June 1941; Foreign Minister Matsuoka then wanted to break the pact, but Russian forces in the east remained strong, and Japan decided to wait for a favorable opportunity to fight with Russia, which in fact never came. In April 1945, certain of German defeat, Russia exercised her right to renounce the pact, and although Japan maintained that the Soviet Union should adhere to the pact for its full five years, the Soviet Union declared war on Japan in August 1945.

Lensen, G. A. *The Strange Neutrality* (Tallahassee, Fla., 1972).
Lu, D. J. *From the Marco Polo Bridge to Pearl Harbor* (Washington, 1961).

Russo-Japanese War (Nichiro sensō) 日露戦争

The Russo-Japanese War was brought about by the conflict of Japanese and

Russian ambitions in northeast Asia and more directly by the Russian failure to withdraw from Manchuria, which she had occupied at the time of the Boxer rebellion (*q.v.*). Negotiations to reach a general agreement over these problems failed, and backed up by the Anglo-Japanese Alliance (*q.v.*), the Japanese severed diplomatic relations on 6 February 1904. Japan initiated hostilities on February 8, and war was declared on February 10. On April 13 the Japanese secured the straits between Japan and Korea with a naval victory at Port Arthur; land forces then advanced from Korea into Manchuria. Other forces advanced into the Liaotung Peninsula, and Port Arthur itself fell after a bitter siege lasting June 1904 – January 1905. After driving the Russians back toward Mukden in September 1904, Japanese troops under the command of Ōyama Iwao won several long, hard-fought battles. The final one to take Mukden in March 1905 involved over 400,000 Japanese troops and 350,000 Russians, and in all 200,000 men were killed or injured. This marked what was in effect a Russian defeat, and Russia's situation was worsened in May by the virtual annihilation of her Baltic Fleet in the Straits of Tsushima by Admiral Tōgō's fleet. Peace talks had been carried on almost throughout the war, but by this time both sides wished for a speedy end to hostilities: Japan for reasons of financial and military exhaustion, Russia due to domestic political upheavals and threatened revolution. The desire for peace was supported by other powers, and U.S. mediation ultimately led to the signing of the Portsmouth Treaty (*q.v.*). The war gave Japan a dominant position in Korea and rights in Manchuria and had worldwide significance as the first defeat of a European power by an Asian country. It also stimulated Chinese nationalism and further weakened the tsarist regime.

Asakawa, K. *The Russo-Japanese Conflict, Its Causes and Issues* (London, 1904).
Okamoto, S. *The Japanese Oligarchy and the Russo-Japanese War* (New York, 1970).
Warner, D., and P. Warner. *The Tide at Sunrise* (New York, 1974).

Ryūkyū Islands (Ryūkyū rettō)
琉球列島

Chain of islands off the southwest of Japan, of which the largest island is Okinawa. The Ryūkyūs are inhabited by a people closely related to the Japanese culturally and racially. During the Tokugawa period the Ryūkyū kingdom was a tributary state of China although an extensive trade, mostly in sugar, was carried on with Satsuma *han*, which claimed political supervision over this "autonomous kingdom." The islands' status was unclear in international law, and after the Restoration the Japanese initiated a policy of integrating the islands into Japan both in name and in reality. In 1874 Japan declared the establishment of Ryūkyū *han*, and conflict with China over the islands' status led to the Formosan expedition (*q.v.*). Eventually in 1879 the Japanese overruled Chinese and Ryūkyūan objections and established Okinawa Prefecture. The assimilation policy was accelerated after Chinese objections petered out with the Sino-Japanese War, but it was only in 1920 that the islands were fully integrated into mainland Japan's political and administrative system. Even so, such measures as land tax reform, conscription, and educational modernization were carried out far later than in other parts of Japan, and standards were inferior. The situation remained in many ways colonial with many Ryūkyūans not regarding themselves as one with mainland Japanese who effectively monopolized most influential posts in the islands. The Ryūkyūs were the scene of bitter fighting toward the end of the Pacific War (*q.v.*); Okinawa fell in June 1945 and was used as a base from which to conduct operations against Japan. After Japan's defeat the islands were placed under U.S. military jurisdiction, which in 1950 was converted to civilian administration. Under the San Francisco Peace Treaty (*q.v.*) they were made U. N. trust territories although Japan held residual sovereignty. There were some calls for total independence for the islands, but from the early 1950s there were increasing calls for their reversion to Japan. A form of Ryūkyūan self-government had been initiated after 1952, but it was extremely limited. The Japanese constitution was not enacted, the U.S. controlled all external relations, and the islands remained effectively under U.S. rule. The islands were the site of several huge U.S. bases and held a strategic position in the Korean War, but an increasing antimilitary opposition arose both within the islands and on the Japanese mainland and contributed to general agitation for the islands' return. The prolonged separation clearly caused serious economic, social, and personal problems. Although the northernmost Amami group were returned to Japan in 1953 since they had been part of Kagoshima Prefecture, it was not until May 1972, after a long campaign, that Okinawa again became part of Japan with its own prefectural government. U.S. and Japanese forces remain, however, and are the subject of considerable disquiet among residents. Agriculture, notably sugar, sweet potato, and pineapple production, remains economically most important, but manufacturing is increasing in the islands although they continue to import many things from Japan. The islands are also a favorite tourist destination for Japanese.

Kerr, G. H. *Okinawa* (Rutland, Vt., 1958).
McCune, S. *The Ryūkyū Islands* (Newton Abbot, Devon, 1975).
Watanabe, A. *The Okinawa Problem* (Melbourne, 1970).

S

Saga Rebellion (Saga no ran)
佐賀の乱

In February 1874 Etō Shinpei led a rebellion of discontented samurai in Saga calling for the invasion of Korea and revival of the old "feudal" system. Looked-for support from Satsuma and Tosa was not forthcoming, and the rebellion was quickly crushed by government forces. Etō and the other leaders were arrested and put to death.

Clement, E. W. "The Saga and Satsuma Rebellions," *Transactions of the Asiatic Society of Japan* 5 (Dec. 1922).

Saigō Takamori 1828–1877 西郷隆盛

Despite lower samurai status Saigō became involved in Satsuma domain affairs under the patronage of Shimazu Nariakira. He was initially strongly antiforeign. Due to his support for Hitotsubashi Keiki in the shōgunal succession dispute (*q.v.*) Saigō was banished to Ōshima in 1859 under the Ansei purge (*q.v.*) but was pardoned in 1862, only to be banished again by Shimazu Hisamitsu until 1864. He then served as Satsuma's agent in Kyoto and became closely involved in national politics. He supported the Bakufu in its disputes with Chōshū but in 1866 played a major part in the conclusion of the Satsuma-Chōshū alliance (*q.v.*) and from then on was a leading figure in the movement to destroy the Bakufu. Saigō was one of the main figures behind the 1868 coup d'état, and as leader of the imperial forces in the Boshin War (*q.v.*) he negotiated the peaceful surrender of Edo castle. He initially participated in *han* reforms but in 1871 became state councillor in the central government. He was also appointed commander in chief of the Imperial Guard. Saigō, with Itagaki and Ōkuma, was probably the most influential government figure remaining in Japan during the absence of the Iwakura mission (*q.v.*). He strongly supported the invasion of Korea (*q.v.*), and when the decision to provoke Korea to hostilities was overturned, he resigned from the central government and returned to Satsuma. In 1876 he opened a private school, and the number of his followers in the area increased rapidly. Discontents also gathered around him, and in 1877 he eventually put himself at the head of the Satsuma rebellion (*q.v.*). With the failure of the rebellion Saigō committed suicide in September 1877, but he maintained after death a reputation as the champion and embodiment of the samurai spirit, an image which is still current. With Ōkubo and

Kido, Saigō is regarded as one of the three major figures behind the Meiji Restoration.

Furukawa, T. "Saigō Takamori," in Japan National Commission for UNESCO, ed., *The Modernization of Japan,* vol. 8 (Tokyo, 1967).
Morris, I. *The Nobility of Failure* (London, 1975).
Mushakōji, S. (ed. and tr. M. Sakamoto). *Great Saigō: The Life of Takamori Saigō* (Tokyo, 1942).
Stephan, J. "Saigō Takamori and the Satsuma Rebellion," *HPJ* 3 (1965).

Saigō Tsugumichi 1843–1902 (Viscount, 1884; Marquis, 1895) 西郷従道

Satsuma samurai and younger brother of Saigō Takamori, Saigō fought in the Boshin War (*q.v.*) and studied military organization in Europe 1869–1870. After his return he remained in the army, leading the Formosan expedition (*q.v.*) and also commanding the Imperial Guard against his brother's rebellion in 1877. He was state councillor 1878–1885, minister of education 1878, war minister 1878–1880, and agriculture and commerce minister 1881–1884. From 1884 Saigō was identified with the navy rather than the army and eventually became admiral of the fleet in 1898. He served as navy minister 1885–1886, 1887–1890, and 1893–1898; agriculture and commerce minister 1886; home minister 1890–1891 and 1898–1900; and war minister 1894–1895. He was also briefly privy councillor in 1892 and the same year sponsored the founding of the Kokumin Kyōkai (National Association), a pro-government group in the Diet. In his last years Saigō was regarded as a *genrō,* but his political influence never reached the level of such men as Yamagata Aritomo.

Saionji Kinmochi 1849–1940 (Marquis, 1884; Prince, 1920) 西園寺公望

Member of a Kyoto court family, Saionji participated in expeditions in the 1868 civil war and then studied French and law in Paris 1871–1880. After his return he founded the Meiji Law School, and an interest in popular rights led him to become president of the *Tōyō Jiyū Shinbun* (Oriental Liberal Paper) edited by Nakae Chōmin and Matsuda Masahisa until an imperial decree forced him to cut his involvement. Throughout his political career he was closely identified with Itō Hirobumi, with whom he visited Europe 1882–1883. After periods as envoy to Austria, Belgium, and Germany, Saionji was a member of the Privy Council before being education minister 1894–1896 and 1898 and acting foreign minister 1895–1896. He participated in the founding of the Seiyūkai and acted as prime minister for Itō in 1900 and 1901. In 1900–1903 he was president of the Privy Council and in July 1903 succeeded Itō as Seiyūkai president. Saionji's first cabinet governed January 1906–July 1908. It was a time of some industrial and social unrest, but Saionji, liberal compared with Katsura Tarō with whom he alternated as prime minister 1902–1913, permitted the founding of the first Socialist party. He toured Manchuria, and the South Manchurian Railway Company (*q.v.*) was established; other Japanese railways were nationalized. Agreements were negotiated with France and Russia to consolidate Japan's position in East Asia. As prime minister for a second time August 1911–December 1912 Saionji advocated nonintervention in the Chinese revolution. His retrenchment policies ended in resignation after his refusal to finance two extra divisions for the army. In 1914 Saionji resigned as leader of the Seiyūkai, but as a *genrō* (*q.v.*) from 1912 he remained a major figure in Japanese politics. His support for constitutional politics and party government made him unpopular with the army and bureaucracy, and he frequently conflicted with Yamagata Aritomo, but as Yamagata's influence waned, Saionji became the dominant *genrō*. As the only *genrō* survivor from 1924 he continued to be consulted on major issues although his influence waned in the 1930s. In 1919 Saionji was Japan's chief delegate to the Paris peace conference.

Bailey, J. H. "Prince Saionji and the Popu-

lar Rights Movement of the 1880s," *JAS* 21, no. 1 (Nov. 1961).
Mayer Oakes, T., tr. *The Saionji-Harada Memoirs* (Detroit, 1968).
Ōmura, B. *Japan's "Grand Old Man" Prince Saionji* (London, 1938).
Takekoshi, Y. *Prince Saionji* (Kyoto, 1933).

Saitō Makoto 1858–1936 (Baron, 1907; Viscount, 1925) 斎藤実
Samurai from Mizusawa *han* (Iwate Prefecture) and close friend of Gotō Shinpei, Saitō graduated from the Naval Academy in 1879 and became a full admiral in 1912. As deputy navy minister 1898–1905 and navy minister 1906–1914 he worked for naval expansion but was forced to resign over the Siemens scandal (*q.v.*) and went on the reserve list. In August 1919 he became governor-general of Korea. A bomb was thrown at him soon after his arrival, but he escaped injury. His policy as governor was to replace military by civilian government, but his measures did not in any way weaken Japanese control over the colony. He left to act as Japanese delegate at the Geneva arms limitation conference in 1927 and was also privy councillor 1927–1929, but he was again governor-general of Korea 1929–1931. Saitō was appointed prime minister in May 1932 after the May 15 incident (*q.v.*). He presided over a so-called "cabinet of national unity" with representatives from the parties, bureaucracy, and military. Saitō's foreign policy included the recognition of Manchukuo (*q.v.*) and Japan's subsequent withdrawal from the League of Nations, although attempts were made afterwards to introduce a more conciliatory foreign policy. At home, funds were allocated for the relief of rural distress, but this policy suffered under the demands for increased military expenditure, and the parties in the Diet became increasingly hostile to the cabinet. Army hostility to cabinet policies worsened the situation. Two members of the cabinet resigned over lack of official discipline, and this, in conjunction with the involvement of Finance Ministry officials in the Imperial Rayon scandal (*q.v.*), brought the resignation of the cabinet in July 1934. Saitō became Lord Privy Seal in 1935 but was assassinated in the February 26 rising (*q.v.*).

Young, A. M. *Imperial Japan, 1926–1938* (London, 1938).

Sakai Incident (Sakai jiken) 堺事件
On 8 March 1868 antiforeign Tosa samurai killed 11 French sailors at Sakai (Osaka) and wounded three others. The French envoy, Léon Roches, demanded apologies from national and *han* governments, execution of the offenders, and $150,000 compensation. The new government, which accepted responsibility for foreign relations, conceded the demands; 11 samurai committed suicide by government order, and nine were exiled.

Sakai Toshihiko 1871–1933 堺利彦
A native of Fukuoka Prefecture, Sakai worked as a schoolteacher and journalist on various papers before joining the *Yorozu Chōhō* (*q.v.*) in 1899. A close follower of Kōtoku Shūsui, he turned from liberalism to socialism and in 1903 left the *Yorozu Chōhō* to edit the *Heimin Shinbun* (Commoners' Newspaper), where his passionate pacifism, to which he remained committed until his death, led him into prison. In 1906–1907 he was among the leaders of the first Japan Socialist Party. Remaining close to Kōtoku, he became an adherent of direct action and was imprisoned 1908–1910 after the red flag incident (*q.v.*). He subsequently founded the Baibunsha, a company which published the theoretical journal *Shinshakai* (New Society) and subsequently other journals, and aimed to support and maintain cooperation between Socialists during the period of suppression following the High Treason trial (*q.v.*). From 1917 Sakai shifted to revolutionary Marxism and in 1922 became the first chairman of the illegal Japan Communist Party. He soon advocated its dissolution because of government suppression, and his attempts to concentrate on building mass Marxist organizations led to his arrest in 1923 and brief imprisonment in 1926. Sakai's attitudes were criticized by the Comintern,

and he did not participate in the refounded J. C. P., becoming a leading member of the Rōnō faction in the Japanese capitalism debate (*q.v.*). Sakai was involved with legal left-wing Socialist parties such as the Musan Taishūtō of 1928–1929 and the Tokyo Musantō, for which he was an unsuccessful Diet candidate in 1930, and was adviser to others. He was also a member of Tokyo municipal assembly.

Beckmann, G. M., and G. Okubo *The Japanese Communist Party, 1922–1945* (Stanford, 1969).
Notehelfer, F. G. *Kōtoku Shūsui: Portrait of a Japanese Radical* (Cambridge, 1971).

Sakamoto Ryōma 1835–1867 坂本龍馬
Samurai from Tosa *han*, Sakamoto studied in Edo but returned to Tosa in 1858 and became a leader of the antiforeign and pro-emperor movements there. In 1862 he fled the *han* and returned to Edo, where he met Katsu Kaishū. For a while he worked closely with Katsu, notably in promoting naval and shipping training. Under Satsuma sponsorship he subsequently set up shipping and trading operations in Nagasaki; his activities included the importing of arms for anti-Bakufu *han*. Sakamoto achieved great stature as a national leader of the anti-Bakufu movement (*q.v.*), helping to bring about the Satsuma-Chōshū alliance (*q.v.*). From April 1867 Sakamoto was reinstated by his *han;* the trading company was organized and expanded with Tosa support. Sakamoto was largely responsible for Tosa daimyō Yamanouchi Yōdō's moderate proposals for a peaceful restoration of imperial rule, which he submitted late in 1867. He was assassinated by Bakufu supporters in December 1867.

Jansen, M. B. *Sakamoto Ryōma and the Meiji Restoration* (Princeton, 1961).

Sakhalin (Karafuto) 樺太
Large island north of Japan which from 1807 came under direct Bakufu jurisdiction. From 1855 Sakhalin was in joint Russo-Japanese possession, but a treaty of May 1875 awarded Sakhalin to Russia in return for Japanese possession of the Kurile Islands. During the Russo-Japanese War, Japan occupied Sakhalin and under the Portsmouth Treaty was awarded the island south of the 50th parallel. The islands were administered by the Karafuto Office, and the territory was developed largely as a source of timber and wood pulp; more valuable oil, coal, and fishing resources were in the north. In 1920 Japan occupied northern Sakhalin in retaliation for the Nikolaevsk massacre (*q.v.*), but it was evacuated in May 1925 in return for mineral, forest, and other concessions. Japanese-owned Sakhalin was occupied by Russia in August 1945; a secret clause of the Yalta agreement (*q.v.*) had awarded the whole island to Russia. Japan renounced her claims under the San Francisco Peace Treaty (*q.v.*) but maintains that Sakhalin's status has yet to be determined under international law.

Stephan, J. *Sakhalin: A History* (Oxford, 1971).

Sakoku Policy. See SECLUSION

Sakuma Shōzan (Zōzan) 1811–1864 佐久間象山
Samurai from Matsuyo domain (now Nagano Prefecture), Sakuma became a Confucian scholar but was also interested in military studies and other forms of Western learning. From the early 1840s he began to call for the establishment of a strict coastal defense network and the continued expulsion of foreigners. Sakuma's adaptation of Neo-Confucianism to foreign technology was reflected in his advocacy of the strengthening of Japan and its defenses by the import of Western skills, the doctrine which was later known as "Eastern morals, Western technology." In 1851 Sakuma opened a school in Edo; among his 500 students were Katsu Kaishū, Yoshida Shōin, Sakamoto Ryōma, Katō Hiroyuki, and Nishimura Shigeki, through whom Sakuma exerted a tremendous influence. Sakuma was under house arrest for nine years following Yoshida

Shōin's attempt to travel to the West and during that time further pursued his Western studies. He now came to the conclusion that the expulsion of foreigners was unrealistic and supported the policy of *kōbu gattai* (*q.v.*) as the best defense against foreign attack. Sakuma was pardoned in 1862 and in 1864 was summoned to Edo to advise the Bakufu but was shortly afterwards assassinated by anti-foreign samurai.

Chang, R. T. *From Prejudice to Tolerance: A Study of the Japanese Image of the West, 1826–1864* (Tokyo, 1970).
_____. "Fujita Tōko and Sakuma Shōzan: Bakumatsu Intellectuals and the West," Ph.D. diss., University of Michigan, 1964.
Harootunian, H. D. *Toward Restoration* (Berkeley, 1970).
Kosaka, M. *Japanese Thought in the Meiji Era* (Tokyo, 1958).

Sakurakai 桜会

The Sakurakai (Cherry Society) was an informal nationalist society formed within the army in autumn 1930. It consisted largely of officers below the rank of lieutenant-colonel, some 60% of them from the general staff. The remainder were mostly at the War Ministry and army educational establishments. Eventually there were some 100 members of varying views, with a strong radical core led by Hashimoto Kingorō and influenced by Kita Ikki and Ōkawa Shūmei. This core considered that the establishment of a military-controlled society in Japan, i.e., "domestic reconstruction," was a prerequisite to advancing Japan's interests in Manchuria and East Asia generally. Sakurakai members were involved in the March and October incidents (*q.v.*), and the society was then disbanded, but although its leaders were dispersed, they were not punished otherwise for their activities.

Crowley, J. B. *Japan's Quest for Autonomy* (Princeton, 1966).
Storry, R. *The Double Patriots* (London, 1957).

Samurai, Rehabilitation of. See Rehabilitation of Samurai

San Francisco Peace Treaty
(Sanfuranshisuko kōwa jōyaku)
サンフランシスコ講和条約

From 1947 there was growing pressure in the U.S. for an end to the Occupation of Japan (*q.v.*). This pressure was stimulated by increasing international tension and U.S. concerns over security in the Pacific. John Foster Dulles was assigned the task of handling the conclusion of a treaty, and in September 1950 the State Department was authorized to initiate informal discussions on the matter. Because of disagreement with the Soviet Union negotiation on the terms of the treaty was carried on on a bilateral basis through diplomatic channels rather than at a conference of allied governments. A nonpunitive, nonrestrictive treaty was drafted by the U.S. after consultation with Britain and presented for signing to an allied conference of 51 nations at San Francisco in September 1951. India, Burma, and Yugoslavia were invited but did not attend. China was not invited due to disagreement over the locus of power. Forty-eight of these countries and Japan signed the treaty on September 8. Under the terms of the treaty Japan was to gain her independence and the Occupation to be concluded, but Japan's territorial claims to Korea, Taiwan, the Pescadores, the Kuriles, South Sakhalin, and the Spratly and Paracel Islands were abandoned; no final disposition of these areas was made in the treaty, however. The Ryūkyū and Bonin islands were to be controlled by the U.S. under a U.N. trusteeship. Japan also renounced her former rights and interests in China and agreed to pay reparations to certain countries. The treaty stated Japan's right to individual and collective defense, and the U.S.-Japan Security Treaty (*q.v.*) was simultaneously signed. The Soviet Union, Poland, and Czechoslovakia objected to the treaty on the grounds that there could be no real peace without China, that the territorial problem was not resolved, and that the security treaty was too closely tied up with the matter. They claimed that declaration of any separate peace by the U.S. and other countries would violate an agreement of "one peace" made in 1942 and therefore refused to sign. Japan remained technically at war with these countries. There was also considerable opposition to the treaty's terms within Japan, but the Japanese were keen to regain independence, and following ratification the treaty came into effect on 28 April 1952. It concluded the Occupation of Japan and World War II in the Pacific. Japan signed a peace agreement with the Chinese Nationalist regime on Taiwan, which remained in force from April 1952 until the Japanese opened diplomatic relations with the People's Republic of China. Agreement was reached with India in June 1952 and with Burma in November 1954. Relations were restored with Yugoslavia in 1952, the U.S.S.R. in October 1956, and Poland and Czechoslovakia in 1957, but no peace treaty has been signed with these countries.

Cohen, B. C. *The Political Process and Foreign Policy* (Princeton, 1957).
Curtis, G. L. "The Dulles-Yoshida Negotiations on the San Francisco Peace Treaty," in A. W. Cordier, ed., *Columbia Essays in International Affairs, the Dean's Papers,* vol. 2 (New York, 1966).
Dower, J. W. *Empire and Aftermath—Yoshida Shigeru and the Japanese Experience, 1878–1954* (Cambridge, Mass., 1979).
Dunn, F. S. *Peacemaking and the Settlement with Japan* (Princeton, 1963).
U.S. Department of State. *Record of Proceedings of Conference for the Conclusion and Signature of the Treaty of Peace with Japan—San Francisco, September 4–8, 1951* (Washington, D.C., 1951)

Sanbetsu Kaigi. See LABOR MOVEMENT

Sanjō Sanetomi 1837–1891 (Prince) 三条実美

Court noble, Sanjō became a leader of the anti-Bakufu, antiforeign movement at court and in 1863 was forced to flee to Chōshū. Reinstated by events, by late 1867 he had returned to Kyoto and then held the highest offices in the new Meiji government. From 1871 Sanjō wielded considerable influence as *dajō daijin,* the government's highest officeholder under the Dajōkan system. With the introduction of the cabinet system in 1885 he became Lord Privy Seal and retained the post until his death. He acted temporarily as prime minister October-December 1889.

Morris, J. *Makers of Japan* (London, 1906).

Sano Manabu 1892–1953 佐野学

Native of Ōita Prefecture, Sano graduated in 1917 from Tokyo University, where he was involved with the Shinjinkai (*q.v.*) and developed an interest in socialism. He afterwards became a lecturer at Waseda University. From 1921 Sano was active in Sōdōmei, and in 1922 he participated in the founding of the Japan Communist Party. In 1923 he became a member of its central committee, but his questioning by police at Waseda the same year led to the arrest of many radicals, and Sano himself fled to the Soviet Union in 1923 to escape arrest. After spending the years 1924–1925 in Shanghai, he returned to Japan to try and rebuild the party, whose dissolution in 1924 he had opposed but in 1926 was imprisoned for 10 months. A strong opponent of Fukumotoism (*q.v.*), Sano was on the party's central executive committee from 1927. He escaped the March 1928 arrests but was arrested in 1929 in Shanghai and brought back to Japan. After a trial 1931–1932 Sano was sentenced to life imprisonment, but his *tenkō* (*q.v.*) in 1933, along with that of Nabeyama Sadachika, had tremendous repercussions on the whole movement. He was released from jail in 1943 and served with the Japanese authorities in Peking. After 1945 he was again professor at Waseda and founded the Japan Political and Economic Research Center. Sano stood unsuccessfully for the Diet in 1947.

Beckmann, G. M., and G. Okubo. *The*

Japanese Communist Party, 1922–1945 (Stanford, 1969).
Scalapino, R. A. *The Japanese Communist Movement, 1920–1966* (Berkeley, 1967).
Swearingen, R., and P. Langer. *Red Flag in Japan* (Cambridge, Mass., 1952).

Sano Tsunetami 1823–1902 (Viscount, 1887; Count, 1895) 佐野常民
Samurai from Hizen, Sano trained in Western learning and in 1866 went for a study tour to France. On his return he worked for naval and technical reform first in his *han* and subsequently at national level, making a major contribution toward the development of Japan's navy. During the Satsuma rebellion he founded a society, the Hakuaisha, to care for the wounded of both sides; this in 1887 became the Japanese Red Cross, and Sano acted as the organization's first president. Sano served in the Genrōin, as finance minister 1880–1881 and was privy councillor 1888–1902, with the exception of a brief spell as agriculture and commerce minister in 1892.

Satō Eisaku 1901–1975 佐藤栄作
Native of Yamaguchi Prefecture, brother of Kishi Nobusuke, and nephew-in-law of Matsuoka Yōsuke, Satō graduated in law from Tokyo University in 1924 and joined the bureaucracy. Entering the Democratic Liberal Party in 1948, he was chief of the cabinet secretariat 1948–1949 before being elected to the Diet in 1949. He then served as head of the party's political affairs section and as its chief secretary. As minister of posts and telecommunications 1951–1952 Satō strengthened government control of broadcasting and was then minister of construction 1952–1953. As party secretary afterwards he was under suspicion of corruption over shipbuilding contracts but was never arrested. Satō joined the Liberal Democratic Party over a year after its founding and then served as finance minister 1958–1960 and minister of international trade and industry 1961–1962. The increase in Satō's factional power allowed him to compete unsuccessfully for the party leadership in July 1964. With bureaucratic and business support, however, he became prime minister in November 1964 and retained the position until June 1972. Satō promised tax reductions, a balance between economic and social development, the development of education, and the return of the southern Kuriles and Okinawa. In 1965 relations with South Korea were reestablished; Satō's maintenance of close relations with the U.S. and extension of the U.S.-Japan Security Treaty in 1970 assisted the eventual return of Okinawa in 1972. At home Satō maintained close contacts with the business and financial world in the pursuit of economic growth and helped to stabilize the conservative hold on power, but his administration was faced by mounting problems. Confronted by the effects of the 1971 dollar crisis, problems over relations with China, pollution, inflation, and the more deleterious effects of economic growth, Satō resigned in 1972. He quickly lost influence in the L.D.P. when Fukuda Takeo, his protégé, did not succeed him as premier. The award of the Nobel Peace Prize to Satō in December 1974 for his antinuclear diplomacy caused considerable controversy.

Fukui, H. *Party in Power* (Canberra, 1970).
Thayer, N. B. *How the Conservatives Rule Japan* (Princeton, 1969).
Yasutomo, D. H. "Satō's China Policy 1964–1966," *Asian Survey* 17, no. 6 (June 1977).

Satow, Sir Ernest M. 1843–1929
British diplomat, Satow arrived in Japan in September 1862 as a student interpreter; he was subsequently interpreter and from 1868 secretary to the Legation. The relative freedom of his position enabled Satow to develop close contacts with many Japanese, especially those of the anti-Bakufu movement (*q.v.*), and he was a source of information and advice both to the British minister, Sir Harry Parkes, and to Japanese. After the Restoration Satow became the leading British expert on the language and literature of Japan, upon which he wrote widely, contributing greatly to

Western understanding of Japan. After 1883 Satow held diplomatic posts in Siam, Uruguay, and Morocco but returned to Japan as British envoy 1895–1900. Apart from his works on Japanese culture Satow's record of his early years in Japan, *A Diplomat in Japan,* is a valuable account of the last years of the Bakufu.

Allen, B. M. *Sir Ernest Satow* (London, 1933).
Satow, E. *A Diplomat in Japan* (London, 1921).

Satsuma 薩摩

In southern Kyūshū, with its castle town at Kagoshima, Satsuma was the large domain of the *tozama* Shimazu daimyō. Sugar trading with the Ryūkyūs and *han* reforms in the early 19th century provided it with a strong economic base, which assisted it later to influence national politics. During the 1850s the daimyō Shimazu Nariakira promoted the introduction of Western armaments and manufacturing into Satsuma. Satsuma involvement in the Namamugi incident (*q.v.*) led to the bombardment of Kagoshima, but the radical *sonnō jōi* movement (*q.v.*) within the *han* was crushed by Shimazu Hisamitsu, father of the next daimyō, and the *han* supported *kōbu gattai (q.v.)* in the early 1860s. Contacts with the West increased, but the anti-Bakufu faction was increasingly dominant, and in 1866 Satsuma concluded an anti-Bakufu alliance with Chōshū (*q.v.*). The two *han* together were the main agents in the Restoration coup and dominated the new government and armed forces for decades. Despite this Satsuma samurai caused the most serious rebellion against the new government, led by Saigō Takamori in 1877.

Beasley, W. G. *The Meiji Restoration* (London, 1973).
______. "Politics and the Samurai Class Structure in Satsuma, 1858–1868," *MAS* 1 (1967).
Sakai, R. K. "Feudal Society and Modern Leadership in Satsuma *han*," *JAS* 16, no. 3 (May 1957).

Satsuma-Chōshū Alliance (Satchō dōmei) 薩長同盟

From the time of Chōshū's conflict with the Bakufu in 1865 Satsuma gradually turned against *kōbu gattai* policies (*q.v.*) and began to act as a channel for the passage of illegal arms to Chōshū. Aided by the mediation of Sakamoto Ryōma and Nakaoka Shintarō of Tosa, in March 1866 Kido Kōin of Chōshū and Saigō Takamori of Satsuma concluded a formal alliance between the two *han*. It was agreed that Satsuma would use its influence to reinstate Chōshū with the court, and to obstruct Bakufu plans for the political oppression of Chōshū; both domains would work to restore the emperor to power. The agreement, which was kept secret, considerably reduced the Bakufu's chances of retaining national leadership. It was followed by agreements with other *han*. Satsuma accordingly refused to assist the Bakufu in its punitive expedition against Chōshū later in 1866.

Craig, A. *Chōshū in the Meiji Restoration* (Cambridge, Mass., 1961).
Jansen, M. B. *Sakamoto Ryōma and the Meiji Restoration* (Princeton, 1961).

Satsuma Rebellion (Seinan sensō) 西南戦争

The Satsuma rebellion of 1877, the greatest of the antigovernment rebellions of the early Meiji years, had its origins in the discontent among conservative ex-samurai with the reforms and foreign policy of the Meiji government. After Saigō Takamori left the government in 1873, he returned to Satsuma, playing no part in national political activity but establishing schools to give military and spiritual training to samurai. His hostility to the new government's policies, especially those which deprived samurai of status and stipend, was communicated to his followers, who by 1877 numbered 2,000 in some 120 "schools" throughout Satsuma. After minor samurai risings in late 1876 the government had plans for administrative reform in Satsuma in hope of forestalling any revolt; as a precautionary measure it attempted to remove arms and munitions from Kagoshima. This move, in conjunction with the discovery of an alleged plot on Saigō's life, sparked off a rising by 1,000 Satsuma men in January 1877, which before long was joined and led by Saigō. The rebels marched northward, with the aim of Saigō's talking to the central government in Tokyo, and by the time Kumamoto was reached, they numbered 13,000. Dogged resistance from the heavily outnumbered Kumamoto garrison halted their progress. Government reinforcements relieved the siege in April, and the rebels were driven back toward Kagoshima. Altogether the government was forced to mobilize some 60,000 troops, and the rising was not put down until September. Saigō committed suicide. The government's modern, conscript army, which, despite little training, could be reinforced by fresh troops and weapons and assisted by modern aids such as the telegraph, proved superior to samurai armed only with traditional weapons and warrior ethos. Nevertheless, the campaign was a severe drain on the government's finances and stimulated inflation. Subsequent samurai opposition to the new government was expressed in political rather than military terms although the armed tradition remained in the nationalist societies and relatively frequent assassinations.

Buck, J. H. "The Satsuma Rebellion of 1877: An Enquiry into Some of Its Military and Political Aspects," Ph.D. diss., American University, 1959.
Mounsey, A. H. *The Satsuma Rebellion* (London, 1879).
Stephan, J. "Saigō Takamori and the Satsuma Rebellion," *HPJ* 3 (1965).

SCAP (Rengōkoku saikō shireikan) 連合国最高司令官

On 14 August 1945 General Douglas MacArthur, the commander in chief of U.S. forces in the Pacific, was appointed Supreme Commander for the Allied Powers (SCAP). MacArthur's headquarters were initially in Yokohama but were transferred to Tokyo on September 8. The Allied Powers General Headquarters (GHQ) *(rengōkoku saikō shireibu),* headed by MacArthur, was subsequently the sole executive authority for the allied powers in relation to the Occupation of Japan, although when the situation permitted SCAP was supposed to consult and advise with the Allied Council for Japan (*q.v.*) on important matters. In fact SCAP took orders only from the U.S. government, and MacArthur's large administration consisted almost exclusively of Americans. His own considerable power and worsening relations between the allies after 1945 meant that as SCAP, MacArthur exercised increasing discretion in policy formulation and implementation. In principle SCAP enforced Occupation policy through the Japanese government, i.e., indirectly, but on occasions more direct methods were utilized. SCAP approval was necessary for all important policy proposals made by the Japanese government. In November 1951 MacArthur was replaced as supreme commander by General Matthew Ridgeway. The GHQ was abolished in April 1952 with implementation of the San Francisco Peace Treaty (*q.v.*). Where necessary functions were transferred to the U.S. Embassy. Ridgeway became supreme commander in the North Pacific.

Ball, W. *Japan, Enemy or Ally?* (New York, 1949).
Kawai, K. *Japan's American Interlude* (Chicago, 1960).
MacArthur, D. *Reminiscences* (London, 1964).
Sebald, W. *With MacArthur in Japan* (New York, 1965).

Seclusion (sakoku) 鎖国

From the 1630s Japan was virtually cut off from outside contact, with the exception of some trade with China and Holland through Deshima (Nagasaki). From the 1790s increasing Western attempts were made to break Japan's isolation, but it was not until the mid-19th century that the increase in Pacific whaling and trading made the U.S. determined to secure from Japan coaling stations and supply and help facilities. The man charged with initiating relations was Commodore Matthew Perry (*q.v.*), whose ultimatum in 1853 caused a domestic political crisis in

Japan. Japanese were divided over whether to maintain seclusion or whether to open ports as a temporary measure, but most agreed that hostilities should be avoided. Eventually under the 1854 Treaty of Kanagawa (*q.v.*) Japan agreed to open ports, provide supplies, help castaways, and later on exchange consuls. This was followed by treaties with other powers and renewed pressure to extend intercourse further. Many Japanese recognized that some foreign contact was inevitable, if not desirable, and the arrival of the persistent Townsend Harris, the U.S. consul, ultimately led to the conclusion of treaties permitting full commercial relations. Imperial refusal to sanction such a treaty provoked a further crisis, which was only solved by the authoritarian measures of Ii Naosuke. Ii's attempts to establish treaties and strengthen the Bakufu meant that increasingly antiforeignism, radical reform, and pro-emperorism became allied with anti-Bakufu attitudes. The slogan *sonnō jōi* (*q.v.*) (revere the emperor and expel the barbarian) became widespread among the Bakufu's opponents. At the time of the crisis over the Harris treaty both Bakufu and court had made a commitment to publicly revoking the treaties and expelling foreigners at a later date; Chōshū attempts to enforce this in 1863 led the Bakufu and Chōshū itself into more trouble with foreigners. Dissatisfaction also led to acts of violence against foreigners 1859–1868. By the mid-1860s not merely the Bakufu but also many of its opponents realized the impossibility of maintaining total isolation, but the antiforeign slogan was retained by the Bakufu's opponents, deliberately utilizing antiforeign sentiment to embarrass the Tokugawa regime. When the new government came to power in 1868, the antiforeign slogan was quickly dropped. Japanese had been permitted to go abroad since 1861, but from the Restoration the country became increasingly open to regular foreign intercourse although relations remained on an unequal basis until treaty revision (*q.v.*) was achieved.

Acta Asiatica 22 (1972) (special issue on seclusion).
Beasley, W. G. *Select Documents on Japanese Foreign Policy, 1853—1868* (London, 1955).

Security Treaty Crisis. See U.S.-JAPAN SECURITY TREATY

Seikanron. See KOREA, INVASION OF

Seinan Rebellion. See SATSUMA REBELLION

Seishō 政商

During the early Meiji period many merchants and industrialists benefited from close contacts with the government, government contracts, and patronage, but those whose government contacts were especially close and profitable came to be known as *seishō*—"political merchants," merchants by grace of political connections. Some built up huge economic empires from this base. The three Tokugawa houses of Mitsui, Ono, and Shimada helped the government with its financial affairs over the difficult period of the Restoration and received extensive patronage. In the years after the Restoration the government used patronage, business privileges, sponsorship, and the cheap sale of its own enterprises to help individual businessmen or companies. This was done either to foster the development of industry or commerce or, sometimes, merely because of personal contacts. Many businessmen benefited from indirect subsidies, but among those who benefited especially from contracts and loans were Iwasaki, Ōkura, Furukawa, Godai, and Fujita. Some of these "political merchants" cut their political contacts as the period progressed, but others continued to utilize them and were often criticized for exploiting them to gain contracts. This government patronage meant that within the government certain individuals were to a certain extent identified with specific businessmen or companies.

The word *seishō* is still sometimes used

to refer to a businessman with strong political affiliations.

Hirschmeier, J. *The Origins of Entrepreneurship in Meiji Japan* (Cambridge, Mass., 1964).

Seitōsha 青鞜社

The Seitōsha (Bluestocking Society) was a literary group formed by university women in 1911 with the aim of publishing a magazine written and edited by women. The founder was Hiratsuka Raichō, and later members included Yamakawa Kikue, Itō Noe, and Kamichika Ichiko. The magazine, *Seitō* (Bluestocking), contained in its first edition an appeal by Hiratsuka for women to recover their rightful place, which set the scene for a lively discussion of the "new Japanese womanhood," and the magazine's criticism of the accepted morality and position of women brought Hiratsuka and her friends intense criticism. The society's maximum membership was 200 to 300, and at its peak the journal sold some 3,000 copies monthly. The emphasis of the society's members gradually turned from literary activities and a belief in personal solutions to the need for social reform and a general advocacy of female emancipation. Leadership passed to Itō Noe, who took over the editorship of *Seitō* until financial difficulties forced it to cease publication in February 1916. The group disbanded, but it had played a major role in initiating a women's emancipation movement, and its traditions were continued in later women's organizations.

Andrew, N. "The Seitōsha: An Early Japanese Women's Organization, 1911–1916," *HPJ* 6 (1972).
Shea, G. T. *Leftwing Literature in Japan: A Brief History of the Proletarian Literary Movement* (Tokyo, 1964).

Seiyū Hontō. See SEIYŪKAI

Seiyūkai 政友会

The first attempt by bureaucratic cabinets to compromise with the political parties in the Diet was marked by the formation of Itō Hirobumi's own party, the Rikken Seiyūkai (Constitutional Society of Political Friends) in 1900. It claimed 152 Diet members, most of them formerly members of the Kenseitō. Under Itō, and under the presidency of Saionji Kinmochi from 1903, the party's leaders followed a policy of compromise with the *hanbatsu* governments. Hara Kei in particular worked hard and successfully to spread the party's influence in the bureaucracy and to build a regional power base by provision of transport and other concrete economic benefits. The party subscribed to vague policy goals in the direction of development of trade, industry, and transport, but its support remained essentially rural. After Hara became president in 1914 the party was for the first time the minority party in the Diet, but it regained its majority in 1917. Under the premiership of Hara Kei from 1918 the party reached its so-called "golden age," but its policies remained essentially conservative; for example, it failed to support universal male suffrage at this time. After Hara's assassination in 1921 the party was led by Takahashi Korekiyo, but a large group split off in 1924 to form the Seiyū Hontō, drastically weakening the party. Under the presidency of Tanaka Giichi from 1925 the party gradually regained its strength; it became increasingly identified with an aggressive foreign policy, opposition to arms limitation, and suppression of the left wing within Japan. Inukai Tsuyoshi's leadership failed to halt this trend to the right in the years 1929–1932. The Seiyūkai had little influence from the mid-1930s, suffering from leadership disputes and fragmentation, and in 1940 all remaining elements of the party dissolved to participate in the formation of the Imperial Rule Assistance Association (*q.v.*).

Berger, G. M. *Parties Out of Power in Japan, 1931–1941* (Princeton, 1977).
Duus, P. *Party Rivalry and Political Change in Taishō Japan* (Cambridge, Mass., 1968).
Hastings, N. S. "The Seiyūkai and Party Government in Japan, 1924–1932," Ph.D. diss., University of Kansas, 1977.

Najita, T. *Hara Kei and the Politics of Compromise* (Cambridge, Mass., 1967).

Sekigunha. See RED ARMY

Sekirankai. See WOMEN'S MOVEMENT

Sekka Bōshidan. See ANTI-BOLSHEVISM LEAGUE

Self-Defense Force (Jieitai) 自衛隊

In July 1950, following the outbreak of the Korean War, General MacArthur authorized the Japanese government to form a 75,000-strong National Police Reserve and to increase the size of the Maritime Safety Board. The stated aim was the maintenance of internal security. Initially an infantry force, the Police Reserve gradually extended its size and scope of operations. In 1952, when the San Francisco Peace Treaty (*q.v.*) and security treaty with the U.S. went into effect, it was renamed the National Safety Force and numbered 110,000 men. In July 1952 this force and the Maritime Safety Board were amalgamated with a newly created air section to form the Self-Defense Force, now numbering 146,000. The force's purpose was the prevention of direct and indirect aggression and where necessary the maintenance of public law and order. The administration of the Self-Defense Force and all other defense matters are the responsibility of the Defense Agency, an external bureau of the Prime Minister's Office. Since 1954 considerable resources have been devoted to the expansion of the S.D.F.; its air, sea, and land divisions are armed with modern equipment and by 1975 comprised some 236,000 men. However, defense spending is small compared with many other countries and has not kept pace with the overall growth in government expenditure. In 1978 defense spending amounted to only 5.5% government expenditure. The S.D.F. could not resist a major invasion, and primary responsibility for external defense still rests with the U.S. under the terms of the security treaty. Since its inception in 1950 the S.D.F. (and its predecessors) has met with considerable opposition on the grounds that its existence violates clause 9 of the constitution of Japan (*q.v.*). Several court cases have raised the question of the constitutionality of the S.D.F., but the Supreme Court has always ruled it to be constitutional. Attempts by Liberal Democratic Party governments to amend the constitution to remove this point of controversy have failed due to their inability to obtain the two-thirds Diet majority necessary for constitutional revision.

Auer, J. E. *The Postwar Rearmament of the Japanese Maritime Forces, 1945–1971* (New York, 1973).
Buck, J. H. "The Japanese Self-Defense Forces," *Asian Survey* 7, no. 9 (Sept. 1967).
Buck, J. H., ed. *The Modern Japanese Military System* (Beverly Hills, 1975).
Emmerson, J. K. *Arms, Yen, and Power, the Japanese Dilemma* (New York, 1971).

Shakai Minshutō 社会民主党

The Shakai Minshutō (Social Democratic Party) was Japan's first Socialist party established in May 1901. Its leaders included Kōtoku Shūsui, Abe Isoo, and Katayama Sen. The party's platform was moderate democratic socialism; members called for pacifism, equality, universal suffrage, some public ownership, and the prosperity of the whole nation, but a refusal to compromise in line with Home Ministry demands led to the party's immediate dissolution.

Shakai Minshutō was also the name given to a small social democratic party led by Hirano Rikizō 1951–1952, which was subsequently absorbed into the Kyōdōtō and then the right-wing Japan Socialist Party.

Totten, G. O. *The Social Democratic Movement in Prewar Japan* (New Haven, 1966).

Shakai Minshūtō 社会民衆党

The Shakai Minshūtō (Social Democratic Party, or Social Masses' Party) was a proletarian party founded in December

1926. Leading members were Abe Isoo, Katayama Tetsu, Nishio Suehiro, Suzuki Bunji, and Matsuoka Komakichi, who became known as the social democratic faction (*shaminkei*) of the interwar proletarian movement. The Shakai Minshūtō was supported by moderate and right-wing Socialists and Sōdōmei and was the biggest proletarian party at the time. Members called for anticommunism, antifascism, and anticapitalism, and also for revision of the government's oppressive legislation but in fact devoted themselves to "safe" activities such as campaigning for help for the unemployed and labor union legislation. The party's compromise with the status quo and condoning of the Manchurian Incident led to internal conflict followed by defections on both wings. The remainder of the party was absorbed into the Shakai Taishūtō in July 1932.

Totten, G. O. *The Social Democratic Movement in Prewar Japan* (New Haven, 1966).

Shakai Taishūtō 社会大衆党

Increasing government suppression of proletarian parties and defections to national socialism stimulated members of the Shakai Minshūtō and the Zenkoku Rōnō Taishūtō (National Labor Farmer Masses' Party) to form a new proletarian party, the Shakai Taishūtō (Social Masses' Party), in July 1932, under the leadership of Abe Isoo and Asō Hisashi. The party announced its opposition to communism, fascism, and capitalism, advocated the conclusion of a nonaggression pact with the Soviet Union and called for international peace, opposing Japan's withdrawal from the League of Nations (*q.v.*). At home it called for industrial harmony, greater cooperation between labor and management, and relief of rural impoverishment. Although nominally a united proletarian front, the party was dominated by center and rightist elements; the absence of much of the Left due to government arrests helped the party to maintain unity, and it also survived potential splits between the factions which had formed it. The Shakai Taishūtō gained an unprecedented 18 Diet seats in the 1936 election, and with 37 seats in 1937 it became the third largest party. From shortly after its formation, however, the party gradually drifted away from social democratic ideals and from 1937 increasingly supported the war. Few members objected when the party dissolved itself into the new structure movement (*q.v.*) in July 1940.

Totten, G. O. *The Social Democratic Movement in Prewar Japan* (New Haven, 1966).

Shanghai Incident (Shanhai jihen) 上海事変

Following the widespread boycotts on Japanese goods after the Manchurian Incident (*q.v.*), the international settlement in Shanghai, always a focal point of Sino-Japanese tension, declared a state of emergency. During garrisoning of the settlement in January 1932 Japanese troops clashed with Chinese forces, and the Japanese overreacted to the clash, bombing areas outside the settlement and bringing in reinforcements to give them control of Shanghai. Japan's action shocked the powers, and China appealed to the League of Nations. Faced with international disapproval and fearful of the effects of continued fighting on the international situation, the Japanese agreed to a cease-fire, and an armistice was concluded on May 5. The incident increased Japan's isolation and worsened still further relations with China.

Crowley, J. B. *Japan's Quest for Autonomy* (Princeton, 1966).
Ogata, S. *Defiance in Manchuria* (Berkeley, 1964).
Thorne, C. *The Limits of Foreign Policy* (London, 1972).
Treat, P. "Shanghai: January 28, 1932," *PHR* 9 (1940).

Shantung Expeditions (Santō shuppei) 山東出兵

Following anti-Japanese boycotts and demonstrations, in May – July 1927 the Tanaka cabinet sent troops to Shantung, ostensibly to protect Japanese residents. The dispatch of the troops was in fact intended to support the Manchurian warlord Chang Tso-lin and hinder the northward advance of Chiang Kai-shek's troops and the possible unification of China. The Nanking government demanded withdrawal of these troops. The Kuomintang northern offensive in fact collapsed, and the Japanese forces had been withdrawn by September in the face of strong criticism at home and abroad. With the reopening of the Kuomintang northern advance the following year, more troops were sent by Japan to Shantung. They occupied the territory near the Shantung Railway, Tsingtao, and Tsinan. In May 1928 these troops clashed with Chinese forces in what became known as the Tsinan incident. A third group of troops was sent to assist in this incident despite China's demands for nonintervention in Chinese affairs and further appeals to the League of Nations. Continuing Japanese control of Tsinan led to a massive anti-Japanese boycott in China and international protests. An agreement was eventually reached in January 1929 and the Japanese troops withdrew.

Bamba, N. *Japanese Diplomacy in a Dilemma* (Vancouver, 1972).

Morton, W. F. "The Tsinan Incident, 1928–1929: Failure of Tanaka's 'Positive Policy' in China," in Columbia University East Asian Institute, *Researches in the Social Sciences on Japan* 2 (1959).

Yoshihashi, T. *Conspiracy at Mukden* (New Haven, 1963).

Shibusawa Eiichi 1841–1931 (Baron, 1900; Viscount, 1920) 渋沢栄一

Member of a rich Saitama farming family, Shibusawa left his home in 1863 and subsequently became a Bakufu retainer, accompanying the shōgun's younger brother to Europe 1867–1868. In 1869 he joined the Finance Ministry and was involved with Inoue Kaoru in such matters as tax reform, currency reform, and banking, but he resigned in 1873 to devote himself to private business. The same year he founded the First National Bank. The champion of the joint stock enterprise, Shibusawa helped organize over 250 industrial and commercial enterprises during his career and in all was connected with over 500. He played a major role in introducing new Western industries and Western techniques in such fields as cotton spinning and in promoting industrial and commercial education. He also went a long way toward making business socially respectable by promoting the Meiji ideal of the patriotic businessman. The enterprises established by Shibusawa are often referred to collectively as the Shibusawa *zaibatsu* although they were less closely interconnected than were other *zaibatsu* enterprises, and Shibusawa never achieved great personal wealth. Shibusawa retired in 1909 from active business organization to devote himself to various social and public enterprises, but he maintained until his death a major advisory role in the business world.

Hirschmeier, J. "Shibusawa Eiichi: Industrial Pioneer," in W. W. Lockwood, ed., *The State and Economic Enterprise in Japan* (Princeton, 1965).

Hoover, W. D. "From Xenophobe to Business Leader," in Japan Culture Institute, ed., *Great Historical Figures of Japan* (Tokyo, 1978).

Obata, K. *An Interpretation of the Life of Viscount Shibusawa* (Tokyo, 1937).

Tsuchiya, T. "Shibusawa Eiichi," *JQ* 12, no. 1 (Jan.-Mar. 1965).

Shidehara Kijūrō 1872–1951 (Baron, 1920) 幣原喜重郎

Native of Osaka, after graduating in law from Tokyo University in 1896, Shidehara joined the Foreign Ministry. He served in various posts before being ambassador to the U.S. 1919–1922, when he was Japan's representative at the Washington Conference (*q.v.*). As foreign minister 1924–1927 and 1929–1931 Shidehara attempted to promote Japan's interests by economic and diplomatic rather than forceful means, by international cooperation and peace and nonintervention in China's achievement of her aspirations. This line was in strong contrast with the "positive" China policy of Tanaka Giichi and became known as conciliatory "Shidehara diplomacy." Support for the London Naval Treaty (*q.v.*) led to criticism of Shidehara for a weak foreign policy. His conciliatory policy was unable to prevent the Manchurian Incident (*q.v.*), and Shidehara resigned late in 1931. He retreated from the forefront of politics, while maintaining his opposition to the political trends of the 1930s, but was recalled to serve as prime minister in October 1945. The cabinet reluctantly presided over the start of the major reforms demanded by the Occupation, including the emperor's renunciation of his divinity and the promulgation of the new constitution. Shidehara had insufficient Diet support to continue his premiership after the general election of April 1946 although he continued as minister of state to 1947. Initially president of the Shinpotō, Shidehara was afterwards a senior figure in the Democratic and Democratic Liberal parties. He was elected to the Diet in 1947 and became president of the House of Representatives in 1949. He died holding this office.

Bamba, N. *Japanese Diplomacy in a Dilemma* (Vancouver, 1972).
Brown, S. D. "Shidehara Kijūrō: The Diplomacy of the Yen," in R. D. Burns and E. M. Bennett, eds., *Diplomats in Crisis: United States-Chinese-Japanese Relations, 1919–1941* (Santa Barbara, 1974).
Takemoto, S. *Failure of Liberalism in Japan: Shidehara Kijūrō's Encounter with Anti-Liberals* (Washington, 1978).

Shigemitsu Mamoru 1887–1957
重光葵
Native of Ōita Prefecture, Shigemitsu graduated from Tokyo University in 1911 and entered the Foreign Ministry. He worked in Tokyo and as a diplomat in various countries before being ambassador to China 1930–1932, where he lost a leg in a bomb attack. As deputy foreign minister 1933–1936 Shigemitsu's attitudes aroused the hostility of the military. He was ambassador to the U.S.S.R. 1936–1938, to Britain 1938–1941 and to the Wang Ching-wei Chinese regime during 1942. He was also foreign minister 1943–1945, and Greater East Asia minister 1944–1945. As foreign minister again August-September 1945 Shigemitsu signed the surrender document on Japan's behalf. Shigemitsu was subsequently sentenced to seven years' imprisonment as a class "A" war criminal but was released in 1950. In 1952 he became president of the new Kaishintō and later entered the Liberal Democratic Party. As foreign minister 1954–1956 Shigemitsu worked to restore Russo-Japanese relations and to obtain Japanese membership in the United Nations.

Coox, A. D. "Shigemitsu Mamoru: The Diplomacy of Crisis," in R. D. Burns and E. M. Bennett, eds., *Diplomats in Crisis: United States-Chinese-Japanese Relations, 1919–1941* (Santa Barbara, 1974).
Shigemitsu, M. *Japan and Her Destiny* (London, 1958).

Shimada Group (Shimada-gumi)
島田組
The Shimada-gumi were Kyoto exchange merchants during the Tokugawa period. They funded the government at the time of the Restoration, helping to stabilize government finances and then, in conjunction with Mitsui and the Ono Group (*q.v.*), acted as official government brokers. Making huge profits from the interest-free use of government funds, Shimada subsequently established a nationwide chain of exchange companies, although even at its peak it did not match the prosperity of Mitsui and Ono. However, in 1874 tighter security regulations for the handling of government funds and the consequent recall of many of these funds proved ruinous to Shimada's exchange business. Unable to survive the collapse of the major part of its enterprises, the group went bankrupt in December.

Hirschmeier, J., and T. Yui, *The Development of Japanese Business, 1600–1973* (London, 1975).

Shimada Saburō 1852–1923 島田三郎
Samurai from Shizuoka Prefecture, Shimada studied at Bakufu schools and the Numazu Military Academy. In 1874 he became editor of the *Yokohama Mainichi Shinbun* (later *Tōkyō Yokohama Mainichi Shinbun*), a paper of which he was later president. Shimada was vocal in the popular rights movement and after a brief bureaucratic career resigned in 1881 and joined the Kaishintō. He was elected to the Diet 14 successive times from 1890 and was associated with the Shinpotō, Kensei Hontō, Dōshikai, and Kenseikai although he kept somewhat detached from the mainstream of politics. He was president of the Diet 1915–1917. Through his journalistic work, his writings, and his parliamentary activity Shimada became known as a fighter for social justice, campaigning for universal suffrage and against prostitution and the pollution produced by the Ashio copper mine (*q.v.*). He was a strong critic of corruption in politics, being closely involved in the impeachment of Hoshi Tōru and the revelation of the Siemens scandal (*q.v.*).

Shimanaka Incident (Shimanaka jiken) 嶋中事件
The December 1960 edition of *Chūō Kōron* (Central Review) (*q.v.*) published an article containing an imaginary execution scene of the imperial family. This was denounced by many as lese majesty, and in February 1961 a young right-winger broke into the house of Shimanaka Hōji, president of the publishing company. He killed a maid and severely wounded Shimanaka's wife. The incident brought public apologies from *Chūō Kōron* for publishing the article. This incident, which occurred the same year as the murder of the Socialist Party chairman Asanuma Inejirō, raised fears of a resurgence of right-wing terrorism.

Shimazu Hisamitsu 1817–1887 (Prince, 1884) 島津久光
Member of the ruling family of Satsuma and half-brother to Shimazu Nariakira. After his son, Tadayoshi, became daimyō of Satsuma in 1858, Shimazu wielded real power in the domain. He continued the program of military strengthening started by Shimazu Nariakira and also his use of able lower-class samurai in higher positions. From 1861 his involvement in national politics meant that he spent much of his time out of Satsuma. He used his forces to suppress extremist antiforeign advocates and established himself as the main promoter of *kōbu gattai* policies (*q.v.*) and a dominant figure at court. Hisamitsu's national influence waned from 1865 with the strengthening of anti-Bakufu trends, but he remained influential. In 1871 he was persuaded to take national office and became *sadaijin,* but overall he did not like the trend of the new government's policies and resigned in 1875 to go into retirement.

Beasley, W. G. *The Meiji Restoration* (London, 1973).

Shimazu Nariakira 1809–1858 島津斉彬
Daimyō of Satsuma from 1851, Shimazu had studied Dutch learning and was known as one of the foremost of the "reforming" daimyō. He was a leading advocate of the policy of building up Japan's economy and defenses. Within Satsuma he promoted men on the basis of ability and embarked on a program of Westernization, which included plans to construct a spinning mill and blast furnace and the adoption of Western military techniques and armaments. A supporter of Tokugawa Keiki in the shōgunal succession dispute (*q.v.*), Shimazu was retired in 1858 and died soon afterwards.

Sakai, R. K. "The Introduction of Western Culture to Satsuma," in Fukuoka UNESCO, *Report of the Second Kyūshū International Cultural Conference* (Fukuoka, 1968).
______. "Shimazu Nariakira and the Emergence of National Leadership in Satsuma," in A. M. Craig and D. H. Shively, eds., *Personality in Japanese History* (Berkeley, 1970).

Shimoda, Treaty of (Shimoda jōyaku) 下田条約

Japan signed treaties at Shimoda with the U.S. and Russia in 1854, but the term *Treaty of Shimoda* usually refers to the revised Treaty of Friendship signed between the U.S. and Japan in June 1857 after negotiations at local level by the U.S. consul Townsend Harris. The treaty allowed for U.S. residence at Shimoda and Hakodate, a vice-consul at Hakodate, the opening of Nagasaki, and currency exchange. It also initiated extraterritoriality (*q.v.*) and permitted U.S. consuls, officials, and their families to purchase directly their immediate needs. The Shimoda Treaty was replaced by the U.S.-Japan Treaty of Amity and Commerce (*q.v.*) the following year.

Beasley, W. G. *Select Documents on Japanese Foreign Policy, 1853–1868* (London, 1955).

Shimonoseki, Bombardment of. See BOMBARDMENT OF SHIMONOSEKI

Shimonoseki Treaty. See SINO-JAPANESE WAR, 1894–1895

Shimoyama Incident (Shimoyama jiken) 下山事件

Following the announcement of massive personnel curtailment in the Japan National Railways as part of the economic stabilization program (*q.v.*) in summer 1949, three serious incidents occurred. On July 5 Shimoyama Sadanori, president of the J.N.R., disappeared. The following day his body was found on a railway line northeast of Tokyo. Neither murder nor suicide have ever been substantiated. On July 15 an unmanned electric train with the operating handle tied down left the rails at Mitaka station in western Tokyo, killing six people on a platform and injuring 14 others, some seriously. Ten Mitaka railway union members, nine of them Communists, were charged with sabotage resulting in death, but in August 1950 all were released except the non-Communist Takeuchi Keisuke, who was sentenced to death. Successive appeals by Takeuchi, who had lost his job under the redundancies, failed, and he died in prison in 1967, still under sentence of death. Then on 17 August 1949 an engineer, assistant engineer, and fireman were killed when a Tokyo-bound train was derailed near Matsukawa, Fukushima Prefecture. Sabotage was proved, and the state accused of conspiracy nine members of the Fukushima branch of the J.N.R. union and 11 persons from the local Toshiba factory, whose members were also facing redundancy. Fifteen of these were Communists. Notwithstanding protestations of innocence, all were found guilty by the district court, but all were later acquitted on appeal, this judgment being confirmed by the Supreme Court in 1963. Antigovernment suits for damages dragged on through the 1960s, and the problem of who did cause the accident remains unsolved. Despite the final verdicts the three incidents served at the time to discredit the J.N.R. union and Communist influence, and the previous vigorous resistance to the J.N.R. reorganization lost much of its force.

Johnson, C. *Conspiracy at Matsukawa* (Berkeley, 1972).
Mainichi Newspapers. *Fifty Years of Light and Dark—The Hirohito Era* (Tokyo, 1975).

Shinagawa Yajirō 1843–1900 (Viscount, 1884) 品川弥二郎

Chōshū samurai, Shinagawa studied under Yoshida Shōin; strong antiforeign sentiments led him to participate in an attack on the British Legation in 1862. He fought in the Boshin War (*q.v.*) and 1870–1876 studied agriculture in Europe. He then worked in the Home Ministry and from 1881 in the Agriculture and Commerce Ministry, where he formed organizations to promote agriculture and industry. After serving as envoy to Germany in 1886, Shinagawa was privy councillor 1888–1891, 1892, and 1899–1900. In 1891 he became home minister under Yamagata. His organization of widespread and violent interference in the February 1892 election caused 25 deaths and nearly 400 injuries and still failed to secure a government majority in the Diet; Shinagawa devoted his subsequent energies to the formation, with Saigō Tsugumichi, of the Kokumin Kyōkai (National Association), a nationalist group supporting nonparty cabinets, which contained many of Yamagata's followers. Shinagawa remained close to Yamagata until his death.

Hackett, R. F. *Yamagata Aritomo in the Rise of Modern Japan, 1838–1922* (Cambridge, Mass., 1971).

Shinjinkai 新人会

Radical group consisting mainly of students and former students of Tokyo University founded in December 1918. Leaders included Akamatsu Katsumaro. The group was patronized by Yoshino Sakuzō and Asō Hisashi and also had close connections with the labor movement, making it a focus for intellectuals, workers, and radicals of various kinds. The Shinjinkai (New Man Society) called for the emancipation of mankind and the rational reform of Japan and to this end held discussion groups, concerned itself with strikes and labor disputes, and organized settlements in slum areas. Many student members became active in left-wing movements subsequently. A journal, *Demokurashii* (Democracy) was published, later renamed *Senku* (Pioneer), *Dōhō* (Brothers), and *Narōdo* (Narod—People). Late in 1921 the Shinjinkai membership was restricted to students and it dominated national student organizations. The membership became more radical, strong connections with Communist organizations developed, and from 1925 members were sporadically arrested. The widespread Communist arrests of 15 March 1928 included many students, and in April 1928 the university ordered the Shinjinkai to disband. It went underground but was formally dissolved in November 1929.

Smith, H. D. *Japan's First Student Radicals* (Cambridge, Mass., 1972).

Shinpeitai Incident (Shinpeitai jiken) 神兵隊事件

Members of the civilian right wing, including members of the Greater Japan Production Party, planned to carry out a coup d'état in July 1933. The activist force, referred to as the Shinpeitai (soldiers of the gods or divine soldiers), hoped to: mobilize over 3,000 people in a demonstration to divert the attention of the police and meanwhile to release from court Inoue Nisshō and other nationalists concurrently being tried; bomb the prime minister's residence while the cabinet was in session; and attack the residence of the Lord Privy Seal and political party headquarters. The group counted on active support from the armed forces to eliminate Japan's leaders and form a new "Shōwa Restoration" (*q.v.*) government under an imperial prince, either Higashikuni or Chichibu. The plot was stopped by police, but no details were released for two years. The trial did not open until 1937, and in 1941 the conspirators were given only short sentences with immediate remission on the grounds of patriotic motives and the failure to execute the plot. Liberal bail terms up to 1941, however, meant that conspirators remained active and influential even before this, although the organizations sponsoring the plot were weakened by its failure.

Storry, R. *The Double Patriots* (London, 1957).

Shinpotō 進歩党

The Shinpotō (Progressive Party) was formed in March 1896 when the Kaishintō under Ōkuma Shigenobu merged with several smaller parties with which it had hitherto cooperated. Initially it numbered 99 Diet members. It advocated responsible government, financial retrenchment, freedom of speech and publication, and a "positive" foreign policy. The Shinpotō gave its support to the second Matsukata cabinet, but increasing divergence of views led Ōkuma and other party members to resign their posts and cut all connection with the cabinet in autumn 1897. The Shinpotō and the Jiyūtō subsequently jointly opposed an increase in the land tax, and this cooperation led to their merger into the Kenseitō in June 1898.

Akita, G. *The Foundations of Constitutional Government in Modern Japan, 1868–1900* (Cambridge, Mass., 1967).

Shintō 神道

The term *Shintō* (way of the gods) is given to the traditional beliefs of Japan. During the Tokugawa period the official position of Shintō declined due to official patronage of Buddhist and Confucian ideas. Some elements of Shintō in effect fused with Buddhism. From the 18th century scholars began to revive Shintō ideology, especially those aspects emphasizing the divine position of the emperor, and this revival had significant ideological implications for the *sonnō jōi* movement (*q.v.*). After the Restoration the new government formally separated Shintō from Buddhism, and for a time it had the position of a state religion dominant in both religious and secular affairs. This privileged position was ended in 1872, but direct government patronage of Shintō was retained to preserve the emperor as a focus of national unity and, indeed, to provide ideological underpinning for the whole Meiji sociopolitical system. During the Meiji period there developed an increasing divergence between state Shintō and sect Shintō. State Shintō referred to those elements of the religion that had a direct bearing on matters of state and the role of the emperor; these came directly under the jurisdiction of the home minister, who was responsible for classifying and financing national and some local shrines. The popular religious beliefs held by Japanese for generations (household Shintō and shrine Shintō) were also ultimately under Home Ministry jurisdiction. Sect Shintō referred to individual religious beliefs, which were the responsibility of private religious organizations. Some of these received official recognition as separate sects; for example, Tenrikyō and Kurozumikyō branched off in the Meiji period. Up to the 1940s there was an increasing emphasis on state Shintō, which became identified with nationalist trends, although the popular religious beliefs and religious life of the people at large changed relatively little. After the war state Shintō was abolished, and all Shintō shrines disestablished to provide a clear separation of church and state. Since then, local shrines have tended to be supported by the community, but state support for national shrines has become a matter of controversy. Despite this complete disestablishment, Shintō rites and festivals continue to be widely observed, and in 1974, over 75% of the population, over 84 million people, declared their adherence to Shintō in some form or other.

Holtom, D. C. *Modern Japan and Shintō Nationalism* (Chicago, 1947).
______. *The National Faith of Japan* (London, 1938).
Kitagawa, J. *Religion in Japanese History* (New York, 1966).
Murakami, S. *Japanese Religion in the Modern Century* (Tokyo, 1980).
Ono, S. *Shintō: The Kami Way* (Tokyo, 1962).

Shipbuilding

When the Tokugawa ban on ocean-going ships was lifted in 1853, the Bakufu as well as various *han* began to construct larger Japanese and Western-style ships. After the Restoration most existing yards were taken over by the government with an eye to their military significance. They were modernized and became the nucleus of the shipbuilding industry. Privately owned yards began to develop from 1876, and with the exception of that at Yokosuka, which was retained for naval construction, the government sold off its yards in the 1880s. However, the technological level remained low, and naval craft in particular were mostly imported. Although legislation in 1896 aimed at promoting shipping and shipbuilding was highly effective, as late as 1913 imports still equaled domestic ship production. Rapidly increasing production during World War I led to the abandonment of protective legislation and a decline in imports and made Japan a world class shipbuilder, but postwar the industry was hit by depression and naval limitation policies. For a time imports again increased, but official encouragement and military aims meant rapid expansion up to 1944. From 1945 the industry was in severe difficulties; not only had it been geared to military production, but strict limitations on production were imposed by the Occupation authorities. A gradual change in policy from 1947 and the Korean War boom led to a revival, in which production for export largely replaced previous naval demand. The shipbuilding encouragement policy led to a major corruption scandal involving leading conservative politicians 1953–1954. Japan has since developed into the world's largest shipbuilder, supplying some 50% of the world's shipping requirements and capable of producing all kinds of ships. Like other shipbuilding nations Japan was hit by the 1970s depression, although less severely than many.

Blumenthal, T. "The Japanese Shipbuilding Industry," in H. Patrick, ed., *Japanese Industrialization and Its Social Consequences* (Berkeley, 1976).
Broadbridge, S. "Shipbuilding and the State in Japan Since the 1850s," *MAS* 11, no. 4 (Oct. 1977).

Shinsanbetsu. See LABOR MOVEMENT

Shipping. See MERCHANT SHIPPING

Shizoku 士族
In 1869 members of the samurai class and quasi-samurai were legally categorized as either *shizoku* or *sotsuzoku*. In 1872 *sotsuzoku* were recategorized as either *shizoku* or *heimin* (common people). The word *shizoku*, therefore, denoted a former samurai, and 3 million Japanese fell into this category in 1873. Outranked only by the nobility (*kazoku*), the *shizoku* were the elite of Japanese society. The introduction of conscription, abolition of sword-bearing, and commutation of stipends (*q.v.*) undermined their traditional privileged position, but the superior nature of their background and education enabled the *shizoku* to dominate the political, economic, and social life of Meiji Japan. However, large numbers of *shizoku* had problems in adapting to post-Restoration society, and the government undertook a major rehabilitation program to assist them. From 1914 the class of an individual was no longer formally registered. The term became no more than an indication of samurai ancestry and was abolished completely in 1947.

Yamamura, K. *A Study of Samurai Income and Entrepreneurship* (Cambridge, Mass., 1974).

Shizoku Jusan. See REHABILITATION OF SAMURAI

Shōgunal Succession Dispute (shōgun keishi mondai) 将軍継嗣問題
During 1857–1858 a political controversy arose over who should succeed the 13th Tokugawa shōgun, Iesada, who was childless. The closest blood claim was that of 11-year-old Tokugawa Yoshitomi of Kii, whose candidature was supported by senior Bakufu officials and *fudai* daimyō. Another faction, led by Matsudaira Keiei and Shimazu Nariakira and supported by members of the Tokugawa related families, reforming *tozama* daimyō, and middle Bakufu officials, supported the candidature of 20-year-old Hitotsubashi Keiki. Keiki had a reputation for ability and progressiveness, and his supporters maintained that he would admit others to consultation and be a suitable shōgun at a time of crisis. An appeal to the court at Kyoto tied the issue up with the controversy over the signing of the Ansei treaties (*q.v.*); the ensuing political crisis led to the regency of Ii Naosuke. Ii decided in favor of Yoshitomi, who succeeded Iesada under the name of Iemochi in 1858. Many of the so-called Hitotsubashi party were purged. Keiki eventually succeeded Iemochi as shōgun in 1866.

Beasley, W. G. *The Meiji Restoration* (London, 1973).

Shōgunate. See TOKUGAWA BAKUFU

Shotai. See KIHEITAI

Shōwa Depression. See DEPRESSION

Shōwa Electrical Scandal (Shōwa Denkō gigoku) 昭和電工疑獄

During September–October 1948 various cabinet ministers and high officials were accused of corruption over the granting of recovery funds to the Shōwa Electrical fertilizer company. Those arrested included former Deputy Prime Minister Nishio Suehiro. The charges contributed to the discrediting of the Ashida Hitoshi cabinet which resigned on October 7. On December 7 Ashida himself was arrested. Out of the total of 64 charged 62 had been acquitted by 1958. Hinohara, the president of the company, and Kurusu, former finance minister, were found guilty of corruption in 1962. Despite the acquittals the affair was at the time a major embarrassment to the Socialist Party.

Shōwa Emperor (Shōwa tennō) 1901– 昭和天皇

The eldest son of the Taishō emperor, Crown Prince Hirohito acted as regent for his father from November 1921, after a brief and historic tour abroad. In January 1924 he married Princess Nagako, daughter of Prince Kuni. Hirohito succeeded his father as emperor in December 1926 and took the reign name of Shōwa. Although the keystone of the "emperor system" (*q.v.*), the Shōwa emperor's belief in democratic politics led him to play little active political role although such inactivity could not be total. He is generally regarded as having enforced the suppression of the February 26 rising in 1936 (*q.v.*) and the final decision for surrender in 1945. In January 1946 the emperor publicly renounced his claim to divinity and has subsequently reigned as a constitutional monarch, living secluded from politics but acting as "the symbol of the state" and performing ceremonial functions. In 1971 he again visited Europe. His eldest son and crown prince is Akihito.

Kanrōji, O. *Hirohito: An Intimate Portrait of the Japanese Emperor* (New York, 1975).
Mosley, L. *Hirohito: Emperor of Japan* (London, 1966)
Reischauer, E. O. *The Emperor of Japan* (New York, 1975).

Shōwa Kenkyūkai 昭和研究会

The Shōwa Kenkyūkai (Shōwa Research Association) was a research group formed in November 1936 to advise Prince Konoe on national policy. It consisted of academics, bureaucrats, and journalists, most of them progressive and liberal; members included Rōyama Masamichi and Miki Kiyoshi. The policy of international cooperation in East Asia and also national unity and cooperation within the country advocated by the group became an integral part of the ideology of the new structure movement (*q.v.*). Opinions within the group became increasingly divided, and it was also criticized for leftist tendencies. The group disbanded with the formation of the Imperial Rule Assistance Association (*q.v.*).

Fletcher, W. M. "Ideologies of Political and Economic Reform and Fascism in Prewar Japan: Ryū Shintarō, Rōyama Masamichi, and the Shōwa Research Association," Ph.D. diss., Yale University, 1975.

Shōwa Restoration (Shōwa ishin) 昭和維新

The term *Shōwa Restoration* (*Shōwa ishin*) was widely used by radical nationalists and right-wing elements during the early Shōwa period, and a Shōwa Restoration was the declared aim of several of the attempted coups d'état by young officers in the early 1930s. The phrase denoted a radical, if vague, reform of the domestic polity to restore the "true relationship" between the emperor and his people, to promote the national spirit, and to achieve government according to the "imperial way"; in effect, it meant abolition of the political parties and of democratic institutions. The use of the word *ishin,* the same word used for the Meiji Restoration, gave the term added significance.

Shillony, B-A. *Revolt in Japan: The Young Officers and the February 26, 1936, Incident* (Princeton, 1973).
Storry, R. *The Double Patriots* (London, 1957).

Siberian Intervention (Shiberia shuppei) シベリア出兵

The possibility of intervention in Siberia was discussed in Japan soon after the 1917 Russian Revolution, and in August 1918 the Terauchi cabinet announced that 12,000 troops would be sent to cooperate with French, British, American, and Canadian troops in assisting Czech forces in the area. Japan in fact sent some 74,000 men in all, claiming a "special position" in the area and the need to protect the Manchurian railway. Major ports in eastern Siberia were occupied, and the new Hara cabinet proved unable to control or withdraw the troops. By June 1920 all other foreign troops had been withdrawn in the face of the Soviet advance, but the Japanese extended their occupation to northern Sakhalin in retaliation for the Nikolaevsk massacre (*q.v.*). Increasing criticism both at home and abroad ultimately led to withdrawal of the troops from Siberia in October 1922. It was only in 1925 that northern Sakhalin was returned to the Soviet Union and diplomatic relations restored.

Hosoya, C. "Origin of the Siberian Intervention, 1917–1918," *Annals of the Hitotsubashi Academy* 9, no. 1 (Oct. 1958).
Morley, J. W. *The Japanese Thrust into Siberia, 1918* (New York, 1959).
White, J. A. *The Siberian Intervention* (Princeton, 1950).

Siemens Scandal (Shiimensu jiken) シーメンス事件

In January 1914 it was revealed during the trial of an official of the Siemens Company in Berlin that the company had engaged in bribery to obtain contracts in Japan. The opposition parties in the Diet initiated a widely supported move to force the resignation of the Yamamoto cabinet on grounds of corruption over naval contracts. Investigations revealed corruption in the navy and in Mitsui Bussan in dealings both with Siemens and with the British company, Vickers. The cabinet survived a no-confidence motion, but the House of Peers rejected its budget proposals, cutting back on the navy budget, and the Yamamoto cabinet resigned in March.

Najita, T. *Hara Kei in the Politics of Compromise* (Cambridge, Mass., 1967).

Silk

During the Tokugawa period silk production developed as a cash crop for farmers, and in the 1860s it became a staple export, assisted by an outbreak of silkworm disease in Europe. Foreign demand raised the price and therefore the production of silk and led to progressive improvements in scale and technique of production. The government encouraged the establishment of reeling plants from 1870, notably at Maebashi and Tomioka, to introduce Western techniques and stimulate exports by standardizing quality. New techniques did spread but large filatures began to appear only after 1890. Unlike cotton mills these were in general sited outside cities, and much of their labor remained village-based. By the early 1890s silk accounted for over 30% of Japan's total exports by value and this level was retained to 1914, assisted by a tripling of production over the years 1894–1914. Even after 1914 silk remained a crucial export item. Mechanization was far slower in other processes such as weaving and dyeing, so most silk exports continued to be of raw silk. The actual production of cocoons as well continued to be largely on a farming sidework basis; as late as 1929 it was estimated that 40% of farm households were raising silk cocoons as a secondary occupation. Therefore, when silk exports were hit by world depression in the late 1920s, it was the farmers who suffered. The price of raw silk slumped and by 1931 was a mere 30% of its 1925 level; the fall exacerbated rural distress already severe due to a fall in rice prices. Raw silk production and exports never recovered and a previously lucrative rural side employment declined, although many farmers still produced cocoons in the postwar period. During the 1930s exports of silk were largely of woven fabrics. Postwar the silk industry has declined rapidly in significance due to the growth in artificial fibres.

Lockwood, W. W. *The Economic Development of Japan* (Princeton, 1968).
Ohara, K. *Japanese Trade and Industry in the Meiji-Taishō Era* (Tokyo, 1959).
Uyehara, S. *The Industry and Trade of Japan* (London, 1926).

Silver Standard. See CURRENCY

Sino-Japanese Military Agreement. See JAPAN-CHINA JOINT DEFENSE AGREEMENT

Sino-Japanese Peace and Friendship Treaty (Nitchū heiwa yūkō jōyaku) 日中平和友好条約
On 12 August 1978 the foreign ministers of Japan and the People's Republic of China concluded a peace and friendship treaty, which came into force after the exchange of ratifications on October 23. China's demands that an antihegemony clause aimed at the Soviet Union be included in the treaty and Japan's reluctance to be pushed into an anti-Soviet stance delayed conclusion of the treaty, but the support of the U.S., the Soviet attitude on the territorial problem, and the anxiety of Japanese businessmen to expand trade with China eventually brought Japan to overcome her objections. The treaty therefore contains the anti-hegemony clause and also the statement desired by Japan that the treaty will not influence the position of either signatory vis-à-vis a third power. The conclusion of the treaty provoked intense criticism of Japan from the U.S.S.R.

Hosoya, C. "Japan's 'Omnidirectional' Course," *Japan Echo* 5, no. 4 (1978).
Irie, M. "The Politics of the Peace and Friendship Treaty," *Japan Echo* 5, no. 4 (1978).

Sino-Japanese Treaty of Commerce and Navigation. See SINO-JAPANESE WAR, 1894–1895

Sino-Japanese War, 1894–1895 (Nisshin sensō) 日清戦争
In 1894 the Korean government requested China for aid against the Tonghak rebels, and under the terms of the 1885 Tientsin Treaty (*q.v.*) the Japanese also sent troops. The two powers' conflict over reforms demanded by Japan in Korea was merely a symptom of a far more fundamental clash of basic rights and interests in the country. Mediation by the Western powers failed, and hostilities broke out on July 23. War was formally declared on August 1. Japan had an initial numerical advantage in forces stationed in Seoul and was better prepared. By mid-September Japan had occupied Pyongyang, defeating China's best land forces. She advanced into Manchuria overland and was also dominant at sea and by early 1895 threatened Tientsin and Peking. The Chinese initiated moves for peace and on March 20 a peace conference was opened at Shimonoseki. The Japanese delegation was led by Itō Hirobumi and Mutsu Munemitsu, China's by Li Hung-chang and Li Ching-fang. After an assassination attempt on Li Hung-chang an armistice was declared on March 30. The Treaty of Shimonoseki was signed on April 17. The terms included recognition of the independence of Korea; cession of Formosa, the Pescadores, and the Liaotung Penin-

sula to Japan; the opening of four more treaty ports in China; an indemnity of 200 million taels to be paid by China to Japan; and the Japanese occupation of Weihaiwei until China complied with the terms. The treaty also provided for a new Treaty of Commerce and Navigation, which was concluded in July 1896. This treaty awarded Japan most-favored nation treatment, permitted navigation on the Yangtze, and allowed Japan to manufacture goods on Chinese soil. After the triple intervention (*q.v.*) Japan returned the Liaotung Peninsula to China, but the Shimonoseki Treaty was ratified as it stood, a separate treaty relating to Liaotung being concluded. Despite the triple intervention Japan's victory established her as a power to be reckoned with in East Asia. For China the war was economically, politically, and territorially disastrous, and the settlement paved the way for further encroachments by Japan and other powers. The Treaty of Commerce and Navigation was revoked by the Chinese Nationalist government in 1929.

Chen, T-M. "The Sino-Japanese War, 1894–1895: Its Origin, Development, and Diplomatic Background," Ph.D. diss., University of California, Berkeley, 1944.
Dotson, L. O. "The Sino-Japanese War of 1894–1895: A Study in Asia Power Politics," Ph.D. diss., Yale University, 1951.
Jansen, M. B. *Japan and China: From War to Peace, 1894–1972* (Chicago, 1975).
Kajima, M. *The Diplomacy of Japan, 1894–1922,* vol. 1, *Sino-Japanese War and Triple Intervention* (Tokyo, 1976).

Sino-Japanese War, 1937–1945 (Nitchū sensō) 日中戦争

At the time of the Marco Polo Bridge incident of July 1937 (*q.v.*) there was dissent within the Japanese army as to whether to extend the conflict or to reserve Japanese strength for a fight with Russia. Reinforcements were eventually sent, and on August 13 these clashed with Chinese troops at Shanghai, initiating full-scale war. War was never declared, however, and the Japanese referred to the fighting first as the North China incident and from September as the China incident. Nevertheless, in November 1937 an imperial headquarters (*daihon'ei*) was established, and in January 1938 Prime Minister Konoe announced that Japan would cease all contact with the Chinese Nationalist government. In April 1938 the National Mobilization Law (*q.v.*) was passed. The Japanese believed that the war could be quickly terminated, and their initial advance was rapid, enabling them to take Peking, Tientsin, Nanking (December 1937), Suchow (March 1938), and Canton (October 1938). Chiang Kai-shek was forced to move his Nationalist (Kuomintang) government to Chungking, but resistance continued although the Nationalists were weakened by the loss of the main industrial areas and had increasing problems in maintaining contact with the outside world. Nominally at least Kuomintang and Chinese Communist forces fought together to expel the Japanese, but Chiang remained highly suspicious that their participation in the war against Japan would strengthen the internal position of the Communists and often failed to provide them with adequate support and cooperation. Nevertheless from 1938 Communist-led guerrillas began to inflict considerable damage on Japanese forces. By the end of that year Japan had already put into the war effort more men and resources than she had originally anticipated would be necessary; the sheer size of the country posed huge obstacles, and Japan was forced to concentrate on holding cities and major lines of communication. Even in the so-called occupied areas her control was weak, and guerrilla activity was carried on on a wide scale. From the early stages of the war Japan had established puppet regimes in the occupied areas, but the state of the war dictated more serious attempts in this direction. In the hope of coming to terms, a collaborationist government was established in Nanking in March 1940 under the former Kuomintang leader Wang Ching-wei. With the conclusion of the Japan-China Basic Treaty (*q.v.*) the Japanese formally recognized the Nanking regime as the government of China, but it never gained credence within the country, and the minimal Japanese concessions which might have helped it came too late to do so. Her inability to extricate herself from the situation in China spurred Japan's advance into Southeast Asia and plunged her into the Pacific War (*q.v.*) after December 1941. This posed an extra strain on Japanese resources, and by early 1943 the Japanese were forced by the situation in the Pacific to relax their all-out effort to conclude the China war. In the remaining two years of the war the Japanese made little headway. Wang Ching-wei was gradually incapacitated by illness and was dead by the end of 1944, and although his regime continued to exist until the end of the war, the areas under its control were eventually turned over to the Nationalists. Although the strength of the Kuomintang forces waned, the Japanese army was worst hit by the assaults of guerrillas in rural areas, many of them Communist-led. Moves to reach a peace settlement were unsuccessful, and after Japan's acceptance of the Potsdam declaration (*q.v.*) Japan formally surrendered to Chiang Kai-shek on 9 September 1945.

Boyle, J. H. *China and Japan at War, 1938–1945: The Politics of Collaboration* (Stanford, 1972).
Coox, A. D. "Recourse to Arms: The Sino-Japanese Conflict, 1937–1945," in A. D. Coox and H. Conroy, eds., *China and Japan: Search for Balance Since World War I* (Santa Barbara, 1978).
Dorn, F. *The Sino-Japanese War, 1937–1941* (New York, 1974).

Social Democratic Party. See SHAKAI MINSHUTŌ; SHAKAI MINSHŪTŌ

Social Masses' Party. See SHAKAI MINSHŪTŌ; SHAKAI TAISHŪTŌ.

Social Security. See SOCIAL WELFARE

Social Welfare

Relief regulations passed by the Dajōkan 1864–1875 consolidated the diverse relief practices of the Tokugawa period and provided emergency relief for children, the old, and the sick. They were supplemented in 1879 by regulations which provided assistance for the help of war-wounded or bereaved. The numbers receiving such relief were never very large, and a decision by the Diet in 1890 that the family and community should bear the responsibility for helping those in need meant that the number receiving relief actually declined. Following World War I members of the left wing and the labor movement began to call for provisions relating to such things as sickness, accident, and unemployment insurance. A greater understanding of poverty, repeated economic crises, pressure from local welfare commissioners, and then the increase in military dominance led to the enactment of various welfare legislation measures during the 1920s and 1930s. In 1921 unemployment bureaus were established. The Health Insurance Law of 1922 (implemented 1927) provided the first occupational illness, accident, and injury insurance. It was initially applied to workplaces with over five employees and became the nucleus of national medical insurance. The sphere of application was enlarged in 1934, and the National Health Insurance Law of 1938 catered to those not covered by existing schemes, including farmers and their families, whose physical deterioration was a worry for army recruitment. The law provided for insurance schemes in voluntary groups, but the state's contribution was small, meaning a heavy burden on the individual. Depression likewise stimulated the 1933 Law for Prevention of Cruelty to Children and supplementary legislation, making the welfare of children up to 14 the direct responsibility of the state in cases where assistance was deemed necessary. Similarly the Mothers' and Children's Protection Law of 1937 was also aimed at the provision of a healthy army. Occupational pension schemes were introduced during the 1930s and a general welfare pension scheme during the Pacific War. Postwar legislation attempted to move toward a more complete system of public welfare and social security. The 1946 Daily Life

Security Law (*seikatsu hogo hō*) laid down a minimum standard of living to be guaranteed by the state, but such a stipulated standard has posed the problems of continual upgrading and of assessment of nonmaterial standards of life. The development of old age pensions has been slow, with much of the population initially uncovered. The aim of the 1959 National Pension Law is to cover the whole population, mostly on a contributory basis, but it will be several decades before this can take full effect. Other insurance and relief schemes relate to the handicapped and the unemployed. The whole concept of social welfare provisions as relief or charity has been rejected, but despite the extension of social welfare provisions the proportion of national income devoted to such purposes remains very small in comparison with other highly developed countries. The pension system remains immature, and it is only in the more advanced sectors of health and medical care that provision is comparable with that provided in other highly industrialized countries. Contributions remain high in most sectors and benefits inadequate. Much is left to the individual's own savings capacity. Apart from legislation covering material benefits there is also legislation which attempts to provide for the general welfare of Japan's population. Most important is perhaps the Child Welfare Law of 1947, which stipulates the responsibility of the state and public bodies as well as of the child's guardian for the protection and education of all children. This kind of policy has led to the growth of welfare centers, welfare workers, and other such facilities.

Bennett, J. W., and S. B. Levine. "Industrialization and Social Deprivation: Welfare, Environment, and the Post-Industrial Society in Japan," in H. Patrick, ed. *Japanese Industrialization and Its Social Consequences* (Berkeley, 1976).
Emi, K. *Essays on the Service Industry and Social Security in Japan* (Tokyo, 1978).
Lee, Y-G. "The Development and the Contemporary System of Social Security in Japan: Historical Trends and Present Day Issues," Ph.D. diss., Manchester University, 1972.
Sagrista Freitas, A. "Social Security in Japan: Its Evolution, Present Status and Economic Implications," Ph.D. diss., Cornell University, 1963.
Taira, K. "Public Assistance in Japan," *JAS* 27, no. 1 (Nov. 1967).

Socialist Movement

Socialist ideas first entered Japan in the 1880s. Parties using the name "Socialist" appeared at this time, and there were the small-scale beginnings of a labor movement. Early in the 1890s groups discussing social problems appeared; search for a solution to social ills led to an increasing interest in Socialist ideas, and in 1898 Christian Socialists and left-wing liberals came together to form the Society for the Study of Socialism (Shakaishugi Kenkyūkai). This developed into the tiny Socialist Society (Shakaishugi Kyōkai) in 1900 after non-Socialists withdrew from participation. This activity around 1900 was closely involved with attempts at labor organization. In 1901 the Shakai Minshutō (Social Democratic Party), Japan's first Socialist party, was formed, but it was immediately banned by the government. Government suppression meant inevitably that many Socialists distanced themselves from labor activities and turned to research, propaganda, and journalistic activities, and there was a flood of Socialist literature. Many leading Socialists wrote for the paper *Yorozu Chōhō* (*q.v.*), but commitment to pacifism led to disputes with the management and to the development of the Socialists' own Heiminsha (*q.v.*). In these early years the movement had a strong Christian and social democratic bias, but the trend was toward increasing radicalism and internationalism. Despite a growing divergence within the movement, Socialists of all kinds came together to form the Japan Socialist Party of 1906–1907. However, a widening rift between direct actionists, led by Kōtoku Shūsui, Yamakawa Hitoshi, and Sakai Toshihiko and supporters of parliamentary action, mostly Christian Socialists led by Katayama Sen, led to the banning of the party and a split which weakened a movement already small. The

1910 High Treason trial (*q.v.*) initiated an era of far worse oppression, during which most Socialists were forced into relative inactivity. International developments, especially the Russian Revolution, and the prevailing postwar depression in both urban and rural areas revived more open activity. It appeared that despite suppression left-wing movements could be a successful form of protest, and with the increase in labor activity socialism began to gain some backing outside the almost purely middle-class elements that had hitherto advocated Socialist ideas. In 1920 Socialists of all kinds came together to form the Japan Socialist League (Nihon Shakaishugi Dōmei). Apart from established Socialists such as Yamakawa Hitoshi the league included members of student organizations such as the Shinjinkai (*q.v.*) and of labor organizations such as the Yūaikai (*q.v.*). This postwar enthusiasm marked the conversion of the intelligentsia to socialism—initiating a theoretical emphasis which is even now conspicuous among the Japanese left wing—and the beginnings of a lively proletarian cultural movement. However, the unity manifested by the Socialist League 1920–1921 was not long maintained. The labor movement, which at this time was the main platform for Socialist ideas, was riven by disputes between anarcho-syndicalists, democratic Socialists, and Bolsheviks. Although anarchism declined after 1922 the labor and Socialist movement failed to regain any real unity during the 1920s and 1930s. The Japan Communist Party was first founded in 1922, although it was only legalized in 1945, and communism gained a strong hold on certain sections of organized labor and the intelligentsia. After the enactment of universal male suffrage in 1925, the Socialist movement turned from the formation of propaganda and research organizations and labor organization to the founding of proletarian political parties. The movement split basically into three strands—often summed up as right wing, left wing, and centrist Socialists—which, despite organizational changes, maintained a continuity up to the war. There was therefore a series of parties of various shades of socialism; the party movement was characterized by continuous splits and mergers—also reflected in organized labor—and inner division on ideological and personal grounds was a major cause of weakness. Government suppression, mostly of the left wing, was extreme, and drove more moderate Socialist elements further to the right to avoid similar persecution. By the 1930s the Left of the movement was virtually destroyed by persecution and *tenkō* (recantation) (*q.v.*). This destruction did assist the formation in 1932 of the moderate Shakai Taishūtō, which maintained a comparative unity until its dissolution in 1940. Despite considerable election success in 1936, this party, like all the others, failed to achieve a mass basis of support. Especially after 1937 there was a strong revival of the connection of socialism with nationalism, first suggested in the nationalist-popular rights connection of the 1880s, and for many the step from socialism to national socialism was not a difficult one. Remaining Socialists in effect rarely offered viable opposition either to the conservative political parties or to army and right-wing elements, either in terms of ideology or in practical policies to deal with prevailing problems. Socialism ceased to be a significant force during the years of the Pacific War. After 1945 the Japan Communist Party was reestablished, and more moderate elements formed the Japan Socialist Party, which has since remained the major left-wing party. The late 1940s experienced a Socialist upsurge in conjunction with labor activity, but the "red purge" (*q.v.*) led to a decline in more left-wing elements, which became active again only after the mid 1950s. Right-wing Socialists formed the Democratic Socialist Party in 1960. Despite ups and downs in the strength of the Socialist parties relative to each other, their joint position overall relative to the Liberal Democratic Party, while sufficient to block constitutional amendments, has shown little marked improvement. After the June 1980 election the Japan Socialist Party, Japan Communist Party, and Democratic Socialist Party together commanded only 168 seats out of 511 in the House of Representatives. Socialist ideas remain popular among certain sectors of the Japanese population—notably the intelligentsia—but they do not appear to have gained the widespread popular base necessary to put Socialist parties in power, and ideological differences mean that Socialist groups rarely act together. (See also individual organizations.)

Colbert, E. S. *The Left Wing in Japanese Politics* (New York, 1952).
Cole, A. B., G. O. Totten, and C. H. Uyehara. *Socialist Parties in Postwar Japan* (New Haven, 1966).
Totten, G. O. *The Social Democratic Movement in Prewar Japan* (New Haven, 1966).

Socialist Society. See SOCIALIST MOVEMENT

Society for the Study of Politics. See POLITICAL STUDIES ASSOCIATION

Society for the Study of Socialism. See SOCIALIST MOVEMENT

Society of Those Who Survive. See YŪZONSHA

Sōdōmei. See LABOR MOVEMENT

Soejima Taneomi 1828–1905 (Count, 1884) 副島種臣

Hizen samurai, Soejima studied English in Nagasaki and joined the anti-Bakufu movement (*q.v.*). After the Restoration he participated in the drafting of the *Seitaisho*, an 1868 government document laying down the proposed lines of government organization. He was state councillor 1869–1871, and as foreign minister 1871–1873 he adopted an assertive foreign policy over the Maria Luz incident (*q.v.*) and the assassination of Ryūkyūan fishermen on Taiwan, which ultimately led to the Formosan expedition (*q.v.*). In 1873 Soejima led a mission to China to discuss the problem of Taiwan, but he resigned from the government the same year over the invasion of Korea (*q.v.*). In 1874, in conjunction with Itagaki Taisuke, Soejima submitted a petition for an elected Diet, but he played no further part in the popular rights movement. He became court adviser in 1886 and sat in the Privy Council 1888–1905, serving as its vice-president 1891–1892. Soejima was briefly home minister in 1892 but resigned over election interference. In 1891 he founded the Tōhō Kyōkai (Eastern Society) to study East Asian affairs.

McWilliams, W. C. "East Meets East: The Soejima Mission to China, 1873," *MN* 30, no. 3 (Autumn 1975).
———. "Soejima Taneomi: Statesman of Early Meiji Japan, 1868–1874," Ph.D. diss., University of Kansas, 1973.

Sōhyō. See LABOR MOVEMENT

Sōka Gakkai. See BUDDHISM

Soldiers of the Gods Incident. See SHINPEITAI INCIDENT

Sonnō jōi 尊王攘夷

There was a renewed interest in ideas relating to the position of the emperor in the Japanese state from the 18th century, and during the mid-19th century the concept of reverence for the emperor (*sonnō*) as a focus of national loyalty gained currency. Opposition to intercourse with foreign countries and rejection of foreigners (*jōi*) had its origins in the Confucian idea of clarification of status between countries, but by the 1850s the slogan embraced all shades of antiforeignism. From 1858, when the shōgun was forced to pursue a policy of opening the country, the two phrases were increasingly linked to form the loyalist war cry against the Bakufu, which was unable to resist foreign encroachment and whose members disputed power with the emperor. Although in the 1860s it became widely apparent that foreigners could not be repulsed and *jōi* views declined as a dominant characteristic of the anti-Bakufu movement, many loyalists retained the slogan *sonnō jōi* (revere the emperor and expel the barbarian) as an anti-Bakufu rallying cry. *Sonnō* ideals culminated in the 1868 Restoration, but a small number of people continued seriously to advocate antiforeignism into the early Meiji period.

Beasley, W. G. *The Meiji Restoration* (London, 1973).
Brown, D. M. *Nationalism in Japan* (Berkeley, 1955).

Sorge Incident (Zoruge jiken) ゾルゲ事件

In autumn 1941 Japanese police arrested members of a spy ring organized by Richard Sorge, adviser to the German Embassy in Tokyo and Far Eastern representative of the Comintern. All leading members of the ring were arrested, including Sorge himself and Ozaki Hotsumi, both of whom were sentenced to death in 1943 and executed in November 1944. Several others died in prison. Figures close to Konoe Fumimaro including Inukai Ken and Saionji Kinkazu were also arrested but were released. The ring had operated since 1933–1934 relaying information on Japanese politics, diplomacy, economics, and military matters to the U.S.S.R., including the information that Japan would strike southward and not at Russia.

Deakin, F. W., and G. R. Storry. *The Case of Richard Sorge* (London, 1966).
Johnson, C. *An Instance of Treason: Ozaki Hotsumi and the Sorge Spy Ring* (Stanford, 1964).

South Manchurian Railway Company (Minamimanshū Tetsudō Kabushiki-gaisha) 南満州鉄道株式会社

A southern branch of the Chinese Eastern Railway from Changchun to Port Arthur and Dairen was constructed by Russia after her lease of the Liaotung Peninsula (*q.v.*) in 1898. These rights passed to Japan in 1905, and in June 1906 their exploitation was entrusted to the new South Manchurian Railway Company, in which the government owned half the capital and appointed the chief officers. The company ran the railway and extended the line to support Japanese industrial development and exploitation in the area; it administered the railway zone, collecting taxes and providing public utilities; it also invested in and promoted industry, commerce, agriculture, and mining. Its role was therefore that of a powerful government organ playing a major role in promoting Japanese economic, political, and military influence in Manchuria and whose leading members, which included Gotō Shinpei, Matsuoka Yōsuke and Ōkawa Shūmei, were men of influence and power in both countries. The company's research section was a major source of information on Manchuria, which was used, among others, by army intelligence. After 1931 the company was increasingly the instrument of the Kwantung Army (*q.v.*), but it remained until 1937 the chief channel for Japanese investment in Manchuria. By 1936 it was a vast corporation with 22 subsidiary companies, but overextension of its interests meant that it was increasingly supplemented by other "official" companies. The Manchurian Heavy Industries Corporation of 1937 took over many of its concerns, excluding the railways, but the company remained important until its demise in 1945.

Jones, F. C. *Manchuria Since 1931* (London, 1949).
Young, C. W. *Japan's Special Position in Manchuria* (rprt. New York, 1971).
———. *Japanese Jurisdiction in the South Manchurian Railway Areas* (Baltimore, 1931).

Southeast Asia, Japanese Invasion of. See JAPANESE INVASION OF SOUTHEAST ASIA

Soviet-Japanese Neutrality Pact. See RUSSO-JAPANESE NEUTRALITY PACT

"Special Procurements" (tokuju)
特需

The purchase of military and other requirements in Japan during the Korean War (*q.v.*) by United Nations (mostly U.S.) forces is often referred to as "special procurements." The international Korean War boom waned after April 1951, but it continued in Japan, and these dollar purchases paid for many of Japan's imports, enabling Japan to reequip industries despite a low level of exports. At their peak in 1952 these purchases amounted to 32% of Japan's foreign currency income and 62% of her dollar income. The demand stimulated a production boom, especially in steel and other areas of heavy industry, which in turn led to a consumer boom in 1953. Japan experienced a major trade boom 1954–1956. Dollar purchases continued after the war in the form of procurement orders by Americans stationed in Japan and dollar-aided purchases by other Asian areas. From the mid-1950s the amount gradually decreased, but these procurements played a key role in Japan's economic recovery.

Allen, G. C. *A Short Economic History of Modern Japan* (London, 1962).
Cohen, J. B. *Japan's Postwar Economy* (Bloomington, Ind., 1958).

Spiritual Mobilization. See NATIONAL SPIRITUAL MOBILIZATION

State Shintō. See SHINTŌ

Steel Industry. See IRON AND STEEL INDUSTRY

Stipends, Commutation of. See COMMUTATION OF STIPENDS

Stock Exchange

Some organized exchange institutions existed during the Tokugawa period, mostly for rice. Bonds and stocks came into increasing use after the Restoration, and in 1874 the government resolved to establish stock exchanges in Tokyo and Osaka. On the basis of regulations issued in 1876–1878 exchanges were established in these cities in 1878 and afterwards in several other cities. The exchanges were designed to be profit making, and their dealings were initially mostly in specie and government bonds, but after the 1890s dealings in shares gradually increased. However, most company funding was achieved through banks rather than through the open market, and much stock exchange dealing was purely speculative. Largely with the aim of controlling speculation and abuses the exchanges were subject to several reorganizations in the prewar period. In 1943 they were reorganized as semipublic concerns and placed under strict government control. Their level of activity declined during the war period, and they were closed completely from 9 August 1945, although some unofficial activity did continue. In 1949 the exchanges at Tokyo and Osaka were reopened as non-profit-making organizations under the control of registered members to deal in the stocks and shares of member companies and organizations. Subsequently other provincial stock exchanges were also reopened. Speculative dealing has been curbed and the range of operations extended, but a large proportion of industrial and commercial capital is still raised by bank loans. The Tokyo Stock Exchange now accounts for two-thirds of all stock exchange transactions in Japan.

Adams, T. F. M. *Japanese Securities Markets* (Tokyo, 1953).
Adams, T. F. M., and I. Hoshii. *Financial History of the New Japan* (Tokyo, 1972).
Bank of Japan. *The Japanese Financial System* (Tokyo, 1978).

Student Movement

There were sporadic student protests in the Meiji period, but it was only after World War I that the rise of the Socialist and democratic movements stimulated any extensive organization of students.

The Shinjinkai (*q.v.*) and nearly 70 other student groups formed a national organization, the Students Social Science Federation, in 1922. Student groups influenced by socialism discussed Marxism and the problems of social science; others engaged in practical activities as well, such as welfare programs and cooperation with labor and political groups. Organized students led the resistance to the introduction of military training in colleges in 1925. The considerable strength of communism in the student movement of the 1920s meant that much of its leadership was subject to persecution or arrest, and various student organizations were banned from the late 1920s. After the early 1930s remaining elements of student organization were absorbed into state-sponsored student organizations. Student activism revived in the postwar period, initially giving its attention to purely educational matters. After a lively movement opposing the raising of fees for educational institutions, a national association, Zengakuren (*q.v.*), was formed in 1948. Increasingly dominated by the left, Zengakuren vigorously opposed curtailments of academic freedom, the strengthening of the powers of police and central government, rearmament, and nuclear warfare. Organized students played a major antigovernment role during the crisis over the U.S.-Japan Security Treaty in 1960. Since then the movement has remained strongly left wing, but the influence of the Japan Communist Party over it has declined. Ideological schisms dealt a severe blow to the unity of the movement; the subsequent trend was toward greater nonsectarianism and increasing resort to violence by anti-Communist radical factions, which has brought down a certain amount of police suppression on much of the movement as a whole. Organized students played a major role in the extensive university unrest of the late 1960s, and in general since 1960 student discontent has concentrated on widespread dissatisfaction with the actual universities.

Battistini, L. *The Postwar Student Struggle in Japan* (Tokyo, 1956).
Krauss, E. S. *Japanese Radicals Revisited* (Berkeley, 1974).
Smith, H. D. *Japan's First Student Radicals* (Cambridge, Mass., 1972).
Tsurumi, K. "Student Movements in 1960 and 1969: Continuity and Change," in S. Takayanagi and K. Miura, eds., *Postwar Trends in Japan* (Tokyo, 1975).

Suffrage Movement (fusen undō)
普選運動

In the early years after the enactment of the Meiji constitution (*q.v.*) a property qualification for suffrage operated, and although the level was subsequently reduced, it was only in May 1925 that universal male suffrage was instituted. After 1892 there was a succession of organizations campaigning for universal suffrage, and in 1900 a petition was presented to the Diet. The issue was one which was strongly supported by Socialists, but increasingly those elements which believed in direct action ceased to support the cause and agitation in this direction declined during the last years of the Meiji period. Calls for suffrage revived from 1915 under the influence of such men as Yoshino Sakuzō and became especially strong after the rice riots of 1918 (*q.v.*). The parties in the Diet were slow to support universal male suffrage. It was first proposed in the Diet in 1902, and in 1911 a male suffrage bill actually passed the Lower House, but it was rejected by the House of Peers. Of the major parties the Kenseikai endorsed universal suffrage in 1919, but it was only in 1924 that it gained the support of the Seiyūkai. Meanwhile, outside the Diet suffrage was supported by the labor movement, and demonstrations were held to promote the campaign; one in Tokyo in 1920 attracted 75,000 people. For several successive years suffrage bills were presented in the Diet, but even the Seiyūkai Hara cabinet, of whom hopes had been high, openly opposed universal suffrage. Labor support temporarily declined due to the dominance of anarcho-syndicalism in the labor movement, but there was a resurgence in the campaign after 1923. Kenseikai and Seiyūkai came together in the movement for the protection of constitutional government (*q.v.*) and open support for universal male suffrage, and in 1925 the new Katō cabinet passed a bill giving the vote to all males over 25. This increased the electorate from 3 million to 12½ million. A women's suffrage movement (*q.v.*) continued to agitate after this, but it was only after the war that women achieved the vote.

Duus, P. "The Universal Manhood Suffrage Issue (1919–1925): From Popular Protest to Party Policy," *HPJ* 1 (1961).
Griffin, E. G. "The Adoption of Universal Manhood Suffrage in Japan," Ph.D. diss., Columbia University, 1965.
———. "The Universal Suffrage Issue in Japanese Politics, 1918–1925," *JAS* 31, no. 2 (Feb. 1972).

Suiheisha. See BURAKU EMANCIPATION MOVEMENT

Sumitomo Zaibatsu 住友財閥
The Sumitomo family developed considerable interests in mining during the Tokugawa period; their biggest operation was the Besshi copper mine in Ehime, and they acted as official copper suppliers to the Bakufu. Business declined at the time of the Restoration but recovered under the direction of Hirose Saihei, who introduced Western technology and organizational practices at Besshi, which then became a base from which Sumitomo interests could diversify. Sumitomo founded its own bank in 1895, and by 1914 interests included trading, mining, banking, warehousing, metal processing, and manufacturing. In 1921 the enterprises comprising the concern were reorganized under a family-owned holding company, and Sumitomo developed into one of the four great prewar *zaibatsu* (*q.v.*). The nature of its interests meant that it played a significant role in time of war. Sumitomo's concerns remained relatively concentrated in heavy industry, and, unlike some other *zaibatsu*, its concerns were tied by organic rather than financial interconnectedness. Although subject to the postwar dissolution policy, Sumitomo interests remain powerful in many of the same fields as before.

Hirschmeier, J. *The Origins of Entrepreneurship in Meiji Japan* (Cambridge, Mass., 1964).
Sumitomo Bank. *The Sumitomo Bank Ltd.—History of 60 Years* (Osaka, 1955).

Supreme Command. See INDEPENDENCE OF THE SUPREME COMMAND

Suzuki Bunji 1885–1946 鈴木文治
A native of Miyagi Prefecture, Suzuki graduated from Tokyo University and worked as a journalist. Under the influence of Abe Isoo and Yoshino Sakuzō he became interested in social problems. He also joined the Christian church and subsequently changed to full-time church work. In 1912 he founded the Yūaikai (*q.v.*). Suzuki's philosophy was one of Christian-based social reformism, and it was with the aim of bringing harmony between labor and capital that he approached the founding of the Yūaikai, but after visiting the U.S. in 1916, he increasingly emphasized the need to strengthen the organization into something more akin to the American Federation of Labor. His continuing emphasis on labor-capital harmony, however, led to a rift with many of his more radical, leading followers. Suzuki was converted to socialism in 1919, but although he remained president of the Yūaikai and its successor, Sōdōmei, until 1930, and was four times Japan's representative to the International Labor Organization, his overwhelming dominance of the labor movement was gone. Suzuki was also a leading figure on the anti-Communist right wing of the proletarian movement and was elected to the Diet in 1928 for the Shakai Minshūtō and in 1936 and 1937 for the Shakai Taishūtō. He ran for election for the Japan Socialist Party in 1946 but died during the campaign.

Large, S. S. "The Japanese Labor Movement, 1912–1919: Suzuki Bunji and

the *Yūaikai*," *JAS* 29, no. 3 (May 1970).
______. *The Yūaikai, 1912–1919* (Tokyo, 1972).

Suzuki Kantarō 1868–1948 (Baron, 1935) 鈴木貫太郎

Native of Chiba Prefecture, Suzuki graduated from the Naval Academy and culminated a naval career by becoming full admiral in 1923, commander of the combined fleet in 1924, and chief of the Naval General Staff 1925–1929. Transferring to the reserve, he then served as privy councillor 1929–1940 and concurrently as Grand Chamberlain from 1929, but he resigned the latter post after sustaining serious injury in the February 26 rising (*q.v.*). During the Pacific War Suzuki was vice-president of the Privy Council 1940–1944, then its president 1944–1945. In April 1945 he succeeded Koiso Kuniaki as prime minister. The war situation was already disastrous for Japan, and the cabinet was divided between desire for peace and the army's demands for a final battle on Japanese soil. The cabinet eventually attempted unsuccessfully to obtain Russian mediation in ending the war. After the bombing of Hiroshima and Nagasaki, the cabinet accepted the Potsdam declaration (*q.v.*) and unconditional surrender. Suzuki resigned the following day, August 15. Suzuki served again as president of the Privy Council 1945–1946.

Butow, R. J. C. *Japan's Decision to Surrender* (Stanford, 1954).

Suzuki Zenkō 1911– 鈴木善幸

Native of Iwate Prefecture, Suzuki studied at the marine training college attached to the Ministry of Agriculture and Forestry, then worked in various organizations concerned with the fishing industry. In 1947 he was elected to the Diet and served as a member of both the Japan Socialist Party and the Shakai Kakushintō (Social Renovation Party) before joining the Liberal Democratic Party. As chairman of the Diet's standing committee on local administration, his skillful handling of the problems resulting from Kishi's attempts to reform the powers of the police began to gain him political recognition. As a leading member of the Ikeda faction he served as minister of posts in 1960, then as cabinet secretary and minister of state 1964–1965. As welfare minister under Satō 1965–1966 Suzuki made major moves toward the improvement of health insurance provisions. His negotiating abilities and political tact meant that he was generally trusted and assisted him to major posts in the party machine; he served as the party's chief of general affairs 1968–1971 and 1972–1974. Following a spell as minister of agriculture under Fukuda 1976–1977 Suzuki, though a power in the party, held no cabinet post, but his assumption of the leadership of the Ōhira faction following Ōhira's sudden death in June 1980 led to his being officially chosen as the L.D.P. leader on 15 July 1980. He formed his first cabinet on 18 July 1980.

Syndicalism. See ANARCHISM

T

Taft-Katsura Agreement (Katsura-Tafuto kyōtei) 桂・タフト協定

In July 1905 Prime Minister Katsura Tarō and W. H. Taft, the U.S. Secretary of War, exchanged confidential notes. These notes gave mutual assurances of the status quo in the Philippines and Japan's suzerainty in Korea, and the desirability of Japan, the U.S., and Britain cooperating to achieve peace in the Far East. The notes meant that Japan was assured that the U.S. would not oppose the expansion of Japan's powers in Korea and its ultimate annexation. The text of the memorandum was revealed in 1924, but there is disagreement over whether it amounted to a full international pact, or whether it was merely an exchange of views. The memorandum was followed by the Root-Takahira agreement (*q.v.*)

Chay, J. "The Taft-Katsura Memorandum Reconsidered," *PHR* 37 (1968).
Esthus, R. A. "The Taft-Katsura Agreement—Reality or Myth?" *Journal of Modern History* 31 (1959).

Taguchi Ukichi 1855–1905 田口卯吉
The son of an Edo Bakufu retainer, Taguchi joined the Finance Ministry in 1872 as a translator. While working there he studied economics and in 1878 published a book supporting free trade in Japan, which made him well known as a liberal economist. In 1877 he had also published the first volume of *A Short History of Japanese Civilization,* a pioneer work in cultural history. In 1878 Taguchi left the government and in 1879 founded the *Tōkyō Keizai Zasshi* (Tokyo Economic Journal) which consistently advocated liberal, free trade economic policies and attacked the government's protectionism. Taguchi's publishing company also pioneered the publication of source materials. Taguchi attempted to put into practice his economic theories through direct involvement with business, notably in railways, mines, banking, and the stock exchange. He worked as a local assemblyman and in 1894 was elected to the Diet. Taguchi left various works on economics and history.

Beasley, W. G., and E. G. Pulleyblank, eds., *Historians of China and Japan* (London, 1961).

Taigyaku Jiken. See HIGH TREASON INCIDENT

Taisei Yokusankai. See IMPERIAL RULE ASSISTANCE ASSOCIATION

Taishō Democracy (Taishō demokurashii) 大正デモクラシー
The term *Taishō democracy* is used to refer to the generally liberal trends apparent in the years following the accession of the Taishō emperor in 1912, which were marked by a relative decline in the political dominance of such elites as the *genrō* (*q.v.*), the military, and the Privy Council, and a relative increase in that of the Diet and the political parties. After the Taishō political crisis (*q.v.*) the ideas of liberal thinkers such as Yoshino Sakuzō and Minobe Tatsukichi gained increasing popularity; their emphasis on the importance of the individual and of democracy was reflected in demands for the greater participation of the people in politics, for universal suffrage, reform of the House of Peers, and arms limitation. The cabinet of Hara Kei in 1918 initiated over a decade of party governments, although few of these proved willing or able to stand up for long to the pressures exerted by other elites given competing powers under the Meiji constitution (*q.v.*). The older established parties in power reacted to the threat posed by the new proletarian parties with suppression; they became increasingly identified with the status quo, and political parties as a whole became increasingly alienated from the people. Their own characteristics and the framework within which they operated led to the decline of the parties as an independent political force from the beginning of the Shōwa period. The so-called "democracy" of the Taishō period is often contrasted with the "fascism" of the Shōwa period, and the nature of the relationship between these two phenomena remains a matter of historical controversy. The relative political liberalism of this period was accompanied by more liberal trends in other fields.

Duus, P. *Party Rivalry and Political Change in Taishō Japan* (Cambridge, Mass., 1968).
Morley, J. *Dilemmas of Growth in Prewar Japan* (Princeton, 1971).
Silberman, B. S., and H. D. Harootunian, eds., *Japan in Crisis: Essays in Taishō Democracy* (Princeton, 1974).

Taishō Emperor (Taishō tennō) 1879–1926 大正天皇
Yoshihito, the third son of the Meiji emperor, became crown prince in 1889 and succeeded his father as the 123rd emperor in July 1912. His reign was given the name of Taishō (Great Justice). Unlike

his father, the Taishō emperor played little active role in political affairs, and the position of the emperor became increasingly a symbolic one. From early in his reign he suffered from mental and physical illness and lived in seclusion. This led to the crown prince, Hirohito (the present emperor), being appointed regent in 1921.

Young, A. M. *Japan Under Taishō Tennō, 1912–1926* (New York, 1929).

Taishō Political Crisis (Taishō seihen) 大正政変

In December 1912 the second Saionji cabinet was forced by the resignation of its army minister to resign following its refusal to grant money for two extra army divisions. There was a public outcry at the ability of the army to bring down a cabinet in this way and at lack of civilian control over the military, and the issue, which had started as one of financial policy, was escalated into a controversy over the constitution and the nature of the Japanese political system. The appointment of Katsura Tarō, a leading figure of the military clique, as prime minister to succeed Saionji worsened the situation. Katsura formed a cabinet with difficulty, utilizing imperial power, but the violent outburst of popular and Diet discontent known as the movement for the protection of constitutional government (*q.v.*) continued. Katsura postponed the Diet session, suspended the Diet, and even announced his intention of forming a political party, but his cabinet eventually resigned in February 1913.

Hackett, R. F. "Yamagata and the Taishō Crisis, 1912–1913," in S. D. Brown, ed. *Studies on Asia* (Lincoln, Nebr., 1962).
Najita, T. *Hara Kei in the Politics of Compromise* (Cambridge, Mass., 1967).

Taiwan 台湾

The island of Formosa (Taiwan) was part of China under the Ch'ing dynasty and in 1874 was invaded by Japanese in a retaliatory expedition for attacks on Ryūkyūan fishermen by natives of the island. Along with the Pescadores the island was ceded to Japan in 1895 under the Treaty of Shimonoseki following the Sino-Japanese War (*q.v.*). The Japanese takeover met with resistance in the center and south of the island from Chinese attempting to establish a republic, and bandit and partisan resistance continued until 1902. In addition, native attacks and uprisings were frequent long after this, and mutual protection had to be maintained by a chain of household and neighborhood organizations working in concert. Japan was initially undecided as to the nature of her colonial policy in Formosa although the initial resistance determined much of the nature of Japanese rule. The post of governor-general was established in 1895; the governor had total control over all matters on the island, and the post was at first held by a general combining both military and civil administrative functions. In 1898–1906 this post was held by Kodama Gentarō, who, in conjunction with the civilian administrator Gotō Shinpei, laid the basis for subsequent rule of the island. Under Kodama a colonial civil service was established, communications and transport services initiated, and provision made for health facilities and a police force. A land survey was carried out and a self-sufficient financial foundation achieved on the basis of an official camphor monopoly and exports of sugar and rice to Japan. The harshness of the regime produced a certain amount of anti-Japanese agitation, and especially after World War I there was considerable pressure for reform. In 1919 the Japanese did establish rule by a civilian administration although a separate military authority continued to exist, and policy became slightly more liberal. After 1921 there were still calls for home rule, but they achieved nothing, and overall there was very little agitation perhaps because of economic prosperity. From 1928 changes in policy marked a move toward giving Taiwanese equal rights with mainland Japanese, but full equality was never achieved. The governor-general retained all power of legislation, and there were no political parties. These gestures toward liberalization were accompanied by attempts to integrate Taiwan by the imposition of Japanese laws and customs, but this had limited success. The keystone of Japanese colonial policy in Taiwan remained making the island economically self-sufficient to enable it to contribute to the national interests of Japan itself. The Bank of Taiwan was established to control investment in the island, but increasingly it lent unwisely to mainland Japan, and the suspension of its dealings initiated the 1927 financial crisis (*q.v.*). Although by 1941 industrial output in Taiwan amounted to 40% by value of total production, rice and sugar remained the staples of the colony's economy throughout the prewar period. Economic ties with Japan became very close during the 1930s, and there is no doubt that some Taiwanese benefited from the flourishing economy. Taiwan held a strategic position in the war against China and after 1937 was also used as a base for Japanese operations. The 1943 Cairo declaration (*q.v.*) stated China's right to the island, which was taken over by the Chinese at the end of the war and subsequently became the seat of the Nationalist government. Japan formally abandoned her claim to sovereignty under the San Francisco Peace Treaty (*q.v.*).

Ch'en, C. C. "Japanese Socio-Political Control in Taiwan, 1895–1945," Ph.D. diss., Harvard University, 1973.
Kerr, G. H. *Formosa—Licensed Revolution and the Home Rule Movement, 1895–1945* (Honolulu, 1974).
Sih, P. K. T. *Taiwan in Modern Times* (n.p., 1973).
Tsurumi, E. P. "Taiwan Under Kodama Gentarō and Gotō Shinpei," *HPJ* 4 (1967).

Taiyō 太陽
A monthly magazine published in Tokyo 1895–1928 (bimonthly 1896–1899), *Taiyō* (Sun) contained a wide range of articles on both general and specialist topics. As a forum in which a variety of people expressed their views and philosophies of political, economic, and social matters, *Taiyō* was the most prominent general journal in the years up to World War I and was highly influential. It subsequently lost much of its influence to *Chūō Kōron* (Central Review) and *Kaizō* (Reconstruction) (*q.v.*).

Takahashi Korekiyo 1854–1936 (Baron, 1907; Viscount, 1920) 高橋是清
Takahashi was a native of Edo but was adopted into a Sendai family shortly after birth. He was sent by his domain to study in America 1867–1869 and after returning worked in the bureaucracy. In 1892 he joined the Bank of Japan and became its vice-president in 1898. For his raising of foreign loans during the Russo-Japanese War, Takahashi was appointed to the House of Peers in 1905. In 1906 he became president of the Yokohama Specie Bank and in 1911 president of the Bank of Japan. In 1913 he joined the Seiyūkai and served as finance minister 1913–1914. He was also finance minister under Hara Kei from 1918 until 1921, when he succeeded Hara as Seiyūkai president and prime minister, acting as his own finance minister. Internal disunity quickly brought the fall of the cabinet in June 1922. In 1924 Takahashi resigned his peerage and place in the House of Peers as part of the movement for the protection of constitutional government (*q.v.*). He was elected to the Diet and served as agriculture and commerce minister 1924–1925. In 1925 he passed the Seiyūkai presidency to Tanaka Giichi but was recalled by Tanaka to serve as finance minister April–June 1927 in an attempt to deal with the 1927 financial crisis (*q.v.*). Takahashi also served as finance minister 1931–1934 and 1934–1936; he reimposed the embargo on exports of gold and followed a policy of deficit financing to promote recovery from depression, a policy which ultimately benefited the military. Takahashi was one of the victims of the February 26 rising (*q.v.*) in 1936.

Duus, P. *Party Rivalry and Political Change in Taishō Japan* (Cambridge, Mass., 1968).
Fukuda, I. "Korekiyo Takahashi—Japan's

Sage of Finance," *CJ* 1, no. 4 (Mar. 1933).

Takahira-Root Agreement. See ROOT-TAKAHIRA AGREEMENT

Takano Fusatarō. See LABOR MOVEMENT

Takashima Shūhan 1798–1866
高島秋帆
A samurai from Nagasaki, Takashima had contact with the Dutch there from his youth and studied Dutch learning. A belief that Japan's existing defenses were inadequate to resist foreign encroachments led him to become an expert in Western gunnery and military methods. His attempts to put his ideas into practice marked the first serious adoption of Western military methods in Japan. Takashima tried to get the Bakufu to recognize the importance of Western defense methods and eventually visited Edo in 1841 to demonstrate infantry drill and gunnery exercises. Reactionary pressure led to his being placed under house arrest 1846–1853, but he resumed his activities after Perry's visit.

Sansom, G. B. *The Western World and Japan* (London, 1950).

Takasugi Shinsaku 1839–1867
高杉晋作
Chōshū samurai, Takasugi studied under Yoshida Shōin and became involved in *han* and national politics. He illegally visited Shanghai in 1862. Initially strongly antiforeign, Takasugi later concentrated his activities on bringing about the end of the Bakufu. It was Takasugi who originated the idea of the *shotai,* Chōshū's irregular troops; he himself formed the Kiheitai (*q.v.*) in 1863, and until his death he played a major role in the organization of the forces for both political and military purposes. Takasugi was responsible for negotiating peace with the powers after the bombardment of Shimonoseki (*q.v.*), but he was twice forced to leave Chōshū because of conservative dominance there. With the loyalist seizure of power in the domain in 1865 his position was assured, and with Kido Kōin he became one of the main arbiters of *han* policy. He continued to act as the domain's expert on Western military science, devoting his efforts to the import of arms and raising of troops and was largely responsible for Chōshū's success against the Bakufu's punitive expedition in 1866. Takasugi died of illness in May 1867.

Craig, A. M. *Chōshū in the Meiji Restoration* (Cambridge, Mass., 1961).
Huber, T. M. "Chōshū Activists in the Meiji Restoration: The Thought and Action of Yoshida Shōin (1830–1859), Kusaka Genzui (1840–1864), and Takasugi Shinsaku (1839–1867)," Ph.D. diss., University of Chicago, 1975.

Takebashi Rising. See TAKEHASHI RISING

Takechi Zuizan 1829–1865 武市瑞山
Gōshi from Tosa, Takechi was a master of fencing and in 1854 opened a school in Kōchi where he trained most of Tosa's loyalist leaders. He then taught in Edo in the late 1850s. Tosa's foremost advocate of *sonnō jōi* (*q.v.*) views, Takechi returned to Tosa to found the Tosa Kinnōtō (Tosa Loyalist Party) in 1860. Takechi's supporters played a major role in *han* government, and as leader of the loyalists and close to Yamanouchi, the daimyō, he himself played a major role in the national and local politics of the early 1860s. From autumn 1863 a more moderate faction gained ascendancy in Tosa; Takechi lost the sympathy of the daimyō and was imprisoned for political assassination and forgery. He was eventually ordered to commit suicide.

Jansen, M. B. "Takechi Zuizan and the Tosa Loyalist Party," *JAS* 18, no. 2 (Feb. 1959).

Takehashi Rising (Takehashi sōdō) 竹橋騒動

On 23 August 1878 members of the artillery section of the Imperial Guard, discontented over reductions in pay and delay in the payment of rewards for services in the Satsuma rebellion, attempted a revolt. The rebels were stationed at the Takehashi (Takebashi) barracks in Tokyo. Several soldiers who tried to halt the revolt were killed, including a battalion commander, and the rebels fired on the residence of the finance minister and advanced toward the Akasaka Palace, with the aim of burning it down and taking prisoner leading statesmen. The authorities, however, had got wind of the plot, and it was quickly put down. After a court-martial in October 218 soldiers were punished, 53 of them shot. The rising was a considerable shock to the Meiji government; it revealed a residue of *shizoku* discontent and lack of total loyalty among Japan's elite forces and resulted in a strengthening of military discipline and the ultimate banning of soldiers from political activity. It was immediately responsible for the *Gunjin Kunkai* (Admonition to Soldiers and Sailors) of 1878 which stressed such virtues as loyalty and bravery and warned against political activity. It also stimulated the *Gunjin Chokuyu* (Imperial Rescript to Soldiers and Sailors) of 1882. This rescript used imperial sanction to reinforce these ideas of loyalty and obedience in accordance with the traditional samurai ethic.

Crowley, J. B. "From Closed Door to Empire: The Formation of the Meiji Military Establishment," in B. S. Silberman and H. D. Harootunian, eds., *Modern Japanese Leadership* (Tucson, 1966).

Hackett, R. F. *Yamagata Aritomo in the Rise of Modern Japan, 1838–1922* (Cambridge, Mass., 1971).

Takigawa Incident. See KYOTO UNIVERSITY

Tanaka Giichi 1863–1929 (Baron, 1920) 田中義一

Chōshū samurai, Tanaka graduated from the Military Academy and entered the army. He studied in Russia 1898–1902 and was on the Manchurian army staff during the Russo-Japanese War. Within the army he was closely identified with Yamagata Aritomo. In 1910 he played a leading part in founding a unified reservists' association (*q.v.*) to inculcate *bushidō* values and loyalty to imperial rule. In 1911 he became chief of the Military Affairs Bureau, where his calls for army expansion helped to bring down the Saionji cabinet. As vice chief of staff from 1915 Tanaka advocated a strong continental policy and in 1917 prompted the founding of a national youth organization, again to reinforce support for military values. As war minister 1918–1921 he continued his work of strengthening national defense and promoted Japan's involvement in the Siberian intervention (*q.v.*). In 1921 he became a full general and was again war minister 1923–1924. Tanaka succeeded Yamagata as leader of the Chōshū military clique and in 1925 went on the reserve list to enter politics and become president of the Seiyūkai. In 1926 he became a member of the House of Peers. Tanaka became prime minister in April 1927 and retained the post until July 1929, acting as his own foreign and colonization minister. The cabinet's immediate task was to deal with the 1927 financial crisis (*q.v.*), for which Tanaka called in Takahashi Korekiyo to act as finance minister. At home Tanaka clamped down on the left wing, especially the Communist Party, arresting many thousands; he amended the Peace Preservation Law (*q.v.*) by imperial decree to include the death penalty and extended police surveillance over the whole country. Abroad the Tanaka cabinet adopted a "strong" and "positive" policy to promote Japan's continental interests, as announced at the Eastern Conference (*q.v.*); this policy included sending the Shantung expeditions (*q.v.*). Tanaka's moves aroused strong international criticism and violent anti-Japanese movements in China, and the murder of Chang Tso-lin (*q.v.*) eventually brought about the fall of the cabinet. Tanaka died shortly afterwards.

Bamba, N. *Japanese Diplomacy in a Dilemma* (Vancouver, 1972).

Etō, S. "The Policy-Making Process of the Proposed Interception of the Peking-Mukden Railway—Tanaka Diplomacy and Its Background," *Acta Asiatica* 14 (1968).
Morton, W. F. *Tanaka Giichi and Japan's China Policy* (Folkestone, Kent, 1980).
Smethurst, R. J. *A Social Basis for Prewar Japanese Militarism* (Berkeley, 1974).

Tanaka Kakuei 1918–
田中角栄
Native of Niigata Prefecture, Tanaka received some engineering education and built up his own transport and construction companies. He was first elected to the Diet in 1947 for the Japan Democratic Party, then joined the Japan Liberal Party. He was arrested for corruption and in 1949 was elected while in prison but was later acquitted. Subsequently in the Liberal Democratic Party, Tanaka was close to Satō and through the 1960s held important posts in the party. He was also minister of posts and telecommunications 1957–1958, finance minister 1962–1965, and minister of international trade and industry 1971–1972. By political maneuvering and extensive use of money, Tanaka had built up the L.D.P.'s biggest faction and in July 1972 beat Fukuda Takeo for the post of president of the L.D.P. and therefore became prime minister, the youngest since the war. Initially Tanaka had considerable support because of his unorthodox background and status as a self-made man. His *Plan for Remodeling the Japanese Archipelago* published in June 1972 was a design to utilize the benefits of economic growth to improve life in Japan, but it was shelved due to inflation and the oil shock of autumn 1973. Tanaka's reestablishment of diplomatic relations with the People's Republic of China in September 1972 is regarded as his major achievement as prime minister. Decreasing popularity and criticism of his financial dealings inside and outside politics caused Tanaka's resignation in December 1974. Tanaka was arrested in July 1976 and charged with corruption to the tune of ¥500 million in connection with the Lockheed scandal (*q.v.*). Proceedings started in January 1977 and still continue.

Tanaka, K. *Building a New Japan* (Tokyo, 1973).

Tanaka Memorial (Tanaka memorandamu) 田中メモランダム
The Tanaka memorial was a report supposedly submitted by Prime Minister Tanaka Giichi to the emperor outlining Japan's continental strategy on the basis of discussions at the Eastern Conference (*q.v.*). The report was first revealed in China and may well have been a Chinese compilation; its authenticity was denied by Japanese, and doubts were cast upon it at the Tokyo war crimes trials. Nevertheless, it had been widely circulated both in China and in other countries by 1929, and wide credence was given to it as proof of planned Japanese aggression, especially in view of incidents during the 1930s, which seemed to bear it out.

Northeastern Affairs Research Society. *Tanaka's Secret Memorial to the Japanese Emperor* (n.d., n.p.).
Stephan, J. J. "The Tanaka Memorial, 1927: Authentic or Spurious?" *MAS* 7 (1973).
Willoughby, W. W. *Japan's Case Examined* (Baltimore, 1940).

Tanaka Shōzō 1841–1913 田中正造
Native of Tochigi Prefecture and village headman, Tanaka was active in the popular rights movement and expounded these ideas in the *Tochigi Shinbun*, which he founded in 1899. In 1880 he became a member of Tochigi Prefectural Assembly and in 1886 its chairman. He opposed the ruthless public works plans of Governor Mishima Michitsune and was imprisoned for a time. In 1890 Tanaka was elected to the Diet as a Kaishintō member. During the 1890s he devoted most of his energies to appeals to the government to solve the Ashio copper mine pollution problem (*q.v.*) without much success. His strategy included mass demonstrations by residents of the polluted area and a direct appeal to the emperor in December 1901. Tanaka

resigned from the Diet in 1901, despairing at its inability to help him stop the pollution, and his subsequent efforts were devoted to opposing those measures which were suggested by the government and helping farmers by such measures as flood control works.

Strong, K. *Ox Against the Storm* (Tenterden, Kent, 1977).

Tani Kanjō 1837–1911 (Viscount, 1884) 谷干城

Tosa samurai, Tani fought against the Bakufu in the Boshin War and then worked to reform the *han* administration before joining the War Ministry in 1871. He fought in the campaigns of the 1870s and as head of the Kumamoto garrison played a major role in suppressing the Satsuma rebellion (*q.v.*). He rose in the army to become a general and head of the Military Academy but resigned because of disagreement with the policies of Yamagata Aritomo. Tani acted as head of the Peers' School from 1884 and then minister of agriculture and commerce 1885–1886, but he resigned over the "excessive" Westernization policies expounded by Inoue Kaoru and the latter's treaty revision proposals. In 1890 he became a member of the House of Peers where his consistent criticism of the government's "betrayal" of Japanese nationalism included opposition to the Russo-Japanese War. Tani was one of the early bureaucratic exponents of *nōhonshugi* (*q.v.*) ideals; he consistently objected to state sponsorship of industry and commerce and stressed the need to establish independent owner-farmers for reasons of military strength and self-sufficiency and as a foil to dangerous ideas. Throughout his life he remained a strong opponent of the popular rights movement.

Havens, T. R. H. *Farm and Nation in Modern Japan: Agrarian Nationalism, 1870–1940* (Princeton, 1974).

Taxation

During the Tokugawa period there was no national taxation system. The main source of income of both Bakufu and daimyō came from land tax on land directly owned by these authorities. In some places this was a crippling burden on farmers. Increasingly as the period progressed, this income was supplemented by taxes on such things as crops other than rice, houses, transit, and commerce, as well as *goyōkin* (forced loans) largely from merchants. The changes in taxation were an important factor undermining the economic base of the Tokugawa system. After the Restoration the government reformed the land tax (*q.v.*), and it remained the staple source of central government income until past 1900 partly because initially there was little alternative, partly as a stimulus to industrialization by penalizing agriculture to help commerce and industry. It remained a heavy burden on farmers, and on many occasions there were calls for reduction in the land tax rate. To supplement this, other taxes included those on *sake* and tobacco introduced during the Matsukata deflation. Other taxes added or increased to sizable proportions subsequently included income tax (1887), business taxes, customs, and taxes on beer, sugar, salt, woven goods, and inheritance. By 1900 some 20% of government income came from indirect taxation, but after 1905 income and business taxes were reduced so that by 1913 indirect taxation accounted for 69% total government income. Tax reforms after World War I indicated that the Japanese government was beginning to regard taxation as not only an instrument of economic policy and revenue raising but also as a means for achieving certain noneconomic aims, but the change was not yet a major one. Further reforms in the late 1920s affected the form rather than substance of taxation. The burden of military build-up and war in the 1930s meant that from 1935 tax reform became a priority to rationalize the whole pattern of taxation and the mélange of laws governing it. This eventually came in 1940. The basic aim of this reform was to create a system ensuring the rise in revenue necessitated by the war situation, and the key was the increase in income tax, which in 1939 had supplied 31% total taxation and monopoly revenue. The massive increase in income tax rates and lowering of exemption levels hit many. Corporation and other direct tax levels were also gradually raised, and despite rises in indirect taxation also direct taxation increased in importance. For greater efficiency regional taxes were more absorbed into the national tax structure. This revised system was subject to many further reforms during the war to meet the unprecedented levels of expenditure. Much of it remained operational through the early years of the Occupation, with adjustments for Occupation policy and massive inflation. Following the recommendations of the American Shoup mission, from 1950 a fundamental reform of the tax system was initiated. Despite wartime changes, the mainstay of government revenue up to this time was still taxes on consumption and circulation. The new emphasis was on direct taxation, especially income and property taxes, decentralization, reduction in consumption taxes, and abolition of circulation taxes. Reform rationalized the whole taxation system with the aim of promoting Japan's economic recovery. Despite reforms since then the system has remained substantially unchanged. In 1978 income and corporation tax together provided nearly 75% of the government's tax income.

Hayashi, T. *Guide to Japanese Taxes* (Tokyo, 1977).
Shiomi, S. *Japan's Finance and Taxation, 1940–1956* (New York, 1957).

Teijin Scandal. See IMPERIAL RAYON SCANDAL

Teiseitō 帝政党

In March 1882 the government sponsored the founding of a political party, the Rikken Teiseitō (Constitutional Imperial Party) to offset the influence of the Jiyūtō and Kaishintō. Under its leader, Fukuchi Gen'ichirō, the party advocated an "emperor-given" constitution, sovereignty lying with the emperor, and limited franchise. Its views were expressed in the *Tokyo Nichi Nichi*. The Teiseitō established regional affiliates, but its organization was weak, and it never attracted more than a few adherents from among conservative and landed elements. It disbanded in September 1883.

Huffman, J. L. "Fukuchi Gen'ichirō, Journalist-Intellectual in Early Meiji Japan," Ph.D. diss., University of Michigan, 1972).

Telegraph

The telegraph was first demonstrated in Japan by Commodore Perry, but real development began only after its enthusiastic adoption by the Meiji government. By late 1869 it connected Tokyo and Yokohama, and by 1873 an Aomori-Tokyo-Nagasaki route had been completed. Rapid development of the telegraph was due both to its low capital cost and to an awareness of its value for administrative centralization and military purposes. For the same reasons all trunk lines and most branch lines were kept under government control, administered by the Ministry of Industry and later the Ministry of Communications. Through the 1870s the trunk routes were expanded and the telegraph proved its military value at the time of the Satsuma rebellion (*q.v.*). Trunk routes were virtually complete by 1880 although it was only later that a comprehensive network connecting the smaller towns and villages was completed. Overseas cables to Vladivostok and Shanghai were opened in 1871. A telephone system was started under government control in 1890, but it was slow to compete with the telegraph, and only in the Taishō period did it become widely used. In 1952 both telegraph and telephone were transferred to a public corporation, the Japan Telegraph and Telephone Corporation (Denden Kōsha).

Shibusawa, K. *Japanese Society in the Meiji Era* (Tokyo, 1958).
Smith, T. C. *Political Change and Industrial Development in Japan: Government Enterprise, 1868–1880* (Stanford, 1955).

Telephone. See TELEGRAPH

Television. See BROADCASTING

Tenancy

Despite legal prohibitions tenancy increased toward the end of the Tokugawa period largely due to increasing rural poverty as a result of commercialization and inflation. By the Restoration some 20% cultivated land was tenanted. The land tax (*q.v.*) reform of the 1870s fixed ownership and tax levels, but it failed to control rents, which were largely paid in kind. High tax and rent levels, commercialization, and deflationary policies in the 1880s accelerated the concentration of land ownership and a rich-poor polarization in the villages. By 1907 some 45 % cultivated land was tenanted. Much of it was owned by absentee landlords, who found it more profitable to let land than to cultivate it. Especially up to World War I, though, many resident landlords did play a positive role in the development of their communities and the fostering of efficient agriculture. In the years after 1900 many landlords ceased to play their traditional role, and improved education led an increasing number of tenants to join together in disputes over rent levels and other causes of distress. These increased sharply after 1918 when depression set in following the prosperity of the early years of the war, in conjunction with poor harvests; protest became more organized, with the formation of farmers' unions, and many large-scale disputes occurred, mostly in the more industrialized southwestern areas. Tenants were in many of these disputes relatively successful. A Tenancy Arbitration Law in 1924 allowed for legal arbitration, and this remained in force until 1951, but it proved to act in favor of landlords rather than tenants. Tenant impoverishment continued; disputes decreased in the late 1920s, only to revive in the early 1930s. These disputes were by and large small scale, concentrated in the more backward northeastern areas. Many were sparked off by attempted eviction, and they often ended in violence. Typical was that of Akutsumura, Tochigi, in 1931–1932, when tenants' demands for rent reduction met with organized intimidation by landlords, and clashes between tenants and members of the right-wing Greater Japan Production Party resulted in three deaths and 109 prosecutions. Tenants were relatively unsuccessful in the disputes of the early 1930s, but conditions improved after the Manchurian Incident, and landlords suffered from the subsequent government measures attempting to ensure food supply in time of war. The view that absentee and nonfarming landholding was a prop for aggressive militarism in Japan led to the postwar land reform (*q.v.*). In mid-1947 it was estimated that 18% of the total of tenanted land was held by absentee landlords and a further 24% by nonfarmers. By the land reform the proportion of cultivated land held by tenants was reduced to only 10%, and this figure has since further decreased.

Dore, R. P. *Land Reform in Japan* (London, 1959).
Wakukawa, S. "The Japanese Farm Tenancy System," in D. G. Haring, ed., *Japan's Prospect* (Cambridge, Mass., 1946).
Waswo, A. *Japanese Landlords* (Berkeley, 1977).

Tenkō 転向

The word *tenkō* (about-face, conversion) is used to refer to fundamental change in a way of thinking, especially the widespread "conversions" of Communists and other antigovernment radicals during the 1930s, who underwent self-criticism and gave public adherence to the ideological position promoted by the state. Conversions were brought about by force, threats to the individual's family, or just by force of circumstances. In June 1933 former Japan Communist Party leaders Nabeyama Sadachika and Sano Manabu issued a declaration of change of faith from prison. Within a month over 30% of all Communists in prison followed suit. Some became violently anti-Communist, others merely refrained from political activity, but this wave of *tenkō* (plus repression) effectively removed the J.C.P. as a viable force until after the war.

Mitchell, R. *Thought Control in Prewar Japan* (Ithaca, 1976).
Steinhoff, P. G. "Tenkō: Ideology and Social Integration in Prewar Japan," Ph.D. diss., Harvard University, 1969.
Tsurumi, K. *Social Change and the Individual: Japan Before and After Defeat in World War II* (Princeton, 1970).

Tennōsei. See EMPEROR SYSTEM

Tenrikyō. See SHINTŌ

Terashima (Terajima) Munenori 1832–1893 (Count, 1884) 寺島宗則
Satsuma samurai, Terashima studied Dutch learning and medicine, taught at the Kaiseijo (*q.v.*), and visited the West 1862 and 1865–1866. In 1868 he joined the new government where he specialized in foreign affairs. He was envoy to England 1872–1873, then foreign minister 1873–1879. During this time he dealt with such matters as the Maria Luz incident (*q.v.*), the Sakhalin-Kurile exchange treaty, and the opening of relations with Korea. He was also state councillor 1873–1881. After being education minister 1879–1880 and president of the Genrōin (*q.v.*) in 1881, Terashima served as envoy to the U.S. 1882–1883. He was afterwards court adviser from 1885 and vice-president of the Privy Council 1888–1891.

Terauchi Masatake 1852–1919 (Viscount, 1907; Count, 1911) 寺内正毅
Chōshū samurai, Terauchi fought in the Boshin War (*q.v.*) and on the recommendation of Ōmura Masujirō studied at Osaka Military School. He joined the army, and although he lost the use of one hand fighting in the Satsuma rebellion, he concentrated on administrative posts and rose to become general in 1906 and field marshal in 1916. He was head of the Military Academy from 1887 and bureau chief at the general staff from 1892. As the first director general of military education 1898–1900, Terauchi reformed the whole system of military training. He served as deputy chief of staff 1900–1902 and was then war minister 1902–1911 and chairman of the committee founding the South Manchurian Railway Company (*q.v.*). As resident general and first governor-general of Korea 1910–1916 Terauchi instituted a harsh military regime in the colony and ruthlessly suppressed all opposition. Known as the protégé of Yamagata Aritomo, Terauchi was appointed prime minister in October 1916. He headed a nonparty cabinet although he compromised to gain Seiyūkai support in the Diet. The cabinet attempted to expand Japan's continental interests by such measures as the Nishihara loans (*q.v.*), the Lansing-Ishii agreement (*q.v.*), and intervention in Siberia, but at home it was criticized for its *hanbatsu* politics (*q.v.*) and its economic policies, which included tax increases for military expansion and worsened an already serious economic situation of rampant inflation. Terauchi remained throughout a supporter of authoritarian, nonparty rule. The cabinet resigned after the rice riots (*q.v.*) in September 1918 with Terauchi already seriously ill. He died shortly after.

Tientsin Treaty (Tenshin jōyaku) 天津条約
In December 1884, in what was known as the Kōshin incident, the Korean Independence Party led by Kim Ok-kyun and Pak Yong-hyō carried out a coup against the pro-Chinese regime in Korea, supported by the Japanese envoy, Takezoe, and Japanese liberals. Their new regime was quickly deposed after the advent of 3,000 Chinese troops, many of its members were executed, and Pak and Kim fled to Japan. Several Japanese were killed or injured, the legation was burnt, and Takezoe fled to Inchon (Chemulpo). In a treaty with Japan concluded in January 1885 Korea apologized, promising to punish the offenders and pay $110,000

compensation. Takezoe was recalled. Subsequently Itō Hirobumi went to China to negotiate with Li Hung-chang a basic settlement over Korea reducing the likelihood of future similar clashes. Under the April 1885 Treaty of Tientsin, also known as the Li-Itō convention, Japan and China agreed to withdraw troops from Korea within four months, not to send military instructors, and to provide prior written notification when sending troops in the future. It was under the terms of this treaty that Japan entered the Sino-Japanese War 1894–1895 (*q.v.*).

Conroy, H. *The Japanese Seizure of Korea, 1868–1910* (Philadelphia, 1960).
Cook, H. F. "Kim Ok-kyun and the Background of the 1884 Emeute," Ph.D. diss., Harvard University, 1969.

Toba-Fushimi, Battle of. See BOSHIN WAR

Tōgō Heihachirō 1848–1934 (Count, 1907) 東郷平八郎
Satsuma samurai, Tōgō was in the Satsuma navy and then the national navy. After studying in England as a naval cadet 1871–1878, he had become a rear-admiral by the end of the Sino-Japanese War. Promoted to full admiral and commander of the fleet in the Russo-Japanese War (*q.v.*), Tōgō's defeat of Russia's Baltic fleet in the Battle of the Japan Sea (Straits of Tsushima) at the end of the war in May 1905 made him widely known. Chief of the Naval General Staff 1905–1909, Tōgō was afterwards supreme military councillor, admiral of the fleet in 1913, and supervisor of the crown prince's studies 1914–1921. Tōgō remained a senior figure in the Japanese navy until his death and was influential in his opposition to the London Naval Treaty (*q.v.*) in 1930.

Blond, G. *Admiral Tōgō* (London, 1961).
Falk, B. A. *Tōgō and the Rise of Japanese Sea Power* (London, 1936).
Ogasawara, N. *Life of Admiral Tōgō* (Tokyo, 1934).

Tōgō Shigenori 1882–1950 東郷茂徳
Native of Kagoshima Prefecture, after graduating from Tokyo University in 1908, Tōgō joined the Foreign Ministry. He was Japan's representative in Germany 1937–1938 and as envoy to Russia 1938–1940 had to deal with the Nomonhan incident (*q.v.*) and the problem of fishing rights. He also attempted to conclude a nonaggression pact. 1941 he became foreign minister under Tōjō and was responsible for the negotiations with the U.S., whose breakdown culminated in the Pacific War (*q.v.*), but he resigned in September 1942, opposing the establishment of the Greater East Asia Ministry (*q.v.*). Tōgō became a member of the House of Peers but undertook little political activity until acting again as foreign minister and Greater East Asia minister under Suzuki April-August 1945 when he made every effort to end the war. He was tried as a class "A" war criminal and was sentenced to 20 years' imprisonment but died in prison.

Suzuki, T. "Shigenori Tōgō; The Man and His Career," *CJ* 10, no. 12 (Dec. 1941).
Tōgō, S. *The Cause of Japan* (New York, 1956).

Tōhō Kaigi. See EASTERN CONFERENCE

Tōjō Hideki 1884–1948 東条英機
Native of Tokyo, after graduating from the Military Academy, Tōjō entered the army. He was chief of the military police in the Kwantung Army (*q.v.*) in 1935, chief of staff of the Kwantung Army in 1937, and deputy minister of war in 1938 and was regarded as one of the leaders of the *tōsei* faction (*q.v.*). Tōjō served as war minister 1940–1941; he persistently refused to sanction the withdrawal of Japanese troops from China and regarded war with the U.S. as inevitable. His attitude helped to bring down the Konoe cabinet, and he succeeded him as prime minister in October 1941, while still commissioned. Tōjō also acted as his own war minister and briefly as his own home

minister. After the outbreak of war with America Tōjō devoted his efforts to strengthening central control and reinforcing public support behind the war effort by such measures as "recommended" candidates in the 1942 election. He established the Greater East Asia Ministry (*q.v.*) for unified administration of colonies and occupied territories and tried unsuccessfully to gain the support of the latter by such measures as the Greater East Asia Conference (*q.v.*). Tōjō tried to control the cabinet by monopolizing all the important posts, and he also acted as munitions minister in a new ministry set up in November 1943 to enable greater command of war supplies. He acted briefly also as agriculture and commerce minister, and in February 1944 became chief of staff as well, in the hope of coordinating war planning. At the same time the navy minister became chief of the naval general staff, but Tōjō never achieved control over the navy. Tōjō's assumption of such massive administrative responsibilities only partially overcame existing organizational weaknesses; he failed to adjust his policies to the worsening war situation, which stimulated an increasingly coordinated movement against him, eventually forcing his resignation in July 1944. After an unsuccessful suicide attempt Tōjō was tried as a class "A" war criminal and hanged in December 1948. Tōjō's aggressive stance and considerable personal influence (both formal and informal) made him the most hated figure during the Pacific War among Japan's enemies.

Berger, G. M. "Conflict, Compromise, and Tragedy: Konoe Fumimaro and Tōjō Hideki," in Japan Culture Institute, ed., *Great Historical Figures of Japan* (Tokyo, 1978).
Browne, C. *Tōjō: The Last Banzai* (New York, 1967).
Butow, R. J. C. *Tōjō and the Coming of War* (Princeton, 1961).

Tokonami Takejirō 1867–1935
床次竹二郎
Native of Kagoshima, Tokonami graduated in 1890 from Tokyo University and entered the Home Ministry. While a bureaucrat he became a follower of Hara Kei, and in 1915 Tokonami was elected to the Diet as a Seiyūkai member. As director of railways and home minister under Hara 1918–1921 Tokonami promoted the formation of the Kyōchōkai (*q.v.*). He remained home minister 1921–1922. His desire to support the Kiyoura cabinet in 1924 led Tokonami and his followers to break away from Seiyūkai to form the Seiyū Hontō. Hope of becoming prime minister led Tokonami to merge the Seiyū Hontō with the Kenseikai in 1927 to form the Minseitō. Tokonami was adviser to the new party but left that in 1928 to found and lead the Shinsei Club. In 1929 he rejoined the Seiyūkai and was railways minister 1931–1932. In 1934 persistent political opportunism led Tokonami to accept the post of communications minister under Okada against the wishes of the Seiyūkai, which struck him off the party register.

Duus, P. *Party Rivalry and Political Change in Taishō Japan* (Cambridge, Mass., 1968).

Tokugawa Bakufu 徳川幕府
The name *Bakufu* was traditionally given to a military government headed by a shōgun, the emperor's military deputy. In 1603 Tokugawa Ieyasu was awarded the title of shōgun, and the Tokugawa family's administration at Edo remained the de facto government of Japan until the Meiji Restoration of 1868; the imperial court at Kyoto was virtually devoid of political influence. The system of Tokugawa Bakufu rule is often referred to as centralized feudalism. The influence of the Tokugawa family was based on the fact that it was the largest landholder; in conjunction with its direct retainers it owned over 25% of all land, including major mines, ports, and cities. The rest of the land was alloted to daimyō, feudal lords who held over 10,000 *koku* of land and who were not subvassals. The Bakufu could increase, decrease, or exchange domains (*han*) as well, and during the early years of the period this was frequently done for punitive, strategic, and other motives. Apart

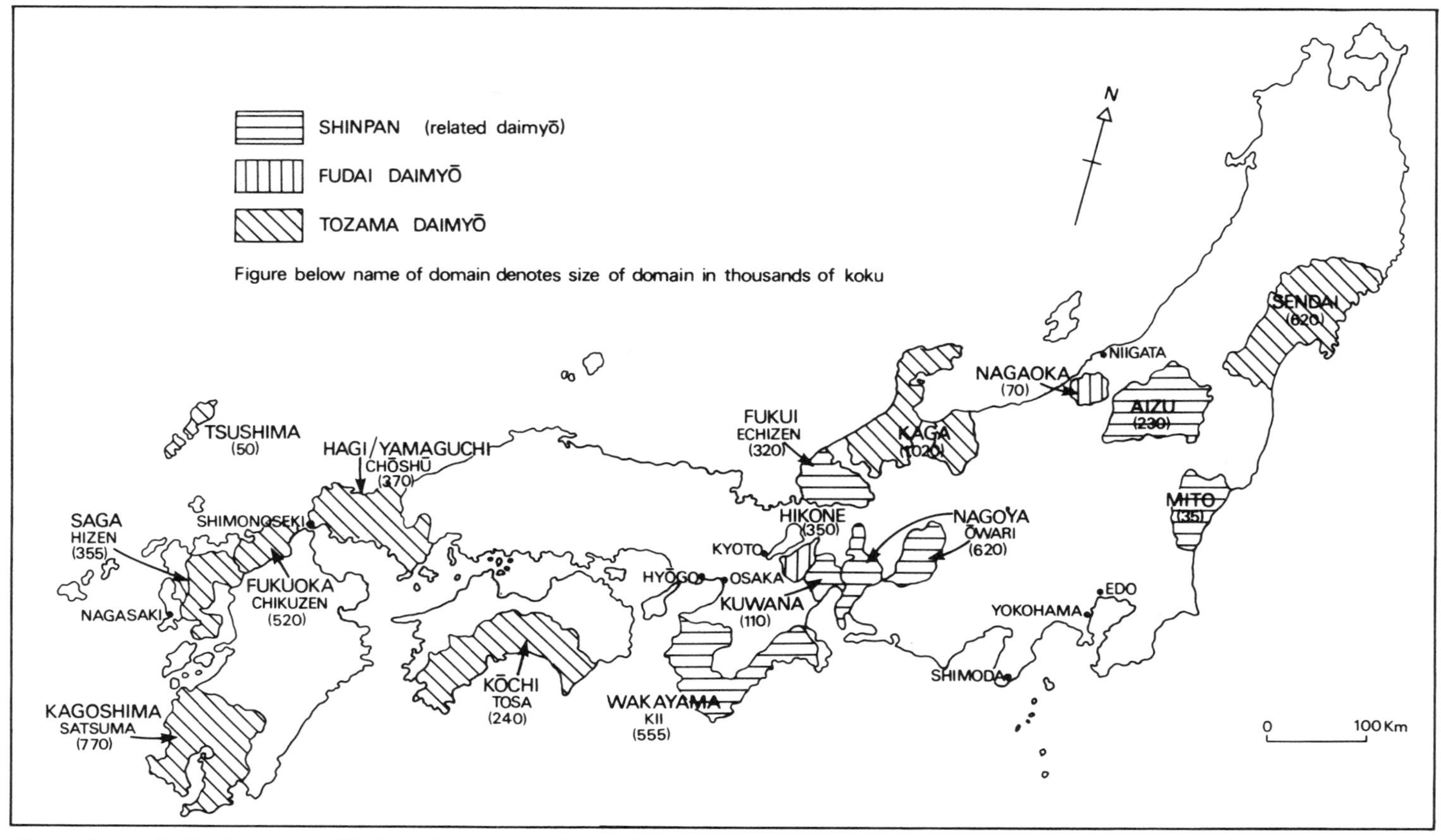

Map 3. JAPAN. Major Domains of Political Importance during the Bakumatsu Period

from families related to the Tokugawa (*sanke* and *shinpan*) the daimyō fell into two categories. The *fudai* were hereditary vassal families of the Tokugawa since before the latter had achieved national power, and only they were eligible for office within the Bakufu, including the highest post of *rōjū* (senior councillor). The *tozama* (outside lords) were not vassals of the Tokugawa house, having submitted only after Ieyasu's victory. The *tozama* owned less than 40% of land, their domains being concentrated at the country's extremities due to the strategic disposition of Tokugawa and *fudai* domains in central areas. All daimyō were subject to detailed regulation of their lives by the Bakufu and to strict control by such mechanisms as the *sankin kōtai* (alternate attendance) system. Within their domains, however, daimyō had considerable autonomy. Society at large was divided into a strict social hierarchy of samurai (warrior), farmer, artisan, merchant, and outcaste. The samurai class from which daimyō and shōgun came (the imperial court was outside the hierarchy) was the ruling class. Only its members could hold feudal vassal status and office in domain or Bakufu administration. Traditionally, samurai held fiefs in land from their lord, but an increasing trend toward a stipend system detached samurai from the land and concentrated land possession in the hands of daimyō and shōgun. The activities and way of life of all the lower classes were also strictly detailed, but as the period progressed the line between classes became less well defined, leading to the emergence of such groups as *gōshi* (rural samurai). Certain doctrines of Neo-Confucianism were emphasized by the regime to provide ideological underpinning to this rigidly hierarchical political and social structure. Total seclusion from foreign intercourse was aimed at preventing subversion from outside. The long-term weakness of the Tokugawa Bakufu was that it had little political, and no economic, status as a national government. Barriers were placed on the exercise of ability and economic and political changes, such as, for example, the rise of the merchant class, meant that status, wealth, income and occupation became decreasingly commensurate with each other. It was the internal strains ultimately caused by the continuing attempt to maintain Tokugawa power through the restriction to a minimum of all political, social, and economic change in conjunction with pressure from abroad that was largely responsible for the fall of the system in 1868.

Bolitho, H. *Treasures Among Men* (New Haven, 1974).

Hall, J. W., and M. B. Jansen, eds., *Studies in the Institutional History of Early Modern Japan* (Princeton, 1968).

Sheldon, C. D. *The Rise of the Merchant Class in Tokugawa Japan, 1600–1868* (Locust Valley, N.Y., 1958).

Totman, C. *The Collapse of the Tokugawa Bakufu, 1862–1868* (Honolulu, 1979).

______. *Politics in the Tokugawa Bakufu, 1600–1843* (Cambridge, Mass., 1967).

Tsukahira, T. G. *Feudal Control in Tokugawa Japan: The Sankin Kōtai System* (Cambridge, Mass., 1966).

Tokugawa Keiki (Yoshinobu) 1837–1913 (Prince, 1902) 徳川慶喜
Seventh son of Tokugawa Nariaki of Mito adopted into the Hitotsubashi family in 1847, Keiki was strongly supported as successor to the shōgun, Iesada, in the 1857–1858 shōgunal succession dispute (*q.v.*) and under the Ansei purge (*q.v.*) was ordered into retirement and put under house arrest. Pardoned after the death of Ii Naosuke, in summer 1862 he became guardian to the shōgun, Iemochi. He spent much time in Kyoto in promoting a *kōbu gattai (q.v.)* policy, instituted reforms in the hope of maintaining Bakufu power, and tried to develop Japan's relations with the West. In summer 1866 Keiki succeeded Iemochi as head of the Tokugawa family, formally taking the title of shōgun early in 1867. He continued his policy of trying to strengthen the Bakufu and the Tokugawa family by reform and relied closely on the advice of the French envoy Léon Roches. Lack of success led him to resign his office in

November 1867 to make way for an imperial council of daimyō (*taisei hōkan*), but this move was insufficient to satisfy his more radical opponents. After the battle of Toba-Fushimi, Keiki was declared an imperial rebel, but unlike some of his supporters he was reluctant to provoke civil war and soon surrendered to the imperial forces. He was succeeded as head of the Tokugawa house by Iesato but was awarded a large fief in Suruga (Shizuoka Prefecture). Keiki was pardoned in 1869 but did not resume political activity, although he retained considerable personal influence. His life is recorded in a biography by Shibusawa Eiichi.

Medzini, M. *French Policy in Japan During the Closing Years of the Tokugawa Regime* (Cambridge, Mass., 1971).
Morris, J. *Makers of Japan* (London, 1906).
Totman, C. "Tokugawa Yoshinobu and Kōbugattai: A Study of Political Inadequacy," *MN* 30 (1975).

Tokugawa Nariaki. See MITO

Tokugawa Shōgunate. See TOKUGAWA BAKUFU

Tokutomi Sohō. See MINYŪSHA

Tokyo 東京

Edo, in the Kantō area, was the seat of the shōgunate in the Tokugawa period. By 1868 it had a population of over 1 million, of which a relatively large proportion were samurai. In September 1868 Edo was renamed Tokyo (eastern capital), and the administration and emperor were effectively established there from 1869.

As the seat of the administration and increasingly as a business center, the city grew rapidly and had a population of 2 million in 1920; many peripheral areas came under the jurisdiction of the metropolitan administration. Much of the city was destroyed in the 1923 Kantō earthquake (*q.v.*); it was mostly rebuilt by 1930, only to have many of its buildings again destroyed by bombing during the later stages of the Pacific War. Much of the population fled to the countryside. Postwar recovery was rapid. By 1955 the population had exceeded the prewar level, and the estimated population of Tokyo metropolitan area in October 1979 was over 11½ million. The rate of increase has slowed since 1970, and decline in manufacturing industry in the Tokyo area means some population decrease in certain areas of the capital.

Smith, H. D. "Tokyo and London: Comparative Conceptions of the City," in A. Craig, ed., *Japan, A Comparative View* (Princeton, 1979).
______. "Tokyo as an Idea: An Exploration of Japanese Urban Thought Until 1945," *JJS* 4, no. 1 (1978).

Tokyo College. See WASEDA UNIVERSITY

Tokyo Nichi Nichi. See NEWSPAPERS

Tokyo University (Tōkyō daigaku) 東京大学

Tokyo University was Japan's first institution to bear the name of university and was established in 1877 from a merger of the former Kaiseijo (*q.v.*) and the Tokyo Medical School, both founded by the Bakufu. Directly administered by the Education Ministry, it was the first modern, Western-style institution of higher education, pursuing both teaching and research. It had four faculties, of medicine, law, literature, and science and ran a four-year course. Initially there were many foreign teachers, mostly British and American, although the format of the university's education was German-influenced. With the addition of the Engineering College (*kōbu daigakkō*) in 1886, it became the Imperial University (the word *Tokyo* was added 1897 to distinguish it from Kyoto Imperial University), and under this name it became the orthodox channel for a successful career in the bureaucracy, an institution clearly aimed at the education of officials and technicians for state purposes. Despite this, a minority of its students were in the forefront of the radical students' movement in the early 1920s. Renamed Tokyo University in 1947, the institution retains a strong hold on the bureaucracy and many other prestigious jobs.

Tokyo War Crimes Trial. See INTERNATIONAL MILITARY TRIBUNAL OF THE FAR EAST

Tonarigumi. See NEIGHBORHOOD ASSOCIATIONS

Tōsei Faction (tōseiha) 統制派
With the *kōdō* faction, the *tōsei* (control) faction dominated the army during the 1930s. Initially led by Nagata Tetsuzan, later leading members were Ishiwara Kanji, Mutō Akira, and Tōjō Hideki. Less interested than the *kōdō* faction in internal reconstruction, members of the *tōseiha* concentrated on the formation of a state geared to war and expansion in Manchuria and China. Dominated by members of the War Ministry and General Staff, the group came to believe after the October incident in 1931 (*q.v.*) that the use of force was undesirable and that their desired aims could be achieved by working with bureaucrats and big business within the status quo. *Kōdō* faction acts were considered to be a breach of army discipline and to endanger Japan's continental strategy. *Tōsei* faction members monopolized the leadership of the army after Araki Sadao resigned as war minister in 1934, and the removal of Mazaki Jinzaburō from the post of director general of military education led to *kōdō* retaliation in the Aizawa incident (*q.v.*). Subsequent *tōsei* moves to control and disperse *kōdō* members contributed to the February 26 incident of 1936 (*q.v.*). Their powerful positions assisted *tōsei* faction members subsequently to remain the dominant influence on army affairs; this influence culminated in Tōjō's premiership.

Crowley, J. B. *Japan's Quest for Autonomy* (Princeton, 1966).
______. "Japanese Army Factionalism in the 1930s," *JAS* 21, no. 3 (May 1962).
Lory, H. *Japan's Military Masters* (New York, 1943).
Storry, R. *The Double Patriots* (London, 1957).

Tōyama Mitsuru 1855–1944 頭山満
Samurai from Fukuoka, in the early 1870s Tōyama banded together with other discontented samurai and was imprisoned after the Hagi rebellion but was released in 1877. He was active in the popular rights movement but from 1881 was a leading figure in the Genyōsha (*q.v.*), which increasingly espoused nationalist and Pan-Asianist views. In the Genyōsha and later in the Kokuryūkai (*q.v.*), Tōyama exercised a dominant influence over Hiraoka Kōtarō and Uchida Ryōhei, the nominal leaders of these organizations, and became the outstanding right-wing nationalist leader of the Meiji-Taishō periods. Strongly opposing the treaty revision proposals of the 1880s and later supporting the war with Russia, Tōyama was openly involved in activities which included attempts to improve Japan's continental position by assistance for antigovernment movements in China and Korea. He was close to Sun Yat-sen, and although he later had considerable doubts concerning Chinese nationalism and its effects on Japan's interests, he maintained an interest in and connections with China until his death. Tōyama's charismatic personality and connections meant he had an influence far beyond that suggested by any formal position. His close contacts with those in positions of power in politics and business as well as in all levels of the right-wing and nationalist movements meant not only that he had a tremendous, if covert, influence on major political and economic decisions but also acted as an intermediary for unofficial contact between government and business and groups at lower levels.

Jansen, M. B. *The Japanese and Sun Yat-sen* (Cambridge, Mass., 1954).
Ogata, T. "Mitsuru Tōyama," *CJ* 9, no. 7 (July 1940).

Transcendental Cabinets. See CABINET SYSTEM

Treaty Revision (jōyaku kaisei) 条約改正

Japan's relations with foreign powers from 1858 were governed by the unequal Ansei treaties modeled on the U.S.-Japan Treaty of Amity and Commerce of 1858 (*q.v.*), which stipulated extraterritoriality (*q.v.*) for foreigners in Japan, most-favored nation treatment, and lack of tariff autonomy. Revision of these treaties became the main object of early Meiji diplomacy, and many of Japan's domestic reforms were aimed at achieving foreign acceptance of Japan on an equal basis. In 1871–1873 the Iwakura mission (*q.v.*) unsuccessfully attempted to negotiate revision. In 1878 Terashima Munenori signed an agreement with the U.S. to restore Japan's tariff autonomy, but implementation was subject to the conclusion of similar agreements with other countries, which were not forthcoming. Domestic opposition to agreements dealing only with tariffs was also strong. Over the years 1885–1887 Inoue Kaoru, who as foreign minister pursued an enthusiastic policy of Westernization, conferred with the major powers in Tokyo and reached an agreement whereby tariffs charged by Japan could be raised (without achieving tariff autonomy), foreigners would have equal dwelling and possession rights with Japanese, the legal system would be Westernized along approved lines, and extraterritoriality would be eliminated as long as foreign judges sat in any court trying foreigners. The agreement was opposed both within the government (especially by Tani Kanjō and Boissonade, French legal adviser to the government) and outside, by members of the popular rights movement claiming that internal democracy was necessary to obtain complete revision, and by nationalists criticizing the excessive Westernization. In July 1887 the negotiations were indefinitely postponed, and Inoue resigned. Inoue's successor, Ōkuma Shigenobu, initiated separate negotiations with each country; he improved Inoue's proposals by limiting the inclusion of foreign judges to the Supreme Court and making unnecessary the foreign approval of a new legal code. Nevertheless, when the terms were revealed, opposition was tremendous; Ōkuma was wounded in a bomb attack in October 1889, the agreement was abandoned, and the cabinet resigned. Subsequent Foreign Ministers Aoki Shūzō and Enomoto Takeaki were no more successful, but in July 1894 Mutsu Munemitsu succeeded in concluding the Anglo-Japanese Treaty of Commerce and Navigation. This was done, however, only by dint of leaving aside the tariff problem. The treaty, which was to come into force five years after ratification, allowed for complete liberalization domestically and the abolition of extraterritoriality. Treaties with the other powers were concluded shortly afterwards. Significantly, this first treaty was signed shortly before the start of the Sino-Japanese War. Tariff autonomy was eventually achieved in 1911 after these treaties expired.

Center for East Asian Cultural Studies. *Meiji Japan Through Contemporary Sources,* vol. 3 (Tokyo, 1972).
Jones, F. D. *Extraterritoriality in Japan and the Diplomatic Relations Resulting in Its Abolition, 1853–1899* (New Haven, 1931).
Morley, J. W., ed., *Japan's Foreign Policy, 1868–1941: A Research Guide* (New York, 1974).

Tripartite Pact (Nichidokui sankoku dōmei) 日独伊三国同盟

A step toward closer Japanese-German relations was taken in the Anti-Comintern Pact (*q.v.*) of 1936. Some further attempts were made to strengthen cooperation in 1938–1939, but eventually only Germany and Italy signed an alliance treaty because of naval opposition in Japan. Negotiations were broken off after the conclusion of the German-Soviet Non-Aggression Pact but reopened in 1940 under the second Konoe cabinet. Konoe's foreign minister, Matsuoka, was confident of a German victory in Europe and pushed the case for alliance. On 27 September 1940 the Tripartite Pact was signed in Berlin. Technically it was not a full military alliance, but it pledged one signatory to assist in all possible ways if another signatory was attacked by a power not currently involved in the wars in Europe or China (excluding the Soviet Union). Japan asserted the purely defensive nature of the pact. She hoped that it would improve relations with Russia and secure her northern borders, thus protecting a southward advance. For Germany the pact implied help against a protracted war with Britain. However, the pact was not successful in assisting Japan to avoid the U.S.'s impeding Japan's southward advance and worsened relations with the U.S. Italy abandoned the pact after defeat in 1943, and it ceased to exist with the fall of Germany in May 1945.

Hosoya, C. "The Tripartite Pact, 1939–1940," in J. W. Morley, ed., *Deterrent Diplomacy—Japan, Germany, and the U.S.S.R., 1935–1940* (New York, 1976).
Ikle, F. W. *German-Japanese Relations, 1936–1940* (New York, 1966).
Meskill, J. M. *Hitler and Japan: The Hollow Alliance* (New York, 1966).
Presseisen, E. L. *Germany and Japan, A Study in Totalitarian Diplomacy, 1933–1941* (The Hague, 1958).

Triple Intervention (sankoku kanshō) 三国干渉
A week after the signing of the Shimonoseki Treaty at the end of the Sino-Japanese War (*q.v.*) in April 1895, Russia, France, and Germany delivered a joint ultimatum to Japan to return the Liaotung Peninsula (*q.v.*) to China on the grounds that the cession endangered Peking and invalidated Korean independence. Russia played a major role in the intervention (although German instigation has also been claimed); Britain refused to participate. The Japanese government failed to gain diplomatic support from other powers such as Britain and the U.S. and on May 4 reluctantly agreed to comply with the demand. In a separate treaty China agreed to pay 30 million taels for the return of Liaotung. Within a few years Russia had herself leased the Liaotung Peninsula from China. The incident left a legacy of bitterness against the powers involved, and by suggesting to Japan that military strength was the only means of commanding international respect and prestige, it pushed her toward subsequent aggressive policies.

Asakawa, K. *The Russo-Japanese Conflict* (London, 1904).
Ikle, F. W. "The Triple Intervention: Japan's Lesson in the Diplomacy of Imperialism," *MN* 22, nos. 1–2 (1967).
Kajima, M. *The Diplomacy of Japan, 1894–1922,* vol. 1, *Sino-Japanese War and Triple Intervention* (Tokyo, 1978).
Langer, W. L. *The Diplomacy of Imperialism, 1890–1902* (New York, 1935).
Nish, I. H. "Britain and the Three-Power Intervention," in J. Chapman and J-P. Lehmann, eds., *BAJS Proceedings 5,* pt. 1 (Sheffield, 1980).

Tsinan Incident. See SHANTUNG EXPEDITIONS

Tsuda Mamichi (Masamichi) 1829–1903 (Baron, 1900) 津田真道
Samurai from Tsuyama domain (Okayama Prefecture), Tsuda studied Western learning and weaponry, at one time under Sakuma Shōzan, and taught in the Bakufu's school of Western learning. In 1862–1865 he studied economics and law in Holland, where he became close to Nishi Amane. On his return he compiled from his lecture notes the first Japanese book on Western law and taught at the Kaiseijo (*q.v.*). After the Restoration he was employed in the Justice, Foreign, and War ministries on legal matters. In 1876 Tsuda became a member of the Genrōin. He worked as a judge before acting as vice-president of the Diet 1890–1891. In 1896–1903 he sat in the House of Peers. As a member of the Meirokusha (*q.v.*) Tsuda played a major role in the introduction of Western thought to Japan and the development of legal thought in Japan during the Meiji period.

Braisted, W. K., tr. and ed., *Meiroku Zasshi* (Cambridge, Mass., 1976).

Tsuda Sōkichi 1873–1961 津田左右吉
Native of Gifu Prefecture, Tsuda graduated in 1893 from Tokyo College (later Waseda University) and worked as a researcher in the history and geography of Korea and Manchuria at the South Manchurian Railway Company (*q.v.*) before becoming professor at Waseda in 1919. He was also interested in Japan's early and intellectual history and from 1913 published a succession of books on these subjects. In his detailed research works on the ancient classics, the *Kojiki* and the *Nihon Shoki,* Tsuda suggested that they could not be regarded as objective history but had been written later to justify the claims of the imperial line. Tsuda's academic achievements were widely acclaimed but he came under attack from nationalists and the right wing and in 1940 four of his books were banned. In 1942 he was charged with lese majesty. Tsuda continued his writing activities after the war.

Tsuda, S. (tr. F. Matsuda) *An Enquiry into the Japanese Mind as Mirrored in Literature* (Tokyo, 1970).
Tsuda, S. (tr. Y. Mori) *What Is the Oriental Culture?* (Tokyo, 1955).

Tsuda Umeko 1865–1929 津田梅子
Native of Tokyo and daughter of the progressive Western scholar, Tsuda Sen, in 1871 Tsuda went to study in the U.S. as one of the first group of girls to study abroad; she returned to Japan in 1882. From 1885 Tsuda taught English at the Peeresses' School and in this capacity studied abroad again 1889–1892. In 1900 she resigned to found her own Girls' English School (now Tsuda Women's University) and remained the head of the school until illness forced her to retire in 1917. She was a leader in the movement for specialized and higher education for women and also played a considerable role in the promotion of English education.

Tsuda, U. *Leaves from Japanese Literature* (Tokyo, 1906).

Tsushima 対島
The islands of Tsushima lie in the strait between Japan and Korea and are now part of Nagasaki Prefecture. During the Tokugawa period the daimyō of Tsushima possessed exclusive rights over Japan's trade with Korea and special rights as the agent for diplomatic relations between the two countries. In 1861 Russian forces landed on the islands, nominally to undertake ship repairs. Nevertheless they constructed barracks and appeared ready to stay indefinitely in the hope of taking over the islands. There were several clashes with the islands' inhabitants. With the aid of British pressure the Japanese government persuaded them to leave, and jurisdiction over the islands was not subsequently disputed. The Straits of Tsushima were the scene of a major naval battle in the Russo-Japanese War.

Lensen, G. A. *The Russian Push Toward Japan* (Princeton, 1959).

Twenty-One Demands (taika nijūikkajō yōkyū) 対華21ヵ条要求
In an attempt to reach an overall settlement with China which would enable her to consolidate her position, on 18 January 1915 Japan presented to President Yüan Shih-k'ai a list of 21 demands. The demands were divided into five groups. They included transfer of former German rights in Shantung to Japan (who already occupied the area), extension of the leases and privileges in South Manchuria and Eastern Inner Mongolia which Japan had inherited from Russia in 1905, joint Sino-Japanese administration of the Hanyehping Iron Works (*q.v.*), and a Chinese promise not to alienate any port or island to a third country. The fifth group of demands infringed directly on Chinese sovereignty and included the appointment of Japanese political, military, and economic advisers, joint policing in troubled areas, construction of railways by Japan, and special economic rights in Fukien Province. China understandably opposed the demands, temporized on negotiations as far as possible, and appealed for foreign

support, but many of the powers were involved in war in Europe, and China received little help. Increasing criticism in China and Japan as well over the handling of the issue meant that Japan delivered a revised draft, excluding the fifth group, as an ultimatum. This was accepted by China on May 19, and notes and treaties were subsequently exchanged. Japan had gained considerable concessions, but her handling of the affair damaged her international reputation, and the concessions were worth little without a stable government in China. For China the date of acceptance became a day of national humiliation, and she subsequently attempted to refute this agreement. Shantung was eventually returned to China in 1922.

Dull, P. S. "Count Katō Kōmei and the Twenty-One Demands," *PHR* 19, no. 2 (May 1950).
Jansen, M. B. *Japan and China: From War to Peace, 1894–1972* (Chicago, 1975).
Shao, H-P. "From the Twenty-One Demands to the Sino-Japanese Military Agreements, 1915–1918: Ambivalent Relations," in A. D. Coox and H. Conroy, eds., *China and Japan: Search for Balance Since World War I* (Santa Barbara, 1978).

U

Uchida Ryōhei 1874–1937 内田良平
Native of Fukuoka, Uchida was closely involved in the Genyōsha (*q.v.*) and active in Korea before the Sino-Japanese War. From 1901 he directed the operations of the Kokuryūkai (*q.v.*) under the patronage and protection of Tōyama Mitsuru. Uchida was a bitter opponent of Russia, advocating war after the triple intervention (*q.v.*) and strongly opposing the terms of the Portsmouth Peace Treaty (*q.v.*). He supported Pan-Asianism and the rise of Asia under Japanese leadership and to this end worked to secure the annexation of Korea and supported the 1911 Chinese revolution. Uchida was also connected with smaller nationalist societies. He developed an increasing interest in domestic renovation and was a strong opponent of the more democratic trends of the Taishō period. He was arrested in 1925 on a charge of plotting to assassinate Prime Minister Katō but was acquitted. He was one of the bitterest opponents of the London Naval Treaty (*q.v.*). In 1931 Uchida founded the Greater Japan Production Party although he also remained leader of the Kokuryūkai until his death. He became ill in 1932 and was afterwards an invalid but overall was a leading figure in the right-wing movement from the late Meiji period until the 1930s.

Han, S. I. "Uchida Ryōhei and Japanese Continental Expansionism, 1874–1916," Ph.D. diss., Claremont Graduate School, 1974.
Storry, R. *The Double Patriots* (London, 1957).

Uchimura Kanzō 1861–1930 内村鑑三
Son of a Takasaki domain samurai but born in Edo, from 1877 Uchimura attended Sapporo Agricultural School (now Hokkaidō University). In 1878 he was baptized a Christian. After brief bureaucratic employment as a scientist Uchimura studied theology in America 1884–1888. After his return to Japan he taught at various schools, but his refusal to bow to the Imperial Rescript on Education (*q.v.*) led to accusations of lese majesty and his discharge from the First High School in 1891. Christianity was subsequently criticized as being contrary to the *kokutai* (*q.v.*). Uchimura subsequently concentrated on writing and preaching, working for the *Yorozu Chōhō* (*q.v.*) and afterwards founding his own journals, the *Tōkyō Dokuritsu Zasshi* (Tokyo Independent Journal) of 1898 and *Seisho no Kenkyū* (Bible Study) based on his lectures on the Bible. Through the latter and through the study group he led, Uchimura exercised

a tremendous influence as an evangelist and a pacifist. From early on he gave his allegiance to no particular church, making him the leader of the "no-church movement"; he claimed to serve the two *J*'s, Japan and Jesus. He wrote widely and his influence even on non-Christians was considerable.

Arima, T. "Uchimura Kanzō: A Study of Post Meiji Japanese Intelligentsia," *HPJ* 1 (1961).
Howes, J. F. "Uchimura Kanzō: The Bible and War," in N. Bamba and J. F. Howes, eds., *Pacifism in Japan* (Kyoto, 1978).
———. "Uchimura Kanzō: Japanese Prophet," in D. A. Rustow, ed., *Philosophers and Kings* (New York, 1970).
Kamei, K. "Uchimura Kanzō, Intolerant Believer," *Japan Interpreter* 10, no. 1 (Summer 1975).
Kawashima, M. "Uchimura Kanzō and Non-Churchism," Ph.D. diss., Claremont Graduate School, 1975.
Uchimura, K. *How I Became a Christian* (rprt. Tokyo, 1971).

Ueki Emori 1857–1892 植木枝盛
A samurai from Tosa, Ueki went to Tokyo in 1873 to study and then became a journalist. He met Itagaki Taisuke and becoming convinced of the need for a representative assembly entered the Risshisha (*q.v.*), and he remained at the center of the democratic movement as a propagandist through the 1870s and 1880s. He also participated in the founding of the Jiyūtō. In 1890 he was elected to the Diet. Ueki's main contribution to the popular rights movement was as a theorist, and he drafted many of the Jiyūtō's manifestoes and petitions, as well as a draft constitution. Ueki's advocacy of natural rights led him to be relatively radical, urging the people to demand and defend rights such as freedom of speech and thought and calling for limitations on the power of government. He believed such freedom would serve to strengthen the country. He envisaged a constitutional monarchy, a federal government, and a unicameral assembly, with all who paid taxes having the right to vote.

Ike, N. *The Beginnings of Political Democracy in Japan* (Baltimore, 1950).

Ugaki Kazushige 1868–1956 宇垣一成
Native of Okayama Prefecture, Ugaki graduated from the Military Academy in 1890 and had a successful army career. A protégé of Tanaka Giichi, Ugaki held various posts in the general staff, that of director general of military education and then became deputy minister of war in 1923. As war minister 1924–1927 he utilized the arms limitation policy to demobilize four divisions and rationalize and modernize Japan's forces, although his critics, including Araki Sadao and his followers, labeled him a "political" general. After acting as governor of Korea April–December 1927, Ugaki was again war minister 1929–1931, but his involvement with the March incident (*q.v.*) forced the resignation of the cabinet. As governor-general of Korea 1931–1936 he attempted to improve agricultural productivity as well as promoting expansion in heavy and military industries. Support from the elder statesmen of Japanese politics and the political parties led to his being asked to form a cabinet in 1937, but this was blocked by the army. After a brief spell as minister of foreign and colonial affairs in 1938 Ugaki resigned over policy toward China and subsequently retired from political activity. After the war he was purged until 1952 and in 1953 was elected to the House of Councillors with the largest number of votes from the national constituency, but illness already made him politically inactive.

Baba, T. "General Ugaki as Foreign Minister," *CJ* 7, no. 2 (Sept. 1938).
Crowley, J. B. *Japan's Quest for Autonomy* (Princeton, 1966).
Yoshihashi, T. *Conspiracy at Mukden* (New Haven, 1963).

Ultranationalism
From the 1880s Japanese such as

Miyake Setsurei responded to excessive Westernization by advocating *kokusuishugi* (emphasis on national essence—national characteristics) and Japanism. Nationalist societies such as the Genyōsha (*q.v.*) also emerged out of opposition to the government, but these gave much of their attention to improving Japan's position on the Continent and in Asia. During the Meiji period advocates of *kokusuishugi* were motivated by an attempt to maintain traditional national characteristics, but increasingly they became opposed to modernization and hostile to all that it embraced, including left-wing and social movements. Traditionalism and antiforeignism became the hallmark of nationalist groups in the 1920s and 1930s, and more and more they turned toward an emphasis on domestic reconstruction. By the 1930s what are generally termed ultranationalist groups included a highly disparate selection of ideologies: conservatives, professional patriots, agrarianists, state Socialists, and genuine social revolutionaries. It included both the influential older societies such as the Kokuryūkai (*q.v.*), small groups of extremists, and adherents of such influential thinkers as Kita Ikki and Ōkawa Shūmei. In the early 1930s many of these disparate ideas found fertile ground in the army; contemporary rural distress contributed to the dominance of ideas which were only in part a continuation of the *kokusuishugi* of the Meiji period. The postwar attack on organized nationalism included the dispersion of existing ultranationalist groups, which for a time, at least, had been discredited by Japan's defeat. Small groups proclaiming the need to preserve Japanese traditions and characteristics have reappeared. The word *chōkokkashugi* is also used as a more literal translation of the English "ultranationalism."

Brown, D. M. *Nationalism in Japan* (Berkeley, 1955).
Jansen, M. B. "Ultranationalism in Japan," *Political Quarterly* 27 (June 1956).
Maruyama, M. *Thought and Behavior in Modern Japanese Politics* (London, 1963).
Morris, I. *Nationalism and the Right Wing in Japan* (London, 1960).
Storry, R. *The Double Patriots* (London, 1957).

Umezu Yoshijirō 1882–1949
梅津美治郎

Native of Ōita Prefecture, after graduating from the Military Academy in 1903, Umezu's more important army posts included that of chief of general affairs at the War Ministry. In 1935 as commander of the Japanese occupying forces in north China, he concluded the Umezu-Ho agreement, whereby the Kuomintang promised to withdraw their offices and forces from Hopei. This was part of Japanese strategy to separate the area from Kuomintang rule. After being vice-minister of war 1936–1938 in September 1939 Umezu was appointed commander of the Kwantung Army (*q.v.*) and delegate to Manchukuo. In July 1944 he became chief of staff and in this capacity signed the surrender instrument after Japan's defeat. Umezu was sentenced to life imprisonment as a class "A" war criminal but died shortly after.

Unequal Treaties. See EXTRATERRITORIALITY; U.S.-JAPAN TREATY OF AMITY AND COMMERCE

Universities

The first modern educational institution to use the name university was the state-run university at Tokyo in 1877. It later became the Imperial University and then Tokyo Imperial University to distinguish it from the other imperial universities established at places such as Kyoto and Kyūshū. The imperial universities, which were utilitarian in design and geared to the needs of the state, were few in number in accordance with the highly elitist education system and extremely prestigious. Tokyo especially was the university of many of Japan's leaders. Development of private institutions of higher education was hindered by lack of full legal status as universities, financial weakness, and lack of any widespread liberal educational tradition, but in 1903 the law was amended to permit private institutions to qualify as universities; such schools as Keiō and Waseda did so. Further legal changes in 1918 led to rapid expansion in the interwar period, especially in the private sector. Over the period 1918–1945 the number of students enrolled in institutes of higher education increased by 250%. During the 1920s the interests of private and state universities grew closer: universities possessed considerable autonomy and academic freedom, and it was the state universities which were the main advocates of this. Central control tightened in the late 1920s, however, and university education was strictly supervised from the early 1930s. After the war, with the reform of the educational system, the existing universities, colleges, higher schools, and normal (teacher training) schools were absorbed into universities providing four-year courses; two-year course universities (so-called *tanki*) were also established. Many universities went coeducational. Freedom of learning and university autonomy is now guaranteed by law. The postwar demand for higher education has led to a huge increase in the number of universities. In 1945 there were 48 universities with over 100,000 students, but in 1979 there were 443 universities with four-year courses, and 518 *tanki*—national, prefectural, municipal and private—with nearly 2 million students. Well over 30% of high school graduates proceeded to university education. There remains a considerable disparity in quality between the various universities and their reputations. Competition to get into the better universities continues from the prewar period, giving rise to ruthless competition and tremendous pressure on school children. Women are acutely disadvantaged in terms of university education; in 1979 under 25% of students of four-year courses were women. Many of the private institutions suffer from acute shortage of funds and therefore of facilities, and with a few exceptions it is the nonprivate universities which provide the best, as well as the cheapest and most prestigious, education.

Blewett, J. J. *Higher Education in Postwar Japan* (Tokyo, 1965).

Journal of Social and Political Ideas in Japan 5, nos. 2–3 (Dec. 1969) (special issue on University and Society).

Koya, A. *Higher Education and Business Recruitment in Japan* (New York, 1969).

Nagai, M. *Higher Education in Japan: Its Takeoff and Crash* (Tokyo, 1971).

Ninomiya, A. *Private Universities in Japan* (Tokyo, 1977).

Pempel, T. J. *Patterns of Japanese Policy-Making: Experiences from Higher Education* (Boulder, 1978).

______. "The Politics of Enrollment Expansion in Japanese Universities," *JAS* 33 (Nov. 1973).

U.S.-Japan Security Treaty (Nichibei anzen hoshō jōyaku [Anpo]) 日米安全保障条約

As part of the peace settlement between Japan and the U.S., a security treaty was concluded between the two countries in September 1951 to take effect from April 1952. The treaty encountered considerable opposition in Japan, where the question of rearmament was raised, but conclusion of the treaty while Japan was still an occupied country meant that ratification was no problem. International criticism of the treaty, which brought Japan into the U.S. camp, was especially strong and led to a refusal by some countries to sign the San Francisco Peace Treaty (*q.v.*). The treaty stated the U.S.'s right to station troops in Japan to protect Japan, maintain peace in East Asia, and on request of the Japanese government to quell internal disturbances. Bases in Japan were to be granted to other countries only with the agreement of the U.S. In the late 1950s there was considerable pressure to change the treaty and opposition to its existence. Protracted negotiations for renewal of the treaty by Prime Minister Kishi gave the Left time to organize a protest, and the signing of the revised treaty in January 1960 initiated a major political crisis. The new treaty deleted the clause permitting U.S. troops to intervene in internal law and order in Japan, as well as that relating to U.S. approval for other countries' bases in Japan, but the remaining clauses still allowed Japan's use as a base for U.S. activity in East Asia, implying enemy status for China. Opposition to Japanese rearmament and fear of involvement in U.S. military activity caused a storm of protest throughout Japan. As well as intense opposition outside, there was a bitter struggle for ratification in the Diet, and opposition Diet members resorted to nonparliamentary means such as sit-ins to delay ratification of the treaty past the deadline of April 26. On May 19 police entered the Diet to enforce the necessary Diet extension, which meant automatic ratification on June 19. Opposition politicians subsequently boycotted Diet proceedings, demanding Kishi's resignation and dissolution of the Diet. May-June saw unprecedented popular resentment expressed in a succession of massive strikes and violent demonstrations by labor, Socialists, and students. The issue of the pending visit of President Eisenhower turned this domestic crisis into a major problem in U.S.-Japanese relations. On June 10 Eisenhower's press secretary was forced to escape by helicopter from a mob at Haneda airport. On June 15 there was a violent clash between riot police and students who had invaded the Diet building; hundreds of students and police were hurt and a 20-year-old female student, Kanba Michiko, who was crushed to death, became a martyr to the movement. Eisenhower's planned visit for June 19 was canceled. The treaty gained automatic ratification on midnight June 19, and instruments of ratification were exchanged on June 23. Kishi immediately resigned, and the opposition movement lost all momentum, but the security treaty crisis (known in Japan as *Anpo*) stands out as one of the most severe political and mass upheavals of postwar Japan. The treaty has since been automatically renewed.

Packard, G.R. *Protest in Tokyo—The Security Treaty Crisis of 1960* (Princeton, 1966).

Ro, C. W. "The Origins and Interpretation of the 1951 U.S.-Japanese Security Treaty," Ph.D. diss., Southern Illinois University, 1977.

Weinstein, M. E. *Japan's Postwar Defense Policy, 1947–1968* (New York, 1971).

U.S.-Japan Treaty of Amity and Commerce (Nichibei shūkō tsūshō jōyaku) 日米修好通商条約

Following negotiations with Townsend Harris the U.S.-Japan Treaty of Amity and Commerce was concluded in July 1858. This became the model for similar treaties signed with Holland, Russia, Britain, and France by October 1858. All treaties came into force in summer 1859. They are referred to collectively by the Japanese as the "Ansei treaties" or "treaties with five powers." The treaties' major provisions were the opening of Edo, Osaka, Hakodate, Kanagawa (Yokohama), Nagasaki, Niigata, and Hyōgo (Kobe) to foreigners; consular courts and extraterritorial rights for foreigners; fixed tariff rates on goods imported into Japan; and most-favored nation treatment. The shōgunate signed these treaties without imperial approval, which provoked a political crisis. Reform of the "unequal" treaties, or "treaty revision," became the main object of Japanese foreign policy in the first half of the Meiji period.

Beasley, W. G. *The Meiji Restoration* (London, 1973).

______. *Select Documents on Japanese Foreign Policy, 1853–1868* (London, 1955).

McMaster, J. "Alcock and Harris: Foreign Diplomacy in Bakumatsu Japan," *MN* 22, nos. 3–4 (1967).

U.S.-Japan Treaty of Friendship. See KANAGAWA TREATY

V

Versailles Peace Treaty (Berusaiyu heiwa jōyaku) ベルサイユ平和条約

After World War I the allies held a conference at Versailles, near Paris, starting in January 1919, to decide the terms of a peace treaty with Germany. Japan's delegation was led by Saionji Kinmochi and included Makino Nobuaki; despite the small scale of her military activities Japan's position was influential. She hoped to take over German rights in Shantung and the German-held islands north of the equator. During the war Japan had concluded secret agreements with China following the Twenty-One Demands (*q.v.*). The final peace treaty awarded Japan the unexpired part of the Kiaochow lease and mining and railway rights formerly owned by Germany, but China refused to accede to these concessions and would not sign the treaty. Japan therefore remained in occupation of Shantung instead of handing it back to China, and the problem was not solved until the time of the Washington Conference (*q.v.*). The treaty also awarded Japan the islands formerly held by Germany, the Marianas, Carolines, and Marshalls, under a League of Nations mandate. Apart from the terms relating to Germany the conference also provided for the establishment of the League of Nations (*q.v.*) in the hope of preserving peace in the postwar period. Although Japan possessed a permanent seat on the council of the league and full representation elsewhere, her failure to get a racial equality clause inserted into the league's charter aroused considerable resentment. The system was further invalidated by the nonparticipation of the U.S..

Mayer, A. J. *Politics and Diplomacy of Peacemaking: Containment and Counterrevolution at Versailles, 1918–1919* (London, 1968).

Young, A. M. *Japan Under Taishō Tennō* (New York, 1929).

Violation of the Rights of the Supreme Command. See INDEPENDENCE OF THE SUPREME COMMAND

W

Wakatsuki Reijirō 1866–1949 (Baron, 1931) 若槻礼次郎

Native of Shimane Prefecture, after graduating from Tokyo University in 1892, Wakatsuki entered the Finance Ministry, rising to the position of deputy finance minister. He served as finance minister 1912–1913 and 1914–1915. Initially a member of the Dōshikai, Wakatsuki became vice-president of the Kenseikai and after the movement for the protection of constitutional government (*q.v.*) was home minister under Katō 1924–1926. He succeeded Katō as Kenseikai president and prime minister in January 1926, but his cabinet was strongly criticized over its financial measures and Shidehara's foreign policy. Wakatsuki resigned in April 1927 after conflicting with the Privy Council over his measures to deal with the 1927 financial crisis (*q.v.*). He joined the Minseitō as adviser and was Japan's chief delegate to the London Naval Conference (*q.v.*) where his agreement to ratios less than those demanded by the navy made him the object of much hostility. Wakatsuki succeeded Hamaguchi as Minseitō president and prime minister in April 1931 and attempted to enforce financial and administrative retrenchment against a background of deep world depression. He was unable to control the army and the spread of fighting after the Manchurian Incident and resigned in December

1931 in the face of demands within the cabinet for a cabinet of national unity to cope with the crisis at home and abroad. Wakatsuki maintained a position as elder statesman after resigning as Minseitō president in 1934.

Young, A. M. *Imperial Japan, 1926–1938* (London, 1938).

Wang Ching-wei. See JAPAN-CHINA BASIC TREATY

Wang Yang-ming. See CONFUCIANISM

Wanpaoshan Incident. See ANTI-JAPANESE MOVEMENT (CHINA)

Waseda University (Waseda Daigaku) 早稲田大学

In 1882 Ōkuma Shigenobu founded a private school known as the Tokyo College (Tōkyō Senmon Gakkō). The college's motto was "independence of learning," and because of its political connections with the Kaishintō and hostility to "official" education, it was initially subject to police harassment. The college became a major institution for the training of men for nongovernmental careers such as journalism. In 1902 it was renamed Waseda University and with Keiō was the first private university to be officially accredited as such. Waseda retains its position as one of the leading private universities, as well as its nongovernment tradition. Waseda students were in the forefront of militant student activism in the 1920s and 1960s.

Washington Conference (Washinton kaigi) ワシントン会議

Between November 1921 and February 1922 representatives of the powers met in Washington to discuss naval arms limitation and Pacific and East Asian affairs. In December 1921 Britain, France, Japan, and the U.S. concluded a Four-Power Pact, whereby each signatory agreed to respect the rights of the others in the area and to consult mutually in case of crisis. This agreement replaced the Anglo-Japanese Alliance (*q.v.*), which was permitted to lapse. In February 1922 five other European countries joined these four in concluding a Nine-Power Pact, which subscribed to Chinese integrity and an "open door" policy. An attempt to achieve a naval balance providing for international security resulted in the signing of the Washington Naval Limitation Treaty also in February 1922. This provided for a 10-year stop on the building of capital ships, size limitation on certain ships and armaments, a standstill in Pacific fortifications, and a 5:5:3 ratio on capital ships for Britain, the U.S., and Japan. Japan had desired a 10:10:7 ratio, and the treaty was signed despite a split in the Japanese delegation. This treaty was the most important interwar disarmament treaty, but it was never unreservedly accepted in Japan, and there was increasing opposition to it within the navy. Japan announced her intention of abandoning this treaty in 1934. At the Washington conference Japan also agreed to restore Chinese sovereignty in Shantung in exchange for Chinese ratification of her economic privileges there.

Asada, S. "Japan's 'Special Interests' and the Washington Conference, 1921–1922," *American Historical Review* 67 (Oct. 1961).
Dingman, R. *Power in the Pacific* (Chicago, 1976).
Ichihashi, Y. *The Washington Conference and After* (rprt. New York, 1969).
Nish, I. H. "Japan and Naval Aspects of the Washington Conference," in W. G. Beasley, ed., *Modern Japan: Aspects of History, Literature, and Society* (London, 1975).

Weber-Komura Memorandum. See KOMURA-WEBER MEMORANDUM

Welfare Ministry (Kōseishō) 厚生省

The establishment of a welfare ministry was discussed from the 1920s, but the real impetus for its actual founding in January 1938 was the army's concern over the condition of its recruits. It took over from the Home Ministry functions relating to welfare facilities, unemployment, medical care, and labor, and its activities during the war period were regarded as crucial to the efficient pursuit of the war. Whatever the motivations behind its foundation, the ministry did play a role in improving the lot of the people. In 1947 the ministry's functions relating to labor were transferred to the new Labor Ministry.

Women's Movement

In the early Meiji period some enlightened intellectuals such as Fukuzawa Yukichi advocated improvement of the position of women, and by the early 1880s women such as Fukuda Hideko were active in the popular rights movement. In 1886 Yajima Kajiko founded the Tokyo Women's Temperance Association (from 1893 the Japan Christian Women's Temperance Association), which campaigned not only for temperance but also for the abolition of prostitution. Legislation in 1889 and 1900 forbade political activity by women, and this became a primary target for the protests of female Socialists and advocates of emancipation. Other women, less concerned with emancipation, turned to public welfare activities. The Patriotic Women's Association (Aikoku Fujinkai) founded by Okumura Ioko in 1901 was intended to assist wounded soldiers and bereaved families. Sponsored by the state, it initially consisted almost exclusively of upper-class women, but by 1919 it had a million members although it engaged in little activity at local level. In contrast, the Seitōsha (*q.v.*) of 1911 advocated the awakening and self-awareness of women, marking the beginning of an intellectual, middle-class-dominated women's protest movement, which continued into the 1930s. The 1919 New Women's Society (Shin Fujin Kyōkai) of Hiratsuka Raichō and Ichikawa Fusae was part of this tradition. With its successor, the Women's Suffrage League, it campaigned for the right to political activity and the vote. Activity among working-class women remained small. The Yūaikai (*q.v.*) permitted women to participate in its activities, and in 1921 Socialist women came together to form the Sekirankai (Red Wave Society), but all the proletarian women's groups, though militant, remained small, and the mass of working-class women were not involved. Only on a few occasions did the proletarian groups form a united front with the moderate campaigners, and the membership of these groups as a whole never matched that of the state-sponsored women's organizations. The Patriotic Women's Association had achieved a membership of 3 million by 1937, campaigning on a slogan of service to the nation. Its chief competitor was the Greater Japan National Defense Women's Association (Dainihon Kokubō Fujinkai), whose founding was sponsored by the army in 1932 to strengthen Japan's national unity and to prepare for national mobilization by military and state service and by the reinforcement of army-approved ideas. By 1938 it claimed almost 8 million members and was an important instrument for army control at local levels. Both organizations competed in activities such as disaster relief, savings campaigns, and comfort for the wounded and bereaved, and the competition led to increasing friction. In February 1942 they were amalgamated into the Greater Japan Women's Association (Dainihon Fujinkai) as one of the integral organizations of the new political structure under the Imperial Rule Assistance Association (*q.v.*). All married women, and unmarried women over 20, had to join, and members cooperated in the war effort by such activities as civil defense and savings programs. By March 1943 the association claimed over 19 million members, but its hold over many of them was never very tight, and divisions persisted within the organization. In June 1945 it was reorganized as a people's volunteer force and subsequently disbanded. There had been no place for antigovernment groups in the 1930s and early 1940s, which saw the state-sponsored reassertion of the traditional status of Japanese women, but after 1945 the middle-class, proletarian, and Christian groups which had been suppressed prewar reemerged; numerous national and local groups for women were founded and were active in a variety of spheres. Women's legal and constitutional status was radically changed postwar, and the granting of the vote to women meant that the main object of women's agitation during the 1950s was prostitution, a campaign in which the Women's Christian Temperance Association played a leading role. Recently, more radical groups have appeared, including Women's Liberation, but they remain small. Despite equality under the constitution much legal and social discrimination against women is still practiced, but its less obvious nature has made protest, if anything, more difficult.

Havens, T. R. H. *Valley of Darkness* (New York, 1978).
Koyama, T. *The Changing Social Position of Women in Japan* (Paris, 1961).
Lebra, J., J. Paulson, and E. Powers, eds., *Women in Changing Japan* (Boulder, 1976).
Smethurst, R. J. *A Social Basis for Prewar Japanese Militarism* (Berkeley, 1970).
Tanaka, K. *Short History of the Women's Movement in Modern Japan* (Tokyo, 1974).

Women's Suffrage Movement (fujin sanseiken undō) 婦人参政権運動

The Public Meeting and Political Societies Law of 1890 and the Peace Police Law of 1900 (*q.v.*) forbade political activity by women; this restriction was therefore the first target of female political activists. In the years after 1900 women Socialists campaigned without success for the repeal of this clause, but their agitation declined after the High Treason trial (*q.v.*). The campaign was revived by the New Women's Association after World War I, and in March 1922 a partial amendment of the law permitted women to attend and hold political meetings although they could not join or form political parties. In 1921 the association also submitted a petition for the right to vote. In 1924 various women's groups came together to form a united group, which in 1925 took the name Women's Suffrage League (Federation to Secure Women's Suffrage). This middle-class-dominated group petitioned to the Diet for the right to vote, but the new Universal Male Suffrage Act of 1925 excluded women from the vote. Disappointment at this failure meant that many women turned their attention to the formation of groups affiliated with the different proletarian parties, enabling them to participate as far as possible in the proletarian party movement, but in 1928 proletarian women's groups joined with the league to form a united front; mass meetings were held, literature distributed, and a petition with 32,000 signatures presented to the Diet. However, proletarian groups withdrew from joint action, and with government suppression of the Left the united front was gone. Annual petitions for the vote were submitted up to the 1930s, but women's groups were increasingly absorbed into the state-sponsored organizations, and remaining ones were disbanded in 1940. Reform of the election law in 1945 gave women the right to vote and to be elected.

Totten, G. O. *The Social Democratic Movement in Prewar Japan* (New Haven, 1966).

World War I (Daichiji sekai taisen) 第一次世界大戦

Japan invoked the terms of the Anglo-Japanese Alliance (*q.v.*) and declared war on Germany on 23 August 1914. She immediately occupied the German-leased territories in Shantung (China) and German-run railways and mines, and also the German-owned islands in the Pacific, the Marshalls, Marianas, and Carolines. Japan took little further part in the conflict as a belligerent, assisting only by sea patrols. She utilized the preoccupation of the other powers to extend her influence in China by such moves as the Twenty-One Demands (*q.v.*) and negotiated with other powers for assurances of support for her claims in East Asia and the Pacific. Economically the war rescued Japan from depression and stimulated a considerable boom. She supplied the belligerents with armaments and was able to supply goods other than arms which could no longer be provided by the belligerents, for example, cotton in India, a market which had previously been monopolized by Britain. There was a remarkable growth in the carrying trade, in foreign trade as a whole, and in Japan's gold reserves. Although some Japanese were vastly enriched by the war, many failed to benefit from the boom which this stimulated, and the rampant inflation culminated in the rice riots (*q.v.*) of 1918. The unrest also stimulated labor and left-wing activity. Overall, Japan failed to utilize the economic benefits accruing from the war in a way that would help her in the long run. Most were dissipated in the 1920–1921 depression. Japan's participation in the war enabled her to join the allies at the Versailles Peace Conference.

Dua, R. P. *Anglo-Japanese Relations During the First World War* (New Delhi, 1972).
Kobayashi, U. *The Basic Industries and Social History of Japan, 1914–1918* (New Haven, 1930).
Spinks, C. N. "Japan's Entry into World War I," *PHR* 5, no. 4 (Dec. 1936).

World War II. See PACIFIC WAR

Y

Yalta Agreement (Yaruta kyōtei)
ヤルタ協定
In February 1945 Stalin, Roosevelt, and Churchill met at Yalta in the Crimea. They concluded a secret agreement whereby Russia promised to enter the war against Japan two to three months after the defeat of Germany. Russia was promised in return the return of southern Sakhalin and neighboring islands, maintenance of the status quo vis-à-vis Outer Mongolia, possession of the Kuriles, and certain concessions in Manchuria. On the basis of this agreement Russia broke the neutrality pact with Japan and declared war in August 1945. The territorial problem hindered the resumption of diplomatic relations between Russia and Japan and still prevents the signing of a peace treaty.

Dallek, R. *Franklin D. Roosevelt and American Foreign Policy, 1932–1945* (New York, 1979).
Stettinius, E. R. *Roosevelt and the Russians: The Yalta Conference* (Garden City, N.Y., 1949).

Yamagata Aritomo 1838–1922 (Count, 1884; Marquis, 1895; Prince, 1907)
山県有朋
Member of Chōshū lower samurai family, Yamagata studied under Yoshida Shōin and participated in the *sonnō jōi* (*q.v.*) movement. He was a commander in the Kiheitai (*q.v.*) and also fought in the Boshin War (*q.v.*). In 1869–1870 he studied Western military systems in Europe and on his return devoted his efforts to military reform in Japan; he was the major figure behind the introduction of conscription (*q.v.*) in 1872. Yamagata was war minister 1873–1878, then chief of staff 1878–1882 and 1884–1885; in this capacity he drafted the Imperial Rescript to Soldiers and Sailors of 1882, which was aimed at inculcating in the forces a samurai spirit proof against the popular rights movement. He was also *sangi* 1874–1885. In 1883 he became home minister and retained the post until 1890, except for nine months in 1889. In this capacity and also as prime minister 1889–1891, Yamagata was the main architect of the new local government system introduced at this time. During his first cabinet came the Imperial Rescript on Education (*q.v.*), and the first elections and Diet were held. Conflict between Diet and government was bitter, and Yamagata eventually resigned. He then acted as justice minister 1892–1893 and president of the Privy Council in 1893 before returning to command the First Army during the Sino-Japanese War. He was also briefly war minister in 1895. Yamagata was again prime minister 1898–1900, and the period was marked by his efforts to restrict the activity of political parties and opposition

to government by such measures as the Peace Police Law (*q.v.*), extension of the role of the Privy Council, and the stipulation that forces' ministers must be serving officers. He strongly opposed party activity, believing that cabinets should be transcendental, and remained the focus of the military and conservative cliques in government, his mantle later being inherited by Katsura Tarō. After retiring as prime minister, Yamagata was chief of staff 1904–1906, president of the Privy Council 1905–1922 (except for June-October 1909), and a member of the Supreme War Council from 1898. As a *genrō* from 1891 he remained a major influence on Japanese politics almost until his death and was especially dominant after the death of Itō.

Hackett, R. F. "The Meiji Leaders and Modernization: The Case of Yamagata Aritomo," in M. B. Jansen, ed., *Changing Japanese Attitudes Toward Modernization* (Princeton, 1965).
______. *Yamagata Aritomo* (Cambridge, Mass., 1971).
______. "Yamagata and the Taishō Crisis, 1912–1913," in S. D. Brown, ed., *Studies on Asia* (Lincoln, Nebr., 1962).

Yamagata-Lobanov Agreement (Yamagata-Robanofu kyōtei) 山県・ロバノフ協定

Following the Komura-Weber memorandum (*q.v.*), on 9 June 1896 Yamagata Aritomo signed an agreement with the Russian foreign minister, Lobanov, in which both countries recognized the independence of Korea and guaranteed loans and assistance for internal reform if necessary by mutual agreement. Secret clauses related to the stationing of troops of both countries in Korea and the dispatch of troops to maintain order and communications; in the latter case the respective spheres of operation were defined, but only vaguely. The agreement in effect gave Russia greater influence in Korea and Japan time for military preparation, but the basic friction remained. This agreement was later extended into the Nishi-Rosen agreement (*q.v.*).

Hackett, R. F. *Yamagata Aritomo in the Rise of Modern Japan* (Cambridge, Mass., 1971).

Yamakawa Hitoshi 1880–1958 山川均

Native of Kurashiki, Okayama Prefecture, later husband of Yamakawa Kikue, Yamakawa was initially interested in Christianity and briefly studied at Dōshisha but then turned to socialism and was involved with the Heiminsha (*q.v.*). In 1906 he participated in the founding of the Japan Socialist Party. He subsequently supported anarchism and in all was four times in prison before returning to Okayama after the High Treason trial (*q.v.*). He became a Marxist, and after returning to Tokyo in 1916, where he joined Sakai Toshihiko's Baibunsha, he became a focal figure in the Socialist movement and a leading Marxist theorist. In 1922 Yamakawa joined the Japan Communist Party but called for the formation of a united proletarian front with a single party rather than a vanguard party which was useless without mass consciousness. On this basis he supported the dissolution of the J.C.P. in 1923, and his views, often termed "Yamakawaism," remained dominant in the party until replaced by Fukumotoism (*q.v.*) early in 1926. Yamakawa's attempts to pursue his ideas led him in 1928 to sever all connection with the J.C.P.; he became the leading theorist of the Rōnō faction in the Japanese capitalism debate (*q.v.*). He was arrested in 1937, and his case was still under appeal at the time of his release in 1945. He reemerged as a leading figure in left-wing politics, still advocating the formation of a popular front, and although he was not formally affiliated to any party, he was a strong influence on the Japan Socialist Party. He stood unsuccessfully for the Diet in 1947.

Beckmann, G. M., and G. Ōkubo. *The Japanese Communist Party, 1922–1945* (Stanford, 1969).
Colbert, E. *The Left Wing in Japanese Politics* (New York, 1952).
Swift, T. D. "Yamakawa Hitoshi and the Dawn of Japanese Socialism," Ph.D. diss., University of California, Berkeley, 1970.

Yamakawa Kikue 1890–1980 山川菊栄
Native of Tokyo and wife of Yamakawa Hitoshi, Yamakawa graduated from Tsuda Women's College and was then active in the women's movement and Socialist movement. In 1920 she joined the Japan Socialist League. She worked closely with Yamakawa Hitoshi and in 1921 formed a proletarian women's Socialist group, the Sekirankai, with women who included Itō Noe and Sakai Magara. Through the 1920s Yamakawa played a key role in the women's movement both as a Socialist theorist and as an activist. In 1947 she became the first head of the Labor Ministry's Women's and Minors' Bureau. She wrote widely on women's problems and socialism and also translated August Bebel's *Die Frau und der Sozialismus* (Women and Socialism) into Japanese.

Yamamoto Gonnohyōe (Gonbei) 1852–1933 (Baron, 1902; Count, 1907) 山本権兵衛
Satsuma samurai, Yamamoto fought in the 1868 civil war and in 1874 graduated from naval school. He was a major influence in the navy during the Sino-Japanese War and achieved the rank of admiral in 1904. As navy minister in successive cabinets 1898–1906 Yamamoto tried to expand the navy and also played a major role in supervising naval activity in the Russo-Japanese War. In February 1913 Yamamoto became prime minister following the Taishō political crisis (*q.v.*). With Seiyūkai support he carried out financial and administrative reform and retrenchment; reserve as well as serving officers became eligible for the posts of war and navy minister. The cabinet resigned in April 1914 following criticism over the Siemens scandal (*q.v.*) and political difficulties following naval cuts imposed on the budget by the House of Peers. Yamamoto went on the reserve list. He was again asked to form a cabinet in August 1923, but he did not succeed until the following month following the emergency imposed by the Kantō earthquake (*q.v.*). The cabinet's main task was to restore law and order and start rebuilding the devastated area, but it lost support in the Diet and any unity it had hitherto possessed. Yamamoto resigned in January 1924, accepting responsibility for an attack on the life of the crown prince, the so-called Toranomon incident. Overall Yamamoto played a considerable role in building up the navy and to the end of his life remained a real power in the navy and leader of the Satsuma political clique.

Najita, T. *Hara Kei and the Politics of Compromise* (Cambridge, Mass., 1967).
Young, A. M. *Japan Under Taishō Tennō, 1912–1926* (New York, 1929).

Yamamoto Isoroku 1884–1943 山本五十六
A native of Niigata Prefecture, Yamamoto graduated from the Naval Academy in 1904 and then studied at Harvard. As deputy navy minister in 1937 Yamamoto was politically unpopular because of his belief that conflict with the U.S., U.S.S.R., and Britain was unwise, this despite his earlier opposition to naval arms limitation; he also opposed alliance with Germany. Despite this he was appointed commander in chief of the combined fleet in 1939. In this capacity, despite personal reservations concerning Japan's overall strategy, he became the architect of Japan's naval and air policy in the Pacific, including the successful attack on Pearl Harbor of 1941. He correctly foresaw that Japan had no hope of success in a lengthy struggle. Even after the decline in Japan's fortunes after the Battle of Midway, Yamamoto remained a personal source of inspiration to Japanese forces. A special mission was detailed to shoot him down over the Solomon Islands in April 1943, and his death was a serious blow to Japanese morale and strategy.

Agawa, H. (tr. J. Bester). *The Reluctant Admiral: Yamamoto and the Imperial Navy* (Tokyo, 1979).
Potter, J. D. *Admiral of the Pacific* (London, 1965).

Yanagida Kunio 1875–1962 柳田国男
Native of Hyōgo Prefecture, Yanagida graduated from Tokyo University in 1900

and entered the bureaucracy. In 1914–1919 he was chief secretary to the House of Peers, but he then resigned and took up employment with Asahi newspapers. In his youth Yanagida was closely identified with the poetic world, but he then began to study Japanese ethnography and folklore, devoting himself to it full time after 1932, and it is here that his most important contribution lies. Apart from editing journals and founding research groups and associations devoted to local history, Yanagida's huge number of published works, starting in 1909, laid the basis for modern research into Japanese culture, folklore, and dialect. He was a privy councillor 1946–1947 and a leading member of the Japanese Academy.

Morse, R. A. "The Search for Japan's National Character and Distinctiveness: Yanagida Kunio (1875–1962) and the Folklore Movement," Ph.D. diss., Princeton University, 1975.

Tsurumi, K. *Yanagida Kunio's Work as a Model of Endogenous Development* (Tokyo, 1975).

Yanagida, K. (tr. F. H. Mayer and Y. Ishiwara) *About Our Ancestors: The Japanese Family System* (Tokyo, 1970).

(Other of Yanagida's works have also been translated into English.)

Yanaihara (Yanaibara) Tadao 1893–1961 矢内原忠雄

Native of Ehime Prefecture, after graduating in economics from Tokyo University, Yanaihara worked for Sumitomo and from 1920 taught at Tokyo, where he became a professor in 1923. His teaching specialized in the field of colonial policy in Japan and elsewhere; his standpoint was a Christian Socialist one, strongly influenced by the ideas of Uchimura Kanzō, Nitobe Inazō, and Yoshino Sakuzō. In 1937 Yanaihara came under attack both from right-wing colleagues and from the government for articles in the *Chūō Kōron* (Central Review) critical of Japan's foreign policy; he was eventually forced to resign from the university. He spent the war years on Christian and pacifist activities but returned to Tokyo in 1945. He taught international economics, founded and became head of the Social Science Research Institute, and was president of Tokyo University 1951–1957. He left many works, mostly on imperialist and colonial policy and on Christianity.

Fujita, W. "Yanaihara Tadao, Disciple of Uchimura Kanzō and Nitobe Inazō," in N. Bamba and J. F. Howes, eds., *Pacifism in Japan* (Kyoto, 1978).

Yanaihara, T. *Pacific Islands Under Japanese Mandate* (rprt. Westport, Conn., 1976).

———. *Religion and Democracy in Modern Japan* (Tokyo, 1948).

Yasuda Zenjirō 1838–1921 安田善次郎

Native of Toyama Prefecture, Yasuda went to Edo and in 1864 started his own business as a money changer, in which he built up a considerable reputation. He benefited from the disruption of the Restoration period and by astute dealing in government notes amassed a considerable fortune. He also handled government business. In 1876 he helped to found the Third National Bank and in 1880 his own private Yasuda Bank, and his involvement with other banking institutions as well made him by the 1890s Japan's leading banker. He founded Japan's first life insurance company and in the 1890s extended his interests into other spheres, especially railways. Despite his early involvement Yasuda later avoided government contacts as far as possible. He established an unlimited partnership, the Hozensha, which acted as a holding company and was the focal point for control over the group's various enterprises, and by the time of Yasuda's death in 1921 the group was regarded as one of the four great *zaibatsu* (*q.v.*). Yasuda was at this time the richest man in Japan, controlling 19 banks with ¥18 million assets and with huge investments in various other areas. The Yasuda *zaibatsu* continued to grow after Yasuda's death but was founded on banking capital, and its lack of a strong industrial sector was a weakness only partially compensated for by a strong financial interest in other concerns, notably those of the Asano group. As of 1945 the Yasuda group comprised some 55 companies. It was severely affected by the dissolution program but although the Yasuda family lost control many of the enterprises have resumed their former connections.

Hirschmeier, J. *The Origins of Entrepreneurship in Meiji Japan* (Cambridge, Mass., 1964).
Yamamura, K. *A Study of Samurai Income and Entrepreneurship* (Cambridge, Mass., 1974).

Yasuda Zaibatsu. See YASUDA ZENJIRŌ

Yellow Peril (kōkaron) 黄禍論
In the late 19th century the idea of the "yellow peril," the rise of the yellow races endangering the position of the white, was used in relation to China, but the idea of the rise of the yellow races led by Japan endangering and overrunning the West gained substance in the 1890s. In spring 1895 Wilhelm II of Germany stated that the rise of the yellow races led by Japan would destroy European culture and European powers should unite in resistance to this threat, with Russia in the vanguard. Although this statement was tied up with plans to promote German interest by Russian advance in the east, a fear of the potential economic, military, and cultural threat posed by the nonwhite races did become more widespread after the Sino-Japanese War. Japan's opponents used her victory in the Russo-Japanese War to spread the idea of the yellow peril among people already shocked by the victory of a yellow, non-Christian race over a white, Christian one, although Japan's supporters pointed out that the "white peril" was already a reality in Asia. Discrimination against Japanese immigrants in the U.S. and the refusal to insert a racial equality clause in the League of Nations charter reinforced the Japanese view that the yellow peril idea was not dead.

Diosy, A. *The New Far East* (London, 1904).
Lehmann, J-P. *The Image of Japan: From Feudal Isolation to World Power, 1850–1905* (London, 1978).

Yen. See CURRENCY

Yokohama 横浜
Under the Ansei treaties of 1858 it was agreed that Kanagawa would be opened to foreign trade, but the Japanese persuaded Western diplomats to agree to change this to the fishing village of Yokohama. This was desired by the Bakufu to isolate the foreign community from the main road and to enable greater control. The "village" expanded fast, developed a large foreign settlement, and within a year or two handled much of Japan's export trade. It was a focus for foreign residence and Japanese-foreign contacts before and after the Restoration. In 1899 Yokohama was given city status. Apart from being a trading center and port, industry also developed, and by 1923 the population was about a half million. It was largely destroyed first by the 1923 Kantō earthquake (*q.v.*) and subsequently by wartime bombing but has recovered postwar and forms, with Tokyo, a huge urban complex. Yokohama is still Japan's biggest international trading port, and has a population of over 2½ million.

Black, J. R. *Young Japan* (London, 1880).
Paske-Smith, M. *Western Barbarians in Japan and Formosa in Tokugawa Days, 1603–1868* (Kobe, 1930).
Poole, O. M. *The Death of Old Yokohama* (London, 1968).

Yokohama Incident. See CHŪŌ KŌRON; KAIZŌ

Yokoi Shōnan 1809–1869 横井小楠
Native of Kumamoto Prefecture, in 1839–1840 Yokoi studied in Edo, where he met such scholars as Fujita Tōko and in 1847 opened a Confucian school in

Kumamoto. He subsequently became a leading advocate of Japan's rulers' opening the country to trade and cooperating with lower samurai and rich farmers to strengthen the economy, but his efforts to stimulate reform failed. In 1858 he went to Fukui *han* as adviser to the daimyō Matsudaira Shungaku (Yoshinaga), who from this time became influential in national politics. Under Yokoi's influence a strongly mercantilist policy was introduced in Fukui; trade and industry were encouraged and the army strengthened. Politically influential, he supported *kōbu gattai* (*q.v.*). In 1863 conservative extremists attempted to assassinate Yokoi; he returned to Kumamoto but was deprived of samurai status and stipend for fleeing a fight leaving two companions wounded. However, he was reinstated and gained high office after the Restoration before being killed by conservatives in 1869.

Chang, R. T. "Yokoi Shōnan's View of Christianity," *MN* 21, nos. 3–4 (1966).
Hiraishi, N. "Universalism in Late Tokugawa Japan: The 'Confucian' Thought of Yokoi Shōnan," *Annals of the Institute of Social Science (Tokyo)* 16 (1975).
Miyauchi, D. Y. "Yokoi Shōnan (1809–1869), a National Political Adviser from Kumamoto *Han* in Late Tokugawa Japan," *JAH* 3 (1969).

Yokoyama Gennosuke 1870–1915 横山源之助
Native of Toyama Prefecture, Yokoyama studied law and in 1894 joined the *Mainichi Shinbun*. Under the influence of such men as Shimada Saburō, the paper's president, he became interested in social problems, and from 1896 conducted a series of investigations into poverty in various parts of the country. The results of his investigations appeared in 1898 in *Nihon no Kasō Shakai* (The Lower Strata of Japanese Society), a major exposé of poverty and bad working conditions, which, despite its weaknesses, is still a valuable historical source. Apart from this work Yokoyama wrote widely on social and labor problems; he played a major role in revealing the existence of poverty in late Meiji Japan and became a model for later social researchers.

Chūbachi, M., and K. Taira. "Poverty in Modern Japan," in H. Patrick, ed., *Japanese Industrialization and Its Social Consequences* (Berkeley, 1976).

Yomiuri Shinbun. See NEWSPAPERS

Yonai Mitsumasa 1880–1948 米内光政
Native of Iwate Prefecture, Yonai graduated from the Naval Academy. He became commander in chief of the combined fleet in 1936 and full admiral in 1937. As navy minister 1937–1939 he supported a policy of friendship with America and Britain, opposing alliance with the Axis powers. Despite military opposition he was appointed prime minister in January 1940 but was caused increasing problems by army dominance, the rise of Germany in Europe and calls for an Axis alliance, proposals from Konoe and others for a new political structure, and Japan's policies in southeast Asia. When his war minister demanded cooperation with the new structure movement (*q.v.*) Yonai in return demanded the war minister's resignation, but the army's refusal to recommend a successor led to the cabinet's resignation in July 1940. Yonai returned as navy minister in four cabinets from July 1944 to the disbanding of the forces' ministries in December 1945, and during this time he actively sought an end to the fighting.

Butow, R. C. *Japan's Decision to Surrender* (Stanford, 1954).
Nishijima, Y. "Navy Minister Yonai," *CJ* 6, no. 2 (Sept. 1937).

Yorozu Chōhō 万朝報
The daily paper *Yorozu Chōhō* (also *Manchōhō*) was founded in 1892 by Kuroiwa Ruikō (1862–1920), a journalist and translator from Tosa. Its circulation expanded, helped largely by serialization of foreign novels, but it also contained many articles on socialism, social problems, and the labor movement. It attacked

hanbatsu politics (*q.v.*) and called for social justice and around 1900 was the most influential progressive paper, counting among its reporters such men as Kōtoku Shūsui, Sakai Toshihiko, and Uchimura Kanzō. In 1903 Kuroiwa began to support the idea of a Russo-Japanese war, and their commitment to pacifism brought the resignation of many of these men. The *Yorozu Chōhō* remained a leading liberal paper, but it declined rapidly after the death of Kuroiwa and had lost most of its influence by the time it was taken over by another paper in 1940.

Notehelfer, F. G. *Kōtoku Shūsui: Portrait of a Japanese Radical* (Cambridge, 1971).

Yoshida Shigeru 1878–1967 吉田茂
Born in Tokyo of a Kōchi family, son of Takeuchi Tsuna and later son-in-law to Makino Nobuaki, after graduating from Tokyo University in 1906, Yoshida entered the Foreign Ministry and after various assignments abroad was appointed consul-general at Mukden in 1925. In this capacity he attended the Eastern Conference (*q.v.*), where he advocated a strong policy in China. In 1928 he became deputy foreign minister and was subsequently ambassador to Italy and then Britain 1936–1938. He was strongly identified in military eyes with liberalism and friendship with Britain and the U.S. and on one occasion during the war was arrested by the military police. From 1938 Yoshida avoided political participation, but in September 1945 he became foreign minister. In May 1946, following the sudden purging of Hatoyama, Yoshida succeeded him as president of the Japan Liberal Party and prime minister. Supported by various conservative parties, Yoshida remained in power until October 1954, with the exception of May 1947–October 1948. As prime minister for much of the Occupation period Yoshida initially complied with major reforms such as the new constitution and land reform (*q.v.*). During the years after his resumption of power in 1948 he allied with the more conservative elements among the Occupation authorities, although he did not always agree with Occupation policy, and although it is difficult to assess the degree of his influence, he would appear to have possessed considerable power, exercised through his considerable personal dynamism and domination. Yoshida strongly supported the economic stabilization program (*q.v.*) and also promoted the so-called "reverse course" policies from the late 1940s, including the "red purge" (*q.v.*), rearmament by the setting-up of what later became the Self-Defense Force, and the security treaty with the U.S. which accompanied the conclusion of the San Francisco Peace Treaty (*q.v.*). Yoshida remained a staunch supporter of the Chinese Nationalist government on Taiwan until his death. After the end of the Occupation Yoshida depurged many Japanese, further strengthened Japan's armed forces, and increased government centralization. Yoshida was strongly opposed by Hatoyama after the latter returned to politics, and a combination of opponents within the conservative parties combined with a decline in his popular appeal eventually brought about Yoshida's resignation, but he remained a powerful influence on conservative politics, with something of the status of an elder statesman. The policies followed by Yoshida during his period in office in effect established the guidelines for the policies followed by subsequent Liberal Democratic governments.

Dower, J. W. *Empire and Aftermath: Yoshida Shigeru and the Japanese Experience, 1878–1954* (Cambridge, Mass., 1979).
Wildes, H. E. *Typhoon in Tokyo* (New York, 1954).
Yoshida, S. *Japan's Decisive Century* (New York, 1967).
———. *Yoshida Memoirs* (London, 1961).

Yoshida Shōin 1830–1859 吉田松陰
Lower samurai from Chōshū, Yoshida studied and traveled in various places in Japan and became a *rōnin* for disobedience to his domain. After being pardoned in 1853, he went to Edo and moved in anti-

foreign and pro-emperor circles. He studied under Sakuma Shōzan, who encouraged him to attempt to escape on one of Commodore Perry's ships in 1854, for which Yoshida was again imprisoned in Chōshū. He was released in 1856 and though still under house arrest taught privately, supervising his own school, the Shōka Sonjuku, during 1858. Although strongly influenced by Confucianism and a desire to maintain Japan's ancient traditions, Yoshida's fervent patriotism led him to call for the adoption of Western science and technology to protect Japan. He aimed to inculcate samurai ideals into his students and arouse loyalty to both emperor and nation, and the logical culmination of his ideas was opposition to a Bakufu so weak that it was unable to protect the nation. Among Yoshida's students were Takasugi Shinsaku, Kido Kōin, Shinagawa Yajirō, Yamagata Aritomo, and Itō Hirobumi, and through them his influence was tremendous, both in Chōshū and in the nation as a whole. Yoshida opposed the U.S.-Japan Treaty of Amity and Commerce of 1858 (*q.v.*) and the other Ansei treaties and early in 1859 was arrested for planning the assassination of a Bakufu official, for which he was subsequently executed.

Earl, D. M. *Emperor and Nation in Japan* (Seattle, 1964).
Harootunian, H. D. *Toward Restoration* (Berkeley, 1970).
Van Straelen, H. *Yoshida Shōin, Forerunner of the Meiji Restoration: A Biographical Study* (Leiden, 1952).

Yoshino Sakuzō 1878–1933 吉野作造

A member of a Miyagi Prefecture merchant family, Yoshino graduated from Tokyo University in 1904. As a student he was strongly influenced by Ebina Danjō. After teaching in China and studying abroad, he became professor of political history at Tokyo in 1913. Yoshino started writing on politics soon after graduating, and during the early Taishō period he became the theoretical leader of the intelligentsia during the era of Taishō democracy (*q.v.*), although he became increasingly subject to criticism from both right and left wing. Nevertheless, his influence on political thought in the whole interwar period was considerable. Yoshino's beliefs were embodied in *minponshugi* (people as the base-ism). He believed that democracy (*minshushugi*) implied that sovereignty resided with the people and was therefore irrelevant to Japan, where sovereignty resided with the emperor, although this did not necessarily imply direct imperial rule. *Minponshugi* implied that the welfare of the people was the basic concern of the state and its government and that all decisions relating to government must be based on public opinion. Through the pages of such journals as *Chūō Kōron* (Central Review) Yoshino called for universal suffrage and restriction of the powers of non-Dietary bodies such as Privy Council, House of Peers, and the army. In 1918 he founded the Reimeikai (Dawn Society), a group of like-minded intellectuals, and he had a strong influence over the early Shinjinkai (*q.v.*) as well as early proletarian parties . In 1924 he resigned his professorship to write political articles in the Asahi newspaper but quickly resumed his post after being indicted for one of his articles. He was also responsible for founding the Meiji Culture Research Association in 1924, which under his guidance produced *Meiji Bunka Zenshū* (Complete Works on Meiji Culture), a major reference work. Yoshino wrote widely on politics, history, and law at both academic and popular levels.

Najita, T. "Some Reflections on Idealism in the Political Thought of Yoshino Sakuzō," in B. S. Silberman and H. D. Harootunian, eds., *Japan in Crisis* (Princeton, 1974).
Perry, W. S. "Yoshino Sakuzō, 1878–1933, Exponent of Democratic Ideals in Japan," Ph.D. diss., Stanford University, 1956.
Silberman, B. S. "The Political Theory and Program of Yoshino Sakuzō," *Journal of Modern History* 31 (Dec. 1959).
Takeda, K. "Yoshino Sakuzō," *JQ* 12, no. 4 (Oct.-Dec. 1965).

Youth Organizations
Village youth groups in Japan date back to the Tokugawa period, but from the mid-Meiji period such groups flourished. Under the influence of Tanaka Giichi in September 1915 a national council for these groups was set up with the official aim of using them for physical and moral training. Although there was no official army control, the youth groups were strongly connected with local reservists' associations and were used to instill patriotism, military popularity, and ideas of national unity, as well as for the traditional community service. A full national organization was established in 1924, and in 1934 this was renamed the Greater Japan Youth Association (Dainihon Seinendan). Left-wing organizations also tried to establish youth groups and sections to spread their ideas, such as the All Japan Proletarian Youth League (Zen Nihon Musan Seinen Dōmei) of 1926–1928, which had strong connections with the Communist Party, but although such organizations were often vocal, they failed to obtain mass participation on the scale of the "official" youth organizations, and their development was brought to a halt by persecution of the left wing. The official organizations gained in strength through the 1930s, and in January 1941 the Greater Japan Youth Association absorbed all other youth groups. Over the next eighteen months its membership rose from 4½ million to 14 million young people. It was engaged in the same voluntary activities as previously, but it was also used to reinforce war aims, to perform urgent tasks, and to bring the idea of the war home. The association was abolished at the end of the war, and the state has since played little part in sponsoring youth organization.

Havens, T. R. H. *Valley of Darkness* (New York, 1978).
Smethurst, R. J. *A Social Basis for Prewar Japanese Militarism* (Berkeley, 1974).

Yūaikai 友愛会
In August 1912 Suzuki Bunji established a mutual aid society named the Yūaikai (Friendly Society). From the initial 13 workers participating, the number gradually increased, including both intellectuals and workers, and the Yūaikai developed various welfare activities relating to health, education, and legal advice and established branches outside Tokyo. In June 1916 a women's section was established, and by spring 1917 the society's membership was over 20,000. From late 1912 a regular journal was published; from 1914 this took the name *Rōdō oyobi Sangyō* (Labor and Industry). From the initial emphasis on mutual aid and harmony between capital and labor, the Yūaikai turned to more active political and labor organization, and against the background of increasing unrest from 1917, it became involved in strikes. The increasing drive for unionism counterbalanced by fear of government repression led to conflict within the movement, and during Suzuki's absence 1918–1919 political activism by the Yūaikai became more marked. By his return dominance had passed from his more moderate line, but Suzuki accepted the change into a full labor union organization and remained among the leadership. In line with its new direction the Yūaikai rejected participation in the Kyōchōkai (*q.v.*) and in 1919 changed its name to Dainihon Rōdō Sōdōmei Yūaikai (Greater Japan Labor Federation Friendly Society). The dropping of the word *Yūaikai* in 1921 created Sōdōmei (Nihon Rōdō Sōdōmei), one of the leading national labor organizations of the interwar period. The Yūaikai left a major legacy to subsequent labor organizations in terms of experience, international contact, and political activism.

Large, S. S. "The Japanese Labor Movement, 1912–1919: Suzuki Bunji and the Yūaikai," *JAS* 29, no. 3 (May 1970).
———. *The Yūaikai, 1912–1919* (Tokyo, 1972).

Yūbin Hōchi. See NEWSPAPERS

Yūzonsha 猶存社
The Yūzonsha (Society of Those Who

Still Remain) was a right-wing society founded in August 1919 by Ōkawa Shūmei and Mitsukawa Kametarō. Kita Ikki subsequently joined, and other members included Nishida Mitsugu. The society aimed to remodel the Japanese empire and liberate the peoples of Asia. Kita's writings were distributed and promoted by the society. The Yūzonsha disbanded in 1923 after a split between Kita and Ōkawa, but its tradition was carried on in other groups.

Wilson, G. M. "Kita Ikki, Ōkawa Shūmei, and the Yūzonsha: A Study in the Genesis of Shōwa Nationalism," *HPJ* 2 (1963).

———. *Radical Nationalist in Japan: Kita Ikki, 1883–1937* (Cambridge, Mass., 1969).

Z

Zaibatsu 財閥

The word *zaibatsu* (financial clique) refers to the huge concerns which dominated the Japanese economy up to 1945, the biggest of which were Mitsui, Mitsubishi, Sumitomo, and Yasuda. The origins of these groups were diverse, but the older ones all benefited in some way from contacts with and patronage from the Meiji government, many being started by the so-called *seishō* (political merchants) (*q.v.*). The pattern of *zaibatsu* development varied tremendously, but certain patterns were common to most. The undertaking of government policy in the early years after the Restoration led to the establishment of nuclear enterprises, for example, shipping in the case of Mitsubishi; and very often government protection had enabled the achievement of a monopoly in a certain field by the 1880s. This monopolistic position helped extreme capital accumulation enabling the firm to branch out; many also benefited by acquiring government businesses when they were sold off in the early 1880s, and these then became the nucleus of the producing sectors. Increasingly, operations extended into all fields, and the owning family could acquire a network of financial, industrial, and commercial holdings sufficiently large to survive periods of acute depression. Expansion was assisted by internal financing through the group's own bank, which in effect was a base camp for enlargement, the extension of credit acting as central leverage to extend control. Close connection between the concern's various enterprises was maintained by such means as interlocking directorships and mutual shareholding. Ownership was vested in the *zaibatsu* family, which used such methods as strategic marriages and "feudal" personal relationships to maintain control. From the early 20th century most of the concerns were reorganized on a pyramidal basis with a holding company (limited or unlimited partnership) acting as a central focus for the group. Shares in the holding company normally remained in the hands of the *zaibatsu* family although management was increasingly handed over to others. *Zaibatsu* influence was further extended by the wielding of rights over small independent companies. One major characteristic which differentiates the *zaibatsu* from their counterparts in other countries is the fact that they were held together by finance rather than technology. Although many *zaibatsu* attempted to break the "political merchant" image in the 1890s, they did maintain close contacts with both politicians and bureaucrats. In the 1930s they became targets for the criticism of both Left and Right, notably from anticapitalist nationalist elements, which caused them to tailor their interests to fit those of the government. At the same time new *zaibatsu* such as Nissan arose whose development was closely tied up with the political trends of the time. They specialized in military and heavy chemical industries and the development of Korea and Manchuria. However, these were weakened as economic concerns by their rapid expansion, inadequate managerial personnel and capital resources, and dependence on quick capital raising through the open market rather than using their own banks. The monopolistic positions of the various *zaibatsu* were considered by the Occupation authorities to have provided a major prop for Japanese militarism and aggression, and as part of the democratization program from 1945 a major program of *zaibatsu* dissolution (*q.v.*) and antimonopolistic legislation was embarked upon. (See also individual *zaibatsu*.)

Bisson, T. A. "The *Zaibatsu*'s Wartime Role," *Pacific Affairs* 18, no. 4 (Dec. 1945).
Hirschmeier, J. *The Origins of Entrepreneurship in Meiji Japan* (Cambridge, Mass., 1964).
Shibagaki, K. "The Early History of the *Zaibatsu*," *Developing Economies* 4, no. 4 (Dec. 1966).
Yamamura, K. "*Zaibatsu* Prewar and *Zaibatsu* Postwar," *JAS* 23, no. 4 (Aug. 1964).

Zaibatsu Dissolution (zaibatsu kaitai) 財閥解体

After Japan's surrender the Occupation authorities advocated a policy of disbanding the monopolistic economic combines, notably the *zaibatsu* (*q.v.*), and removing *zaibatsu* families from control of these organizations, on the grounds that the existence of such combines had assisted the development of aggressive militarism in Japan. Late in 1945 all *zaibatsu* capital was frozen, and legislation in April 1946 provided for the establishment of the Holding Companies Liquidation Commission, which subsequently engaged in the compulsory purchase of shares held by 83 holding companies of varying importance. Banks and financial institutions were excluded. Many *zaibatsu* family members and former officials were also purged. Legislation was introduced to prevent excessive concentrations of economic power. The Anti-Monopoly Law of April 1947 prohibited holding companies, private monopoly, cartel agreements, unfair dealings and competition, shareholding above certain designated levels, as well as containing other related provisions. A Fair Trade Commission supervised the enforcement of the law. The December 1947 Deconcentration Law (Law for the Exclusion of Excessive Concentrations of Economic Power) was aimed at disbanding existing organizations considered dangerously monopolistic. Under its provisions the Holding Companies Liquidation Commission designated 325 companies as excessive concentrations of economic strength to be split up into their constituent parts or controlled in other ways. Some of the designated companies were obvious candidates, but the inclusion of many on the list was totally unexpected. These proposals, made in February 1948, caused alarm in Japan, where they were regarded as a U.S. scheme to inflict severe damage on Japanese business, and among conservatives in America. Protest in both countries at the radical proposals meant that in December 1949 the Deconcentration Review Board stated that it had recommended the reorganization of only 19 major companies on the list and that the program would stop there. Although the power of the *zaibatsu* families was broken by the reforms, the program caused little fundamental damage to the economy; in fact it can be argued what dissolution took place stimulated market competition, strengthened company executives, and assisted the diffusion of technology. However, the failure to touch banks, subsequent legal reform, and government policy since the Occupation mean that many of the connections between companies dissolved at the time have been revived. New business groupings known as *keiretsu* have appeared, although they are less dominant in the economy than previously, and excessive concentrations of economic strength are still considered by many to exist on a wide scale.

Bisson, T. A. *Zaibatsu Dissolution in Japan* (Berkeley, 1954).
Hadley, E. F. *Antitrust in Japan* (Princeton, 1970).

Zengakuren 全学連
Various elements of the student movement came together in September 1948 to form Zengakuren (short for All Japan Federation of Student Self-Government Associations). By 1949 it boasted 300,000 members in over 145 colleges. Strongly influenced by the Japan Communist Party, Zengakuren vigorously opposed the government on both academic and nonacademic matters. A split in the J.C.P. led to a decline, but it revived 1956–1958 and by 1959 again boasted 300,000 members, although many of them were not active. Communist influence remained considerable, but the mainstream of Zengakuren was now opposed to the J.C.P. Zengakuren opposed the government on such matters as the development of moral education and the introduction of an efficiency rating system for teachers, and its radical core was in the vanguard of opposition to renewal of the security treaty in 1960, though often at odds with other opponents of the treaty. After the crisis many students lost interest in the movement, and control reverted to the hands of hard-core radicals. Faced with a decline of interest, Zengakuren became divided into factions, and this was followed by a succession of splinter groups throughout the whole student movement. The importance of Zengakuren again increased during the student unrest of the late 1960s, but it has since again declined.

Dowsey, S. J., ed. *Zengakuren, Japan's Revolutionary Students* (Berkeley, 1970).
Packard, G. R. *Protest in Tokyo* (Princeton, 1966).
Sunada, I. "The Thought and Behavior of *Zengakuren:* Trends in the Japanese Student Movement," *Asian Survey* 9, no. 6 (June 1969).

Zenkoku Rōnō Taishūtō. See RŌDŌ NŌMINTŌ

Zenkoku Sangyōbetsu Rōdō Kumiai Rengō. See LABOR MOVEMENT

Zennihon Rōdō Kumiai Kaigi. See LABOR MOVEMENT

Zennihon Rōdō Sōdōmei. See LABOR MOVEMENT

Zenrō Kaigi. See LABOR MOVEMENT

APPENDIX 1
Era Names

During the Tokugawa period, years were reckoned according to era names (*nengō*), which from 1868 were made concurrent with the reign of a single emperor. Despite the change from the lunar calendar in 1873 and increasing use of the Western calendar, years are still frequently referred to according to era names.

Tenpo	1830–1844
Kōka	1844–1848
Kaei	1848–1854
Ansei	1854–1860
Man'en	1860–1861
Bunkyū	1861–1864
Genji	1864–1865
Keiō	1865–1868
Meiji	1868–1912
Taishō	1912–1926
Shōwa	1926–

NOTE: The year in which an era begins is counted both as the first year of that era and as the final year of the previous era.

APPENDIX 2
Emperors Since 1817

Ninkō	1817–1846
Kōmei	1846–1867
Meiji	1867–1912
Taishō	1912–1926
Shōwa	1926–

NOTE: The first date in each case is the date of accession.

APPENDIX 3

Population of Japan, 1872–1977 (excluding overseas territories of the Japanese empire, to nearest thousand)

Date	Population in Millions
1872	33.110
1875	33.997
1880	35.929
1885	37.869
1890	40.453
1895	42.271
1900	44.826
1905	47.678
1910	50.985
1915	54.936
1920	55.963
1925	59.737
1930*	64.450
1935*	69.254
1940*	73.114
1945*	71.998
1950*	83.200
1955*	89.276
1960*	93.419
1965*	98.275
1970*	103.720
1975*	111.940
1977	114.154

*Denotes year of census.

NOTE: Figures prior to 1872 are of very doubtful accuracy and are not given here. Even the official figures cited here are generally regarded as inexact prior to the introduction of full census taking.

Figures given are for those with official registration (*honseki*) in Japan proper and are according to Naikaku Tōkeikyoku (Cabinet Statistics Bureau), *Nihon Teikoku Tōkei Nenkan* (Statistical Yearbook of Imperial Japan), 1882–1941; Tōkei Iinkai Jimukyoku and Sōrifu Tōkeikyoku (Executive Office, Statistics Commission and Bureau of Statistics, Prime Minister's Office), *Nihon Tōkei Nenkan* (Japan Statistical Yearbook), 1949–

APPENDIX 4
Development of Political Parties in Modern Japan

The following figures are intended to clarify the major developments in national political organizations, where frequent splintering, name changing, and regrouping are apt to cause confusion. The figures are intended to show only the most important developments; numerous smaller groups and factions have therefore been omitted, especially with reference to the period before 1940. Party titles adhere to the usage adopted in the main body of the text. Figure 1—*Major Prewar Political Parties*—uses Japanese titles since these are normally used in English texts relating to the period; translations are given for these names where feasible. Writings on postwar politics tend to use the English names of political parties; therefore this order has been reversed in Figure 2—*Major Postwar Political Parties.* There are exceptions in both cases, however, notably the Japan Communist Party and Kōmeitō.

———→	indicates one organization becoming the major, or an important, element in another
- - - - - -→	indicates the membership of an earlier organization becoming the major element in a new organization
. . . .	illegal organization

Figure 1. Major Prewar Political Parties

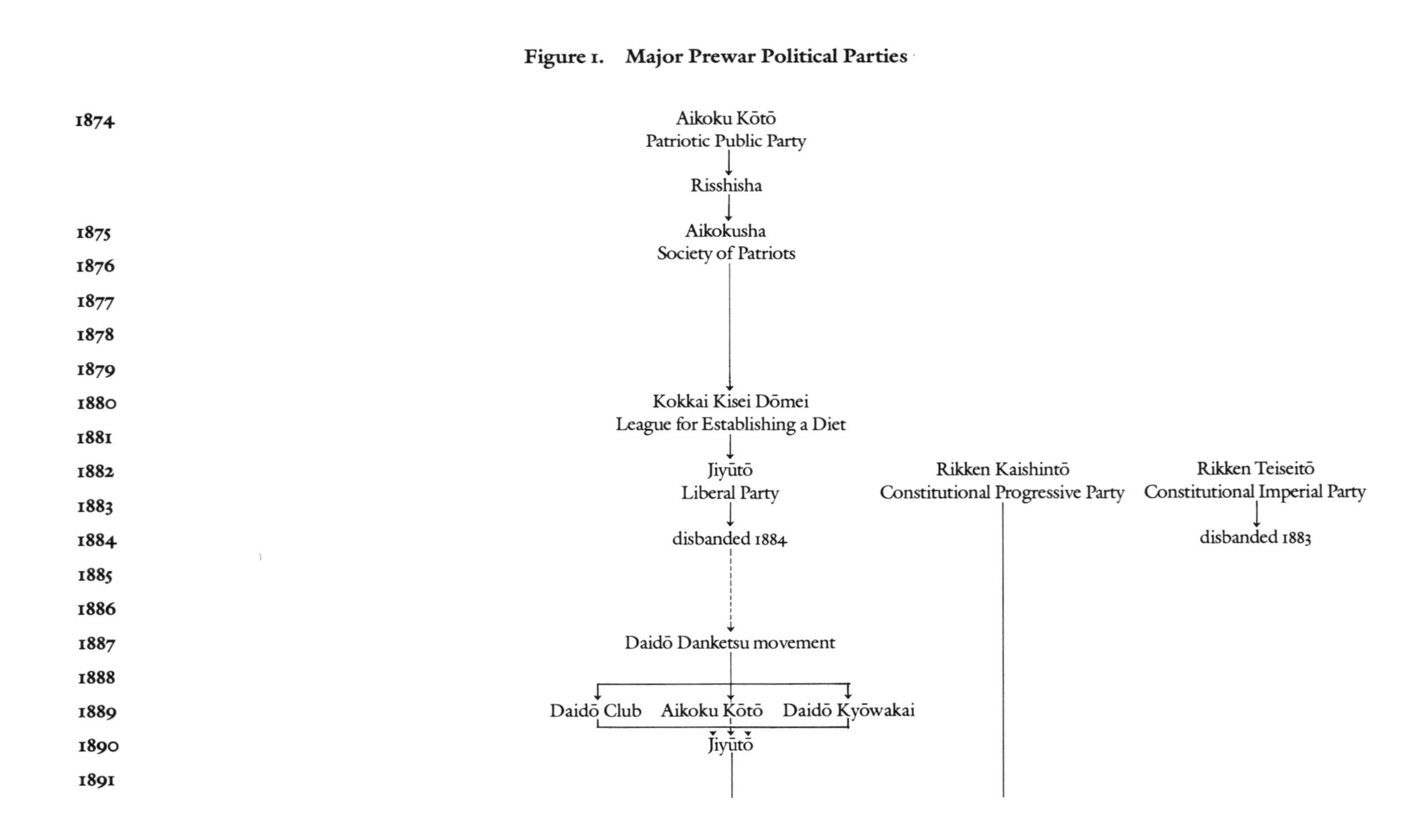

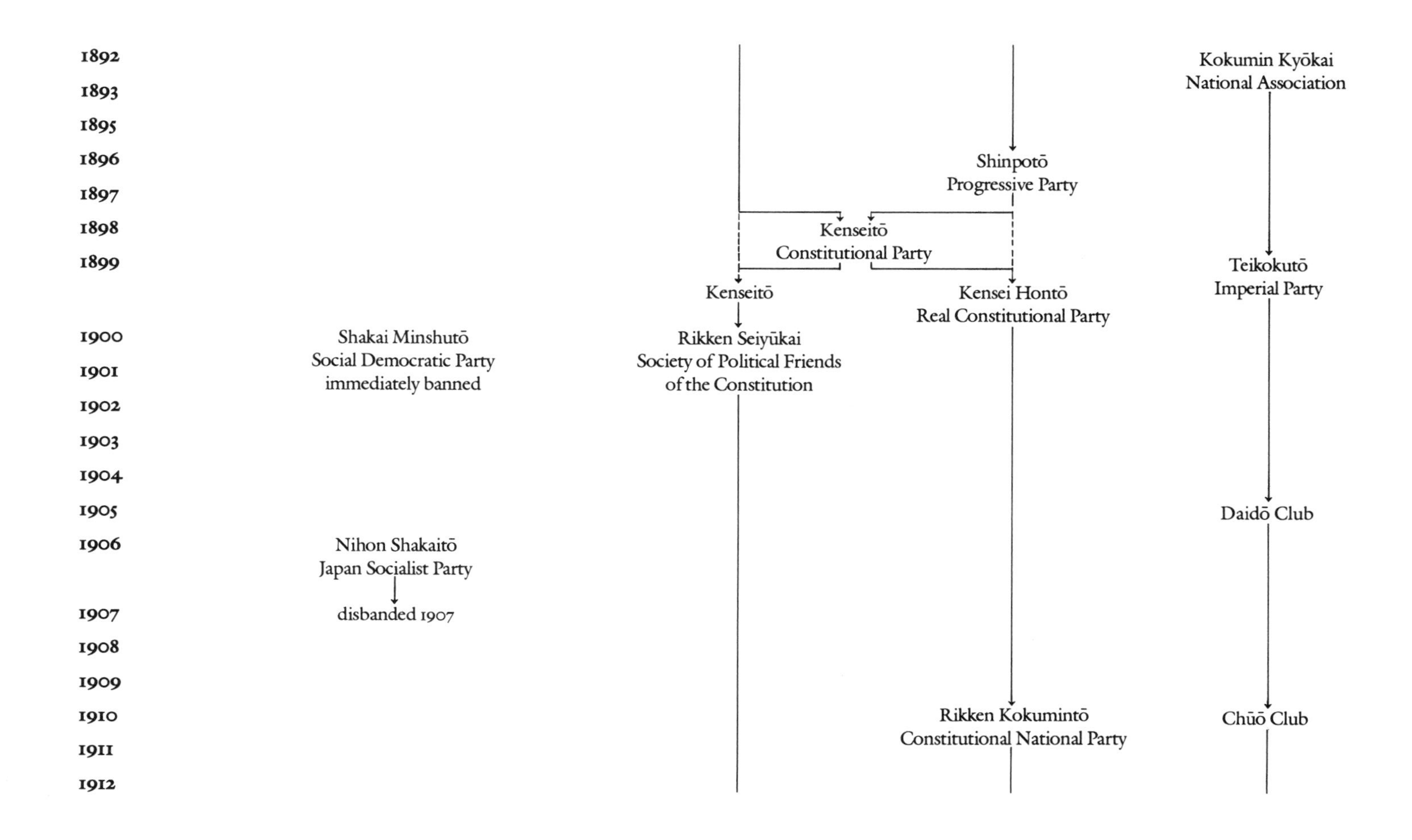
1892
1893
1895
1896
1897
1898
1899
1900
1901
1902
1903
1904
1905
1906
1907
1908
1909
1910
1911
1912
Kokumin Kyōkai
National Association
Shinpotō
Progressive Party
Kenseitō
Constitutional Party
Teikokutō
Imperial Party
Kenseitō
Kensei Hontō
Real Constitutional Party
Shakai Minshutō
Social Democratic Party
immediately banned
Rikken Seiyūkai
Society of Political Friends
of the Constitution
Daidō Club
Nihon Shakaitō
Japan Socialist Party
disbanded 1907
Rikken Kokumintō
Constitutional National Party
Chūō Club

Figure 1. Major Prewar Political Parties (continued)

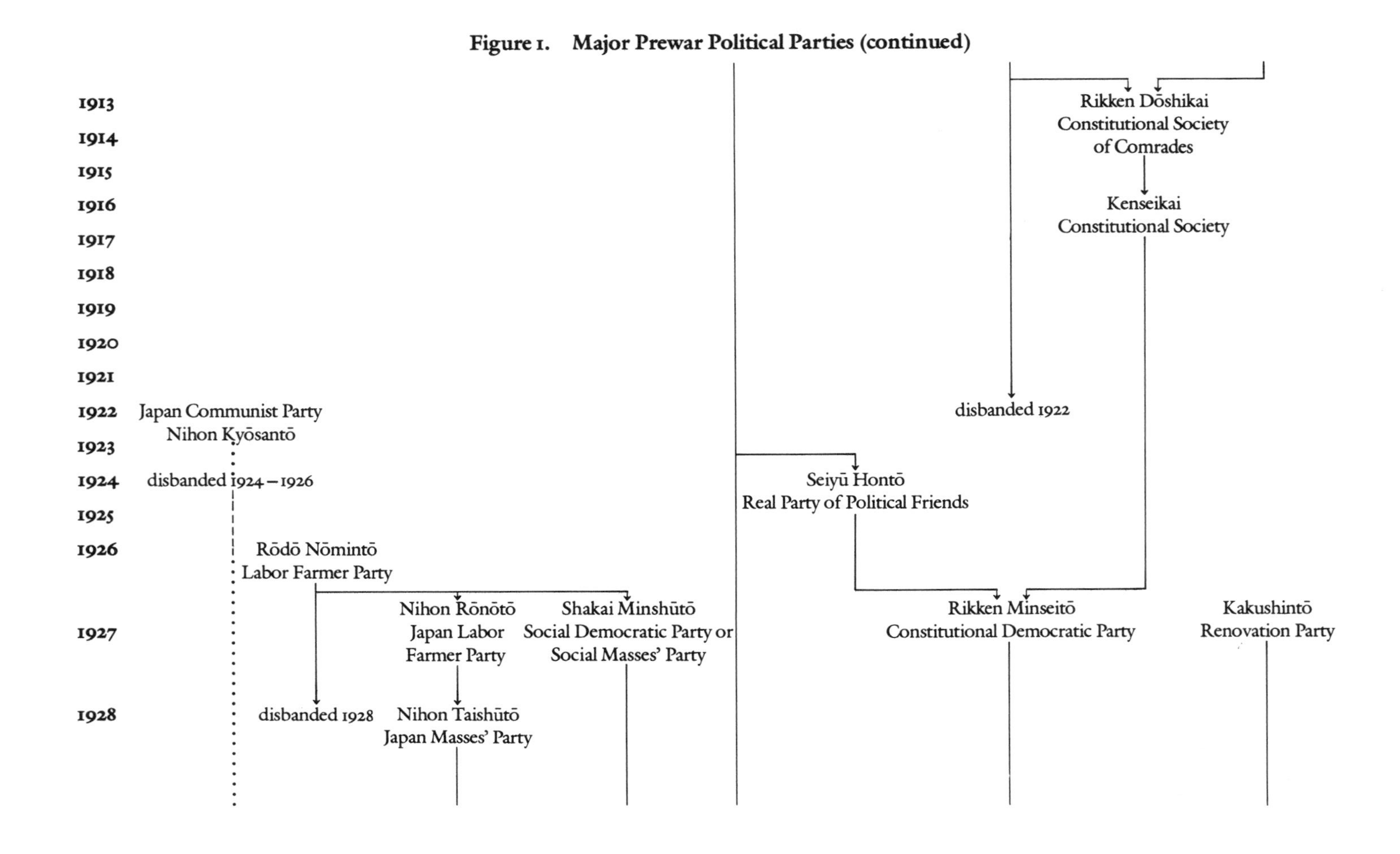

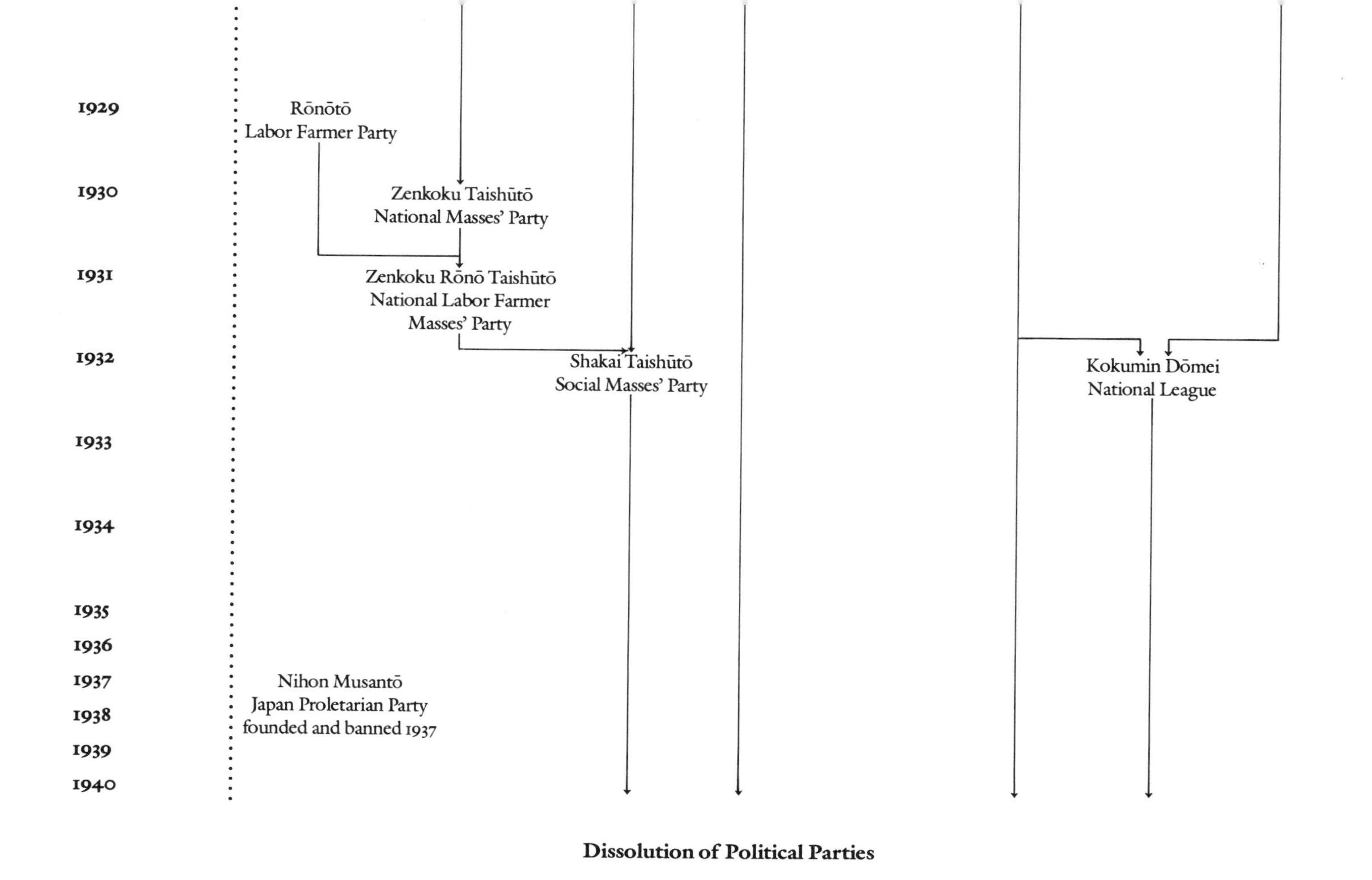
1929
1930
1931
1932
1933
1934
1935
1936
1937
1938
1939
1940
Rōnōtō
Labor Farmer Party
Zenkoku Taishūtō
National Masses' Party
Zenkoku Rōnō Taishūtō
National Labor Farmer
Masses' Party
Shakai Taishūtō
Social Masses' Party
Kokumin Dōmei
National League
Nihon Musantō
Japan Proletarian Party
founded and banned 1937
Dissolution of Political Parties

Figure 2. Major Postwar Political Parties

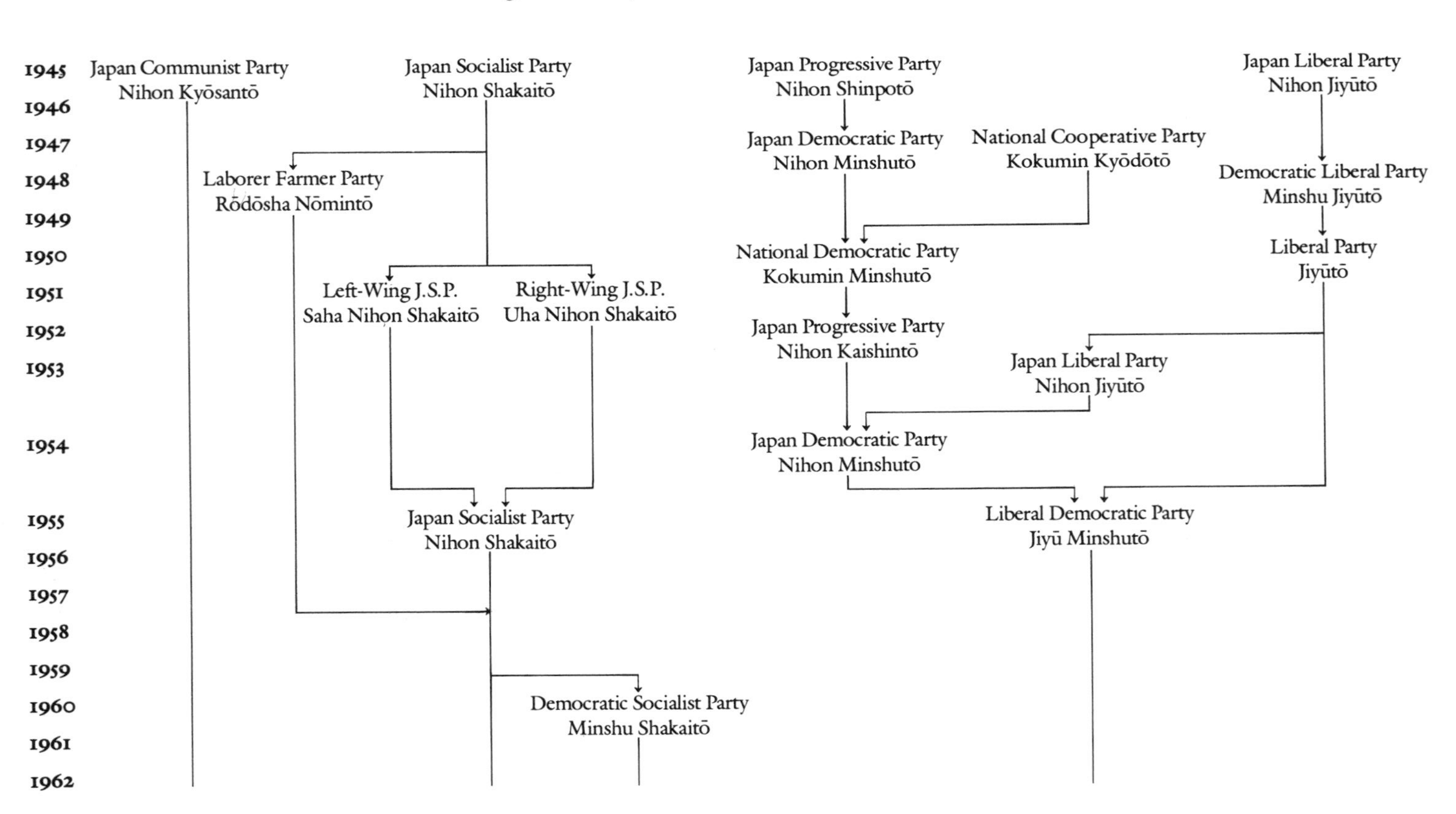

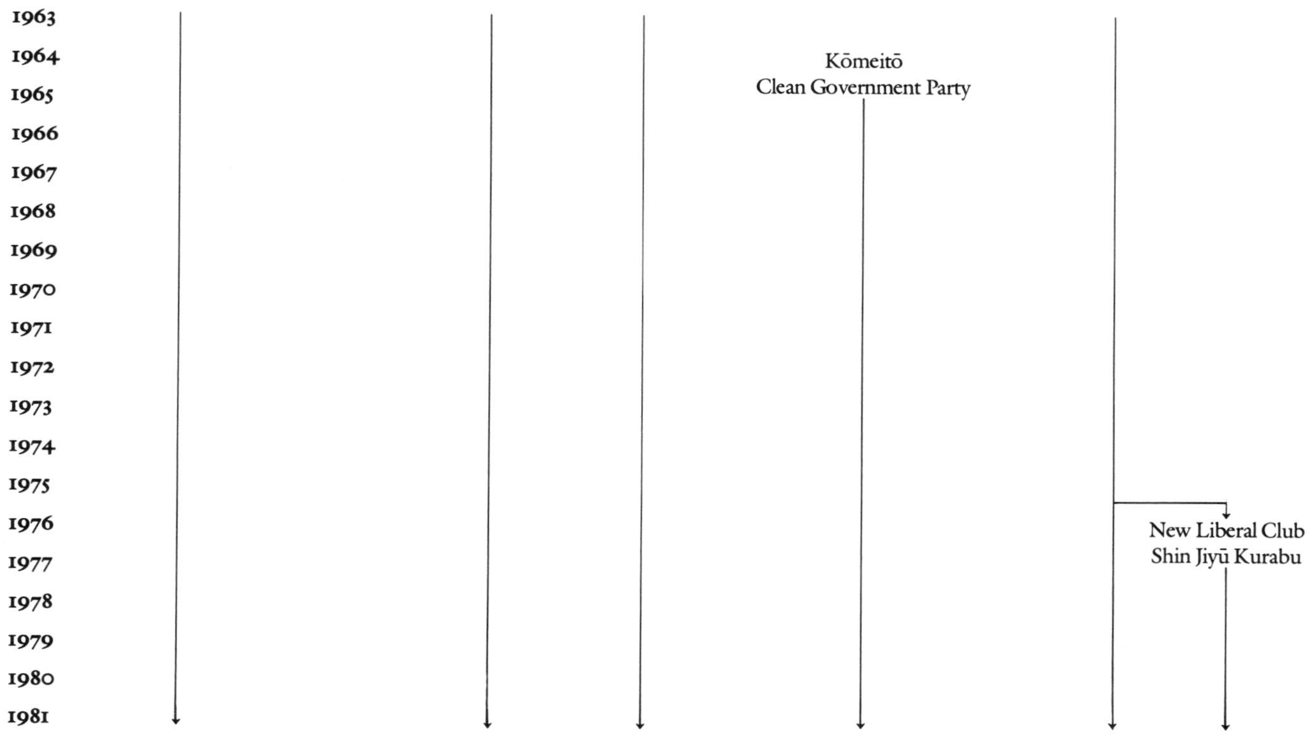

1963
1964
1965
1966
1967
1968
1969
1970
1971
1972
1973
1974
1975
1976
1977
1978
1979
1980
1981

Kōmeitō
Clean Government Party

New Liberal Club
Shin Jiyū Kurabu

APPENDIX 5

Japanese Cabinets Since the Introduction of the Cabinet System in 1885

The date given for each cabinet is that on which it took office and that on which it formally handed over power to its successor, although in the latter case the whole cabinet or the prime minister may have resigned, or died, prior to this. Where no date is given for a minister's tenure of office, he served for the whole period of the cabinet. An asterisk (*) denotes deputy premier during some period.

First Itō Cabinet
22 Dec. 1885–30 Apr. 1888

Prime Minister	Itō Hirobumi
Foreign Affairs	Inoue Kaoru (22 Dec. 1885–16 Sept. 1887)
	Itō Hirobumi (16 Sept. 1887–1 Feb. 1888)
	Ōkuma Shigenobu (1 Feb. 1888–30 Apr. 1888)
Home Affairs	Yamagata Aritomo
Finance	Matsukata Masayoshi
War	Ōyama Iwao
Navy	Saigō Tsugumichi (22 Dec. 1885–10 July 1886, 1 July 1887–30 Apr. 1888)
	Ōyama Iwao (10 July 1886–1 July 1887)
Justice	Yamada Akiyoshi
Education	Mori Arinori
Agriculture and Commerce	Tani Kanjō (22 Dec. 1885–26 July 1887, but from 16 Mar. 1886–24 June 1887 either Saigō or Yamagata was acting minister)
	Hijikata Hisamoto (26 July 1887–16 Sept. 1887)
	Kuroda Kiyotaka (16 Sept. 1887–30 Apr. 1888)
Communications	Enomoto Takeaki
Chief of Cabinet Secretariat	Tanaka Mitsuaki
Director of Legislative Bureau	Yamao Yōzō (23 Dec. 1885–7 Feb. 1888)
	Inoue Kowashi (7 Feb. 1888–30 Apr. 1888)

Kuroda Cabinet
30 Apr. 1888–24 Dec. 1889

Prime Minister	Kuroda Kiyotaka (Sanjō Sanetomi was acting prime minister 25 Oct.–24 Dec. 1889)
Foreign Affairs	Ōkuma Shigenobu
Home Affairs	Yamagata Aritomo (30 Apr. 1888–3 Dec. 1888)
	Matsukata Masayoshi (3 Dec. 1888–3 Oct. 1889)
	Yamagata Aritomo (3 Oct. 1889–24 Dec. 1889)
Finance	Matsukata Masayoshi
War	Ōyama Iwao
Navy	Saigō Tsugumichi
Justice	Yamada Akiyoshi
Education	Mori Arinori (30 Apr. 1888–12 Feb. 1889)
	Ōyama Iwao (16 Feb. 1889–22 Mar. 1889)
	Enomoto Takeaki (22 Mar. 1889–24 Dec. 1889)
Agriculture and Commerce	Enomoto Takeaki (30 Apr. 1888–25 July 1889)
	Inoue Kaoru (25 July 1889–24 Dec. 1889)
Communications	Enomoto Takeaki (30 Apr. 1888–22 Mar. 1889)
	Gotō Shōjirō (22 Mar. 1889–24 Dec. 1889)
Hanretsu	Itō Hirobumi
Chief of Cabinet Secretariat	Komaki Banchō
Chief of Legislative Bureau	Inoue Kowashi

First Yamagata Cabinet
24 Dec. 1889–6 May 1891

Prime Minister	Yamagata Aritomo
Foreign Affairs	Aoki Shūzō
Home Affairs	Yamagata Aritomo (24 Dec. 1889–17 May 1890)
	Saigō Tsugumichi (17 May 1890–6 May 1891)
Finance	Matsukata Masayoshi
War	Ōyama Iwao
Navy	Saigō Tsugumichi (24 Dec. 1889–17 May 1890)
	Kabayama Sukenori (17 May 1890–6 May 1891)
Justice	Yamada Akiyoshi (24 Dec. 1889–25 Dec. 1890, 7 Feb. 1891–6 May 1891)
	Ōki Takatō (25 Dec. 1890–7 Feb. 1891)
Education	Enomoto Takeaki (24 Dec. 1889–17 May 1890)
	Yoshikawa Akimasa (17 May 1890–6 May 1891)

Agriculture and Commerce	Iwamura Michitoshi (24 Dec. 1889–17 May 1890)
	Mutsu Munemitsu (17 May 1890–6 May 1891)
Communications	Gotō Shōjirō
Hanretsu	Ōki Takatō
Chief of Cabinet Secretariat	Subu Kōhei
Chief of Legislative Bureau	Inoue Kowashi

First Matsukata Cabinet
6 May 1891–8 Aug. 1892

Prime Minister	Matsukata Masayoshi
Foreign Affairs	Aoki Shūzō (6 May 1891–29 May 1891)
	Enomoto Takeaki (29 May 1891–8 Aug. 1892)
Home Affairs	Saigō Tsugumichi (6 May 1891–1 June 1891)
	Shinagawa Yajirō (1 June 1891–11 Mar. 1892)
	Soejima Taneomi (11 Mar. 1892–8 June 1892)
	Matsukata Masayoshi (8 June 1892–14 July 1892)
	Kōno Togama (14 July 1892–8 Aug. 1892)
Finance	Matsukata Masayoshi
War	Ōyama Iwao (6 May 1891–17 May 1891)
	Takashima Tomonosuke (17 May 1891–8 Aug. 1892)
Navy	Kabayama Sukenori
Justice	Yamada Akiyoshi (6 May 1891–1 June 1891)
	Tanaka Fujimaro (1 June 1891–23 June 1892)
	Kōno Togama (23 June 1892–8 Aug. 1892)
Education	Yoshikawa Akimasa (6 May 1891–1 June 1891)
	Ōki Takatō (1 June 1891–8 Aug. 1892)
Agriculture and Commerce	Mutsu Munemitsu (6 May 1891–14 Mar. 1892)
	Kōno Togama (14 Mar. 1892–14 July 1892)
	Sano Tsunetami (14 July 1892–8 Aug. 1892)
Communications	Gotō Shōjirō
Chief of Cabinet Secretariat	Hirayama Narinobu
Chief of Legislative Bureau	Ozaki Saburō

Second Itō Cabinet
8 Aug. 1892–18 Sept. 1896

Prime Minister	Itō Hirobumi (Inoue Kaoru was acting prime minister 28 Nov. 1892–6 Feb. 1893; and Kuroda Kiyotaka 21

	Mar. – 1 Apr. 1896, 5 June – 13 July 1896, 31 Aug. – 18 Sept. 1896)
Foreign Affairs	Mutsu Munemitsu (8 Aug. 1892 – 5 June 1895, 3 Apr. 1896 – 30 May 1896)
	Saionji Kinmochi (5 June 1895 – 3 Apr. 1896, 30 May 1896 – 18 Sept. 1896)
Home Affairs	Inoue Kaoru (8 Aug. 1892 – 15 Oct. 1894, but Yoshikawa Akimasa was acting minister 2 May 1894 – 25 June 1894)
	Yoshikawa Akimasa (3 Feb. 1896 – 14 Apr. 1896)
	Nomura Yasushi (15 Oct. 1894 – 3 Feb. 1896)
	Itagaki Taisuke (14 Apr. 1896 – 18 Sept. 1896)
Finance	Watanabe Kuniaki (8 Aug. 1892 – 17 Mar. 1895, 27 Aug. 1895 – 18 Sept. 1896)
	Matsukata Masayoshi (17 Mar. 1895 – 27 Aug. 1895)
War	Ōyama Iwao (8 Aug. 1892 – 9 Oct. 1894, 26 May 1895 – 18 Sept. 1896)
	Saigō Tsugumichi (9 Oct. 1894 – 7 Mar. 1895, 28 Apr. 1895 – 8 May 1895)
	Yamagata Aritomo (7 Mar. 1895 – 28 Apr. 1895, 8 May 1895 – 26 May 1895)
Navy	Nire Kagenori (8 Aug. 1892 – 11 Mar. 1893)
	Saigō Tsugumichi (11 Mar. 1893 – 18 Sept. 1896)
Justice	Yamagata Aritomo (8 Aug. 1892 – 11 Mar. 1893)
	Yoshikawa Akimasa (16 Mar. 1893 – 18 Sept. 1896)
Education	Kōno Togama (8 Aug. 1892 – 7 Mar. 1893)
	Inoue Kowashi (7 Mar. 1893 – 29 Aug. 1894)
	Yoshikawa Akimasa (29 Aug. 1894 – 3 Oct. 1894)
	Saionji Kinmochi (3 Oct. 1894 – 18 Sept. 1896)
Agriculture and Commerce	Gotō Shōjirō (8 Aug. 1892 – 22 Jan. 1894)
	Enomoto Takeaki (22 Jan. 1894 – 18 Sept. 1896)
Communications	Kuroda Kiyotaka (8 Aug. 1892 – 17 Mar. 1895)
	Watanabe Kunitake (17 Mar. 1895 – 9 Oct. 1895)
	Shirane Sen'ichi (9 Oct. 1895 – 18 Sept. 1896)
Colonization (est. 1 Apr. 1896)	Takashima Tomonosuke
Hanretsu	Kuroda Kiyotaka (17 Mar. 1895 – 18 Sept. 1896)
Chief of Cabinet Secretariat	Itō Miyoji
Chief of Legislative Bureau	Suematsu Kenchō

Second Matsukata Cabinet
18 Sept. 1896 – 12 Jan. 1898

Prime Minister	Matsukata Masayoshi (Kuroda Kiyotaka was acting prime minister 14 Apr. 1897 – 8 June 1897)
Foreign Affairs	Saionji Kinmochi (18 Sept. 1896 – 22 Sept. 1896)
	Ōkuma Shigenobu (22 Sept. 1896 – 6 Nov. 1897)
	Nishi Tokujirō (6 Nov. 1897 – 12 Jan. 1898)
Home Affairs	Itagaki Taisuke (18 Sept. 1896 – 20 Sept. 1896)
	Kabayama Sukenori (20 Sept. 1896 – 12 Jan. 1898)
Finance	Matsukata Masayoshi
War	Ōyama Iwao (18 Sept. 1896 – 20 Sept. 1896)
	Takashima Tomonosuke (20 Sept. 1896 – 12 Jan. 1898)
Navy	Saigō Tsugumichi
Justice	Yoshikawa Akimasa (18 Sept. 1896 – 26 Sept. 1896)
	Kiyoura Keigo (26 Sept. 1896 – 12 Jan. 1898)
Education	Saionji Kinmochi (18 Sept. 1896 – 28 Sept. 1896)
	Hachisuka Mochiaki (28 Sept. 1896 – 6 Nov. 1897)
	Hamao Arata (6 Nov. 1897 – 12 Jan. 1898)
Agriculture and Commerce	Enomoto Takeaki (18 Sept. 1896 – 29 Mar. 1897)
	Ōkuma Shigenobu (29 Mar. 1897 – 6 Nov. 1897)
	Yamada Nobumichi (8 Nov. 1897 – 12 Jan. 1898)
Communications	Shirane Sen'ichi (18 Sept. 1896 – 26 Sept. 1896)
	Nomura Yasushi (26 Sept. 1896 – 12 Jan. 1898)
Colonization	Takashima Tomonosuke (18 Sept. 1896 – 2 Sept. 1897, when the ministry was abolished)
Chief of Cabinet Secretariat	Takahashi Kenzō (18 Sept. 1896 – 8 Oct. 1897)
	Hirayama Narinobu (8 Oct. 1897 – 12 Jan. 1898)
Chief of Legislative Bureau	Kōmuchi Tomotsune (18 Sept. 1896 – 28 Oct. 1897)
	Ume Kenjirō (28 Oct. 1897 – 12 Jan. 1898)

Third Itō Cabinet
12 Jan. 1898 – 30 June 1898

Prime Minister	Itō Hirobumi
Foreign Affairs	Nishi Tokujirō
Home Affairs	Yoshikawa Akimasa
Finance	Inoue Kaoru
War	Katsura Tarō
Navy	Saigō Tsugumichi
Justice	Sone Arasuke
Education	Saionji Kinmochi (12 Jan. 1898 – 30 Apr. 1898)
	Toyama Shōichi (30 Apr. 1898 – 30 June 1898)
Agriculture and Commerce	Itō Miyoji (12 Jan. 1898 – 26 Apr. 1898)
	Kaneko Kentarō (26 Apr. 1898 – 30 June 1898)
Communications	Suematsu Kenchō
Chief of Cabinet Secretariat	Samejima Takenosuke
Chief of Legislative Bureau	Ume Kenjirō

First Ōkuma Cabinet
30 June 1898 – 8 Nov. 1898

Prime Minister	Ōkuma Shigenobu
Foreign Affairs	Ōkuma Shigenobu
Home Affairs	Itagaki Taisuke
Finance	Matsuda Masahisa
War	Katsura Tarō
Navy	Saigō Tsugumichi
Justice	Daitō Gitetsu
Education	Ozaki Yukio (30 June 1898 – 27 Oct. 1898)
	Inukai Tsuyoshi (27 Oct. 1898 – 8 Nov. 1898)
Agriculture and Commerce	Ōishi Masami
Communications	Hayashi Yūzō
Chief of Cabinet Secretariat	Taketomi Tokitoshi
Chief of Legislative Bureau	Kōmuchi Tomotsune

Second Yamagata Cabinet
8 Nov. 1898 – 19 Oct. 1900

Prime Minister	Yamagata Aritomo
Foreign Affairs	Aoki Shūzō
Home Affairs	Saigō Tsugumichi
Finance	Matsukata Masayoshi
War	Katsura Tarō
Navy	Yamamoto Gonnohyōe
Justice	Kiyoura Keigo
Education	Kabayama Sukenori
Agriculture and Commerce	Sone Arasuke
Communications	Yoshikawa Akimasa
Chief of Cabinet Secretariat	Yasuhiro Ban'ichirō
Chief of Legislative Bureau	Hirata Tōsuke

Fourth Itō Cabinet
19 Oct. 1900 – 2 June 1901

Prime Minister	Itō Hirobumi (19 Oct. 1900 – 2 May 1901, with Saionji Kinmochi acting or caretaker prime minister 27 Oct. 1900 – 12 Dec. 1900, 2 May 1901 – 2 June 1901)
Foreign Affairs	Katō Takaaki
Home Affairs	Suematsu Kenchō
Finance	Watanabe Kunitake (19 Oct. 1900 – 14 May 1901)
	Saionji Kinmochi (14 May 1901 – 2 June 1901)
War	Katsura Tarō (19 Oct. 1900 – 23 Dec. 1900)
	Kodama Gentarō (23 Dec. 1900 – 2 June 1901)
Navy	Yamamoto Gonnohyōe
Justice	Kaneko Kentarō
Education	Matsuda Masahisa
Agriculture and Commerce	Hayashi Yūzō
Communications	Hoshi Tōru (19 Oct. 1900 – 22 Dec. 1900)
	Hara Kei (22 Dec. 1900 – 2 June 1901)
Hanretsu	Saionji Kinmochi
Chief of Cabinet Secretariat	Samejima Takenosuke
Chief of Legislative Bureau	Okuda Yoshindo

First Katsura Cabinet
2 June 1901 – 7 Jan. 1906

Prime Minister	Katsura Tarō
Foreign Affairs	Sone Arasuke (2 June 1901 – 21 Sept. 1901)
	Komura Jūtarō (21 Sept. 1901 – 3 July 1905, 18 Oct. 1905 – 4 Nov. 1905, 2 – 7 Jan. 1906)
	Katsura Tarō (3 July – 18 Oct. 1905, 4 Nov. 1905 – 2 Jan. 1906)
Home Affairs	Utsumi Tadakatsu (2 June 1901 – 15 July 1903)
	Kodama Gentarō (15 July – 12 Oct. 1903)
	Katsura Tarō (12 Oct. 1903 – 20 Feb. 1904)
	Yoshikawa Akimasa (20 Feb. 1904 – 16 Sept. 1905)
	Kiyoura Keigo (16 Sept. 1905 – 7 Jan. 1906)
Finance	Sone Arasuke
War	Kodama Gentarō (2 June 1901 – 27 Mar. 1902)
	Terauchi Masatake (27 Mar. 1902 – 7 Jan. 1906)
Navy	Yamamoto Gonnohyōe

Justice	Kiyoura Keigo (2 June 1901 – 22 Sept. 1903)
	Hatano Takanao (22 Sept. 1903 – 7 Jan. 1906)
Education	Kikuchi Dairoku (2 June 1901 – 17 July 1903)
	Kodama Gentarō (17 July 1903 – 22 Sept. 1903)
	Kubota Yuzuru (22 Sept. 1903 – 14 Dec. 1905)
	Katsura Tarō (14 Dec. 1905 – 7 Jan. 1906)
Agriculture and Commerce	Hirata Tōsuke (2 June 1901 – 17 July 1903)
	Kiyoura Keigo (17 July 1903 – 7 Jan. 1906)
Communications	Yoshikawa Akimasa (2 June 1901 – 17 July 1903)
	Sone Arasuke (17 July – 22 Sept. 1903)
	Ōura Kanetake (22 Sept. 1903 – 7 Jan. 1906)
Chief of Cabinet Secretariat	Shibata Kamon
Chief of Legislative Bureau	Okuda Yoshindo (2 June 1901 – 26 Sept. 1902)
	Ichiki Kitokurō (26 Sept. 1902 – 7 Jan. 1906)

First Saionji Cabinet
7 Jan. 1906 – 14 July 1908

Prime Minister	Saionji Kinmochi
Foreign Affairs	Katō Takaaki (7 Jan. 1906 – 3 Mar. 1906)
	Saionji Kinmochi (3 Mar. 1906 – 19 May 1906, 30 Aug. 1906 – 18 Sept. 1906)
	Hayashi Tadasu (19 May – 30 Aug. 1906, 18 Sept. 1906 – 14 July 1908)
Home Affairs	Hara Kei
Finance	Sakatani Yoshio (7 Jan. 1906 – 14 Jan. 1908)
	Matsuda Masahisa (14 Jan. 1908 – 14 July 1908)
War	Terauchi Masatake
Navy	Saitō Makoto
Justice	Matsuda Masahisa (7 Jan. 1906 – 25 Mar. 1908)
	Senke Takatomi (25 Mar. 1908 – 14 July 1908)
Education	Saionji Kinmochi (7 Jan. 1906 – 27 Mar. 1906)
	Makino Nobuaki (27 Mar. 1906 – 14 July 1908)
Agriculture and Commerce	Matsuoka Yasutake
Communications	Yamagata Isaburō (7 Jan. 1906 – 14 Jan. 1908)
	Hara Kei (14 Jan. – 25 Mar. 1908)
	Hotta Masayasu (25 Mar. 1908 – 14 July 1908)

Chief of Cabinet Secretariat	Ishiwatari Bin'ichi (7 Jan. 1906 – 4 Jan. 1908)
	Minami Hiroshi (4 Jan. 1908 – 14 July 1908)
Chief of Legislative Bureau	Okano Keijirō

Second Katsura Cabinet 14 July 1908 – 30 Aug. 1911

Prime Minister	Katsura Tarō
Foreign Affairs	Terauchi Masatake (14 July 1908 – 27 Aug. 1908)
	Komura Jūtarō (27 Aug. 1908 – 30 Aug. 1911)
Home Affairs	Hirata Tōsuke
Finance	Katsura Tarō
War	Terauchi Masatake
Navy	Saitō Makoto
Justice	Okabe Nagamoto
Education	Komatsubara Eitarō
Agriculture and Commerce	Ōura Kanetake (14 July 1908 – 26 Mar. 1910, 3 Sept. 1910 – 30 Aug. 1911)
	Komatsubara Eitarō (28 Mar. – 3 Sept. 1910)
Communications	Gotō Shinpei
Chief of Cabinet Secretariat	Shibata Kamon
Chief of Legislative Bureau	Yasuhiro Ban'ichirō

Second Saionji Cabinet 30 Aug. 1911 – 21 Dec. 1912

Prime Minister	Saionji Kinmochi
Foreign Affairs	Uchida Kōsai (Hayashi Tadasu was acting minister 30 Aug. 1911 – 16 Oct. 1911)
Home Affairs	Hara Kei
Finance	Yamamoto Tatsuo
War	Ishimoto Shinroku (30 Aug. 1911 – 2 Apr. 1912)
	Uehara Yūsaku (5 Apr. 1912 – 21 Dec. 1912)
Navy	Saitō Makoto
Justice	Matsuda Masahisa
Education	Haseba Sumitaka (Makino Nobuaki was acting minister 9 Nov. – 21 Dec. 1912)
Agriculture and Commerce	Makino Nobuaki
Communications	Hayashi Tadasu
Chief of Cabinet Secretariat	Minami Hiroshi
Chief of Legislative Bureau	Okano Keijirō

Third Katsura Cabinet 21 Dec. 1912 – 20 Feb. 1913

Prime Minister	Katsura Tarō
Foreign Affairs	Katsura Tarō (21 Dec. 1912 – 29 Jan. 1913)
	Katō Takaaki (29 Jan. 1913 – 20 Feb. 1913)

Home Affairs	Ōura Kanetake
Finance	Wakatsuki Reijirō
War	Kigoshi Yasutsuna
Navy	Saitō Makoto
Justice	Matsumuro Itaru
Education	Shibata Kamon
Agriculture and Commerce	Nakakōji Ren
Communications	Gotō Shinpei
Chief of Cabinet Secretariat	Egi Tasuku
Chief of Legislative Bureau	Ichiki Kitokurō

First Yamamoto Cabinet
20 Feb. 1913 – 16 Apr. 1914

Prime Minister	Yamamoto Gonnohyōe
Foreign Affairs	Makino Nobuaki
Home Affairs	Hara Kei
Finance	Takahashi Korekiyo
War	Kigoshi Yasutsuna (20 Feb. 1913 – 24 June 1913)
	Kusunose Yukihiko (24 June 1913 – 16 Apr. 1914)
Navy	Saitō Makoto
Justice	Matsuda Masahisa (20 Feb. 1913 – 11 Nov. 1913)
	Okuda Yoshindo (11 Nov. 1913 – 16 Apr. 1914)
Education	Okuda Yoshindo (20 Feb. 1913 – 6 Mar. 1914)
	Ōoka Ikuzō (6 Mar. 1914 – 16 Apr. 1914)
Agriculture and Commerce	Yamamoto Tatsuo
Communications	Motoda Hajime
Chief of Cabinet Secretariat	Yamanouchi Kazutsugu
Chief of Legislative Bureau	Okano Keijirō (20 Feb. 1913 – 20 Sept. 1913)
	Kuratomi Yūzaburō (20 Sept. 1913 – 16 Apr. 1914)

Second Ōkuma Cabinet
16 Apr. 1914 – 9 Oct. 1916

Prime Minister	Ōkuma Shigenobu
Foreign Affairs	Katō Takaaki (6 Apr. 1914 – 10 Aug. 1915)
	Ōkuma Shigenobu (10 Aug. – 13 Oct. 1915)
	Ishii Kikujirō (13 Oct. 1915 – 9 Oct. 1916)
Home Affairs	Ōkuma Shigenobu (16 Apr. 1914 – 7 Jan. 1915, 30 July – 10 Aug. 1915)
	Ōura Kanetake (7 Jan. – 30 July 1915)
	Ichiki Kitokurō (10 Aug. 1915 – 9 Oct. 1916)
Finance	Wakatsuki Reijirō (16 Apr. 1914 – 10 Aug. 1915)
	Taketomi Tokitoshi (10 Aug. 1915 – 9 Oct. 1916)

Army	Oka Ichinosuke (16 Apr. 1914 – 30 Mar. 1916)
	Ōshima Ken'ichi (30 Mar. 1916 – 9 Oct. 1916)
Navy	Yasuhiro Rokurō (16 Apr. 1914 – 10 Aug. 1915)
	Katō Tomosaburō (10 Aug. 1915 – 9 Oct. 1916)
Justice	Ozaki Yukio
Education	Ichiki Kitokurō (16 Apr. 1914 – 10 Aug. 1915)
	Takada Sanae (10 Aug. 1915 – 9 Oct. 1916)
Agriculture and Commerce	Ōura Kanetake (16 Apr. 1914 – 7 Jan. 1915)
	Kōno Hironaka (7 Jan. 1915 – 9 Oct. 1916)
Communications	Taketomi Tokitoshi (16 Apr. 1914 – 10 Aug. 1915)
	Minoura Katsundo (10 Aug. 1915 – 9 Oct. 1916)
Chief of Cabinet Secretariat	Egi Tasuku
Chief of Legislative Bureau	Takahashi Sakue

Terauchi Cabinet
9 Oct. 1916 – 29 Sept. 1918

Prime Minister	Terauchi Masatake
Foreign Affairs	Terauchi Masatake (9 Oct. 1916 – 21 Nov. 1916)
	Motono Ichirō (21 Nov. 1916 – 23 Apr. 1918)
	Gotō Shinpei (23 Apr. 1918 – 29 Sept. 1918)
Home Affairs	Gotō Shinpei (9 Oct. 1916 – 23 Apr. 1918)
	Mizuno Rentarō (23 Apr. 1918 – 29 Sept. 1918)
Finance	Terauchi Masatake (9 Oct. 1916 – 6 Dec. 1916)
	Katsuta Kazue (6 Dec. 1916 – 29 Sept. 1918)
War	Ōshima Ken'ichi
Navy	Katō Tomosaburō
Justice	Matsumuro Itaru
Education	Okada Ryōhei
Agriculture and Commerce	Nakakōji Ren
Communications	Den Kenjirō
Chief of Cabinet Secretariat	Kodama Hideo
Chief of Legislative Bureau	Arimatsu Hideyoshi

Hara Cabinet
29 Sept. 1918 – 13 Nov. 1921

Prime Minister	Hara Kei (Uchida Kōsai was acting prime minister 4 – 13 Nov. 1921)
Foreign Affairs	Uchida Kōsai
Home Affairs	Tokonami Takejirō
Finance	Takahashi Korekiyo

War	Tanaka Giichi (29 Sept. 1918 – 9 June 1921) Yamanashi Hanzō (9 June 1921 – 13 Nov. 1921)
Navy	Katō Tomosaburō (Hara Kei was acting minister 12 Oct. – 4 Nov. 1921; Uchida Kōsai 5 – 13 Nov. 1921)
Justice	Hara Kei (29 Sept. 1918 – 15 May 1920) Ōki Enkichi (15 May 1920 – 13 Nov. 1921)
Education	Nakahashi Tokugorō
Agriculture and Commerce	Yamamoto Tatsuo
Communications	Noda Utarō
Railways (est. 15 May 1920)	Motoda Hajime
Chief of Cabinet Secretariat	Takahashi Mitsutake
Chief of Legislative Bureau	Yokota Sennosuke

Takahashi Cabinet
13 Nov. 1921 – 12 June 1922

Prime Minister	Takahashi Korekiyo
Foreign Affairs	Uchida Kōsai
Home Affairs	Tokonami Takejirō
Finance	Takahashi Korekiyo
War	Yamanashi Hanzō
Navy	Katō Tomosaburō (Takahashi Korekiyo was acting minister 13 Nov. 1921 – 10 Mar. 1922)
Justice	Ōki Enkichi
Education	Nakahashi Tokugorō
Agriculture and Commerce	Yamamoto Tatsuo
Communications	Noda Utarō
Railways	Motoda Hajime
Chief of Cabinet Secretariat	Mitsuchi Chūzō
Chief of Legislative Bureau	Yokota Sennosuke (13 Nov. 1921 – 28 Mar. 1922) Baba Eiichi (28 Mar. 1922 – 12 June 1922)

Katō Tomosaburō Cabinet
12 June 1922 – 2 Sept. 1923

Prime Minister	Katō Tomosaburō (Uchida Kōsai was acting prime minister 25 Aug. – 2 Sept. 1923)
Foreign Affairs	Uchida Kōsai
Home Affairs	Mizuno Rentarō
Finance	Ichiki Otohiko
War	Yamanashi Hanzō
Navy	Katō Tomosaburō (12 June 1922 – 15 May 1923) Takarabe Takeshi (15 May 1923 – 2 Sept. 1923)
Justice	Okano Keijirō
Education	Kamata Eikichi
Agriculture and Commerce	Arai Kentarō
Communications	Maeda Toshisada
Railways	Ōki Enkichi

Chief of Cabinet Secretariat	Miyata Mitsuo
Chief of Legislative Bureau	Baba Eiichi

Second Yamamoto Cabinet
2 Sept. 1923 – 7 Jan. 1924

Prime Minister	Yamamoto Gonnohyōe
Foreign Affairs	Yamamoto Gonnohyōe (2 – 19 Sept. 1923)
	Ijūin Hikokichi (19 Sept. 1923 – 7 Jan. 1924)
Home Affairs	Gotō Shinpei
Finance	Inoue Junnosuke
War	Tanaka Giichi
Navy	Takarabe Takeshi
Justice	Den Kenjirō (2 – 6 Sept. 1923)
	Hiranuma Kiichirō (6 Sept. 1923 – 7 Jan. 1924)
Education	Inukai Tsuyoshi (2 – 6 Sept. 1923)
	Okano Keijirō (6 Sept. 1923 – 7 Jan. 1924)
Agriculture and Commerce	Den Kenjirō (2 Sept. 1923 – 24 Dec. 1923)
	Okano Keijirō (24 Dec. 1923 – 7 Jan. 1924)
Communications	Inukai Tsuyoshi
Railways	Yamanouchi Kazutsugu
Chief of Cabinet Secretariat	Kabayama Sukehide
Chief of Legislative Bureau	Matsumoto Jōji

Kiyoura Cabinet
7 Jan. 1924 – 11 June 1924

Prime Minister	Kiyoura Keigo
Foreign Affairs	Matsui Keishirō
Home Affairs	Mizuno Rentarō
Finance	Katsuta Kazue
War	Ugaki Kazushige
Navy	Murakami Kakuichi
Justice	Suzuki Kisaburō
Education	Egi Kazuyuki
Agriculture and Commerce	Maeda Toshisada
Communications	Fujimura Yoshirō
Railways	Komatsu Kenjirō
Chief of Cabinet Secretariat	Kobashi Ichita
Chief of Legislative Bureau	Satake Sango

First Katō Takaaki Cabinet
11 June 1924 – 2 Aug. 1925

Prime Minister	Katō Takaaki
Foreign Affairs	Shidehara Kijūrō
Home Affairs	Wakatsuki Reijirō
Finance	Hamaguchi Osachi
War	Ugaki Kazushige
Navy	Takarabe Takeshi
Justice	Yokota Sennosuke (11 June 1924 – 5 Feb. 1925)
	Takahashi Korekiyo (5 – 9 Feb. 1925)
	Ogawa Heikichi (9 Feb. 1925 – 2 Aug. 1925)

Education	Okada Ryōhei
Agriculture and Commerce	Takahashi Korekiyo (11 June 1924–1 Apr. 1925, when the ministry was abolished)
Agriculture and Forestry (est. 1 Apr. 1925)	Takahashi Korekiyo (1–17 Apr. 1925) Okazaki Kunisuke (17 Apr. 1925–2 Aug. 1925)
Commerce and Industry (est. 1 Apr. 1925)	Takahashi Korekiyo (1–17 Apr. 1925) Noda Utarō (17 Apr. 1925–2 Aug. 1925)
Communications	Inukai Tsuyoshi (11 June 1924–30 May 1925) Adachi Kenzō (31 May 1925–2 Aug. 1925)
Railways	Sengoku Mitsugu
Chief of Cabinet Secretariat	Egi Tasuku
Chief of Legislative Bureau	Tsukamoto Seiji

Second Katō Takaaki Cabinet
2 Aug. 1925–30 Jan. 1926

Prime Minister	Katō Takaaki (Wakatsuki Reijirō was acting prime minister 26–30 Jan. 1926)
Foreign Affairs	Shidehara Kijūrō
Home Affairs	Wakatsuki Reijirō
Finance	Hamaguchi Osachi
War	Ugaki Kazushige
Navy	Takarabe Takeshi
Justice	Egi Tasuku
Education	Okada Ryōhei
Agriculture and Forestry	Hayami Seiji
Commerce and Industry	Kataoka Naoharu
Communications	Adachi Kenzō
Railways	Sengoku Mitsugu
Chief of Cabinet Secretariat	Tsukamoto Seiji
Chief of Legislative Bureau	Yamakawa Tadao

First Wakatsuki Cabinet
30 Jan. 1926–20 Apr. 1927

Prime Minister	Wakatsuki Reijirō
Foreign Affairs	Shidehara Kijūrō
Home Affairs	Wakatsuki Reijirō (30 Jan. 1926–3 June 1926) Hamaguchi Osachi (3 June 1926–16 Dec. 1926, 15 Mar. 1927–20 Apr. 1927) Adachi Kenzō (16 Dec. 1926–15 Mar. 1927)
Finance	Hamaguchi Osachi (30 Jan. 1926–3 June 1926) Hayami Seiji (3 June 1926–14 Sept. 1926) Kataoka Naoharu (14 Sept. 1926–20 Apr. 1927)
War	Ugaki Kazushige
Navy	Takarabe Takeshi
Justice	Egi Tasuku

Education	Okada Ryōhei
Agriculture and Forestry	Hayami Seiji (30 Jan. 1926 – 3 June 1926)
	Machida Chūji (3 June 1926 – 20 Apr. 1927)
Commerce and Industry	Kataoka Naoharu (30 Jan. 1926 – 14 Sept. 1926)
	Fujisawa Ikunosuke (14 Sept. 1926 – 20 Apr. 1927)
Communications	Adachi Kenzō
Railways	Sengoku Mitsugu (30 Jan. 1926 – 3 June 1926)
	Inoue Tadashirō (3 June 1926 – 20 Apr. 1927)
Chief of Cabinet Secretariat	Tsukamoto Seiji
Chief of Legislative Bureau	Yamakawa Tadao

Tanaka Giichi Cabinet
20 Apr. 1927 – 2 July 1929

Prime Minister	Tanaka Giichi
Foreign Affairs	Tanaka Giichi
Home Affairs	Suzuki Kisaburō (20 Apr. 1927 – 4 May 1928)
	Tanaka Giichi (4 – 23 May 1928)
	Mochizuki Keisuke (23 May 1928 – 2 July 1929)
Finance	Takahashi Korekiyo (20 Apr. 1927 – 2 June 1927)
	Mitsuchi Chūzō (2 June 1927 – 2 July 1929)
War	Shirakawa Yoshinori
Navy	Okada Keisuke
Justice	Hara Yoshimichi
Education	Mitsuchi Chūzō (20 Apr. 1927 – 2 June 1927)
	Mizuno Rentarō (2 June 1927 – 25 May 1928)
	Katsuta Kazue (25 May 1928 – 2 July 1929)
Agriculture and Forestry	Yamamoto Teijirō
Commerce and Industry	Nakahashi Tokugorō
Communications	Mochizuki Keisuke (20 Apr. 1927 – 23 May 1928)
	Kuhara Fusanosuke (23 May 1928 – 2 July 1929)
Railways	Ogawa Heikichi
Colonization (est. 10 June 1929)	Tanaka Giichi
Chief of Cabinet Secretariat	Hatoyama Ichirō
Chief of Legislative Bureau	Maeda Yonezō

Hamaguchi Cabinet
2 July 1929 – 14 Apr. 1931

Prime Minister	Hamaguchi Osachi (Shidehara Kijūrō was acting prime minister 15 Nov. 1930 – 9 Mar. 1931)

Foreign Affairs	Shidehara Kijūrō
Home Affairs	Adachi Kenzō
Finance	Inoue Junnosuke
War	Ugaki Kazushige (2 July 1929 – 16 June 1930, 10 Dec. 1930 – 14 Apr. 1931)
	Abe Nobuyuki (16 June 1930 – 10 Dec. 1930)
Navy	Takarabe Takeshi (2 July 1929 – 3 Oct. 1930, but Hamaguchi was acting minister 26 Nov. 1929 – 19 May 1930)
	Abo Kiyokazu (3 Oct. 1930 – 14 Apr. 1931)
Justice	Watanabe Chifuyu
Education	Kobashi Ichita (2 July 1929 – 29 Nov. 1929)
	Tanaka Ryūzō (29 Nov. 1929 – 14 Apr. 1931)
Agriculture and Forestry	Machida Chūji
Commerce and Industry	Tawara Magoichi
Communications	Koizumi Matajirō
Railways	Egi Tasuku
Colonization	Matsuda Genji
Hanretsu	Abe Nobuyuki (16 June – 10 Dec. 1930)
Chief of Cabinet Secretariat	Suzuki Fujiya
Chief of Legislative Bureau	Kawasaki Takukichi

Second Wakatsuki Cabinet
14 Apr. 1931 – 13 Dec. 1931

Prime Minister	Wakatsuki Reijirō
Foreign Affairs	Shidehara Kijūrō
Home Affairs	Adachi Kenzō
Finance	Inoue Junnosuke
War	Minami Jirō
Navy	Abo Kiyokazu
Justice	Watanabe Chifuyu
Education	Tanaka Ryūzō
Agriculture and Forestry	Machida Chūji
Commerce and Industry	Sakurauchi Yukio
Communications	Koizumi Matajirō
Railways	Egi Tasuku (14 Apr. 1931 – 10 Sept. 1931)
	Hara Shūjirō (10 Sept. 1931 – 13 Dec. 1931)
Colonization	Hara Shūjirō (14 Apr. 1931 – 10 Sept. 1931)
	Wakatsuki Reijirō (10 Sept. 1931 – 13 Dec. 1931)
Chief of Cabinet Secretariat	Kawasaki Takukichi
Chief of Legislative Bureau	Takenouchi Sakuhei (15 Apr. 1931 – 9 Nov. 1931)
	Saitō Takao (9 Nov. 1931 – 13 Dec. 1931)

Inukai Cabinet
13 Dec. 1931 – 26 May 1932

Prime Minister	Inukai Tsuyoshi (Takahashi Korekiyo acted as caretaker prime minister 16 – 26 May 1932)

Foreign Affairs	Inukai Tsuyoshi (13 Dec. 1931–14 Jan. 1932)
	Yoshizawa Kenkichi (14 Jan. 1932–26 May 1932)
Home Affairs	Nakahashi Tokugorō (13 Dec. 1931–16 Mar. 1932)
	Inukai Tsuyoshi (16–25 Mar. 1932)
	Suzuki Kisaburō (25 Mar. 1932–26 May 1932)
Finance	Takahashi Korekiyo
War	Araki Sadao
Navy	Ōsumi Mineo
Justice	Suzuki Kisaburō (13 Dec. 1931–25 Mar. 1932)
	Kawamura Takeji (25 Mar. 1932–26 May 1932)
Education	Hatoyama Ichirō
Agriculture and Forestry	Yamamoto Teijirō
Commerce and Industry	Maeda Yonezō
Communications	Mitsuchi Chūzō
Railways	Tokonami Takejirō
Colonization	Hata Toyosuke
Chief of Cabinet Secretariat	Mori Kaku
Chief of Legislative Bureau	Shimada Toshio

Saitō Cabinet
26 May 1932–8 July 1934

Prime Minister	Saitō Makoto
Foreign Affairs	Saitō Makoto (26 May 1932–6 July 1932)
	Uchida Kōsai (6 July 1932–14 Sept. 1933)
	Hirota Kōki (14 Sept. 1933–8 July 1934)
Home Affairs	Yamamoto Tatsuo
Finance	Takahashi Korekiyo
War	Araki Sadao (26 May 1932–23 Jan. 1934)
	Hayashi Senjūrō (23 Jan. 1934–8 July 1934)
Navy	Okada Keisuke (26 May 1932–9 Jan. 1933)
	Ōsumi Mineo (9 Jan. 1933–8 July 1934)
Justice	Koyama Matsukichi
Education	Hatoyama Ichirō (26 May 1932–3 Mar. 1934)
	Saitō Makoto (3 Mar. 1934–8 July 1934)
Agriculture and Forestry	Gotō Fumio
Commerce and Industry	Nakajima Kumakichi (26 May 1932–9 Feb. 1934)
	Matsumoto Jōji (9 Feb. 1934–8 July 1934)
Communications	Minami Hiroshi
Railways	Mitsuchi Chūzō
Colonization	Nagai Ryūtarō
Chief of Cabinet Secretariat	Shibata Zenzaburō (26 May 1932–13 Mar. 1933)
	Horikiri Zenjirō (13 Mar. 1933–8 July 1934)

Chief of Legislative Bureau	Horikiri Zenjirō (26 May 1932–13 Mar. 1933)
	Kurosaki Teizō (13 Mar. 1933–8 July 1934)

Okada Cabinet
8 July 1934–9 Mar. 1936

Prime Minister	Okada Keisuke (Gotō Fumio was acting prime minister 26–29 Feb. 1936)
Foreign Affairs	Hirota Kōki
Home Affairs	Gotō Fumio
Finance	Fujii Sanenobu (8 July 1934–26 Nov. 1934)
	Takahashi Korekiyo (27 Nov. 1934–26 Feb. 1936)
	Machida Chūji (27 Feb. 1936–9 Mar. 1936)
War	Hayashi Senjūrō (8 July 1934–5 Sept. 1935)
	Kawashima Yoshiyuki (5 Sept. 1935–9 Mar. 1936)
Navy	Ōsumi Mineo
Justice	Ohara Naoshi
Education	Matsuda Genji (8 July 1934–1 Feb. 1936)
	Kawasaki Takukichi (2 Feb. 1936–9 Mar. 1936)
Agriculture and Forestry	Yamazaki Tatsunosuke
Commerce and Industry	Machida Chūji
Communications	Tokonami Takejirō (8 July 1934–8 Sept. 1935)
	Okada Keisuke (9–12 Sept. 1935)
	Mochizuki Keisuke (12 Sept. 1935–9 Mar. 1936)
Railways	Uchida Nobuya
Colonization	Okada Keisuke (8 July 1934–25 Oct. 1934)
	Kodama Hideo (25 Oct. 1934–9 Mar. 1936)
Chief of Cabinet Secretariat	Kawada Isao (8 July 1934–20 Oct. 1934)
	Yoshida Shigeru (20 Oct. 1934–11 May 1935)
	Shirane Takesuke (11 May 1935–9 Mar. 1936)
Chief of Legislative Bureau	Kanamori Tokujirō (8 July 1934–11 Jan. 1936)
	Ōhashi Hachirō (11 Jan. 1936–9 Mar. 1936)

Hirota Cabinet
9 Mar. 1936–2 Feb. 1937

Prime Minister	Hirota Kōki
Foreign Affairs	Hirota Kōki (9 Mar.–2 Apr. 1936)
	Arita Hachirō (2 Apr. 1936–2 Feb. 1937)
Home Affairs	Ushio Keinosuke
Finance	Baba Eiichi

War	Terauchi Hisaichi
Navy	Nagano Osami
Justice	Hayashi Raizaburō
Education	Ushio Keinosuke (9–25 Mar. 1936)
	Hirao Hachisaburō (25 Mar. 1936–2 Feb. 1937)
Agriculture and Forestry	Shimada Toshio
Commerce and Industry	Kawasaki Takukichi (9–27 Mar. 1936)
	Ogawa Gōtarō (28 Mar. 1936–2 Feb. 1937)
Communications	Tanomogi Keikichi
Railways	Maeda Yonezō
Colonization	Nagata Hidejirō
Chief of Cabinet Secretariat	Fujinuma Shōhei
Chief of Legislative Bureau	Tsugita Daizaburō

Hayashi Cabinet
2 Feb. 1937–4 June 1937

Prime Minister	Hayashi Senjūrō
Foreign Affairs	Hayashi Senjūrō (2 Feb. 1937–3 Mar. 1937)
	Satō Naotake (3 Mar. 1937–4 June 1937)
Home Affairs	Kawarada Kakichi
Finance	Yūki Toyotarō
War	Nakamura Kōtarō (2–9 Feb. 1937)
	Sugiyama Gen (9 Feb. 1937–4 June 1937)
Navy	Yonai Mitsumasa
Justice	Shiono Suehiko
Education	Hayashi Senjūrō
Agriculture and Forestry	Yamazaki Tatsunosuke
Commerce and Industry	Godō Takuo
Communications	Yamazaki Tatsunosuke (2–10 Feb. 1937)
	Kodama Hideo (10 Feb. 1937–4 June 1937)
Railways	Godō Takuo
Colonization	Yūki Toyotarō
Chief of Cabinet Secretariat	Ōhashi Hachirō
Chief of Legislative Bureau	Kawagoe Takeo

First Konoe Cabinet
4 June 1937–5 Jan. 1939

Prime Minister	Konoe Fumimaro
Foreign Affairs	Hirota Kōki (4 June 1937–26 May 1938)
	Ugaki Kazushige (26 May–30 Sept. 1938)
	Konoe Fumimaro (30 Sept.–29 Oct. 1938)
	Arita Hachirō (29 Oct. 1938–5 Jan. 1939)
Home Affairs	Baba Eiichi (4 June 1937–14 Dec. 1937)
	Suetsugu Nobumasa (14 Dec. 1937–5 Jan. 1939)
Finance	Kaya Okinori (4 June 1937–26 May 1938)
	Ikeda Shigeaki (26 May 1938–5 Jan. 1939)
War	Sugiyama Gen (4 June 1937–3 June 1938)
	Itagaki Seishirō (3 June 1938–5 Jan. 1939)

Navy	Yonai Mitsumasa
Justice	Shiono Suehiko
Education	Yasui Eiji (4 June 1937–22 Oct. 1937)
	Kido Kōichi (22 Oct. 1937–26 May 1938)
	Araki Sadao (26 May 1938–5 Jan. 1939)
Agriculture and Forestry	Arima Yoriyasu
Commerce and Industry	Yoshino Shinji (4 June 1937–26 May 1938)
	Ikeda Shigeaki (26 May 1938–5 Jan. 1939)
Communications	Nagai Ryūtarō
Railways	Nakajima Chikuhei
Colonization	Ōtani Sonyū (4 June 1937–25 June 1938)
	Ugaki Kazushige (25 June–30 Sept. 1938)
	Konoe Fumimaro (30 Sept.–29 Oct. 1938)
	Hatta Yoshiaki (29 Oct. 1938–5 Jan. 1939)
Welfare (est. 11 Jan. 1938)	Kido Kōichi
Chief of Cabinet Secretariat	Kazami Akira
Chief of Legislative Bureau	Taki Masao (4 June 1937–25 Oct. 1937)
	Funada Naka (25 Oct. 1937–5 Jan. 1939)

Hiranuma Cabinet
5 Jan. 1939–30 Aug. 1939

Prime Minister	Hiranuma Kiichirō
Foreign Affairs	Arita Hachirō
Home Affairs	Kido Kōichi
Finance	Ishiwata Sōtarō
War	Itagaki Seishirō
Navy	Yonai Mitsumasa
Justice	Shiono Suehiko
Education	Araki Sadao
Agriculture and Forestry	Sakurauchi Yukio
Commerce and Industry	Hatta Yoshiaki
Communications	Shiono Suehiko (5 Jan. 1939–7 Apr. 1939)
	Tanabe Harumichi (7 Apr. 1939–30 Aug. 1939)
Railways	Maeda Yonezō
Colonization	Hatta Yoshiaki (5 Jan. 1939–7 Apr. 1939)
	Koiso Kuniaki (7 Apr. 1939–30 Aug. 1939)
Welfare	Hirose Hisatada
Hanretsu	Konoe Fumimaro
Chief of Cabinet Secretariat	Tanabe Harumichi (5 Jan. 1939–7 Apr. 1939)
	Ōta Kōzō (7 Apr. 1939–30 Aug. 1939)
Chief of Legislative Bureau	Kurosaki Teizō

Abe Cabinet
30 Aug. 1939–16 Jan. 1940

Prime Minister	Abe Nobuyuki
Foreign Affairs	Abe Nobuyuki (30 Aug.–25 Sept. 1939)
	Nomura Kichisaburō (25 Sept. 1939–16 Jan. 1940)
Home Affairs	Ohara Naoshi

Finance	Aoki Kazuo
War	Hata Shunroku
Navy	Yoshida Zengo
Justice	Miyagi Chōgorō
Education	Kawarada Kakichi
Agriculture and Forestry	Godō Takuo (30 Aug. 1939–16 Oct. 1939)
	Sakai Tadamasa (16 Oct. 1939–16 Jan. 1940)
Commerce and Industry	Godō Takuo
Communications	Nagai Ryūtarō
Railways	Nagai Ryūtarō (30 Aug. 1939–29 Nov. 1939)
	Nagata Hidejirō (29 Nov. 1939–16 Jan. 1940)
Colonization	Kanemitsu Tsuneo
Welfare	Ohara Naoshi (30 Aug. 1939–29 Nov. 1939)
	Akita Kiyoshi (29 Nov. 1939–16 Jan. 1940)
Chief of Cabinet Secretariat	Endō Ryūsaku
Chief of Legislative Bureau	Karasawa Toshiki

Yonai Cabinet
16 Jan. 1940–22 July 1940

Prime Minister	Yonai Mitsumasa
Foreign Affairs	Arita Hachirō
Home Affairs	Kodama Hideo
Finance	Sakurauchi Yukio
War	Hata Shunroku
Navy	Yoshida Zengo
Justice	Kimura Naotatsu
Education	Matsuura Shinjirō
Agriculture and Forestry	Shimada Toshio
Commerce and Industry	Fujihara Ginjirō
Communications	Katsu Masanori
Railways	Matsuno Tsuruhei
Colonization	Koiso Kuniaki
Welfare	Yoshida Shigeru
Chief of Cabinet Secretariat	Ishiwata Sōtarō
Chief of Legislative Bureau	Hirose Hisatada

Second Konoe Cabinet
22 July 1940–18 July 1941

Prime Minister	Konoe Fumimaro
Foreign Affairs	Matsuoka Yōsuke (Konoe was acting minister 12 Mar.–22 Apr. 1941)
Home Affairs	Yasui Eiji (22 July 1940–21 Dec. 1940)
	Hiranuma Kiichirō (21 Dec. 1940–18 July 1941)
Finance	Kawada Isao
War	Tōjō Hideki
Navy	Yoshida Zengo (22 July 1940–5 Sept. 1940)

	Oikawa Koshirō (5 Sept. 1940–18 July 1941)
Justice	Kazami Akira (22 July 1940–21 Dec. 1940)
	Yanagawa Heisuke (21 Dec. 1940–18 July 1940)
Education	Hashida Kunihiko
Agriculture and Forestry	Konoe Fumimaro (22–24 July 1940)
	Ishiguro Tadaatsu (24 July 1940–11 June 1941)
	Ino Tetsuya (11 June 1941–18 July 1941)
Commerce and Industry	Kobayashi Ichizō (22 July 1940–4 Apr. 1941, but Kawada Isao was acting minister 31 Aug. 1940–2 Nov. 1940)
	Toyoda Teijirō (4 Apr. 1941–18 July 1941)
Communications	Murata Shōzō
Railways	Murata Shōzō (22 July 1940–28 Sept. 1940)
	Ogawa Gōtarō (28 Sept. 1940–18 July 1941)
Colonization	Matsuoka Yōsuke (22 July 1940–28 Sept. 1940)
	Akita Kiyoshi (28 Sept. 1940–18 July 1941)
Welfare	Yasui Eiji (22 July 1940–28 Sept. 1940)
	Kanemitsu Tsuneo (28 Sept. 1940–18 July 1941)
Ministers of State	Hiranuma Kiichirō (6–21 Dec. 1940)
	Hoshino Naoki (6 Dec. 1940–4 Apr. 1941)
	Ogura Masatsune (2 Apr. 1941–18 July 1941)
	Suzuki Teiichi (4 Apr. 1941–18 July 1941)
Hanretsu	Hoshino Naoki (22 July 1940–6 Dec. 1940)
Chief of Cabinet Secretariat	Tomita Kenji
Chief of Legislative Bureau	Murase Naokai

Third Konoe Cabinet
18 July 1941–18 Oct. 1941

Prime Minister	Konoe Fumimaro
Foreign Affairs	Toyoda Teijirō
Home Affairs	Tanabe Harumichi
Finance	Ogura Masatsune
War	Tōjō Hideki
Navy	Oikawa Koshirō
Justice	Konoe Fumimaro (18–25 July 1941)
	Iwamura Michiyo (25 July 1941–18 Oct. 1941)
Education	Hashida Kunihiko
Agriculture and Forestry	Ino Tetsuya
Commerce and Industry	Sakonji Masazō

Communications	Murata Shōzō
Railways	Murata Shōzō
Colonization	Toyoda Teijirō
Welfare	Koizumi Chikahiko
Ministers of State	Hiranuma Kiichirō
	Suzuki Teiichi
	Yanagawa Heisuke
Chief of Cabinet Secretariat	Tomita Kenji
Chief of Legislative Bureau	Murase Naokai

Tōjō Cabinet
18 Oct. 1941–22 July 1944

Prime Minister	Tōjō Hideki
Foreign Affairs	Tōgō Shigenori (18 Oct. 1941–1 Sept. 1942)
	Tōjō Hideki (1–17 Sept. 1942)
	Tani Masayuki (17 Sept. 1942–20 Apr. 1943)
	Shigemitsu Mamoru (20 Apr. 1943–22 July 1944)
Home Affairs	Tōjō Hideki (18 Oct. 1941–17 Feb. 1942)
	Yuzawa Michio (17 Feb. 1942–20 Apr. 1943, but Tōjō was acting minister 25 Nov. 1942–4 Jan. 1943)
	Andō Kisaburō (20 Apr. 1943–22 July 1944)
Finance	Kaya Okinori (18 Oct. 1942–19 Feb. 1944)
	Ishiwata Sōtarō (19 Feb. 1944–22 July 1944)
War	Tōjō Hideki
Navy	Shimada Shigetarō (18 Oct. 1941–17 July 1944)
	Nomura Naokuni (17–22 July 1944)
Justice	Iwamura Michiyo
Education	Hashida Kunihiko (18 Oct. 1941–20 Apr. 1943)
	Tōjō Hideki (20–23 Apr. 1943)
	Okabe Nagakage (23 Apr. 1943–22 July 1944)
Agriculture and Forestry	Ino Hiroya (18 Oct. 1941–20 Apr. 1943)
	Yamazaki Tatsunosuke (20 Apr. 1943–1 Nov. 1943, when the ministry was abolished)
Agriculture and Commerce (est. 1 Nov. 1943)	Yamazaki Tatsunosuke (1 Nov. 1943–19 Feb. 1944)
	Uchida Nobuya (19 Feb. 1944–22 July 1944)
Commerce and Industry	Kishi Nobusuke (18 Oct. 1941–8 Oct. 1943)
	Tōjō Hideki (8 Oct. 1943–1 Nov. 1943, when the ministry was abolished)
Munitions (est. 1 Nov. 1943)	Tōjō Hideki

Communications	Terajima Ken (18 Oct. 1941–8 Oct. 1943) Hatta Yoshiaki (8 Oct. 1943–1 Nov. 1943, when the ministry was abolished)
Transport and Communications (est. 1 Nov. 1943)	Hatta Yoshiaki (1 Nov. 1943–19 Feb. 1944) Gotō Keita (19 Feb. 1943–22 July 1944)
Railways	Terajima Ken (18 Oct. 1941–2 Dec. 1941) Hatta Yoshiaki (2 Dec. 1941–1 Nov. 1943, when the ministry was abolished)
Colonization	Tōgō Shigenori (18 Oct. 1941–2 Dec. 1941) Ino Hiroya (2 Dec. 1941–1 Nov. 1942, when the ministry was abolished)
Greater East Asia (est. 1 Nov. 1942)	Aoki Kazuo
Welfare	Koizumi Chikahiko
State	Suzuki Teiichi Andō Kisaburō (9 June 1942–20 Apr. 1943) Aoki Kazuo (17 Sept. 1942–1 Nov. 1942 Ōasa Tadao (20 Apr. 1943–22 July 1944) Gotō Fumio (26 May 1943–22 July 1944) Kishi Nobusuke (8 Oct. 1943–22 July 1944) Fujihara Ginjirō (17 Nov. 1943–22 July 1944)
Chief of Cabinet Secretariat	Hoshino Naoki
Chief of Legislative Bureau	Moriyama Toshikazu

Koiso Cabinet
22 July 1944–7 Apr. 1945

Prime Minister	Koiso Kuniaki
Foreign Affairs	Shigemitsu Mamoru
Home Affairs	Ōdachi Shigeo
Finance	Ishiwata Sōtarō (22 July 1944–21 Feb. 1945) Tsushima Juichi (21 Feb. 1945–7 Apr. 1945)
War	Sugiyama Gen
Navy	Yonai Mitsumasa
Justice	Matsuzaka Hiromasa
Education	Ninomiya Harushige (22 July 1944–26 Jan. 1945) Kodama Hideo (acting minister 26 Jan.–10 Feb. 1945, then minister 10 Feb.–7 Apr. 1945)
Agriculture and Commerce	Shimada Toshio
Munitions	Fujihara Ginjirō (22 July 1944–19 Dec. 1944) Yoshida Shigeru (19 Dec. 1944–7 Apr. 1945)
Transport and Communications	Maeda Yonezō
Greater East Asia	Shigemitsu Mamoru

Welfare	Hirose Hisatada (22 July 1944–10 Feb. 1945)
	Aikawa Katsuroku (10 Feb. 1945–7 Apr. 1945)
State	Machida Chūji
	Ogata Taketora
	Kodama Hideo (22 July 1944–10 Feb. 1945)
	Kobayashi Seizō (19 Dec. 1944–1 Mar. 1945)
	Hirose Hisatada (10–21 Feb. 1945)
	Ishiwata Sōtarō (21 Feb. 1945–7 Apr. 1945)
Chief of Cabinet Secretariat	Miura Kunio (22–29 July 1944)
	Tanaka Takeo (29 July 1944–10 Feb. 1945)
	Hirose Hisatada (10–21 Feb. 1945)
	Ishiwata Sōtarō (21 Feb. 1945–7 Apr. 1945)
Chief of Legislative Bureau	Miura Kunio

Suzuki Kantarō Cabinet
7 Apr. 1945–17 Aug. 1945

Prime Minister	Suzuki Kantarō
Foreign Affairs	Suzuki Kantarō (7–9 Apr. 1945)
	Tōgō Shigenori (9 Apr 1945–17 Aug. 1945)
Home Affairs	Abe Genki
Finance	Hirose Toyosaku
War	Anami Korechika
Navy	Yonai Mitsumasa
Justice	Matsuzaka Hiromasa
Education	Ōta Kōzō
Agriculture and Commerce	Ishiguro Tadaatsu
Munitions	Toyoda Teijirō
Transport and Communications	Toyoda Teijirō (7–11 Apr. 1945)
	Kobiyama Naoto (11 Apr.–19 May 1945, when the ministry was abolished)
Transport (est. 19 May 1945)	Kobiyama Naoto (19 May 1945–17 Aug. 1945)
Greater East Asia	Suzuki Kantarō (7–9 Apr. 1945)
	Tōgō Shigenori (9 Apr. 1945–17 Aug. 1945)
Welfare	Okada Tadahiko
State	Sakurai Heigorō
	Shimomura Hiroshi
	Sakonji Masazō
	Yasui Tōji (11 Apr. 1945–17 Aug. 1945)
Chief of Cabinet Secretariat	Sakomizu Hisatsune
Chief of Legislative Bureau	Murase Naokai

Higashikuni Cabinet
17 Aug. 1945–9 Oct. 1945

Prime Minister	Higashikuni Naruhiko
Foreign Affairs	Shigemitsu Mamoru (17 Aug. 1945–17 Sept. 1945)
	Yoshida Shigeru (17 Sept. 1945–9 Oct. 1945)
Home Affairs	Yamazaki Iwao
Finance	Tsushima Juichi
War	Higashikuni Naruhiko (17–23 Aug. 1945)
	Shimomura Sadamu (23 Aug. 1945–9 Oct. 1945)
Navy	Yonai Mitsumasa
Justice	Iwata Chūzō
Education	Matsumura Kenzō (17–18 Aug. 1945)
	Maeda Tamon (18 Aug. 1945–9 Oct. 1945)
Agriculture and Commerce	Sengoku Kōtarō (17 Aug. 1945–26 Aug. 1945, when the ministry was abolished)
Agriculture and Forestry (est. 26 Aug. 1945)	Sengoku Kōtarō
Munitions	Nakajima Chikuhei (17 Aug. 1945–26 Aug. 1945, when the ministry was abolished)
Commerce and Industry (est. 26 Aug. 1945)	Nakajima Chikuhei
Transport	Kobiyama Naoto
Greater East Asia	Shigemitsu Mamoru (17 Aug. 1945–26 Aug. 1945, when the ministry was abolished)
Welfare	Matsumura Kenzō
State	Konoe Fumimaro
	Ogata Taketora
	Obata Toshishirō (19 Aug. 1945–9 Oct. 1945)
Chief of Cabinet Secretariat	Ogata Taketora
Chief of Legislative Bureau	Murase Naokai

Shidehara Cabinet
9 Oct. 1945–22 May 1946

Prime Minister	Shidehara Kijūrō
Foreign Affairs	Yoshida Shigeru
Home Affairs	Horikiri Zenjirō (9 Oct. 1945–13 Jan. 1946)
	Mitsuchi Chūzō (13 Jan. 1946–22 May 1946)
Finance	Shibusawa Keizō
War	Shimomura Sadamu (9 Oct. 1945–1 Dec. 1945, when the ministry was abolished)
First Demobilization (est. 1 Dec. 1945)	Shidehara Kijūrō
Navy	Yonai Mitsumasa (9 Oct.–1 Dec. 1945, when the ministry was abolished)

Second Demobilization (est. 1 Dec. 1945)	Shidehara Kijūrō
Justice	Iwata Chūzō
Education	Maeda Tamon (9 Oct. 1945–13 Jan. 1946)
	Abe Yoshishige (13 Jan. 1946–22 May 1946)
Agriculture and Forestry	Matsumura Kenzō (9 Oct. 1945–13 Jan. 1946)
	Soejima Senpachi (13 Jan. 1946–22 May 1946)
Commerce and Industry	Ogasawara Sankurō
Transport	Tanaka Takeo (9 Oct. 1945–13 Jan. 1946)
	Mitsuchi Chūzō (13–26 Jan. 1946)
	Murakami Giichi (26 Jan. 1946–22 May 1946)
Welfare	Ashida Hitoshi
State	Matsumoto Jōji
	Kobayashi Ichizō (30 Oct. 1945–9 Mar. 1946)
	Tsugita Daisaburō (13 Jan. 1946–22 May 1946)
	Ishiguro Takeshige (26 Feb.–22 May 1946)
	Narahashi Wataru (26 Feb.–22 May 1946)
Chief of Cabinet Secretariat	Tsugita Daisaburō (9 Oct. 1945–13 Jan. 1946)
	Narahashi Wataru (13 Jan. 1946–22 May 1946)
Chief of Legislative Bureau	Narahashi Wataru (9 Oct. 1945–13 Jan. 1946)
	Ishiguro Takeshige (13 Jan.–19 Mar. 1946)
	Irie Toshirō (19 Mar. 1946–22 May 1946)

First Yoshida Cabinet
22 May 1946–24 May 1947

Prime Minister	Yoshida Shigeru
Foreign Affairs	Yoshida Shigeru
Home Affairs	Ōmura Seiichi (22 May 1946–31 Jan. 1947)
	Uehara Etsujirō (31 Jan. 1947–24 May 1947)
Finance	Ishibashi Tanzan
First Demobilization	Yoshida Shigeru (22 May 1946–15 June 1946, when the ministry was abolished)
Second Demobilization	Yoshida Shigeru 22 May 1946–15 June 1946, when the ministry was abolished)
Justice	Kimura Tokutarō
Education	Tanaka Kōtarō (22 May 1946–31 Jan. 1947)

	Takahashi Seiichirō (31 Jan. 1947–24 May 1947)
Agriculture and Forestry	Wada Hiroo (22 May 1946–30 Jan. 1947)
	Yoshida Shigeru (31 Jan.–15 Feb. 1947)
	Kimura Kozaemon (15 Feb. 1947–24 May 1947)
Commerce and Industry	Hoshijima Nirō (22 May 1946–31 Jan. 1947)
	Ishii Mitsujirō (31 Jan. 1947–24 May 1947)
Transport	Hiratsuka Tsunejirō (22 May 1946–31 Jan. 1947)
	Masuda Kaneshichi (31 Jan. 1947–24 May 1947)
Communications (est. 1 July 1946)	Hitotsumatsu Sadayoshi (1 July 1946–24 May 1947)
Welfare	Kawai Yoshinari
State:	
President of the Demobilization Agency (est. 15 June 1946)	*Shidehara Kijūrō (15 June 1946–24 May 1947)
President of Administrative Management Bureau (est. 26 Nov. 1946)	Saitō Takao (28 Nov. 1946–24 May 1947)
Director General of Economic Stabilization Board and Director of Price Board (est. 12 Aug. 1946)	Zen Keinosuke (12 Aug. 1946–31 Jan. 1947)
	Ishibashi Tanzan (31 Jan.–20 Mar. 1947)
	Takase Sōtarō (20 Mar. 1947–24 May 1947)
Without Portfolio	Shidehara Kijūrō (22 May–15 June 1946)
	Hitotsumatsu Sadayoshi (22 May–1 July 1946)
	Saitō Takao (22 May–28 Nov. 1946)
	Uehara Etsujirō (22 May 1946–31 Jan. 1947)
	Kanamori Tokujirō (19 June 1946–24 May 1947)
	Hoshijima Nirō (31 Jan. 1947–24 May 1947)
	Tanaka Man'itsu (26 Feb. 1947–24 May 1947)
Chief of Cabinet Secretariat	Hayashi Jōji
Chief of Legislative Bureau	Irie Toshirō

Katayama Cabinet
24 May 1947–10 Mar. 1948

Prime Minister	Katayama Tetsu
Foreign Affairs	*Ashida Hitoshi (1 June 1947–10 Mar. 1948)
Home Affairs	Kimura Kozaemon (1 June 1947–31 Dec. 1947, when the ministry was abolished)

Finance	Yano Shōtarō (24 May 1947–25 June 1947) Kurusu Takeo (25 June 1947–10 Mar. 1948)
Justice	Suzuki Yoshio (24 May 1947–15 Feb. 1948, when the ministry was abolished)
Attorney General (est. 15 Feb. 1948)	Suzuki Yoshio
Education	Morito Tatsuo
Agriculture and Forestry	Hirano Rikizō (24 May 1947–4 Nov. 1947) Katayama Tetsu (4 Nov.–13 Dec. 1947) Hatano Kanae (13 Dec. 1947–10 Mar. 1948)
Commerce and Industry	Mizutani Chōzaburō
Transport	Tomabechi Gizō (24 May 1947–4 Dec. 1947) Kitamura Tokutarō (4 Dec. 1947–10 Mar. 1948)
Communications	Miki Takeo
Welfare	Hitotsumatsu Sadayoshi
Labor (est. 1 Sept. 1947)	Yonekubo Mitsusuke
State:	
President of Administrative Management Bureau	Saitō Takao
Director of Economic Stabilization Board and Director of Price Board	Wada Hiroo
President of Demobilization Agency	Sasamori Junzō (24 May 1947–15 Oct. 1947, when the agency was abolished)
President of Construction Board (est. 1 Jan. 1948)	Kimura Kozaemon
Director of Reparations Agency (est. 1 Feb. 1948)	Sasamori Junzō
Chairman of Local Finance Committee (est. 1 Jan. 1948)	Takeda Giichi
Without Portfolio	Yonekubo Mitsusuke (24 May–1 Sept. 1947) Takeda Giichi (24 May 1947–7 Jan. 1948) Hayashi Heima (1 June–25 Nov. 1947) Nishio Suehiro (1 June 1947–10 Mar. 1948) Sasamori Junzō (15 Oct. 1947–1 Feb. 1948)
Chief of Cabinet Secretariat	Nishio Suehiro (1 June 1947–10 Mar. 1948)
Chief of Legislative Bureau	Satō Tatsuo (14 June 1947–15 Feb. 1948, when the bureau was abolished)

Ashida Cabinet
10 Mar. 1948 – 15 Oct. 1948

Prime Minister	Ashida Hitoshi
Foreign Affairs	Ashida Hitoshi
Finance	Kitamura Tokutarō
Attorney General	Suzuki Yoshio
Education	Morito Tatsuo
Agriculture and Forestry	Nagae Kazuo
Commerce and Industry	Mizutani Chōzaburō
Transport	Okada Seiichi
Communications	Tomiyoshi Eiji
Welfare	Takeda Giichi
Labor	Katō Kanjū
Construction (est. 10 July 1948)	Hitotsumatsu Sadayoshi
State:	
Director of Administrative Management Agency	Funada Kyōji
Director of Economic Stabilization Board and Director of Price Board	Kurusu Takeo
President of Construction Board	Hitotsumatsu Sadayoshi (10 Mar. 1948 – 9 July 1948, when the board was abolished)
Director of Reparations Agency	Funada Kyōji
Chairman of Local Finance Committee	Nomizo Masaru
Director of Central Economic Investigation Agency (est. 1 Aug. 1948)	Kurusu Takeo
Without Portfolio	*Nishio Suehiro (10 Mar. – 6 July 1948) Tomabechi Gizō
Chief of Cabinet Secretariat	Tomabechi Gizō

Second Yoshida Cabinet
15 Oct. 1948 – 16 Feb. 1949

Prime Minister	Yoshida Shigeru
Foreign Affairs	Yoshida Shigeru
Finance	Izumiyama Sanroku (15 Oct. 1948 – 14 Dec. 1948) Ōya Shinzō (14 Dec. 1948 – 16 Feb. 1949)
Attorney General	Yoshida Shigeru (15 Oct. – 7 Nov. 1948) Ueda Shunkichi (7 Nov. 1948 – 16 Feb. 1949)
Education	Shimojō Yasumaro
Agriculture and Forestry	Sutō Hideo
Commerce and Industry	Ōya Shinzō
Transport	Ozawa Saeki
Communications	Furuhata Tokuya
Welfare	*Hayashi Jōji
Labor	Masuda Kaneshichi
Construction	Masutani Hideji

State:	
Director of Administrative Management Agency	Ueda Shunkichi (15 Oct.–10 Nov. 1948) Kudō Tetsuo (10 Nov. 1948–16 Feb. 1949)
Director of Economic Stabilization Board and Director of Price Board	Izumiyama Sanroku (10 Nov.–14 Dec. 1948) Sutō Hideo (14 Dec. 1948–16 Feb. 1949)
Director of Reparations Agency	Inoue Tomoharu
Chairman of Local Finance Committee	Iwamoto Nobuyuki
Director of Central Economic Investigation Agency	Izumiyama Sanroku (15 Oct.–14 Dec. 1948) Sutō Hideo (14 Dec. 1948–16 Feb. 1949)
Without Portfolio	Mori Kōtarō
Chief of Cabinet Secretariat	Satō Eisaku

Third Yoshida Cabinet
16 Feb. 1949–30 Oct. 1952

Prime Minister	Yoshida Shigeru (Masutani Hideji was acting premier 31 Aug.–14 Sept. 1951)
Foreign Affairs	Yoshida Shigeru (16 Feb. 1949–30 Apr. 1952) Okazaki Katsuo (30 Apr. 1952–30 Oct. 1952)
Finance	Ikeda Hayato
Attorney General	Ueda Shunkichi (16 Feb. 1949–28 June 1950) Ōhashi Takeo (28 June 1950–26 Dec. 1951) Kimura Tokutarō (26 Dec. 1951–1 Aug. 1952, when the post was abolished with the reestablishment of the Justice Ministry)
Justice (re-est. 1 Aug. 1952)	Kimura Tokutarō
Education	Takase Sōtarō (16 Feb. 1949–6 May 1950) Amano Teiyū (6 May 1950–12 Aug. 1952) Okano Kiyohide (12 Aug. 1952–30 Oct. 1952)
Agriculture and Forestry	Mori Kōtarō (16 Feb. 1949–28 June 1950) Hirokawa Kōzen (28 June 1950–4 July 1951) Nemoto Ryūtaro (4 July–26 Dec. 1951) Hirokawa Kōzen (26 Dec. 1951–30 Oct. 1952)
Commerce and Industry	Inagaki Heitarō (16 Feb. 1949–24 May 1949, when the ministry was abolished)
International Trade and Industry (est. 25 May 1949)	Inagaki Heitarō (25 May 1949–17 Feb. 1950) Ikeda Hayato (17 Feb.–11 Apr. 1950) Takase Sōtarō (11 Apr.–28 June 1950) Yokoo Shigemi (28 June 1950–4 July 1951) Takahashi Ryūtarō (4 July 1951–30 Oct. 1952)

Transport	Ōya Shinzō (16 Feb. 1949–28 June 1950) Yamazaki Takeshi (28 June 1950–26 Dec. 1951) Murakami Giichi (26 Dec. 1951–30 Oct. 1952)
Communications	Ozawa Saeki (16 Feb. 1949–31 May 1949, when the ministry was abolished)
Posts (est. 1 June 1949)	Ozawa Saeki (1 June 1949–28 June 1950) Tamura Bunkichi (28 June 1950–4 July 1951) Satō Eisaku (4 July 1951–30 Oct. 1952)
Telecommunications (est. 1 June 1949)	Ozawa Saeki (1 June 1949–28 June 1950) Tamura Bunkichi (28 June 1950–4 July 1951) Satō Eisaku (4 July 1951–31 July 1952, when the ministry was abolished)
Welfare	*Hayashi Jōji (16 Feb. 1949–28 June 1950) Kurokawa Takeo (28 June 1950–4 July 1951) Hashimoto Ryōgo (4 July 1951–18 Jan. 1952) Yoshitake Eiichi (18 Jan. 1952–30 Oct. 1952)
Labor	Suzuki Masabumi (16 Feb. 1949–28 June 1950) Hori Shigeru (28 June 1950–26 Dec. 1951) Yoshitake Eiichi (26 Dec. 1951–30 Oct. 1952)
Construction	Masutani Hideji (16 Feb. 1949–6 May 1950) Masuda Kaneshichi (6 May 1950–4 July 1951) Noda Uichi (4 July 1951–30 Oct. 1952)
State:	
Director Administrative Management Agency	Honda Ichirō (16 Feb. 1949–28 June 1950) Okano Kiyohide (28 June–12 July 1950) Hirokawa Kōzen (12 July 1950–4 July 1951) Hashimoto Ryōgo (4 July 1951–18 Jan. 1952) Kimura Tokutarō (18 Jan.–28 Feb. 1952) Noda Uichi (28 Feb. 1952–30 Oct. 1952)
Director of Economic Stabilization Board, Director of Price Board, and Director of Central Economic Investigation Agency	Aoki Takayoshi (16 Feb. 1949–28 June 1950) Sutō Hideo (28 June 1950–1 Aug. 1952, when all were abolished)
Director Economic Council Agency (est. 1 Aug. 1952)	Sutō Hideo (1 Aug. 1952–2 Sept. 1952) Yamazaki Takeshi (2 Sept. 1952–30 Oct. 1952)
Director of Reparations Agency	Higai Senzō (16 Feb.–11 Mar. 1949) Yamaguchi Kikuichirō (11 Mar. 1949–28 June 1950)

	Masuda Kaneshichi (28 June 1950–7 June 1951) Sutō Hideo (7 June–4 July 1951) Noda Uichi (4 July–26 Dec. 1951) Okazaki Katsuo (26 Dec. 1951–28 Apr. 1952, when the agency was abolished)
Chairman Local Finance Commission (abolished 1 June 1949)	Kimura Kozaemon (16 Feb. 1949–31 May 1949; the commission was abolished the following day)
Director Local Autonomy Agency (est. 1 June 1949)	Kimura Kozaemon (1 June 1949–24 Jan. 1950) Honda Ichirō (24 Jan.–28 June 1950) Okano Kiyohide (28 June 1950–1 Aug. 1952, when the agency was abolished)
Director Autonomy Agency (est. 1 Aug. 1952)	Okano Kiyohide
Director Hokkaidō Development Agency (est. 1 June 1950)	Masuda Kaneshichi (1 June 1950–7 June 1951) Sutō Hideo (7 June–4 July 1951) Noda Uichi (4 July 1951–30 Oct. 1952)
Acting Director National Safety Agency (est. 1 Aug. 1952)	Yoshida Shigeru
Without Portfolio	Yamaguchi Kikuichirō (16 Feb. 1949–11 Mar. 1949) Masuda Kaneshichi (24 June 1949–6 May 1950) Higai Senzō (3 Nov. 1949–28 June 1950) *Hayashi Jōji (28 June 1950–13 Mar. 1951) Masutani Hideji (4 July 1951–26 Dec. 1951) Nakayama Toshihiko (2 Sept. 1951–30 Oct. 1952) Yamazaki Takeshi (26 Dec. 1951–1 Sept. 1952) Ōhashi Takeo (27 Dec. 1951–1 Aug. 1952) Ōnogi Hidejirō (2 Sept. 1952–30 Oct. 1952) Yamagata Katsumi (2 Sept. 1952–30 Oct. 1952)
Chief of Cabinet Secretariat	Masuda Kaneshichi (16 Feb. 1949–6 May 1950) Okazaki Katsuo (6 May 1950–26 Dec. 1951) Hori Shigeru (26 Dec. 1951–30 Oct. 1952)
Chief of Legislative Bureau (re-est. 1 Aug. 1952)	Satō Tatsuo

Fourth Yoshida Cabinet
30 Oct. 1952–21 May 1953

Prime Minister	Yoshida Shigeru
Foreign Affairs	Okazaki Katsuo

Finance	Mukai Tadaharu
Justice	Inukai Ken
Education	Okano Kiyohide
Agriculture and Forestry	Ogasawara Sankurō (30 Oct.–5 Dec. 1952)
	Hirokawa Kōzen (5 Dec. 1952–3 Mar. 1953)
	Tago Kazutami (3 Mar.–21 May 1953)
International Trade and Industry	Ikeda Hayato (30 Oct.–29 Nov. 1952)
	Ogasawara Sankurō (29 Nov. 1952–21 May 1953)
Transport	Ishii Mitsujirō
Posts and Telecommunications	Takase Sōtarō
Welfare	Yamagata Katsumi
Labor	Totsuka Kuichirō
Construction	Satō Eisaku (30 Oct. 1952–10 Feb. 1953)
	Totsuka Kuichirō (10 Feb.–21 May 1953)
State:	
Director Administrative Management Agency	Honda Ichirō
Director Economic Council Agency	Ikeda Hayato (30 Oct.–29 Nov. 1952)
	Ogasawara Sankurō (29 Nov. 1952–3 Mar. 1953)
	Mizuta Mikio (3 Mar.–21 May 1953)
Director Autonomy Agency	Honda Ichirō
Director Hokkaidō Development Agency	Satō Eisaku (30 Oct. 1952–10 Feb. 1953)
	Totsuka Kuichirō (10 Feb.–21 May 1953)
Director National Safety Agency	Kimura Tokutarō
Without Portfolio	Hayashiya Kamejirō
	*Ogata Taketora
	Ōnogi Hidejirō
Chief of Cabinet Secretariat	Ogata Taketora (30 Oct. 1952–24 Mar. 1953)
	Fukunaga Kenji (24 Mar.–21 May 1953)
Chief of Legislative Bureau	Satō Tatsuo

Fifth Yoshida Cabinet
21 May 1953–10 Dec. 1954

Prime Minister	Yoshida Shigeru (Ogata Taketora was acting premier 26 Sept.–17 Nov. 1954)
Foreign Affairs	Okazaki Katsuo
Finance	Ogasawara Sankurō
Justice	Inukai Ken (21 May 1953–22 Apr. 1954)
	Katō Ryōgorō (22 Apr.–19 June 1954)
	Ohara Naoshi (21 June–10 Dec. 1954)
Education	Ōdachi Shigeo
Agriculture and Forestry	Uchida Nobuya (21 May–22 June 1953)
	Hori Shigeru (22 June 1953–10 Dec. 1954)
International Trade and Industry	Okano Kiyohide (21 May 1953–8 Jan. 1954)
	Aichi Kiichi (8 Jan.–10 Dec. 1954)

Transport	Ishii Mitsujirō
Posts and Telecommunications	Tsukada Jūichirō
Welfare	Yamagata Katsumi (21 May 1953–9 Jan. 1954) Kusaba Ryūen (9 Jan. 1954–10 Dec. 1954)
Labor	Kosaka Zentarō
Construction	Totsuka Kuichirō (21 May 1953–16 June 1954) Ozawa Saeki (16 June–10 Dec. 1954)
State:	
Director Administrative Management Agency	Tsukada Jūichirō
Director Economic Council Agency	Okano Kiyohide (21 May 1953–8 Jan. 1954) Aichi Kiichi (8 Jan.–10 Dec. 1954)
Director Autonomy Agency	Tsukada Jūichirō
Director Hokkaidō Development Agency	Totsuka Kuichirō (21 May 1953–14 Jan. 1954) Ōno Banboku (14 Jan.–27 July 1954) *Ogata Taketora (27 July–10 Dec. 1954)
Director National Safety Agency	Kimura Tokutarō
Director Defense Agency (superseded National Safety Agency 9 June 1954)	Kimura Tokutarō (1 July–10 Dec. 1954)
Chairman National Public Safety Commission (est. June 1954)	Kosaka Zentarō (1 July–30 Sept. 1954) Ohara Naoshi (1 Oct.–10 Dec. 1954)
Without Portfolio	Ōnogi Hidejirō (21 May 1953–9 Jan. 1954) Ōno Banboku (21 May 1953–14 Jan. 1954) *Ogata Taketora (21 May 1953–27 July 1954) Andō Masazumi (21 May 1953–24 Nov. 1954) Katō Ryōgorō (9 Jan.–22 Apr. 1954, 19 June–10 Dec. 1954) Fukunaga Kenji (24 Sept.–10 Dec. 1954)
Chief of Cabinet Secretariat	Fukunaga Kenji
Chief of Legislative Bureau	Satō Tatsuo

First Hatoyama Cabinet
10 Dec. 1954–19 Mar. 1955

Prime Minister	Hatoyama Ichirō
Foreign Affairs	*Shigemitsu Mamoru
Finance	Ichimada Hisato
Justice	Hanamura Shirō
Education	Andō Masazumi
Agriculture and Forestry	Kōno Ichirō
International Trade and Industry	Ishibashi Tanzan
Transport	Miki Takeo
Posts and Telecommunications	Takechi Yūki
Welfare	Tsurumi Yūsuke
Labor	Chiba Saburō
Construction	Takeyama Yūtarō

State:	
Director Administrative Management Agency	Nishida Takao
Director Economic Council Agency	Takasaki Tatsunosuke
Director Autonomy Agency	Nishida Takao
Director Hokkaidō Development Agency	Miyoshi Hideyuki
Director Defense Agency	Ōmura Seiichi
Chairman National Public Safety Commission	Ōasa Tadao
Chief of Cabinet Secretariat	Nemoto Ryūtarō
Chief of Legislative Bureau	Hayashi Shūzō

Second Hatoyama Cabinet
19 Mar. 1955–22 Nov. 1955

Prime Minister	Hatoyama Ichirō
Foreign Affairs	*Shigemitsu Mamoru
Finance	Ichimada Hisato
Justice	Hanamura Shirō
Education	Matsumura Kenzō
Agriculture and Forestry	Kōno Ichirō
International Trade and Industry	Ishibashi Tanzan
Transport	Miki Takeo
Posts and Telecommunications	Matsuda Takechiyo
Welfare	Kawasaki Hideji
Labor	Nishida Takao
Construction	Takeyama Yūtarō
State:	
Director Administrative Management Agency	Kawashima Shōjirō
Director Economic Council Agency	Takasaki Tatsunosuke (19 Mar. 1955–20 July 1955, when the agency was abolished)
Director Economic Planning Agency (est. 20 July 1955)	Takasaki Tatsunosuke
Director Autonomy Agency	Kawashima Shōjirō
Director Hokkaidō Development Agency	Ōkubo Tomejirō
Director Defense Agency	Sugihara Arata (19 Mar.–31 July 1955) Sunada Shigemasa (31 July–22 Nov. 1955)
Chairman National Public Safety Commission	Ōasa Tadao
Chief of Cabinet Secretariat	Nemoto Ryūtarō
Chief of Legislative Bureau	Hayashi Shūzō

Third Hatoyama Cabinet
22 Nov. 1955–23 Dec. 1956

Prime Minister	Hatoyama Ichirō
Foreign Affairs	*Shigemitsu Mamoru
Finance	Ichimada Hisato

Justice	Makino Ryōzō
Education	Kiyose Ichirō
Agriculture and Forestry	Kōno Ichirō
International Trade and Industry	Ishibashi Tanzan
Transport	Yoshino Shinji
Posts and Telecommunications	Murakami Isamu
Welfare	Kobayashi Eizō
Labor	Kuraishi Tadao
Construction	Baba Motoharu
State:	
Director Administrative Management Agency	Kōno Ichirō
Director Economic Planning Agency	Takasaki Tatsunosuke
Director Autonomy Agency	Ōta Masataka
Director Hokkaidō Development Agency	Shōriki Matsutarō
Director Defense Agency	Funada Naka
Chairman National Public Safety Commission	Ōasa Tadao
Director Science and Technology Agency (est. 19 May 1956) and Chairman Atomic Power Commission (est. 1 Jan. 1956)	Shōriki Matsutarō
Chief of Cabinet Secretariat	Nemoto Ryūtarō
Chief of Legislative Bureau	Hayashi Shūzō

Ishibashi Cabinet
23 Dec. 1956–25 Feb. 1957

Prime Minister	Ishibashi Tanzan (Kishi Nobusuke was acting premier 31 Jan.–25 Feb. 1957)
Foreign Affairs	Kishi Nobusuke
Finance	Ikeda Hayato
Justice	Nakamura Umekichi
Education	Nadao Hirokichi
Agriculture and Forestry	Ide Ichitarō
International Trade and Industry	Mizuta Mikio
Transport	Miyazawa Taneo
Posts and Telecommunications	Ishibashi Tanzan (23–27 Dec. 1956) Hirai Tarō (27 Dec. 1956–25 Feb. 1957)
Welfare	Kanda Hiroshi
Labor	Matsuura Shūtarō
Construction	Nanjō Tokuo
State:	
Director Administrative Management Agency	Ōkubo Tomejirō
Director Economic Planning Agency	Uda Kōichi
Director Autonomy Agency	Tanaka Isaji
Director Hokkaidō Development Agency	Ishibashi Tanzan (23–27 Dec. 1956) Kawamura Matsusuke (27 Dec. 1956–25 Feb. 1957)

Director Defense Agency	Ishibashi Tanzan (23 Dec. 1956–2 Feb. 1957)
	Kodaki Akira (2–25 Feb. 1957)
Chairman National Public Safety Commission	Ōkubo Tomejirō
Director Science and Technology Agency and Chairman Atomic Power Commission	Uda Kōichi
Chief of Cabinet Secretariat	Ishida Hirohide
Chief of Legislative Bureau	Hayashi Shūzō

First Kishi Cabinet
25 Feb. 1957–12 June 1958

Prime Minister	Kishi Nobusuke
Foreign Affairs	Kishi Nobusuke (25 Feb.–10 July 1957)
	Fujiyama Aiichirō (10 July 1957–12 June 1958)
Finance	Ikeda Hayato (25 Feb.–10 July 1957)
	Ichimada Hisato (10 July 1957–12 June 1958)
Justice	Nakamura Umekichi (25 Feb.–10 July 1957)
	Karasawa Toshiki (10 July 1957–12 June 1958)
Education	Nadao Hirokichi (25 Feb.–10 July 1957)
	Matsunaga Tō (10 July 1957–12 June 1958)
Agriculture and Forestry	Ide Ichitarō (25 Feb.–10 July 1957)
	Akagi Munenori (10 July 1957–12 June 1958)
International Trade and Industry	Mizuta Mikio (25 Feb–10 July 1957)
	Maeo Shigesaburō (10 July 1957–12 June 1958)
Transport	Miyazawa Taneo (25Feb–10July 1957)
	Nakamura Sannojō (10 July 1957–12 June 1958)
Posts and Telecommunications	Hirai Tarō (25 Feb.–10 July 1957)
	Tanaka Kakuei (10 July 1957–12 June 1958)
Welfare	Kanda Hiroshi (25 Feb.–10 July 1957)
	Horiki Kenzō (10 July 1957–12 June 1958)
Labor	Matsuura Shūtarō (25 Feb.–10 July 1957)
	Ishida Hirohide (10 July 1957–12 June 1958)
Construction	Nanjō Tokuo (25 Feb.–10 July 1957)
	Nemoto Ryūtarō (10 July 1957–12 June 1958)
State:	
Director Administrative Management Agency	Ōkubo Tamejirō (25 Feb.–10 July 1957)
	*Ishii Mitsujirō (10 July 1957–12 June 1958)
Director Economic Planning Agency	Uda Kōichi (25 Feb.–10 July 1957)
	Kōno Ichirō (10 July 1957–12 June 1958)

Director Autonomy Agency	Tanaka Isaji (25 Feb.–10 July 1957) Kōri Yūichi (10 July 1957–12 June 1958)
Director Hokkaidō Development Agency	Kawamura Matsusuke (25 Feb.–30 Apr. 1957) Kajima Morinosuke (30 Apr.–10 July 1957) *Ishii Mitsujirō (10 July 1957–12 June 1958)
Director Defense Agency	Kodaki Akira (25 Feb.–10 July 1957) Tsushima Juichi (10 July 1957–12 June 1958)
Chairman National Public Safety Commission	Ōkubo Tomejirō (25 Feb.–10 July 1957) Shōriki Matsutarō (10 July 1957–12 June 1958)
Director of Science and Technology Agency and Chairman of Atomic Power Commission	Uda Kōichi (25 Feb.–10 July 1957) Shōriki Matsutarō (10 July 1957–12 June 1958)
Without Portfolio	*Ishii Mitsujirō (25 Feb.–10 July 1957)
Chief of Cabinet Secretariat	Ishida Hirohide (25 Feb.–10 July 1957) Aichi Kiichi (10 July 1957–12 June 1958)
Director of Legislative Bureau	Hayashi Shūzō
Director of General Affairs, Prime Minister's Office (est. 1 Aug. 1957)	Imamatsu Jirō

Second Kishi Cabinet
12 June 1958–19 July 1960

Prime Minister	Kishi Nobusuke (Masutani Hideji was acting premier 11 July–11 Aug. 1959, 16–24 Jan. 1960)
Foreign Affairs	Fujiyama Aiichirō
Finance	Satō Eisaku
Justice	Aichi Kiichi (12 June 1958–18 June 1959) Ino Hiroya (18 June 1959–19 July 1960)
Education	Nadao Hirokichi (12 June 1958–12 Jan. 1959) Hashimoto Ryōgo (12 Jan.–18 June 1959) Matsuda Takechiyo (18 June 1959–19 July 1960)
Agriculture and Forestry	Miura Kunio (12 June 1958–18 June 1959) Fukuda Takeo (18 June 1959–19 July 1960)
International Trade and Industry	Takasaki Tatsunosuke (12 June 1958–18 June 1959) Ikeda Hayato (18 June 1959–19 July 1960)
Transport	Nagano Mamoru (12 June 1958–24 Apr. 1959) Shigemune Yūzō (24 Apr.–18 June 1959) Narahashi Wataru (18 June 1959–19 July 1960)
Posts and Telecommunications	Terao Yutaka (12 June 1958–18 June 1959) Uetake Haruhiko (18 June 1959–19 July 1960)
Welfare	Hashimoto Ryōgo (12 June 1958–12 Jan. 1959)

	Sakata Michita (12 Jan.–18 June 1959) Watanabe Yoshio (18 June 1959–19 July 1960)
Labor	Kuraishi Tadao (12 June 1958–18 June 1959) Matsuno Raizō (18 June 1959–19 July 1960
Construction	Endō Saburō (12 June 1958–18 June 1959) Murakami Isamu (18 June 1959–19 July 1960)
Local Autonomy (est. 1 July 1960)	Ishihara Kanichirō
State:	
Director Administrative Management Agency	Yamaguchi Kikuichirō (12 June 1958–18 June 1959) *Masutani Hideji (18 June 1959–19 July 1960)
Director Economic Planning Agency	Miki Takeo (12 June–31 Dec. 1958) Takasaki Tatsunosuke (31 Dec. 1958–12 Jan. 1959) Sekō Kōichi (12 Jan.–18 June 1959) Kanno Watarō (18 June 1959–19 July 1960)
Director Autonomy Agency	Aoki Masashi (12 June–28 Oct. 1958, 12 Jan.–18 June 1959) Aichi Kiichi (28 Oct. 1958–12 Jan. 1959) Ishihara Kanichirō (12 Jan. 1959–1 July 1960, when the agency became a ministry)
Director Hokkaidō Development Agency	Yamaguchi Kikuichirō (12 June 1958–18 June 1959) Murakami Isamu (18 June 1959–19 July 1960)
Director Defense Agency	Satō Gisen (12 June 1958–12 Jan. 1959) Ino Shigejirō (12 Jan.–18 June 1959) Akagi Munenori (18 June 1959–19 July 1960)
Chairman National Public Safety Commission	Aoki Masashi (12 June 1958–18 June 1959) Ishihara Kanichirō (18 June 1959–19 July 1960)
Director Science and Technology Agency and Chairman Atomic Power Commission	Miki Takeo (12 June–31 Dec. 1958) Takasaki Tatsunosuke (31 Dec. 1958–18 June 1959) Nakasone Yasuhiro (18 June 1959–19 July 1960)
Chairman Capital Region Development Commission	Endō Saburō (12 June 1958–18 June 1959) Murakami Isamu (18 June 1959–19 July 1960)
Without Portfolio	Ikeda Hayato (12 June–31 Dec. 1958)
Chief of Cabinet Secretariat	Akagi Munenori (12 June 1958–18 June 1959) Shiina Etsusaburō (18 June 1959–19 July 1960)

Chief of Legislative Bureau	Hayashi Shūzō
Director General Affairs, Prime Minister's Office	Matsuno Raizō (12 June 1958–18 June 1959) Fukuda Tokuyasu (18 June 1959–19 July 1960)

First Ikeda Cabinet
19 July 1960–8 Dec. 1960

Prime Minister	Ikeda Hayato
Foreign Affairs	Kosaka Zentarō
Finance	Mizuta Mikio
Justice	Kojima Tetsuzō
Education	Araki Masuo
Agriculture and Forestry	Nanjō Tokuo
International Trade and Industry	Ishii Mitsujirō
Transport	Minami Yoshio
Posts and Telecommunications	Suzuki Zenkō
Welfare	Nakayama Masa
Labor	Ishida Hirohide
Construction	Hashimoto Tomisaburō
Local Autonomy	Yamazaki Iwao (19 July–13 Oct. 1960) Sutō Hideo (13 Oct.–8 Dec. 1960)
State:	
Director Administrative Management Agency	Takahashi Shintarō
Director Economic Planning Agency	Sakomizu Hisatsune
Director Hokkaidō Development Agency	Nishikawa Jingorō
Director Defense Agency	Esaki Masumi
Chairman National Public Safety Commission	Yamazaki Iwao (19 July–13 Oct. 1960) Sutō Hideo (13 Oct–8 Dec. 1960)
Director Science and Technology Agency and Chairman Atomic Power Commission	Araki Masuo
Chairman Capital Region Development Commission	Hashimoto Tomisaburō
Chief of Cabinet Secretariat	Ōhira Masayoshi
Chief of Legislative Bureau	Hayashi Shūzō
Director General Affairs, Prime Minister's Office	Fujieda Sensuke

Second Ikeda Cabinet
8 Dec. 1960–9 Dec. 1963

Prime Minister	Ikeda Hayato (Sutō Hideo was acting premier, 19–30 June 1961; Satō Eisaku, 16–30 Nov. 1961; Kawajima Shōjiro, 4–25 Nov. 1962; Kōno Ichirō 23 Sept.–6 Oct. 1963, 24–28 Nov. 1963)

Foreign Affairs	Kosaka Zentarō (8 Dec. 1960–18 July 1962)
	Ōhira Masayoshi (18 July 1962–9 Dec. 1963)
Finance	Mizuta Mikio (8 Dec. 1960–18 July 1962)
	Tanaka Kakuei (18 July 1962–9 Dec. 1963)
Justice	Ueki Kōshirō (8 Dec. 1960–18 July 1962)
	Nakagaki Kunio (18 July 1962–18 July 1963)
	Kaya Okinori (18 July–9 Dec. 1963)
Education	Araki Masuo (8 Dec. 1960–18 July 1963)
	Nadao Hirokichi (18 July–9 Dec. 1963)
Agriculture and Forestry	Sutō Hideo (8 Dec. 1960–18 July 1961)
	Kōno Ichirō (18 July 1961–18 July 1962)
	Shigemasa Seishi (18 July 1962–18 July 1963)
	Akagi Munenori (18 July–9 Dec. 1963)
International Trade and Industry	Shiina Etsusaburō (8 Dec. 1960–18 July 1961)
	Satō Eisaku (18 July 1961–18 July 1962)
	Fukuda Hajime (18 July 1962–9 Dec. 1963)
Transport	Kogure Budayū (8 Dec. 1960–18 July 1961)
	Saitō Noboru (18 July 1961–18 July 1962)
	Ayabe Kentarō (18 July 1962–9 Dec. 1963)
Posts and Telecommunications	Kogane Yoshiteru (8 Dec. 1960–18 July 1961)
	Sakomizu Hisatsune (18 July 1961–18 July 1962)
	Teshima Sakae (18 July 1962–8 Jan. 1963)
	Ozawa Kyūtarō (8 Jan.–18 July 1963)
	Koike Shinzō (18 July–9 Dec. 1963)
Welfare	Furui Yoshimi (8 Dec. 1960–18 July 1961)
	Nadao Hirokichi (18 July 1961–18 July 1962)
	Nishimura Eiichi (18 July 1962–18 July 1963)
	Kobayashi Takeji (18 July–9 Dec. 1963)
Labor	Ishida Hirohide (8 Dec. 1960–18 July 1961)
	Fukunaga Kenji (18 July 1961–18 July 1962)
	Ōhashi Takeo (18 July 1962–9 Dec. 1963)
Construction	Nakamura Umekichi (8 Dec. 1960–18 July 1962)
	Kōno Ichirō (18 July 1962–9 Dec. 1963)
Local Autonomy	Yasui Ken (8 Dec. 1960–18 July 1962)
	Shinoda Kōsaku (18 July 1962–18 July 1963)
	Hayakawa Takashi (18 July–9 Dec. 1963)

State:	
Director Administrative Management Agency	Ozawa Saeki (8 Dec. 1960–18 July 1961) Kawajima Shōjirō (18 July 1961–18 July 1963) Yamamura Shinjirō (18 July–9 Dec. 1963)
Director Economic Planning Agency	Sakomizu Hisatsune (8 Dec. 1960–18 July 1961) Fujiyama Aiichirō (18 July 1961–18 July 1962) Miyazawa Kiichi (18 July 1962–9 Dec. 1963)
Director Hokkaidō Development Agency	Ozawa Saeki (8 Dec. 1960–18 July 1961) Kawajima Shōjirō (18 July 1961–18 July 1963) Satō Eisaku (18 July–9 Dec. 1963)
Director Defense Agency	Nishimura Naomi (8 Dec. 1960–18 July 1961) Fujieda Sensuke (18 July 1961–18 July 1962) Shiga Kenjirō (18 July 1962–18 July 1963) Fukuda Tokuyasu (18 July 1963–9 Dec. 1963)
Chairman National Public Safety Commission	Yasui Ken (8 Dec. 1960–18 July 1962) Shinoda Kōsaku (18 July 1962–18 July 1963) Hayakawa Takashi (18 July–9 Dec. 1963)
Director Science and Technology Agency and Chairman Atomic Power Commission	Ikeda Masanosuke (8 Dec. 1960–18 July 1961) Miki Takeo (18 July 1961–18 July 1962) Kondō Tsuruyo (18 July 1962–18 July 1963) Satō Eisaku (18 July–9 Dec. 1963)
Chairman Capital Region Development Commission	Nakamura Umekichi (8 Dec. 1960–18 July 1962) Kawajima Shōjirō (18 July 1962–2 Nov. 1962 Kōno Ichirō (2 Nov. 1962–9 Dec. 1963)
Chairman Kinki Region Development Commission	Kōno Ichirō (10 July–9 Dec. 1963)
Chief of Cabinet Secretariat	Ōhira Masayoshi (8 Dec. 1960–18 July 1962) Kurogane Yasumi (18 July 1962–9 Dec. 1963)
Chief of Legislative Bureau (renamed Cabinet Legal Office 1 July 1962)	Hayashi Shūzō
Director of General Affairs, Prime Minister's Office	Fujieda Sensuke (8 Dec. 1960–18 July 1961) Kodaira Hisao (18 July 1961–18 July 1962) Tokuyasu Jitsuzō (18 July 1962–18 July 1963) Noda Takeo (18 July–9 Dec. 1963)

Third Ikeda Cabinet
9 Dec. 1963–9 Nov. 1964

Prime Minister	Ikeda Hayato
Foreign Affairs	Ōhira Masayoshi (9 Dec. 1963–18 July 1964)
	Shiina Etsusaburō (18 July–9 Nov. 1964)
Finance	Tanaka Kakuei
Justice	Kaya Okinori (9 Dec. 1963–18 July 1964)
	Takahashi Hitoshi (18 July–9 Nov. 1964)
Education	Nadao Hirokichi (9 Dec. 1963–18 July 1964)
	Aichi Kiichi (18 July–9 Nov. 1964)
Agriculture and Forestry	Akagi Munenori
International Trade and Industry	Fukuda Hajime (9 Dec. 1963–18 July 1964)
	Sakurauchi Yoshio (18 July–9 Nov. 1964)
Transport	Ayabe Kentarō (9 Dec. 1963–18 July 1964)
	Matsuura Shūtarō (18 July–9 Nov. 1964)
Posts and Telecommunications	Koike Shinzō (9 Dec. 1963–18 July 1964)
	Tokuyasu Jitsuzō (18 July–9 Nov. 1964)
Welfare	Kobayashi Takeji (9 Dec. 1963–18 July 1964)
	Kanda Hiroshi (18 July–9 Nov. 1964)
Labor	Ōhashi Takeo (9 Dec. 1963–18 July 1964)
	Ishida Hirohide (18 July–9 Nov. 1964)
Construction	Kōno Ichirō (9 Dec. 1963–18 July 1964)
	Koyama Osanori (18 July–9 Nov. 1964)
Local Autonomy	Hayakawa Takashi (9 Dec. 1963–25 Mar. 1964)
	Akazawa Masamichi (25 Mar.–18 July 1964)
	Yoshitake Eichi (18 July–9 Nov. 1964)
State:	
Director Administrative Management Agency	Yamamura Shinjirō (9 Dec. 1963–18 July 1964)
	Masuhara Keikichi (18 July–9 Nov. 1964)
Director Economic Planning Agency	Miyazawa Kiichi (9 Dec. 1963–18 July 1964)
	Takahashi Mamoru (18 July–9 Nov. 1964)
Director Hokkaidō Development Agency	Satō Eisaku (9 Dec. 1963–18 July 1964)
	Masuhara Keikichi (18 July–9 Nov. 1964)
Director Defense Agency	Fukuda Tokuyasu (9 Dec. 1963–18 July 1964)
	Koizumi Junya (18 July–9 Nov. 1964)
Chairman National Public Safety Commission	Hayakawa Takashi (9 Dec. 1963–25 Mar. 1964)
	Akazawa Masamichi (25 Mar.–18 July 1964)
	Yoshitake Eichi (18 July–9 Nov. 1964)

Director Science and Technology Agency and Chairman Atomic Power Commission	Satō Eisaku (9 Dec. 1963–18 July 1964) Aichi Kiichi (18 July–9 Nov. 1964)
Chairman Capital Region Development Commission and Kinki Region Development Commission	Kōno Ichirō (9 Dec. 1965–18 July 1964) Koyama Osanori (18 July–9 Nov. 1964)
Without Portfolio	Kōno Ichirō (18 July–9 Nov. 1964, with responsibility for the Olympic Games)
Chief of Cabinet Secretariat	Kurogane Yasumi (9 Dec. 1963–18 July 1964) Suzuki Zenkō (18 July–9 Nov. 1964)
Chief of Cabinet Legal Office	Hayashi Shūzō
Director of General Affairs, Prime Minister's Office	Noda Takeo (9 Dec. 1963–18 July 1964) Usui Sōichi (18 July–9 Nov. 1964)

First Satō Cabinet
9 Nov. 1964–17 Feb. 1967

Prime Minister	Satō Eisaku (Kōno Ichirō was acting premier 10–17 Jan. 1965)
Foreign Affairs	Shiina Etsusaburō (9 Nov. 1964–3 Dec. 1966) Miki Takeo (3 Dec. 1966–17 Feb. 1967)
Finance	Tanaka Kakuei (9 Nov. 1964–3 June 1965) Fukuda Takeo (3 June 1965–3 Dec. 1966) Mizuta Mikio (3 Dec. 1966–17 Feb. 1967)
Justice	Takahashi Hitoshi (9 Nov. 1964–3 June 1965) Ishii Mitsujirō (3 June 1965–3 Dec. 1966) Tanaka Isaji (3 Dec. 1966–17 Feb. 1967)
Education	Aichi Kiichi (9 Nov. 1964–3 June 1965) Nakamura Umekichi (3 June 1965–1 Aug. 1966) Arita Kiichi (1 Aug.–3 Dec. 1966) Kennoki Toshihiro (3 Dec. 1966–17 Feb. 1967)
Agriculture and Forestry	Akagi Munenori (9 Nov. 1964–3 June 1965) Sakata Eiichi (3 June 1965–1 Aug. 1966) Matsuno Raizō (1 Aug.–3 Dec. 1966) Kuraishi Tadao (3 Dec. 1966–17 Feb. 1967)
International Trade and Industry	Sakurauchi Yoshio (9 Nov. 1964–3 June 1965) Miki Takeo (3 June 1965–3 Dec. 1966) Kanno Watarō (3 Dec. 1966–17 Feb. 1967)
Transport	Matsuura Shūtarō (9 Nov. 1964–3 June 1965) Nakamura Torata (3 June 1965–1 Aug. 1966) Arafune Seijūrō (1 Aug.–14 Oct. 1966) Fujieda Sensuke (14 Oct.–3 Dec. 1966) Ōhashi Takeo (3 Dec. 1966–17 Feb. 1967)

Posts and Telecommunications	Tokuyasu Jitsuzō (9 Nov. 1964–3 June 1965) Kōri Yūichi (3 June 1965–1 Aug. 1966) Shintani Torasaburō (1 Aug.–3 Dec. 1966) Kobayashi Takeji (3 Dec. 1966–17 Feb. 1967)
Welfare	Kanda Hiroshi (9 Nov. 1964–3 June 1965) Suzuki Zenkō (3 June 1965–3 Dec. 1966) Bō Hideo (3 Dec. 1966–17 Feb. 1967)
Labor	Ishida Hirohide (9 Nov. 1964–3 June 1965) Kodaira Hisao (3 June 1965–1 Aug. 1966) Yamate Mitsuo (1 Aug.–3 Dec. 1966) Hayakawa Takashi (3 Dec. 1966–17 Feb. 1967)
Construction	Koyama Osanori (9 Nov. 1964–3 June 1965) Setoyama Mitsuo (3 June 1965–1 Aug. 1966) Hashimoto Tomisaburō (1 Aug.–3 Dec. 1966) Nishimura Eiichi (3 Dec. 1966–17 Feb. 1967)
Local Autonomy	Yoshitake Eichi (9 Nov. 1964–3 June 1965) Nagayama Tadanori (3 June 1965–1 Aug. 1966) Shiomi Toshitsugu (1 Aug.–3 Dec. 1966) Fujieda Sensuke (3 Dec. 1966–17 Feb. 1967)
State:	
Director Administrative Management Agency	Masuhara Keikichi (9 Nov. 1964–3 June 1965) Fukuda Tokuyasu (3 June 1965–1 Aug. 1966) Tanaka Shigeho (1 Aug.–3 Dec. 1966) Matsudaira Isao (3 Dec. 1966–17 Feb. 1967)
Director Economic Planning Agency	Takahashi Mamoru (9 Nov. 1964–3 June 1965) Fujiyama Aiichirō (3 June 1965–4 Nov. 1966) Satō Eisaku (4 Nov.–3 Dec. 1966) Miyazawa Kiichi (3 Dec. 1966–17 Feb. 1967)
Director Hokkaidō Development Agency	Masuhara Keikichi (9 Nov. 1964–3 June 1965) Fukuda Tokuyasu (3 June 1965–1 Aug. 1966)

	Maeo Shigesaburō (1 Aug.–3 Dec. 1966) Nikaidō Susumu (3 Dec. 1966–17 Feb. 1967)
Director Defense Agency	Koizumi Junya (9 Nov. 1964–3 June 1965) Matsuno Raizō (3 June 1965–1 Aug. 1966) Kanbayashiyama Eikichi (1 Aug.–3 Dec. 1966) Masuda Kaneshichi (3 Dec. 1966–17 Feb. 1967)
Chairman National Public Safety Commission	Yoshitake Eichi (9 Nov. 1964–3 June 1965) Nagayama Tadanori (3 June 1965–1 Aug. 1966) Shiomi Toshitsugu (1 Aug.–3 Dec. 1966) Fujieda Sensuke (3 Dec. 1966–17 Feb. 1967)
Director Science and Technology Agency and Chairman Atomic Power Commission	Aichi Kiichi (9 Nov. 1964–3 June 1965) Uehara Shōkichi (3 June 1965–1 Aug. 1966) Arita Kiichi (1 Aug.–3 Dec. 1966) Nikaidō Susumu (3 Dec. 1966–17 Feb. 1967)
Chairman Capital Region Development Commission and Kinki Region Development Commission	Koyama Osanori (9 Nov. 1964–3 June 1965) Setoyama Mitsuo (3 June 1965–1 Aug. 1966) Hashimoto Tomisaburō (1 Aug.–3 Dec. 1966) Nishimura Eiichi (3 Dec. 1966–17 Feb. 1967)
Chairman Chūbu Region Development Commission (est. 1 July 1966)	Setoyama Mitsuo (1 July–1 Aug. 1966) Hashimoto Tomisaburō (1 Aug.–3 Dec. 1966) Nishimura Eiichi (3 Dec. 1966–17 Feb. 1967)
Chief of Cabinet Secretariat (Minister of State from 28 June 1966)	Hashimoto Tomisaburō (28 June–1 Aug. 1966) Aichi Kiichi (1 Aug.–3 Dec. 1966) Fukunaga Kenji (3 Dec. 1966–17 Feb. 1967)
Director of General Affairs, Prime Minister's Office (Minister of State from 19 May 1965)	Usui Sōichi (19 May–3 June 1965) Yasui Ken (3 June 1965–1 Aug. 1966) Mori Kiyoshi (1 Aug.–3 Dec. 1966) Tsukahara Toshio (3 Dec. 1966–17 Feb. 1967)
Without Portfolio	Kōno Ichirō (9 Nov. 1964–3 June 1965)
Chief of Cabinet Secretariat	Hashimoto Tomisaburō (9 Nov. 1964–28 June 1966, from which date post filled by a Minister of State)

Director of General Affairs, Prime Minister's Office	Usui Sōichi (9 Nov. 1964–19 May 1965, from which date post filled by a Minister of State)
Chief of Cabinet Legal Office	Takatsuji Masami

Second Satō Cabinet
17 Feb. 1967–14 Jan. 1970

Prime Minister	Satō Eisaku (Miki Takeo was acting premier 30 June–2 July 1967, 7–9 Sept. 1967, 8–21 Oct. 1967; Masuda Kaneshichi, 20–30 Sept. 1967, 12–20 Nov. 1967; Hori Shigeru, 17–26 Nov. 1969)
Foreign Affairs	Miki Takeo (17 Feb. 1967–30 Nov. 1968)
	Aichi Kiichi (30 Nov. 1968–14 Jan. 1970)
Finance	Mizuta Mikio (17 Feb. 1967–30 Nov. 1968)
	Fukuda Takeo (30 Nov. 1968–14 Jan. 1970)
Justice	Tanaka Isaji (17 Feb. 1967–25 Nov. 1967)
	Akama Bunzō (25 Nov. 1967–30 Nov. 1968)
	Saigō Kichinosuke (30 Nov. 1968–14 Jan. 1970)
Education	Kennoki Toshihiro (17 Feb.–25 Nov. 1967)
	Nadao Hirokichi (25 Nov. 1967–30 Nov. 1968)
	Sakata Michita (30 Nov. 1968–14 Jan. 1970)
Agriculture and Forestry	Kuraishi Tadao (17 Feb. 1967–23 Feb. 1968)
	Nishimura Naomi (23 Feb.–30 Nov. 1968)
	Hasegawa Shirō (30 Nov. 1968–14 Jan. 1970)
International Trade and Industry	Kanno Watarō (17 Feb.–25 Nov. 1967)
	Shiina Etsusaburō (25 Nov. 1967–30 Nov. 1968)
	Ōhira Masayoshi (30 Nov. 1968–14 Jan. 1970)
Transport	Ōhashi Takeo (17 Feb.–25 Nov. 1967)
	Nakasone Yasuhiro (25 Nov. 1967–30 Nov. 1968)
	Harada Ken (30 Nov. 1968–14 Jan. 1970)
Posts and Telecommunications	Kobayashi Takeji (17 Feb. 1967–30 Nov. 1968)
	Kōmoto Toshio (30 Nov. 1968–14 Jan. 1970)
Welfare	Bō Hideo (17 Feb.–25 Nov. 1967)
	Sonoda Sunao (25 Nov. 1967–30 Nov. 1968)

	Saitō Noboru (30 Nov. 1968–14 Jan. 1970)
Labor	Hayakawa Takashi (17 Feb.–25 Nov. 1967)
	Ogawa Heiji (25 Nov. 1967–30 Nov. 1968)
	Hara Kenzaburō (30 Nov. 1968–14 Jan. 1970)
Construction	Nishimura Eiichi (17 Feb.–25 Nov. 1967)
	Hori Shigeru (25 Nov. 1967–30 Nov. 1968)
	Tsubokawa Shinzō (30 Nov. 1968–14 Jan. 1970)
Local Autonomy	Fujieda Sensuke (17 Feb.–25 Nov. 1967)
	Akazawa Masamichi (25 Nov. 1967–30 Nov. 1968)
	Noda Takeo (30 Nov. 1968–14 Jan. 1970)
State:	
Director Administrative Management Agency	Matsudaira Isao (17 Feb.–25 Nov. 1967)
	Kimura Takeo (25 Nov. 1967–30 Nov. 1968)
	Araki Masuo (30 Nov. 1968–14 Jan. 1970)
Director Economic Planning Agency	Miyazawa Kiichi (17 Feb. 1967–30 Nov. 1968)
	Kanno Watarō (30 Nov. 1968–14 Jan. 1970)
Director Hokkaidō Development Agency	Nikaidō Susumu (17 Feb.–25 Nov. 1967)
	Kimura Takeo (25 Nov. 1967–30 Nov. 1968)
	Noda Takeo (30 Nov. 1968–14 Jan. 1970)
Director Defense Agency	Masuda Kaneshichi (17 Feb. 1967–30 Nov. 1968)
	Arita Kiichi (30 Nov. 1968–14 Jan. 1970)
Chairman National Public Safety Commission	Fujieda Sensuke (17 Feb.–25 Nov. 1967)
	Akazawa Masamichi (25 Nov. 1967–30 Nov. 1968)
	Araki Masuo (30 Nov. 1968–14 Jan. 1970)
Director Science and Technology Agency and Chairman Atomic Power Commission	Nikaidō Susumu (17 Feb.–25 Nov. 1967)
	Nabeshima Naotsugu (25 Nov. 1967–30 Nov. 1968)
	Kiuchi Shirō (30 Nov. 1968–14 Jan. 1970)
Chairman Capital Region Development Commission, Kinki Region Development Commission, and Chūbu Region Development Commission	Nishimura Eiichi (17 Feb.–25 Nov. 1967)
	Hori Shigeru (25 Nov. 1967–30 Nov. 1968)
	Tsubokawa Shinzō (30 Nov. 1968–14 Jan. 1970)
Chief of Cabinet Secretariat	Fukunaga Kenji (17 Feb.–22 June 1967)
	Kimura Toshio (22 June 1967–30 Nov. 1968)
	Hori Shigeru (30 Nov. 1968–14 Jan. 1970)

Director of General Affairs, Prime Minister's Office	Tsukahara Toshio (17 Feb.–25 Nov. 1967) Tanaka Tatsuo (25 Nov. 1967–30 Nov. 1968) Tokonami Tokuji (30 Nov. 1968–14 Jan. 1970)
Chief of Cabinet Legal Office	Takatsuji Masami

Third Satō Cabinet
14 Jan. 1970–7 July 1972

Prime Minister	Satō Eisaku (Hori Shigeru was acting premier, 18–27 Oct. 1970, 1 July 1972; Maeo Shigesaburō, 5–10 Jan. 1972)
Foreign Affairs	Aichi Kiichi (14 Jan. 1970–5 July 1971) Fukuda Takeo (5 July 1971–7 July 1972)
Finance	Fukuda Takeo (14 Jan. 1970–5 July 1971) Mizuta Mikio (5 July 1971–7 July 1972)
Justice	Kobayashi Takeji (14 Jan. 1970–9 Feb. 1971) Akita Daisuke (9–17 Feb. 1971) Ueki Kōshirō (17 Feb.–5 July 1971) Maeo Shigesaburō (5 July 1971–7 July 1972)
Education	Sakata Michita (14 Jan. 1970–5 July 1971) Takami Saburō (5 July 1971–7 July 1972)
Agriculture and Forestry	Kuraishi Tadao (14 Jan. 1970–5 July 1971) Akagi Munenori (5 July 1971–7 July 1972)
International Trade and Industry	Miyazawa Kiichi (14 Jan. 1970–5 July 1971) Tanaka Kakuei (5 July 1971–7 July 1972)
Transport	Hashimoto Tomisaburō (14 Jan. 1970–5 July 1971) Niwa Kyōshirō (5 July 1971–7 July 1972)
Posts and Telecommunications	Ide Ichitarō (14 Jan. 1970–5 July 1971) Hirose Masao (5 July 1971–7 July 1972)
Welfare	Uchida Tsuneo (14 Jan. 1970–5 July 1971) Saitō Noboru (5 July 1971–7 July 1972)
Labor	Nohara Masakatsu (14 Jan. 1970–5 July 1971) Hara Kenzaburō (5 July 1971–28 Jan. 1972) Tsukahara Toshio (28 Jan.–7 July 1972)
Construction	Nemoto Ryūtarō (14 Jan. 1970–5 July 1971) Nishimura Eiichi (5 July 1971–7 July 1972)
Local Autonomy	Akita Daisuke (14 Jan. 1970–5 July 1971) Tokai Motosaburō (5 July 1971–7 July 1972)

State:	
Director Administrative Management Agency	Araki Masuo (14 Jan. 1970–5 July 1971) Nakamura Torata (5 July 1971–7 July 1972)
Director Economic Planning Agency	Satō Ichirō (14 Jan. 1970–5 July 1971) Kimura Toshio (5 July 1971–7 July 1972)
Director Hokkaidō Development Agency	Nishida Shinichi (14 Jan. 1970–5 July 1971) Tokai Motosaburō (5 July 1971–7 July 1972)
Director Defense Agency	Nakasone Yasuhiro (14 Jan. 1970–5 July 1971) Masuhara Keikichi (5 July–2 Aug. 1971) Nishimura Naomi (2 Aug.–3 Dec. 1971) Esaki Masumi (3 Dec. 1971–7 July 1972)
Chairman National Public Safety Commission	Araki Masuo (14 Jan. 1970–5 July 1971) Nakamura Torata (5 July 1971–7 July 1972)
Director Science and Technology Agency and Chairman Atomic Power Commission	Nishida Shinichi (14 Jan. 1970–5 July 1971) Hiraizumi Wataru (5 July–16 Nov. 1971) Kiuchi Shirō (16 Nov. 1971–7 July 1972)
Chairman Capital Region Development Commission, Kinki Region Development Commission, and Chūbu Region Development Commission	Nemoto Ryūtarō (14 Jan. 1970–5 July 1971) Nishimura Eiichi (5 July 1971–7 July 1972)
Chief of Cabinet Secretariat	Hori Shigeru (14 Jan. 1970–5 July 1971) Takeshita Noboru (5 July 1971–7 July 1972)
Director of General Affairs, Prime Minister's Office	Yamanaka Sadanori
Director Environment Agency (est. 1 July 1971)	Yamanaka Sadanori (1–5 July 1971) Ōishi Buichi (5 July 1971–7 July 1972)
Director Okinawa Development Agency (est. 15 May 1972)	Yamanaka Sadanori (15 May–7 July 1972)
Chief of Cabinet Legal Office	Takatsuji Masami

First Tanaka Kakuei Cabinet
7 July 1972–22 Dec. 1972

Prime Minister	Tanaka Kakuei (Miki Takeo was acting premier 31 Aug.–3 Sept. 1972, 25–30 Sept. 1972)
Foreign Affairs	Ōhira Masayoshi
Finance	Ueki Kōshirō
Justice	Kōri Yūichi
Education	Inaba Osamu
Agriculture and Forestry	Adachi Tokurō
International Trade and Industry	Nakasone Yasuhiro
Transport	Sasaki Hideyo
Posts and Telecommunications	Tanaka Kakuei (7–12 July 1972) Miike Makoto (12 July–22 Dec. 1972)

Welfare	Shiomi Shunji
Labor	Tamura Hajime
Construction	Kimura Takeo
Local Autonomy	Fukuda Hajime
State:	
Director Administrative Management Agency	Hamano Seigo
Director Economic Planning Agency	Arita Kiichi (12 July–22 Dec. 1972)
Director Hokkaidō Development Agency	Fukuda Hajime
Director Defense Agency	Masuhara Keikichi
Chairman National Public Safety Commission	Kimura Takeo
Director Science and Technology Agency and Chairman Atomic Power Commission	Nakasone Yasuhiro
Chairman Capital Region Development Commission, Kinki Region Development Commission, and Chūbu Region Development Commission	Kimura Takeo
Chief of Cabinet Secretariat	Nikaidō Susumu
Director of General Affairs, Prime Minister's Office	Honna Takeshi
Director Environment Agency	Koyama Osanori
Director Okinawa Development Agency	Honna Takeshi
Without Portfolio	*Miki Takeo
Chief of Cabinet Legal Office	Yoshikuni Ichirō

Second Tanaka Kakuei Cabinet
22 Dec. 1972–9 Dec. 1974

Prime Minister	Tanaka Kakuei (Miki Takeo was acting premier, 29 July–6 Aug. 1973, 26 Sept.–11 Oct. 1973; Hori Shigeru, 7–14 Jan. 1974; Nishimura Eiichi, 19 Aug. 1974, 12–27 Sept. 1974, 28 Oct.–8 Nov. 1974)
Foreign Affairs	Ōhira Masayoshi (22 Dec. 1972–16 July 1974)
	Kimura Toshio (16 July–9 Dec. 1974)
Finance	Aichi Kiichi (22 Dec. 1972–25 Nov. 1973)
	Fukuda Takeo (25 Nov. 1973–16 July 1974)
	Ōhira Masayoshi (16 July–9 Dec. 1974)
Justice	Tanaka Isaji (22 Dec. 1972–25 Nov. 1973)
	Nakamura Umekichi (25 Nov. 1973–11 Nov. 1974)
	Hamano Seigo (11 Nov.–9 Dec. 1974)
Education	Okuno Seisuke (22 Dec. 1972–11 Nov. 1974)
	Mihara Asao (11 Nov.–9 Dec. 1974)

Agriculture and Forestry	Sakurauchi Yoshio (22 Dec. 1972–25 Nov. 1973)
	Kuraishi Tadao (25 Nov. 1973–9 Dec. 1974)
International Trade and Industry	Nakasone Yasuhiro
Transport	Shintani Torasaburō (22 Dec. 1972–25 Nov. 1973)
	Tokunaga Masatoshi (25 Nov. 1973–11 Nov. 1974)
	Etō Akira (11 Nov.–9 Dec. 1974)
Posts and Telecommunications	Kuno Chūji (22 Dec. 1972–25 Nov. 1973)
	Harada Ken (25 Nov. 1973–11 Nov. 1974)
	Kashima Toshio (11 Nov.–9 Dec. 1974)
Welfare	Saitō Kunikichi (22 Dec. 1972–11 Nov. 1974)
	Fukunaga Kenji (11 Nov.–9 Dec. 1974)
Labor	Katō Tsunetarō (22 Dec. 1972–25 Nov. 1973)
	Hasegawa Takashi (25 Nov. 1973–11 Nov. 1974)
	Ōkubo Takeo (11 Nov.–9 Dec. 1974)
Construction	Kanemaru Shin (22 Dec. 1972–25 Nov. 1973)
	Kameoka Takao (25 Nov. 1973–11 Nov. 1974)
	Ozawa Tatsuo (11 Nov.–9 Dec. 1974)
Local Autonomy	Esaki Masumi (22 Dec. 1972–25 Nov. 1973)
	Machimura Kingo (25 Nov. 1973–11 Nov. 1974)
	Fukuda Hajime (11 Nov.–9 Dec. 1974)
State:	
Director Administrative Management Agency	Fukuda Takeo (22 Dec. 1972–25 Nov. 1973)
	Hori Shigeru (25 Nov. 1973–16 July 1974)
	Hosoda Kichizō (16 July–9 Dec. 1974)
Director Economic Planning Agency	Kosaka Zentarō (22 Dec. 1972–25 Nov. 1973)
	Uchida Tsuneo (25 Nov. 1973–11 Nov. 1974)
	Kuranari Tadashi (11 Nov.–9 Dec. 1974)
Director Hokkaidō Development Agency	Esaki Masumi (22 Dec. 1972–25 Nov. 1973)
	Machimura Kingo (25 Nov. 1973–11 Nov. 1974)
	Fukuda Hajime (11 Nov.–9 Dec. 1974)
Director Defense Agency	Masuhara Keikichi (22 Dec. 1972–29 May 1973)
	Yamanaka Sadanori (29 May 1973–11 Nov. 1974)
	Uno Sōsuke (11 Nov.–9 Dec. 1974)

Chairman National Public Safety Commission	Esaki Masumi (22 Dec. 1972–25 Nov. 1973)
	Machimura Kingo (25 Nov. 1973–11 Nov. 1974)
	Fukuda Hajime (11 Nov.–9 Dec. 1974)
Director Science and Technology Agency and Chairman Atomic Power Commission	Maeda Kazuo (22 Dec. 1972–25 Nov. 1973)
	Moriyama Kinji (25 Nov. 1973–11 Nov. 1974)
	Adachi Tokurō (11 Nov.–9 Dec. 1974)
Chairman Capital Region Development Commission, Kinki Region Development Commission, and Chūbu Region Development Commission	Kanemaru Shin (22 Dec. 1972–25 Nov. 1973)
	Kameoka Takao (25 Nov. 1973–26 June 1974, when all three commissions were abolished)
Chief of Cabinet Secretariat	Nikaidō Susumu (22 Dec. 1972–11 Nov. 1974)
	Takeshita Noboru (11 Nov.–9 Dec. 1974)
Director of General Affairs, Prime Minister's Office	Tsubokawa Shinzō (22 Dec. 1972–25 Nov. 1973)
	Kosaka Tokusaburō (25 Nov. 1973–9 Dec. 1974)
Director Environment Agency	*Miki Takeo (22 Dec. 1972–12 July 1974)
	Mōri Matsuhei (12 July–9 Dec. 1974)
Director Okinawa Development Agency	Tsubokawa Shinzō (22 Dec. 1972–25 Nov. 1973)
	Kosaka Tokusaburō (25 Nov. 1973–9 Dec. 1974)
Director National Land Agency (est. 26 June 1974)	Nishimura Eiichi (26 June–11 Nov. 1974)
	Niwa Hyōsuke (11 Nov.–9 Dec. 1974)
Without Portfolio	Nishimura Eiichi (24–25 June 1974)
Chief of Cabinet Legal Office	Yoshikuni Ichirō

Miki Cabinet
9 Dec. 1974–24 Dec. 1976

Prime Minister	Miki Takeo
Foreign Affairs	Miyazawa Kiichi (9 Dec. 1974–15 Sept. 1976)
	Kosaka Zentarō (15 Sept.–24 Dec. 1976)
Finance	Ōhira Masayoshi
Justice	Inaba Osamu
Education	Nagai Michio
Agriculture and Forestry	Abe Shintarō (9 Dec. 1974–15 Sept. 1976)
	Ōishi Buichi (15 Sept.–9 Dec. 1976)
International Trade and Industry	Kōmoto Toshio
Transport	Kimura Mutsuo (9 Dec. 1974–15 Sept. 1976)
	Ishida Hirohide (15 Sept.–9 Dec. 1976)
Posts and Telecommunications	Murakami Isamu (9 Dec. 1974–15 Sept. 1976)
	Fukuda Tokuyasu (15 Sept.–9 Dec. 1976)

Welfare	Tanaka Masami (22 Dec. 1974–15 Sept. 1976)
	Hayakawa Takashi (15 Sept.–9 Dec. 1976)
Labor	Hasegawa Takashi (22 Dec. 1974–15 Sept. 1976)
	Urano Sachio (15 Sept.–9 Dec. 1976)
Construction	Kariya Tadao (22 Dec. 1974–15 Jan. 1976)
	Takeshita Noboru (19 Jan.–15 Sept. 1976)
	Chiyūma Tatsui (15 Sept.–9 Dec. 1976)
Local Autonomy	Fukuda Hajime (22 Dec. 1974–15 Sept. 1976)
	Amano Hiroyoshi (15 Sept.–9 Dec. 1976)
State:	
Director Administrative Management Agency	Matsuzawa Yūzō (22 Dec. 1974–15 Sept. 1976)
	Arafune Seijūrō (15 Sept.–9 Dec. 1976)
Director Economic Planning Agency	*Fukuda Takeo (22 Dec. 1974–5 Nov. 1976)
	Noda Uichi (6 Nov.–9 Dec.1976)
Director Hokkaidō Development Agency	Fukuda Hajime (22 Dec. 1974–15 Sept. 1976)
	Amano Kimiyoshi (15 Sept.–9 Dec. 1976)
Director Defense Agency	Sakata Michita
Chairman National Public Safety Commission	Fukuda Hajime (22 Dec. 1974–15 Sept. 1976)
	Amano Kimiyoshi (15 Sept.–9 Dec. 1976)
Director Science and Technology Agency	Sasaki Yoshitake (22 Dec. 1974–15 Sept. 1976)
	Maeda Masao (15 Sept.–9 Dec. 1976)
Chief of Cabinet Secretariat	Ide Ichitarō
Director of General Affairs, Prime Minister's Office	Ueki Mitsunori (22 Dec. 1974–15 Sept. 1976)
	Nishimura Shōji (15 Sept.–9 Dec. 1976)
Director Environment Agency	Ozawa Tatsuo (22 Dec. 1974–15 Sept. 1976)
	Marumo Shigesada (15 Sept.–9 Dec. 1976)
Director Okinawa Development Agency	Ueki Mitsunori (22 Dec. 1974–15 Sept. 1976)
	Nishimura Shōji (15 Sept.–9 Dec. 1976)
Director National Land Agency	Kanemaru Shin (22 Dec. 1974–15 Sept. 1976)
	Amano Kōsei (15 Sept.–9 Dec. 1976)
Chief of Cabinet Legal Office	Yoshikuni Ichirō (22 Dec. 1974–15 Sept. 1976)
	Sanada Hideo (15 Sept.–9 Dec. 1976)

Fukuda Cabinet
24 Dec. 1976–7 Dec. 1978

Prime Minister	Fukuda Takeo (Nishimura Eiichi was acting premier 19–25 Mar. 1977, 6–18 Aug. 1977)

Foreign Affairs	Hatoyama Iichirō (24 Dec. 1976–28 Nov. 1977)
	Sonoda Sunao (28 Nov. 1977–7 Dec. 1978)
Finance	Bō Hideo (24 Dec. 1976–28 Nov. 1977)
	Murayama Tatsuo (28 Nov. 1977–7 Dec. 1978)
Justice	Fukuda Hajime (24 Dec. 1976–4 Oct. 1977)
	Setoyama Mitsuo (4 Oct. 1977–7 Dec. 1978)
Education	Kaifu Toshiki (24 Dec. 1976–28 Nov. 1977)
	Sunada Shigetami (28 Nov. 1977–7 Dec. 1978)
Agriculture and Forestry	Suzuki Zenkō (24 Dec. 1976–28 Nov. 1977)
	Nakagawa Ichirō (28 Nov. 1977–7 Dec. 1978)
International Trade and Industry	Tanaka Tatsuo (24 Dec. 1976–28 Nov. 1977)
	Kōmoto Toshio (28 Nov. 1977–7 Dec. 1978)
Transport	Tamura Hajime (24 Dec. 1976–28 Nov. 1977)
	Fukunaga Kenji (28 Nov. 1977–7 Dec.1978)
Posts and Telecommunications	Komiyama Jūshirō (24 Dec. 1976–28 Nov. 1977)
	Hattori Yasushi (28 Nov. 1977–7 Dec. 1978)
Welfare	Watanabe Michio (24 Dec. 1976–28 Nov. 1977)
	Ozawa Tatsuo (28 Nov. 1977–7 Dec. 1978)
Labor	Ishida Hirohide (24 Dec. 1976–28 Nov. 1977)
	Fujii Katsushi (28 Nov. 1977–7 Dec. 1978)
Construction	Hasegawa Shirō (24 Dec. 1976–28 Nov. 1977)
	Sakurauchi Yoshio (28 Nov. 1977–7 Dec. 1978)
Local Autonomy	Ogawa Heiji (24 Dec. 1976–28 Nov. 1977)
	Katō Takanori (28 Nov. 1977–7 Dec. 1978)

State:

Director Administrative Management Agency	Nishimura Eiichi (24 Dec. 1976–28 Nov. 1977)
	Arafune Seijūrō (28 Nov. 1977–7 Dec. 1978)

Director Economic Planning Agency, with responsibility for overall transport policy	Kuranari Tadashi (24 Dec. 1976–28 Nov. 1977)
	Miyazawa Kiichi (28 Nov. 1977–7 Dec. 1978)
Director Hokkaidō Development Agency	Ogawa Heiji (24 Dec. 1976–28 Nov. 1977)
	Katō Takanori (28 Nov. 1977–7 Dec. 1978)
Director Defense Agency	Mihara Asao (24 Dec. 1976–28 Nov. 1977)
	Kanemaru Shin (28 Nov. 1977–7 Dec. 1978)
Chairman National Public Safety Commission	Ogawa Heiji (24 Dec. 1976–28 Nov. 1977)
	Katō Takanori (28 Nov. 1977–7 Dec. 1978)
Director Science and Technology Agency and Chairman Atomic Power Commission	Uno Sōsuke (24 Dec. 1976–28 Nov. 1977)
	Kumagai Tasaburō (28 Nov. 1977–7 Dec. 1978)
Chief of Cabinet Secretariat	Sonoda Sunao (24 Dec. 1976–28 Nov. 1977)
	Abe Shintarō (28 Nov. 1977–7 Dec. 1978)
Director of General Affairs, Prime Minister's Office	Fujita Masaaki (24 Dec. 1976–28 Nov. 1977)
	Inamura Sakonshirō (28 Nov. 1977–7 Dec. 1978)
Director Environment Agency	Ishihara Shintarō (24 Dec. 1976–28 Nov. 1977)
	Yamada Hisanari (28 Nov. 1977–7 Dec. 1978)
Director Okinawa Development Agency	Fujita Masaaki (24 Dec. 1976–28 Nov. 1977)
	Inamura Sakonshirō (28 Nov. 1977–7 Dec. 1978)
Director National Land Agency	Tazawa Kichirō (24 Dec. 1976–28 Nov. 1977)
	Sakurauchi Yoshio (28 Nov. 1977–7 Dec. 1978)
Without Portfolio	Ushiba Nobuhiko (28 Nov. 1977–7 Dec. 1978)
Chief of Cabinet Legal Office	Sanada Hideo

Ōhira Cabinet
7 Dec. 1978–18 July 1980

Prime Minister	Ōhira Masayoshi (Itō Masayoshi acted as caretaker prime minister 12 June–18 July 1980)
Foreign Affairs	Sonoda Sunao
Finance	Kaneko Ippei
Justice	Furui Yoshimi
Education	Naitō Yosaburō
Agriculture and Forestry	Watanabe Michio
International Trade and Industry	Esaki Masumi

Transport	Moriyama Kinji
Posts and Telecommunications	Shirahama Nikichi
Welfare	Hashimoto Ryūtarō
Labor	Kurihara Yūkō
Construction	Tokai Motosaburō
Local Autonomy	Shibuya Naozō
State:	
Director Administrative Management Agency	Kanai Motohiko
Director Economic Planning Agency, with responsibility for overall transport policy	Kosaka Tokusaburō
Director Hokkaidō Development Agency	Shibuya Naozō
Director Defense Agency	Yamashita Ganri
Chairman National Public Safety Commission	Shibuya Naozō
Director Science and Technology Agency and Chairman Atomic Power Commission	Kaneko Iwazō
Chief of Cabinet Secretariat	Tanaka Rokusuke
Director of General Affairs, Prime Minister's Office	Mihara Asao
Director Environment Agency	Uemura Senichirō
Director Okinawa Development Agency	Mihara Asao
Director National Land Agency	Nakano Shirō
Chief of Cabinet Legal Office	Sanada Hideo

Suzuki Zenkō Cabinet
18 July 1980 –

Prime Minister	Suzuki Zenkō
Foreign Affairs	Itō Masayoshi
Finance	Watanabe Michio
Justice	Okuno Seisuke
Education	Tanaka Tatsuo
Agriculture and Forestry	Kameoka Takao
International Trade and Industry	Tanaka Rokusuke
Transport	Shiokawa Masajirō
Posts and Telecommunications	Yamanouchi Ichirō
Welfare	Saitō Kunikichi (18 July – 19 Sept. 1980) Sonoda Sunao
Labor	Fujio Masayuki
Construction	Saitō Shigeyoshi
Local Autonomy	Ishiba Jirō (18 July – 16 Dec. 1980) Abiko Tōkichi
State:	
Director Administrative Management Agency	Nakasone Yasuhiro
Director Economic Planning Agency, with responsibility for overall transport policy	Kōmoto Toshio

Director Hokkaidō Development Agency	Hata Kenzaburō
Director Defense Agency	Ōmura Jūji
Chairman National Public Safety Commission	Ishiba Jirō
Director Science and Technology Agency and Chairman Atomic Power Commission	Nakagawa Ichirō
Chief of Cabinet Secretariat	Miyazawa Kiichi
Director of General Affairs, Prime Minister's Office	Nakayama Tarō
Director Environment Agency	Kujiraoka Hyōsuke
Director Okinawa Development Agency	Nakayama Tarō
Director National Land Agency	Hara Kenzaburō
Chief of Cabinet Legal Office	Tsunoda Reijirō

Glossary

This glossary includes those Japanese words and phrases which most commonly appear in English-language texts relating to the history of modern Japan. Some of the words and phrases receive fuller explanation in the main text of the dictionary.

Anpo 安保 Abbreviation for Nichibei Anpo Jōyaku (U.S.–Japan Security Treaty signed in 1951). Especially used with reference to the protests against the renewal of the treaty in 1960.

bakufu 幕府 "Military government." The administration headed by the shōgun.

bakuhan 幕藩 Abbreviation for *bakufu-han*. Commonly used to refer to the social, political, and economic system existing under the Tokugawa shōgun.

bakumatsu 幕末 The last days of the Tokugawa regime (1850s–1860s).

***Bansho Torishirabejo* (also *Bansho Shirabejo*)** 蕃書取調所 "Place for the investigation of barbarian writings." Name given to the Bakufu's institute of Western learning, later renamed the Kaiseijo.

bunmei kaika 文明開化 "Civilization and enlightenment."

buraku 部落 Hamlet.

burakumin 部落民 "Hamlet people." Members of Japan's outcast class. (See also *eta* and *hinin*.)

bushi 武士 Warrior, samurai.

bushidō 武士道 The way of the warrior, the samurai ethic.

chitsuroku shobun 秩禄処分 Commutation of stipends.

chō 町 Measure of area, approximately 2.45 acres.

chokugo 勅語 Imperial rescript (i.e., proclamation).

chokuyu 勅諭 Imperial injunction.

chōnin 町人 Merchant, townsman.

Daihon'ei 大本営 Imperial Headquarters.

daimyō 大名 Feudal lord in direct vassalage to the shōgun heading a domain of over 10,000 *koku*.

dainagon 大納言 Chief councillor of state (early *Dajōkan* system of government).

Dainihon 大日本 Greater Japan. Frequently used to refer to Japan and later the Japanese empire in the years up to 1945.

dajō daijin 太政大臣 Highest official of *Dajōkan* system of administration 1871–1885, equivalent to later prime minister.

Dajōkan (also Daijōkan, Dajōkwan) 太政官 The executive body of the early Meiji government 1868–1885, which gave its name to the whole structure of government during this period.

dekasegi 出稼 "Working away from home." Employment away from one's home with the aim of supplementing family income, in theory on a temporary rather than permanent basis.

eta えた Outcast. The word *burakumin* is now frequently used instead of *eta*.

fu 府 City, urban district. First established as a unit of local government during the Meiji period, the term is still used for the urban districts of Osaka and Kyoto.

fudai 譜代 Used to denote a daimyō already in hereditary vassalage to the Tokugawa family at the time of its seizure of power.

fukoku kyōhei 富国強兵 "Rich country, strong army." Slogan used in the early Meiji period to indicate the Westernization policies adopted to strengthen Japan.

Gaimushō 外務省 Foreign Ministry.

gakkō 学校 School, college.

Gakusei 学制 Education Law (1872).

gekokujō 下剋上 "The low achieving victory over the high." The replacement of a lord by his retainer, hence the domination of a senior by his junior.

genbun itchi 言文一致 Unification of the written and spoken languages.

genrō 元老 "Elder statesman." Used specifically to refer to the group of men who unofficially wielded power during the late Meiji and Taishō periods.

Genrōin 元老院 "Senate." The deliberative assembly established prior to the Imperial Diet 1875–1890.

ginkō 銀行 Bank.

gōnō 豪農 Wealthy farmer.

gōshi 郷士 Rural samurai, originally one permitted to live outside a castle town.

goshinpei 御親兵 Imperial troops, later reorganized under the name *Konoehei.*

goyōkin 御用金 Forced loans or levies imposed by the feudal authorities during the Tokugawa period, mostly on merchants.

gozen kaigi 御前会議 Conference of senior statesmen held in the presence of the emperor, often translated as "imperial conference."

gun 郡 Local government unit, subdivision of a prefecture.

gunbatsu 軍閥 Military clique or faction, also sometimes translated as "militarists."

gunken seido 郡県制度 "Prefectural system." Used to denote a centralized administrative system, as in Imperial China, in contrast to the feudal system (*hōken seido*) of Tokugawa Japan.

ha 派 Faction.

haihan chiken 廃藩置県 Abolition of the domains and establishment of prefectures (1871).

han 藩 Domain held in fief by a daimyō. Also translated "clan" and "fief."

hanbatsu 藩閥 "Domain/clan faction." Used specifically to refer to the domination of Japanese politics in the late Meiji and Taishō periods by men from Satsuma and Chōshū.

hanseki hōkan 版籍奉還 Return of lands and people to the emperor, the first step toward the abolition of the domains taken in 1869.

hatamoto 旗本 Direct retainer of the shōgun with a fief or stipend of less than 10,000 *koku*, thereby ranking below a *fudai* daimyō.

heimin 平民 Commoner. From 1869 the mass of the population not designated nobility (*kazoku*) or warriors (*shizoku, sotsuzoku*) were classed as *heimin.*

hinin 非人 "Nonperson." Formerly used to designate certain members of Japan's outcasts; the term *burakumin* is now normally used.

hōken seido 封建制度 "Feudal system." Used to denote an administration based on the holding of fiefs as in Tokugawa Japan, in contrast to the prefectural system (*gunken seido*).

Hōmushō 法務省 Ministry of Justice (title after 1952).

hyōjungo 標準語 Standard language.

ie 家 Family, house.

ishin 維新 "Renovation." The term is widely translated as restoration as in "Meiji Restoration" and "Shōwa Restoration."

Jingikan 神祇官 Bureau of Shrines, the nominal locus of supreme power under the early *Dajōkan* system of administration to 1871.

jiyū minken undō 自由民権運動 Freedom and people's rights movement (1870s–1880s).

jōi 攘夷 "Expel the barbarian." Antiforeign slogan widely adopted in conjunction with the phrase *sonnō* (revere the emperor) by opponents of the Bakufu from the mid-1850s.

jūshin 重臣 Senior statesman. Used especially in the 1930s and 1940s when so-called senior statesmen gathered in conference to select a new prime minister and decide on major state matters, a role previously exercised by the *genrō.*

kaikoku 開国 "Open the country." Used specifically to refer to a desire to reopen relations with other countries before the conclusion of the Ansei treaties in 1858.

Kaitakushi 開拓史 Colonization Board responsible for the administration of Hokkaidō 1869–1882 (full title Hokkaidō *Kaitakushi*).

kami 神 Superior being, spirit, god.

kamon 家門 Daimyō from a family collateral to the Tokugawa house and bearing the name of Matsudaira.

kana 仮名(かな) Phonetic syllabaries used in conjunction with characters for writing Japanese. There are two of these: *hiragana*, the cursive syllabary, and *katakana*, the square syllabary.

kanji 漢字 Chinese characters.

Kansai 関西 "West of the barrier." The Kyoto-Osaka area.

Kantō 関東 "East of the barrier." The Tokyo-Yokohama area.

karō 家老 Principal official/retainer of a domain.

kazoku 華族 Nobility, consisting until 1884 of *kuge* (court nobility) and former daimyō, and subsequently denoting members of the new Western-style peerage.

kazoku kokka 家族国家 "Family state." The idea of the nation as one family headed by the emperor, which was an integral part of the "emperor system" ideology before 1945.

keiretsu 系列 "Chain, order." Term used to refer to conglomerates of economic interest which have developed since 1945.

ken 県 Prefecture, first established as a local government unit in former Tokugawa lands in 1868 and subsequently extended to embrace the whole country excluding urban areas and Hokkaidō.

Kenpeitai (sometimes just *Kenpei*) 憲兵隊(憲兵) Military police.

kikan 機関 Agency, organ. Used especially to denote small organizations engaged in undercover trading or intelligence activities during the war years 1937–1945.

kizoku 貴族 Nobility.

Kizokuin 貴族院 House of Peers (1890–1947).

kōbu gattai 公武合体 "Unity of the Court and Bakufu." Used to denote the policies of those who, in the late 1850s and early 1860s, sought accommodation between the Bakufu and leading daimyō.

kobun 子分 See *oyabun kobun*

kōdō 皇道 The imperial way.

koku 石 Unit of capacity equal to 4.96 bushels and the major unit for the measurement of rice.

kokudaka 石高 "Amount of *koku*." The yield of rice gained from an enfeoffment during the Tokugawa period, hence the measurement indicating the size or valuation of a fief or stipend.

kokugaku 国学 "National learning, nativism." The study of Japan's origins and Shintō beliefs through the medium of the native classics which developed from the mid-Tokugawa period.

kokutai 国体 "National polity."

Konoehei 近衛兵 Imperial Guard.

ku 区 Ward (administrative subdivision of a city).

kuge 公家 Court nobility of the Tokugawa period. *Kuge* became one element in the post-Restoration nobility.

Kyōikurei 教育令 Education Ordinance (1879).

Mankan kōkan 満韓交換 "Manchuria in exchange for Korea." Used to denote the policies of the late 19th and early 20th centuries which attempted a Russo-Japanese rapprochement by ensuring Japanese domination in Korea in return for that of Russia in Manchuria.

minponshugi 民本主義 "People as the base-ism." Often translated "democracy" but specifically democratic ideals as expounded in the thought of Yoshino Sakuzō.

minshushugi 民主主義 Democracy.

miso 味噌 Fermented bean paste, one of the staples of the traditional Japanese diet.

Naidaijin 内大臣 "Inner Minister." Usually translated "Lord Keeper of the Privy Seal." Court official acting as adviser to the emperor 1885-1945.

Naikaku Kanbō Chōkan 内閣官房長官 Chief of the Cabinet Secretariat (term used after 1947).

Naikaku Shokikanchō 内閣書記官長 Chief of the Cabinet Secretariat (term used until 1947).

Naimushō 内務省 Home Ministry (1873–1947).

narikin 成金 Nouveau riche, especially those profiting from the World War I boom.

Nihon 日本 Japan. Prewar the pronunciation *Nippon* was common.

nōhonshugi 農本主義 "Agriculture as the base-ism." An ideological trend emphasizing agriculture prevalent in Japan before the Pacific War; often translated "agrarianism."

ōdō 王道 The kingly way.

ōsei fukko 王政復古 Restoration of imperial rule achieved by the overthrow of the Bakufu and return to the emperor of government responsibility in 1868.

***oyabun kobun* (also *oyakata kogata*)** 親分子分(親方子方) A leader and his followers, a boss and his henchmen.

rangaku 蘭学 "Dutch learning." During the Tokugawa period most Western study was achieved through the medium of Dutch books: *rangaku* refers both to the study of the Dutch language and to wider Western learning.

rin 厘 Unit of currency equivalent to one-tenth of a *sen* and one-thousandth of a *yen*, out of use since the prewar period due to inflation.

rōdō 労働 Labor.

rōjū 老中 Bakufu elder, *fudai* daimyō appointed as senior councillor to the shōgun.

rōnin 浪人 Masterless samurai. During the late Tokugawa period many samurai illegally left their domains, often to engage in anti-Bakufu activities, and hence became *rōnin*. (The term is now also used to refer to a student waiting to retake university entrance examinations following initial failure.)

ryō 両 Unit of currency in use during the Tokugawa period and replaced by the *yen* in 1872.

sadaijin 左大臣 "Minister of the Left." Senior official under *Dajōkan* system of administration.

Sain 左院 "Department of the Left." Body headed by the Minister of the Left under the *Dajōkan* system.

sake 酒 Rice wine.

samurai 侍 Feudal retainer, member of the warrior class.

sangi 参議 State councillor under the *Dajōkan* system of government 1869–1885.

Sangiin 参議院 House of Councillors (Upper House) of the Japanese Diet under the 1947 constitution.

sanke 三家 "Three houses." The three senior branches of the Tokugawa family whose domains lay in Kii, Owari, and Mito.

sankin kōtai 参勤交代 Alternate residence. The system whereby the Bakufu forced the various daimyō to spend much of their time in Edo rather than in their own domains, used to reinforce Bakufu control over them.

sanyo 参与 Councillor under *Dajōkan* system of administration 1868–1869.

seii taishōgun 征夷大将軍 "Barbarian-subduing great general." Normally abbreviated to shōgun.

Seiin 正院 Highest decision-making body under the *Dajōkan* governmental system 1871–1877.

seikanron 征韓論 "Advocacy of the subjugation of Korea." Refers to the calls for the invasion of Korea, which led to a major government split in 1873.

seishō 政商 "Political merchant." Used especially to refer to those businessmen who benefited from government connections during the Meiji period.

sen 銭 Unit of currency equivalent to one-hundredth of a *yen*, now no longer in use due to inflation.

Shihōshō 司法省 Justice Ministry (term used 1871–1947).

Shikan Gakkō (Rikugun Shikan Gakkō) 士官学校(陸軍士官学校) Military Academy (1874–1945).

shinbun 新聞 Newspaper.

shinōkōshō 士農工商 "Warrior, farmer, artisan, merchant." The four classes of Tokugawa society whose rigid hierarchy formed the basis of political, economic, and social organization.

shinpan 親藩 "Related *han*." Those domains headed by collaterals or relatives of the Tokugawa family.

shishi 志士 "Men of spirit." Used especially to refer to the loyalist patriots of the late Tokugawa period.

shizoku 士族 Warrior families, gentry. From 1869 former members of the warrior class were designated *shizoku*.

shizoku jusan 士族授産 Rehabilitation of the samurai. The policies adopted in the early Meiji period to reduce economic, political, and social problems caused by dispossessed samurai following the reduction and abolition of stipends.

shō 省 Ministry.

shōgun 将軍 Abbreviation of *seii taishōgun*—"barbarian-subduing great general," a title initially awarded to the emperor's military deputy. From 1192 the holders of the title were often the effective rulers of Japan. It was held by members of the Tokugawa family from 1603 until political power was officially restored to the emperor in 1868.

shokusan kōgyō 殖産興業 "Increase in production and founding of industries." Phrase used to describe the government's industrialization policy in the early Meiji period.

shotai 諸隊 Auxiliary units formed in Chōshū from 1863 to reinforce regular troops in case of foreign or Bakufu attack.

shōya 庄屋 Village headman.

Shūgiin 衆議院 House of Representatives (Lower House) of the Imperial Diet under the Meiji constitution from 1890 and of the National Diet under the 1947 constitution. A word with the same pronunciation but with different characters was also used for a samurai assembly existing 1869–1873.

shuntō 春闘 "Spring offensive." The campaign for wage increases mounted annually by the labor union movement since 1956 when the Spring Offensive Joint Action Committee was formed.

sonnō 尊王 "Revere the emperor." Slogan used by advocates of the return to the emperor of governmental responsibility during the later Tokugawa period.

sonnō jōi 尊王攘夷 "Revere the emperor, expel the barbarian." Slogan used by opponents of the Bakufu following the yielding to Western pressure for the establishment of relations in 1858.

sotsuzoku 卒族 Term used to designate former lower members of the warrior class and quasi-samurai 1869–1872. In 1872 *sotsuzoku* were reclassified as either *shizoku* or *heimin*.

Tainichi Rijikai (Rengōkoku Tainichi Rijikai) 対日理事会 (連合国対日理事会) Allied Council for Japan.

tairiku rōnin 大陸浪人 "Continental adventurer." Used mostly to refer to members of the Kokuryūkai and other nationalist societies of the pre-1945 period engaged in undercover activities in mainland Asia to enhance Japan's influence.

tairō 大老 "Great elder." Normally translated regent. Chief minister of the Bakufu, usually appointed in times of crisis to take precedence over the *rōjū* (senior councillors).

taisei hōkan 大政奉還 Return of responsibility for administration from the shōgun to the emperor by Tokugawa Keiki in 1867.

Taisei Yokusankai 大政翼賛会 Imperial Rule Assistance Association, the nuclear body of the new political structure established in 1940.

tenkō 転向 About-face, conversion. Used especially with reference to the "conversion" of Communists to the prevailing orthodoxy during the 1930s.

tennōsei 天皇制 Emperor system. The governmental structure and official ideology of pre-1945 Japan.

terakoya 寺子屋 Temple schools, which were the main source of education for the general populace during the Tokugawa period.

tōbaku 討幕 "Overthrow of the Bakufu." Used to denote the anti-Bakufu movement of the 1860s.

tonarigumi 隣組 Neighborhood association.

tondenhei 屯田兵 "Farming troops." Term used in the modern period to refer to the combination of agricultural and militia activity operative in Hokkaidō from the 1870s.

tozama 外様 "Outside lord." Daimyō who was not a hereditary vassal of the Tokugawa family.

udaijin 右大臣 "Minister of the Right." Senior official under the *Dajōkan* system of administration.

Uin 右院 "Department of the Right." Government organ headed by the Minister of the Right and responsible for administration under the *Dajōkan* system 1869–1875.

yen 円 Unit of currency introduced in 1872 and equivalent to 1 *ryō* of the old currency.

yōgaku 洋学 Western learning.

zaibatsu 財閥 "Financial clique." The major concentrations of economic interests which dominated the Japanese economy up to 1945.

Japanese-English Index

This index does not claim to be fully comprehensive. It includes the characters for those words, items, and individuals which have an entry in the main body of the text or in the glossary, and, in addition, the characters for the emperors, era names, and places appearing in the appendices. The intention is purely to provide a convenient source of reference for beginners in the use of Japanese-language sources. Entries are arranged according to the number of strokes in the first character of an entry.

Two Strokes

九州	Kyūshū
乃木希典	Nogi Maresuke
二・二六事件	February 26 uprising
十一月事件	November incident
十月事件	October incident

Three Strokes

万延	Man'en
万朝報	Yorozu Chōhō
三井財閥	Mitsui *zaibatsu*
三木武夫	Miki Takeo
三木清	Miki Kiyoshi
三月事件	March incident
三宅雪嶺	Miyake Setsurei
三条実美	Sanjō Sanetomi
三国干渉	Triple intervention
三重	Mie
三島通庸	Mishima Michitsune
三家	*sanke*
三浦梧楼	Miura Gorō
三菱財閥	Mitsubishi *zaibatsu*
三野村利左衛門	Minomura Rizaemon
下山事件	Shimoyama incident
下田条約	Shimoda, Treaty of
下剋上	*gekokujō*
下関	Shimonoseki
千島	Kurile Islands

山本五十六	Yamamoto Isoroku
山本権兵衛	Yamamoto Gonnohyōe
山形	Yamagata
山東	Shantung
山東出兵	Shantung expeditions
山県有朋	Yamagata Aritomo
山県・ロバノフ協定	Yamagata-Lobanov agreement
山梨	Yamanashi

Four Strokes

五・一五事件	May 15 incident
五代友厚	Godai Tomoatsu
五ヵ条の誓文	Charter Oath
天津	Tientsin
天津条約	Tientsin Treaty
天保	Tenpo (era)
天皇制	Emperor system
天皇機関説	Emperor organ theory
内大臣	Lord Keeper of the Privy Seal
内田良平	Uchida Ryōhei
内村鑑三	Uchimura Kanzō
内務省	Home Ministry
内閣官房長官	Chief of Cabinet Secretariat (after 1947)
内閣書記官長	Chief of Cabinet Secretariat (until 1947)
中上川彦次郎	Nakamigawa Hikojirō
中央公論	*Chūō Kōron*
中江兆民	Nakae Chōmin
中村正直	Nakamura Masanao
中国に関する9ヵ国条約	Nine-Power Pact
中野正剛	Nakano Seigō
井上日召	Inoue Nisshō
井上哲次郎	Inoue Tetsujirō
井上毅	Inoue Kowashi
井上準之助	Inoue Junnosuke
井上馨(聞多)	Inoue Kaoru (Bunda)
井伊直弼	Ii Naosuke
屯田兵	*tondenhei*
元田永孚	Motoda Eifu
元老	*genrō*
元老院	Genrōin
元治	Genji (era)
文久	Bunkyū (era)
文明開化	Civilization and enlightenment
仁川	Chemulpo (Inchon)
仁孝	Ninkō (era)
公武合体	*kōbu gattai*
公明党	Kōmeitō
公家	*kuge*
円	*yen*
区	*ku*
友愛会	Yūaikai
太政大臣	*dajō daijin*
太政官	*Dajōkan*
太政官制	*Dajōkan* system

Five Strokes

Seven Strokes

Eight Strokes

Seventeen Strokes

臨時外交調査委員会	Advisory Council on Foreign Relations
薩長同盟	Satsuma-Chōshū alliance
薩摩	Satsuma
鍋山貞親	Nabeyama Sadachika

Eighteen Strokes

藩	*han*
藩閥	*hanbatsu*
藩閥政治	*hanbatsu* politics
藤田伝三郎	Fujita Denzaburō
鎖国	Seclusion

Nineteen Strokes

蘭学	Dutch learning
蘆溝橋事件	Marco Polo Bridge incident
譜代	*fudai*

Twenty Strokes

攘夷	*jōi*

Kana

カイロ宣言	Cairo declaration
ケロッグ不戦条約	Kellogg Pact
サン・フランシスコ講和条約	San Francisco Peace Treaty
シベリア出兵	Siberian intervention
シーメンス事件	Siemens scandal
ゾルゲ事件	Sorge incident
ノモンハン事件	Nomonhan incident
ベルサイユ平和条約	Versailles Peace Treaty
ポツダム宣言	Potsdam declaration
ポーツマス条約	Portsmouth Treaty
マリア・ルス号事件	Maria Luz incident
ヤルタ協定	Yalta agreement
リットン調査団	Lytton commission
レッド・パージ	"Red purge"
ロッキード事件	Lockheed scandal
ロンドン海軍軍縮会議	London naval conference
ワシントン会議	Washington conference

Designer: Randall Goodall
Compositor: Innovative Media
Printer: Vail-Ballou Press
Binder: Vail-Ballou Press
Text: 9/10 Galliard
Display: Univers 75 Black Roman